COUNT LEO NIKOLAEVICH TOLSTOY, the you
brothers, was born in 1828 at Yasnaya Polyana, his fath.
estate in Tula province, about two hundred miles from Moscow.
His mother died when he was two, and his father when he was
nine. He revered their memory, and they were the inspiration
for his portraits of Princess Mary and Nicholas Rostov in *War
and Peace*. Both his mother and father belonged to the Russian
nobility, and Tolstoy always remained highly conscious of his
aristocratic status, even when towards the end of his life he
embraced and taught doctrines of Christian equality and the
brotherhood of man.

He served in the army in the Caucasus and the Crimea,
where as an artillery officer at the siege of Sevastopol he wrote
his first stories and impressions. After leaving the army he
travelled and studied educational theories, which deeply
interested him. In 1862 he married Sophia Behrs and for the
next fifteen years lived a tranquil and productive life as a
country gentleman and author. *War and Peace* was finished in
1869 and *Anna Karenina* in 1877. He had thirteen children. In
1879, after undergoing a severe spiritual crisis, he wrote the
autobiographical *A Confession*, and from then on he became a
'Tolstoyan', seeking to propagate his views on religion, morality,
non-violence, and renunciation of the flesh. He continued to
write, but chiefly in the form of parables, tracts and morality
plays – written 'with the left hand of Tolstoy' as a Russian
critic has put it – though he also composed a late novel,
*Resurrection*, and one of his finest long tales, *Hadji Murat*.
Because of his new beliefs and disciples, and his international
fame as pacifist and sage, relations with his wife became
strained and family life increasingly difficult. At last in 1910,
at the age of 82, he left his home and died of pneumonia at a
local railway station.

HENRY GIFFORD, formerly Professor of English and Com-
parative Literature at the University of Bristol, has written
widely on Russian literature. His publications include *The Novel
in Russia* (1964) and *Tolstoy* (Past Masters, 1982).

# THE WORLD'S CLASSICS

===

## LEO TOLSTOY

# *War and Peace*

### VOLUME ONE

===

Translated by
**LOUISE AND AYLMER MAUDE**

Edited by
**HENRY GIFFORD**

Oxford  New York

OXFORD UNIVERSITY PRESS

1983

Oxford University Press, Walton Street, Oxford OX2 6DP

London Glasgow New York Toronto
Delhi Bombay Calcutta Madras Karachi
Kuala Lumpur Singapore Hong Kong Tokyo
Nairobi Dar es Salaam Cape Town
Melbourne Auckland

and associates in

Beirut Berlin Ibadan Mexico City Nicosia

War and Peace first published 1868–9
This translation first published by Oxford University Press 1922–3
Two-volume World's Classics paperback edition first published 1983

Introduction, Chronology, Select Bibliography and Notes
© Henry Gifford 1983

British Library Cataloguing in Publication Data

Tolstoi, L. N.
War and peace.—(The World's classics)
Vol. 1
I. Title   II. Maude, Louise
III. Maude, Aylmer   IV. Gifford, Henry
V. Voina i mir. English
891.73′3[F]   PG3366.V6
ISBN 0-19-281582-2

Library of Congress Cataloging in Publication Data

Tolstoy, Leo, graf, 1828–1910.
War and peace.
(The World's classics)
Translation of: Voina i mir.
First published in this translation in 1922–1923.
Bibliography: v. 1, p.
I. Maude, Louise Shanks, 1855–1939.   II. Maude,
Aylmer, 1858–1938.   III. Gifford, Henry.   IV. Title.
PG3366.V6 1983   891.73′3   82–14117

ISBN 0-19-281582-2 (pbk. : v. 1)
ISBN 0-19-281614-4 (pbk. : v. 2)

Set by New Western Printing Ltd.
Printed in Great Britain by
Hazell Watson & Viney Limited
Aylesbury, Bucks

# CONTENTS

## VOLUME ONE

### WAR AND PEACE

## VOLUME TWO

### WAR AND PEACE

# INTRODUCTION

WAR AND PEACE was not immediately or universally recognized by its readers as a world's classic. It came out by instalments between 1865 and 1869, in a time of fierce controversy; and there were complaints from both left and right about its being tendentious. Tolstoy's contemporaries could few of them stand back and see the grand design of the book; they were distracted by questions of genre – was this a novel of family life? an historical chronicle, not without its distortions? or a panoramic 'poem' like Gogol's *Dead Souls*? Tolsty rejected all these definitions when in 1868 he published 'Some Words About *War and Peace*' (to be found at the end of this volume). He claimed that the best things in the fiction of his countrymen had never conformed to the known genres. But many of his readers found it difficult to adjust to the changed perspective in a novel that started with the domestic life of a few families and moved steadily into the domain of a national epic. They were even more perplexed when, half-way through it, passages of theoretical argument about history and free will began to grow in frequency, until the Second Epilogue left fiction behind altogether, and hammered out a paradoxical thesis.

Tolstoy tells us in 'Some Words' that he wrote the novel during 'five years of uninterrupted and exceptionally strenuous labour under the best conditions of life'. It was certainly strenuous labour, as the many drafts that have survived witness; and the only interruptions it suffered were those incidental to raising a family – he had married in 1862 – and farming his estate. He claimed in a letter of 1863 to be at the height of his powers; and never had Tolstoy felt so much at harmony with himself. The 'best conditions of life' meant virtual seclusion on his estate of Yasnaya Polyana. He wanted explicitly in this novel to celebrate the life of the Russian nobility (a term including what we should call the gentry) and the solid agrarian order which found itself under challenge in a new phase of Russian history following the Emancipation of the Serfs in 1861. Yasnaya Polyana and all it stood for was very precious to Tolstoy. The atmosphere of the place is palpable when he writes of the Rostovs and their country pursuits at Otradnoe.

The challenge, of which Tolstoy was keenly aware, to his own cherished traditions came from the so-called 'new men' who began to dominate the intellectual scene after the defeat of Russia in the Crimean War, during which the repressive Tsar Nicholas I had died. The years ensuing were remarkable, even by Russian standards, for their ideological conflict. The leading journal then was *The Contemporary*, edited by the poet Nekrasov, who had been glad to publish Tolstoy's own work from *Childhood* (1852) onwards, and regarded him as a writer of exceptional promise – an opinion shared by Turgenev. But Nekrasov had come increasingly under the influence of two associates, Chernyshevsky and Dobrolyubov, former seminarists whose militant views were odious to Tolstoy. Dogmatically, they put their trust in progress, in the rationality of man once freed from superstition and the constraints of despotism, and in the organization of society on scientific principles. Tolstoy, though himself an unresting inquirer, was no friend to intellectuals: we have only to consider his attitude in *War and Peace* to Speransky. In 1863 Chernyshevsky, although in prison, had been able to publish a novel, *What Is To Be Done?*, which portrayed an emancipated woman who dreams of a radiant future. Tolstoy resented it as an attack on the family, and the many admirers of Chernyshevsky's novel among the intelligentsia could see plainly his polemical intention in *War and Peace*.

At the beginning of the 1860s, after having dropped out of literature for a while, Tolstoy made a start on a novel about the Decembrists. These were the liberal conspirators from the aristocracy who on 14 December 1825 rose against Nicholas I on his accession. In 1856 at the beginning of a new reign those who had survived thirty years of exile in Siberia were allowed to return. Tolstoy was interested in these revolutionaries of an earlier generation. He abandoned his novel about the Decembrists, but Pierre in *War and Peace*, as the First Epilogue reveals, took a leading part in one of the circles leading up to the insurrection, and he admits to Prince Andrew's son that his friend too would have shared their ideas. In these two representatives of the aristocracy, before the modern age which he opposed, Tolstoy could realize the life of thinking men who had liberated themselves from ideology. Prince Andrew tired of Speransky's notions, Freemasonry ceased to enchant Pierre.

The novel about the Decembrists was never written. Now Tolstoy turned to the beginning of the century, when Napoleon filled the western horizon of Russia. He began by narrating the fortunes of a few aristocratic families in those years from 1805. The first instalment to appear bore the title *1805*, but it was not until a few months later, in March 1865, that Tolstoy recorded in his diary a new vision of what his novel might be. At one early stage he had thought of calling it *All's Well That Ends Well*, which would seem to tilt the balance towards the domestic, with the war as a temporary disturbance of its peaceful waters. But now he had become absorbed in reading about Napoleon and Alexander, and the idea that came upon him 'like a cloud of joy and of the consciousness of being able to make something great' was that he would write 'the psychological history of the romance between Alexander and Napoleon'. Alexander puzzled him, so intelligent, sensitive, a potentially great man who wavered between liberalism when he supported Speransky, and military harshness when he replaced him by Arakcheev. Tolstoy sees 'confusion outwardly' in Alexander, and yet, within, a spiritual brightness. Reading about the two leaders he had come to see 'all the baseness, all the phrase-making, all the senselessness, all the contradictions of the people surrounding them, and of themselves' – particularly of Napoleon, whom already he condemned as insincere, unfeeling, and self-deluded. Napoleon 'is not interesting, but only the people surrounding him and on whom he acted'. All this gave rise to 'great thoughts' and when Tolstoy conceived his work at this stage as a 'poem' he was aware of its epic possibilities.

He had now become a historical novelist in the most profound sense. His readers might complain that he appeared to forget the original characters of his story, as he came more and more to expatiate upon public events and public figures, and later to challenge the historians and argue with military experts. They had expected a family chronicle, of the kind Tolstoy himself had read in Trollope's work, with admiration for the novelist's mastery, though he soon recognized how much Trollope dealt in the conventional. Tolstoy had a good knowledge of the contemporary English novel, and some respect for it. *War and Peace*, however, developed on lines of its own, and Tolstoy was right when he insisted that it could not be placed in any accepted category.

For the reader in our time, with all the study that has been made of Tolstoy's working methods when he wrote this novel, it no longer perplexes, and the design is fairly simple to see. We know from Russian critics of this century like Shklovsky and Eykhenbaum how he handled his sources, and what transformations the story underwent as it grew in his mind. There is an excellent account of all this in the book by R. F. Christian, *Tolstoy's 'War and Peace': A Study* (Oxford, 1962). For many years the English reader, encouraged in this view by Henry James and his disciple Percy Lubbock, failed to perceive the coherence of Tolstoy's novel. It was indeed open to the winds of his time – Tolstoy allowed no barriers between art and daily living. The world of Alexander's era is not distanced by reminders of its pastness as that of the Regency is in *Vanity Fair*, or Middlemarch in the late 1820s and early 1830s by George Eliot contemplating it fifty years later. Tolstoy writes of the past (though with some deliberate historical colouring) in terms of the present, and *War and Peace* is a novel of the 1860s like any other of that contentious decade, even if the issues are presented in a wider perspective. For this reason it is a developing work, that deepened with Tolstoy's awareness of moral and historical problems. But the flood through all its branches is channelled and controlled. The ideas of the novel – though it adds up to more than its ideas – are linked in a firm structure.

Tolstoy's own experience entered deeply into the novel. His family were quick to recognize many of the people and situations, although no character is to be identified wholly with its prototype. He changed more in a character than a letter or two in the surname (the old Prince Nicholas Bolkonsky from his grandfather Prince Nicholas Volkonsky, or his daughter from Tolstoy's own mother, also Mary, and like her plain and wealthy). Tolstoy's portraits are always subtly enhanced so that, as William James once remarked, 'life indeed seems less real than his tale of it.' Natasha with her extraordinary openness to life is more than an amalgam of Tolstoy's sister-in-law and his wife.

The battle scenes owe much to what he had seen himself in the Crimean War, when at Sevastopol he was present in the dangerous Fourth Bastion. The *Sevastopol Sketches* describing life under siege there have been worked up into the immense and crowded canvas of Napoleon's campaigns in 1805 and 1812. Many years later Tolstoy spoke of his debt to Stendhal who in *La Chartreuse de Parme* depicted the battle of Waterloo as experienced by the bewildered Fabrice, a participant who has utterly lost his bearings. The character of warfare had changed little from Austerlitz to Tolstoy's own time: the weapons had made no striking advance, communications remained slow, intelligence was haphazard; the signals network of a modern army did not exist. The military experts (whom, like experts of every kind, Tolstoy held in contempt) were displeased with his calm dismissal of military science. They could not fail to resent the many gibes at pedantic German theorists (many soldiers of high rank under the imperial regime were German in origin). Prince Andrew, just before Borodino, overhears a brief exchange between the great theorist of war, Clausewitz, and a compatriot. It revolts him by its lack of sensitivity to the suffering in war, which is seen purely in a technical light. However, General Dragomirov, a military critic of *War and Peace* who dissented strongly from Tolstoy's conclusions about the futility of strategic studies, had to admit that his battle scenes could give 'invaluable practical lessons'. Tolstoy, in a way that very few military historians ever did, showed the experience of war for those taking part in it.

The brush with Clausewitz belongs to a grand strategy pursued throughout the novel. Tolstoy develops his own campaign parallel with Kutuzov's. Each is concerned to repel the foreign invader. Tolstoy's prejudice against Napoleon (and the way he often manipulates his source material exposes the prejudice) is not mere resentment of the national enemy. Napoleon represents the inhumanity that Tolstoy is already beginning to find in modern civilization. Whereas Kutuzov, deliberately set up as the moral opposite to Napoleon, has a natural compassion, it never occurs to Napoleon that war is anything but magnificent theatre with himself in the leading role, that destiny which he has manufactured and wants to serve him. Kutuzov's wisdom is contrasted with Napoleon's delusions of grandeur. And the insincerity, the lack of any real concern for their fellow-men that marks the court circle in Petersburg – so unlike the warm-hearted Rostovs in Moscow – finds its reflection in French manners and its clichés in French speech. Tolstoy knows that for him the genuine is the Russian. The French and the Germans alike are out of touch with actualities. Here, I think, more comes into play than patriotic bias. Tolstoy is pitting the natural against the contrived.

Tolstoy's point of view, consistent and at times heavily stressed, does lead to some tampering with sources. Although he claims in 'Some Words About *War and Peace*' to have 'accumulated a whole library of materials', his reading was somewhat narrowly selective and, in the way of genius, desultory. He made use of two standard Russian histories, by Mikhaylovsky-Danilevsky (1844) and Bogdanovich (1859–60); also of Thiers's *Histoire du Consulat et de l'Empire* (1845–62), which for twenty years held the field against other French accounts of Napoleon. All three works could make available for him vividly recorded scenes. But he explains in 'Some Words' that 'the tasks of artists and historians are quite different'. The historian is dominated by his single idea of a character (though we might argue that Tolstoy is dominated by a single idea of Napoleon); whereas the artist, aware that nothing in life is answerable to tidy schemes, has to approach the historical event from another side (and people show new aspects of themselves under the force of events). 'Either from his own experience, or from letters, memoirs, and accounts, the artist realizes a certain event to himself . . .'. Tolstoy began his preparations for *War and*

*Peace* by seeking out the reminiscences of those who had witnessed his chosen period, their letters and diaries – whatever would help him to 'realize to himself' how it had actually looked and felt. This intimate approach was not approved of by all critics.

Turgenev, who made many objections to *War and Peace* that qualified his admiration, thought he could see a deliberate sleight of hand in the method. 'Tolstoy', he wrote, 'astonishes the reader by the pointed toe of Alexander's boot, by Speransky's laugh, making one assume that he must know *everything*...'. The way in which Tolstoy claimed intimacy with his characters and the period as a whole offended the survivors of that age. Old Prince Vyazemsky, long before the friend of Pushkin, himself the son of a leading figure in Catherine's reign, and witness (much like Pierre) of Borodino, was not alone in thinking that Tolstoy had impugned the patriotism of the aristocracy in 1812. There were complaints from others who had known the time that Tolstoy failed to catch the tone and the manners. The son of the egregious Count Rostopchin, Governor-General of Moscow in 1812, was among those who protested at Tolstoy's distortions.

The most memorable episode concerning Rostopchin is that when, shortly before the abandonment of Moscow, he sets the mob on to lynching the unfortunate Vereshchagin, who is to be punished as 'the villain who has caused the ruin of Moscow'. Viktor Shklovsky has carefully examined Tolstoy's narrative in relation to his sources. The actual event is little changed by Tolstoy. He does not put into Rostopchin's mouth words that contradict what eyewitnesses heard, though the scene is made more vivid by repetitions: thus (in the Russian text) Rostopchin four times gives the order 'Cut him down!' In the same way, Tolstoy constantly reminds the reader of Vereshchagin's appearance – 'the young man in the fur-lined coat'; he emphasizes the 'long thin neck', and shows how in Vereshchagin's terror 'A vein in the young man's long thin neck swelled like a cord and went blue behind the ear, and suddenly his face flushed.' Tolstoy brings out magnificently the human pathos of the scene, with the unwilling crowd that 'moaned and heaved forward, but again paused', Vereshchagin's 'timid yet theatrical voice', the worse theatre of Rostopchin's incitations to 'cut him down', and the moment at which 'the barrier of human feeling, strained to the utmost...suddenly broke.' Vereshchagin's 'plaintive moan of reproach' – his cry when struck by the blunt side of the soldier's sabre – is fatal to him, and it is 'drowned by the threatening and angry roar of the crowd'.

The account of Rostopchin's confused feelings in his carriage as he leaves the mob is, of course, wholly of Tolstoy's invention. At the memory of Vereshchagin's words 'Count! One God is above us both!' – Tolstoy tells us 'a disagreeable shiver ran down his back. But this was only a momentary feeling and Count Rostopchin smiled disdainfully at himself. "I had other duties," thought he. "The people had to be appeased ...".'. There is no knowing whether Rostopchin entertained such thoughts. Yet the situation would seem to demand them, if he is to live with himself now this outrage has happened. The imaginative truth of this scene is irresistible.

Tolstoy's treatment of Napoleon, as we have noted, is hostile from the beginning, when he had first set down his impressions of the 'romance between Alexander and Napoleon'. Tolstoy felt an antipathy to Napoleon, as he did to the able minister Speransky, because they were plebeians (and no doubt his aversion to Chernyshevsky and Dobrolyubov can be felt here), but even more because they were, in Tolstoy's view, unreal. Napoleon in *War and Peace* appears as a stage emperor, surrounded by burlesque kings of his own creation, and nullified by his own rhetoric. It is hard to believe that Pushkin should have called this mountebank a 'sovereign of our thoughts', or Manzoni have written at Napoleon's death in 1821: 'two centuries/The one armed against the other,/Submissive turned to him/As if they waited on destiny.' Tolstoy denies him all military skill (though it is true that Napoleon lacked his usual flair at Borodino). Since Napoleon has not the root of the matter in him, he is worthless.

Here the philosophy that shaped the novel must be considered. Tolstoy, as we have seen, brought to the interpretation of this history the weight of his own experience. He had become convinced that the outcome of a battle hangs on the plain soldier who does what instinct tells him is right in a moment of crisis. In this way Captain Tushin with a single battery is able to save the army from defeat at Schön Graben – and is afterwards blamed for abandoning a gun, until Prince Andrew speaks up for him. Later in the book Tolstoy formulates the principle: 'Only unconscious action bears fruit, and he who plays a part in an historic event never understands its significance.' The point of view, as so often in Tolstoy's maxims, is exaggerated; but Tolstoy is able to illustrate this time and again in his account of action – particularly in the experience of Nicholas Rostov. And the submission to events, so unavoidable for the soldier in the thick of an engagement, is something that generals must understand, if they are to fulfil the role that Tolstoy allows to them. Thus Bagration at the same battle does not issue orders, except to confirm what is really happening, but 'owing to the tact Bagration showed, his presence was very valuable'. He is an excellent commander, because he concerns himself with the one thing he can influence, the morale of his troops.

The supreme example of this quality is, of course, Kutuzov, who, worldly and self-indulgent old man that he is, yet remains devoted to the mission he has been chosen to carry out. Kutuzov had been appointed commander-in-chief, after Barclay de Tolly was forced to give up Smolensk, by an unwilling Alexander who bowed to popular pressure. When Pushkin, a strong partisan of Barclay, argued his case in 1836, he did not deny that Kutuzov was the man necessary at the moment.

Only Kutuzov could propose the battle of Borodino; only Kutuzov could yield Moscow to the enemy; only Kutuzov could continue in that wise active inactivity, lulling Napoleon to sleep when Moscow burned and awaiting the fatal moment; because Kutuzov alone was invested with the people's confidence, which so marvellously he justified.

Pushkin's testimony is valuable, because it shows the popular view of Kutuzov, which Tolstoy was right to trust, whatever the quibbles of historians. He probably exaggerates the degree of 'wise passiveness' (to use Wordsworth's term) that Kutuzov displays, but essentially the truth was such. Kutuzov in *War and Peace* dozes through the councils of war, ignores the voices dissenting from him, gives every sign of senility; but all the time he is listening to the groundswell of what the Russian people, soldiers and partisans, have to tell him about the war. He becomes the spokes-man of Russian instinct, and it triumphs against all expectation.

Napoleon was no truly great man, because greatness cannot exist 'where simplicity, goodness and truth are absent'. Pierre has long searched for these qualities, which are, of course, manifested in Kutuzov. But Pierre finds them in a common soldier (more accurately, a very uncommon one), Platon Karataev. Whereas Tolstoy's Kutuzov convinces, Platon has not impressed many readers as he did Strakhov, Tolstoy's critic and confidant, for whom this holy fool symbolized 'the strength and beauty of the Russian people'. Tolstoy wanted Platon to be so taken, but whether he achieved the artistic triumph that Strakhov claimed is ques-tionable. Platon represents the very opposite of Prince Andrew, whose pride of intellect and readiness to censure have to be purged in suffering. It is as if Tolstoy sought relief through the conception of Platon from the wearisome struggle with ideas that engaged Prince Andrew and Pierre. This meek peasant is able to give Pierre 'that tranquillity of mind, that inner harmony, which had so impressed him in the soldiers at the battle of Borodino'. Platon lives entirely in the moment, babbling and inconsequential. Yet he is always wise in his unreason. At this time Dostoevsky had just created the image of the 'underground man', set up like Platon (whose name, Plato, could not be more ironically chosen) to counter a life-denying logic. But while the 'underground man' takes obstinate satisfaction in his own meanness, Platon knows nothing of himself; and his love for his neighbour, though unfailing, is involuntary and quite impersonal. Most readers are embarrassed by what they consider to be a rare case of Tolstoy caught faking.

It is only with Platon that he fails to convince in his insistence on the value of 'unconscious' action. The term 'unconsciousness' is disputable, since Kutuzov, for instance, may be called in a deeper sense conscious of what was happening. Tolstoy everywhere places his trust in the primacy of feeling, in the capacity for acting on the spur of the moment when the moment is properly understood. Thus, Nicholas at Voronezh forgets his pledge to Sonya (not spontaneously given) and falls in love with a transformed Princess Mary, when 'a new life-force takes possession of her.' Thus Natasha, who had been so busy organizing the conveyance of the family possessions from Moscow, suddenly insists that the carts should be unloaded to take wounded men. These, and a hundred episodes like them, are persuasive because the decision seems to flow inevitably from the character's awareness.

However, in his quarrel with the historians Tolstoy has not the same authority. We can understand what Turgenev meant when he spoke of 'our genius and crank [taking] the bit between his teeth'. Tolstoy distrusted the historians (who fell under his general ban on specialists) because in the first place they relied upon written reports of warfare which he knew from experience to bear little relation to the facts. Nicholas, called without irony 'a truthful young man', finds that he has to make up a story of what he might have done at Schön Graben, because his hearers would not have accepted the literal truth. Tolstoy's scepticism spreads also to the explanations that historians give of all human affairs. He is very high-handed, and inaccurate, in his account of historical procedures in the Second Epilogue, because his knowledge of the subject was somewhat hastily gathered. But the underlying question still has to be answered: How are we to account for the upheavals of 1812, that drove millions of men to the east, plundering, burning and slaughtering on their way, and then as suddenly drove them back to the west? Tolstoy was aware of the vast labyrinth of connections that lead up to and flow from every action. Perhaps this is especially a novelist's awareness, since for the novelist the world is made up of countless arresting particulars. There are good reasons, as Isaiah Berlin has shown in *The Hedgehog and the Fox*, for attending seriously to Tolstoy's arguments. Their tone may be brutally dogmatic, yet these are matters of great importance that he discusses, and his attention to them added profundity to his novel, even though the way in which they are presented throws the book to some extent out of balance.

Tolstoy's prejudices, to which his contemporaries were so sensitive, cannot be said to have warped the essential truth of *War and Peace*. Even if, as Konstantin Leontiev complained, his characters think the thoughts of Tolstoy's day rather than their own, there is in the book that permanent truth of feeling which Wordsworth believed to be the concern of poetry. Tolstoy has no rival among the novelists in his capacity to realize life, to reveal human beings in their egotism and their ability at times to fulfil themselves innocently and in harmony with the world. *War and Peace*, though depicting cruelty and disaster on a huge scale, can be fairly described as an essay in harmony. It affirms that man is inescapably a moral creature, and that he achieves his fulfilment in unpretentiously being himself.

HENRY GIFFORD

# NOTE ON THE TRANSLATION

AYLMER MAUDE and his wife Louise, the translators responsible for the *Centenary Edition of Tolstoy's Works* (Oxford, 1928–37), knew both Tolstoy and Russia intimately. Louise was born in Moscow and lived there for forty years; Aylmer Maude spent two years at a Moscow school, and stayed in Russia for twenty-three years. He met Tolstoy in 1888, and became a friend and a disciple, though with some reservations. Tolstoy often expressed his gratitude to them both for their service as translators, because they were fully competent in both languages, meticulous throughout, and devoted to his work. Maude's *Life of Tolstoy* (Oxford, 1930) remains a valuable account by one who understood him well, and had played a useful part in one of Tolstoy's most cherished projects – the resettlement of the Dukhobors in Canada.

The Maudes' translation has appeared hitherto in three volumes, consisting in all of fifteen books and two Epilogues. These have now been aligned with the standard Russian text in four books and fifteen parts, after a few minor adjustments.

The translation was accompanied by footnotes, and other more detailed notes at the end of each volume. Many of these have been preserved, some augmented, others altogether replaced, and certain new notes have been written. Of particular interest are the original notes on Russian manners and customs, from Maude's long familiarity with the people.

# SELECT BIBLIOGRAPHY

*The Centenary Edition of Tolstoy* in 21 vols. (Oxford, 1928–37) has translations by Louise and Aylmer Maude of his principal works. The World's Classics paperback editions include *Anna Karenina* and *The Raid and Other Stories*.

Tolstoy's *Letters* have been edited in 2 vols. by R. F. Christian (London, 1978).

There are biographies by Aylmer Maude in 2 vols. (Oxford, 1930), E. J. Simmons in 2 vols. (Boston, Mass., 1945–6; Vintage paperback, 1960) and Henri Troyat (London, 1960; Penguin paperback, 1970).

Critical studies include John Bayley, *Tolstoy and the Novel* (London, 1966), R. F. Christian, *Tolstoy: A Critical Introduction* (Cambridge, 1969), Henry Gifford, *Tolstoy* (Oxford: Past Masters, 1982), Malcolm Jones, ed., *New Essays on Tolstoy* (Cambridge, 1978), Ralph E. Matlaw, ed., *Tolstoy: A Collection of Critical Essays* (New Jersey, 1967).

The following have special reference to *War and Peace*: Isaiah Berlin, *The Hedgehog and the Fox* (London, 1953; reprinted in his *Russian Thinkers*, London, 1978); R. F. Christian, *Tolstoy's 'War and Peace'*: A Study (Oxford, 1962).

For contemporary criticisms of *War and Peace* see A. V. Knowles, ed., *Tolstoy: The Critical Heritage* (London, 1978).

# CHRONOLOGY OF LEO TOLSTOY

1828    28 August (O.S.): born at Yasnaya Polyana, province of Tula, fourth son of Count Nikolay Tolstoy. Mother dies 1830, father 1837.

1844–7  Studies at University of Kazan (Oriental Languages, then Law). Leaves without graduating.

1851    Goes to Caucasus with elder brother. Participates in army raid on local village. Begins to write *Childhood* (publ. 1852).

1854    Commissioned. *Boyhood.** Active service on Danube; gets posting to Sevastopol.

1855    After its fall returns to Petersburg, already famous for his first two *Sevastopol Sketches*. Literary and social life in the capital.

1856    Leaves army. *A Landlord's Morning*.

1857    Visits Western Europe. August: returns to Yasnaya Polyana.

1859    His interest and success in literature wane. Founds on his estate a school for peasant children. *Three Deaths; Family Happiness*.

1860–1  Second visit to Western Europe, in order to study educational methods.

1861    Serves as Arbiter of the Peace, to negotiate land settlements after Emancipation of Serfs.

1862    Death of two brothers. Marries Sophia Behrs, daughter of a Moscow physician. There were to be thirteen children of the marriage, only eight growing up. Publishes educational magazine *Yasnaya Polyana*.

1863    *The Cossacks; Polikushka*. Begins *War and Peace*.

1865–6  *1805* (first part of *War and Peace*).

1866    Unsuccessfully defends at court martial soldier who had struck officer.

1869    *War and Peace* completed; final vols. published.

1870    Studies drama and Greek.

1871–2  Working on *Primer* for children.

1872    *A Prisoner in the Caucasus*.

1873    Goes with family to visit new estate in Samara. Publicizes Samara famine. Begins *Anna Karenina* (completed 1877).

* Tolstoy's works are dated, unless otherwise indicated, according to the year of publication.

# PRINCIPAL CHARACTERS
## AND GUIDE TO PRONUNCIATION

THE names by which the principal characters are usually known are given in capitals. The stressed syllable is marked with an acute accent; ë is pronounced *yo*, and always stressed. The stress on some of the principal place-names is also given below.

## THE BEZÚKHOVS

COUNT Cyril BEZÚKHOV·

PIERRE, his son, legitimized after his father's death, becomes Count Peter BEZÚKHOV.

Princess CATICHE, Pierre's cousin.

## THE ROSTÓVS*

COUNT Ilyá ROSTÓV.

COUNTESS Nataly ROSTÓVA, his wife.

Count NICHOLAS Rostóv (Nikólenka), their elder son.

Count Peter Rostóv (PÉTYA), their second son.

Countess VÉRA Rostóva, their elder daughter.

Countess Nataly Rostóva (NATÁSHA), their younger daughter.

SÓNYA, a poor member of the Rostóv family circle.

BERG, Alphonse Kárlich, an officer of German extraction who marries Véra.

## THE BOLKÓNSKYS

PRINCE Nicholas BOLKÓNSKY, a retired General-in-Chief.

PRINCE ANDREW Bolkónsky, his son.

PRINCESS MARY (Másha) Bolkónskaya, his daughter.

Princess Elizabeth Bolkónskaya (LISE), Andrew's wife.

TÍKHON, Prince N. Bolkónsky's attendant.

ALPÁTYCH, his steward.

## THE KURÁGINS

PRINCE VASÍLI Kurágin.

Prince HIPPOLYTE Kurágin, his elder son.

* So stressed by Maude, probably on the analogy of the place-name; but A. B. Goldenveizer (*Vblízi Tolstogo*, Moscow 1959, p. 371) reports that Tolstoy himself always stressed it Róstov.

Prince ANATOLE Kurágin, his younger son.

Princess HÉLÈNE Kurágina (Lëlya), his daughter, who marries Pierre.

Princess ANNA MIKHÁYLOVNA Drubetskáya.

Prince BORÍS Drubetskóy (Bóry), her son.

JULIE Karágina, an heiress who marries Borís.

MÁRYA DMÍTRIEVNA Akhrosímova (*le terrible dragon*).

BILÍBIN, a diplomat.

DENÍSOV, Vasíli Dmítrich (Váska), an hussar officer.

Lavrúshka, his batman.

DÓLOKHOV (Fédya), an officer and desperado.

Count Rostopchín, Governor of Moscow.

ANNA PÁVLOVNA Scherer (Annette), Maid of Honour to the ex-Empress Márya Fëdorovna.

Shinshín, a relation of Countess Rostóva's.

Timókhin, an infantry officer.

Túshin, an artillery officer.

Platon KARATÁEV, a peasant.

| | |
|---|---|
| Boguchárovo | Shevárdino |
| Borodinó ←important Battle of novel! | Smolénsk |
| Málo–Yaroslávets | Torzhók |
| Mytíshchi | Vorónezh |
| Ryazán | Vyázma |

austerlitz

# DATES OF PRINCIPAL EVENTS

## 1805

o.s.

| | |
|---|---|
| 11 Oct.* | Kutuzov inspects regiment near Braunau. *Le malheureux Mack* arrives. |
| 23 Oct. | The Russian army crosses the Enns. |
| 24 Oct. | Fight at Amstetten. |
| 28 Oct. | The Russian army crosses the Danube. |
| 30 Oct. | Defeats Mortier at Dürrenstein. |
| 4 Nov. | Napoleon writes to Murat from Schönbrunn. Battle of Schön Graben. |
| 19 Nov. | The Council of War at Ostralitz. |
| 20 Nov. | Battle of Austerlitz. |

## 1807

| | |
|---|---|
| 27 Jan. | Battle of Preussisch-Eylau. |
| 2 June | Battle of Friedland. |
| 13 June | The Emperors meet at Tilsit. |

## 1812

| | |
|---|---|
| 17 May | Napoleon leaves Dresden. |
| 12 June | Napoleon crosses the Niemen and enters Russia. |
| 14 June | Alexander sends Balashev to Napoleon. |
| 13 July | The Pavlograd hussars in action at Ostrovna. |
| 4 Aug. | Alpatych at Smolensk hears distant firing. |
| 5 Aug. | Bombardment of Smolensk. |
| 7 Aug. | Prince Nicholas Bolkonsky leaves Bald Hills for Bogucharovo. |
| 8 Aug. | Kutuzov appointed Commander-in-Chief. |
| 10 Aug. | Prince Andrew's column abreast of Bald Hills. |
| 17 Aug. | Kutuzov reaches Tsarevo-Zaymishche and takes command of the army. |
| | Nicholas Rostov rides to Bogucharovo. |
| 24 Aug. | Battle of the Shevardino Redoubt. |
| 26 Aug. | Battle of Borodino. |

\* To adjust nineteenth-century old-style dates to our western calendar twelve days have to be added in each case.

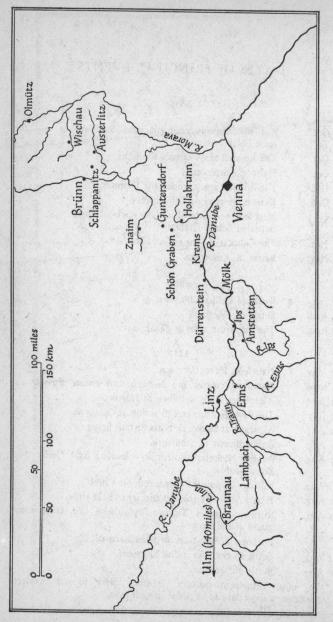

100 miles

150 km

Olmütz

Wischau

Austerlitz

Schlappanitz

Brünn

Znaim

Guntersdorf

Schön Graben

Hollabrunn

R. Morava

Krems

R. Danube

Vienna

Dürrenstein

Mölk

Ips

Amstetten

R. Ips

R. Enns

Linz

Enns

R. Traun

Lambach

Braunau

R. Danube

R. Inn

Ulm (140 miles)

1. THE 1805 CAMPAIGN

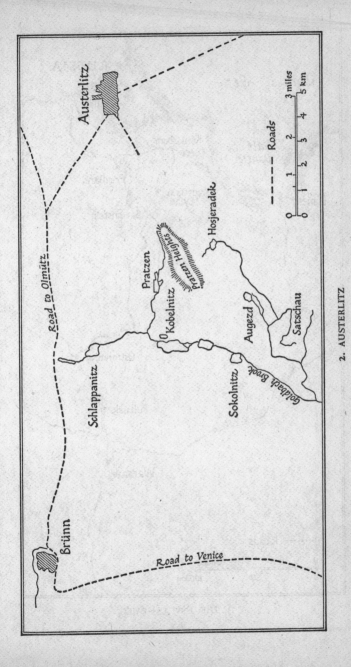

Austerlitz

Road to Olmütz

Brünn

Road to Venice

Schlappanitz

Pratzen

Kobelnitz

Pratzen Heights

Hosjeradek

Sokolnitz

Goldbach Brook

Augezd

Satschau

Roads

3 miles

5 km

2. AUSTERLITZ

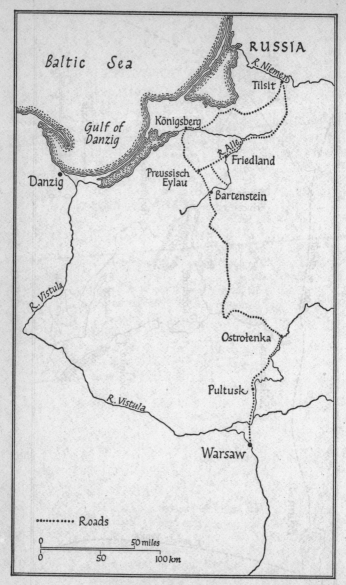

Baltic Sea

RUSSIA

R. Niemen

Tilsit

Gulf of
Danzig

Königsberg

R. Alle

Friedland

Danzig

Preussisch
Eylau

Bartenstein

R. Vistula

Ostrołenka

R. Vistula

Pultusk

Warsaw

.......... Roads

0        50 miles
0        50        100 km

3. THE 1807 CAMPAIGN

# CHAPTER CONTENTS

## VOLUME ONE

## BOOK ONE

### PART I

### PART II

## BOOK TWO

### PART I

### PART II

## PART III

## PART V

(Continued in Volume Two)

# WAR AND PEACE

\*

## BOOK ONE

# PART ONE

## 1

'WELL, Prince, so Genoa and Lucca are now just family estates of the Buonapartes.* But I warn you, if you don't tell me that this means war, if you still try to defend the infamies and horrors perpetrated by that Antichrist – I really believe he is Antichrist – I will have nothing more to do with you and you are no longer my friend, no longer my "faithful slave", as you call yourself! But how do you do? I see I have frightened you – sit down and tell me all the news.'

It was in July 1805, and the speaker was the well-known Anna Pavlovna Scherer, maid of honour and favourite of the Empress Marya Fëdorovna. With these words she greeted Prince Vasili, a man of high rank and importance, who was the first to arrive at her reception. Anna Pavlovna had had a cough for some days. She was, as she said, suffering from *la grippe; grippe* being then a new word in St Petersburg, used only by the *élite*.

All her invitations without exception, written in French, and delivered by a scarlet-liveried footman that morning, ran as follows:

If you have nothing better to do, Count (or Prince), and if the prospect of spending an evening with a poor invalid is not too terrible, I shall be very charmed to see you to-night between 7 and 10.

Annette Scherer.

'Heavens! what a virulent attack!' replied the prince, not in the least disconcerted by this reception. He had just entered, wearing an embroidered court uniform, knee-breeches and shoes, and had stars on his breast and a serene expression on his flat face. He spoke in that refined French in which our grandfathers not only spoke but thought, and with the gentle, patronizing intonation natural to a man of importance who had grown old in society and at court. He went up to Anna Pavlovna, kissed her hand, presenting to her his bald, scented and shining head, and complacently seated himself on the sofa.

'First of all, dear friend, tell me how you are. Set your friend's mind at rest,' said he without altering his tone, beneath the

3

politeness and affected sympathy of which indifference and even irony could be discerned.

'Can one be well while suffering morally? Can one be calm in times like these if one has any feeling?' said Anna Pavlovna. 'You are staying the whole evening, I hope?'

'And the fête at the English Ambassador's? To-day is Wednesday. I must put in an appearance there,' said the prince. 'My daughter is coming for me to take me there.'

'I thought to-day's fête had been cancelled. I confess all these festivities and fireworks are becoming wearisome.'

'If they had known that you wished it, the entertainment would have been put off,' said the prince, who, like a wound-up clock, by force of habit said things he did not even wish to be believed.

'Don't tease! Well, and what has been decided about Novosiltsev's dispatch?* You know everything.'

'What can one say about it?' replied the prince in a cold, listless tone. 'What has been decided? They have decided that Buonaparte has burnt his boats, and I believe that we are ready to burn ours.'

Prince Vasili always spoke languidly, like an actor repeating a stale part. Anna Pavlovna Scherer on the contrary, despite her forty years, overflowed with animation and impulsiveness. To be an enthusiast had become her social vocation and, sometimes even when she did not feel like it, she became enthusiastic in order not to disappoint the expectations of those who knew her. The subdued smile which, though it did not suit her faded features, always played round her lips, expressed, as in a spoilt child, a continual consciousness of her charming defect, which she neither wished, nor could, nor considered it necessary, to correct.

In the midst of a conversation on political matters Anna Pavlovna burst out:

'Oh, don't speak to me of Austria. Perhaps I don't understand things, but Austria never has wished, and does not wish, for war. She is betraying us! Russia alone must save Europe. Our gracious sovereign recognizes his high vocation and will be true to it. That is the one thing I have faith in! Our good and wonderful sovereign has to perform the noblest rôle on earth, and he is so virtuous and noble that God will not forsake him. He will fulfil his vocation and crush the hydra of revolution, which has become more terrible than ever in the person of this murderer and villain! We alone must avenge the blood of the just one ... Whom, I ask you, can we rely on ...? England with her commercial spirit will not and cannot understand the Emperor Alexander's loftiness of soul. She has refused to evacuate Malta. She wanted to find, and still seeks, some secret motive in our actions. What answer did

4

Novosiltsev get? None. The English have not understood and cannot understand the self-abnegation of our Emperor who wants nothing for himself, but only desires the good of mankind. And what have they promised? Nothing! And what little they have promised they will not perform! Prussia has always declared that Buonaparte is invincible and that all Europe is powerless before him...And I don't believe a word that Hardenberg says, or Haugwitz either. This famous Prussian neutrality is just a trap. I have faith only in God and the lofty destiny of our adored monarch. He will save Europe!'

She suddenly paused, smiling at her own impetuosity.

'I think,' said the prince with a smile, 'that if you had been sent instead of our dear Wintzingerode you would have captured the King of Prussia's consent by assault. You are so eloquent. Will you give me a cup of tea?'

'In a moment. A *propos*,' she added, becoming calm again, 'I am expecting two very interesting men to-night, le Vicomte de Mortemart, who is connected with the Montmorencys through the Rohans, one of the best French families. He is one of the genuine *émigrés*, the good ones. And also the Abbé Morio. Do you know that profound thinker? He has been received by the Emperor. Had you heard?'

'I shall be delighted to meet them,' said the prince. 'But tell me,' he added with studied carelessness as if it had only just occurred to him, though the question he was about to ask was the chief motive of his visit, 'is it true that the Dowager Empress wants Baron Funke to be appointed first secretary at Vienna? The baron by all accounts is a poor creature.'

Prince Vasili wished to obtain this post for his son, but others were trying through the Dowager Empress Marya Fëdorovna to secure it for the baron.

Anna Pavlovna almost closed her eyes to indicate that neither she nor anyone else had a right to criticize what the Empress desired or was pleased with.

'Baron Funke has been recommended to the Dowager Empress by her sister,' was all she said, in a dry and mournful tone.

As she named the Empress, Anna Pavlovna's face suddenly assumed an expression of profound and sincere devotion and respect, mingled with sadness, and this occurred every time she mentioned her illustrious patroness. She added that her Majesty had deigned to show Baron Funke *beaucoup d'estime*, and again her face clouded over with sadness.

The prince was silent and looked indifferent. But, with the womanly and courtier-like quickness and tact habitual to her, Anna

Pavlovna wished both to rebuke him (for daring to speak as he had done of a man recommended to the Empress) and at the same time to console him, so she said—

'Now about your family. Do you know that since your daughter came out everyone has been enraptured by her? They say she is amazingly beautiful.'

The prince bowed to signify his respect and gratitude.

'I often think,' she continued after a short pause, drawing nearer to the prince and smiling amiably at him as if to show that political and social topics were ended and the time had come for intimate conversation – 'I often think how unfairly sometimes the joys of life are distributed. Why has fate given you two such splendid children? I don't speak of Anatole, your youngest. I don't like him,' she added in a tone admitting of no rejoinder and raising her eyebrows. 'Two such charming children. And really you appreciate them less than anyone, and so you don't deserve to have them.'

And she smiled her ecstatic smile.

'I can't help it,' said the prince. 'Lavater would have said I lack the bump of paternity.'

'Don't joke; I mean to have a serious talk with you. Do you know I am dissatisfied with your younger son? Between ourselves' (and her face assumed its melancholy expression) 'he was mentioned at her Majesty's and you were pitied . . .'

The prince answered nothing, but she looked at him significantly, awaiting a reply. He frowned.

'What would you have me do?' he said at last. 'You know I did all a father could for their education, and they have both turned out fools. Hippolyte is at least a quiet fool, but Anatole is an active one. That is the only difference between them.' He said this smiling in a way more natural and animated than usual, so that the wrinkles round his mouth very clearly revealed something unexpectedly coarse and unpleasant.

'And why are children born to such men as you? If you were not a father there would be nothing I could reproach you with,' said Anna Pavlovna, looking up pensively.

'I am your faithful slave, and to you alone I can confess that my children are the bane of my life. It is the cross I have to bear. That is how I explain it to myself. It can't be helped!'

He said no more, but expressed his resignation to cruel fate by a gesture. Anna Pavlovna meditated.

'Have you never thought of marrying your prodigal son Anatole?' she asked. 'They say old maids have a mania for match-making, and though I don't feel that weakness in myself as yet,

I know a little person who is very unhappy with her father. She is a relation of yours, Princess Marya Bolkonskaya.

Prince Vasili did not reply though, with the quickness of memory and perception befitting a man of the world, he indicated by a movement of the head that he was considering this information.

'Do you know,' he said at last, evidently unable to check the sad current of his thoughts, 'that Anatole is costing me forty thousand rubles a year? And', he went on after a pause, 'what will it be in five years, if he goes on like this?' Presently he added: 'That's what we fathers have to put up with ... Is this princess of yours rich?'

'Her father is very rich and stingy. He lives in the country. He is the well-known Prince Bolkonsky who had to retire from the army under the late Emperor, and was nicknamed "the King of Prussia". He is very clever but eccentric, and a bore. The poor girl is very unhappy. She has a brother; I think you know him, he married Lisa Meinen lately. He is an aide-de-camp of Kutuzov's and will be here to-night.'

'Listen, dear Annette,' said the prince, suddenly taking Anna Pavlovna's hand and for some reason drawing it downwards. 'Arrange that affair for me and I shall always be your most devoted slave – *slafe* with an f, as a village elder of mine writes in his reports. She is rich and of good family and that's all I want.'

And with the familiarity and easy grace peculiar to him, he raised the maid of honour's hand to his lips, kissed it, and swung it to and fro as he lay back in his arm-chair, looking in another direction.

'*Attendez*,' said Anna Pavlovna, reflecting, 'I'll speak to Lisa, young Bolkonsky's wife, this very evening, and perhaps the thing can be arranged. It shall be on your family's behalf that I'll start my apprenticeship as old maid.'

2

ANNA PAVLOVNA'S drawing-room was gradually filling. The highest Petersburg society was assembled there: people differing widely in age and character but alike in the social circle to which they belonged. Prince Vasili's daughter, the beautiful Hélène, came to take her father to the ambassador's entertainment; she wore a ball dress and her badge as maid of honour. The youthful little Princess Bolkonskaya, known as *la femme la plus séduisante de Pétersbourg*, was also there. She had been married during the previous winter, and being pregnant did not go to any large gatherings, but only to small receptions. Prince Vasili's son, Hippolyte, had come with Mortemart, whom he introduced. The Abbé Morio and many others had also come.

To each new arrival Anna Pavlovna said, 'You have not yet seen my aunt,' or 'You do not know my aunt?' and very gravely conducted him or her to a little old lady, wearing large bows of ribbons in her cap, who had come sailing in from another room as soon as the guests began to arrive; and slowly turning her eyes from the visitor to her aunt, Anna Pavlovna mentioned each one's name and then left them.

Each visitor performed the ceremony of greeting this old aunt whom not one of them knew, not one of them wanted to know, and not one of them cared about; Anna Pavlovna observed these greetings with mournful and solemn interest and silent approval. The aunt spoke to each of them in the same words, about their health and her own, and the health of her Majesty, 'who, thank God, was better to-day.' And each visitor, though politeness prevented his showing impatience, left the old woman with a sense of relief at having performed a vexatious duty and did not return to her the whole evening.

The young Princess Bolkonskaya had brought some work in a gold-embroidered velvet bag. Her pretty little upper lip, on which a delicate dark down was just perceptible, was too short for her teeth, but it lifted all the more sweetly, and was especially charming when she occasionally drew it down to meet the lower lip. As is always the case with a thoroughly attractive woman, her defect – the shortness of her upper lip and her half open mouth – seemed to be her own special and peculiar form of beauty. Everyone brightened at the sight of this pretty young woman, so soon to become a mother, so full of life and health, and carrying her burden so lightly. Old men and dull dispirited young ones who looked at her, after being in her company and talking to her a little while, felt as if they too were becoming, like her, full of life and health. All who talked to her, and at each word saw her bright smile and the constant gleam of her white teeth, thought that they were in a specially amiable mood that day.

The little princess went round the table with quick short swaying steps, her workbag on her arm, and gaily spreading out her dress sat down on a sofa near the silver samovar, as if all she was doing was a pleasure to herself and to all around her. 'I have brought my work,' said she in French, displaying her bag and addressing all present. 'Mind, Annette, I hope you have not played a wicked trick on me,' she added, turning to her hostess. 'You wrote that it was to be quite a small reception, and just see how

8

badly I am dressed.' And she spread out her arms to show her short-waisted, lace-trimmed, dainty grey dress, girdled with a broad ribbon just below the breast.

'*Soyez tranquille, Lise*, you will always be prettier than anyone else,' replied Anna Pavlovna.

'You know,' said the princess in the same tone of voice and still in French, turning to a general, 'my husband is deserting me? He is going to get himself killed. Tell me what this wretched war is for?' she added, addressing Prince Vasili, and without waiting for an answer she turned to speak to his daughter, the beautiful Hélène.

'What a delightful woman this little princess is!' said Prince Vasili to Anna Pavlovna.

One of the next arrivals was a stout, heavily built young man with close-cropped hair, spectacles, the light-coloured breeches fashionable at that time, a very high ruffle and a brown dress-coat. The stout young man was an illegitimate son of Count Bezukhov, a well-known grandee of Catherine's time who now lay dying in Moscow. The young man had not yet entered either the military or civil service, as he had only just returned from abroad where he had been educated, and this was his first appearance in society. Anna Pavlovna greeted him with the nod she accorded to the lowest hierarchy in her drawing-room. But in spite of this lowest grade greeting, a look of anxiety and fear, as at the sight of something too large and unsuited to the place, came over her face when she saw Pierre enter. Though he was certainly rather bigger than the other men in the room her anxiety could only have reference to the clever though shy, but observant and natural, expression which distinguished him from everyone else in that drawing-room.

'It is very good of you, Monsieur Pierre, to come and visit a poor invalid,' said Anna Pavlovna, exchanging an alarmed glance with her aunt as she conducted him to her.

Pierre murmured something unintelligible, and continued to look round as if in search of something. On his way to the aunt he bowed to the little princess with a pleased smile, as to an intimate acquaintance.

Anna Pavlovna's alarm was justified, for Pierre turned away from the aunt without waiting to hear her speech about her Majesty's health. Anna Pavlovna in dismay detained him with the words:

'Do you know the Abbé Morio? He is a most interesting man.'

'Yes, I have heard of his scheme for perpetual peace, and it is very interesting but hardly feasible.'

'You think so?' rejoined Anna Pavlovna in order to say something and get away to attend to her duties as hostess. But Pierre now committed a reverse act of impoliteness. First he had left a lady before she had finished speaking to him, and now he continued to speak to another who wished to get away. With his head bent, and his big feet spread apart, he began explaining his reasons for thinking the abbé's plan chimerical.

'We will talk of it later,' said Anna Pavlovna with a smile.

And having got rid of this young man who did not know how to behave, she resumed her duties as hostess and continued to listen and watch, ready to help at any point where the conversation might happen to flag. As the foreman of a spinning-mill when he has set the hands to work, goes round and notices, here a spindle that has stopped or there one that creaks or makes more noise than it should, and hastens to check the machine or set it in proper motion, so Anna Pavlovna moved about her drawing-room, approaching now a silent, now a too noisy group, and by a word or slight rearrangement kept the conversational machine in steady, proper and regular motion. But amid these cares her anxiety about Pierre was evident. She kept an anxious watch on him when he approached the group round Mortemart to listen to what was being said there, and again when he passed to another group whose centre was the abbé.

Pierre had been educated abroad, and this reception at Anna Pavlovna's was the first he had attended in Russia. He knew that all the intellectual lights of Petersburg were gathered there and, like a child in a toy shop, did not know which way to look, afraid of missing any clever conversation that was to be heard. Seeing the self-confident and refined expression on the faces of those present he was always expecting to hear something very profound. At last he came up to Morio. Here the conversation seemed interesting and he stood waiting for an opportunity to express his own views, as young people are fond of doing.

3

ANNA PAVLOVNA'S reception was in full swing. The spindles hummed steadily and ceaselessly on all sides. With the exception of the aunt, beside whom sat only one elderly lady, who with her thin careworn face was rather out of place in this brilliant society, the whole company had settled into three groups. One, chiefly masculine, had formed round the abbé. Another, of young people, was grouped round the beautiful Princess Hélène, Prince Vasili's daughter, and the little Princess Bolkonskaya, very pretty and rosy, though rather too plump for her age. The third group was gathered round Mortemart and Anna Pavlovna.

The vicomte was a nice-looking young man with soft features and polished manners, who evidently considered himself a celebrity but out of politeness modestly placed himself at the disposal of the circle in which he found himself. Anna Pavlovna was obviously serving him up as a treat to her guests. As a clever *maître d'hôtel* serves up as a specially choice delicacy a piece of meat that no one who had seen it in the kitchen would have cared to eat, so Anna Pavlovna served up to her guests, first the vicomte and then the abbé, as peculiarly choice morsels. The group about Mortemart immediately began discussing the murder of the Duc d'Enghien.* The vicomte said that the Duc d'Enghien had perished by his own magnanimity, and that there were particular reasons for Buona-parte's hatred of him.

'Ah, yes! Do tell us all about it, vicomte,' said Anna Pavlovna, with a pleasant feeling that there was something *à la Louis* XV in the sound of that sentence: '*Contez nous cela, vicomte.*'

The vicomte bowed and smiled courteously in token of his willingness to comply. Anna Pavlovna arranged a group round him, inviting everyone to listen to his tale.

'The vicomte knew the duc personally,' whispered Anna Pavlovna to one of the guests. 'The vicomte is a wonderful *raconteur*,' said she to another. 'How evidently he belongs to the best society,' said she to a third; and the vicomte was served up to the company in the choicest and most advantageous style, like a well-garnished joint of roast beef on a hot dish.

The vicomte wished to begin his story and gave a subtle smile.

'Come over here, Hélène, dear,' said Anna Pavlovna to the beautiful young princess who was sitting some way off, the centre of another group.

The princess smiled. She rose with the same unchanging smile with which she had first entered the room – the smile of a perfectly beautiful woman. With a slight rustle of her white dress trimmed with moss and ivy, with a gleam of white shoulders, glossy hair and sparkling diamonds, she passed between the men who made way for her, not looking at any of them but smiling on all, as if graciously allowing each the privilege of admiring her beautiful figure and shapely shoulders, back, and bosom – which in the fashion of those days were very much exposed – and she seemed to bring the glamour of a ball-room with her as she moved towards Anna Pavlovna. Hélène was so lovely that not only did she not show any trace of coquetry, but on the contrary she even appeared

11

shy of her unquestionable and all too victorious beauty. She seemed to wish, but to be unable, to diminish its effect.

'How lovely!' said everyone who saw her; and the vicomte lifted his shoulders and dropped his eyes as if startled by something extraordinary when she took her seat opposite and beamed upon him also with her unchanging smile.

'Madame, I doubt my ability before such an audience,' said he, smilingly inclining his head.

The princess rested her bare round arm on a little table and considered a reply unnecessary. She smilingly waited. All the time the story was being told she sat upright, glancing now at her beautiful round arm, altered in shape by its pressure on the table, now at her still more beautiful bosom, on which she readjusted a diamond necklace. From time to time she smoothed the folds of her dress, and whenever the story produced an effect she glanced at Anna Pavlovna, at once adopted just the expression she saw on the maid of honour's face, and again relapsed into her radiant smile.

The little princess had also left the tea-table and followed Hélène.

'Wait a moment, I'll get my work... Now then, what are you thinking of?' she went on, turning to Prince Hippolyte. 'Fetch me my work-bag.'

There was a general movement as the princess, smiling and talking merrily to everyone at once, sat down and gaily arranged herself in her seat.

'Now I am all right,' she said, and asking the vicomte to begin, she took up her work.

Prince Hippolyte, having brought the work-bag, joined the circle and moving a chair close to hers seated himself beside her.

Le charmant Hippolyte was surprising by his extraordinary resemblance to his beautiful sister, but yet more by the fact that in spite of this resemblance he was exceedingly ugly. His features were like his sister's, but while in her case everything was lit up by a joyous, self-satisfied, youthful, and constant smile of animation, and by the wonderful classic beauty of her figure, his face on the contrary was dulled by imbecility and a constant expression of sullen self-confidence, while his body was thin and weak. His eyes, nose, and mouth all seemed puckered into a vacant, wearied grimace, and his arms and legs always fell into unnatural positions.

'It's not going to be a ghost story?' said he, sitting down beside the princess and hastily adjusting his lorgnette, as if without this instrument he could not begin to speak.

'Why no, my dear fellow,' said the astonished narrator, shrugging his shoulders.

'Because I hate ghost stories,' said Prince Hippolyte in a tone which showed that he only understood the meaning of his words after he had uttered them.

He spoke with such self-confidence that his hearers could not be sure whether what he said was very witty or very stupid. He was dressed in a dark-green dress coat, knee-breeches of the colour of *cuisse de nymphe effrayée*, as he called it, shoes and silk stockings.

The vicomte told his tale very neatly. It was an anecdote, then current, to the effect that the Duc d'Enghien had gone secretly to Paris to visit Mademoiselle George;* that at her house he came upon Bonaparte, who also enjoyed the famous actress's favours, and that in his presence Napoleon happened to fall into one of the fainting fits to which he was subject, and was thus at the duc's mercy. The latter spared him, and this magnanimity Bonaparte subsequently repaid by death.

The story was very pretty and interesting, especially at the point where the rivals suddenly recognized one another; and the ladies looked agitated.

'Charming!' said Anna Pavlovna with an inquiring glance at the little princess.

'Charming!' whispered the little princess, sticking the needle into her work as if to testify that the interest and fascination of the story prevented her from going on with it.

The vicomte appreciated this silent praise and smiling gratefully prepared to continue, but just then Anna Pavlovna, who had kept a watchful eye on the young man who so alarmed her, noticed that he was talking too loudly and vehemently with the abbé, so she hurried to the rescue. Pierre had managed to start a conversation with the abbé about the balance of power, and the latter, evidently interested by the young man's simple-minded eagerness, was explaining his pet theory. Both were talking and listening too eagerly and too naturally, which was why Anna Pavlovna disapproved.

'The means are ... the balance of power in Europe and the rights of the people,' the abbé was saying. 'It is only necessary for one powerful nation like Russia – barbaric as she is said to be – to place herself disinterestedly at the head of an alliance having for its object the maintenance of the balance of power in Europe, and it would save the world!'

'But how are you to get that balance?' Pierre was beginning.

At that moment Anna Pavlovna came up, and looking severely at Pierre, asked the Italian how he stood the Russian climate. The Italian's face instantly changed and assumed an offensively affected, sugary expression, evidently habitual to him when conversing with women.

'I am so enchanted by the brilliancy of the wit and culture of the society, more especially of the feminine society, in which I have had the honour of being received, that I have not yet had time to think of the climate,' said he.

Not letting the abbé and Pierre escape, Anna Pavlovna, the more conveniently to keep them under observation, brought them into the larger circle.

Just then another visitor entered the drawing-room: Prince Andrew Bolkonsky, the little princess's husband. He was a very handsome young man, of medium height, with firm, clear-cut features. Everything about him, from his weary, bored expression to his quiet, measured step, offered a most striking contrast to his lively little wife. It was evident that he not only knew everyone in the drawing-room, but had found them to be so tiresome that it wearied him to look at or listen to them. And among all these faces that he found so tedious, none seemed to bore him so much as that of his pretty wife. He turned away from her with a grimace that distorted his handsome face, kissed Anna Pavlovna's hand, and screwing up his eyes scanned the whole company.

'You are off to the war, Prince?' said Anna Pavlovna.

'General Kutuzov,' said Bolkonsky, speaking French and stressing the last syllable of the general's name like a Frenchman, 'has been pleased to take me as an aide-de-camp. . . .'

'And Lise, your wife?'

'She will go to the country.'

'Are you not ashamed to deprive us of your charming wife?'

'André,' said his wife, addressing her husband in the same coquettish manner in which she spoke to other men, 'the vicomte has been telling us such a tale about Mademoiselle George and Buonaparte!'

Prince Andrew screwed up his eyes and turned away. Pierre, who from the moment Prince Andrew entered the room had watched him with glad, affectionate eyes, now came up and took his arm. Before he looked round Prince Andrew frowned again, expressing his annoyance with whoever was touching his arm, but when he saw Pierre's beaming face he gave him an unexpectedly kind and pleasant smile.

'There now! . . . So you, too, are in the great world?' said he to Pierre.

'I knew you would be here,' replied Pierre. 'I will come to supper with you. May I?' he added in a low voice so as not to disturb the vicomte who was continuing his story.

'No, impossible!' said Prince Andrew, laughing and pressing Pierre's hand to show that there was no need to ask the question. He wished to say something more, but at that moment Prince Vasili and his daughter got up to go and the two young men rose to let them pass.

'You must excuse me, dear Vicomte,' said Prince Vasili to the Frenchman, holding him down by the sleeve in a friendly way to prevent his rising. 'This unfortunate fête at the ambassador's deprives me of a pleasure, and obliges me to interrupt you. I am very sorry to leave your enchanting party,' said he, turning to Anna Pavlovna.

His daughter, Princess Hélène, passed between the chairs lightly holding up the folds of her dress, and the smile shone still more radiantly on her beautiful face. Pierre gazed at her with rapturous, almost frightened, eyes as she passed him.

'Very lovely,' said Prince Andrew.

'Very,' said Pierre.

In passing, Prince Vasili seized Pierre's hand and said to Anna Pavlovna:

'Educate this bear for me! He has been staying with me a whole month and this is the first time I have seen him in society. Nothing is so necessary for a young man as the society of clever women.'

4

ANNA PAVLOVNA smiled and promised to take Pierre in hand. She knew his father to be a connexion of Prince Vasili's. The elderly lady who had been sitting with the old aunt rose hurriedly and overtook Prince Vasili in the ante-room. All the affectation of interest she had assumed had left her kindly and tear-worn face and it now expressed only anxiety and fear.

'How about my son Boris, Prince?' said she, hurrying after him into the ante-room. 'I can't remain any longer in Petersburg. Tell me what news I may take back to my poor boy.'

Although Prince Vasili listened reluctantly and not very politely to the elderly lady, even betraying some impatience, she gave him an ingratiating and appealing smile, and took his hand that he might not go away.

'What would it cost you to say a word to the Emperor, and then he would be transferred to the Guards at once?' said she.

'Believe me, Princess, I am ready to do all I can,' answered Prince Vasili, 'but it is difficult for me to ask the Emperor. I should advise you to appeal to Rumyantsev through Prince Golitsin. That would be the best way.'

The elderly lady was a Princess Drubetskaya, belonging to one of the best families in Russia, but she was poor, and having long been out of society had lost her former influential connexions. She had now come to Petersburg to procure an appointment in the Guards for her only son. It was, in fact, solely to meet Prince Vasili that she had obtained an invitation to Anna Pavlovna's reception, and had sat listening to the vicomte's story. Prince Vasili's words frightened her, an embittered look clouded her once handsome face, but only for a moment; then she smiled again and clutched Prince Vasili's arm more tightly.

'Listen to me, Prince,' said she. 'I have never yet asked you for anything and I never will again, nor have I ever reminded you of my father's friendship for you; but now I entreat you for God's sake to do this for my son – and I shall always regard you as a benefactor,' she added hurriedly. 'No, don't be angry, but promise! I have asked Golitsin and he has refused. Be the kindhearted man you always were,' she said, trying to smile though tears were in her eyes.

'Papa, we shall be late,' said Princess Hélène, turning her beautiful head and looking over her classically moulded shoulder as she stood waiting by the door.

Influence in society, however, is capital which has to be economized if it is to last. Prince Vasili knew this, and having once realized that if he asked on behalf of all who begged of him, he would soon be unable to ask for himself, he became chary of using his influence. But in Princess Drubetskaya's case he felt, after her second appeal, something like qualms of conscience. She had reminded him of what was quite true; he had been indebted to her father for the first steps in his career. Moreover, he could see by her manner that she was one of those women – mostly mothers – who having once made up their minds, will not rest until they have gained their end, and are prepared if necessary to go on insisting day after day and hour after hour, and even to make scenes. This last consideration moved him.

'My dear Anna Mikhaylovna,' said he with his usual familiarity and weariness of tone, 'it is almost impossible for me to do what you ask; but to prove my devotion to you and how I respect your father's memory, I will do the impossible – your son shall be transferred to the Guards. Here is my hand on it. Are you satisfied?'

'My dear benefactor! This is what I expected from you – I knew your kindness!' He turned to go.

'Wait – just a word! When he has been transferred to the Guards...' she faltered, 'You are on good terms with Michael Ilarionovich Kutuzov*...recommend Boris to him as adjutant! Then I shall be at rest, and then...'

Prince Vasili smiled.

'No, I won't promise that. You don't know how Kutuzov is pestered since his appointment as Commander-in-Chief. He told me himself that all the Moscow ladies have conspired to give him all their sons as adjutants.'

'No, but do promise! I won't let you go! My dear benefactor...'

'Papa,' said his beautiful daughter in the same tone as before, 'we shall be late.'

'Well, *au revoir*! Good-bye! You hear her?'

'Then to-morrow you will speak to the Emperor?'

'Certainly; but about Kutuzov, I don't promise.'

'Do promise, do promise, Vasili!' cried Anna Mikhaylovna as he went, with the smile of a coquettish girl, which at one time probably came naturally to her, but was now very ill-suited to her care-worn face.

Apparently she had forgotten her age and by force of habit employed all the old feminine arts. But as soon as the prince had gone her face resumed its former cold, artificial expression. She returned to the group where the vicomte was still talking, and again pretended to listen, while waiting till it would be time to leave. Her task was accomplished.

'And what do you think of this latest comedy, the coronation at Milan?' asked Anna Pavlovna, 'and of the comedy of the people of Genoa and Lucca laying their petitions before Monsieur Buonaparte, and Monsieur Buonaparte sitting on a throne and granting the petitions of the nations? Adorable! It is enough to make one's head whirl! It is as if the whole world had gone crazy.'

Prince Andrew looked Anna Pavlovna straight in the face with a sarcastic smile.

' "*Dieu me la donne, gare à qui la touche!*"* (Bonaparte's words at his coronation). They say he was very fine when he said that,' he remarked, repeating the words in Italian: ' "*Dio la dona, gai a qui la tocca!*" '

'I hope this will prove the last drop that will make the glass run over,' Anna Pavlovna continued. 'The sovereigns will not be able to endure this man who is a menace to everything.'

'The sovereigns? I do not speak of Russia,' said the vicomte, polite but hopeless: 'The sovereigns, madame...What have they done for Louis XVII, for the Queen, or for Madame Elizabeth? Nothing!' and he became more animated. 'And believe me, they are reaping the reward of their betrayal of the Bourbon cause. The sovereigns! Why, they are sending ambassadors to compliment the usurper.'

And sighing disdainfully, he again changed his position.

Prince Hippolyte, who had been gazing at the vicomte for some time through his lorgnette, suddenly turned completely round towards the little princess, and having asked for a needle began tracing the Condé coat-of-arms on the table. He explained this to her with as much gravity as if she had asked him to do it.

'*Bâton de gueules, engrêlé de gueules d'azur – maison Condé,*'\* said he.

The princess listened, smiling.

'If Buonaparte remains on the throne of France a year longer,' the vicomte continued, with the air of a man who, in a matter with which he is better acquainted than anyone else, does not listen to others but follows the current of his own thoughts, 'things will have gone too far. By intrigues, violence, exile, and executions, French society – I mean good French society – will have been for ever destroyed, and then . . .'

He shrugged his shoulders and spread out his hands. Pierre wished to make a remark for the conversation interested him, but Anna Pavlovna, who had him under observation, interrupted:

'The Emperor Alexander,' said she, with the melancholy which always accompanied any reference of hers to the Imperial family, 'has declared that he will leave it to the French people themselves to choose their own form of government; and I believe that once free from the usurper, the whole nation will certainly throw itself into the arms of its rightful king,' she concluded, trying to be amiable to the royalist emigrant.

'That is doubtful,' said Prince Andrew. 'Monsieur le Vicomte quite rightly supposes that matters have already gone too far. I think it will be difficult to return to the old régime.'

'From what I have heard,' said Pierre, blushing and breaking into the conversation, 'almost all the aristocracy has already gone over to Bonaparte's side.'

'It is the Buonapartists who say that,' replied the vicomte without looking at Pierre. 'At the present time it is difficult to know the real state of French public opinion.'

'Bonaparte has said so,' remarked Prince Andrew with a sarcastic smile.

It was evident that he did not like the vicomte and was aiming his remarks at him, though without looking at him.

'"I showed them the path to glory, but they did not follow it",' Prince Andrew continued after a short silence, again quoting

Napoleon's words. ' "I opened my antechambers and they crowded in." I do not know how far he was justified in saying so.'

'Not in the least,' replied the vicomte. 'After the murder of the duc even the most partial ceased to regard him as a hero. If to some people,' he went on, turning to Anna Pavlovna, 'he ever was a hero, after the murder of the duc there was one martyr more in heaven and one hero less on earth.'

Before Anna Pavlovna and the others had time to smile their appreciation of the vicomte's epigram, Pierre again broke into the conversation, and though Anna Pavlovna felt sure he would say something inappropriate, she was unable to stop him.

'The execution of the Duc d'Enghien,' declared Monsieur Pierre, 'was a political necessity, and it seems to me that Napoleon showed greatness of soul by not fearing to take on himself the whole responsibility of that deed.'

'*Dieu! Mon Dieu!*' muttered Anna Pavlovna in a terrified whisper.

'What, Monsieur Pierre . . . Do you consider that assassination shows greatness of soul?' said the little princess, smiling and drawing her work nearer to her.

'Oh! Oh!' exclaimed several voices.

'Capital!' said Prince Hippolyte in English, and began slapping his knee with the palm of his hand.

The vicomte merely shrugged his shoulders. Pierre looked solemnly at his audience over his spectacles and continued.

'I say so,' he continued desperately, 'because the Bourbons fled from the Revolution leaving the people to anarchy, and Napoleon alone understood the Revolution and quelled it, and so for the general good, he could not stop short for the sake of one man's life.'

'Won't you come over to the other table?' suggested Anna Pavlovna.

But Pierre continued his speech without heeding her.

'No,' cried he, becoming more and more eager, 'Napoleon is great because he rose superior to the Revolution, suppressed its abuses, preserved all that was good in it – equality of citizenship and freedom of speech and of the press – and only for that reason did he obtain power.'

'Yes, if having obtained power, without availing himself of it to commit murder he had restored it to the rightful king, I should have called him a great man,' remarked the vicomte.

'He could not do that. The people only gave him power that he might rid them of the Bourbons and because they saw that he was a great man. The Revolution was a grand thing!' continued Monsieur Pierre, betraying by this desperate and provocative

19

proposition his extreme youth and his wish to express all that was in his mind.

'What? Revolution and regicide a grand thing?... Well, after that... But won't you come to this other table?' repeated Anna Pavlovna.

'Rousseau's *Contrat social*,' said the vicomte with a tolerant smile.

'I am not speaking of regicide, I am speaking about ideas.'

'Yes: ideas of robbery, murder, and regicide,' again interjected an ironical voice.

'Those were extremes, no doubt, but they are not what is most important. What is important are the rights of man, emancipation from prejudices, and equality of citizenship, and all these ideas Napoleon has retained in full force.'

'Liberty and Equality,' said the vicomte contemptuously, as if at last deciding seriously to prove to this youth how foolish his words were, '– high-sounding words which have long been discredited. Who does not love Liberty and Equality? Even our Saviour preached liberty and equality. Have people since the Revolution become happier? On the contrary. We wanted liberty, but Buonaparte has destroyed it.'

Prince Andrew kept looking with an amused smile from Pierre to the vicomte and from the vicomte to their hostess. In the first moment of Pierre's outburst Anna Pavlovna, despite her social experience, was horror-struck. But when she saw that Pierre's sacrilegious words had not exasperated the vicomte, and had convinced herself that it was impossible to stop him, she rallied her forces and joined the vicomte in a vigorous attack on the orator.

'But, my dear Monsieur Pierre,' said she, 'how do you explain the fact of a great man executing a duke – or even an ordinary man – who is innocent and untried?'

'I should like,' said the vicomte, 'to ask how Monsieur explains the 18th Brumaire; was not that an imposture? It was a swindle, and not at all like the conduct of a great man!'

'And the prisoners he killed in Africa?* That was horrible!' said the little princess, shrugging her shoulders.

'He's a low fellow, say what you will,' remarked Prince Hippolyte.

Pierre, not knowing whom to answer, looked at them all and smiled. His smile was unlike the half-smile of other people. When he smiled his grave, even rather gloomy look was instantaneously replaced by another – a childlike, kindly, even rather silly look, which seemed to ask forgiveness.

The vicomte, who was meeting him for the first time, saw clearly that this young Jacobin was not so terrible as his words suggested. All were silent.

'How do you expect him to answer you all at once?' said Prince Andrew. 'Besides, in the actions of a statesman one has to distinguish between his acts as a private person, as a general, and as an emperor. So it seems to me.'

'Yes, yes, of course!' Pierre chimed in, pleased at the arrival of this reinforcement.

'One must admit,' continued Prince Andrew, 'that Napoleon as a man was great on the bridge of Arcole,* and in the hospital at Jaffa where he gave his hand to the plague-stricken; but ... but there are other acts which it is difficult to justify.'

Prince Andrew, who had evidently wished to tone down the awkwardness of Pierre's remarks, rose and made a sign to his wife that it was time to go.

Suddenly Prince Hippolyte started up making signs to everyone to attend, and asking them all to be seated began:

'I was told a charming Moscow story to-day, and must treat you to it. Excuse me, Vicomte – I must tell it in Russian or the point will be lost ...' And Prince Hippolyte began to tell his story in such Russian as a Frenchman would speak after spending about a year in Russia. Everyone waited, so emphatically and eagerly did he demand their attention to his story.

'There is in Moscow a lady, *une dame*, and she is very stingy. She must have two footmen behind her carriage, and very big ones. That was her taste. And she had a lady's maid, also big. She said ...'

Here Prince Hippolyte paused, evidently collecting his ideas with difficulty.

'She said ... Oh yes! She said, "girl," to the maid, "put on a livery, get up behind the carriage, and come with me while I make some calls." '

Here Prince Hippolyte spluttered and burst out laughing long before his audience, which produced an effect unfavourable to the narrator. Several persons, among them the elderly lady and Anna Pavlovna, did however smile.

'She went. Suddenly there was a great wind. The girl lost her hat and her long hair came down ...' Here he could contain himself no longer and went on, between gasps of laughter: 'And the whole world knew ...'

And so the anecdote ended. Though it was unintelligible why he had told it, or why it had to be told in Russian, still Anna Pavlovna and the others appreciated Prince Hippolyte's social tact in so agreeably ending Pierre's unpleasant and unamiable outburst. After the anecdote the conversation broke up into insignificant small talk about the last and next balls, about theatricals, and who would meet whom, and when and where.

## 5

HAVING thanked Anna Pavlovna for her charming soirée, the guests began to take their leave.

Pierre was ungainly. Stout, above the average height, broad, with huge red hands, he did not know, as the saying is, how to enter a drawing-room and still less how to leave one; that is, how to say something particularly agreeable before going away. Besides this he was absent-minded. When he rose to go, he took up instead of his own, the general's three-cornered hat, and held it, pulling at the plume, till the general asked him to restore it. All his absent-mindedness and inability to enter a room and converse in it was however redeemed by his kindly, simple, and modest expression. Anna Pavlovna turned towards him and, with a Christian mildness that expressed forgiveness of his indiscretion, nodded and said: 'I hope to see you again, but I also hope you will change your opinions, my dear Monsieur Pierre.'

When she said this, he did not reply and only bowed, but again everybody saw his smile, which said nothing, unless perhaps, 'Opinions are opinions, but you see what a capital, good-natured fellow I am.' And everyone, including Anna Pavlovna, felt this.

Prince Andrew had gone out into the hall, and turning his shoulders to the footman who was helping him on with his cloak, listened indifferently to his wife's chatter with Prince Hippolyte who had also come into the hall. Prince Hippolyte stood close to the pretty, pregnant princess, and stared fixedly at her through his eyeglass.

'Go in, Annette, or you will catch cold,' said the little princess, taking leave of Anna Pavlovna. 'It is settled,' she added in a low voice.

Anna Pavlovna had already managed to speak to Lisa about the match she contemplated between Anatole and the little princess's sister-in-law.

'I rely on you, my dear,' said Anna Pavlovna, also in a low tone. 'Write to her and let me know how her father looks at the matter. Au revoir!' – and she left the hall.

Prince Hippolyte approached the little princess and, bending his face close to her, began to whisper something.

22

Two footmen, the princess's and his own, stood holding a shawl and a cloak, waiting for the conversation to finish. They listened to the French sentences which to them were meaningless, with an air of understanding but not wishing to appear to do so. The princess as usual spoke smilingly and listened with a laugh.

'I am very glad I did not go to the ambassador's,' said Prince Hippolyte, '– so dull. It has been a delightful evening, has it not? Delightful!'

'They say the ball will be very good,' replied the princess, drawing up her downy little lip. 'All the pretty women in society will be there.'

'Not all, for you will not be there; not all,' said Prince Hippolyte smiling joyfully; and snatching the shawl from the footman, whom he even pushed aside, he began wrapping it round the princess. Either from awkwardness or intentionally (no one could have said which) after the shawl had been adjusted he kept his arm around her for a long time, as though embracing her.

Still smiling, she gracefully moved away, turning and glancing at her husband. Prince Andrew's eyes were closed: he seemed weary and sleepy.

'Are you ready?' he asked his wife, looking past her.

Prince Hippolyte hurriedly put on his cloak, which in the latest fashion reached to his very heels, and stumbling in it, ran out into the porch following the princess, whom a footman was helping into the carriage.

'*Princesse, au revoir,*' cried he, stumbling with his tongue as well as with his feet.

The princess, picking up her dress, was taking her seat in the dark carriage, her husband was adjusting his sabre; Prince Hippolyte, under pretence of helping, was in everyone's way.

'Allow me, sir,' said Prince Andrew in Russian in a cold, disagreeable tone to Prince Hippolyte who was blocking his path.

'I am expecting you, Pierre,' said the same voice, but gently and affectionately.

The postillion started, the carriage wheels rattled. Prince Hippolyte laughed spasmodically as he stood in the porch waiting for the vicomte whom he had promised to take home.

'Well, *mon cher,*' said the vicomte, having seated himself beside Hippolyte in the carriage, 'your little princess is very nice, very nice indeed, quite French,' and he kissed the tips of his fingers. Hippolyte burst out laughing.

'Do you know, you are a terrible chap for all your innocent airs,' continued the vicomte. 'I pity the poor husband, that little officer who gives himself the airs of a monarch.'

Hippolyte spluttered again, and amid his laughter said, 'And you were saying that the Russian ladies are not equal to the French? One has to know how to deal with them.'

Pierre, arriving before the others, went into Prince Andrew's study like one quite at home, and from habit immediately lay down on the sofa, took from the shelf the first book that came to his hand (it was Caesar's *Commentaries*) and resting on his elbow, began reading it in the middle.

'What have you done to Mlle Scherer? She will be quite ill now,' said Prince Andrew, as he entered the study rubbing his small white hands.

Pierre turned his whole body, making the sofa creak. He lifted his eager face to Prince Andrew, smiled, and waved his hand.

'That abbé is very interesting but he does not see the thing in the right light ... In my opinion perpetual peace is possible, but – I do not know how to express it ... not by a balance of political power....'

It was evident that Prince Andrew was not interested in such abstract conversation.

'One can't everywhere say all one thinks, *mon cher*. Well, have you at last decided on anything? Are you going to be a guardsman or a diplomatist?' asked Prince Andrew after a momentary silence.

Pierre sat up on the sofa, with his legs tucked under him.

'Really, I don't yet know. I don't like either the one or the other.'

'But you must decide on something! Your father expects it.'

Pierre at the age of ten had been sent abroad with an abbé as tutor, and had remained away till he was twenty. When he returned to Moscow his father dismissed the abbé and said to the young man, 'Now go to Petersburg, look round, and choose your profession. I will agree to anything. Here is a letter to Prince Vasili, and here is money. Write to me all about it, and I will help you in everything.' Pierre had already been choosing a career for three months, and had not decided on anything. It was about this choice that Prince Andrew was speaking. Pierre rubbed his forehead.

'But he must be a freemason,' said he, referring to the abbé whom he had met that evening.

'That is all nonsense,' Prince Andrew again interrupted him, 'let us talk business. Have you been to the Horse Guards?'

'No, I have not: but this is what I have been thinking and wanted to tell you. There is a war now against Napoleon. If it were a war for freedom I could understand it and should be the

24

first to enter the army; but to help England and Austria against the greatest man in the world is not right.'

Prince Andrew only shrugged his shoulders at Pierre's childish words. He put on the air of one who finds it impossible to reply to such nonsense, but it would in fact have been difficult to give any other answer than the one Prince Andrew gave to this naïve question.

'If no one fought except on his own conviction, there would be no wars,' he said.

'And that would be splendid,' said Pierre.

Prince Andrew smiled ironically.

'Very likely it would be splendid, but it will never come about....'

'Well, why are you going to the war?' asked Pierre.

'What for? I don't know. I must. Besides that I am going ...'. He paused. 'I am going because the life I am leading here does not suit me!'

6

THE rustle of a woman's dress was heard in the next room. Prince Andrew shook himself as if waking up, and his face assumed the look it had had in Anna Pavlovna's drawing-room. Pierre removed his feet from the sofa. The princess came in. She had changed her gown for a house dress as fresh and elegant as the other. Prince Andrew rose and politely placed a chair for her.

'How is it,' she began, as usual in French, settling down briskly and fussily in the easy chair, 'how is it Annette never got married? How stupid you men all are not to have married her! Excuse me for saying so, but you have no sense about women. What an argumentative fellow you are, Monsieur Pierre!'

'And I am still arguing with your husband. I can't understand why he wants to go to the war,' replied Pierre, addressing the princess with none of the embarrassment so commonly shown by young men in their intercourse with young women.

The princess started. Evidently Pierre's words touched her to the quick.

'Ah, that is just what I tell him!' said she. 'I don't understand it; I don't in the least understand why men can't live without wars. How is it that we women don't want anything of the kind, don't need it? Now you shall judge between us. I always tell him: here he is uncle's aide-de-camp, a most brilliant position. He is so well known, so much appreciated by everyone. The other day at the Apraksins' I heard a lady asking, "Is that the famous Prince

Andrew?" I did indeed.' She laughed. 'He is so well received every-where. He might easily become aide-de-camp to the Emperor. You know the Emperor spoke to him most graciously. Annette and I were speaking of how to arrange it. What do you think?'

Pierre looked at his friend, and noticing that he did not like the conversation, gave no reply.

'When are you starting?' he asked.

'Oh, don't speak of his going, don't! I won't hear it spoken of,' said the princess in the same petulantly playful tone in which she had spoken to Hippolyte in the drawing-room and which was so plainly ill-suited to the family circle of which Pierre was almost a member. 'To-day when I remembered that all these delightful associations must be broken off ... and then you know, André ...' (she looked significantly at her husband) 'I'm afraid, I'm afraid!' she whispered, and a shudder ran down her back.

Her husband looked at her as if surprised to notice that some-one besides Pierre and himself was in the room, and addressed her in a tone of frigid politeness.

'What is it you are afraid of, Lise? I don't understand,' said he.

'There, what egotists men all are: all, all egotists! Just for a whim of his own, goodness only knows why, he leaves me and locks me up alone in the country.'

'With my father and sister, remember,' said Prince Andrew gently.

'Alone all the same, without *my* friends. . . . And he expects me not to be afraid.'

Her tone was now querulous and her lip drawn up, giving her not a joyful, but an animal, squirrel-like expression. She paused as if she felt it indecorous to speak of her pregnancy before Pierre, though the gist of the matter lay in that.

'I still can't understand what you are afraid of,' said Prince Andrew slowly, not taking his eyes off his wife.

The princess blushed, and raised her arms with a gesture of despair.

'No, Andrew, I must say you have changed. Oh, how you have ...'

'Your doctor tells you to go to bed earlier,' said Prince Andrew. 'You had better go.'

The princess said nothing, but suddenly her short downy lip quivered. Prince Andrew rose, shrugged his shoulders, and walked about the room.

Pierre looked over his spectacles with naïve surprise, now at him and now at her, moved as if about to rise too, but changed his mind.

'Why should I mind Monsieur Pierre being here?' exclaimed the little princess suddenly, her pretty face all at once distorted by a tearful grimace. 'I have long wanted to ask you, Andrew, why you have changed so to me? What have I done to you? You are going to the war and have no pity for me. Why is it?'

'Lise!' was all Prince Andrew said. But that one word expressed an entreaty, a threat, and above all conviction that she would herself regret her words. But she went hurriedly:

'You treat me like an invalid or a child. I see it all! Did you behave like that six months ago?'

'Lise, I beg you to desist,' said Prince Andrew still more emphatically.

Pierre who had been growing more and more agitated as he listened to all this, rose and approached the princess. He seemed unable to bear the sight of tears, and was ready to cry himself.

'Calm yourself, Princess! It seems so to you because ... I assure you I myself have experienced ... and so ... because ... No, excuse me! An outsider is out of place here ... No, don't distress yourself ... Good-bye!'

Prince Andrew caught him by the hand.

'No, wait, Pierre! The princess is too kind to wish to deprive me of the pleasure of spending the evening with you.'

'No, he thinks only of himself,' muttered the princess without restraining her angry tears.

'Lise!' said Prince Andrew drily, raising his voice to the pitch which indicates that patience is exhausted.

Suddenly the angry, squirrel-like expression of the princess's pretty face changed into a winning and piteous look of fear. Her beautiful eyes glanced askance at her husband's face, and her own assumed the timid, deprecating expression of a dog when it rapidly but feebly wags its drooping tail.

'Mon Dieu, mon Dieu!' she muttered, and lifting her dress with one hand she went up to her husband and kissed him on the forehead.

'Good-night, Lise,' said he, rising and courteously kissing her hand as he would have done to a stranger.

The friends were silent. Neither cared to begin talking. Pierre continually glanced at Prince Andrew; Prince Andrew rubbed his forehead with his small hand.

'Let us go and have supper,' he said with a sigh, going to the door.

They entered the elegant, newly decorated, and luxurious dining-room. Everything from the table-napkins to the silver, china, and glass, bore that imprint of newness found in the households of the newly married. Half-way through supper Prince Andrew leant his elbows on the table, and with a look of nervous agitation such as Pierre had never before seen on his face, began to talk – as one who has long had something on his mind and suddenly determines to speak out.

'Never, never marry, my dear fellow! That's my advice: never marry till you can say to yourself that you have done all you are capable of, and until you have ceased to love the woman of your choice and have seen her plainly as she is, or else you will make a cruel and irrevocable mistake. Marry when you are old and good for nothing – or all that is good and noble in you will be lost. It will all be wasted on trifles. Yes! Yes! Yes! Don't look at me with such surprise. If you marry expecting anything from yourself in the future you will feel at every step that for you all is ended, all is closed except the drawing-room where you will be ranged side by side with a court lackey and an idiot! ... But what's the good? ...' and he waved his arm.*

Pierre took off his spectacles, which made his face seem different and the good-natured expression still more apparent, and gazed at his friend in amazement.

'My wife,' continued Prince Andrew, 'is an excellent woman, one of those rare women with whom a man's honour is safe; but, O God, what would I not give now to be unmarried! You are the first and only one to whom I mention this, because I like you.'

As he said this Prince Andrew was less than ever like that Bolkonsky who had lolled in Anna Pavlovna's easy chairs and with half-closed eyes had uttered French phrases between his teeth. Every muscle of his thin face was now quivering with nervous excitement; his eyes, in which the fire of life had seemed extinguished, now flashed with brilliant light. It was evident that the more lifeless he seemed at ordinary times, the more impassioned he became in these moments of almost morbid irritation.

'You don't understand why I say this,' he continued, 'but it is the whole story of life. You talk of Bonaparte and his career,' said he (though Pierre had not mentioned Bonaparte), 'but Bonaparte when he worked went step by step towards his goal. He was free, he had nothing but his aim to consider, and he reached it. But tie yourself up with a woman, and like a chained convict you lose all freedom! And all you have of hope and strength merely weighs you down and torments you with regret. Drawing-rooms, gossip, balls, vanity, and triviality – these are the enchanted circle I cannot escape from. I am now going to the war, the greatest war there ever was, and I know nothing and am fit for nothing. I am very amiable and have a caustic wit,' continued Prince

Andrew, 'and at Anna Pavlovna's they listen to me. And that stupid set without whom my wife cannot exist, and those women ... If you only knew what those society women are, and women in general! My father is right. Selfish, vain, stupid, trivial in everything – that's what women are when you see them in their true colours! When you meet them in society it seems as if there were something in them, but there's nothing, nothing, nothing! No, don't marry, my dear fellow; don't marry!' concluded Prince Andrew.

'It seems funny to me,' said Pierre, 'that *you, you* should consider yourself incapable and your life a spoilt life. You have everything before you, everything. And you ...'

He did not finish his sentence, but his tone showed how highly he thought of his friend and how much he expected of him in the future.

'How can he talk like that?' thought Pierre. He considered his friend a model of perfection because Prince Andrew possessed in the highest degree just the very qualities Pierre lacked, and which might be best described as strength of will. Pierre was always astonished at Prince Andrew's calm manner of treating everybody, his extraordinary memory, his extensive reading (he had read everything, knew everything, and had an opinion about everything), but above all at his capacity for work and study. And if Pierre was often struck by Andrew's lack of capacity for philosophical meditation (to which he himself was particularly addicted), he regarded even this not as a defect but as a sign of strength.

Even in the best, most friendly and simplest relations of life, praise and commendation are essential, just as grease is necessary to wheels that they may run smoothly.

'My part is played out,' said Prince Andrew. 'What's the use of talking about me? Let us talk about you,' he added after a silence, smiling at his reassuring thoughts.

That smile was immediately reflected on Pierre's face.

'But what is there to say about me?' said Pierre, his face relaxing into a careless, merry smile. 'What am I? An illegitimate son!' He suddenly blushed crimson, and it was plain that he had made a great effort to say this. 'Without a name and without means ... And it really ...' But he did not say what 'it really' was. 'For the present I am free and am all right. Only I haven't the least idea what I am to do; I wanted to consult you seriously.'

Prince Andrew looked kindly at him, yet his glance – friendly and affectionate as it was – expressed a sense of his own superiority.

'I am fond of you, especially as you are the one live man among our whole set. Yes, you're all right! Choose what you will; it's all the same. You'll be all right anywhere. But look here: give up visiting those Kuragins and leading that sort of life. It suits you so badly – all this debauchery, dissipation, and the rest of it!'

'What would you have, my dear fellow?' answered Pierre, shrugging his shoulders. 'Women, my dear fellow; women!'

'I don't understand it,' replied Prince Andrew. 'Women who are *comme il faut*, that's a different matter; but the Kuragins' set of women, "women and wine", I don't understand!'

Pierre was staying at Prince Vasili Kuragin's and sharing the dissipated life of his son Anatole, the son whom they were planning to reform by marrying him to Prince Andrew's sister.

'Do you know?' said Pierre, as if suddenly struck by a happy thought, 'seriously, I have long been thinking of it ... Leading such a life I can't decide or think properly about anything. One's head aches, and one spends all one's money. He asked me for to-night, but I won't go.'

'You give me your word of honour not to go?'

'On my honour!'

It was past one o'clock when Pierre left his friend. It was a cloudless, northern, summer night. Pierre took an open cab intending to drive straight home. But the nearer he drew to the house the more he felt the impossibility of going to sleep on such a night. It was light enough to see a long way in the deserted street and it seemed more like morning or evening than night. On the way Pierre remembered that Anatole Kuragin was expecting the usual set for cards that evening, after which there was generally a drinking bout, finishing with visits of a kind Pierre was very fond of.

'I should like to go to Kuragin's,' thought he.

But he immediately recalled his promise to Prince Andrew not to go there. Then, as happens to people of weak character, he desired so passionately once more to enjoy that dissipation he was so accustomed to, that he decided to go. The thought immediately occurred to him that his promise to Prince Andrew was of no account, because before he gave it he had already promised Prince Anatole to come to his gathering; 'besides,' thought he, 'all such "words of honour" are conventional things with no definite meaning, especially if one considers that by to-morrow one may be dead, or something so extraordinary may happen to one that honour and dishonour will be all the same!' Pierre often indulged in reflections of this sort, nullifying all his decisions and intentions. He went to Kuragin's.

Reaching the large house near the Horse Guards' barracks, in which Anatole lived, Pierre entered the lighted porch, ascended the stairs, and went in at the open door. There was no one in the ante-room; empty bottles, cloaks, and over-shoes were lying about; there was a smell of alcohol, and sounds of voices and shouting in the distance.

Cards and supper were over, but the visitors had not yet dispersed. Pierre threw off his cloak and entered the first room, in which were the remains of supper. A footman, thinking no one saw him. was drinking on the sly what was left in the glasses. From the third room came sounds of laughter, the shouting of familiar voices, the growling of a bear, and general commotion. Some eight or nine young men were crowding anxiously round an open window. Three others were romping with a young bear, one pulling him by the chain and trying to set him at the others.

'I bet a hundred on Stevens!' shouted one.

'Mind, no holding on!' cried another.

'I bet on Dolokhov!' cried a third. 'Kuragin, you part our hands.'*

'There, leave Bruin alone; here's a bet on.'

'At one draught, or he loses!' shouted a fourth.

'Jacob, bring a bottle!' shouted the host, a tall handsome fellow who stood in the midst of the group, without a coat, and with his fine linen shirt unfastened in front. 'Wait a bit, you fellows. ... Here is Petya! Good man!' cried he, addressing Pierre.

Another voice, from a man of medium height with clear blue eyes, particularly striking among all these drunken voices by its sober ring, cried from the window: 'Come here; part the bets!' This was Dolokhov, an officer of the Semënov regiment, a notorious gambler and duellist, who was living with Anatole. Pierre smiled, looking about him merrily.

'I don't understand. What's it all about?'

'Wait a bit, he is not drunk yet! A bottle here,' said Anatole, and taking a glass from the table he went up to Pierre.

'First of all you must drink!'

Pierre drank one glass after another, looking from under his brows at the tipsy guests who were again crowding round the window, and listening to their chatter. Anatole kept on refilling Pierre's glass while explaining that Dolokhov was betting with Stevens, an English naval officer, that he would drink a bottle of rum sitting on the outer ledge of the third-floor window with his legs hanging out.

'Go on, you must drink it all,' said Anatole, giving Pierre the last glass, 'or I won't let you go!'

'No, I won't, said Pierre, pushing Anatole aside, and he went up to the window.

Dolokhov was holding the Englishman's hand and clearly and distinctly repeating the terms of the bet, addressing himself particularly to Anatole and Pierre.

Dolokhov was of medium height, with curly hair and light blue eyes. He was about five-and-twenty. Like all infantry officers he wore no moustache, so that his mouth, the most striking feature of his face, was clearly seen. The lines of that mouth were remarkably finely curved. The middle of the upper lip formed a sharp wedge and closed firmly on the firm lower one, and something like two distinct smiles played continually round the two corners of the mouth; this, together with the resolute, insolent intelligence of his eyes, produced an effect which made it impossible not to notice his face. Dolokhov was a man of small means and no connexions. Yet though Anatole spent tens of thousands of rubles, Dolokhov lived with him and had placed himself on such a footing that all who knew them, including Anatole himself, respected him more than they did Anatole. Dolokhov could play all games and nearly always won. However much he drank he never lost his clear-headedness. Both Kuragin and Dolokhov were at that time notorious among the rakes and scapegraces of Petersburg.

The bottle of rum was brought. The window frame which prevented anyone from sitting on the outer sill, was being forced out by two footmen, who were evidently flurried and intimidated by the directions and shouts of the gentlemen around.

Anatole with his swaggering air strode up to the window. He wanted to smash something. Pushing away the footmen he tugged at the frame, but could not move it. He smashed a pane.

'You have a try, Hercules,' said he, turning to Pierre.

Pierre seized the crossbeam, tugged, and wrenched the oak frame out with a crash.

'Take it right out, or they'll think I'm holding on,' said Dolokhov.

'Is the Englishman bragging.... Eh? Is it all right?' said Anatole.

'First rate,' said Pierre, looking at Dolokhov, who with a bottle of rum in his hand was approaching the window, from which the light of the sky, the dawn merging with the afterglow of sunset, was visible.

Dolokhov, the bottle of rum still in his hand, jumped onto the window-sill. 'Listen!' cried he, standing there and addressing those in the room. All were silent.

'I bet fifty imperials' – he spoke French that the Englishman might understand him, but he did not speak it very well – 'I bet fifty imperials . . . or do you wish to make it a hundred?' added he, addressing the Englishman.

'No, fifty,' replied the latter.

'All right. Fifty imperials . . . that I will drink a whole bottle of rum without taking it from my mouth, sitting outside the window on this spot' (he stooped and pointed to the sloping ledge outside the window), 'and without holding on to anything. Is that right?'

'Quite right,' said the Englishman.

Anatole turned to the Englishman and taking him by one of the buttons of his coat and looking down at him – the Englishman was short – began repeating the terms of the wager to him in English.

'Wait!' cried Dolokhov, hammering with the bottle on the window-sill to attract attention. 'Wait a bit, Kuragin. Listen! If anyone else does the same, I will pay him a hundred imperials. Do you understand?'

The Englishman nodded, but gave no indication whether he intended to accept this challenge or not. Anatole did not release him, and though he kept nodding to show that he understood, Anatole went on translating Dolokhov's words into English. A thin young lad, an hussar of the Life Guards, who had been losing that evening, climbed on the window-sill, leaned over, and looked down.

'Oh! Oh Oh!' he muttered, looking down from the window at the stones of the pavement.

'Shut up!' cried Dolokhov, pushing him away from the window. The lad jumped awkwardly back into the room, tripping over his spurs.

Placing the bottle on the window-sill where he could reach it easily, Dolokhov climbed carefully and slowly through the window and lowered his legs. Pressing against both sides of the window, he adjusted himself on his seat, lowered his hands, moved a little to the right and then to the left and took up the bottle. Anatole brought two candles and placed them on the window-sill, though it was already quite light. Dolokhov's back in his white shirt, and his curly head, were lit up from both sides. Everyone crowded to the window, the Englishman in front. Pierre stood smiling but silent. One man, older than the others present, suddenly pushed forward with a scared and angry look and wanted to seize hold of Dolokhov's shirt.

'I say, this is folly! He'll be killed,' said this more sensible man. Anatole stopped him.

'Don't touch him! You'll startle him and then he'll be killed. Eh? . . . What then? . . . Eh?'

Dolokhov turned round, and again holding on with both hands, arranged himself on his seat.

'If anyone comes meddling again,' said he, emitting the words separately through his thin compressed lips, 'I will throw him down there. Now then!'

Saying this he again turned round, dropped his hands, took the bottle and lifted it to his lips, threw back his head, and raised his free hand to balance himself. One of the footmen who had stooped to pick up some broken glass, remained in that position without taking his eyes from the window and from Dolokhov's back. Anatole stood erect with staring eyes. The Englishman looked on sideways pursing up his lips. The man who had wished to stop the affair ran to a corner of the room and threw himself on a sofa with his face to the wall. Pierre hid his face, from which a faint smile forgot to fade though his features now expressed horror and fear. All were still. Pierre took his hand from his eyes, Dolokhov still sat in the same position, only his head was thrown further back till his curly hair touched his shirt collar, and the hand holding the bottle was lifted higher and higher and trembled with the effort. The bottle was emptying perceptibly and rising still higher and his head tilting yet further back. 'Why is it so long?' thought Pierre. It seemed to him that more than half an hour had elapsed. Suddenly Dolokhov made a backward movement with his spine, and his arm trembled nervously; this was sufficient to cause his whole body to slip as he sat on the sloping ledge. As he began slipping down, his head and arm wavered still more with the strain. One hand moved as if to clutch the window-sill, but refrained from touching it. Pierre again covered his eyes and thought he would never open them again. Suddenly he was aware of a stir all around. He looked up: Dolokhov was standing on the window-sill with a pale but radiant face.

'It's empty!'

He threw the bottle to the Englishman, who caught it neatly. Dolokhov jumped down. He smelt strongly of rum.

'Well done! . . . Fine fellow! . . . There's a bet for you! . . . Devil take you!' came from different sides.

The Englishman took out his purse and began counting out the money. Dolokhov stood frowning and did not speak. Pierre jumped upon the window-sill.

'Gentlemen, who wishes to bet with me? I'll do the same thing!' he suddenly cried. 'Even without a bet there! Tell them to bring me a bottle. I'll do it. . . . Bring a bottle!'

'Let him do it, let him do it,' said Dolokhov, smiling.

'What next? Have you gone mad? ... No one would let you ... Why, you go giddy even ón a staircase,' exclaimed several voices.

'I'll drink it! Let's have a bottle of rum!' shouted Pierre, banging the table with a determined and drunken gesture and preparing to climb out of the window.

They seized him by his arms; but he was so strong that everyone who touched him was sent flying.

'No, you'll never manage him that way,' said Anatole. 'Wait a bit and I'll get round him ... Listen! I'll take your bet to-morrow, but now we are all going to ——'s.'

'Come on then,' cried Pierre. 'Come on! ... And we'll take Bruin with us.'

And he caught the bear, took it in his arms, lifted it from the ground, and began dancing round the room with it.

7

PRINCE VASILI kept the promise he had given to Princess Drubetskaya who had spoken to him on behalf of her only son Boris on the evening of Anna Pavlovna's soirée. The matter was mentioned to the Emperor, an exception made, and Boris transferred into the regiment of Semënov Guards with the rank of cornet. He received however no appointment to Kutuzov's staff despite all Anna Mikhaylovna's endeavours and entreaties. Soon after Anna Pavlovna's reception Anna Mikhaylovna returned to Moscow and went straight to her rich relations the Rostovs, with whom she stayed when in the town and where her darling Bory, who had only just entered a regiment of the line and was being at once transferred to the Guards as a cornet, had been educated from childhood and lived for years at a time. The Guards had already left Petersburg on the 10th of August, and her son, who had remained in Moscow for his equipment, was to join them on the march to Radzivilov.*

It was St Natalia's day and the name-day of two of the Rostovs – the mother and the youngest daughter – both named Nataly. Ever since the morning carriages with six horses had been coming and going continually, bringing visitors to the Countess Rostova's big house on the Povarskaya, so well known to all Moscow. The countess herself and her handsome eldest daughter were in the drawing-room with the visitors who came to congratulate, and who constantly succeeded one another in relays.

The countess was a woman of about forty-five, with a thin oriental type of face, evidently worn out with child-bearing – she had had twelve. A langour of motion and speech, resulting from weakness, gave her a distinguished air which inspired respect. Princess Anna Mikhaylovna Drubetskaya, who as a member of the household was also seated in the drawing-room, helped to receive and entertain the visitors. The young people were in one of the inner rooms, not considering it necessary to take part in receiving the visitors. The count* met the guests and saw them off, inviting them all to dinner.

'I am very, very grateful to you, *mon cher*' (or '*ma chère*' – he called everyone without exception and without the slightest variation in his tone, 'my dear', whether they were above or below him in rank) – 'I thank you for myself and for our two dear ones whose name-day we are keeping. But mind you come to dinner or I shall be offended, *ma chère*! On behalf of the whole family I beg you to come, *mon cher*!' These words he repeated to everyone without exception or variation, and with the same expression on his full, cheerful, clean-shaven face, the same firm pressure of the hand and the same quick, repeated bows. As soon as he had seen a visitor off he returned to one of those who were still in the drawing-room, drew a chair towards him or her, and jauntily spreading out his legs and putting his hands on his knees with the air of a man who enjoys life and knows how to live, he swayed to and fro with dignity, offered surmises about the weather, or touched on questions of health, sometimes in Russian and sometimes in very bad but self-confident French; then again, like a man weary but unflinching in the fulfilment of duty, he rose to see some visitors off, and stroking his scanty grey hairs over his bald patch, also asked them to dinner. Sometimes on his way back from the ante-room he would pass through the conservatory and pantry into the large marble dining-hall, where tables were being set out for eighty people; and looking at the footmen, who were bringing in silver and china, moving tables, and unfolding damask table-linen, he would call Dmitri Vasilevich, a man of good family and the manager of all his affairs, and while looking with pleasure at the enormous table would say: 'Well, Dmitri, you'll see that things are all as they should be? That's right! The great thing is the serving, that's it.' And with a complacent sigh he would return to the drawing-room.

'Marya Lvovna Karagina and her daughter!' announced the countess's gigantic footman in his bass voice, entering the drawing-room. The countess reflected a moment and took a pinch from a gold snuff-box with her husband's portrait on it.

'I'm quite worn out by these callers. However, I'll see her and

36

no more. She is so affected. Ask her in,' she said to the footman in a sad voice, as if saying: 'Very well, finish me off.'

A tall, stout, proud-looking woman, with a round-faced smiling daughter, entered the drawing-room, their dresses rustling.

'Dear Countess, what an age ... She has been laid up, poor child ... at the Razumovskys' ball ... and Countess Apraksina.... I was so delighted ...', came the sounds of animated feminine voices, interrupting one another and mingling with the rustling of dresses and the scraping of chairs. Then one of those conversations began which last out until, at the first pause, the guests rise with a rustle of dresses and say, 'I am so delighted ... mamma's health ... and Countess Apraksina ...', and then again rustling, pass into the ante-room, put on cloaks or mantles, and drive away. The conversation was on the chief topic of the day: the illness of the wealthy and celebrated beau of Catherine's day, Count Bezukhov, and about his illegitimate son Pierre, the one who had behaved so improperly at Anna Pavlovna's reception.

'I am so sorry for the poor count,' said the visitor. 'He is in such bad health, and now this vexation about his son is enough to kill him!'

'What is that?' asked the countess as if she did not know what the visitor alluded to, though she had already heard about the cause of Count Bezukhov's distress some fifteen times.

'That's what comes of a modern education,' exclaimed the visitor. 'It seems that while he was abroad this young man was allowed to do as he liked, and now in Petersburg I hear he has been doing such terrible things that he has been expelled by the police.'

'You don't say so!' replied the countess.

'He chose his friends badly,' interposed Anna Mikhaylovna. 'Prince Vasili's son, he and a certain Dolokhov have, it is said, been up to heaven only knows what! And they have had to suffer for it. Dolokhov has been degraded to the ranks and Bezukhov's son sent back to Moscow. Anatole Kuragin's father managed somehow to get his son's affair hushed up, but even he was ordered out of Petersburg.'

'But what have they been up to?' asked the countess.

'They are regular brigands, especially Dolokhov,' replied the visitor. 'He is a son of Marya Ivanovna Dolokhova, such a worthy woman, but there, just fancy! Those three got hold of a bear somewhere, put it in a carriage, and set off with it to visit some actresses! The police tried to interfere, and what did the young men do? They tied a policeman and the bear back to back and put the bear into the Mokya Canal. And there was the bear swimming about with the policeman on his back!'

'What a nice figure the policeman must have cut, my dear!' shouted the count, dying with laughter.

'Oh, how dreadful! How can you laugh at it, Count?'

Yet the ladies themselves could not help laughing.

'It was all they could do to rescue the poor man,' continued the visitor. 'And to think it is Cyril Vladimirovich Bezukhov's son who amuses himself in this sensible manner! And he was said to be so well educated and clever. This is all that his foreign education has done for him! I hope that here in Moscow no one will receive him, in spite of his money. They wanted to introduce him to me, but I quite declined: I have my daughters to consider.'

'Why do you say this young man is so rich?' asked the countess, turning away from the girls, who at once assumed an air of inattention. 'His children are all illegitimate. I think Pierre also is illegitimate.'

The visitor made a gesture with her hand.

'I should think he has a score of them.'

Princess Anna Mikhaylovna intervened in the conversation, evidently wishing to show her connexions and knowledge of what went on in society.

'The fact of the matter is,' said she significantly, and also in a half whisper, 'everyone knows Count Cyril's reputation.... He has lost count of his children, but this Pierre was his favourite.'

'How handsome the old man still was only a year ago!' remarked the countess. 'I have never seen a handsomer man.'

'He is very much altered now,' said Anna Mikhaylovna. 'Well, as I was saying, Prince Vasili is the next heir through his wife, but the count is very fond of Pierre, looked after his education, and wrote to the Emperor about him; so that in case of his death – and he is so ill that he may die at any moment, and Dr Lorrain has come from Petersburg – no one knows who will inherit his immense fortune, Pierre or Prince Vasili. Forty thousand serfs and millions of rubles! I know it all very well for Prince Vasili told me himself. Besides, Cyril Vladimirovich is my mother's second cousin. He's also my Bory's godfather,' she added, as if she attached no importance at all to the fact.

'Prince Vasili arrived in Moscow yesterday. I hear he has come on some inspection business,' remarked the visitor.

'Yes, but between ourselves,' said the princess, 'that is a pretext. The fact is he has come to see Count Cyril Vladimirovich, hearing how ill he is.'

'But do you know, my dear, that was a capital joke,' said the count; and seeing that the elder visitor was not listening, he turned to the young ladies. 'I can just imagine what a funny figure that policeman cut!'

And as he waved his arms to impersonate the policeman, his portly form again shook with a deep ringing laugh, the laugh of one who always eats well and, in particular, drinks well. 'So, do come and dine with us!' he said.

8

A SILENCE ensued. The countess looked at her callers, smiling affably, but not concealing the fact that she would not be distressed if they now rose and took their leave. The visitor's daughter was already smoothing down her dress with an inquiring look at her mother, when suddenly from the next room were heard the footsteps of boys and girls running to the door and the noise of a chair falling over, and a girl of thirteen, hiding something in the folds of her short muslin frock, darted in and stopped short in the middle of the room. It was evident that she had not intended her flight to bring her so far. Behind her in the doorway appeared a student with a crimson coat-collar, an officer of the Guards, a girl of fifteen, and a plump rosy-faced boy in a short jacket.

The count jumped up and, swaying from side to side, spread his arms wide and threw them round the little girl who had run in.

'Ah, here she is!' he exclaimed laughing. 'My pet, whose name-day it is. My dear pet!'

'*Ma chère*, there is a time for everything,' said the countess with feigned severity. 'You spoil her, Ilya,' she added, turning to her husband.

'How do you do, my dear? I wish you many happy returns of your name-day,' said the visitor. 'What a charming child,' she added, addressing the mother.

This black-eyed, wide-mouthed girl, not pretty but full of life, with childish bare shoulders which after her run heaved and shook her bodice, with black curls tossed backward, thin bare arms, little legs in lace-frilled drawers, and feet in low slippers – was just at that charming age when a girl is no longer a child, though the child is not yet a young woman. Escaping from her father she ran to hide her flushed face in the lace of her mother's mantilla – not paying the least attention to her severe remark – and began to laugh. She laughed, and in fragmentary sentences tried to explain about a doll which she produced from the folds of her frock.

'Do you see? ... My doll.... Mimi.... You see....' was all Natasha managed to utter (to her everything seemed funny). She leaned against her mother and burst into such a loud, ringing fit of laughter that even the prim visitor could not help joining in.

'Now then, go away and take your monstrosity with you,' said the mother, pushing away her daughter with pretended sternness, and turning to the visitor she added: 'She is my youngest girl.'

Natasha, raising her face for a moment from her mother's mantilla, glanced up at her through tears of laughter, and again hid her face.

The visitor, compelled to look on at this family scene, thought it necessary to take some part in it.

'Tell me, my dear,' said she to Natasha, 'is Mimi a relation of yours? A daughter, I suppose?'

Natasha did not like the visitor's tone of condescension to childish things. She did not reply, but looked at her seriously.

Meanwhile the younger generation: Boris, the officer, Anna Mikhaylovna's son; Nicholas, the undergraduate, the count's eldest son; Sonya, the count's fifteen-year-old niece, and little Petya, his youngest boy, had all settled down in the drawing-room and were obviously trying to restrain within the bounds of decorum the excitement and mirth that shone in all their faces. Evidently in the back rooms, from which they had dashed out so impetuously, the conversation had been more amusing than the drawing-room talk of society scandals, the weather, and Countess Apraksina. Now and then they glanced at one another, hardly able to suppress their laughter.

The two young men, the student and the officer, friends from childhood, were of the same age and both handsome fellows, though not alike. Boris was tall and fair, and his calm and handsome face had regular, delicate features. Nicholas was short with curly hair and an open expression. Dark hairs were already showing on his upper lip, and his whole face expressed impetuosity and enthusiasm. Nicholas blushed when he entered the drawing-room. He evidently tried to find something to say, but failed. Boris on the contrary at once found his footing, and related quietly and humorously how he had known that doll Mimi when she was still quite a young lady, before her nose was broken; how she had aged during the five years he had known her, and how her head had cracked right across the skull. Having said this he glanced at Natasha. She turned away from him and glanced at her younger brother, who was screwing up his eyes and shaking with suppressed laughter, and unable to control herself any longer, she jumped up and rushed from the room as fast as her nimble little feet would carry her. Boris did not laugh.

'You were meaning to go out weren't you, mamma? Do you want the carriage?' he asked his mother with a smile.

'Yes, yes, go and tell them to get it ready,' she answered, returning his smile.

Boris quietly left the room and went in search of Natasha. The plump boy ran after them angrily, as if vexed that their programme had been disturbed.

## 9

THE only young people remaining in the drawing-room, not counting the young lady visitor and the countess's eldest daughter (who was four years older than her sister and behaved already like a grown-up person), were Nicholas and Sonya, the niece. Sonya was a slender little brunette with a tender look in her eyes which were veiled by long lashes, thick black plaits coiling twice round her head, and a tawny tint in her complexion and especially in the colour of her slender but graceful and muscular arms and neck. By the grace of her movements, by the softness and flexibility of her small limbs, and by a certain coyness and reserve of manner, she reminded one of a pretty, half-grown kitten which promises to become a beautiful little cat. She evidently considered it proper to show an interest in the general conversation by smiling, but in spite of herself her eyes under their thick long lashes watched her cousin who was going to join the army, with such passionate girlish adoration that her smile could not for a single instant impose upon anyone, and it was clear that the kitten had settled down only to spring up with more energy and again play with her cousin as soon as they too could, like Natasha and Boris, escape from the drawing-room.

'Ah yes, my dear,' said the count, addressing the visitor and pointing to Nicholas, 'his friend Boris has become an officer, and so for friendship's sake he is leaving the university and me, his old father, and entering the military service, my dear. And there was a place and everything waiting for him in the Archives Department! Isn't that friendship?' remarked the count in an inquiring tone.

'But they say that war has been declared,' replied the visitor.

'They've been saying so a long while,' said the count, 'and they'll say so again and again, and that will be the end of it. My dear, there's friendship for you,' he repeated. 'He's joining the hussars.'

The visitor, not knowing what to say, shook her head.

'It's not at all from friendship,' declared Nicholas, flaring up and turning away as if from a shameful aspersion. 'It is not from friendship at all; I simply feel that the army is my vocation.'

He glanced at his cousin and the young lady visitor; and they were both regarding him with a smile of approbation.

'Schubert, the colonel of the Pavlograd Hussars, is dining with us to-day. He has been here on leave and is taking Nicholas back with him. It can't be helped!' said the count, shrugging his shoulders and speaking playfully of a matter that evidently distressed him.

'I have already told you, papa,' said his son, 'that if you don't wish to let me go, I'll stay. But I know I am no use anywhere except in the army; I am not a diplomat nor a government clerk. – I don't know how to hide what I feel.' As he spoke he kept glancing with the flirtatiousness of a handsome youth at Sonya and the young lady visitor.

The little kitten, feasting her eyes on him, seemed ready at any moment to start her gambols again and display her kittenish nature.

'All right, all right!' said the old count. 'He always flares up! This Buonaparte has turned all their heads; they all think of how he rose from an ensign and became Emperor. Well, well, God grant it,' he added, not noticing his visitor's sarcastic smile.

The elders began talking about Bonaparte. Julie Karagina turned to young Rostov.

'What a pity you weren't at the Arkharovs' on Thursday. I was so dull without you,' said she, giving him a tender smile.

The young man, flattered, sat down nearer to her with a coquettish smile, and engaged the smiling Julie in a confidential conversation without at all noticing that his involuntary smile had stabbed the heart of Sonya, who blushed and smiled unnaturally. In the midst of his talk he glanced round at her. She gave him a passionately angry glance, and hardly able to restrain her tears and maintain the artificial smile on her lips, she got up and left the room. All Nicholas's animation vanished. He waited for the first pause in the conversation, and then with a distressed face left the room to find Sonya.

'How plainly all these young people wear their hearts on their sleeves!' said Anna Mikhaylovna, pointing to Nicholas as he went out. '*Cousinage — dangereux voisinage*,' she added.

'Yes,' said the countess when the brightness these young people had brought into the room had vanished; and as if answering a question no one had put but which was always in her mind, 'and how much suffering, how much anxiety one has had to go through that we might rejoice in them now! And yet really the anxiety is greater now than the joy. One is always, always anxious! Especially just at this age, so dangerous both for girls and boys.'

'It all depends on the bringing up,' remarked the visitor.

'Yes, you're quite right,' continued the countess. 'Till now I have always, thank God, been my children's friend and had their full confidence,' said she, repeating the mistake of so many parents who imagine that their children have no secrets from them. 'I know I shall always be my daughters' first confidante, and that if Nicholas, with his impulsive nature, does get into mischief (a boy can't help it) he will all the same never be like those Petersburg young men.'

'Yes, they are splendid, splendid youngsters,' chimed in the count, who always solved questions that seemed to him perplexing by deciding that everything was splendid. 'Just fancy: wants to be an hussar. What's one, to do, my dear?'

'What a charming creature your younger girl is,' said the visitor; 'a little volcano!'

'Yes, a regular volcano,' said the count. 'Takes after me! And what a voice she has; though she's my daughter, I tell the truth when I say she'll be a singer, a second Salomoni! We have engaged an Italian to give her lessons.'

'Isn't she too young? I have heard that it harms the voice to train it at that age.'

'Oh no, not at all too young!' replied the count. 'Why, our mothers used to be married at twelve or thirteen.'

'And she's in love with Boris already. Just fancy!' said the countess with a gentle smile, looking at Boris's mother, and went on, evidently concerned with a thought that always occupied her: 'Now you see if I were to be severe with her and to forbid it ... goodness knows what they might be up to on the sly' (she meant that they would be kissing), 'but as it is, I know every word she utters. She will come running to me of her own accord in the evening and tell me everything. Perhaps I spoil her, but really that seems the best plan. With her elder sister I was stricter.'

'Yes, I was brought up quite differently,' remarked the handsome elder daughter Countess Vera, with a smile.

But the smile did not enhance Vera's beauty as smiles generally do; on the contrary it gave her an unnatural, and therefore unpleasant, expression. Vera was good-looking, not at all stupid, quick at learning, was well brought up, and had a pleasant voice; what she said was true and appropriate, yet, strange to say, everyone – the visitors and countess alike – turned to look at her as if wondering why she had said it, and they all felt awkward.

'People are always too clever with their eldest children and try to make something exceptional of them,' said the visitor.

'What's the good of denying it, my dear? Our dear countess was too clever with Vera,' said the count. 'Well, what of that? She's turned out splendidly all the same,' he added, winking at Vera.

The guests got up and took their leave, promising to return to dinner.

'What manners! I thought they would never go,' said the countess, when she had seen her guests out.

10

WHEN Natasha ran out of the drawing-room she only went as far as the conservatory. There she paused and stood listening to the conversation in the drawing-room, waiting for Boris to come out. She was already growing impatient, and stamped her foot, ready to cry at his not coming at once, when she heard the young man's discreet steps approaching neither quickly nor slowly. At this Natasha dashed swiftly among the flower-tubs and hid there.

Boris paused in the middle of the room, looked round, brushed a little dust from the sleeve of his uniform, and going to a mirror examined his handsome face. Natasha, very still, peered out from her ambush, waiting to see what he would do. He stood a little while before the glass, smiled, and walked toward the other door. Natasha was about to call him but changed her mind. 'Let him look for me,' thought she. Hardly had Boris gone than Sonya, flushed, in tears, and muttering angrily, came in at the other door. Natasha checked her first impulse to run out to her, and remained in her hiding place, watching – as under an invisible cap – to see what went on in the world. She was experiencing a new and peculiar pleasure. Sonya, muttering to herself, kept looking round towards the drawing-room door. It opened and Nicholas came in.

'Sonya, what is the matter with you? How can you?' said he, running up to her.

'It's nothing, nothing; leave me alone!' sobbed Sonya.

'Ah, I know what it is.'

'Well, if you do, so much the better, and you can go back to her!'

'So-o-onya! Look here! How can you torture me and yourself like that, for a mere fancy?' said Nicholas taking her hand.

Sonya did not pull it away, and left off crying. Natasha, not stirring and scarcely breathing, watched from her ambush with sparkling eyes. 'What will happen now?' thought she.

'Sonya! What is anyone in the world to me? You alone are everything!' said Nicholas. 'And I will prove it to you.'

'I don't like you to talk like that.'

'Well then, I won't; only forgive me, Sonya!' He drew her to him and kissed her.

'Oh, how nice,' thought Natasha; and when Sonya and Nicholas had gone out of the conservatory she followed and called Boris to her.

'Boris, come here,' said she with a sly and significant look. 'I have something to tell you. Here, here!' and she led him into the conservatory to the place among the tubs where she had been hiding.

Boris followed her, smiling.

'What is the *something*?' asked he.

She grew confused, glanced round, and seeing the doll she had thrown down on one of the tubs, picked it up.

'Kiss the doll,' said she.

Boris looked attentively and kindly at her eager face, but did not reply.

'Don't you want to? Well then, come here,' said she, and went further in among the plants and threw down the doll. 'Closer, closer!' she whispered.

She caught the young officer by his cuffs, and a look of solemnity and fear appeared on her flushed face.

'And me? Would you like to kiss me?' she whispered almost inaudibly, glancing up at him from under her brows, smiling, and almost crying from excitement.

Boris blushed.

'How funny you are!' he said, bending down to her and blushing still more, but he waited and did nothing.

Suddenly she jumped up onto a tub to be higher than he, embraced him so that both her slender bare arms clasped him above his neck, and tossing back her hair, kissed him full on the lips.

Then she slipped down among the flower pots on the other side of the tubs and stood, hanging her head.

'Natasha,' he said, 'you know that I love you, but . . .'

'You are in love with me?' Natasha broke in.

'Yes, I am, but please don't let us do like that . . . In another four years . . . then I will ask for your hand.'

Natasha considered.

'Thirteen, fourteen, fifteen, sixteen,' she counted on her slender little fingers. 'All right! Then it's settled?'

45

A smile of joy and satisfaction lit up her eager face.

'Settled!' replied Boris.

'For ever?' said the little girl. 'Till death itself?'

She took his arm and with a happy face went with him into the adjoining sitting-room.

## 11

AFTER receiving her visitors the countess was so tired that she gave orders to admit no more, but the porter was told to be sure to invite to dinner all who came 'to congratulate'. The countess wished to have a tête-à-tête talk with the friend of her childhood, Princess Anna Mikhaylovna, whom she had not seen properly since she returned from Petersburg. Anna Mikhaylovna, with her tear-worn but pleasant face, drew her chair nearer to that of the countess.

'With you I will be quite frank,' said Anna Mikhaylovna. 'There are not many left of us old friends! That 's why I so value your friendship.'

Anna Mikhaylovna looked at Vera and paused. The countess pressed her friend's hand.

'Vera,' she said to her eldest daughter who was evidently not a favourite, 'how is it you have so little tact? Don't you see you are not wanted here? Go to the other girls, or . . .'

The handsome Vera smiled contemptuously but did not seem at all hurt.

'If you had told me sooner, mamma, I should have gone,' she replied as she rose to go to her own room.

But as she passed the sitting-room she noticed two couples sitting, one pair at each window. She stopped and smiled scornfully. Sonya was sitting close to Nicholas who was copying out some verses for her, the first he had ever written. Boris and Natasha were at the other window and ceased talking when Vera entered. Sonya and Natasha looked at Vera with guilty, happy faces.

It was pleasant and touching to see these little girls in love; but apparently the sight of them roused no pleasant feeling in Vera.

'How often have I asked you not to take my things?' she said. 'You have a room of your own,' and she took the inkstand from Nicholas.

'In a minute, in a minute,' he said, dipping his pen.

'You always manage to do things at the wrong time,' continued Vera. 'You came rushing into the drawing-room so that everyone felt ashamed of you.'

46

Though what she said was quite just, perhaps for that very reason no one replied, and the four simply looked at one another. She lingered in the room with the inkstand in her hand.

'And at your age what secrets can there be between Natasha and Boris, or between you two? It's all nonsense!'

'Now? Vera, what does it matter to you?' said Natasha in defence, speaking very gently.

She seemed that day to be more than ever kind and affectionate to everyone.

'Very silly,' said Vera. 'I am ashamed of you. Secrets indeed!'

'All have secrets of their own,' answered Natasha, getting warmer. 'We don't interfere with you and Berg.'

'I should think not,' said Vera, 'because there can never be anything wrong in my behaviour. But I'll just tell mamma how you are behaving with Boris.'

'Natalya Ilyinichna behaves very well to me,' remarked Boris. 'I have nothing to complain of.'

'Don't, Boris! You are such a diplomat that it is really tiresome,' said Natasha in a mortified voice that trembled slightly. (She used the word 'diplomat', which was just then much in vogue among the children, in the special sense they attached to it.) 'Why does she bother me?' And she added, turning to Vera, 'You'll never understand it, because you've never loved anyone. You have no heart! You are a Madame de Genlis and nothing more,' (this nickname, bestowed on Vera by Nicholas, was considered very stinging) 'and your greatest pleasure is to be unpleasant to people! Go and flirt with Berg as much as you please,' she finished quickly.

'I shall at any rate not run after a young man before visitors . . .'

'Well, now you've done what you wanted,' put in Nicholas, '—said unpleasant things to everyone and upset them. Let's go to the nursery.'

All four, like a flock of scared birds, got up and left the room.

'The unpleasant things were said to me,' remarked Vera, 'I said none to anyone.'

'Madame de Genlis! Madame de Genlis!' shouted laughing voices through the door.

The handsome Vera, who produced such an irritating and unpleasant effect on everyone, smiled, and evidently unmoved by what had been said to her, went to the looking-glass and arranged her hair and scarf. Looking at her own handsome face she seemed to become still colder and calmer.

*

In the drawing-room the conversation was still going on.

'Ah, my dear,' said the countess, 'my life is not all roses either. Don't I know that at the rate we are living our means won't last long? It's all the Club and his easy-going nature. Even in the country do we get any rest? Theatricals, hunting, and heaven knows what besides! But don't let's talk about me; tell me how you managed everything. I often wonder at you, Annette, – how at your age you can rush off alone in a carriage to Moscow, to Petersburg, to those ministers and great people, and know how to deal with them all! It's quite astonishing. How did you get things settled? I couldn't possibly do it.'

'Ah, my love,' answered Anna Mikhaylovna, 'God grant you never know what it is to be left a widow without means and with a son you love to distraction! One learns many things then,' she added with a certain pride. 'That lawsuit taught me much. When I want to see one of those big people I write a note: "Princess So-and-So desires an interview with So-and-So," and then I take a cab and go myself two, three, or four times – till I get what I want. I don't mind what they may think of me.'

'Well, and to whom did you apply about Bory?' asked the countess. 'You see yours is already an officer in the Guards, while my Nicholas is going as a cadet. There's no one to interest himself for him. To whom did you apply?'

'To Prince Vasili. He was so kind. He at once agreed to everything, and put the matter before the Emperor,' said Princess Anna Mikhaylovna enthusiastically, quite forgetting all the humiliation she had endured to gain her end.

'Has Prince Vasili aged much?' asked the countess. 'I have not seen him since we acted together at the Rumyantsovs' theatricals. I expect he has forgotten me. He paid me attentions in those days,' said the countess, with a smile.

'He is just the same as ever,' replied Anna Mikhaylovna, 'over-flowing with amiability. His position has not turned his head at all. He said to me, "I am sorry I can do so little for you, dear Princess. I am at your command." Yes, he is a fine fellow and a very kind relation. But, Nataly, you know my love for my son: I would do anything for his happiness! And my affairs are in such a bad way that my position is now a terrible one,' continued Anna Mikhaylovna, sadly, dropping her voice. 'My wretched lawsuit takes all I have and makes no progress. Would you believe it, I have literally not a penny and don't know how to equip Boris.' She took out her handkerchief and began to cry. 'I need five hundred rubles, and have only one twenty-five ruble note. I am in such a state . . . My only hope now is in Count Cyril Vladimirovich

Bezukhov. If he will not assist his godson – you know he is Bory's godfather – and allow him something for his maintenance, all my trouble will have been thrown away . . . I shall not be able to equip him.'

The countess's eyes filled with tears and she pondered in silence.

'I often think, though perhaps it's a sin,' said the princess, 'that here lives Count Cyril Vladimirovich Bezukhov so rich, all alone . . . that tremendous fortune . . . and what is his life worth? It's a burden to him, and Bory's life is only just beginning. . . .'

'Surely he will leave something to Boris,' said the countess.

'Heaven only knows, my dear! These rich grandees are so selfish. Still, I will take Boris and go to see him at once, and I shall speak to him straight out. Let people think what they will of me, it's really all the same to me when my son's fate is at stake.' The princess rose. 'It's now two o'clock and you dine at four. There will just be time.'

And like a practical Petersburg lady who knows how to make the most of time, Anna Mikhaylovna sent someone to call her son, and went into the ante-room with him.

'Good-bye, my dear,' said she to the countess who saw her to the door, and added in a whisper so that her son should not hear, 'Wish me good luck.'

'Are you going to Count Cyril Vladimirovich, my dear?' said the count coming out from the dining-hall into the ante-room, and he added: 'If he is better, ask Pierre to dine with us. He has been to the house, you know, and danced with the children. Be sure to invite him, my dear. We will see how Taras distinguishes himself to-day. He says Count Orlov never gave such a dinner as ours will be!'

## 12

'MY dear Boris,' said Princess Anna Mikhaylovna to her son as Countess Rostova's carriage in which they were seated drove over the straw-covered street and turned into the wide courtyard of Count Cyril Vladimirovich Bezukhov's house. 'My dear Boris,' said the mother, drawing her hand from beneath her old mantle and laying it timidly and tenderly on her son's arm, 'be affectionate and attentive to him. Count Cyril Vladimirovich is your godfather after all, and your future depends on him. Remember that, my dear, and be nice to him, as you so well know how to be.'

'If only I knew that anything besides humiliation would come of it . . .' answered her son coldly. 'But I have promised and will do it for your sake.'

Although the hall-porter saw someone's carriage standing at the entrance, after scrutinizing the mother and son (who without asking to be announced had passed straight through the glass porch between the rows of statues in niches) and looking significantly at the lady's old cloak, he asked whether they wanted the count or the princesses, and hearing that they wished to see the count, said his excellency was worse to-day, and that his excellency was not receiving anyone.

'We may as well go back,' said the son in French.

'My dear!' exclaimed his mother imploringly, again laying her hand on his arm as if that touch might soothe or rouse him.

Boris said no more, but looked inquiringly at his mother without taking off his cloak.

'My friend,' said Anna Mikháylovna in gentle tones, addressing the hall-porter, 'I know Count Cyril Vladímirovich is very ill... that's why I have come...I am a relation. I shall not disturb him, my friend...I only need see Prince Vasíli Sergéevich: he is staying here, is he not? Please announce me.'

The hall-porter sullenly pulled a bell that rang upstairs, and turned away.

'Princess Drubetskáya to see Prince Vasíli Sergéevich,' he called to a footman dressed in knee-breeches, shoes, and a swallow-tail coat, who ran downstairs and looked over from the half-way landing.

The mother smoothed the folds of her dyed silk dress before a large Venetian mirror in the wall, and in her trodden-down shoes briskly ascended the carpeted stairs.

'My dear,' she said to her son, once more stimulating him by a touch, 'you promised me!'

The son, lowering his eyes, followed her quietly.

They entered the large hall, from which one of the doors led to the apartments assigned to Prince Vasíli.

Just as the mother and son, having reached the middle of the hall, were about to ask their way of an elderly footman who had sprung up as they entered, the bronze handle of one of the doors turned and Prince Vasíli came out – wearing a velvet coat with a single star on his breast, as was his custom when at home – taking leave of a good-looking, dark-haired man. This was the celebrated Petersburg doctor, Lorrain.

'Then it is certain?' said the prince.

'Prince, *humanum est errare*, but...' replied the doctor, swallowing his r's, and pronouncing the Latin words with a French accent.

'Very well, very well...'

Seeing Anna Mikhaylovna and her son, Prince Vasili dismissed the doctor with a bow and approached them silently and with a look of inquiry. The son noticed that an expression of profound sorrow suddenly clouded his mother's face, and he smiled slightly.

'Ah Prince! In what sad circumstances we meet again! And how is our dear invalid?' said she, as though unaware of the cold offensive look fixed on her.

Prince Vasili stared at her and at Boris questioningly and perplexed. Boris bowed politely. Prince Vasili without acknowledging the bow turned to Anna Mikhaylovna, answering her query by a movement of the head and lips indicating very little hope for the patient.

'Is it possible?' exclaimed Anna Mikhaylovna. 'Oh, how awful! It is terrible to think. . . . This is my son,' she added, indicating Boris. 'He wanted to thank you himself.'

Boris again bowed politely.

'Believe me, Prince, a mother's heart will never forget what you have done for us.'

'I am glad I was able to do you a service, my dear Anna Mikhaylovna,' said Prince Vasili, arranging his lace frill, and in tone and manner, here in Moscow to Anna Mikhaylovna whom he had placed under an obligation, assuming an air of much greater importance than he had done in Petersburg at Anna Scherer's reception.

'Try to serve well and show yourself worthy,' added he, addressing Boris with severity. 'I am glad. . . . Are you here on leave?' he went on in his usual tone of indifference.

'I am awaiting orders to join my new regiment, your excellency,' replied Boris, betraying neither annoyance at the prince's brusque manner nor a desire to enter into conversation, but speaking so quietly and respectfully that the prince gave him a searching glance.

'Are you living with your mother?'

'I am living at Countess Rostova's,' replied Boris, again adding, 'your excellency.'

'That is, with Ilya Rostov who married Nataly Shinshina,' said Anna Mikhaylovna.

'I know, I know,' answered Prince Vasili in his monotonous voice. 'I never could understand how Nataly made up her mind to marry that unlicked bear! A perfectly absurd and stupid fellow, and a gambler too, I am told.'

'But a very kind man, Prince,' said Anna Mikhaylovna with a pathetic smile, as though she too knew that Count Rostov deserved this censure, but asked him not to be too hard on the poor old man. 'What do the doctors say?' asked the princess after a pause, her worn face again expressing deep sorrow.

'They give little hope,' replied the prince.

'And I should so like to thank *Uncle* once more for all his kindness to me and to Boris. He is his godson,' she added, her tone suggesting that this fact ought to give Prince Vasili much satisfaction.

Prince Vasili became thoughtful and frowned. Anna Mikhaylovna saw that he was afraid of finding in her a rival for Count Bezukhov's fortune, and hastened to reassure him.

'If it were not for my sincere affection and devotion to *Uncle*,' said she, uttering the word with peculiar assurance and unconcern, 'I know his character: noble, upright ... but you see he has no one with him except the young princesses. . . . They are still young. . . .' She bent her head and continued in a whisper: 'Has he performed his final duty,* Prince? How priceless are those last moments! It can make things no worse, and it is absolutely necessary to prepare him if he is so ill. We women, Prince,' and she smiled tenderly, 'always know how to say these things. I absolutely must see him, however painful it may be for me. I am used to suffering.'

Evidently the prince understood her, and also understood, as he had done at Anna Pavlovna's, that it would be difficult to get rid of Anna Mikhaylovna.

'Would not such a meeting be too trying for him, dear Anna Mikhaylovna?' said he. 'Let us wait until evening. The doctors are expecting a crisis.'

'But one cannot delay, Prince, at such a moment! Consider that the welfare of his soul is at stake. Ah, it is awful: the duties of a Christian . . .'

A door of one of the inner rooms opened and one of the princesses, the count's niece, entered with a cold stern face. The length of her body was strikingly out of proportion to her short legs. Prince Vasili turned to her.

'Well, how is he?'

'Still the same; but what can you expect, this noise . . .' said the princess, looking at Anna Mikhaylovna as at a stranger.

'Ah, my dear, I hardly knew you,' said Anna Mikhaylovna with a happy smile, ambling lightly up to the count's niece. 'I have come, and am at your service to help you nurse *my uncle*. I imagine what you have gone through,' and she sympathetically turned up her eyes.

The princess gave no reply and did not even smile, but left the room at once. Anna Mikhaylovna took off her gloves, and occupying the position she had conquered, settled down in an arm-chair, inviting Prince Vasili to take a seat beside her.

'Boris,' she said to her son with a smile, 'I shall go in to see the count, my uncle; but you, my dear, had better go to Pierre meanwhile and don't forget to give him the Rostovs' invitation. They ask him to dinner. I suppose he won't go?' she continued, turning to the prince.

'On the contrary,' replied the prince, who had plainly become depressed, 'I shall be only too glad if you relieve me of that young man ... Here he is, and the count has not once asked for him.'

He shrugged his shoulders. A footman conducted Boris down one flight of stairs and up another, to Pierre's rooms.

## 13

PIERRE, after all, had not managed to choose a career for himself in Petersburg, and had been expelled from there for riotous conduct and sent to Moscow. The story told about him at Count Rostov's was true. Pierre had taken part in tying a policeman to a bear. He had now been for some days in Moscow and was staying as usual at his father's house. Though he expected that the story of his escapade would be already known in Moscow and that the ladies about his father – who were never favourably disposed towards him – would have used it to turn the count against him, he nevertheless on the day of his arrival went to his father's part of the house. Entering the drawing-room, where the princesses spent most of their time, he greeted the ladies, two of whom were sitting at embroidery frames while a third read aloud. It was the eldest who was reading – the one who had met Anna Mikhaylovna. The two younger ones were embroidering: both were rosy and pretty and they differed only in that one had a little mole on her lip which made her much prettier. Pierre was received as if he were a corpse or a leper. The eldest princess paused in her reading and silently stared at him with frightened eyes; the second assumed precisely the same expression; while the youngest, the one with the mole, who was of a cheerful and lively disposition, bent over her frame to hide a smile probably evoked by the amusing scene she foresaw. She drew her wool down through the canvas and, scarcely able to refrain from laughing, stooped as if trying to make out the pattern.

'How do you do, cousin?' said Pierre. 'You don't recognize me?'

'I recognize you only too well, too well.'

'How is the count? Can I see him?' asked Pierre, awkwardly as usual, but unabashed.

'The count is suffering physically and mentally, and apparently you have done your best to increase his mental sufferings.'

'Can I see the count?' Pierre again asked.

'H'm ... If you wish to kill him, to kill him outright, you can see him ... Olga, go and see whether uncle's beef-tea is ready – it is almost time,' she added, giving Pierre to understand that they were busy, and busy making his father comfortable, while evidently he, Pierre, was only busy causing him annoyance.

Olga went out. Pierre stood looking at the sisters; then he bowed and said:

'Then I will go to my rooms. You will let me know when I can see him.'

And he left the room, followed by the low but ringing laughter of the sister with the mole.,

Next day Prince Vasili had arrived and settled in the count's house. He sent for Pierre and said to him:

'My dear fellow, if you are going to behave here as you did in Petersburg, you will end very badly; that is all I have to say to you. The count is very, very, ill, and you must not see him at all.'

Since then Pierre had not been disturbed and had spent the whole time in his rooms upstairs.

When Boris appeared at his door Pierre was pacing up and down his room, stopping occasionally at a corner to make menacing gestures at the wall, as if running a sword through an invisible foe, and glaring savagely over his spectacles, and then again resuming his walk, muttering indistinct words, shrugging his shoulders, and gesticulating.

'England is done for,' said he, scowling and pointing his finger at someone unseen. 'Mr Pitt, as a traitor to the nation and to the rights of man, is sentenced to ...' But before Pierre – who at that moment imagined himself to be Napoleon in person and to have just effected the dangerous crossing of the straits of Dover and captured London – could pronounce Pitt's sentence, he saw a well-built and handsome young officer entering his room. Pierre paused. He had left Moscow when Boris was a boy of fourteen, and had quite forgotten him, but in his usual impulsive and hearty way he took Boris by the hand with a friendly smile.

'Do you remember me?' asked Boris quietly with a pleasant smile. 'I have come with my mother to see the count, but it seems he is not well.'

'Yes, it seems he is ill. People are always disturbing him,' answered Pierre, trying to remember who this young man was.

Boris felt that Pierre did not recognize him but did not consider it necessary to introduce himself, and without experiencing the least embarrassment looked Pierre straight in the face.

'Count Rostov asks you to come to dinner to-day,' said he, after a considerable pause which made Pierre feel uncomfortable.

'Ah, Count Rostov!' exclaimed Pierre joyfully. 'Then you are his son, Ilya? Only fancy, I didn't know you at first. Do you remember how we went to the Sparrow Hills with Madame Jacquot? ... It's such an age ...'

'You are mistaken,' said Boris deliberately, with a bold and slightly sarcastic smile. 'I am Boris, son of Princess Anna Mikhaylovna Drubetskaya. Rostov, the father, is Ilya, and his son is Nicholas. I never knew any Madame Jacquot.'

Pierre shook his head and arms as if attacked by mosquitoes or bees.

'Oh dear, what am I thinking about? I've mixed everything up. One has so many relatives in Moscow! So you are Boris? Of course. Well, now we know where we are. And what do you think of the Boulogne expedition? The English will come off badly, you know, if Napoleon gets across the Channel. I think the expedition is quite feasible. If only Villeneuve doesn't make a mess of things!'

Boris knew nothing about the Boulogne expedition; he did not read the papers and it was the first time he had heard Villeneuve's name.

'We here in Moscow are more occupied with dinner parties and scandal than with politics,' said he in his quiet ironical tone. 'I know nothing about it and have not thought about it. Moscow is chiefly busy with gossip,' he continued. 'Just now they are talking about you and your father.'

Pierre smiled in his good-natured way as if afraid for his companion's sake that the latter might say something he would afterwards regret. But Boris spoke distinctly, clearly and drily, looking straight into Pierre's eyes.

'Moscow has nothing else to do but gossip,' Boris went on. 'Everybody is wondering to whom the count will leave his fortune, though he may perhaps outlive us all, as I sincerely hope he will. ...'

'Yes, it is all very horrid,' interrupted Pierre, 'very horrid.'

Pierre was still afraid that this officer might inadvertently say something disconcerting to himself.

'And it must seem to you,' said Boris flushing slightly, but not changing his tone or attitude, 'it must seem to you that everyone is trying to get something out of the rich man?'

'So it does,' thought Pierre.

'But I just wish to say, to avoid misunderstandings, that you are quite mistaken if you reckon me or my mother among such people. We are very poor, but for my own part at any rate, for the very reason that your father is rich I don't regard myself as a relation of his, and neither I nor my mother would ever ask or take anything from him.'

For a long time Pierre could not understand, but when he did, he jumped up from the sofa, seized Boris under the elbow in his quick, clumsy way, and blushing far more than Boris, began to speak with a feeling of mingled shame and vexation.

'Well, this is strange! Do you suppose I ... who could think? ... I know very well ...'

But Boris again interrupted him.

'I am glad I have spoken out fully. Perhaps you did not like it? You must excuse me,' said he, putting Pierre at ease instead of being put at ease by him, 'but I hope I have not offended you. I always make it a rule to speak out.... Well, what answer am I to take? Will you come to dinner at the Rostovs?'

And Boris, having apparently relieved himself of an onerous duty and extricated himself from an awkward situation and placed another in it, became quite pleasant again.

'No, but I say,' said Pierre, calming down, 'you are a wonderful fellow! What you have just said is good, very good. Of course you don't know me. We have not met for such a long time ... not since we were children. You might think that I ... I understand, quite understand. I could not have done it myself, I should not have had the courage, but it's splendid. I am very glad to have made your acquaintance. It's queer,' he added after a pause, 'that you should have suspected me!' He began to laugh. 'Well, what of it! I hope we'll get better acquainted,' and he pressed Boris's hand. 'Do you know, I have not once been in to see the count. He has not sent for me ... I am sorry for him as a man, but what can one do?'

'And so you think Napoleon will manage to get an army across?' asked Boris with a smile.

Pierre saw that Boris wished to change the subject, and being of the same mind he began explaining the advantages and disadvantages of the Boulogne expedition.

A footman came in to summon Boris – the princess was going. Pierre, in order to make Boris's better acquaintance, promised to come to dinner, and warmly pressing his hand looked affectionately over his spectacles into Boris's eyes. After he had gone Pierre continued pacing up and down the room for a long time, no longer piercing an imaginary foe with his imaginary sword, but smiling at the remembrance of that pleasant intelligent and resolute young man.

As often happens in early youth, especially to one who leads a lonely life, he felt an unaccountable tenderness for this young man and made up his mind that they would be friends.

Prince Vasili saw the princess off. She held a handkerchief to her eyes and her face was tearful.

'It is dreadful, dreadful!' she was saying, 'but cost me what it may I shall do my duty. I will come and spend the night. He must not be left like this. Every moment is precious. I can't think why his nieces put it off. Perhaps God will help me to find a way to prepare him! ... Adieu, Prince! May God support you ...'

'*Adieu, ma bonne,*' answered Prince Vasili turning away from her.

'Oh, he is in a dreadful state,' said the mother to her son when they were in the carriage. 'He hardly recognizes anybody.'

'I don't understand, Mamma – what his attitude is to Pierre?' asked the son.

'The will will show that, my dear; our fate also depends on it ...'

'But why do you expect that he will leave us anything?'

'Ah my dear! He is so rich, and we are so poor!'

'Well, that is hardly a sufficient reason, Mamma ...'

'Oh Heaven! How ill he is!' exclaimed the mother.

14

AFTER Anna Mikhaylovna had driven off with her son to visit Count Cyril Vladimirovich Bezukhov, Countess Rostova sat for a long time all alone applying her handkerchief to her eyes. At last she rang.

'What is the matter with you, my dear?' she said crossly to the maid who kept her waiting some minutes. 'Don't you wish to serve me? Then I'll find you another place.'

The countess was upset by her friend's sorrow and humiliating poverty, and was therefore out of sorts, a state of mind which with her always found expression in calling her maid 'my dear' and speaking to her with exaggerated politeness.

'I am very sorry, ma'am,' answered the maid.

'Ask the count to come to me.'

The count came waddling in to see his wife with a rather guilty look as usual.

'Well, little Countess? What a *sauté* of game *au madère* we

57

are to have, my dear! I tasted it. The thousand rubles I paid for Taras were not ill-spent. He is worth it!'

He sat down by his wife, his elbows on his knees and his hands ruffling his grey hair.

'What are your commands, little Countess?'

'You see, my dear ... What's that mess?' she said, pointing to his waistcoat. 'It's the *sauté*, most likely,' she added with a smile. 'Well, you see, Count, I want some money.'

Her face became sad.

'Oh, little Countess!' ... and the count began bustling to get out his pocket-book.

'I want a great deal, Count! I want five hundred rubles,' and taking out her cambric handkerchief she began wiping her husband's waistcoat.

'Yes, immediately, immediately! Hey, who's there?' he called out in a tone only used by persons who are certain that those they call will rush to obey the summons. 'Send Dmitri to me!'

Dmitri, a man of good family who had been brought up in the count's house and now managed all his affairs, stepped softly into the room.

'This is what I want, my dear fellow,' said the count to the deferential young man who had entered. 'Bring me ...' he reflected a moment, 'yes, bring me seven hundred rubles, yes! But mind, don't bring me such tattered and dirty notes as last time, but nice clean ones for the countess.'

'Yes, Dmitri, clean ones, please,' said the countess, sighing deeply.

'When would you like them, your Excellency?' asked Dmitri. 'Allow me to inform you ... But, don't be uneasy,' he added, noticing that the count was beginning to breathe heavily and quickly which was always a sign of approaching anger. 'I was forgetting ... Do you wish it brought at once?'

'Yes, yes; just so! Bring it. Give it to the countess.'

'What a treasure that Dmitri is,' added the count with a smile when the young man had departed. 'There is never any "impossible" with him. That's a thing I hate! Everything is possible.'

'Ah, money, Count, money! How much sorrow it causes in the world,' said the countess. 'But I am in great need of this sum.'

'You, my little Countess, are a notorious spendthrift,' said the count, and having kissed his wife's hand he went back to his study.

When Anna Mikhaylovna returned from Count Bezukhov's the money, all in clean notes, was lying ready under a handkerchief on the countess's little table, and Anna Mikhaylovna noticed that something was agitating her.

'Well, my dear?' asked the countess.

'Oh, what a terrible state he is in! One would not know him, he is so ill! I was only there a few moments and hardly said a word . . .'

'Annette, for heaven's sake don't refuse me,' the countess began, with a blush that looked very strange on her thin, dignified, elderly face, and she took the money from under the handkerchief.

Anna Mikhaylovna instantly guessed her intention and stooped to be ready to embrace the countess at the appropriate moment.

'This is for Boris from me for his outfit.'

Anna Mikhaylovna was already embracing her and weeping. The countess wept too. They wept because they were friends, and because they were kind-hearted, and because they – friends from childhood – had to think about such a base thing as money, and because their youth was over. . . . But those tears were pleasant to them both.

15

COUNTESS ROSTOVA, with her daughters and a large number of guests, was already seated in the drawing-room. The count took the gentlemen into his study, and showed them his choice collection of Turkish pipes. From time to time he went out to ask: 'Hasn't she come yet?' They were expecting Marya Dmitrievna Akhrosimova,* known in society as *le terrible dragon*, a lady distinguished not for wealth or rank, but for common sense and frank plainness of speech. Marya Dmitrievna was known to the Imperial family as well as to all Moscow and Petersburg, and both cities wondered at her, laughed privately at her rudeness, and told good stories about her, while none the less all without exception respected and feared her.

In the count's room, which was full of tobacco-smoke, they talked of the war that had been announced in a manifesto, and about the recruiting. None of them had yet seen the manifesto, but they all knew it had appeared. The count sat on the sofa between two guests who were smoking and talking. He neither smoked nor talked, but bending his head first to one side and then to the other watched the smokers with evident pleasure and listened to the conversation of his two neighbours, whom he egged on against each other.

One of them was a sallow, clean-shaven civilian with a thin and wrinkled face, already growing old, though he was dressed like a most fashionable young man. He sat with his legs up on the sofa as if quite at home, and having stuck an amber mouthpiece far into his mouth, was inhaling the smoke spasmodically and screwing up his eyes. This was an old bachelor, Shinshin, a cousin of the countess's, a man with 'a sharp tongue' as they said in Moscow society. He seemed to be condescending to his companion. The latter, a fresh, rosy officer of the Guards, irreproachably washed, brushed and buttoned, held his pipe in the middle of his mouth and with red lips gently inhaled the smoke, letting it escape from his handsome mouth in rings. This was Lieutenant Berg, an officer in the Semënov regiment with whom Boris was to travel to join the army, and about whom Natasha had teased her elder sister Vera, speaking of Berg as her 'intended'. The count sat between them and listened attentively. His favourite occupation when not playing boston, a card game he was very fond of, was that of listener, especially when he succeeded in setting two loquacious talkers at one another.

'Well then, old chap, *mon très honorable* Alphonse Karlovich,' said Shinshin, laughing ironically and mixing the most ordinary Russian expressions with the choicest French phrases – which was a peculiarity of his speech, '*Vous comptez vous faire des rentes sur l'État*; you want to make something out of your company?'

'No, Peter Nikolaevich; I only want to show that in the cavalry the advantages are far less than in the infantry. Just consider my own position now, Peter Nikolaevich ...'

Berg always spoke quietly, politely, and with great precision. His conversation always related entirely to himself; he would remain calm and silent when the talk related to any topic that had no direct bearing on himself. He could remain silent for hours without being at all put out of countenance himself or making others uncomfortable, but as soon as the conversation concerned himself he would begin to talk circumstantially and with evident satisfaction.

'Consider my position, Peter Nikolaevich. Were I in the cavalry I should get not more than two hundred rubles every four months, even with the rank of lieutenant; but as it is I receive two hundred and thirty,' said he, looking at Shinshin and the count with a joyful, pleasant smile, as if it were obvious to him that his success must always be the chief desire of everyone else.

'Besides that, Peter Nikolaevich, by exchanging into the Guards I shall be in a more prominent position,' continued Berg, 'and vacancies occur much more frequently in the Foot Guards. Then just think what can be done with two hundred and thirty rubles! I even manage to put a little aside and to send something to my father,' he went on, emitting a smoke ring.

'*La balance y est*.... A German knows how to skin a flint, as the proverb says,' remarked Shinshin, moving his pipe to the other side of his mouth and winking at the count.

The count burst out laughing. The other guests seeing that Shinshin was talking came up to listen. Berg, oblivious of irony or indifference continued to explain how by exchanging into the Guards he had already gained a step on his old comrades of the Cadet Corps; how in war-time the company commander might get killed and he, as senior in the company, might easily succeed to the post; how popular he was with everyone in the regiment, and how satisfied his father was with him. Berg evidently enjoyed narrating all this, and did not seem to suspect that others, too, might have their own interests. But all he said was so prettily sedate, and the *naïveté* of his youthful egotism was so obvious, that he disarmed his hearers.

'Well, my boy, you'll get along wherever you go – foot or horse – that I'll warrant,' said Shinshin, patting him on the shoulder and taking his feet off the sofa.

Berg smiled joyously. The count, followed by his guests, went into the drawing-room.

\*

It was just the moment before a big dinner when the assembled guests, expecting the summons to *zakúska,*\* avoid engaging in any long conversation but think it necessary to move about and talk, in order to show that they are not at all impatient for their food. The host and hostess look towards the door, and now and then glance at one another, and the visitors try to guess from these glances who, or what, they are waiting for – some important relation who has not yet arrived, or a dish that is not yet ready.

Pierre had come just at dinner-time, and was sitting awkwardly in the middle of the drawing-room on the first chair he had come across, blocking the way for everyone. The countess tried to make him talk, but he went on naïvely looking around through his spectacles as if in search of somebody and answered all her questions in monosyllables. He was in the way and was the only one who did not notice the fact. Most of the guests, knowing of the affair with the bear, looked with curiosity at this big, stout, quiet man, wondering how such a clumsy, modest fellow could have played such a prank on a policeman.

'You have only lately arrived?' the countess asked him.

'*Oui, madame,*' replied he, looking around him.

'You have not yet seen my husband?'

'*Non, madame.*' He smiled quite inappropriately.

61

'You have been in Paris recently I believe? I suppose it's very interesting.'

'Very interesting.'

The countess exchanged glances with Anna Mikhaylovna. The latter understood that she was being asked to entertain this young man, and sitting down beside him she began to speak about his father; but he answered her, as he had the countess, only in monosyllables. The other guests were all conversing with one another. 'The Razumovskys... It was charming... You are very kind... Countess Apraksina...' was heard on all sides. The countess rose and went into the ball-room.

'Marya Dmitrievna?' came her voice from there.

'Herself,' came the answer in a rough voice, and Marya Dmitrievna entered the room.

All the unmarried ladies and even the married ones except the very oldest rose. Marya Dmitrievna paused at the door. Tall and stout, holding high her fifty-year-old head with its grey curls, she stood surveying the guests, and leisurely arranged her wide sleeves as if rolling them up. Marya Dmitrievna always spoke in Russian.

'Health and happiness to her whose name-day we are keeping and to her children,' she said, in her loud, full-toned voice which drowned all others. 'Well, you old sinner,' she went on, turning to the count who was kissing her hand, 'you're feeling dull in Moscow, I daresay? Nowhere to hunt with your dogs? But what is to be done, old man? Just see how these nestlings are growing up,' and she pointed to the girls. 'You must look for husbands for them, whether you like it or not.'

'Well,' said she, 'how's my Cossack?' (Marya Dmitrievna always called Natasha a Cossack), and she stroked the child's arm as she came up fearless and gay to kiss her hand. 'I know she's a scamp of a girl, but I like her.'

She took a pair of pear-shaped ruby earrings from her huge reticule, and having given them to the rosy Natasha, who beamed with the pleasure of her saint's-day fête, turned away at once and addressed herself to Pierre.

'Eh, eh, friend! Come here a bit,' said she, assuming a soft high tone of voice. 'Come here, my friend, ...' and she ominously tucked up her sleeves still higher. Pierre approached, looking at her in a childlike way through his spectacles.

'Come nearer, come nearer, friend! I used to be the only one to tell your father the truth when he was in favour, and in your case it's my evident duty.'

She paused. All were silent, expectant of what was to follow, for this was clearly only a prelude.

'A fine lad! My word! A fine lad!...His father lies on his death-bed and he amuses himself setting a policeman astride a bear! For shame, sir, for shame! It would be better if you went to the war.'

She turned away and gave her hand to the count, who could hardly keep from laughing.

'Well, I suppose it is time we were at table?' said Marya Dmitrievna.

The count went in first with Marya Dmitrievna, the countess followed on the arm of a colonel of hussars, a man of importance to them because Nicholas was to go with him to the regiment; then came Anna Mikhaylovna with Shinshin. Berg gave his arm to Vera. The smiling Julie Karagin went in with Nicholas. After them other couples followed, filling the whole dining-hall, and last of all the children, tutors, and governesses, followed singly. The footmen began moving about, chairs scraped, the band struck up in the gallery, and the guests settled down in their places. Then the strains of the count's household band were replaced by the clatter of knives and forks, the voices of visitors, and the soft steps of the footmen. At one end of the table sat the countess with Marya Dmitrievna on her right and Anna Mikhaylovna on her left, the other lady visitors were farther down. At the other end sat the count, with the hussar colonel on his left and Shinshin and the other male visitors on his right. Midway down the long table on one side sat the grown-up young people: Vera beside Berg, and Pierre beside Boris; and on the other side the children, tutors, and governesses. From behind the crystal decanters and fruit-dishes the count kept glancing at his wife and her tall cap with its light-blue ribbons, and busily filled his neighbours' glasses, not neglecting his own. The countess in turn, without omitting her duties as hostess, threw significant glances from behind the pineapples at her husband whose face and bald head seemed by their redness to contrast more than usual with his grey hair. At the ladies' end an even chatter of voices was heard all the time, at the men's end the voices sounded louder and louder, especially that of the colonel of hussars, who growing more and more flushed, ate and drank so much that the count held him up as a pattern to the other guests. Berg with tender smiles was saying to Vera that love is not an earthly but a heavenly feeling. Boris was telling his new friend Pierre who the guests were and exchanging glances with Natasha, who was sitting opposite. Pierre spoke little but examined the new faces, and ate a great deal. Of the two soups he chose turtle with savoury patties and went on to the game without omitting a single dish or one of the wines.

These latter the butler thrust mysteriously forward wrapped in a napkin from behind the next man's shoulders and whispered: 'Dry Madeira'... 'Hungarian'... or 'Rhine-wine' as the case might be. Of the four crystal glasses engraved with the count's monogram that stood before his plate, Pierre held out one at random and drank with enjoyment, gazing with ever-increasing amiability at the other guests. Natasha, who sat opposite, was looking at Boris as girls of thirteen look at the boy they are in love with and have just kissed for the first time. Sometimes that same look fell on Pierre, and that funny lively little girl's look made him inclined to laugh without knowing why.

Nicholas sat at some distance from Sonya, beside Julie Karagin, to whom he was again talking with the same involuntary smile. Sonya wore a company smile but was evidently tormented by jealousy; now she turned pale, now she blushed and strained every nerve to overhear what Nicholas and Julie were saying to one another. The governess kept looking round uneasily as if preparing to resent any slight that might be put upon the children. The German tutor was trying to remember all the dishes, wines, and kinds of dessert, in order to send a full description of the dinner to his people in Germany; and he felt greatly offended when the butler with a bottle wrapped in a napkin passed him by. He frowned, trying to appear as if he did not want any of that wine, but was mortified because no one would understand that it was not to quench his thirst or from greediness that he wanted it, but simply from a conscientious desire for knowledge.

16

AT the men's end of the table the talk grew more and more animated. The colonel told them that the declaration of war had already appeared in Petersburg and that a copy, which he had himself seen, had that day been forwarded by courier to the commander-in-chief.

'And why the deuce are we going to fight Bonaparte?' remarked Shinshin. 'He has stopped Austria's cackle and I fear it will be our turn next.'

The colonel was a stout, tall, plethoric German, evidently devoted to the service and patriotically Russian. He resented Shinshin's remark.

'It is for the reasson, my goot sir,' said he, speaking with a German accent, 'for the reasson zat ze Emperor knows zat. He declares in ze manifessto zat he cannot fiew wiz indifference ze danger vreatening Russia and zat ze safety and dignity of ze Empire as vell as ze sanctity of its *alliances...*', he spoke this last word with particular emphasis as if in it lay the gist of the matter.

Then with the unerring official memory that characterized him he repeated from the opening words of the manifesto:

'*...and the wish, which constitutes the Emperor's sole and absolute aim – to establish peace in Europe on firm foundations – has now decided him to despatch part of the army abroad and to create a new condition for the attainment of that purpose.*'

'Zat, my dear sir, is vy...' he concluded, drinking a tumbler of wine with dignity and looking to the count for approval.

'*Connaissez-vous le proverbe:* "*Jerome, Jerome, do not roam, but turn spindles at home!*"?' said Shinshin, puckering his brows and smiling. '*Cela nous convient à merveille.* Suvorov now – he knew what he was about; yet they beat him *à plate couture,*\* and where are we to find Suvorovs now? *Je vous demande un peu,*' said he, continually changing from French to Russian.

'Ve must vight to the last tr-r-op of our plood!' said the colonel, thumping the table; 'and ve must tie for our Emperor, and zen all vill pe vell. And ve must discuss it as little as po-o-ossible'... he dwelt particularly on the word *possible*...'as po-o-ossible,' he ended, again turning to the count. 'Zat is how ve old hussars look at it, and zere's an end of it! And how do you, a young man and a young hussar, how do you judge of it?' he added, addressing Nicholas, who when he heard that the war was being discussed had turned from his partner with eyes and ears intent on the colonel.

'I am quite of your opinion,' replied Nicholas, flaming up, turning his plate round and moving his wine glasses about with as much decision and desperation as though he were at that moment facing some great danger. 'I am convinced that we Russians must die or conquer,' he concluded, conscious – as were others – after the words were uttered that his remarks were too enthusiastic and emphatic for the occasion and were therefore awkward.

'What you said just now was splendid!' said his partner Julie.

Sonya trembled all over and blushed to her ears and behind them and down to her neck and shoulders while Nicholas was speaking.

Pierre listened to the colonel's speech and nodded approvingly.

'That's fine,' said he.

'The young man's a real hussar!' shouted the colonel, again thumping the table.

'What are you making such a noise about over there?' Marya Dmitrievna's deep voice suddenly inquired from the other end of the table. 'What are you thumping the table for?' she demanded of the hussar, 'and why are you exciting yourself? Do you think the French are here?'

'I am speaking ze truce,' replied the hussar with a smile.

'It's all about the war,' the count shouted down the table. 'You know my son's going, Marya Dmitrievna? My son is going.'

'I have four sons in the army but still I don't fret. It is all in God's hands. You may die in your bed or God may spare you in a battle,' replied Marya Dmitrievna's deep voice, which easily carried the whole length of the table.

'That's true!'

Once more the conversations concentrated, the ladies' at the one end and the men's at the other.

'You won't ask,' Natasha's little brother was saying; 'I know you won't ask!'

'I will,' replied Natasha.

Her face suddenly flushed with reckless and joyous resolution. She half rose, by a glance inviting Pierre, who sat opposite, to listen to what was coming, and turning to her mother:

'Mamma!' rang out the clear contralto notes of her childish voice, audible the whole length of the table.

'What is it?' asked the countess, startled; but seeing by her daughter's face that it was only mischief, she shook a finger at her sternly with a threatening and forbidding movement of her head.

The conversation was hushed.

'Mamma! What sweets are we going to have?' and Natasha's voice sounded still more firm and resolute.

The countess tried to frown, but could not. Marya Dmitrievna shook her fat finger.

'Cossack!' she said threateningly.

Most of the guests, uncertain how to regard this sally, looked at the elders.

'You had better take care!' said the countess.

'Mamma! What sweets are we going to have?' Natasha again cried boldly, with saucy gaiety, confident that her prank would be taken in good part.

Sonya and fat little Petya doubled up with laughter.

'You see! I *have* asked,' whispered Natasha to her little brother and to Pierre, glancing at him again.

'Ice-pudding, but you won't get any,' said Marya Dmitrievna.

Natasha saw there was nothing to be afraid of and so she braved even Marya Dmitrievna.

'Marya Dmitrievna! What kind of ice-pudding? I don't like ice-cream.'

'Carrot-ices.'

'No! What kind, Marya Dmitrievna? What kind?' she almost screamed; 'I want to know!'

Marya Dmitrievna and the countess burst out laughing, and all the guests joined in. Everyone laughed, not at Marya Dmitrievna's answer but at the incredible boldness and smartness of this little girl who had dared to treat Marya Dmitrievna in this fashion.

Natasha only desisted when she had been told that there would be pineapple ice. Before the ices champagne was served round. The band again struck up, the count and countess kissed, and the guests, leaving their seats, went up to 'congratulate' the countess, and reached across the table to clink glasses with the count, with the children, and with one another. Again the footmen rushed about, chairs scraped, and in the same order in which they had entered but with redder faces, the guests returned to the drawing-room and to the count's study.

<h2 style="text-align:center">17</h2>

THE card-tables were drawn out, sets made up for boston, and the count's visitors settled themselves, some in the two drawing-rooms, some in the sitting-room, some in the library.

The count, holding his cards fanwise, kept himself with difficulty from dropping into his usual after-dinner nap, and laughed at everything. The young people, at the countess's instigation, gathered round the clavichord and harp. Julie by general request played first. After she had played a little air with variations on the harp, she joined the other young ladies in begging Natasha and Nicholas, who were noted for their musical talent, to sing something. Natasha, who was treated as though she were grown up, was evidently very proud of this but at the same time felt shy.

'What shall we sing?' she asked.

'"The Brook,"' suggested Nicholas.

'Well then let's be quick. Boris, come here,' said Natasha. 'But where is Sonya?'

She looked round and seeing that her friend was not in the room ran to look for her.

Running into Sonya's room and not finding her there, Natasha ran to the nursery, but Sonya was not there either. Natasha concluded that she must be on the chest in the passage. The chest in the passage was the place of mourning for the younger female generation in the Rostov household. And there in fact was Sonya lying face downward on Nurse's dirty feather-bed on the top of the chest, crumpling her gauzy pink dress under her, hiding her face with her slender fingers, and sobbing so convulsively that her bare little shoulders shook. Natasha's face which had been so radiantly happy all that saint's-day, suddenly changed: her eyes became fixed, and then a shiver passed down her broad neck and the corners of her mouth drooped.

'Sonya! What is it?... What is the matter?... Oo... Oo... Oo...!' And Natasha's large mouth widened, making her look quite ugly, and she began to wail like a baby without knowing why, except that Sonya was crying. Sonya tried to lift her head to answer but could not, and hid her face still deeper in the bed. Natasha wept, sitting on the blue-striped feather-bed and hugging her friend. With an effort Sonya sat up and began wiping her eyes and explaining.

'Nicholas is going away in a week's time, his... papers... have come... he told me himself... but still I should not cry,' and she showed a paper she held in her hand – with the verses Nicholas had written, 'still, I should not cry, but you can't... no one can understand... what a soul he has!'

And she began to cry again because he had such a noble soul.

'It's all very well for you... I am not envious... I love you and Boris also,' she went on, gaining a little strength; 'he is nice ... there are no difficulties in your way... But Nicholas is my cousin... one would have to... the Metropolitan himself*... and even then it can't be done. And besides, if she tells Mamma' (Sonya looked upon the countess as her mother and called her so) 'that I am spoiling Nicholas's career and am heartless and ungrateful, while truly... God is my witness,' and she made the sign of the cross, 'I love her so much, and all of you, only Vera... And what for? What have I done to her? I am so grateful to you that I would willingly sacrifice everything, only I have nothing...'

Sonya could not continue, and again hid her face in her hands and in the feather-bed. Natasha began consoling her, but her face showed that she understood all the gravity of her friend's trouble.

'Sonya,' she suddenly exclaimed, as if she had guessed the true reason of her friend's sorrow, 'I'm sure Vera has said something to you since dinner? Hasn't she?'

'Yes, these verses Nicholas wrote himself and I copied some others, and she found them on my table and said she'd show them to Mamma, and that I was ungrateful, and that Mamma would never allow him to marry me, but that he'll marry Julie. You see how he's been with her all day... Natasha, what have I done to deserve it?'

And again she began to sob, more bitterly than before. Natasha

68

lifted her up, hugged her, and smiling through her tears, began comforting her.

'Sonya, don't believe her, darling! Don't believe her! Do you remember how we and Nicholas, all three of us, talked in the sitting-room after supper? Why, we settled how everything was to be. I don't quite remember how, but don't you remember that it could all be arranged and how nice it all was? There's Uncle Shinshin's brother has married his first cousin! And we are only second cousins, you know. And Boris says it is quite possible. You know I have told him all about it. And he is so clever and so good!' said Natasha. 'Don't you cry, Sonya, dear love, darling Sonya;' and she kissed her and laughed. 'Vera's spiteful; never mind her! And all will come right and she won't say anything to Mamma. Nicholas will tell her himself, and he doesn't care at all for Julie.'

Natasha kissed her on the hair.

Sonya sat up. The little kitten brightened, its eyes shone, and it seemed ready to lift its tail, jump down on its soft paws, and begin playing with the ball of worsted as a kitten should.

'Do you think so? ... Really? Truly?' she said, quickly smoothing her frock and hair.

'Really, truly!' answered Natasha, pushing in a crisp lock that had strayed from under her friend's plaits.

Both laughed.

'Well, let's go and sing "The Brook".'

'Come along!'

'Do you know, that fat Pierre who sat opposite me is so funny!' said Natasha, stopping suddenly. 'I feel so happy!'

And she set off at a run along the passage.

Sonya, shaking off some down which clung to her and tucking away the verses in the bosom of her dress close to her bony little chest, ran after Natasha down the passage into the sitting-room with flushed face and light, joyous steps. At the visitors' request the young people sang the quartette 'The Brook', with which everyone was delighted. Then Nicholas sang a song he had just learnt.

> At night time in the moon's fair glow,
>   How sweet, as fancies wander free,
> To feel that *in this world there's one*
> *Who still is thinking but of thee!*
>
> That while her fingers touch the harp
>   Wafting sweet music o'er the lea,
> It is for thee thus swells her heart,
>   Sighing its message out to thee....
>
> A day or two, then bliss unspoilt,
>   But oh! till then I cannot live!...

He had not finished the last verse before the young people began to get ready to dance in the large hall, and the sound of the feet and the coughing of the musicians were heard from the gallery.

*

Pierre was sitting in the drawing-room where Shinshin had engaged him, as a man recently returned from abroad, in a political conversation in which several others joined but which bored Pierre. When the music began Natasha came in and walking straight up to Pierre said, laughing and blushing:

'Mamma told me to ask you to join the dancers.'

'I am afraid of mixing the figures,' Pierre replied; 'but if you will be my teacher ...' And lowering his big arm he offered it to the slender little girl.

While the couples were arranging themselves and the musicians tuning up, Pierre sat down with his little partner. Natasha was perfectly happy; she was dancing with a *grown-up* man, who had been *abroad*. She was sitting in a conspicuous place and talking to him like a grown-up lady. She had a fan in her hand that one of the ladies had given her to hold. Assuming quite the pose of a society woman (heaven knows when and where she had learnt it) she talked with her partner, fanning herself and smiling over the fan.

'Dear, dear! Just look at her!' exclaimed the countess as she crossed the ball-room, pointing to Natasha.

Natasha blushed and laughed.

'Well, really, Mamma! Why should you? What is there to be surprised at?'

In the midst of the third *écossaise* there was a clatter of chairs being pushed back in the sitting-room where the count and Marya Dmitrievna had been playing cards with the majority of the more distinguished and older visitors. They now, stretching themselves after sitting so long, and replacing their purses and pocket-books, entered the ball-room. First came Marya Dmitrievna and the count, both with merry countenances. The count, with playful ceremony somewhat in *ballet* style, offered his bent arm to Marya Dmitrievna. He drew himself up, a smile of debonair gallantry lit up his face, and as soon as the last figure of the *écossaise* was ended, he clapped his hands to the musicians and shouted up to their gallery, addressing the first violin:

'Simën! Do you know the *Daniel Cooper*?'

This was the count's favourite dance, which he had danced in his youth. (Strictly speaking, *Daniel Cooper* was one figure of the *anglaise*.)

'Look at Papa!' shouted Natasha to the whole company, and

quite forgetting that she was dancing with a grown-up partner she bent her curly head to her knees and made the whole room ring with her laughter.

And indeed everybody in the room looked with a smile of pleasure at the jovial old gentleman, who standing beside his tall and stout partner, Marya Dmitrievna, curved his arms, beat time, straightened his shoulders, turned out his toes, tapped gently with his foot, and by a smile that broadened his round face more and more, prepared the onlookers for what was to follow. As soon as the provocatively gay strains of *Daniel Cooper* (somewhat resembling those of a merry peasant dance) began to sound, all the doorways of the ball-room were suddenly filled by the domestic serfs – the men on one side and the women on the other – who with beaming faces had come to see their master making merry.

'Just look at the master! A regular eagle he is!' loudly remarked the nurse, as she stood in one of the doorways.

The count danced well and knew it. But his partner could not and did not want to dance well. Her enormous figure stood erect, her powerful arms hanging down (she had handed her reticule to the countess), and only her stern but handsome face really joined in the dance. What was expressed by the whole of the count's plump figure, in Marya Dmitrievna found expression only in her more and more beaming face and quivering nose. But if the count, getting more and more into the swing of it, charmed the spectators by the unexpectedness of his adroit manœuvres and the agility with which he capered about on his light feet, Marya Dmitrievna produced no less impression by slight exertions – the least effort to move her shoulders or bend her arms when turning, or stamp her foot – which everyone appreciated in view of her size and habitual severity. The dance grew livelier and livelier. The other couples could not attract a moment's attention to their own evolutions and did not even try to do so. All were watching the count and Marya Dmitrievna. Natasha kept pulling everyone by sleeve or dress, urging them to 'look at Papa!' though as it was they never took their eyes off the couple. In the intervals of the dance the count, breathing deeply, waved and shouted to the musicians to play faster. Faster, faster and faster; lightly, more lightly and yet more lightly whirled the count, flying round Marya Dmitrievna, now on his toes, now on his heels; until, turning his partner round to her seat, he executed the final *pas*, raising his light foot backwards, bowing his perspiring head, smiling, and making a wide sweep with his arm, amid a thunder of applause and laughter led by Natasha. Both partners stood still, breathing heavily and wiping their faces with their cambric handkerchiefs.

'That's how we used to dance in our time, *ma chère*,' said the count.

'That *was* a *Daniel Cooper!*' exclaimed Marya Dmitrievna, tucking up her sleeves and puffing heavily.

— 18 —

WHILE in the Rostovs' ball-room the sixth *anglaise* was being danced, to a tune in which the weary musicians blundered, and while tired footmen and cooks were getting the supper, Count Bezukhov had a sixth stroke. The doctors pronounced recovery impossible. After a mute confession, Communion was administered to the dying man, preparations made for the sacrament of Unction, and in his house there was the bustle and thrill of suspense usual at such moments. Outside the house, beyond the gates, a group of undertakers, who hid whenever a carriage drove up, waited in expectation of an important order for an expensive funeral. The Military Governor of Moscow, who had been assiduous in sending aides-de-camp to inquire after the count's health, came himself that evening to bid a last farewell to the celebrated grandee of Catherine's court, Count Bezukhov.

The magnificent reception-room was crowded. Everyone stood up respectfully when the Military Governor, having stayed about half an hour alone with the dying man, passed out, slightly acknowledging their bows and trying to escape as quickly as possible from the glances fixed on him by the doctors, clergy, and relatives of the family. Prince Vasili, who had grown thinner and paler during the last few days, escorted him to the door, repeating something to him several times in low tones.

When the Military Governor had gone, Prince Vasili sat down all alone on a chair in the ball-room, crossing one leg high over the other, leaning his elbow on his knee and covering his face with his hand. After sitting so for a while he rose, and, looking about him with frightened eyes, went with unusually hurried steps down the long corridor leading to the back of the house, to the room of the eldest princess.

Those who were in the dimly-lit reception-room spoke in nervous whispers, and whenever anyone went into or came from the dying man's room, grew silent and gazed with eyes full of curiosity at his door, which creaked slightly when opened.

'The limits of human life . . . are fixed and may not be o'erpassed,' said an old priest to a lady who had taken a seat beside him and was listening naïvely to his words.

'I wonder, is it not too late to administer Unction?' asked the lady, adding the priest's clerical title, as if she had no opinion of her own on the subject.

'Ah madam, it is a great sacrament,' replied the priest, passing his hand over the thin grizzled strands of hair combed back across his bald head.

'Who was that? The Military Governor himself?' was being asked at the other side of the room. 'How young-looking he is!'

'Yes, and he is over sixty. I hear the count no longer recognizes anyone? They wished to administer the sacrament of Unction.'

'I knew someone who received that sacrament seven times.'

The second princess had just come from the sick room with her eyes red from weeping and sat down beside Doctor Lorrain, who was sitting in a graceful pose under a portrait of Catherine, leaning his elbow on a table.

'Beautiful,' said the doctor in answer to a remark about the weather. 'The weather is beautiful, Princess; and besides, in Moscow one feels as if one were in the country.'

'Yes, indeed,' replied the princess with a sigh. 'So he may have something to drink?'

Lorrain considered.

'Has he taken his medicine?'

'Yes.'

The doctor glanced at his watch.

'Take a glass of boiled water and put a pinch of cream of tartar,' and he indicated with his delicate fingers what he meant by a pinch.

'Dere has neffer been a gase,' a German doctor was saying to an aide-de-camp, 'dat one liffs after de sird sdroke.'

'And what a well-preserved man he was!' remarked the aide-de-camp. 'And who will inherit his wealth?' he added in a whisper.

'It von't go begging,' replied the German with a smile.

Everyone again looked towards the door, which creaked as the second princess went in with the drink she had prepared according to Lorrain's instructions. The German doctor went up to Lorrain.

'Do you think he can last till morning?' asked the German, addressing Lorrain in French which he pronounced badly.

Lorrain, pursing up his lips, waved a severely negative finger before his nose.

'To-night, not later,' said he in a low voice, and he moved away with a decorous smile of self-satisfaction at being able clearly to understand and state the patient's condition.

Meanwhile Prince Vasili had opened the door into the princess's room.

In this room it was almost dark; only two tiny lamps were burning before the icons and there was a pleasant scent of flowers and burnt pastilles. The room was crowded with small pieces of furniture, whatnots, cupboards, and little tables. The quilt of a high, white feather-bed was just visible behind a screen. A small dog began to bark.

'Ah, is it you, cousin?'

She rose and smoothed her hair, which was as usual so extremely smooth that it seemed to be made of one piece with her head and covered with varnish.

'Has anything happened?' she asked. 'I am so terrified.'

'No, there is no change. I only came to have a talk about business, Catiche,' muttered the prince, seating himself wearily on the chair she had just vacated. 'You have made the place warm, I must say,' he remarked. 'Well, sit down: let's have a talk.'

'I thought perhaps something had happened,' she said with her unchanging stonily severe expression; and, sitting down opposite the prince, she prepared to listen.

'I wished to get a nap, *mon cousin*, but I can't.'

'Well, my dear?' said Prince Vasili, taking her hand and bending it downwards as was his habit.

It was plain that this 'well?' referred to much that they both understood without naming.

The princess, who had a straight, rigid body, abnormally long for her legs, looked directly at Prince Vasili with no sign of emotion in her prominent grey eyes. Then she shook her head and glanced up at the icons with a sigh. This might have been taken as an expression of sorrow and devotion, or of weariness and hope of resting before long. Prince Vasili understood it as an expression of weariness.

'And I?' he said; 'do you think it is easier for me? I am as worn out as a post-horse, but still I must have a talk with you, Catiche, a very serious talk.'

Prince Vasili said no more and his cheeks began to twitch nervously, now on one side now on the other, giving his face an unpleasant expression which was never to be seen on it in a drawing-room. His eyes too seemed strange: at one moment they looked impudently sly and at the next glanced round in alarm.

The princess, holding her little dog on her lap with her thin bony hands, looked attentively into Prince Vasili's eyes evidently resolved not to be the first to break silence, if she had to wait till morning.

'Well, you see, my dear Princess and cousin, Catherine Seménovna,' continued Prince Vasili, returning to his theme, apparently not without an inner struggle; 'at such a moment as this one must think of everything. One must think of the future, of all of you . . . I love you all, like children of my own, as you know.'

The princess continued to look at him without moving, and with the same dull expression.

'And then of course my family has also to be considered,' Prince Vasili went on, testily pushing away a little table without looking at her. 'You know, Catiche, that we – you three sisters, Mamontov, and my wife – are the count's only direct heirs. I know, I know how hard it is for you to talk or think of such matters. It is no easier for me; but, my dear, I am getting on for sixty and must be prepared for anything. Do you know I have sent for Pierre? The count', pointing to his portrait, 'definitely demanded that he should be called.'

Prince Vasili looked questioningly at the princess, but could not make out whether she was considering what he had just said or whether she was simply looking at him.

'There is one thing I constantly pray God to grant, *mon cousin*,' she replied, 'and it is that He would be merciful to him and would allow his noble soul peacefully to leave this . . .'

'Yes, yes, of course,' interrupted Prince Vasili impatiently, rubbing his bald head and angrily pulling back towards him the little table that he had pushed away. 'But . . . in short the fact is . . . you know yourself that last winter the count made a will by which he left all his property, not to us his direct heirs, but to Pierre.'

'He has made wills enough!' quietly remarked the princess. 'But he cannot leave the estate to Pierre. Pierre is illegitimate.'

'But, my dear,' said Prince Vasili suddenly, clutching the little table and becoming more animated and talking more rapidly: 'what if a letter has been written to the Emperor in which the count asks for Pierre's legitimation? Do you understand that in consideration of the count's services, his request would be granted? . . .'

The princess smiled as people do who think they know more about the subject under discussion than those they are talking with.

'I can tell you more,' continued Prince Vasili, seizing her hand, 'that letter was written, though it was not sent, and the Emperor knew of it. The only question is has it been destroyed or not? If not, then as soon as *all is over*,' and Prince Vasili sighed to intimate what he meant by the words *all is over*, 'and the count's papers are opened, the will and letter will be delivered to the Emperor, and the petition will certainly be granted. Pierre will get everything as the legitimate son.'

'And our share?' asked the princess smiling ironically, as if anything might happen, only not that.

'But, my poor Catiche, it is as clear as daylight! He will then be the legal heir to everything and you won't get anything. You must know, my dear, whether the will and letter were written, and whether they have been destroyed or not. And if they have somehow been overlooked, you ought to know where they are, and must find them, because . . .'

'What next?' the princess interrupted, smiling sardonically and not changing the expression of her eyes. 'I am a woman, and you think we are all stupid; but I know this: an illegitimate son cannot inherit . . . *un bâtard!*' she added, as if supposing that this translation of the word would effectively prove to Prince Vasili the invalidity of his contention.

'Well really, Catiche! Can't you understand! You are so intelligent, how is it you don't see that if the count has written a letter to the Emperor begging him to recognize Pierre as legitimate, it follows that Pierre will not be Pierre but will become Bezukhov, and will then inherit everything under the will? And if the will and letter are not destroyed, then you will have nothing but the consolation of having been dutiful *et tout ce qui s'en suit!* That's certain.'

'I know the will was made, but I also know that it is invalid; and you, *mon cousin*, seem to consider me a perfect fool,' said the princess with the expression women assume when they suppose they are saying something witty and stinging.

'My dear Princess Catherine Seménovna,' began Prince Vasili impatiently, 'I came here not to wrangle with you, but to talk about your interests as with a kinswoman, a good, kind, true relation. And I tell you for the tenth time, that if the letter to the Emperor and the will in Pierre's favour are among the count's papers, then, my dear girl, you and your sisters are not heiresses! If you don't believe me, then believe an expert. I have just been talking to Dmitri Onufrich' (the family solicitor) 'and he says the same.'

At this a sudden change evidently took place in the princess's ideas; her thin lips grew white, though her eyes did not change, and her voice when she began to speak passed through such transitions as she herself evidently did not expect.

'That would be a fine thing!' said she. 'I never wanted anything and I don't now.'

She pushed the little dog off her lap and smoothed her dress.

'And this is gratitude – this is recognition for those who have sacrificed everything for his sake!' she cried. 'It's splendid! Fine! I don't want anything, Prince.'

'Yes, but you are not the only one. There are your sisters . . .' replied Prince Vasili.

But the princess did not listen to him.

'Yes, I knew it long ago but had forgotten. I knew that I could expect nothing but meanness, deceit, envy, intrigue, and ingratitude – the blackest ingratitude – in this house . . .'

'Do you or do you not know where that will is?' insisted Prince Vasili, his cheeks twitching more than ever.

'Yes, I was a fool! I still believed in people, loved them, and sacrificed myself. But only the base, the vile succeed! I know who has been intriguing!'

The princess wished to rise, but the prince held her by the hand. She had the air of one who has suddenly lost faith in the whole human race. She gave her companion an angry glance.

'There is still time, my dear. You must remember, Catiche, that it was all done casually in a moment of anger, of illness, and was afterwards forgotten. Our duty, my dear, is to rectify his mistake, to ease his last moments by not letting him commit this injustice, and not to let him die feeling that he is rendering unhappy those who . . .'

'Who sacrificed everything for him,' chimed in the princess, who would again have risen had not the prince still held her fast, 'though he never could appreciate it. No, *mon cousin*,' she added with a sigh, 'I shall always remember that in this world one must expect no reward, that in this world there is neither honour nor justice. In this world one has to be cunning and cruel.'

'Now come, come! Be reasonable. I know your excellent heart.'

'No, I have a wicked heart.'

'I know your heart,' repeated the prince. 'I value your friendship and wish you to have as good an opinion of me. Don't upset yourself, and let us talk sensibly while there is still time, be it a day or be it but an hour. . . . Tell me all you know about the will, and above all where it is. You must know. We will take it at once and show it to the count. He has no doubt forgotten it and will wish to destroy it. You understand that my sole desire is conscientiously to carry out his wishes; that is my only reason for being here. I came simply to help him and you.'

'Now I see it all! I know who has been intriguing – I know!' cried the princess.

'That's not the point, my dear.'

'It's that protégée of yours, that sweet Princess Drubetskaya, that Anna Mikhaylovna whom I would not take for a housemaid . . . the infamous vile woman!'

'Do not let us lose any time . . .'

'Ah, don't talk to me! Last winter she wheedled herself in here and told the count such vile, disgraceful things about us, especially about Sophie – I can't repeat them – that it made the count quite ill and he would not see us for a whole fortnight. I know it was then he wrote this vile, infamous paper, but I thought the thing was invalid.'

'We've got to it at last – why did you not tell me about it sooner?'

'It's in the inlaid portfolio that he keeps under his pillow,' said the princess, ignoring his question. 'Now I know! Yes; if I have a sin, a great sin, it is hatred of that vile woman!' almost shrieked the princess, now quite changed. 'And what does she come worming herself in here for? But I will give her a piece of my mind. The time will come!'

## 19

WHILE these conversations were going on in the reception-room and the princess's room, a carriage containing Pierre (who had been sent for) and Anna Mikhaylovna (who found it necessary to accompany him) was driving into the court of Count Bezukhov's house. As the wheels rolled softly over the straw beneath the windows, Anna Mikhaylovna, having turned with words of comfort to her companion realized that he was asleep in his corner and woke him up. Rousing himself, Pierre followed Anna Mikhaylovna out of the carriage, and only then began to think of the interview with his dying father which awaited him. He noticed that they had not come to the front entrance but to the back door. While he was getting down from the carriage steps two men, who looked like tradespeople, ran hurriedly from the entrance and hid in the shadow of the wall. Pausing for a moment, Pierre noticed several other men of the same kind hiding in the shadow of the house on both sides. But neither Anna Mikhaylovna nor the footman nor the coachman, who could not help seeing these people, took any notice of them. 'It seems to be all right,' Pierre concluded, and followed Anna Mikhaylovna. She hurriedly ascended the narrow dimly-lit stone staircase, calling to Pierre, who was lagging behind, to follow. Though he did not see why it was necessary for him to go to the count at all, still less why he had to go by the back stairs, yet judging by Anna Mikhaylovna's air of assurance and haste, Pierre concluded that it was all absolutely necessary. Half-way up the stairs they were almost knocked over by some men who, carrying pails, came running downstairs, their boots clattering. These men pressed close to the wall to let Pierre and Anna Mikhaylovna pass and did not evince the least surprise at seeing them there.

'Is this the way to the princesses' apartments?' asked Anna Mikhaylovna of one of them.

'Yes,' replied a footman in a bold loud voice, as if anything were now permissible; 'the door to the left, ma'am.'

'Perhaps the count did not ask for me,' said Pierre when he reached the landing. 'I'd better go to my own room.'

Anna Mikhaylovna paused and waited for him to come up.

'Ah, my friend!' she said, touching his arm as she had done her son's when speaking to him that afternoon, 'believe me I suffer no less than you do, but be a man!'

'But really, hadn't I better go away?' he asked, looking kindly at her over his spectacles.

'Ah, my dear friend! Forget the wrongs that may have been done you. Think that he is your father... perhaps in the agony of death.' She sighed. 'I have loved you like a son from the first. Trust yourself to me, Pierre. I shall not forget your interests.'

Pierre did not understand a word, but the conviction that all this had to be grew stronger, and he meekly followed Anna Mikhaylovna who was already opening a door.

This door led into a back ante-room. An old man, a servant of the princesses, sat in a corner knitting a stocking. Pierre had never been in this part of the house and did not even know of the existence of these rooms. Anna Mikhaylovna, addressing a maid who was hurrying past with a decanter on a tray as 'my dear' and 'my sweet', asked about the princesses' health, and then led Pierre along a stone passage. The first door on the left led into the princesses' apartments. The maid with the decanter in her haste had not closed the door (everything in the house was done in haste at that time), and Pierre and Anna Mikhaylovna in passing instinctively glanced into the room, where Prince Vasili and the eldest princess were sitting close together talking. Seeing them pass, Prince Vasili drew back with obvious impatience, while the princess jumped up and with a gesture of desperation slammed the door with all her might.

This action was so unlike her usual composure and the fear depicted on Prince Vasili's face so out of keeping with his dignity, that Pierre stopped and glanced inquiringly over his spectacles at his guide. Anna Mikhaylovna evinced no surprise, she only smiled faintly and sighed, as if to say that this was no more than she had expected.

'Be a man, my friend. I will look after your interests,' said she in reply to his look, and went still faster along the passage.

Pierre could not make out what it was all about, and still less what 'watching over his interests' meant, but he decided that all these things had to be. From the passage they went into a large dimly-lit room adjoining the count's reception-room. It was one of those sumptuous but cold apartments known to Pierre only from the front approach, but even in this room there now stood an empty bath, and water had been spilt on the carpet. They were met by a deacon with a censer and by a servant who passed out on tiptoe without heeding them. They went into the reception-room familiar to Pierre, with two Italian windows opening into the conservatory with its large bust and full-length portrait of Catherine the Great. The same people were still sitting here in almost the same positions as before, whispering to one another. All became silent and turned to look at the pale tear-worn Anna Mikhaylovna as she entered, and at the big stout figure of Pierre who, hanging his head, meekly followed her.

Anna Mikhaylovna's face expressed a consciousness that the decisive moment had arrived. With the air of a practical Petersburg lady she now, keeping Pierre close beside her, entered the room even more boldly than that afternoon. She felt that as she brought with her the person the dying man wished to see her own admission was assured. Casting a rapid glance at all those in the room and noticing the count's confessor there, she glided up to him with a sort of amble, not exactly bowing, yet seeming to grow suddenly smaller, and respectfully received the blessing first of one and then of another priest.

'God be thanked that you are in time,' said she to one of the priests; 'all we relatives have been in such anxiety. This young man is the count's son,' she added more softly. 'What a terrible moment!'

Having said this she went up to the doctor.

'Dear doctor,' said she, 'this young man is the count's son. Is there any hope?'

The doctor cast a rapid glance upwards and silently shrugged his shoulders. Anna Mikhaylovna with just the same movement raised her shoulders and eyes, almost closing the latter, sighed, and moved away from the doctor to Pierre. To him, in a particularly respectful and tenderly sad voice, she said:

'Trust in His mercy!' and pointing out a small sofa for him to sit and wait for her, she went silently towards the door that everyone was watching and it creaked very slightly as she disappeared behind it.

Pierre having made up his mind to obey his monitress implicitly, moved towards the sofa she had indicated. As soon as Anna Mikhaylovna had disappeared he noticed that the eyes of all in the room turned to him with something more than curiosity and sympathy. He noticed that they whispered to one another, casting significant looks at him with a kind of awe and even servility. A deference such as he had never before received was shown him. A strange lady, the one who had been talking to the priests, rose and offered him her seat; an aide-de-camp picked up and returned a glove Pierre had dropped; the doctors became respectfully silent as he passed by, and moved to make way for him. At first Pierre wished to take another seat so as not to trouble the lady, and also to pick up the glove himself and to pass round the doctors who were not even in his way; but all at once he felt that this would not do, and that to-night he was a person obliged to perform some sort of awful rite which everyone expected of him, and that he was therefore bound to accept their services. He took the glove in silence from the aide-de-camp, and sat down in the lady's chair, placing his huge hands symmetrically on his knees in the naïve attitude of an Egyptian statue, and decided in his own mind that all was as it should be, and that in order not to lose his head and do foolish things he must not act on his own ideas to-night, but must yield himself up entirely to the will of those who were guiding him.

Not two minutes had passed before Prince Vasili with head erect majestically entered the room. He was wearing his long coat with three stars on his breast. He seemed to have grown thinner since the morning; his eyes seemed larger than usual when he glanced round and noticed Pierre. He went up to him, took his hand (a thing he never used to do) and drew it downwards as if wishing to ascertain whether it was firmly fixed on.

'Courage, courage, my friend! He has asked to see you. That is well!' and he turned to go.

But Pierre thought it necessary to ask: 'How is ...' and hesitated, not knowing whether it would be proper to call the dying man 'the count', yet ashamed to call him 'father'.

'He had another stroke about half-an-hour ago. Courage, my friend ...'

Pierre's mind was in such a confused state that the word 'stroke' suggested to him a blow from something. He looked at Prince Vasili in perplexity, and only later grasped that a stroke was an attack of illness. Prince Vasili said something to Lorrain in passing and went through the door on tiptoe. He could not walk well on tiptoe and his whole body jerked at each step. The eldest princess followed him, and the priests and deacons and some servants also went in at the door. Through that door was heard a noise of things being moved about, and at last Anna Mikhaylovna, still with the same expression, pale but resolute in the discharge of duty, ran out and touching Pierre lightly on the arm said:

'The divine mercy is inexhaustible! Unction is about to be administered. Come.'

Pierre went in at the door, stepping on the soft carpet, and noticed that the strange lady, the aide-de-camp, and some of the servants, all followed him in, as if there were now no further need for permission to enter that room.

20

PIERRE well knew this large room divided by columns and an arch, its walls hung round with Persian carpets. The part of the room behind the columns, with a high silk-curtained mahogany bedstead on one side and on the other an immense case containing icons, was brightly illuminated with red light like a Russian church during evening service. Under the gleaming icons stood a long invalid chair, and in that chair on snowy white smooth pillows, evidently freshly changed, Pierre saw – covered to the waist by a bright green quilt – the familiar, majestic figure of his father, Count Bezukhov, with that grey mane of hair above his broad forehead which reminded one of a lion, and the deep characteristically noble wrinkles of his handsome, ruddy face. He lay just under the icons; his large thick hands outside the quilt. Into the right hand, which was lying palm downwards, a wax taper had been thrust between forefinger and thumb, and an old servant, bending over from behind the chair, held it in position. By the chair stood the priests, their long hair falling over their magnificent glittering vestments, with lighted tapers in their hands, slowly and solemnly conducting the service. A little behind them stood the two younger princesses holding handkerchiefs to their eyes, and just in front of them their eldest sister, Catiche, with a vicious and determined look steadily fixed on the icons, as though declaring to all that she could not answer for herself should she glance round. Anna Mikhaylovna, with a meek, sorrowful, and all-forgiving expression on her face, stood by the door near the strange lady. Prince Vasili in front of the door, near the invalid chair, a wax taper in his left hand, was leaning his left arm on the carved back of a velvet chair he had turned round for the purpose, and was crossing himself with his right hand, turning his eyes upward each time he touched his forehead. His face wore a calm look of piety and resignation to the will of God. 'If you do not understand these sentiments,' he seemed to be saying, 'so much the worse for you!'

Behind him stood the aide-de-camp, the doctors, and the menservants; the men and women had separated as in church. All were silently crossing themselves, and the reading of the church service, the subdued chanting of deep bass voices, and in the intervals sighs and the shuffling of feet, were the only sounds that could be heard. Anna Mikhaylovna, with an air of importance that showed that she felt she quite knew what she was about, went across the room to where Pierre was standing and gave him a taper. He lit it and, distracted by observing those around him, began crossing himself with the hand that held the taper.

Sophie, the rosy, laughter-loving, youngest princess with the mole, watched him. She smiled, hid her face in her handkerchief, and remained with it hidden for a while; then looking up and seeing Pierre she again began to laugh. She evidently felt unable to look at him without laughing, but could not resist looking at him; so to be out of temptation she slipped quietly behind one of the columns. In the midst of the service the voices of the priests suddenly ceased, they whispered to one another, and the old servant who was holding the count's hand got up and said something to the ladies. Anna Mikhaylovna stepped forward and, stooping over the dying man, beckoned to Lorrain from behind her back. The French doctor held no taper; he was leaning against one of the columns in a respectful attitude implying that he, a foreigner, in spite of all differences of faith, understood the full importance of the rite now being performed and even approved of it. He now approached the sick man with the noiseless step of one in full vigour of life, with his delicate white fingers raised from the green quilt the hand that was free, and turning sideways felt the pulse and reflected a moment. The sick man was given something to drink, there was a stir around him, then the people resumed their places and the service continued. During this interval Pierre noticed that Prince Vasili left the chair on which he had been leaning, and – with an air which intimated that he knew what he was about and if others did not understand him it was so much the worse for them – did not go up to the dying man, but passed by him, joined the eldest princess, and moved with her to the side of the room where stood the high bedstead with its silken hangings. On leaving the bed both Prince Vasili and the princess passed out by a back door, but returned to their places one after the other before the service was concluded. Pierre paid no more attention to this occurrence than to the rest of what went on, having made up his mind once for all that what he saw happening around him that evening was in some way essential.

The chanting of the service ceased, and the voice of the priest was heard respectfully congratulating the dying man on having received the sacrament. The dying man lay as lifeless and immovable as before. Around him everyone began to stir: steps were audible and whispers, among which Anna Mikhaylovna's was the most distinct.

Pierre heard her say:

'Certainly he must be moved onto the bed; here it will be impossible . . .'

The sick man was so surrounded by doctors, princesses, and servants, that Pierre could no longer see the reddish-yellow face with its grey mane – which, though he saw other faces as well, he had not lost sight of for a single moment during the whole service. He judged by the cautious movements of those who crowded round the invalid chair that they had lifted the dying man and were moving him.

'Catch hold of any arm or you'll drop him!' he heard one of the servants say in a frightened whisper. 'Catch hold from underneath. Here!' exclaimed different voices; and the heavy breathing of the bearers and the shuffling of their feet grew more hurried, as if the weight they were carrying were too much for them.

As the bearers, among whom was Anna Mikhaylovna, passed the young man he caught a momentary glimpse between their heads and backs of the dying man's high, stout, uncovered chest and powerful shoulders, raised by those who were holding him under the armpits, and of his grey, curly, leonine head. This head, with its remarkably broad brow and cheekbones, its handsome, sensual mouth, and its cold, majestic expression, was not disfigured by the approach of death. It was the same as Pierre remembered it three months before, when the count had sent him to Petersburg. But now this head was swaying helplessly with the uneven movements of the bearers, and the cold listless gaze fixed itself upon nothing.

After a few minutes' bustle beside the high bedstead, those who had carried the sick man dispersed. Anna Mikhaylovna touched Pierre's hand and said 'Come'. Pierre went with her to the bed on which the sick man had been laid in a stately pose in keeping with the ceremony just completed. He lay with his head propped high on the pillows. His hands were symmetrically placed on the green silk quilt, the palms downwards. When Pierre came up the count was gazing straight at him, but with a look the significance of which could not be understood by mortal man. Either this look meant nothing but that as long as one has eyes they must look somewhere, or it meant too much. Pierre hesitated, not knowing what to do, and glanced inquiringly at his guide. Anna Mikhaylovna made a hurried sign with her eyes, glancing at the sick man's hand and moving her lips as if to send it a kiss. Pierre, carefully stretching his neck so as not to touch the quilt, followed her suggestion and pressed his lips to the large-boned, fleshy hand. Neither the hand nor a single muscle of the count's face stirred. Once more Pierre looked questioningly at Anna Mikhaylovna to see what he was to do next. Anna Mikhaylovna with her eyes indicated a chair that stood beside the bed. Pierre obediently sat down, his eyes asking if he were doing right. Anna Mikhaylovna nodded approvingly. Again Pierre fell into the naïvely symmetrical pose of an Egyptian statue, evidently distressed that his stout and clumsy body took up so much room and doing his utmost to look as small as possible. He looked at the count, who still gazed at the spot where Pierre's face had been before he sat down. Anna Mikhaylovna indicated by her attitude her consciousness of the pathetic importance of these last moments of meeting between the father and son. This lasted about two minutes, which to Pierre seemed an hour. Suddenly the broad muscles and lines of the count's face began to twitch. The twitching increased, the handsome mouth was drawn to one side (only now did Pierre realize how near death his father was), and from that distorted mouth issued an indistinct, hoarse sound. Anna Mikhaylovna looked attentively at the sick man's eyes, trying to guess what he wanted; she pointed first to Pierre, then to some drink, then named Prince Vasili in an inquiring whisper, then pointed to the quilt. The eyes and face of the sick man showed impatience. He made an effort to look at the servant who stood constantly at the head of the bed.

'Wants to turn on the other side,' whispered the servant, and got up to turn the count's heavy body towards the wall.

Pierre rose to help him.

While the count was being turned over, one of his arms fell back helplessly and he made a fruitless effort to pull it forward. Whether he noticed the look of terror with which Pierre regarded that lifeless arm, or whether some other thought flitted across his dying brain, at any rate he glanced at the refractory arm, at Pierre's terror-stricken face, and again at the arm, and on his face a feeble, piteous smile appeared, quite out of keeping with his features, that seemed to deride his own helplessness. At sight of this smile Pierre felt an unexpected quivering in his breast and a tickling in his nose, and tears dimmed his eyes. The sick man was turned onto his side with his face to the wall. He sighed.

'He is dozing,' said Anna Mikhaylovna, observing that one of the princesses was coming to take her turn at watching. 'Let us go.'

Pierre went out.

## 21

THERE was now no one in the reception-room except Prince Vasili and the eldest princess, who were sitting under the portrait of Catherine the Great and talking eagerly. As soon as they saw Pierre and his companion they became silent, and Pierre thought he saw the princess hide something as she whispered:

'I can't bear the sight of that woman.'

'Catiche has had tea served in the small drawing-room,' said Prince Vasili to Anna Mikhaylovna. 'Go and take something, my poor Anna Mikhaylovna, or you will not hold out.'

To Pierre he said nothing, merely giving his arm a sympathetic squeeze below the shoulder. Pierre went with Anna Mikhaylovna into the small drawing-room.

'There is nothing so refreshing after a sleepless night as a cup of this delicious Russian tea,' Lorrain was saying with an air of restrained animation as he stood sipping tea from a delicate Chinese handleless cup before a table on which tea and a cold supper were laid in the small circular room. Around the table all who were at Count Bezukhov's house that night had gathered to fortify themselves. Pierre well remembered this small circular drawing-room with its mirrors and little tables. During balls given at the house, Pierre, who did not know how to dance, had liked sitting in this room to watch the ladies who as they passed through in their ball dresses with diamonds and pearls on their bare shoulders, looked at themselves in the brilliantly lighted mirrors which repeated their reflections several times. Now this same room was dimly lighted by two candles. On one small table tea-things and supper-dishes stood in disorder, and in the middle of the night a motley throng of people sat there, not merry-making, but sombrely whispering, and betraying by every word and movement that they none of them forgot what was happening and what was about to happen in the bedroom. Pierre did not eat anything though he would very much have liked to. He looked inquiringly at his monitress, and saw that she was again going on tiptoe to the reception-room where they had left Prince Vasili and the eldest princess. Pierre concluded that this also was essential, and after a short interval followed her. Anna Mikhaylovna was standing beside the princess, and they were both speaking in excited whispers.

'Permit me, Princess, to know what is necessary and what is not necessary,' said the younger of the two speakers, evidently in the same state of excitement as when she had slammed the door of her room.

'But, my dear Princess,' answered Anna Mikhaylovna blandly but impressively, blocking the way to the bedroom and preventing the other from passing, 'won't this be too much for poor uncle at a moment when he needs repose? Worldly conversation at a moment when his soul is already prepared . . .'

Prince Vasili was seated in an easy chair in his familiar attitude, with one leg crossed high above the other. His cheeks, which were so flabby that they looked heavier below, were twitching violently; but he wore the air of a man little concerned in what the two ladies were saying.

'Come, my dear Anna Mikhaylovna, let Catiche do as she pleases. You know how fond the count is of her.'

'I don't even know what is in this paper,' said the younger of the two ladies, addressing Prince Vasili and pointing to an inlaid portfolio she held in her hand. 'All I know is that his real will is in his writing-table, and this is a paper he has forgotten. . . .'

She tried to pass Anna Mikhaylovna, but the latter sprang so as to bar her path.

'I know, my dear, kind Princess,' said Anna Mikhaylovna, seizing the portfolio so firmly that it was plain she would not let go easily. 'Dear Princess, I beg and implore you, have some pity on him! *Je vous en conjure . . .*'

The princess did not reply. Their efforts in the struggle for the portfolio were the only sounds audible, but it was evident that if the princess did speak, her words would not be flattering to Anna Mikhaylovna. Though the latter held on tenaciously, her voice lost none of its honeyed firmness and softness.

'Pierre, my dear, come here. I think he will not be out of place in a family consultation; is it not so, Prince?'

'Why don't you speak, cousin?' suddenly shrieked the princess, so loud that those in the drawing-room heard her and were startled. 'Why do you remain silent when heaven knows who permits herself to interfere, making a scene on the very threshold of a dying man's room? Intriguer!' she hissed viciously, and tugged with all her might at the portfolio.

But Anna Mikhaylovna went forward a step or two to keep her hold on the portfolio, and changed her grip.

Prince Vasili rose. 'Oh!' said he with reproach and surprise, 'this is absurd! Come, let go I tell you.'

The princess let go.

'And you too!'

But Anna Mikhaylovna did not obey him.

'Let go, I tell you! I will take the responsibility. I myself will go and ask him, I! . . . does that satisfy you?'

87

'But, Prince,' said Anna Mikhaylovna, 'after such a solemn sacrament, allow him a moment's peace! Here, Pierre, tell them your opinion,' said she, turning to the young man who, having come quite close, was gazing with astonishment at the angry face of the princess which had lost all dignity, and at the twitching cheeks of Prince Vasili.

'Remember that you will answer for the consequences,' said Prince Vasili severely. 'You don't know what you are doing.'

'Vile woman!' shouted the princess, darting unexpectedly at Anna Mikhaylovna and snatching the portfolio from her.

Prince Vasili bent his head and spread out his hands.

At this moment that terrible door, which Pierre had watched so long and which had always opened so quietly, burst noisily open and banged against the wall, and the second of the three sisters rushed out wringing her hands.

'What are you doing!' she cried vehemently. 'He is dying and you leave me alone with him!'

Her sister dropped the portfolio. Anna Mikhaylovna, stooping, quickly caught up the object of contention and ran into the bedroom. The eldest princess and Prince Vasili, recovering themselves, followed her. A few minutes later the eldest sister came out with a pale hard face, again biting her underlip. At sight of Pierre her expression showed an irrepressible hatred.

'Yes, now you may be glad!' said she; 'this is what you have been waiting for.' And bursting into tears she hid her face in her handkerchief and rushed from the room.

Prince Vasili came next. He staggered to the sofa on which Pierre was sitting and dropped onto it, covering his face with his hand. Pierre noticed that he was pale and that his jaw quivered and shook as if in an ague.

'Ah, my friend!' said he, taking Pierre by the elbow; and there was in his voice a sincerity and weakness Pierre had never observed in it before. 'How often we sin, how much we deceive, and all for what? I am near sixty, dear friend ... I too ... All will end in death, all! Death is awful ...' and he burst into tears.

Anna Mikhaylovna came out last. She approached Pierre with slow, quiet steps.

'Pierre!' she said.

Pierre gave her an inquiring look. She kissed the young man on his forehead, wetting him with her tears. Then after a pause she said:

'He is no more ...'

Pierre looked at her over his spectacles.

'Come, I will go with you. Try to weep, nothing gives such relief as tears.'

She led him into the dark drawing-room and Pierre was glad no one could see his face. Anna Mikhaylovna left him, and when she returned he was fast asleep with his head on his arm.

In the morning Anna Mikhaylovna said to Pierre:

'Yes, my dear, this is a great loss for us all, not to speak of you. But God will support you: you are young, and are now I hope in command of an immense fortune. The will has not yet been opened. I know you well enough to be sure that this will not turn your head, but it imposes duties on you, and you must be a man.'

Pierre was silent.

'Perhaps later on I may tell you, my dear boy, that if I had not been there, God only knows what would have happened! You know, uncle promised me only the day before yesterday not to forget Boris. But he had no time. I hope, my dear friend, you will carry out your father's wish?'

Pierre understood nothing of all this and colouring shyly looked in silence at Princess Anna Mikhaylovna. After her talk with Pierre, Anna Mikhaylovna returned to the Rostovs' and went to bed. On waking in the morning she told the Rostovs and all her acquaintances the details of Count Bezukhov's death. She said the count had died as she would herself wish to die, that his end was not only touching but edifying. As to the last meeting between father and son, it was so touching that she could not think of it without tears, and did not know which had behaved better during those awful moments – the father who so remembered everything and everybody at the last and had spoken such pathetic words to the son, or Pierre, whom it had been pitiful to see, so stricken was he with grief, though he tried hard to hide it in order not to sadden his dying father. 'It is painful, but it does one good. It uplifts the soul to see such men as the old count and his worthy son,' said she. Of the behaviour of the eldest princess and Prince Vasili she spoke disapprovingly, but in whispers and as a great secret.

22

AT Bald Hills, Prince Nicholas Andreevich Bolkonsky's* estate, the arrival of young Prince Andrew and his wife was daily expected, but this expectation did not upset the regular routine of life in the old prince's household. General-in-Chief Prince Nicholas Andreevich (nicknamed in society 'the King of Prussia'), ever since the Emperor Paul had exiled him to his country estate had lived there continuously with his daughter, Princess Mary, and her companion Mademoiselle Bourienne. Though in the new reign he was free to return to the capitals he still continued to live in the country, remarking that anyone who wanted to see him could come the hundred miles from Moscow to Bald Hills, while he himself needed no one and nothing. He used to say that there are only two sources of human vice – idleness and superstition, and only two virtues – activity and intelligence. He himself undertook his daughter's education, and to develop these two cardinal virtues in her gave her lessons in algebra and geometry till she was twenty, and arranged her life so that her whole time was occupied. He was himself always occupied: writing his memoirs, solving problems in higher mathematics, turning snuff-boxes on a lathe, working in the garden, or superintending the building that was always going on at his estate. As regularity is a prime condition facilitating activity, regularity in his household was carried to the highest point of exactitude. He always came to table under precisely the same conditions, and not only at the same hour but at the same minute. With those about him, from his daughter to his serfs, the prince was sharp and invariably exacting, so that without being a hard-hearted man he inspired such fear and respect as few hard-hearted men would have aroused. Although he was in retirement and had now no influence in political affairs, every high official appointed to the province in which the prince's estate lay considered it his duty to visit him, and waited in the lofty antechamber just as the architect, gardener, or Princess Mary did, till the prince appeared punctually to the appointed hour. Everyone sitting in this antechamber experienced the same feeling of respect and even fear when the enormously high study door opened and showed the figure of a rather small old man, with powdered wig, small withered hands, and bushy grey eyebrows which, when he frowned, sometimes hid the gleam of his shrewd, youthfully glittering eyes.

On the morning of the day that the young couple were to arrive, Princess Mary entered the antechamber as usual at the time appointed for the morning greeting, crossing herself with trepidation and repeating a silent prayer. Every morning she came in like that, and every morning she prayed that the daily interview might pass off well.

An old powdered man-servant who was sitting in the antechamber rose quietly and said in a whisper: 'Please walk in.'

Through the door came the regular hum of a lathe. The princess timidly opened the door which moved noiselessly and easily. She paused at the entrance. The prince was working at the lathe and after glancing round continued his work.

The enormous study was full of things evidently in constant

use. The large table covered with books and plans, the tall glass-fronted bookcase with keys in the locks, the high desk for writing while standing up, on which lay an open exercise-book, and the lathe with tools laid ready to hand and shavings scattered around – all indicated continuous, varied, and orderly activity. The motion of the small foot shod in a Tartar boot embroidered with silver, and the firm pressure of the lean sinewy hand, showed that the prince still possessed the tenacious endurance and vigour of hardy old age. After a few more turns of the lathe he removed his foot from the pedal, wiped his chisel, dropped it into a leather pouch attached to the lathe, and approaching the table, summoned his daughter. He never gave his children a blessing, so he simply held out his bristly cheek (as yet unshaven) and regarding her tenderly and attentively, said severely:

'Quite well? All right then, sit down.' He took the exercise-book containing lessons in geometry written by himself, and drew up a chair with his foot.

'For to-morrow!' said he, quickly finding the page and making a scratch from one paragraph to another with his hard nail.

The princess bent over the exercise-book on the table.

'Wait a bit, here's a letter for you,' said the old man suddenly, taking a letter addressed in a woman's hand from a bag hanging above the table, onto which he threw it.

At the sight of the letter red patches showed themselves on the princess's face. She took it quickly and bent her head over it.

'From Heloïse?'* asked the prince with a cold smile that showed his still sound, yellowish teeth.

'Yes, it's from Julie,' replied the princess with a timid glance and a timid smile.

'I'll let two more letters pass, but the third I'll read,' said the prince sternly; 'I'm afraid you write much nonsense. I'll read the third!'

'Read this if you like, father,' said the princess, blushing still more and holding out the letter.

'The third, I said the third!' cried the prince abruptly, pushing the letter away, and leaning his elbows on the table he drew towards him the exercise-book containing geometrical figures.

'Well, madam,' he began, stooping over the book close to his daughter and placing an arm on the back of the chair on which she sat, so that she felt herself surrounded on all sides by the acrid scent of old age and tobacco, which she had known so long. 'Now, madam, these triangles are equal; please note that the angle ABC....'

The princess looked in a scared way at her father's eyes glittering close to her; the red patches on her face came and went, and it was plain that she understood nothing and was so frightened that her fear would prevent her understanding any of her father's further explanations, however clear they might be. Whether it was the teacher's fault or the pupil's, this same thing happened every day: the princess's eyes drew dim, she could not see and could not hear anything, but was only conscious of her stern father's withered face close to her, of his breath and the smell of him, and could think only of how to get away quickly to her own room to make out the problem in peace. The old man was beside himself: moved the chair on which he was sitting noisily backwards and forwards, made efforts to control himself and not become vehement, but almost always did become vehement, scolded, and sometimes flung the exercise-book away.

The princess gave a wrong answer.

'Well now, isn't she a fool!' shouted the prince, pushing the book aside and turning sharply away; but rising immediately, he paced up and down, lightly touched his daughter's hair and sat down again.

He drew up his chair and continued to explain.

'This won't do, Princess; it won't do,' said he, when Princess Mary, having taken and closed the exercise-book with the next day's lesson, was about to leave: 'Mathematics are most important, madam! I don't want to have you like our silly ladies. Get used to it and you'll like it,' and he patted her cheek. 'It will drive all the nonsense out of your head.'

She turned to go, but he stopped her with a gesture and took an uncut book from the high desk.

'Here is some sort of *Key to the Mysteries*\* that your Heloïse has sent you. Religious! I don't interfere with anyone's belief . . . I have looked at it. Take it. Well, now go. Go.'

He patted her on the shoulder and himself closed the door after her.

Princess Mary went back to her room with the sad, scared expression that rarely left her and which made her plain, sickly face yet plainer. She sat down at her writing-table, on which stood miniature portraits and which was littered with books and papers. The princess was as untidy as her father was tidy. She put down the geometry-book and eagerly broke the seal of her letter. It was from her most intimate friend from childhood; that same Julie Karagin who had been at the Rostovs' name-day party.

Julie wrote in French:

Dear and precious Friend, How terrible and frightful a thing is separation! Though I tell myself that half my life and half my happiness are wrapped up in you, and that in spite of the distance separating us our hearts are united by indissoluble bonds, my heart rebels against fate and in spite of the pleasures and distractions around me I cannot overcome a certain secret sorrow that has been in my heart ever since we parted. Why are we not together as we were last summer, in your big study, on the blue sofa, the confidential sofa? Why cannot I now, as three months ago, draw fresh moral strength from your look, so gentle, calm, and penetrating, a look I loved so well and seem to see before me as I write?

Having read thus far, Princess Mary sighed and glanced into the mirror which stood on her right. It reflected a weak, ungraceful figure and thin face. Her eyes, always sad, now looked with particular hopelessness at her reflection in the glass. 'She flatters me,' thought the princess, turning away and continuing to read. But Julie did not flatter her friend: the princess's eyes – large, deep, and luminous (it seemed as if at times there radiated from them shafts of warm light), were so beautiful that very often in spite of the plainness of her face they gave her an attraction more powerful than that of beauty. But the princess never saw the beautiful expression of her own eyes – the look they had when she was not thinking of herself. As with everyone, her face assumed a forced unnatural expression as soon as she looked in a glass. She went on reading:

All Moscow talks of nothing but war. One of my two brothers is already abroad, the other is with the Guards, who are starting on their march to the frontier. Our dear Emperor has left Petersburg and it is thought intends to expose his precious person to the chances of war. God grant that the Corsican monster who is destroying the peace of Europe may be overthrown by the angel whom it has pleased the Almighty, in His goodness, to give us as sovereign! To say nothing of my brothers, this war has deprived me of one of the associations nearest my heart. I mean young Nicholas Rostov, who with his enthusiasm could not bear to remain inactive and has left the university to join the army. I will confess to you, dear Mary, that in spite of his extreme youth his departure for the army was a great grief to me. This young man, of whom I spoke to you last summer, is so noble-minded and full of that real youthfulness which one seldom finds nowadays among our old men of twenty and, particularly, he is so frank and has so much heart. He is so pure and poetic that my relations with him, transient as they were, have been one of the sweetest comforts to my poor heart, which has already suffered so much. Some day I will tell you about our parting and all that was said then. That is still too fresh. Ah, dear friend, you are happy not to know these poignant joys and sorrows. You are fortunate, for the latter are generally the stronger! I know very well that Count Nicholas is too young ever to be more to me than a friend, but this sweet friendship, this poetic and pure intimacy, were what my heart needed. But enough of this! The chief news, about which all Moscow gossips, is the death of old Count Bezukhov, and his inheritance. Fancy! The three princesses have received very little, Prince Vasili nothing, and it is Monsieur Pierre who has inherited all the property and has besides been recognized as legitimate; so that he is now Count Bezukhov and possessor of the finest fortune in Russia. It is rumoured that Prince Vasili played a very despicable part in this affair and that he returned to Petersburg quite crestfallen.

I confess I understand very little about all these matters of wills and inheritance; but I do know that since this young man, whom we all used to know as plain Monsieur Pierre, has become Count Bezukhov and the owner of one of the largest fortunes in Russia, I am much amused to watch the change in the tone and manners of the mammas burdened by marriageable daughters, and of the young ladies themselves, towards him, though, between you and me, he always seemed to me a poor sort of fellow. As for the past two years people have amused themselves by finding husbands for me (most of whom I don't even know), the matchmaking chronicles of Moscow now speak of me as the future Countess Bezukhova. But you will understand that I have no desire for the post. A *propos* of marriages: do you know that a while ago that *universal auntie* Anna Mikhaylovna told me, under the seal of strict secrecy, of a plan of marriage for you. It is neither more nor less than with Prince Vasili's son Anatole, whom they wish to reform by marrying him to someone rich and *distinguée*, and it is on you that his relations' choice has fallen. I don't know what you will think of it, but I consider it my duty to let you know of it. He is said to be very handsome and a terrible scapegrace. That is all I have been able to find out about him.

But enough of gossip. I am at the end of my second sheet of paper, and mamma has sent for me to go and dine at the Apraksins'. Read the mystical book I am sending you; it has an enormous success here. Though there are things in it difficult for the feeble human mind to grasp, it is an admirable book which calms and elevates the soul. Adieu! Give my respects to monsieur your father and my compliments to Mademoiselle Bourienne. I embrace you as I love you.

JULIE.

P.S. Let me have news of your brother and his charming little wife.

The princess pondered awhile with a thoughtful smile and her luminous eyes lit up so that her face was entirely transformed. Then she suddenly rose and with her heavy tread went up to the table. She took a sheet of paper and her hand moved rapidly over it. This is the reply she wrote, also in French:

Dear and precious Friend, – Your letter of the 13th has given me great delight. So you still love me, my romantic Julie? Separation, of which you say so much that is bad, does not seem to have had its usual effect on you. You complain of our separation. What then should I say, if I *dared* complain, I who am deprived of all who are dear to me? Ah, if we had not religion to console us life would be very sad. Why do you suppose that I should look severely on your affection for that young man? On such matters I am only severe with myself. I understand such feelings in others, and if never having felt them I cannot approve of them, neither do I condemn them. Only it seems to me that Christian love, love of one's neighbour, love of one's enemy, is worthier, sweeter, and better, than the feelings which the beautiful eyes of a young man can inspire in a romantic and loving young girl like yourself.

The news of Count Bezukhov's death reached us before your letter and my father was much affected by it. He says the count was the last representative but one of the great century, and that it is his own turn now, but that he will do all he can to let his turn come as late as possible. God preserve us from that terrible misfortune!

I cannot agree with you about Pierre, whom I knew as a child. He always seemed to me to have an excellent heart, and that is the quality I value most in people. As to his inheritance and the part played by Prince Vasili, it is very sad for both. Ah, my dear friend, our divine Saviour's words, that it is easier for a camel to go through the eye of a needle than for a rich man to enter the Kingdom of God, are terribly true. I pity Prince Vasili but am still more sorry for Pierre. So young, and burdened with such riches – to what temptations he will be exposed! If I were asked what I desire most on earth, it would be to be poorer than the poorest beggar. A thousand thanks, dear friend, for the volume you have sent me and which has such success in Moscow. Yet since you tell me that among some good things it contains others which our weak human understanding cannot grasp, it seems to me rather useless to spend time in reading what is unintelligible and can therefore bear no fruit. I never could understand the fondness some people have for confusing their minds by dwelling on mystical books that merely awaken their doubts and excite their imagination, giving them a bent for exaggeration quite contrary to Christian simplicity. Let us rather read the Epistles and Gospels. Let us not seek to penetrate what mysteries they contain; for how can we, miserable sinners that we are, know the terrible and holy secrets of Providence while we remain in this flesh which forms an impenetrable veil between us and the Eternal? Let us rather confine ourselves to studying those sublime rules which our divine Saviour has left for our guidance here below. Let us try to conform to them and follow them, and let us be persuaded that the less we let our feeble human minds roam, the better we shall please God, who rejects all knowledge that does not come from Him; and the less we seek to fathom what He has been pleased to conceal from us, the sooner will He vouchsafe its revelation to us through His divine Spirit.

My father has not spoken to me of a suitor, but has only told me that he has received a letter and is expecting a visit from Prince Vasili. In regard to this project of marriage for me, I will tell you, dear sweet friend, that I look on marriage as a divine institution to which we must conform. However painful it may be to me, should the Almighty ever lay the duties of wife and mother upon me I shall try to perform them as faithfully as I can, without disquieting myself by examining my feelings towards him whom He may give me for husband.

I have had a letter from my brother, who announces his speedy arrival at Bald Hills with his wife. This pleasure will be but a brief one, however, for he will leave us again to take part in this unhappy war into which we have been drawn God knows how or why. Not only where you are – at the heart of affairs and of the world – is the talk all of war, even here amid field-work and the calm of nature – which townsfolk consider characteristic of the country – rumours of war are heard and painfully felt. My father talks of nothing but marches and counter-marches, things of which I understand nothing; and the day before yesterday during my daily walk through the village I witnessed a heartrending scene . . . It was a convoy of conscripts enrolled from our people and starting to join the army. You should have seen the state of the mothers, wives, and children, of the men who were going, and should have heard the sobs. It seems as though mankind has forgotten the laws of its divine Saviour, Who preached love and forgiveness of injuries – and that men attribute the greatest merit to skill in killing one another.

Adieu, dear and kind friend; may our divine Saviour and his most Holy Mother keep you in their holy and all-powerful care!

MARY.

'Ah, you are sending off a letter, Princess? I have already dispatched mine. I have written to my poor mother,' said the smiling Mademoiselle Bourienne rapidly, in her pleasant mellow tones and with guttural r's. She brought into Princess Mary's strenuous mournful and gloomy world a quite different atmosphere, careless, lighthearted, and self-satisfied.

'Princess, I must warn you,' she added, lowering her voice and evidently listening to herself with pleasure, and speaking with exaggerated *grasseyement*,\* 'the prince has been scolding Michael Ivanovich. He is in a very bad humour, very morose. Be prepared.'

'Ah, dear friend,' replied Princess Mary, 'I have asked you never to warn me of the humour my father is in. I do not allow myself to judge him and would not have others do so.'

The princess glanced at her watch and seeing that she was five minutes late in starting her practice on the clavichord, went into the sitting-room with a look of alarm. Between twelve and two o'clock, as the day was mapped out, the prince rested and the princess played the clavichord.

## 23

THE grey-haired valet was sitting drowsily listening to the snoring of the prince, who was in his large study. From the far side of the house through the closed doors came the sound of difficult passages – twenty times repeated – of a sonata of Dussek's.

Just then a closed carriage and another with a hood drove up to the porch. Prince Andrew got out of the carriage, helped his little wife to alight, and let her pass into the house before him. Old Tikhon, wearing a wig, put his head out of the door of the antechamber, reported in a whisper that the prince was sleeping, and hastily closed the door. Tikhon knew that neither the son's arrival nor any other unusual event must be allowed to disturb the appointed order of the day. Prince Andrew apparently knew this as well as Tikhon; he looked at his watch as if to ascertain whether his father's habits had changed since he was at home last, and, having assured himself that they had not, he turned to his wife.

'He will get up in twenty minutes. Let us go across to Mary's room,' he said.

The little princess had grown stouter during this time, but her eyes and her short, downy, smiling lip lifted when she began to speak just as merrily and prettily as ever.

'Why, this is a palace!' she said to her husband, looking around with the expression with which people compliment their host at a ball. 'Let's come, quick, quick!' And with a glance round, she smiled at Tikhon, at her husband, and at the footman who accompanied them.

'Is that Mary practising? Let's go quietly and take her by surprise.'

Prince Andrew followed her with a courteous but sad expression.

'You've grown older, Tikhon,' he said in passing to the old man, who kissed his hand.

Before they reached the room from which the sounds of the clavichord came, the pretty, fair-haired Frenchwoman, Mademoiselle Bourienne, rushed out apparently beside herself with delight.

'Ah! what joy for the princess!' exclaimed she: 'At last! I must let her know.'

'No, no, please not...You are Mademoiselle Bourienne,' said the little princess, kissing her. 'I know you already through my sister-in-law's friendship for you. She was not expecting us?'

They went up to the door of the sitting-room from which came the sound of the oft-repeated passage of the sonata. Prince Andrew stopped and made a grimace, as if expecting something unpleasant.

The little princess entered the room. The passage broke off in the middle, a cry was heard, then Princess Mary's heavy tread and the sound of kissing. When Prince Andrew went in the two princesses, who had only met once before for a short time at his wedding, were in each other's arms warmly pressing their lips to whatever place they happened to touch. Mademoiselle Bourienne stood near them pressing her hand to her heart, with a beatific smile and obviously equally ready to cry or to laugh. Prince Andrew shrugged his shoulders and frowned, as lovers of music do when they hear a false note. The two women let go of one another, and then as if afraid of being too late, seized each other's hands, kissing them and pulling them away, and again began kissing each other on the face, and then to Prince Andrew's surprise both began to cry and kissed again. Mademoiselle Bourienne also began to cry. Prince Andrew evidently felt ill at ease, but to the two women it seemed quite natural that they should cry, and apparently it never entered their heads that it could have been otherwise at this meeting.

'Ah! my dear!...Ah! Mary!...' they suddenly exclaimed, and then laughed. 'I dreamt last night...' – 'You were not expecting us?...' – 'Ah! Mary, you have got thinner!...' 'And you have grown stouter!...'

'I knew the princess at once,' put in Mademoiselle Bourienne.

'And I had no idea!...' exclaimed Princess Mary. 'Ah Andrew, I did not see you.'

Prince Andrew and his sister, hand in hand, kissed one another, and he told her she was still the same cry-baby as ever. Princess Mary had turned towards her brother, and through her tears the loving warm gentle look of her large luminous eyes, very beautiful at that moment, rested on Prince Andrew's face.

The little princess talked incessantly, her short downy upper lip continually and rapidly touching her rosy nether lip when necessary and drawing up again next moment when her face broke into a smile of glittering teeth and sparkling eyes. She told of an accident they had had on the Spassky Hill which might have been serious for her in her condition, and immediately after that informed them that she had left all her clothes in Petersburg and that heaven knew what she would have to dress in here; and that Andrew had quite changed, and that Kitty Odyntsova had married an old man, and that there was a suitor for Mary, a real one, but that they would talk of that later. Princess Mary was still looking silently at her brother and her beautiful eyes were full of love and sadness. It was plain that she was following a train of thought independent of her sister-in-law's words. In the midst of a description of the last Petersburg fête she addressed her brother:

'So you are really going to the war, Andrew?' she said sighing. Lise sighed too.

'Yes, and even to-morrow,' replied her brother.

'He is leaving me here; God knows why, when he might have had promotion . . .'

Princess Mary did not listen to the end, but continuing her train of thought turned to her sister-in-law with a tender glance at her figure.

'Is it certain?' she asked.

The face of the little princess changed. She sighed and said:

'Yes, quite certain. Ah! it is very dreadful . . .'

Her lip descended. She brought her face close to her sister-in-law's, and unexpectedly again began to cry.

'She needs rest,' said Prince Andrew with a frown. 'Don't you, Lise? Take her to your room and I'll go to father. How is he? Just the same?'

'Yes, just the same. Though I don't know what your opinion will be,' answered the princess joyfully.

'And are the hours the same? And the walks in the avenues? And the lathe?' asked Prince Andrew, with a scarcely perceptible smile which showed that, in spite of all his love and respect for his father, he was aware of his weaknesses.

'The hours are the same, and the lathe, and also the mathematics and my geometry lessons,' said Princess Mary gleefully, as if her lessons in geometry were among the greatest delights of her life.

When the twenty minutes had elapsed and the time had come for the old prince to get up, Tikhon came to call the young prince to his father. The old man made a departure from his usual routine in honour of his son's arrival: he gave orders to admit him to his apartments while he dressed for dinner. The old prince always dressed in old-fashioned style, wearing an antique coat and powdered hair; and when Prince Andrew entered his father's dressing-room (not with the contemptuous look and manner he wore in drawing-rooms, but with the animated face with which he talked to Pierre) the old man was sitting on a large leather-covered chair, wrapped in a powdering mantle, entrusting his head to Tikhon.

'Ah! here's the warrior! Wants to vanquish Buonaparte?' said the old man, shaking his powdered head as much as the tail, which Tikhon was holding fast to plait, would allow.

'You at least must tackle him properly, or else if he goes on like this he'll soon have us, too, for his subjects! How are you?' And he held out his cheek.

The old man was in a good temper after his nap before dinner. (He used to say, that a nap 'after dinner was silver – before dinner, golden'.) He cast happy, sidelong glances at his son from under his thick bushy eyebrows. Prince Andrew went up and kissed his father on the spot indicated to him. He made no reply on his father's favourite topic – making fun of the military men of the day, and more particularly of Bonaparte.

'Yes, father, I have come to you and brought my wife who is pregnant,' said Prince Andrew, following every movement of his father's face with an eager and respectful look. 'How is your health?'

'Only fools and rakes fall ill, my boy. You know me: I am busy from morning till night and abstemious, so of course I am well.'

'Thank God,' said his son smiling.

'God has nothing to do with it! Well, go on,' he continued, returning to his hobby; 'tell me how the Germans have taught you to fight Buonaparte by this new science you call "strategy"?'

Prince Andrew smiled.

'Give me time to collect my wits, father,' said he, with a smile that showed that his father's foibles did not prevent his son from loving and honouring him. 'Why, I have not yet had time to settle down!'

'Nonsense, nonsense!' cried the old man, shaking his pigtail to see whether it was firmly plaited, and grasping his son by the hand. 'The house for your wife is ready. Princess Mary will take her there and show her over, and they'll talk nineteen to the dozen. That's their woman's way! I am glad to have her. Sit down and talk. About Michelsen's army I understand* – Tolstoy's too . . . a simultaneous expedition. . . . But what's the southern army to do? Prussia is neutral . . . I know that. What about Austria?' said he, rising from his chair and pacing up and down the room followed by Tikhon, who ran after him, handing him different articles of clothing. 'What of Sweden? How will they cross Pomerania?'

Prince Andrew, seeing that his father insisted, began – at first reluctantly, but gradually with more and more animation, and from habit changing unconsciously from Russian to French as he went on – to explain the plan of operation for the coming campaign. He explained how an army, ninety thousand strong, was to threaten Prussia so as to bring her out of her neutrality and draw her into the war; how part of that army was to join some Swedish forces at Stralsund; how two hundred and twenty thousand Austrians, with a hundred thousand Russians, were to operate in Italy and on the Rhine; how fifty thousand Russians and as many English were to land at Naples, and how a total force of five hundred thousand men was to attack the French from different sides. The old prince did not evince the least interest during this explanation, but as if he were not listening to it continued to dress while walking about, and three times unexpectedly interrupted. Once he stopped it by shouting: 'The white one, the white one!'

This meant that Tikhon was not handing him the waistcoat he wanted. Another time he interrupted, saying:

'And will she soon be confined?' and shaking his head reproachfully said: 'That's bad! Go on, go on.'

The third interruption came when Prince Andrew was finishing his description. The old man began to sing, in the cracked voice of old age: '*Malbrook s'en va-t-en guerre. Dieu sait quand reviendra.*'

His son only smiled.

'I don't say it's a plan I approve of,' said the son; 'I am only telling you what it is. Napoleon has also formed his plan by now, not worse than this one.'

'Well you've told me nothing new,' and the old man repeated, meditatively and rapidly:

'*Dieu sait quand reviendra.* Go to the dining-room.'

## 24

AT the appointed hour the prince, powdered and shaven, entered the dining-room where his daughter-in-law, Princess Mary, and Mademoiselle Bourienne, were already awaiting him together with his architect, who by a strange caprice of his employer's was admitted to table, though the position of that insignificant individual was such as could certainly not have caused him to expect that honour. The prince, who generally kept very strictly to social distinctions and rarely admitted even important government officials to his table, had unexpectedly selected Michael Ivanovich (who always went into a corner to blow his nose on his checked handkerchief) to illustrate the theory that all men are equals, and had more than once impressed on his daughter that Michael Ivanovich was 'not a whit worse than you or I'. At dinner the prince usually spoke to the taciturn Michael Ivanovich more often than to anyone else.

In the dining-room, which like all the rooms in the house was exceedingly lofty, the members of the household, and the footmen – one behind each chair – stood waiting for the prince to enter. The head butler, napkin on arm, was scanning the setting of the table, making signs to the footmen, and anxiously glancing from the clock to the door by which the prince was to enter. Prince Andrew was looking at a large gilt frame, new to him, containing the genealogical tree of the Princes Bolkonsky, opposite which hung another such frame with a badly-painted portrait (evidently by the hand of the artist belonging to the estate) of a ruling prince, in a crown – an alleged descendant of Rurik and ancestor of the Bolkonskys. Prince Andrew, looking again at that genealogical tree, shook his head, laughing as a man laughs who looks at a portrait so characteristic of the original as to be amusing.

'How thoroughly like him that is!' he said to Princess Mary, who had come up to him.

Princess Mary looked at her brother in surprise. She did not understand what he was laughing at. Everything her father did inspired her with reverence and was beyond question.

'Everyone has his Achilles' heel,' continued Prince Andrew. 'Fancy, with *his* powerful mind, indulging in such nonsense!'

Princess Mary could not understand the boldness of her brother's criticism and was about to reply, when the expected footsteps were heard coming from the study. The prince walked in quickly and jauntily as was his wont, as if intentionally contrasting the briskness of his manners with the strict formality of his house. At that moment the great clock struck two, and another with a shrill tone joined in from the drawing-room. The prince stood still; his lively glittering eyes from under their thick bushy eyebrows sternly scanned all present and rested on the little princess. She felt, as courtiers do when the Tsar enters, the sensation of fear and respect which the old man inspired in all around him. He stroked her hair, and then patted her awkwardly on the back of her neck.

'I'm glad, glad, to see you,' he said, looking attentively into her eyes, and then quickly went to his place and sat down. 'Sit down, sit down! Sit down, Michael Ivanovich!'

He indicated a place beside him to his daughter-in-law. A footman moved the chair for her.

'Ho, ho!' said the old man, casting his eyes on her rounded figure. 'You've been in a hurry. That's bad!'

He laughed in his usual dry, cold, unpleasant way, with his lips only and not with his eyes.

'You must walk, as much as possible, as much as possible,' he said.

The little princess did not, or did not wish to, hear his words.

She was silent and seemed confused. The prince asked her about her father, and she began to smile and talk. He asked about mutual acquaintances, and she became still more animated and chattered away giving him greetings from various people and retailing the town gossip.

'Countess Apraksina, poor thing, has lost her husband and she has cried her eyes out,' she said, growing more and more lively.

As she became animated the prince looked at her more and more sternly, and suddenly, as if he had studied her sufficiently and had formed a definite idea of her, he turned away and addressed Michael Ivanovich.

'Well, Michael Ivanovich, our Buonaparte will be having a bad time of it. Prince Andrew' (he always spoke thus of his son) 'has been telling me what forces are being collected against him! While you and I have never thought much of him.'

Michael Ivanovich did not at all know when 'you and I' had said such things about Bonaparte, but understanding that he was wanted as a peg on which to hang the prince's favourite topic, he looked inquiringly at the young prince, wondering what would follow.

'He is a great tactician!' said the prince to his son, pointing to the architect.

And the conversation again turned on the war, on Bonaparte, and the generals and statesmen of the day. The old prince seemed convinced not only that all the men of the day were mere babies who did not know the A B C of war or of politics, and that Bonaparte was an insignificant little Frenchy, successful only because there were no longer any Potëmkins or Suvorovs left to oppose him; but he was also convinced that there were no political difficulties in Europe and no real war, but only a sort of puppet-show at which the men of the day were playing, pretending to do something real. Prince Andrew gaily bore with his father's ridicule of the new men, and drew him on and listened to him with evident pleasure.

'The past always seems good,' said he, 'but did not Suvorov himself fall into a trap Moreau set him, and from which he did not know how to escape?'

'Who told you that? Who?' cried the prince. 'Suvorov!' And he jerked away his plate, which Tikhon briskly caught. 'Suvorov! ... Consider, Prince Andrew! Two ... Frederick and Suvorov; Moreau! ... Moreau would have been a prisoner if Suvorov had had a free hand; but he had the Hofs-kriegs-wurst-schnapps-Rath* on his hands. It would have puzzled the devil himself! When you get there you'll find out what those Hofs-kriegs-wurst-Raths are! Suvorov couldn't manage them so what chance has Michael Kutuzov? No, my dear boy,' he continued, 'you and your generals won't get on against Buonaparte; you'll have to call in the French, so that birds of a feather may fight together. The German, Pahlen, has been sent to New York in America, to fetch the Frenchman Moreau,* he said, alluding to the invitation made that year to Moreau to enter the Russian service. . . . 'Wonderful! . . . Were the Potëmkins, Suvorovs, and Orlovs Germans? No, lad, either you fellows have all lost your wits, or I have outlived mine. May God help you, but we'll see what will happen. Buonaparte has become a great commander among them! Hm! . . .'

'I don't at all say that all the plans are good,' said Prince Andrew, 'I am only surprised at your opinion of Bonaparte. You may laugh as much as you like, but all the same Bonaparte is a great general!'

'Michael Ivanovich!' cried the old prince to the architect who, busy with his roast meat, hoped he had been forgotten: 'Didn't I tell you Buonaparte was a great tactician? Here, he says the same thing.'

'To be sure, your excellency,' replied the architect.

The prince again laughed his frigid laugh.

'Buonaparte was born with a silver spoon in his mouth. He has got splendid soldiers. Besides he began by attacking Germans. And only idlers have failed to beat the Germans. Since the world began everybody has beaten the Germans. They beat no one – except one another. He made his reputation fighting them.'

And the prince began explaining all the blunders which, according to him, Bonaparte had made in his campaigns and even in politics. His son made no rejoinder, but it was evident that whatever arguments were presented he was as little able as his father to change his opinion. He listened, refraining from a reply, and involuntarily wondered how this old man, living alone in the country for so many years, could know and discuss so minutely and acutely all the recent European military and political events.

'You think I'm an old man and don't understand the present state of affairs?' concluded his father. 'But it troubles me. I don't sleep at night. Come now, where has this great commander of yours shown his skill?' he concluded.

'That would take too long to tell,' answered the son.

'Well, then go off to your Bonaparte! Mademoiselle Bourienne, here's another admirer of that powder-monkey emperor of yours,' he exclaimed in excellent French.

'You know, Prince, I am not a Bonapartist!'

'*Dieu sait quand reviendra*' ... hummed the prince out of tune and, with a laugh still more so, he quitted the table.

The little princess during the whole discussion and the rest of the dinner sat silent, glancing with a frightened look now at her father-in-law and now at Princess Mary. When they left the table she took her sister-in-law's arm and drew her into another room.

'What a clever man your father is,' said she; 'perhaps that is why I am afraid of him.'

'Oh, he is so kind!' answered Princess Mary.

## 25

PRINCE ANDREW was to leave next evening. The old prince, not altering his routine, retired as usual after dinner. The little princess was in her sister-in-law's room. Prince Andrew in a travelling coat without epaulettes had been packing with his valet in the rooms assigned to him. After inspecting the carriage himself and seeing the trunks put in, he ordered the horses to be harnessed. Only those things he always kept with him remained in his room; a small box, a large canteen fitted with silver plate, two Turkish pistols, and a sabre – a present from his father who had brought it from the siege of Ochakov.* All these travelling effects of Prince Andrew's were in very good order: new, clean, and in cloth covers carefully tied with tapes.

When starting on a journey or changing their mode of life, men capable of reflection are generally in a serious frame of mind. At such moments one reviews the past and plans for the future. Prince Andrew's face looked very thoughtful and tender. With his hands behind him he paced briskly from corner to corner of the room looking straight before him and thoughtfully shaking his head. Did he fear going to the war, or was he sad at leaving his wife? – perhaps both, but evidently he did not wish to be seen in that mood, for hearing footsteps in the passage he hurriedly unclasped his hands, stopped at a table as if tying the cover of the small box, and assumed his usual tranquil and impenetrable expression. It was the heavy tread of Princess Mary that he heard.

'I hear you have given orders to harness,' she cried, panting (she had apparently been running), 'and I did so wish to have another talk with you alone! God knows how long we may again be parted. You are not angry with me for coming? You have changed so, Andrusha,' she added, as if to explain such a question.

She smiled as she uttered his pet name, 'Andrusha'. It was

105

obviously strange to her to think that this stern handsome man should be Andrusha – the slender mischievous boy who had been her playfellow in childhood.

'And where is Lise?' he asked, answering her question only by a smile.

'She was so tired that she has fallen asleep on the sofa in my room. Oh, Andrew! What a treasure of a wife you have,' said she, sitting down on the sofa, facing her brother. 'She is quite a child: such a dear, merry child. I have grown so fond of her.'

Prince Andrew was silent, but the princess noticed the ironical and contemptuous look that showed itself on his face.

'One must be indulgent to little weaknesses; who is free from them, Andrew? Don't forget that she has grown up and been educated in society, and so her position now is not a rosy one. We should enter into everyone's situation. *Tout comprendre, c'est tout pardonner.* Think what it must be for her, poor thing, after what she has been used to, to be parted from her husband and be left alone in the country, in her condition! It's very hard.'

Prince Andrew smiled as he looked at his sister, as we smile at those we think we thoroughly understand.

'You live in the country and don't think the life terrible,' he replied.

'I . . . that's different. Why speak of me? I don't want any other life, and can't, for I know no other. But think, Andrew: for a young society woman to be buried in the country during the best years of her life, all alone, – for papa is always busy, and I . . . well, you know what poor resources I have for entertaining a woman used to the best society. There is only Mademoiselle Bourienne. . . .'

'I don't like your Mademoiselle Bourienne at all,' said Prince Andrew.

'No? She is very nice and kind, and above all she's much to be pitied. She has no one, no one. To tell the truth, I don't need her, and she's even in my way. You know I always was a savage, and now am even more so. I like being alone. . . . Father likes her very much. She and Michael Ivanovich are the two people to whom he is always gentle and kind, because he has been a benefactor to them both. As Sterne says: "We don't love people so much for the good they have done us, as for the good we have done them." Father took her when she was homeless after losing her own father. She is very good-natured, and my father likes her way of reading. She reads to him in the evenings and reads splendidly.'

'To be quite frank, Mary, I expect father's character sometimes makes things trying for you, doesn't it?' Prince Andrew asked suddenly.

Princess Mary was first surprised and then aghast at this question.

'For me? For me? ... Trying for me! ...' said she.

'He always was rather harsh; and now I should think he's getting very trying,' said Prince Andrew, apparently speaking lightly of their father in order to puzzle or test his sister.

'You are good in every way, Andrew, but you have a kind of intellectual pride,' said the princess, following the train of her own thoughts rather than the trend of the conversation – 'and that's a great sin. How can one judge father? But even if one might, what feeling except veneration could such a man as my father evoke? And I am so contented and happy with him. I only wish you were all as happy as I am.'

Her brother shook his head incredulously.

'The only thing that is hard for me ... I will tell you the truth, Andrew, – is father's way of treating religious subjects. I don't understand how a man of his immense intellect can fail to see what is as clear as day, and can go so far astray. That is the only thing that makes me unhappy. But even in this I can see lately a shade of improvement. His satire has been less bitter of late, and there was a monk he received and had a long talk with.'

'Ah! my dear, I am afraid you and your monk are wasting your powder,' said Prince Andrew banteringly yet tenderly.

'Ah! *mon ami*, I only pray, and hope that God will hear me. Andrew ...' she said timidly after a moment's silence, 'I have a great favour to ask of you.'

'What is it, dear?'

'No – promise that you will not refuse! It will give you no trouble and is nothing unworthy of you, but it will comfort me. Promise, Andrusha! ...' said she, putting her hand in her reticule but not yet taking out what she was holding inside it, as if what she held were the subject of her request and must not be shown before the request was granted.

She looked timidly at her brother.

'Even if it were a great deal of trouble ...' answered Prince Andrew as if guessing what it was about.

'Think what you please! I know you are just like father. Think as you please, but do this for my sake! Please do! Father's father, our grandfather, wore it in all his wars.' (She still did not take out what she was holding in her reticule.) 'So you promise?'

'Of course. What is it?'

'Andrew, I bless you with this icon and you must promise me you will never take it off. Do you promise?'

'If it does not weigh a hundredweight and won't break my

107

neck ... To please you ...' said Prince Andrew. But immediately, noticing the pained expression his joke had brought to his sister's face, he repented and added: 'I am glad to; really, dear, I am very glad.'

'Against your will He will save and have mercy on you and bring you to Himself, for in Him alone is truth and peace,' said she in a voice trembling with emotion, solemnly holding up in both hands before her brother a small, oval, antique, dark-faced icon of the Saviour in a gold setting, on a finely wrought silver chain.

She crossed herself, kissed the icon, and handed it to Andrew.

'Please, Andrew, for my sake! ...'

Rays of gentle light shone from her large timid eyes. Those eyes lit up the whole of her thin sickly face and made it beautiful. Her brother would have taken the icon, but she stopped him. Andrew understood, crossed himself, and kissed the icon. There was a look of tenderness, for he was touched, but also a gleam of irony on his face.

'Thank you, my dear.' She kissed him on the forehead and sat down again on the sofa. They were silent for a while.

'As I was saying to you, Andrew, be kind and generous as you always used to be. Don't judge Lise harshly,' she began. 'She is so sweet, so good-natured, and her position now is a very hard one.'

'I do not think I have complained of my wife to you, Masha, or blamed her. Why do you say all this to me?'

Red patches appeared on Princess Mary's face and she was silent as if she felt guilty.

'I have said nothing to you, but you have already been talked to. And I am sorry for that,' he went on.

The patches grew deeper on her forehead, neck and cheeks. She tried to say something but could not. Her brother had guessed right: the little princess had been crying after dinner and had spoken of her forebodings about her confinement, and of how she dreaded it, and had complained of her fate, her father-in-law and her husband. After crying she had fallen asleep. Prince Andrew felt sorry for his sister.

'Know this, Masha: I can't reproach, have not reproached, and never shall reproach *my wife* with anything, and I cannot reproach myself with anything in regard to her; and that always will be so in whatever circumstances I may be placed. But if you want to know the truth ... if you want to know whether I am happy? No! Is she happy? No! But why this is so I don't know ...'

As he said this he rose, went to his sister and, stooping, kissed her forehead. His fine eyes lit up with a thoughtful, kindly, and

108

unaccustomed brightness, but he was looking not at his sister but over her head towards the darkness of the open doorway.

'Let us go to her, I must say good-bye. Or – go and wake her, and I'll come in a moment. Petrushka!' he called to his valet: 'Come here, take these away. Put this on the seat and this to the right.'

Princess Mary rose and moved to the door, then stopped and said:

'Andrew, if you had faith you would have turned to God and asked him to give you the love you do not feel, and your prayer would have been answered.'

'Well, maybe!' said Prince Andrew. 'Go, Masha; I'll come immediately.'

On the way to his sister's room, in the passage which connected one wing with the other, Prince Andrew met Mademoiselle Bourienne smiling sweetly. It was the third time that day that, with an ecstatic and artless smile, she had met him in secluded passages.

'Oh! I thought you were in your room,' she said, for some reason blushing and dropping her eyes.

Prince Andrew looked sternly at her and an expression of anger suddenly came over his face. He said nothing to her but looked at her forehead and hair without looking at her eyes, with such contempt that the Frenchwoman blushed and went away without a word. When he reached his sister's room his wife was already awake and her merry voice, hurrying one word after another, came through the open door. She was speaking as usual in French, and as if after long self-restraint she wished to make up for lost time.

'No, but imagine the old Countess Zubova,* with false curls and her mouth full of false teeth, as if she were trying to cheat old age.... Ha, ha, ha! Mary!'

This very sentence about Countess Zubova and this same laugh Prince Andrew had already heard from his wife in the presence of others some five times. He entered the room softly. The little princess, plump and rosy, was sitting in an easy chair with her work in her hands, talking incessantly, repeating Petersburg reminiscences and even phrases. Prince Andrew came up, stroked her hair, and asked if she felt rested after their journey. She answered him, and continued her chatter.

The coach with six horses was waiting at the porch. It was an autumn night, so dark that the coachman could not see the carriage-pole. Servants with lanterns were bustling about in the porch. The immense house was brilliant with lights shining through its lofty windows. The domestic serfs were crowding in the hall, waiting to bid good-bye to the young prince. The members of the household were all gathered in the reception hall: Michael Ivanovich, Mademoiselle Bourienne, Princess Mary, and the little princess. Prince Andrew had been called to his father's study, as the latter wished to say good-bye to him alone. All were waiting for them to come out.

When Prince Andrew entered the study the old man in his old-age spectacles and white dressing-gown, in which he received no one but his son, sat at the table writing. He glanced round.

'Going?' And he went on writing.

'I've come to say good-bye.'

'Kiss me here,' and he touched his cheek: 'Thanks, thanks!'

'What do you thank me for?'

'For not dilly-dallying and not hanging to a woman's apron-strings. The Service before everything. Thanks, thanks!' And he went on writing, so that his quill spluttered and squeaked. 'If you have anything to say, say it. These two things can be done together,' he added.

'About my wife. . . . I am ashamed as it is to leave her on your hands. . . .'

'Why talk nonsense? Say what you want.'

'When her confinement is due, send to Moscow for an *accoucheur* . . . Let him be here. . . .'

The old prince stopped writing and, as if not understanding, fixed his stern eyes on his son.

'I know that no one can help if nature does not do her work,' said Prince Andrew, evidently confused. 'I know that out of a million cases only one goes wrong, but it is her fancy and mine. They have been telling her things. She has had a dream and is frightened.'

'Hm . . . Hm . . .' muttered the old prince to himself, finishing what he was writing. 'I'll do it.'

He signed with a flourish and suddenly turning to his son began to laugh.

'It's a bad business, eh?'

'What is bad, father?'

'The wife!' said the old prince, briefly and significantly.

'I don't understand!' said Prince Andrew.

'Yes, it can't be helped, lad,' said the prince. 'They're all like that; one can't unmarry. Don't be afraid; I won't tell anyone, but you know it yourself.'

He seized his son by the hand with small bony fingers, shook it, looked straight into his son's face with keen eyes which seemed to see through him, and again laughed his frigid laugh.

The son sighed, thus admitting that his father had understood him. The old man continued to fold and seal his letter, snatching up and throwing down the wax, the seal, and the paper, with his accustomed rapidity.

'What's to be done? She's pretty! I will do everything. Make your mind easy,' said he in abrupt sentences while sealing his letter.

Andrew did not speak; he was both pleased and displeased that his father understood him. The old man got up and gave the letter to his son.

'Listen!' said he; 'don't worry about your wife: what can be done shall be. Now listen! Give this letter to Michael Ilarionovich.* I have written that he should make use of you in proper places and not keep you long as an adjutant: a bad position! Tell him I remember and like him. Write and tell me how he receives you. If he is all right – serve him. Nicholas Bolkonsky's son need not serve under anyone if he is in disfavour. Now come here.'

He spoke so rapidly that he did not finish half his words, but his son was accustomed to understand him. He led him to the desk, raised the lid, drew out a drawer, and took out an exercise-book filled with his bold, tall, close handwriting.

'I shall probably die before you. So remember, these are my memoirs; hand them to the Emperor after my death. Now here is a Lombard-bond* and a letter; it is a premium for the man who writes a history of Suvorov's wars. Send it to the Academy. Here are some jottings for you to read when I am gone. You will find them useful.'

Andrew did not tell his father that he would no doubt live a long time yet. He felt that he must not say it.

'I will do it all, father,' he said.

'Well, now, good-bye!' He gave his son his hand to kiss, and embraced him. 'Remember this, Prince Andrew, if they kill you it will hurt me, your old father. . . .' He paused unexpectedly, and then in a querulous voice suddenly shrieked: 'but if I hear that you have not behaved like a son of Nicholas Bolkonsky, I shall be ashamed!'

'You need not have said that to me, father,' said the son with a smile.

The old man was silent.

'I also wanted to ask you,' continued Prince Andrew, 'if I'm killed and if I have a son, do not let him be taken away from you – as I said yesterday . . . let him grow up with you . . . Please.'

'Not let the wife have him?' said the old man, and laughed.

They stood silent, facing one another. The old man's sharp eyes

111

were fixed straight on his son's. Something twitched in the lower part of the old prince's face.

'We've said good-bye. Go!' he suddenly shouted in a loud, angry voice, opening his door.

'What is it? What?' asked both princesses when they saw for a moment at the door Prince Andrew and the figure of the old man in a white dressing-gown, spectacled and wigless, shouting in an angry voice.

Prince Andrew sighed and made no reply.

'Well!' he said, turning to his wife.

And this 'Well!' sounded coldly ironic, as if he were saying: 'Now go through your performance.'

'Andrew, already!' said the little princess, turning pale and looking with dismay at her husband.

He embraced her. She screamed and fell unconscious on his shoulder.

He cautiously released the shoulder she leant on, looked into her face, and carefully placed her in an easy chair.

'Adieu, Mary,' said he gently to his sister, taking her by the hand and kissing her, and then he left the room with rapid steps.

The little princess lay in the arm-chair, Mademoiselle Bourienne chafing her temples. Princess Mary, supporting her sister-in-law, still looked with her beautiful eyes full of tears at the door through which Prince Andrew had gone, and made the sign of the cross in his direction. From the study, like pistol shots, came the frequent sound of the old man angrily blowing his nose. Hardly had Prince Andrew gone when the study door opened quickly, and the stern figure of the old man in the white dressing-gown looked out.

'Gone? That's all right!' said he; and looking angrily at the unconscious little princess, he shook his head reprovingly and slammed the door.

### END OF PART ONE

# PART TWO

## 1

IN October 1805 a Russian army was occupying the villages and towns of the Archduchy of Austria, and yet other regiments freshly arriving from Russia were settling near the fortress of Braunau and burdening the inhabitants on whom they were quartered. Braunau was the head-quarters of the commander-in-chief, Kutuzov.

On October 11th, 1805, one of the infantry regiments that had just reached Braunau had halted half a mile from the town, waiting to be inspected by the commander-in-chief. Despite the un-Russian appearance of the locality and surroundings – fruit gardens, stone fences, tiled roofs, and hills in the distance – and despite the fact that the inhabitants (who gazed with curiosity at the soldiers) were not Russians, the regiment had just the appearance of any Russian regiment preparing for an inspection anywhere in the heart of Russia.

On the evening of the last day's march an order had been received that the commander-in-chief would inspect the regiment on the march. Though the words of the order were not clear to the regimental commander, and the question arose whether the troops were to be in marching order or not, it was decided at a consultation between the battalion commanders, to present the regiment in parade order, on the principle that it is always better to 'bow too low than not bow low enough'. So the soldiers, after a twenty-mile march, were kept mending and cleaning all night long without closing their eyes, while the adjutants and company commanders calculated and reckoned, and by morning the regiment – instead of the straggling, disorderly crowd it had been on its last march the day before – presented a well-ordered array of two thousand men each of whom knew his place and his duty, had every button and every strap in place, and shone with cleanliness. And not only externally was all in order, but had it pleased the commander-in-chief to look under the uniforms he would have found on every man a clean shirt, and in every knapsack, the appointed number of articles, 'awl, soap, and all', as the soldiers say. There was only one circumstance concerning which no one could be at ease. It was the state of the soldiers' boots. More than half the men's boots were in holes. But this defect was not due to any fault of the regimental commander, for in spite of repeated demands boots had not been issued by the Austrian commissariat, and the regiment had marched some seven hundred miles.

The commander of the regiment was an elderly, choleric, stout and thick-set general with grizzled eyebrows and whiskers, and wider from chest to back than across the shoulders. He had on a brand new uniform showing the creases where it had been folded, and thick gold epaulettes which seemed to stand rather than lie down on his massive shoulders. He had the air of a man happily performing one of the most solemn duties of his life. He walked about in front of the line and at every step pulled himself up, slightly arching his back. It was plain that the commander admired his regiment, rejoiced in it, and that his whole mind was engrossed by it, yet his strut seemed to indicate that besides military matters social interests and the fair sex occupied no small part of his thoughts.

'Well, Michael Mitrich, sir?' he said, addressing one of the battalion commanders who smilingly pressed forward (it was plain that they both felt happy). 'We had our hands full last night. However, I think the regiment is not a bad one, eh?'

The battalion commander perceived the jovial irony and laughed.

'It would not be turned off the field even on the Tsaritsin Meadow.'*

'What?' asked the commander.

At that moment, on the road from the town on which signallers had been posted, two men appeared on horseback. They were an aide-de-camp followed by a Cossack.

The aide-de-camp was sent to confirm the order which had not been clearly worded the day before, namely, that the commander-in-chief wished to see the regiment just in the state in which it had been on the march: in their greatcoats, and packs, and without any preparation whatever.

A member of the Hofkriegsrath from Vienna had come to Kutuzov the day before with proposals and demands for him to join up with the army of the Archduke Ferdinand and Mack, and Kutuzov, not considering this junction advisable, meant among other arguments in support of his view, to show the Austrian general the wretched state in which the troops arrived from Russia. With this object he intended to meet the regiment; so the worse the condition it was in, the better pleased the commander-in-chief would be. Though the aide-de-camp did not know these circumstances, he nevertheless delivered the definite order that the men should be in their greatcoats and in marching-order, and that the commander-in-chief would otherwise be dissatisfied. On hearing this the regimental commander hung his head, silently shrugged his shoulders, and spread out his arms with a choleric gesture.

'A fine mess we've made of it!' he remarked.

'There now! Didn't I tell you, Michael Mitrich, that if it was said "on the march" it meant in greatcoats?' said he reproachfully to the battalion commander. Oh, my God!' he added stepping resolutely forward. 'Company commanders!' he shouted in a voice accustomed to command. 'Sergeant-majors! . . . How soon will he be here?' he asked the aide-de-camp with a respectful politeness evidently relating to the personage he was referring to.

'In an hour's time, I should say.'

'Shall we have time to change clothes?'

'I don't know, general. . . .'

The regimental commander, going up to the line himself, ordered the soldiers to change into their greatcoats. The company commanders ran off to their companies, the sergeant-majors began bustling (the greatcoats were not in very good condition), and instantly the squares that had up to then been in regular order and silent, began to sway and stretch and hum with voices. On all sides soldiers were running to and fro, throwing up their knapsacks with a jerk of their shoulders and pulling the straps over their heads, unstrapping their overcoats and drawing the sleeves on with upraised arms.

In half an hour all was again in order, only the squares had become grey instead of black. The regimental commander walked with his jerky steps to the front of the regiment and examined it from a distance.

'Whatever is this? This!' he shouted and stood still. 'Commander of the third company!'

'Commander of the third company wanted by the general! . . . commander to the general . . . third company to the commander.' The words passed along the lines and an adjutant ran to look for the missing officer.

When the eager but misrepeated words had reached their destination in a cry of: 'The general to the third company,' the missing officer appeared from behind his company, and though he was a middle-aged man and not in the habit of running, trotted awkwardly stumbling on his toes towards the general. The captain's face showed the uneasiness of a schoolboy who is told to repeat a lesson he has not learnt. Spots appeared on his nose, the redness of which was evidently due to intemperance, and his mouth twitched nervously. The general looked the captain up and down as he came up panting, slackening his pace as he approached.

'You will soon be dressing your men in petticoats! What is this?' shouted the regimental commander, thrusting forward his jaw and pointing at a soldier in the ranks of the third company in a great-coat of bluish cloth, which contrasted with the others. 'What have you been after? The commander-in-chief is expected and you leave your place? Eh? I'll teach you to dress the men in fancy coats for a parade. . . . Eh . . . ?'

The commander of the company, with his eyes fixed on his superior pressed two fingers more and more rigidly to his cap, as if in this pressure lay his only hope of salvation.

'Well, why don't you speak? Whom have you got there dressed up as a Hungarian?' said the commander with an austere gibe.

'Your Excellency . . .'

'Well, your Excellency what? Your Excellency! But what about your Excellency? . . . nobody knows.'

'Your Excellency, it's the officer Dolokhov, who has been reduced to the ranks,' said the captain softly.

'Well? Has he been degraded into a field-marshal, or into a soldier? If a soldier, he should be dressed in regulation uniform like the others.'

'Your Excellency, you gave him leave yourself, on the march.'

'Gave him leave? Leave? That's just like you young men,' said the regimental commander, cooling down a little. 'Leave indeed. . . . One says a word to you and you . . . What?' he added with renewed irritation, 'I beg you to dress your men decently.'

And the commander, turning to look at the adjutant, directed his jerky steps down the line. He was evidently pleased at his own display of anger and walking up to the regiment wished to find a further excuse for wrath. Having snapped at an officer for an unpolished badge, at another because his line was not straight, he reached the third company.

'H-o-o-w are you standing? Where's your leg? Your leg?' shouted the commander with a tone of suffering in his voice, while there were still five men between him and Dolokhov with his bluish-grey uniform.

Dolokhov slowly straightened his bent knee, looking straight with his clear, insolent eyes in the general's face.

'Why a blue coat? Off with it . . . Sergeant-major! Change his coat . . . the ras . . .'. He did not finish.

'General, I must obey orders, but I am not bound to endure . . .' Dolokhov hurriedly interrupted.

'No talking in the ranks! . . . No talking, no talking!'

'Not bound to endure insults,' Dolokhov concluded in loud, ringing tones.

The eyes of the general and the soldier met. The general became silent, angrily pulling down his tight scarf.

'I request you to have the goodness to change your coat,' he said as he turned away.


## 2

'HE'S coming!' shouted the signaller at that moment.

The regimental commander, flushing, ran to his horse, seized the stirrup with trembling hands, threw his body across the saddle, righted himself, drew his sabre, and with a happy and resolute countenance, opening his mouth awry, prepared to shout. The regiment fluttered like a bird preening its plumage, and became motionless.

'Att-ention!' shouted the regimental commander in a soul-shaking voice which expressed joy for himself, severity for the regiment, and welcome for the approaching chief.

Along the broad country road, edged on both sides by trees, came a high, light-blue Viennese calèche, slightly creaking on its springs and drawn by six horses at a smart trot. Behind the calèche galloped the suite and a convoy of Croats. Beside Kutuzov sat an Austrian general, in a white uniform that looked strange among the Russian black ones. The calèche stopped in front of the regiment. Kutuzov and the Austrian general were talking in low voices, and Kutuzov smiled slightly as treading heavily he stepped down from the carriage just as if those two thousand men breathlessly gazing at him and the regimental commander did not exist.

The word of command rang out, and again the regiment quivered, as with a jingling sound it presented arms. Then amidst a dead silence the feeble voice of the commander-in-chief was heard. The regiment roared, 'Health to your Ex . . . len . . . len . . . lency!' and again all became silent. At first Kutuzov stood still while the regiment moved; then he and the general in white, accompanied by the suite, walked between the ranks.

From the way the regimental commander saluted the commander-in-chief and devoured him with his eyes, drawing himself up obsequiously, and from the way he walked through the ranks behind the generals, bending forward and hardly able to restrain his jerky movements, and from the way he darted forward at every word or gesture of the commander-in-chief, it was evident that he performed his duty as a subordinate with even greater zeal than his duty as a commander. Thanks to the strictness and assiduity of its commander the regiment, in comparison with others that had reached Braunau at the same time, was in splendid condition. There were only 217 sick and stragglers. Everything was in good order except the boots.

Kutuzov walked through the ranks, sometimes stopping to say a few friendly words to officers he had known in the Turkish war, sometimes also to the soldiers. Looking at their boots he several times shook his head sadly, pointing them out to the Austrian general with an expression which seemed to say that he was not blaming anyone, but could not help noticing what a bad state of things it was. The regimental commander ran forward on each such occasion fearing to miss a single word of the commander-in-chief's regarding the regiment. Behind Kutuzov, at a distance that allowed every softly spoken word to be heard, followed some twenty men of his suite. These gentlemen talked among themselves and sometimes laughed. Nearest of all to the commander-in-chief walked a handsome adjutant. This was Prince Bolkonsky. Beside him was his comrade Nesvitsky, a tall staff-officer, extremely stout, with a kindly, smiling, handsome face and moist eyes. Nesvitsky could hardly keep from laughter provoked by a swarthy hussar officer who walked beside him. This hussar, with a grave face and without a smile or a change in the expression of his fixed eyes, watched the regimental commander's back and mimicked his every movement. Each time the commander started and bent forward, the hussar started and bent forward in exactly the same manner, Nesvitsky laughed and nudged the others to make them look at the wag.

Kutuzov walked slowly and languidly past thousands of eyes which were starting from their sockets to watch their chief. On reaching the third company he suddenly stopped. His suite not having expected this, involuntarily came closer to him.

'Ah, Timokhin!' said he, recognizing the red-nosed captain who had been reprimanded on account of the blue greatcoat.

One would have thought it impossible for a man to stretch himself more than Timokhin had done when he was reprimanded by the regimental commander, but now that the commander-in-chief addressed him he drew himself up to such an extent that it seemed he could not have sustained it had the commander-in-chief continued to look at him, and so Kutuzov, who evidently understood his case and wished him nothing but good, quickly turned away, a scarcely perceptible smile flitting over his scarred and puffy face.

'Another Ismail comrade,' said he. 'A brave officer! Are you satisfied with him?' he asked the regimental commander.

And the latter – unconscious that he was being reflected in the hussar officer as in a looking-glass – started, moved forward, and answered: 'Highly satisfied, your Excellency!'

'We all have our weaknesses,' said Kutuzov smiling and walking away from him. 'He used to have a predilection for Bacchus.'

The regimental commander was afraid he might be blamed for this, and did not answer. The hussar at that moment noticed the face of the red-nosed captain and his drawn-in stomach, and mimicked his expression and pose with such exactitude that Nesvitsky could not help laughing. Kutuzov turned round. The officer evidently had complete control of his face, and while Kutuzov was turning managed to make a grimace and then assume a most serious, deferential, and innocent expression.

The third company was the last, and Kutuzov pondered, apparently trying to recollect something. Prince Andrew stepped forward from among the suite and said softly in French:

'You told me to remind you of the officer Dolokhov, reduced to the ranks in this regiment.'

Dolokhov, who had already changed into a soldier's grey greatcoat, did not wait to be called. The shapely figure of the fair-haired soldier, with his clear blue eyes, stepped forward from the ranks, went up to the commander-in-chief, and presented arms.

'Have you a complaint to make?' Kutuzov asked with a slight frown.

'This is Dolokhov,' said Prince Andrew.

'Ah!' said Kutuzov. 'I hope this will be a lesson to you. Do your duty. The Emperor is gracious, and I shan't forget you if you deserve well.'

The clear blue eyes looked at the commander-in-chief just as boldly as they had looked at the regimental commander, seeming by their expression to tear open the veil of convention that separates a commander-in-chief so widely from a private.

'One thing I ask of your Excellency,' Dolokhov said in his firm, ringing, deliberate voice. 'I ask an opportunity to atone for my fault and prove my devotion to his Majesty the Emperor and to Russia!'

Kutuzov turned away. The same smile of the eyes with which he had turned from Captain Timokhin again flitted over his face. He turned away with a grimace as if to say that everything Dolokhov had said to him and everything he could say had long been known to him, that he was weary of it and it was not at all what he wanted. He turned away and went to the carriage.

The regiment broke up into companies, which went to their appointed quarters near Braunau, where they hoped to receive boots and clothes and to rest after their hard marches.

'You won't bear me a grudge, Prokhor Ignatych?' said the regimental commander, overtaking the third company on its way to its quarters and riding up to Captain Timokhin who was walking in front. (The regimental commander's face now that the inspection was happily over beamed with irrepressible delight.) 'It's in the Emperor's service . . . it can't be helped . . . one is sometimes a bit hasty on parade . . . I am the first to apologize, you know me! . . . He was very pleased!' And he held out his hand to the captain.

'Don't mention it, General, as if I'd be so bold!' replied the captain, his nose growing redder as he gave a smile which showed where two front teeth were missing that had been knocked out by the butt end of a gun at Ismail.

'And tell Mr Dolokhov that I won't forget him – he may be quite easy. And tell me, please – I've been meaning to ask – how is he behaving himself, and in general . . .'

'As far as the service goes he is quite punctilious, your Excellency; but his character . . .' said Timokhin.

'And what about his character?' asked the regimental commander.

'It's different on different days,' answered the captain. 'One day he is sensible, well educated and good-natured, and the next he's a wild beast. . . . In Poland, if you please, he nearly killed a Jew.'

'Oh, well, well!' remarked the regimental commander. 'Still, one must have pity on a young man in misfortune. You know he has important connexions . . . Well then, you just . . .'

'I will, your Excellency,' said Timokhin, showing by his smile that he understood his commander's wish.

'Well, of course, of course!'

The regimental commander sought out Dolokhov in the ranks, and reining in his horse, said to him:

'After the next affair . . . epaulettes.'

Dolokhov looked round but did not say anything, nor did the mocking smile on his lips change.

'Well, that's all right,' continued the regimental commander. 'A cup of vodka for the men from me,' he added so that the soldiers could hear. 'I thank you all! God be praised!' and he rode past that company and overtook the next one.

'Well, he's really a good fellow, one can serve under him,' said Timokhin to the subaltern beside him.

'In a word, a hearty one...' said the subaltern, laughing (the regimental commander was nicknamed *King of Hearts*).

The cheerful mood of their officers after the inspection infected the soldiers. The company marched on gaily. The soldiers' voices could be heard on every side.

'And they said Kutuzov was blind of one eye?'

'And so he is! Quite blind!'

'No, friend, he is sharper eyed than you are. Boots and leg-bands* ...he noticed everything...'

'When he looked at my feet, friend...well, thinks I...'

'And that other one with him, the Austrian, looked as if he were smeared with chalk – as white as flour! I suppose they polish him up as they do the guns.'

'I say, Fedeshon!...Did he say when the battles are to begin? You were near him. Everybody said that Buonaparte himself was at Braunau.'

'Buonaparte himself...Just listen to the fool, what he doesn't know! The Prussians are up in arms now. The Austrians, you see, are putting them down. When they've been put down, the war with Buonaparte will begin. And he says Buonaparte is in Braunau! Shows you're a fool. You'd better listen more carefully!'

'What devils these quartermasters are! See, the fifth company is turned into the village already...they will have their buckwheat cooked before we reach our quarters.'

'Give me a biscuit, you devil!'

'And did you give me tobacco yesterday? That's just it, friend! Ah well, never mind, here you are.'

'They might call a halt here or we'll have to do another four miles without eating.'

'Wasn't it fine when those Germans gave us lifts!* You just sit still and are drawn along.'

'And here, friend, the people are quite beggarly. There they all seemed to be Poles – all under the Russian crown – but here they're all regular Germans.'

'Singers to the front!' came the captain's order.

And from the different ranks some twenty men ran to the front. A drummer, their leader, turned round facing the singers, and flourishing his arm began a long-drawn-out soldiers' song, commencing with the words: 'Morning dawned, the sun was rising' and concluding: 'On then, brothers, on to glory, led by Father Kamensky.' This song had been composed in the Turkish campaign and was now being sung in Austria, the only change being that the words 'Father Kamensky' were replaced by 'Father Kutuzov'.

Having jerked out these last words as soldiers do and waved his

121

arms as if flinging something to the ground, the drummer – a lean, handsome soldier of forty – looked sternly at the singers and screwed up his eyes. Then having satisfied himself that all eyes were fixed on him, he raised both arms as if carefully lifting some invisible but precious object above his head and, holding it there for some seconds, suddenly flung it down and began:

'Oh, my bower, oh, my bower . . .!'

'Oh, my bower new . . . !' chimed in twenty voices, and the castanet-player in spite of the burden of his equipment rushed out to the front and walking backwards before the company jerked his shoulders and flourished his castanets as if threatening someone. The soldiers, swinging their arms and keeping time spontaneously, marched with long steps. Behind the company the sound of wheels, the creaking of springs, and the tramp of horses' hoofs were heard. Kutuzov and his suite were returning to the town. The commander-in-chief made a sign that the men should continue to march at ease, and he and all his suite showed pleasure at the sound of the singing and the sight of the dancing soldier and the gay and smartly marching men. In the second file from the right flank, beside which the carriage passed the company, a blue-eyed soldier involuntarily attracted notice. It was Dolokhov marching with particular grace and boldness in time to the song and looking at those driving past as if he pitied all who were not at that moment marching with the company. The hussar cornet of Kutuzov's suite who had mimicked the regimental commander, fell back from the carriage and rode up to Dolokhov.

Hussar cornet Zherkov had at one time, in Petersburg, belonged to the wild set led by Dolokhov. Zherkov had met Dolokhov abroad as a private and had not seen fit to recognize him. But now that Kutuzov had spoken to the gentleman-ranker, he addressed him with the cordiality of an old friend.

'My dear fellow how are you?' said he through the singing, making his horse keep pace with the company.

'How am I?' Dolokhov answered coldly. 'I am as you see.'

The lively song gave a special flavour to the tone of free and easy gaiety with which Zherkov spoke, and to the intentional coldness of Dolokhov's reply.

'And how do you get on with the officers?' inquired Zherkov.

'All right. They are good fellows. And how have you wriggled onto the staff?'

'I was attached; I'm on duty.'

Both were silent.

'She let the hawk fly upward from her wide right sleeve,' went the song, arousing an involuntary sensation of courage and cheerfulness. Their conversation would probably have been different but for the effect of that song.

'Is it true the Austrians have been beaten?' asked Dolokhov.

'The devil only knows! They say so.'

'I'm glad,' answered Dolokhov briefly and clearly, as the song demanded.

'I say, come round some evening and we'll have a game of faro!' said Zherkov.

'Why, have you too much money?'

'Do come.'

'I can't. I've sworn not to. I won't drink and won't play till I get reinstated.'

'Well that's only till the first engagement.'

'We shall see.'

They were again silent.

'Come if you need anything. One can at least be of use on the staff . . .'

Dolokhov smiled. 'Don't trouble. If I want anything, I won't beg – I'll take it!'

'Well, never mind; I only . . .'

'And I only . . .'

'Good-bye.'

'Good health . . .'

> *'It's a long, long way*
> *To my native land . . .'*

Zherkov touched his horse with the spurs; it pranced excitedly from foot to foot uncertain with which to start, then settled down, galloped past the company, and overtook the carriage, still keeping time to the song.

3

ON returning from the review Kutuzov took the Austrian general into his private room, and calling his adjutant, asked for some papers relating to the condition of the troops on their arrival, and the letters that had come from the Archduke Ferdinand, who was in command of the advanced army. Prince Andrew Bolkonsky came into the room with the required papers. Kutuzov and the Austrian member of the Hofkriegsrath were sitting at the table on which a plan was spread out.

'Ah! . . .' said Kutuzov glancing at Bolkonsky as if by this exclamation he was asking the adjutant to wait, and he went on with the conversation in French.

'All I can say, General,' said he with a pleasant elegance of expression and intonation that obliged one to listen to each deliberately spoken word. It was evident that Kutuzov himself listened with pleasure to his own voice. 'All I can say, General, is that if the matter depended on my personal wishes, the will of his Majesty the Emperor Francis would have been fulfilled long ago. I should long ago have joined the archduke. And believe me on my honour that to me personally it would be a pleasure to hand over the supreme command of the army into the hands of a better informed and more skilful general – of whom Austria has so many – and to lay down all this heavy responsibility. But circumstances are sometimes too strong for us, General.'

And Kutuzov smiled in a way that seemed to say, 'You are quite at liberty not to believe me and I don't even care whether you do or not, but you have no grounds for telling me so. And that is the whole point.'

The Austrian general looked dissatisfied, but had no option but to reply in the same tone.

'On the contrary,' he said, in a querulous and angry tone that contrasted with his flattering words, 'on the contrary, your Excellency's participation in the common action is highly valued by his Majesty; but we think the present delay is depriving the splendid Russian troops and their commander of the laurels they have been accustomed to win in their battles,' he concluded his evidently prearranged sentence.

Kutuzov bowed with the same smile.

'But that is my conviction, and judging by the last letter with which his Highness the Archduke Ferdinand has honoured me, I imagine that the Austrian troops, under the direction of so skilful a leader as General Mack have by now already gained a decisive victory and no longer need our aid,' said Kutuzov.

The general frowned. Though there was no definite news of an Austrian defeat, there were many circumstances confirming the unfavourable rumours that were afloat, and so Kutuzov's suggestion of an Austrian victory sounded much like irony. But Kutuzov went on blandly smiling with the same expression, which seemed to say that he had a right to suppose so. And in fact the last letter he had received from Mack's army informed him of a victory and stated that strategically the position of the army was very favourable.

'Give me that letter,' said Kutuzov turning to Prince Andrew. 'Please have a look at it' – and Kutuzov with an ironical smile about the corners of his mouth read to the Austrian general the following passage, in German, from the Archduke Ferdinand's letter.

'We have fully concentrated forces of nearly seventy thousand men with which to attack and defeat the enemy should he cross the Lech. Also, as we are masters of Ulm, we cannot be deprived of the advantage of commanding both sides of the Danube, so that should the enemy not cross the Lech, we can cross the Danube, throw ourselves on his line of communication, recross the river lower down, and frustrate his intention should he try to direct his whole force against our faithful ally. We shall therefore confidently await the moment when the Imperial Russian army will be fully equipped, and shall then, in conjunction with it, easily find a way to prepare for the enemy the fate he deserves.'

Kutuzov sighed deeply on finishing this paragraph and looked at the member of the Hofkriegsrath mildly and attentively.

'But you know the wise maxim, your Excellency, advising one to expect the worst,' said the Austrian general, evidently wishing to have done with jests and to come to business. He involuntarily looked round at the aide-de-camp.

'Excuse me, General,' interrupted Kutuzov, also turning to Prince Andrew. 'Look here, my dear fellow, get from Kozlovsky all the reports from our scouts. Here are two letters from Count Nostitz and here is one from his Highness the Archduke Ferdinand and here are these,' he said, handing him several papers, 'make a neat memorandum in French out of all this, showing all the news we have had of the movements of the Austrian army, and then give it to his Excellency.'

Prince Andrew bowed his head in token of having understood from the first not only what had been said but also what Kutuzov would have liked to tell him. He gathered up the papers and, with a bow to both, stepped softly over the carpet and went out into the waiting-room.

Though not much time had passed since Prince Andrew had left Russia, he had changed greatly during that period. In the expression of his face, in his movements, in his walk, scarcely a trace was left of his former affected languor and indolence. He now looked like a man who has no time to think of the impression he makes on others, but is occupied with agreeable and interesting work. His face expressed more satisfaction with himself and those around him, his smile and glance were brighter and more attractive.

Kutuzov, whom he had overtaken in Poland, had received him very kindly, promised not to forget him, distinguished him above the other adjutants, and had taken him to Vienna and given him the more serious commissions. From Vienna Kutuzov wrote to his old comrade, Prince Andrew's father:

'Your son bids fair to become an officer distinguished by his industry, firmness, and expedition. I consider myself fortunate to have such a subordinate by me.'

On Kutuzov's staff, among his fellow-officers and in the army generally, Prince Andrew had, as he had had in Petersburg society, two quite opposite reputations. Some, a minority, acknowledged him to be different from themselves and from everyone else, expected great things of him, listened to him, admired, and imitated him, and with them Prince Andrew was natural and pleasant. Others, the majority, disliked him and considered him conceited, cold, and disagreeable. But among these people Prince Andrew knew how to take his stand so that they respected and even feared him.

Coming out of Kutuzov's room into the waiting-room with the papers in his hand Prince Andrew came up to his comrade, the aide-de-camp on duty, Kozlovsky, who was sitting at the window with a book.

'Well, Prince?' asked Kozlovsky.

'I am ordered to write a memorandum explaining why we are not advancing.'

'And why is it?'

Prince Andrew shrugged his shoulders.

'Any news from Mack?'

'No.'

'If it were true that he has been beaten news would have come.'

'Probably,' said Prince Andrew moving towards the outer door. But at that instant a tall Austrian general in a greatcoat, with the order of Maria Theresa on his neck and a black bandage round his head, who had evidently just arrived, entered quickly, slamming the door. Prince Andrew stopped short.

'Commander-in-chief Kutuzov?' said the newly-arrived general, speaking quickly with a harsh German accent, looking to both sides and advancing straight towards the inner door.

'The commander-in-chief is engaged,' said Kozlovsky, going hurriedly up to the unknown general and blocking his way to the door. 'Whom shall I announce?'

The unknown general looked disdainfully down at Kozlovsky, who was rather short, as if surprised that anyone should not know him.

'The commander-in-chief is engaged,' repeated Kozlovsky calmly.

The general's face clouded, his lips quivered and trembled. He took out a notebook, hurriedly scribbled something in pencil, tore out the leaf, gave it to Kozlovsky, stepped quickly to the window and threw himself into a chair, gazing at those in the room as if asking, 'Why do they look at me?' Then he lifted his head, stretched his neck as if he intended to say something, but immediately, with affected indifference, began to hum to himself, producing a queer sound which immediately broke off. The door of the private room opened and Kutuzov appeared in the doorway. The general with the bandaged head bent forward as though running away from some danger, and making long quick strides with his thin legs, went up to Kutuzov.

'*Vous voyez le malheureux Mack,*' he uttered in a broken voice. Kutuzov's face as he stood in the open door-way remained perfectly immobile for a few moments. Then wrinkles ran over his face like a wave and his forehead became smooth again, he bowed his head respectfully, closed his eyes, silently let Mack enter his room before him, and closed the door himself behind him.

The report which had been circulated that the Austrians had been beaten and that the whole army had surrendered at Ulm proved to be correct. Within half an hour adjutants had been sent in various directions with orders which showed that the Russian troops, who had hitherto been inactive, would also have to meet the enemy.

Prince Andrew was one of those rare staff-officers whose chief interest lay in the general progress of the war. When he saw Mack and heard the details of his disaster he understood that half the campaign was lost, understood all the difficulties of the Russian army's position, and vividly imagined what awaited it and the part he would have to play. Involuntarily he felt a joyful agitation at the thought of the humiliation of arrogant Austria and that in a week's time he might, perhaps, see and take part in the first Russian encounter with the French since Suvorov met them. He feared that Bonaparte's genius might outweigh all the courage of the Russian troops, and at the same time could not admit the idea of his hero being disgraced.

Excited and irritated by these thoughts Prince Andrew went towards his room to write to his father, to whom he wrote every day. In the corridor he met Nesvitsky with whom he shared a room, and the wag Zherkov; they were as usual laughing.

'Why are you so glum?' asked Nesvitsky noticing Prince Andrew's pale face and glittering eyes.

'There's nothing to be gay about,' answered Bolkonsky.

Just as Prince Andrew met Nesvitsky and Zherkov, there came towards them from the other end of the corridor, Strauch, an Austrian general who was on Kutuzov's staff in charge of the provisioning of the Russian army, and the member of the Hofkriegsrath who had arrived the previous evening. There was room enough in the wide corridor for the generals to pass the three officers quite easily, but Zherkov, pushing Nesvitsky aside with his arm, said in a breathless voice,

'They're coming!...they're coming...Stand aside, make way, please make way!'

The generals were passing by, looking as if they wished to avoid embarrassing attentions. On the face of the wag Zherkov there suddenly appeared a stupid smile of glee which he seemed unable to suppress.

'Your Excellency,' said he in German, stepping forward and addressing the Austrian general, 'I have the honour to congratulate you.'

He bowed his head and scraped first with one foot and then with the other, awkwardly, like a child at a dancing-lesson.

The member of the Hofkriegsrath looked at him severely, but seeing the seriousness of his stupid smile, could not but give him a moment's attention. He screwed up his eyes showing that he was listening.

'I have the honour to congratulate you. General Mack has arrived, quite well, only a little bruised just here,' he added, pointing with a beaming smile to his head.

The general frowned, turned away, and went on.

'*Gott, wie naiv!*' said he angrily, after he had gone a few steps.

Nesvitsky with a laugh threw his arms round Prince Andrew, but Bolkonsky, turning still paler, pushed him away with an angry look and turned to Zherkov. The nervous irritation aroused by the appearance of Mack, the news of his defeat, and the thought of what lay before the Russian army, found vent in anger at Zherkov's untimely jest.

'If you, sir, choose to make a *buffoon* of yourself,' he said sharply, with a slight trembling of the lower jaw, 'I can't prevent your doing so; but I warn you that if you *dare* to play the fool in my presence, I will teach you to behave yourself.'

Nesvitsky and Zherkov were so surprised by this outburst that they gazed at Bolkonsky silently with wide-open eyes.

'What's the matter? I only congratulated them,' said Zherkov.

'I am not jesting with you; please be silent!' cried Bolkonsky, and taking Nesvitsky's arm he left Zherkov, who did not know what to say.

'Come, what's the matter, old fellow?' said Nesvitsky trying to soothe him.

'What's the matter?' exclaimed Prince Andrew standing still in his excitement. 'Don't you understand that either we are officers serving our Tsar and our country, rejoicing in the successes and grieving at the misfortunes of our common cause, or we are merely lackeys who care nothing for their master's business. *Quarante mille hommes massacrés et l'armée de nos alliés détruite, et vous trouvez là le mot pour rire,*' he said, as if strengthening his views by this French sentence. '*C'est bien pour un garçon de rien comme cet individu dont vous avez fait un ami, mais pas pour vous, pas pour vous.* Only a hobbledehoy could amuse himself in this way,' he added in Russian – but pronouncing the word with a French accent – having noticed that Zherkov could still hear him.

He waited a moment to see whether the cornet would answer, but he turned and went out of the corridor.

4

THE Pavlograd hussars were stationed two miles from Braunau. The squadron in which Nicholas Rostov served as a cadet was quartered in the German village of Salzeneck. The best quarters in the village were assigned to cavalry-captain Denisov, the squadron commander, known throughout the whole cavalry division as Vaska Denisov. Cadet Rostov ever since he had overtaken the regiment in Poland had lived with the squadron commander.

On October 11th, the day when all was astir at head-quarters over the news of Mack's defeat, the camp life of the officers of this squadron was proceeding as usual. Denisov, who had been losing at cards all night, had not yet come home when Rostov rode back early in the morning from a foraging expedition. Rostov in his cadet uniform, with a jerk to his horse rode up to the porch, swung his leg over the saddle with a supple youthful movement, stood for a moment in the stirrup as if loth to part from his horse, and at last sprang down and called to his orderly.

'Ah, Bondarenko, dear friend!' said he to the hussar who rushed up headlong to the horse. 'Walk him up and down, my dear fellow,' he continued, with that gay brotherly cordiality which good-hearted young people show to everyone when they are happy.

'Yes, your Excellency,' answered the Ukrainian gaily, tossing his head.

'Mind, walk him up and down well!'

Another hussar also rushed towards the horse, but Bondarenko had already thrown the reins of the snaffle-bridle over the horse's head. It was evident that the cadet was liberal with his tips and that it paid to serve him. Rostov patted the horse's neck and then his flank, and lingered for a moment.

'Splendid! What a horse he will be!' he thought with a smile, and holding up his sabre, his spurs jingling, he ran up the steps of the porch. His landlord, who in a waistcoat and a pointed cap, pitchfork in hand, was clearing manure from the cow-house, looked out, and his face immediately brightened on seeing Rostov. '*Schön gut Morgen! Schön gut Morgen!*' he said winking with a merry smile, evidently pleased to greet the young man.

'*Schon fleissig?*'\* said Rostov with the same gay brotherly smile which did not leave his eager face. '*Hoch Oestreicher! Hoch Russen! Kaiser Alexander hoch!*'\* said he, quoting words often repeated by the German landlord.

The German laughed, came out of the cowshed, pulled off his cap, and waving it above his head cried:

'*Und die ganze Welt hoch!*'

Rostov waved his cap above his head like the German and cried laughing, '*Und vivat die ganze Welt!*' Though neither the German cleaning his cowshed, nor Rostov back with his platoon from foraging for hay, had any reason for rejoicing, they looked at each other with joyful delight and brotherly love, wagged their heads in token of their mutual affection, and parted smiling, the German returning to his cowshed and Rostov going to the cottage he occupied with Denisov.

'What about your master?' he asked Lavrushka, Denisov's orderly, whom all the regiment knew for a rogue.

'Hasn't been in since the evening. Must have been losing,' answered Lavrushka. 'I know by now, if he wins he comes back to brag about it, but if he stays out till morning it means he's lost and will come back in a rage. Will you have coffee?'

'Yes, bring some.'

Ten minutes later Lavrushka brought the coffee. 'He's coming!' said he. 'Now for trouble!' Rostov looked out of the window and saw Denisov coming home. Denisov was a small man with a red face, sparkling black eyes, and black tousled moustache and hair. He wore an unfastened cloak, wide breeches hanging down in creases, and a crumpled shako on the back of his head. He came up to the porch gloomily, hanging his head.

'Lavwuska!' he shouted loudly and angrily, 'take it off, block-head!'

'Well, I am taking it off,' replied Lavrushka's voice.

'Ah, you're up already,' said Denisov, entering the room.

'Long ago,' answered Rostov, 'I have already been for the hay, and have seen Fräulein Mathilde.'

'Weally! And I've been losing, bwother. I lost yesterday like a damned fool!' cried Denisov, not pronouncing his r's. 'Such ill

130

luck! Such ill luck. As soon as you left, it began and went on. Hullo there! Tea!'

Puckering up his face as though smiling, and showing his short strong teeth, he began with the stubby fingers of both hands to ruffle up his thick tangled black hair.

'And what devil made me go to that wat?' (an officer nicknamed 'the rat') he said, rubbing his forehead and whole face with both hands. 'Just fancy, he didn't let me win a single cahd, not one cahd.'

He took the lighted pipe that was offered to him, gripped it in his fist, and tapped it on the floor, making the sparks fly, while he continued to shout.

'He lets one win the singles and collahs it as soon as one doubles it; gives the singles and snatches the doubles!'

He scattered the burning tobacco, smashed the pipe, and threw it away. Then he remained silent for a while, and all at once looked cheerfully with his glittering, black eyes at Rostov.

'If at least we had some women here; but there's nothing foh one to do but dwink. If we could only get to fighting soon. Hullo, who's there?' he said, turning to the door as he heard a tread of heavy boots and the clinking of spurs that came to a stop, and a respectful cough.

'The squadron quartermaster!' said Lavrushka.

Denisov's face puckered still more.

'Wetched!' he muttered, throwing down a purse with some gold in it. 'Wostov, deah fellow, just see how much there is left and shove the purse undah the pillow,' he said, and went out to the quartermaster.

Rostov took the money and, mechanically arranging the old and new coins in separate piles, began counting them.

'Ah! Telyanin! How d'ye do? They plucked me last night,' came Denisov's voice from the next room.

'Where? At Bykov's, at the rat's ... I knew it,' replied a piping voice, and Lieutenant Telyanin, a small officer of the same squadron, entered the room.

Rostov thrust the purse under the pillow and shook the damp little hand which was offered him. Telyanin for some reason had been transferred from the Guards just before this campaign. He behaved very well in the regiment but was not liked; Rostov especially detested him and was unable to overcome or conceal his groundless antipathy to the man.

'Well, young cavalryman, how is my Rook behaving?' he asked. (Rook was a young horse Telyanin had sold to Rostov.)

The lieutenant never looked the man he was speaking to

straight in the face; his eyes continually wandered from one object to another.

'I saw you riding this morning . . .' he added.

'Oh, he's all right, a good horse,' answered Rostov, though the horse for which he had paid seven hundred rubles was not worth half that sum. 'He's begun to go a little lame on the left foreleg,' he added.

'The hoof's cracked! That's nothing. I'll teach you what to do and show you what kind of rivet to use.'

'Yes, please do,' said Rostov.

'I'll show you, I'll show you! It's not a secret. And it's a horse you'll thank me for.'

'Then I'll have it brought round,' said Rostov wishing to avoid Telyanin, and he went out to give the order.

In the passage Denisov, with a pipe, was squatting on the threshold facing the quartermaster who was reporting to him. On seeing Rostov Denisov screwed up his face and pointing over his shoulder with his thumb to the room where Telyanin was sitting, he frowned and gave a shudder of disgust.

'Ugh! I don't like that fellow,' he said, regardless of the quartermaster's presence.

Rostov shrugged his shoulders as much as to say: 'Nor do I, but what's one to do?' and having given his order, he returned to Telyanin.

Telyanin was sitting in the same indolent pose in which Rostov had left him, rubbing his small white hands.

'Well there certainly are disgusting people,' thought Rostov as he entered.

'Have you told them to bring the horse?' asked Telyanin, getting up and looking carelessly about him.

'I have.'

'Let us go ourselves. I only came round to ask Denisov about yesterday's order. Have you got it, Denisov?'

'Not yet. But where are you off to?'

'I want to teach this young man how to shoe a horse,' said Telyanin.

They went through the porch and into the stable. The lieutenant explained how to rivet the hoof and went away to his own quarters.

When Rostov went back there was a bottle of vodka and a sausage on the table. Denisov was sitting there scratching with his pen on a sheet of paper. He looked gloomily in Rostov's face and said:

'I am witing to her.'

He leant his elbows on the table with his pen in his hand, and evidently glad of a chance to say quicker in words what he wanted to write, told Rostov the contents of his letter.

'You see, my fwiend,' he said, 'we sleep when we don't love. We are childwen of the dust ... but one falls in love and one is a God, one is pua' as on the fihst day of cweation ... Who's that now? Send him to the devil, I'm busy!' he shouted to Lavrushka, who went up to him not in the least abashed.

'Who should it be? You yourself told him to come. It's the quartermaster for the money.'

Denisov frowned and was about to shout some reply but stopped.

'Wetched business,' he muttered to himself. 'How much is left in the puhse?' he asked, turning to Rostov.

'Seven new and three old imperials.'

'Oh, it's wetched! Well, what are you standing there for, you sca'cwow? Call the quahtehmasteh,' he shouted to Lavrushka.

'Please, Denisov, let me lend you some: I have some, you know,' said Rostov, blushing.

'Don't like borrowing from my own fellows, I don't,' growled Denisov.

'But if you won't accept money from me like a comrade, you will offend me. Really I have some,' Rostov repeated.

'No, I tell you.'

And Denisov went to the bed to get the purse from under the pillow.

'Where have you put it, Wostov?'

'Under the lower pillow.'

'It's not there.'

Denisov threw both pillows on the floor. The purse was not there.

'That's odd.'

'Wait, haven't you dropped it?' said Rostov, picking up the pillows one at a time and shaking them.

He pulled off the quilt and shook it. The purse was not there.

'Dear me, can I have forgotten? No, I remember thinking that you kept it under your head like treasure,' said Rostov. 'I put it just here. Where is it?' he asked, turning to Lavrushka.

'I haven't been in the room. It must be where you put it.'

'But it isn't! ...'

'You're always like that; you thwow a thing down anywhere and forget it. Feel in your pockets.'

'No, if I hadn't had the thought of treasure,' said Rostov, 'but that's why I remember putting it there.'

133

Lavrushka turned all the bedding over, looked under the bed and under the table, searched everywhere, and stood still in the middle of the room. Denisov silently watched Lavrushka's movements, and when the latter threw up his arms in surprise saying it was nowhere to be found, Denisov glanced at Rostov.

'Wostov, you've not been playing schoolboy twicks....'

Rostov felt Denisov's gaze fixed on him, raised his eyes, and instantly dropped them again. All the blood which had seemed congested somewhere below his throat rushed to his face and eyes. He could not draw breath.

'And there hasn't been anyone in the room except the lieutenant and yourselves. It must be here somewhere,' said Lavrushka.

'Now then, you devil's puppet, look alive and hunt for it!' shouted Denisov suddenly, turning purple and rushing at the man with a threatening gesture. 'If the purse isn't found I'll flog you, I'll flog you all.'

Rostov, his eyes avoiding Denisov, began buttoning his coat, buckled on his sabre, and put on his cap.

'I must have that purse, I tell you,' shouted Denisov, shaking his orderly by the shoulders and knocking him against the wall.

'Denisov, let him alone, I know who has taken it,' said Rostov going towards the door without raising his eyes.

Denisov paused, thought a moment, and evidently understanding what Rostov hinted at, seized his arm.

'Nonsense!' he cried, and the veins on his forehead and neck stood out like cords. 'You are mad, I tell you. I won't allow it. The purse is here! I'll flay this scoundwel alive, and it will be found.'

'I know who has taken it,' repeated Rostov in an unsteady voice, and went to the door.

'And I tell you, don't you dahe to do it!' shouted Denisov, rushing at the cadet to restrain him.

But Rostov pulled away his arm and with as much anger as though Denisov were his worst enemy firmly fixed his eyes directly on his face.

'Do you understand what you're saying?' he said in a trembling voice. 'There was no one else in the room except myself. So that if it is not so, then ...'

He could not finish and ran out of the room.

'Ah, may the devil take you and everybody,' were the last words Rostov heard.

Rostov went to Telyanin's quarters.

'The master is not in, he's gone to head-quarters,' said Telyanin's orderly. 'Has something happened?' he added, surprised at the cadet's troubled face.

'No, nothing.'

'You've only just missed him,' said the orderly.

The head-quarters were situated two miles away from Salzeneck, and Rostov, without returning home, took a horse and rode there. There was an inn in the village which the officers frequented. Rostov rode up to it and saw Telyanin's horse at the porch.

In the second room of the inn the lieutenant was sitting over a dish of sausages and a bottle of wine.

'Ah, you've come here too, young man!' he said, smiling and raising his eyebrows.

'Yes,' said Rostov as if it cost him a great effort to utter the word; and he sat down at the nearest table.

Both were silent. There were two Germans and a Russian officer in the room. No one spoke and the only sounds heard were the clatter of knives and the munching of the lieutenant.

When Telyanin had finished his lunch he took out of his pocket a double purse, and drawing its rings aside with his small, white, turned-up fingers, drew out a gold imperial, and lifting his eyebrows gave it to the waiter.

'Please be quick,' he said.

The coin was a new one. Rostov rose and went up to Telyanin.

'Allow me to look at your purse,' he said in a low, almost inaudible, voice.

With shifting eyes but eyebrows still raised, Telyanin handed him the purse.

'Yes, it's a nice purse. Yes, yes,' he said growing suddenly pale, and added, 'Look at it, young man.'

Rostov took the purse in his hand, examined it and the money in it, and looked at Telyanin. The lieutenant was looking about in his usual way and suddenly seemed to grow very merry.

'If we get to Vienna I'll get rid of it there, but in these wretched little towns there's nowhere to spend it,' said he. 'Well, let me have it, young man, I'm going.'

Rostov did not speak.

'And you? Are you going to have lunch too? They feed you quite decently here,' continued Telyanin. 'Now then, let me have it.'

He stretched out his hand to take hold of the purse. Rostov let go of it. Telyanin took the purse and began carelessly slipping it into the pocket of his riding-breeches with his eyebrows lifted and his mouth slightly open, as if to say, 'Yes, yes, I am putting my purse in my pocket and that's quite simple and is no one else's business.'

'Well, young man?' he said with a sigh, and from under his lifted brows he glanced into Rostov's eyes.

Some flash as of an electric spark shot from Telyanin's eyes to Rostov's and back, and back again and again in an instant.

'Come here,' said Rostov, catching hold of Telyanin's arm and almost dragging him to the window. 'That money is Denisov's; you took it...' he whispered just above Telyanin's ear.

'What? What? How dare you? What?' said Telyanin.

But these words came like a piteous, despairing cry and an entreaty for pardon. As soon as Rostov heard them, an enormous load of doubt fell from him. He was glad, and at the same instant began to pity the miserable man who stood before him, but the task he had begun had to be completed.

'Heaven only knows what the people here may imagine,' muttered Telyanin, taking up his cap and moving towards a small empty room. 'We must have an explanation...'

'I know it and shall prove it,' said Rostov.

'I...'

Every muscle of Telyanin's pale terrified face began to quiver, his eyes still shifted from side to side but with a downward look not rising to Rostov's face, and his sobs were audible.

'Count!...Don't ruin a young fellow...here is this wretched money, take it...' He threw it on the table. 'I have an old father and mother!...'

Rostov took the money, avoiding Telyanin's eyes, and went out of the room without a word. But at the door he stopped and then retraced his steps. 'O God,' he said with tears in his eyes, 'how could you do it?'

'Count,...' said Telyanin drawing nearer to him.

'Don't touch me,' said Rostov, drawing back. 'If you need it, take the money,' and he threw the purse to him and ran out of the inn.

5

THAT same evening there was an animated discussion among the squadron's officers in Denisov's quarters.

'And I tell you, Rostov, that you must apologize to the colonel!' said a tall, grizzly-haired staff-captain with enormous moustaches and many wrinkles on his large features, to Rostov who was crimson with excitement.

The staff-captain, Kirsten, had twice been reduced to the ranks for affairs of honour and had twice regained his commission.

'I will allow no one to call me a liar!' cried Rostov. 'He told me I lied, and I told him he lied. And there it rests. He may keep me on duty every day, or may place me under arrest, but no one can make me apologize, because if he, as commander of this regiment, thinks it beneath his dignity to give me satisfaction, then . . .'

'You just wait a moment, my dear fellow, and listen,' interrupted the staff-captain in his deep bass, calmly stroking his long moustache. 'You tell the colonel in the presence of other officers that an officer has stolen . . .'

'I'm not to blame that the conversation began in the presence of other officers. Perhaps I ought not to have spoken before them, but I am not a diplomatist. That's why I joined the hussars, thinking that here one would not need finesse; and he tells me that I am lying – so let him give me satisfaction . . .'

'That's all right. No one thinks you a coward, but that's not the point. Ask Denisov whether it is not out of the question for a cadet to demand satisfaction of his regimental commander?'

Denisov sat gloomily biting his moustache and listening to the conversation, evidently with no wish to take part in it. He answered the staff-captain's question by a disapproving shake of his head.

'You speak to the colonel about this nasty business before other officers,' continued the staff-captain, 'and Bogdanich' (the colonel was called Bogdanich) 'shuts you up.'

'He did not shut me up, he said I was telling an untruth.'

'Well, have it so, and you talked a lot of nonsense to him and must apologize.'

'Not on any account!' exclaimed Rostov.

'I did not expect this of you,' said the staff-captain seriously and severely. 'You don't wish to apologize, but, man, it's not only to him but to the whole regiment – all of us – you're to blame all round. The case is this: you ought to have thought the matter over and taken advice; but no, you go and blurt it all straight out before the officers. Now what was the colonel to do? Have the officer tried and disgrace the whole regiment? Is that how you look at it? We don't see it like that. And Bogdanich was a brick: he told you you were saying what was not true. It's not pleasant, but what's to be done, my dear fellow? You landed yourself in it. And now, when one wants to smooth the thing over, some conceit prevents your apologizing, and you wish to make the whole affair public. You are offended at being put on duty a bit, but why not apologize to an old and honourable officer? Whatever Bogdanich may be, anyway he is an honourable and brave old colonel! You're quick at taking offence, but you don't mind disgracing the whole regiment!' The staff-captain's voice began to tremble. 'You have been in the regiment next to no time, my lad, you're here to-day and to-morrow you'll be appointed adjutant somewhere and can snap your fingers when it is said, "There are thieves among the Pavlograd officers!" But it's not all the same to us! Am I not right, Denisov? It's not the same!'

Denisov remained silent and did not move, but occasionally looked with his glittering black eyes at Rostov.

'You value your own pride and don't wish to apologize,' continued the staff-captain, 'but we old fellows, who have grown up in and God willing are going to die in the regiment, we prize the honour of the regiment, and Bogdanich knows it. Oh we do prize it, old fellow! And all this is not right, it's not right! You may take offence or not but I always stick to mother truth. It's not right!'

And the staff-captain rose and turned away from Rostov.

'That's twue, devil take it!' shouted Denisov, jumping up. 'Now then, Wostov, now then!'

Rostov, growing red and pale alternately, looked first at one officer and then at the other.

'No, gentlemen, no ... you mustn't think ... I quite understand. You're wrong to think that of me ... I ... for me ... for the honour of the regiment I'd ... Ah well, I'll show that in action, and for me the honour of the flag ... Well, never mind, it's true I'm to blame, to blame all round. Well, what else do you want? ...'

'Come, that's right, Count!' cried the staff-captain, turning round the clapping Rostov on the shoulder with his big hand.

'I tell you,' shouted Denisov, 'he's a fine fellow.'

'That's better, Count,' said the staff-captain, beginning to address Rostov by his title, as if in recognition of his confession. 'Go and apologize, your Excellency. Yes, go!'

'Gentlemen, I'll do anything. No one shall hear a word from me,' said Rostov in an imploring voice, 'but I can't apologize, by God I can't, do what you will! How can I go and apologize like a little boy asking forgiveness?'

Denisov began to laugh.

'It'll be worse for you. Bogdanich is vindictive and you'll pay for your obstinacy,' said Kirsten.

'No, on my word it's not obstinacy! I can't describe the feeling. I can't ...'

'Well it's as you like,' said the staff-captain. 'And what has become of that scoundrel?' he asked Denisov.

'He has weported himself sick, he's to be stwuck off the list to-mowow,' muttered Denisov.

'It is an illness, there's no other way of explaining it,' said the staff-captain.

'Illness or not, he'd better not cwoss my path. I'd kill him!' shouted Denisov in a bloodthirsty tone.

Just then Zherkov entered the room.

'What brings you here?' cried the officers turning to the new-comer.

'We're to go into action, gentlemen! Mack has surrendered with his whole army.'

'It's not true!'

'I've seen him myself!'

'What? Saw the real Mack? With hands and feet?'

'Into action! Into action! Bring him a bottle for such news! But how did you come here?'

'I've been sent back to the regiment all on account of that devil, Mack. An Austrian general complained of me. I congratulated him on Mack's arrival ... What's the matter, Rostov? You look as if you'd just come out of a hot bath.'

'Oh, my dear fellow, we're in such a stew here these last two days.'

The regimental adjutant came in and confirmed the news brought by Zherkov. They were under orders to advance next day.

'We're going into action, gentlemen!'

'Well, thank God! We've been sitting here too long!'

## 6

KUTUSOV fell back towards Vienna,* destroying behind him the bridges over the rivers Inn (at Braunau) and Traun (near Linz). On October 23rd the Russian troops were crossing the river Enns. At mid-day the Russian baggage-train, the artillery, and columns of troops, were defiling through the town of Enns on both sides of the bridge.

It was a warm, rainy, autumnal day. The wide expanse that opened out before the heights on which the Russian batteries stood guarding the bridge, was at times veiled by a diaphanous curtain of slanting rain, and then, suddenly spread out in the sunlight, far-distant objects could be clearly seen glittering as though freshly varnished. Down below, the little town could be seen with its white, red-roofed houses, its cathedral, and its bridge, on both sides of which streamed jostling masses of Russian troops. At the bend of the Danube, vessels, an island, and a castle with a park surrounded by the waters of the confluence of the Enns and the Danube, became visible, and the rocky left bank of the Danube covered with pine forests, with a mystic background of green tree-tops and bluish gorges. The turrets of a convent stood out beyond a wild virgin pine-forest, and far away on the other side of the Enns the enemy's horse patrols could be discerned.

Among the field-guns on the brow of the hill the general in command of the rearguard stood with a staff-officer, scanning the country through his field-glass. A little behind them Nesvitsky, who had been sent to the rearguard by the commander-in-chief, was sitting on the trail of a gun-carriage. A Cossack who accompanied him had handed him a knapsack and a flask, and Nesvitsky was treating some officers to pies and real *doppel-kümmel*. The officers gladly gathered round him, some on their knees, some squatting Turkish fashion on the wet grass.

'Yes, the Austrian prince who built that castle was no fool. It's a fine place! Why are you not eating anything, gentlemen?' Nesvitsky was saying.

'Thank you very much, Prince,' answered one of the officers, pleased to be talking to a staff-officer of such importance. 'It's a lovely place! We passed close to the park and saw two deer... and what a splendid house!'

'Look, Prince,' said another, who would have dearly liked to take another pie but felt shy, and therefore pretended to be examining the countryside – 'See, our infantrymen have already got there. Look there in the meadow behind the village, three of them are dragging something. They'll ransack that castle,' he remarked with evident approval.

'So they will,' said Nesvitsky. 'No, but what I should like,' added he, munching a pie in his moist-lipped handsome mouth, 'would be to slip in over there.'

He pointed with a smile to a turreted nunnery, and his eyes narrowed and gleamed.

'That would be fine, gentlemen!'

The officers laughed.

'Just to flutter the nuns a bit. They say there are Italian girls among them. On my word I'd give five years of my life for it!'

'They must be feeling dull, too,' said one of the bolder officers, laughing.

Meanwhile the staff-officer standing in front pointed out something to the general, who looked through his field-glass.

'Yes, so it is, so it is,' said the general angrily, lowering the field-glass and shrugging his shoulders, 'so it is! They'll be fired on at the crossing. And why are they dawdling there?'

On the opposite side the enemy could be seen by the naked eye, and from their battery a milk-white cloud arose. Then came the distant report of a shot, and our troops could be seen hurrying to the crossing.

Nesvitsky rose puffing, and went up to the general smiling.

'Would not your Excellency like a little refreshment?' he said.

'It's a bad business,' said the general without answering him, 'our men have been wasting time.'

'Hadn't I better ride over, your Excellency?' asked Nesvitsky.

'Yes, please do,' answered the general, and he repeated the order that had already once been given in detail: 'and tell the hussars that they are to cross last and to fire the bridge as I ordered; and the inflammable material on the bridge must be re-inspected.'

'Very good,' answered Nesvitsky.

He called the Cossack with his horse, told him to put away the knapsack and flask, and swung his heavy person easily into the saddle.

'I'll really call in on the nuns,' he said to the officers who watched him smilingly, and he rode off by the winding path down the hill.

'Now then let's see how far it will carry, Captain. Just try!' said the general, turning to an artillery officer. 'Have a little fun to pass the time.'

'Crew, to your guns!' commanded the officer.

In a moment the men came running gaily from their camp fires and began loading.

'One!' came the command.

Number one jumped briskly aside. The gun rang out with a deafening metallic roar, and a whistling grenade flew above the heads of our troops below the hill and fell far short of the enemy, a little smoke showing the spot where it burst.

The faces of officers and men brightened up at the sound. Everyone got up and began watching the movements of our troops below, as plainly visible as if but a stone's throw away, and the movements of the approaching enemy farther off. At the same instant the sun came fully out from behind the clouds, and the clear sound of the solitary shot and the brilliance of the bright sunshine merged in a single joyous and spirited impression.


7


Two of the enemy's shots had already flown across the bridge, where there was a crush. Half-way across stood Prince Nesvitsky, who had alighted from his horse and whose big body was jammed against the railings. He looked back laughing to the Cossack who stood a few steps behind him holding two horses by their bridles. Each time Prince Nesvitsky tried to move on, soldiers and carts pushed him back again and pressed him against the railings, and all he could do was to smile.

'What a fellow you are, friend!' said the Cossack to a convoy-soldier with a wagon, who was pressing onto the infantrymen who were crowded together close to his wheels and his horses. 'What a fellow! You can't wait a moment! Don't you see the General wants to pass?'

But the convoyman took no notice of the word 'General', and shouted at the soldiers who were blocking his way. 'Hi there boys! Keep to the left! Wait a bit.' But the soldiers, crowded together shoulder to shoulder, their bayonets interlocking, moved over the bridge in a dense mass. Looking down over the rails Prince Nesvitsky saw the rapid, noisy little waves of the Enns, which rippling and eddying round the piles of the bridge chased each other along. Looking on the bridge he saw equally uniform living waves of soldiers, shoulder-straps, covered shakos, knapsacks, bayonets, long muskets, and under the shakos faces with broad cheekbones, sunken cheeks, and listless tired expressions, and feet that moved through the sticky mud that covered the planks of the bridge. Sometimes through the monotonous waves of men, like a fleck of white foam on the waves of the Enns, an officer in a cloak, and with a type of face different from that of the men, squeezed his way along; sometimes like a chip of wood whirling in the river, an hussar on foot, an orderly, or a townsman, was carried through the waves of infantry; and sometimes like a log floating down the river, an officers' or company's baggage wagon, piled high, leather-covered, and hemmed in on all sides, moved across the bridge.

'It's as if a dam had burst,' said the Cossack hopelessly. 'Are there many more of you to come?'

'A million all but one!' replied a waggish soldier in a torn coat with a wink, and passed on followed by another, an old man.

'If *he*' (*he* meant the enemy) 'begins popping at the bridge now,' said the old soldier dismally to a comrade, 'you'll forget to scratch yourself.'

That soldier passed on, and after him came another sitting on a cart.

'Where the devil have the leg-bands been shoved to?' said an orderly, running behind the cart and fumbling in the back of it.

And he also passed on with the wagon. Then came some merry soldiers who had evidently been drinking.

'And then, old fellow, he gives him one in the teeth with the butt end of his gun...' a soldier whose greatcoat was well tucked up said gaily, with a wide swing of his arm.

'Yes, the ham was just delicious...' answered another, with a loud laugh. And they, too, passed on, so that Nesvitsky did not learn who had been struck on the teeth, or what the ham had to do with it.

'Bah! How they scurry. He just sends a ball and they think they'll all be killed,' a sergeant was saying angrily and reproachfully.

'As it flies past me, Daddy, the ball I mean,' said a young soldier with an enormous mouth, hardly refraining from laughing, 'I felt like dying of fright. I did, 'pon my word, I got that frightened!' said he, as if bragging of having been frightened.

That one also passed. Then followed a cart unlike any that had gone before. It was a German cart with a pair of horses led by a German, and seemed loaded with a whole houseful of effects. A fine brindled cow with a large udder was attached to the cart behind. A woman with an unweaned baby, an old woman, and a healthy German girl with bright red cheeks, were sitting on some feather-beds. Evidently these fugitives were allowed to pass by special permission. The eyes of all the soldiers turned towards the women, and while the vehicle was passing at foot pace all the soldiers' remarks related to the two young ones. Every face bore almost the same smile, expressing unseemly thoughts about the women.

'Just see, the German sausage is making tracks, too!'

'Sell me the missis,' said another soldier, addressing the German, who angry and frightened, strode energetically along with downcast eyes.

'See how smart she's made herself! Oh, the devils!'

'There, Fedotov, you should be quartered on them!'

'I have seen as much before now, mate!'

'Where are you going?' asked an infantry officer who was eating an apple, also half smiling as he looked at the handsome girl.

The German closed his eyes, signifying that he did not understand.

'Take it if you like,' said the officer, giving the girl an apple.

The girl smiled and took it. Nesvitsky like the rest of the men on the bridge did not take his eyes off the women till they had passed. When they had gone by the same stream of soldiers followed, with the same kind of talk, and at last all stopped. As often happens, the horses of a convoy-wagon became restive at the end of the bridge, and the whole crowd had to wait.

'And why are they stopping? There's no proper order!' said the soldiers. 'Where are you shoving to? Devil take you! Can't you wait? It'll be worse if he fires the bridge. See, here's an officer jammed in too,' – different voices were saying in the crowd, as the men looked at one another, and all pressed towards the exit from the bridge.

Looking down at the waters of the Enns under the bridge, Nesvitsky suddenly heard a sound new to him, of something swiftly approaching . . . something big, that splashed into the water.

'Just see where it carries to!' a soldier near by said sternly, looking round at the sound.

'Encouraging us to get along quicker,' said another uneasily.

The crowd moved on again. Nesvitsky realized that it was a cannon-ball.

'Hey, Cossack, my horse!' he said. 'Now then, you there! get out of the way! Make way!'

With great difficulty he managed to get to his horse, and shouting continually he moved on. The soldiers squeezed themselves to make way for him, but again pressed on him so that they jammed his leg, and those nearest him were not to blame, for they were themselves pressed still harder from behind.

'Nesvitsky, Nesvitsky! you numskull!' came a hoarse voice from behind him.

Nesvitsky looked round, and saw, some fifteen paces away but separated by the living mass of moving infantry, Vaska Denisov, red and shaggy, with his cap on the back of his black head and a cloak hanging jauntily over his shoulder.

'Tell these devils, these fiends, to let me pass!' shouted Denisov evidently in a fit of rage, his coal-black eyes with their bloodshot whites glittering and rolling as he waved his sheathed sabre in a small bare hand as red as his face.

'Ah, Vaska!' joyfully replied Nesvitsky. 'What's up with you?'

'The squadwon can't pass,' shouted Vaska Denisov, showing his white teeth fiercely and spurring his black thoroughbred Arab, which twitched its ears as the bayonets touched it, and snorted, spurting white foam from its bit, tramping the planks of the bridge with his hoofs, and apparently ready to jump over the railings had his rider let him. 'What is this? They're like sheep! Just like sheep! Out of the way! . . . Let us pass! . . . Stop there, you devil with the cart! I'll hack you with my sabre!' he shouted, actually drawing his sabre from its scabbard and flourishing it.

The soldiers crowded against one another with terrified faces, and Denisov joined Nesvitsky.

'How's it you're not drunk to-day?' said Nesvitsky when the other had ridden up to him.

'They don't even give one time to dwink!' answered Vaska Denisov. They keep dwagging the wegiment to and fwo all day. If they mean to fight, let's fight. But the devil knows what this is.'

'What a dandy you are to-day!' said Nesvitsky, looking at Denisov's new cloak and saddle-cloth.

Denisov smiled, took out of his sabretache a handkerchief that diffused a smell of perfume, and put it to Nesvitsky's nose.

'Of course. I'm going into action! I've shaved, bwushed my teeth, and scented myself.'

The imposing figure of Nesvitsky followed by his Cossack, and the determination of Denisov who flourished his sword and shouted frantically, had such an effect that they managed to squeeze through to the farther side of the bridge and stopped the infantry. Beside the bridge Nesvitsky found the colonel to whom he had to deliver the order, and having done this he rode back.

Having cleared the way Denisov stopped at the end of the bridge. Carelessly holding in his stallion that was neighing and pawing the ground eager to rejoin its fellows, he watched his squadron draw nearer. Then the clang of hoofs, as of several horses galloping, resounded on the planks of the bridge, and the squadron, officers in front and men four abreast, spread across the bridge and began to emerge on his side of it.

The infantry who had been stopped crowded near the bridge in the trampled mud, and gazed, with that particular feeling of ill-will, estrangement, and ridicule with which troops of different arms usually encounter one another, at the clean smart hussars who moved past them in regular order.

'Smart lads! Only fit for a fair!' said one.

'What good are they? They're led about just for show!' remarked another.

'Don't kick up the dust, you infantry!' jested an hussar whose prancing horse had splashed mud over some foot-soldiers.

'I'd like to put you on a two-days' march with a knapsack! Your fine cords would soon get a bit rubbed,' said an infantryman, wiping the mud off his face with his sleeve. 'Perched up there, you're more like a bird than a man.'

'There now, Zikin, they ought to put you on a horse. You'd look fine,' said a corporal, chaffing a thin little soldier who bent under the weight of his knapsack.

'Take a stick between your legs, that'll suit you for a horse!' the hussar shouted back.

THE last of the infantry hurriedly crossed the bridge, squeezing together as they approached it as if passing through a funnel. At last the baggage-wagons had all crossed, the crush was less, and the last battalion came onto the bridge. Only Denisov's squadron of hussars remained on the farther side of the bridge facing the enemy, who could be seen from the hill on the opposite bank but was not yet visible from the bridge, for the horizon as seen from the valley through which the river flowed was formed by the rising ground only half a mile away. At the foot of the hill lay waste land over which a few groups of our Cossack scouts were moving. Suddenly on the road at the top of the high ground, artillery and troops in blue uniform were seen. These were the French. A group of Cossack scouts retired down the hill at a trot. All the officers and men of Denisov's squadron, though they tried to talk of other things and to look in other directions, thought only of what was there on the hilltop, and kept constantly looking at the patches appearing on the sky-line, which they knew to be the enemy's troops. The weather had cleared again since noon and the sun was descending brightly upon the Danube and the dark hills around it. It was calm, and at intervals the bugle-calls and the shouts of the enemy could be heard from the hill. There was no one now between the squadron and the enemy except a few scattered skirmishers. An empty space of some seven hundred yards was all that separated them. The enemy ceased firing, and that stern, threatening, inaccessible and intangible line which separates two hostile armies was all the more clearly felt.

'One step beyond that boundary line which resembles the line dividing the living from the dead, lies uncertainty, suffering, and death. And what is there? Who is there? – there beyond that field, that tree, that roof lit up by the sun? No one knows, but one wants to know. You fear and yet long to cross that line, and know that sooner or later it must be crossed and you will have to find out what is there, just as you will inevitably have to learn what lies the other side of death. But you are strong, healthy, cheerful, and excited, and are surrounded by other such excitedly-animated and healthy men.' So thinks, or at any rate feels, anyone who comes in sight of the enemy, and that feeling gives a particular glamour and glad keenness of impression to everything that takes place at such moments.

On the high ground where the enemy was, the smoke of a

cannon rose, and a ball flew whistling over the heads of the hussar squadron. The officers who had been standing together rode off to their places. The hussars began carefully aligning their horses. Silence fell on the whole squadron. All were looking at the enemy in front and at the squadron commander, awaiting the word of command. A second and a third cannon-ball flew past. Evidently they were firing at the hussars, but the balls with rapid rhythmic whistle flew over the heads of the horsemen and fell somewhere beyond them. The hussars did not look round, but at the sound of each shot, as at the word of command, the whole squadron with its rows of faces so alike yet so different, holding its breath while the ball flew past, rose in the stirrups and sank back again. The soldiers without turning their heads glanced at one another, curious to see their comrades' impression. Every face, from Denisov's to that of the bugler, showed one common expression of conflict, irritation, and excitement, around chin and mouth. The quartermaster frowned, looking at the soldiers as if threatening to punish them. Cadet Mironov ducked every time a ball flew past. Rostov on the left flank, mounted on his Rook – a handsome horse despite its game leg – had the happy air of a schoolboy called up before a large audience for an examination in which he feels sure he will distinguish himself. He was glancing at everyone with a clear bright expression, as if asking them to notice how calmly he sat under fire. But despite himself, on his face too that same indication of something new and stern showed round the mouth.

'Who's that curtseying there? Cadet Miwonov! That's not wight! Look at me,' cried Denisov who, unable to keep still on one spot, kept turning his horse in front of the squadron.

The black, hairy, snub-nosed face of Vaska Denisov, and his whole short sturdy figure with the sinewy hairy hand and stumpy fingers in which he held the hilt of his naked sabre, looked just as it usually did, especially towards evening when he had emptied his second bottle; he was only redder than usual. With his shaggy head thrown back like birds when they drink, pressing his spurs mercilessly into the sides of his good horse Bedouin and sitting as though falling backwards in the saddle, he galloped to the other flank of the squadron and shouted in a hoarse voice to the men to look to their pistols. He rode up to Kirsten. The staff-captain on his broad-backed steady mare came at a walk to meet him. His face with its long moustache was serious as always, only his eyes were brighter than usual.

'Well, what about it?' said he to Denisov. 'It won't come to a fight. You'll see – we shall retire.'

'The devil only knows what they're about!' muttered Denisov.

'Ah, Wostov,' he cried noticing the cadet's bright face, 'you've got it at last.'

And he smiled approvingly, evidently pleased with the cadet. Rostov felt perfectly happy. Just then the commander appeared on the bridge. Denisov galloped up to him.

'Your Excellency! Let us attack them! I'll dwive them off.'

'Attack indeed!' said the colonel in a bored voice, puckering up his face as if driving off a troublesome fly. 'And why are you stopping here? Don't you see the skirmishers are retreating? Lead the squadron back.'

The squadron crossed the bridge and drew out of range of fire without having lost a single man. The second squadron that had been in the front line followed them across and the last Cossacks quitted the farther side of the river.

The two Pavlograd squadrons, having crossed the bridge, retired up the hill one after the other. Their colonel, Karl Bogdanich Schubert,* came up to Denisov's squadron and rode at a foot-pace not far from Rostov, without taking any notice of him although they were now meeting for the first time since their encounter concerning Telyanin. Rostov feeling that he was at the front and in the power of a man towards whom he now admitted that he had been to blame, did not lift his eyes from the colonel's athletic back, his nape covered with light hair, and his red neck. It seemed to Rostov that Bogdanich was only pretending not to notice him, and that his whole aim now was to test the cadet's courage, so he drew himself up and looked around him merrily; then it seemed to him that Bogdanich rode so near in order to show him his courage. Next he thought that his enemy would send the squadron on a desperate attack just to punish him – Rostov. Then he imagined how, after the attack, Bogdanich would come up to him as he lay wounded and would magnanimously extend the hand of reconciliation.

The high-shouldered figure of Zherkov, familiar to the Pavlograds as he had but recently left their regiment, rode up to the colonel. After his dismissal from head-quarters Zherkov had not remained in the regiment, saying he was not such a fool as to slave at the front when he could get more rewards by doing nothing on the staff, and had succeeded in attaching himself as an orderly officer to Prince Bagration. He now came to his former chief with an order from the commander of the rearguard.

'Colonel,' he said, addressing Rostov's enemy with an air of gloomy gravity and glancing round at his comrades, 'there is an order to stop and fire the bridge.'

'An order to who?' asked the colonel morosely.

'I don't myself know "to who",' replied the coronet in a serious tone, 'but the prince told me to "go and tell the colonel that the hussars must return quickly and fire the bridge".'

Zherkov was followed by an officer of the suite who rode up to the colonel of hussars with the same order. After him the stout Nesvitsky came galloping up on a Cossack horse that could scarcely carry his weight.

'How's this, Colonel?' he shouted as he approached. 'I told you to fire the bridge, and now someone has gone and blundered; they are all beside themselves over there and one can't make anything out.'

The colonel deliberately stopped the regiment and turned to Nesvitsky.

'You spoke to me of inflammable material,' said he, 'but you said nothing about firing it.'

'But, my dear sir,' said Nesvitsky as he drew up, taking off his cap and smoothing his hair wet with perspiration with his plump hand, 'wasn't I telling you to fire the bridge, when inflammable material had been put in position?'

'I am not your "dear sir," Mr Staff-officer, and you did not tell me to burn the bridge! I know the service, and it is my habit orders strictly to obey. You said the bridge would be burnt, but who would it burn, I could not know by the holy spirit!'

'Ah, that's always the way!' said Nesvitsky with a wave of the hand. 'How did you get here?' said he, turning to Zherkov.

'On the same business. But you *are* damp! Let me wring you out!'

'You were saying, Mr Staff-officer . . .' continued the colonel in an offended tone.

'Colonel,' interrupted the officer of the suite, 'you must be quick or the enemy will bring up his guns to use grape-shot.'

The colonel looked silently at the officer of the suite, at the stout staff-officer, and at Zherkov, and he frowned.

'I will the bridge fire,' he said in a solemn tone, as if to announce that in spite of all the unpleasantness he had to endure he would still do the right thing.

Striking his horse with his long muscular legs as if it were to blame for everything, the colonel moved forward and ordered the second squadron, that in which Rostov was serving under Denisov, to return to the bridge.

'There, it's just as I thought,' said Rostov to himself. 'He wishes to test me!' His heart contracted and the blood rushed to his face. 'Let him see whether I am a coward!' he thought.

Again on all the bright faces of the squadron the serious

expression appeared that they had worn when under fire. Rostov watched his enemy, the colonel, closely – to find in his face confirmation of his own conjecture, but the colonel did not once glance at Rostov, and looked as he always did when at the front, solemn and stern. Then came the word of command.

'Look sharp! Look sharp!' several voices repeated around him.

Their sabres catching in the bridles and their spurs jingling, the hussars hastily dismounted, not knowing what they were to do. The men were crossing themselves. Rostov no longer looked at the colonel, he had no time. He was afraid of falling behind the hussars, so much afraid that his heart stood still. His hand trembled as he gave his horse into an orderly's charge, and he felt the blood rush to his heart with a thud. Denisov rode past him, leaning back and shouting something. Rostov saw nothing but the hussars running all around him, their spurs catching and their sabres clattering.

'Stretchers!' shouted someone behind him.

Rostov did not think what this call for stretchers meant; he ran on, trying only to be ahead of the others; but just at the bridge, not looking at the ground, he came on some sticky, trodden mud, stumbled, and fell on his hands. The others outstripped him.

'At boss zides, Captain,' he heard the voice of the colonel, who, having ridden ahead, had pulled up his horse near the bridge, with a triumphant, cheerful face.

Rostov wiping his muddy hands on his breeches looked at his enemy, and was about to run on, thinking that the farther he went to the front the better. But Bogdanich, without looking at or recognizing Rostov, shouted to him:

'Who's that running on the middle of the bridge? To the right! Come back, Cadet!' he cried angrily; and turning to Denisov, who, showing off his courage, had ridden on to the planks of the bridge:

'Why run risks, Captain? You should dismount,' he said.

'Oh, every bullet has its billet,' answered Vaska Denisov, turning in his saddle.

Meanwhile Nesvitsky, Zherkov, and the officer of the suite were standing together out of range of the shots, watching, now the small group of men with yellow shakos, dark-green jackets braided with cord, and blue riding-breeches, who were swarming near the bridge, and then what was approaching in the distance from the opposite side – the blue uniforms and groups with horses, easily recognizable as artillery.

'Will they burn the bridge or not? Who'll get there first? Will they get there and fire the bridge or will the French get within grape-shot range and wipe them out?' These were the questions each man of the troops on the high ground above the bridge involuntarily asked himself with a sinking heart – watching the bridge and the hussars in the bright evening light and the blue tunics advancing from the other side with their bayonets and guns.

'Ugh! The hussars will get it hot!' said Nesvitsky; 'they are within grape-shot range now.'

'He shouldn't have taken so many men,' said the officer of the suite.

'True enough,' answered Nesvitsky; 'two smart fellows could have done the job just as well.'

'Ah, your Excellency,' put in Zherkov, his eyes fixed on the hussars, but still with that naïve air that made it impossible to know whether he was speaking in jest or in earnest. 'Ah, your Excellency! How you look at things! Send two men? And who then would give us the Vladimir medal and ribbon? But now, even if they do get peppered, the squadron may be recommended for honours and he may get a ribbon. Our Bogdanich knows how things are done.'

'There now!' said the officer of the suite, 'that's grapeshot.'

He pointed to the French guns, the limbers of which were being detached and hurriedly removed.

On the French side, amid the groups with cannon, a cloud of smoke appeared, then a second and a third almost simultaneously, and at the moment when the first report was heard a fourth was seen. Then two reports one after another, and a third.

'Oh! Oh!' groaned Nesvitsky, as if in fierce pain, seizing the officer of the suite by the arm. 'Look! A man has fallen! Fallen, fallen!'

'Two, I think.'

'If I were Tsar I would never go to war,' said Nesvitsky, turning away.

The French guns were hastily reloaded. The infantry in their blue uniforms advanced towards the bridge at a run. Smoke appeared again but at irregular intervals, and grape-shot cracked and rattled onto the bridge. But this time Nesvitsky could not see what was happening there, as a dense cloud of smoke arose from it. The hussars had succeeded in setting it on fire and the French batteries were now firing at them, no longer to hinder them but because the guns were trained and there was someone to fire at.

The French had time to fire three rounds of grape-shot before the hussars got back to their horses. Two were misdirected and the shot went too high, but the last round fell in the midst of a group of hussars and knocked three of them over.

Rostov, absorbed by his relations with Bogdanich, had paused on the bridge, not knowing what to do. There was no one to hew down (as he had always imagined battles to himself), nor could he help to fire the bridge because he had not brought any burning straw with him like the other soldiers. He stood looking about him, when suddenly he heard a rattle on the bridge as if nuts were being spilt, and the hussar nearest to him fell against the rails with a groan. Rostov ran up to him with the others. Again someone shouted, 'Stretchers!' Four men seized the hussar and began lifting him.

'Oooh! For Christ's sake let me alone!' cried the wounded man, but still he was lifted and laid on the stretcher.

Nicholas Rostov turned away and, as if searching for something, gazed into the distance, at the waters of the Danube, at the sky, and at the sun. How beautiful the sky looked; how blue, how calm, and how deep! How bright and glorious was the setting sun! With what soft glitter the waters of the distant Danube shone. And fairer still were the far away blue mountains beyond the river, the nunnery, the mysterious gorges, and the pine forests veiled in mist to their summits ... There was peace and happiness ... 'I should wish for nothing else, nothing, if only I were there,' thought Rostov. 'In myself alone and in that sunshine there is so much happiness; but here ... groans, suffering, fear, and this uncertainty and hurry ... There – they are shouting again, and again are all running back somewhere, and I shall run with them, and it, death, is here above me and around ... Another instant and I shall never again see the sun, this water, that gorge! ...'

At that instant the sun began to hide behind the clouds, and other stretchers came in view before Rostov. And the fear of death and of the stretchers, and love of the sun and of life, all merged into one feeling of sickening agitation.

'O Lord God! Thou who art in that heaven, save, forgive, and protect me!' Rostov whispered.

The hussars ran back to the men who held their horses; their voices sounded louder and calmer, the stretchers disappeared from sight.

'Well, fwiend? So you've smelt powdah!' shouted Vaska Denisov just above his ear.

'It's all over; but I am a coward – yes, a coward!' thought Rostov, and sighing deeply he took Rook, his horse, which stood resting one foot, from the orderly, and began to mount.

'Was that grape-shot?' he asked Denisov.

'Yes and no mistake!' cried Denisov. 'You worked like wegular bwicks and it's nasty work! An attack's pleasant work! Hacking away at the dogs! But this sort of thing is the very devil, with them shooting at you like a target.'

And Denisov rode up to a group that had stopped near Rostov, composed of the colonel, Nesvitsky, Zherkov, and the officer from the suite.

'Well it seems that no one has noticed,' thought Rostov. And this was true. No one had taken any notice, for everyone knew the sensation which the cadet under fire for the first time had experienced.

'Here's something for you to report,' said Zherkov. 'See if I don't get promoted to a sub-lieutenancy.'

'Inform the prince that I the bridge fired!' said the colonel triumphantly and gaily.

'And if he asks about the losses?'

'A trifle,' said the colonel in his bass voice: 'two hussars wounded, and one knocked out,' he added, unable to restrain a happy smile, and pronouncing the phrase 'knocked out' with ringing distinctness.

9

PURSUED by the French army of a hundred thousand men under the command of Bonaparte, encountering a population that was unfriendly to it, losing confidence in its allies, suffering from shortness of supplies, and compelled to act under conditions of war unlike anything that had been foreseen, the Russian army of thirty-five thousand men commanded by Kutuzov was hurriedly retreating along the Danube, stopping where overtaken by the enemy and fighting rearguard actions only as far as necessary to enable it to retreat without losing its heavy equipment. There had been actions at Lambach, Amstetten, and Mölk;* but despite the courage and endurance – acknowledged even by the enemy – with which the Russians fought, the only consequence of these actions was a yet more rapid retreat. Austrian troops that had escaped capture at Ulm and had joined Kutuzov at Braunau, now separated from the Russian army, and Kutuzov was left with only his own weak and exhausted forces. The defence of Vienna was no longer to be thought of. Instead of an offensive, the plan of which, carefully prepared in accord with the modern science of strategics, had been handed to Kutuzov when he was in Vienna by the Austrian Hofkriegsrath, the sole and almost unattainable aim remaining for him was to effect a junction with the forces that were advancing from Russia, without losing his army as Mack had done at Ulm.

On the 28th of October Kutuzov with his army crossed to the left bank of the Danube and took up a position for the first time with the river between himself and the main body of the French. On the 30th he attacked Mortier's division which was on the left bank, and broke it up. In this action for the first time trophies were taken: banners, cannon, and two enemy generals. For the first time, after a fortnight's retreat, the Russian troops had halted and after a fight had not only held the field but had repulsed the French. Though the troops were ill-clad, exhausted, and had lost a third of their number in killed, wounded, sick, and stragglers; though a number of sick and wounded had been abandoned on the other side of the Danube with a letter in which Kutuzov entrusted them to the humanity of the enemy; and though the big hospitals and the houses in Krems converted into military hospitals could no longer accommodate all the sick and wounded, yet the stand made at Krems and the victory over Mortier raised the spirits of the army considerably. Throughout the whole army and at head-quarters most joyful though erroneous rumours were rife of the imaginary approach of columns from Russia, of some victory gained by the Austrians, and of the retreat of the frightened Bonaparte.

Prince Andrew during the battle had been in attendance on the Austrian General Schmidt, who was killed in the action. His horse had been wounded under him and his own arm slightly grazed by a bullet. As a mark of the commander-in-chief's special favour he was sent with the news of this victory to the Austrian Court, now no longer at Vienna (which was threatened by the French) but at Brünn. Despite his apparently delicate build Prince Andrew could endure physical fatigue far better than many very muscular men, and on the night of the battle, having arrived at Krems, excited but not weary, with despatches from Dokhturov to Kutuzov, he was sent immediately with a special despatch to Brünn. To be so sent meant not only a reward but an important step towards promotion.

The night was dark but starry, the road showed black in the snow that had fallen the previous day – the day of the battle. Reviewing his impressions of the recent battle, picturing pleasantly to himself the impression his news of a victory would create, or recalling the send-off given him by the commander-in-chief and his fellow-officers, Prince Andrew was galloping along in a post-chaise enjoying the feelings of a man who has at length begun to attain a long-desired happiness. As soon as he closed his eyes his ears seemed filled with the rattle of the wheels and the sensation of victory. Then he began to imagine that the Russians were running away and that he himself was killed, but he quickly roused himself with a feeling of joy, as if learning afresh that this was not so but that on the contrary the French had run away. He again recalled all the details of the victory and his own calm courage during the battle, and feeling reassured he dozed off ... The dark starry night was followed by a bright cheerful morning. The snow was thawing in the sunshine, the horses galloped quickly, and on both sides of the road were forests of different kinds, fields, and villages.

At one of the post-stations he overtook a convoy of Russian wounded. The Russian officer in charge of the transport lolled back in the front cart, shouting and scolding a soldier with coarse abuse. In each of the long German carts six or more pale, dirty, bandaged men were being jolted over the stony road. Some of them were talking (he heard Russian words), others were eating bread; the more severely wounded looked silently, with the languid interest of sick children, at the envoy hurrying past them.

Prince Andrew told his driver to stop, and asked a soldier in what action they had been wounded. 'Day before yesterday, on the Danube,' answered the soldier. Prince Andrew took out his purse and gave the soldier three gold pieces.

'That's for them all,' he said to the officer who came up. 'Get well soon, lads!' he continued, turning to the soldiers. 'There's plenty to do still.'

'What news, sir?' asked the officer, evidently anxious to start a conversation.

'Good news! ... Go on!' he shouted to the driver, and they galloped on.

It was already quite dark when Prince Andrew rattled over the paved streets of Brünn and found himself surrounded by high buildings, the lights of shops, houses, and street-lamps, fine carriages, and all that atmosphere of a large and active town which is always so attractive to a soldier after camp life. Despite his rapid journey and sleepless night, Prince Andrew when he drove up to the palace felt even more vigorous and alert than he had done the day before. Only his eyes gleamed feverishly and his thoughts followed one another with extraordinary clearness and rapidity. He again vividly recalled the details of the battle, no longer dim, but definite and in the concise form in which he imagined himself stating them to the Emperor Francis. He vividly imagined the casual questions that might be put to him and the answers he would give. He expected to be at once presented to the Emperor.

At the chief entrance to the palace, however, an official came running out to meet him, and learning that he was a special messenger led him to another entrance.

'To the right from the corridor, *Euer Hochgeboren!* There you will find the adjutant on duty,' said the official. 'He will conduct you to the Minister of War.'

The adjutant on duty, meeting Prince Andrew, asked him to wait, and went in to the Minister of War. Five minutes later he returned and bowing with particular courtesy ushered Prince Andrew before him along a corridor to the cabinet where the Minister of War was at work. The adjutant by his elaborate courtesy appeared to wish to ward off any attempt at familiarity on the part of the Russian messenger.

Prince Andrew's joyous feeling was considerably weakened as he approached the door of the minister's room. He felt offended, and without his noticing it the feeling of offence immediately turned into one of disdain which was quite uncalled for. His fertile mind instantly suggested to him a point of view which gave him a right to despise the adjutant and the minister. 'Away from the smell of powder, they probably think it easy to gain victories!' he thought. His eyes narrowed disdainfully, he entered the room of the Minister of War with peculiarly deliberate steps. This feeling of disdain was heightened when he saw the minister seated at a large table reading some papers and making pencil notes on them, and for the first two or three minutes taking no notice of his arrival. A wax candle stood at each side of the minister's bent bald head with its grey temples. He went on reading to the end, without raising his eyes at the opening of the door and the sound of footsteps.

'Take this and deliver it,' said he to his adjutant, handing him the papers and still taking no notice of the special messenger.

Prince Andrew felt that either the actions of Kutuzov's army interested the Minister of War less than any of the other matters he was concerned with, or he wanted to give the Russian special messenger that impression. 'But that is a matter of perfect indifference to me,' he thought. The minister drew the remaining papers together, arranged them evenly, and then raised his head. He had an intellectual and distinctive head, but the instant he turned to Prince Andrew the firm, intelligent expression on his face changed in a way evidently deliberate and habitual to him. His face took on the stupid artificial smile (which does not even attempt to hide its artificiality) of a man who is continually receiving many petitioners one after another.

'From General Field-Marshal Kutuzov?' he asked. 'I hope it is good news? There has been an encounter with Mortier? A victory? It was high time!'

He took the despatch which was addressed to him and began to read it with a mournful expression.

'Oh, my God! Schmidt!' he exclaimed in German. 'What a calamity! What a calamity!'

Having glanced through the despatch he laid it on the table and looked at Prince Andrew, evidently considering something.

'Ah, what a calamity! You say the affair was decisive? But Mortier is not captured.' Again he pondered. 'I'm very glad you have brought good news, though Schmidt's death is a heavy price to pay for the victory. His Majesty will no doubt wish to see you, but not to-day. I thank you! You must have a rest. Be at the levee to-morrow after the parade. However I will let you know.'

The stupid smile, which had left his face while he was speaking, reappeared.

'Au revoir! Thank you very much. His Majesty will probably desire to see you,' he added, bowing his head.

When Prince Andrew left the palace he felt that all the interest and happiness the victory had afforded him had been now left in the indifferent hands of the Minister of War and the polite adjutant. The whole tenor of his thoughts instantaneously changed; the battle seemed the memory of a remote event long past.

10

PRINCE ANDREW stayed at Brünn with Bilibin, a Russian acquaintance of his in the diplomatic service.

'Ah, my dear Prince! I could not have a more welcome visitor,' said Bilibin as he came out to meet Prince Andrew. 'Franz, put the prince's things in my bedroom,' said he to the servant who was ushering Bolkonsky in. 'So you're a messenger of victory, eh? Splendid! And I am sitting here ill, as you see.'

After washing and dressing, Prince Andrew came into the diplomat's luxurious study and sat down to the dinner prepared for him. Bilibin settled down comfortably beside the fire.

After his journey and the campaign during which he had been deprived of all the comforts of cleanliness and all the refinements of life, Prince Andrew felt a pleasant sense of repose among luxurious surroundings such as he had been accustomed to from childhood. Besides it was pleasant, after his reception by the Austrians, to speak if not in Russian (for they were speaking French) at least with a Russian who would, he supposed, share the general

Russian antipathy to the Austrians which was then particularly strong.

Bilibin was a man of thirty-five, a bachelor and of the same circle as Prince Andrew. They had known each other previously in Petersburg, but had become more intimate when Prince Andrew was in Vienna with Kutuzov. Just as Prince Andrew was a young man who gave promise of rising high in the military profession, so to an even greater extent, Bilibin gave promise of rising in his diplomatic career. He was still a young man but no longer a young diplomat, as he had entered the service at the age of sixteen, had been in Paris and Copenhagen, and now held a rather important post in Vienna. Both the foreign minister and our ambassador in Vienna knew him and valued him. He was not one of those many diplomats who are esteemed because they have certain negative qualities, avoid doing certain things, and speak French. He was one of those who, liking work, knew how to do it, and despite his indolence would sometimes spend a whole night at his writing-table. He worked equally well whatever the import of his work. It was not the question 'What for?' but the question 'How?' that interested him. What the diplomatic matter might be he did not care, but it gave him great pleasure to prepare a circular, memorandum, or report, skilfully, pointedly and elegantly. Bilibin's services were valued not only for what he wrote, but also for his skill in dealing and conversing with those in the highest spheres.

Bilibin liked conversation as he liked work, only when it could be made elegantly witty. In society he always awaited an opportunity to say something striking, and took part in a conversation only when that was possible. His conversation was always sprinkled with wittily original, finished phrases of general interest. These sayings were prepared in the inner laboratory of his mind in a portable form as if intentionally, so that insignificant society people might carry them from drawing-room to drawing-room. And in fact Bilibin's witticisms were hawked about in the Viennese drawing-rooms and often had an influence on matters considered important.

His thin, worn, sallow face was covered with deep wrinkles, which always looked as clean and well washed as the tips of one's fingers after a Russian bath. The movement of these wrinkles formed the principal play of expression on his face. Now his forehead would pucker into deep folds and his eyebrows were lifted, then his eyebrows would descend and deep wrinkles would crease his cheeks. His small, deep-set eyes always twinkled and looked out straight.

'Well, now tell me about your exploits,' said he.

Bolkonsky, very modestly without once mentioning himself, described the engagement and his reception by the Minister of War.

'They received me and my news as one receives a dog in a game of skittles,' said he in conclusion.

Bilibin smiled and the wrinkles on his face disappeared.

'*Cependant, mon cher,*' he remarked, examining his nails from a distance and puckering the skin above his left eye, '*malgré la haute estime que je professe pour* the Orthodox Russian army, *j'avoue que votre victoire n'est pas des plus victorieuses.*'

He went on talking in this way in French, uttering only those words in Russian on which he wished to put a contemptuous emphasis.

'Come now! You with all your forces fall on the unfortunate Mortier and his one division, and even then Mortier slips through your fingers! Where's the victory?'

'But seriously,' said Prince Andrew, 'we can at any rate say without boasting that it was a little better than at Ulm...'

'Why didn't you capture one, just one, marshal for us?'

'Because not everything happens as one expects with the smoothness of a parade. We had expected, as I told you, to get at their rear by seven in the morning but had not reached it by five in the afternoon.'

'And why didn't you do it at seven in the morning? You ought to have been there at seven in the morning,' returned Bilibin with a smile. 'You ought to have been there at seven in the morning.'

'Why did you not succeed in impressing on Bonaparte by diplomatic methods that he had better leave Genoa alone?' retorted Prince Andrew in the same tone.

'I know,' interrupted Bilibin, 'you're thinking it's very easy to take marshals, sitting on a sofa by the fire! That is true, but still why didn't you capture him? So don't be surprised if not only the Minister of War but also his Most August Majesty the Emperor and King Francis is not much delighted by your victory. Even I, a poor secretary of the Russian Embassy, do not feel any need, in token of my joy, to give my Franz a *thaler*, or let him go with his *Liebchen* to the Prater... True, we have no Prater here...'

He looked straight at Prince Andrew and suddenly unwrinkled his forehead.

'It is now my turn to ask you "why?" *mon cher*,' said Bolkonsky. 'I confess I do not understand: perhaps there are diplomatic subtleties here beyond my feeble intelligence, but I can't make it out. Mack loses a whole army, the Archduke Ferdinand and the

159

Archduke Karl give no signs of life and make blunder after blunder. Kutuzov alone at last gains a real victory, destroying the spell of the invincibility of the French, and the Minister of War does not even care to hear the details.'

'That's just it, my dear fellow! You see it's *hurrah* for the Tsar, for Russia, for the Orthodox Greek faith! All that is beautiful, but what do we, I mean the Austrian Court, care for your victories? Bring us nice news of a victory by the Archduke Karl or Ferdinand (one archduke's as good as another, as you know) and even if it is only over a fire-brigade of Bonaparte's, that will be another story and we'll fire off some cannon! But this sort of thing seems done on purpose to vex us. The Archduke Karl does nothing, the Archduke Ferdinand disgraces himself. You abandon Vienna, give up its defence – as much as to say: "Heaven is with us, but heaven help you and your capital!" The one general whom we all loved, Schmidt, you expose to a bullet, and then you congratulate us on the victory! Admit that more irritating news than yours could not have been conceived. It's as if it had been done on purpose, on purpose. Besides, suppose you did gain a brilliant victory, if even the Archduke Karl gained a victory, what effect would that have on the general course of events? It's too late now when Vienna is occupied by the French army!'

'What? Occupied? Vienna occupied?'

'Not only occupied, but Bonaparte is at Schönbrunn, and the count, our dear Count Vrbna, goes to him for orders.'

After the fatigues and impressions of the journey, his reception, and especially after having dined, Bolkonsky felt that he could not take in the full significance of the words he heard.

'Count Lichtenfels was here this morning,' Bilibin continued, 'and showed me a letter in which the parade of the French in Vienna was fully described: Prince Murat *et tout le tremblement*...* You see that your victory is not a matter of great rejoicing and that you can't be received as a saviour.'

'Really I don't care about that, I don't care at all,' said Prince Andrew, beginning to understand that his news of the battle before Krems was really of small importance in view of such events as the fall of Austria's capital. 'How is it Vienna was taken? What of the bridge and its celebrated bridge-head and Prince Auersperg? We heard reports that Prince Auersperg was defending Vienna,' said he.

'Prince Auersperg is on this, on our side of the river, and is defending us – doing it very badly I think, but still he is defending us. But Vienna is on the other side. No, the bridge has not yet been taken and I hope it will not be, for it is mined and orders have been given to blow it up. Otherwise we should long ago have been in the mountains of Bohemia, and you and your army would have spent a bad quarter of an hour between two fires.'

'But still this does not mean that the campaign is over,' said Prince Andrew.

'Well, I think it is. The bigwigs here think so too, but they daren't say so. It will be as I said at the beginning of the campaign, it won't be your skirmishing at Dürrenstein, or gunpowder at all that will decide the matter, but those who devised it,' said Bilibin, quoting one of his own *mots*, releasing the wrinkles on his forehead, and pausing. 'The only question is what will come of the meeting between the Emperor Alexander and the King of Prussia in Berlin?* If Prussia joins the allies, Austria's hand will be forced and there will be war. If not it is merely a question of settling where the preliminaries of the new Campo Formio are to be drawn up.'

'What an extraordinary genius!' Prince Andrew suddenly exclaimed, clenching his small hand and striking the table with it, 'and what luck the man has!'

'Buonaparte?' said Bilibin inquiringly, puckering up his forehead to indicate that he was about to say something witty. 'Buonaparte?' he repeated, accentuating the *u*: 'I think, however, now that he lays down laws for Austria at Schönbrunn, *il faut lui faire grâce de l'u!*\* I shall certainly adopt an innovation and call him simply Bonaparte!'

'But joking apart,' said Prince Andrew, 'do you really think the campaign is over?'

'This is what I think. Austria has been made a fool of, and she is not used to it. She will retaliate. And she has been fooled in the first place because her provinces have been pillaged – they say the Holy Russian army loots terribly – her army is destroyed, her capital taken, and all this for the *beaux yeux* of His Sardinian Majesty.* And therefore – this is between ourselves – I instinctively feel that we are being deceived, my instinct tells me of negotiations with France and projects for peace, a secret peace concluded separately.'

'Impossible!' cried Prince Andrew. 'That would be too base.'

'If we live we shall see,' replied Bilibin, his face again becoming smooth as a sign that the conversation was at an end.

When Prince Andrew reached the room prepared for him and lay down in a clean shirt on the feather-bed with its warmed and fragrant pillows, he felt that the battle of which he had brought tidings was far far away from him. The alliance with Prussia, Austria's treachery, Bonaparte's new triumph, to-morrow's levee and parade, and the audience with the Emperor Francis, occupied his thoughts.

He closed his eyes, and immediately a sound of cannonading, of musketry, and the rattling of carriage wheels seemed to fill his ears, and now again drawn out in a thin line the musketeers were descending the hill, the French were firing, and he felt his heart palpitating as he rode forward beside Schmidt with the bullets merrily whistling all around, and he experienced tenfold the joy of living, as he had not done since childhood.

He woke up . . .

'Yes, that all happened!' he said, and smiling happily to himself like a child, he fell into a deep youthful slumber.

11

NEXT day he woke late. Recalling his recent impressions the first thought that came into his mind was that to-day he had to be presented to the Emperor Francis; he remembered the Minister of War, the polite Austrian adjutant, Bilibin, and last night's conversation. Having dressed for his attendance at court in full parade uniform, which he had not worn for a long time, he went into Bilibin's study fresh, animated and handsome, with his hand bandaged. In the study were four gentlemen of the diplomatic corps. With Prince Hippolyte Kuragin, who was a secretary to the embassy, Bolkonsky was already acquainted. Bilibin introduced him to the others.

The gentlemen assembled at Bilibin's were young, wealthy, gay, society men, who here, as in Vienna, formed a special set which Bilibin, their leader, called *les nôtres*. This set, consisting almost exclusively of diplomats, evidently had its own interests which had nothing to do with war or politics but related to high society, to certain women, and to the official side of the service. These gentlemen received Prince Andrew as one of themselves, an honour they did not extend to many. From politeness and to start conversation, they asked him a few questions about the army and the battle, and then the talk went off into merry jests and gossip.

'But the best of it was,' said one, telling of the misfortune of a fellow diplomat, 'that the Chancellor told him flatly that his appointment to London was a promotion and that he was so to regard it. Can you fancy the figure he cut . . .?'

'But the worst of it, gentlemen – I am giving Kuragin away to you – is that that man suffers, and this Don Juan, wicked fellow, is taking advantage of it!'

Prince Hippolyte was lolling in a lounge chair with his legs over its arm. He began to laugh.

'Tell me about that!' he said.

'Oh, you Don Juan! You serpent!' cried several voices.

'You, Bolkonsky, don't know,' said Bilibin turning to Prince Andrew, 'that all the atrocities of the French army (I nearly said of the Russian army) are nothing compared to what this man has been doing among the women!'

'*La femme est la campagne de l'homme,*' announced Prince Hippolyte, and began looking through a lorgnette at his elevated legs.

Bilibin and the rest of 'ours' burst out laughing in Hippolyte's face, and Prince Andrew saw that Hippolyte, of whom – he had to admit – he had almost been jealous on his wife's account, was the butt of this set.

'Oh, I must give you a treat,' Bilibin whispered to Bolkonsky. 'Kuragin is exquisite when he discusses politics – you should see his gravity!'

He sat down beside Hippolyte and wrinkling his forehead began talking to him about politics. Prince Andrew and the others gathered round these two.

'The Berlin cabinet cannot express a feeling of alliance,' began Hippolyte gazing round with importance at the others, 'without expressing ... as in its last note ... you understand ... Besides, unless his Majesty the Emperor derogates from the principle of our alliance ...

'Wait, I have not finished ...' he said to Prince Andrew, seizing him by the arm, 'I believe that intervention will be stronger than non-intervention. And ...' he paused. 'Finally one cannot impute the non-receipt of our despatch of November 18. That is how it will end.' And he released Bolkonsky's arm to indicate that he had now quite finished.

'Demosthenes, I know thee by the pebble thou secretest in thy golden mouth!' said Bilibin, and the mop of hair on his head moved with satisfaction.

Everybody laughed, and Hippolyte louder than anyone. He was evidently distressed, and breathed painfully, but could not restrain the wild laughter that convulsed his usually impassive features.

'Well now, gentlemen,' said Bilibin, 'Bolkonsky is my guest in this house and in Brünn itself. I want to entertain him, as far as I can, with all the pleasures of life here. If we were in Vienna it would be easy, but here, in this wretched Moravian hole, it is more difficult, and I beg you all to help me. Brünn's attractions must be shown him. You can undertake the theatre, I society, and you, Hippolyte, of course the women.'

'We must let him see Amelie, she's exquisite!' said one of 'ours', kissing his finger-tips.

'In general we must turn this bloodthirsty soldier to more humane interests,' said Bilibin.

'I shall scarcely be able to avail myself of your hospitality, gentlemen, it is already time for me to go,' replied Prince Andrew looking at his watch.

'Where to?'

'To the Emperor.'

'Oh! Oh! Oh!'

'Well, *au revoir*, Bolkonsky! Au *revoir*, Prince! Come back early to dinner,' cried several voices. 'We'll take you in hand.'

'When speaking to the Emperor, try as far as you can to praise the way that provisions are supplied and the routes indicated,' said Bilibin, accompanying him to the hall.

'I should like to speak well of them, but as far as I know the facts, I can't,' replied Bolkonsky, smiling.

'Well, talk as much as you can, anyway. He has a passion for giving audiences, but he does not like talking himself and can't do it, as you will see.'


12

AT the levee Prince Andrew stood among the Austrian officers as he had been told to, and the Emperor Francis merely looked fixedly into his face and just nodded to him with his long head. But after it was over the adjutant he had seen the previous day ceremoniously informed Bolkonsky that the Emperor desired to give him an audience. The Emperor Francis received him standing in the middle of the room. Before the conversation began Prince Andrew was struck by the fact that the Emperor seemed confused and blushed as if not knowing what to say.

'Tell me, when did the battle begin?' he asked hurriedly.

Prince Andrew replied. Then followed other questions just as simple: 'Was Kutuzov well? When had he left Krems?' and so on. The Emperor spoke as if his sole aim were to put a given number of questions – the answers to these questions, as was only too evident, did not interest him.

'At what o'clock did the battle begin?' asked the Emperor.

'I cannot inform your Majesty at what o'clock the battle began at the front, but at Dürrenstein, where I was, our attack began after five in the afternoon,' replied Bolkonsky growing more animated and expecting that he would have a chance to give a reliable account, which he had ready in his mind, of all he knew and had seen. But the Emperor smiled and interrupted him.

'How many miles?'

'From where to where, your Majesty?'

'From Dürrenstein to Krems.'

'Three and a half miles, your Majesty.'

'The French have abandoned the left bank?'

'According to the scouts the last of them crossed on rafts during the night.'

'Is there sufficient forage in Krems?'

'Forage had not been supplied to the extent . . .'

The Emperor interrupted him.

'At what o'clock was General Schmidt killed?'

'At seven o'clock, I believe.'

'At seven o'clock? It's very sad, very sad!'

The Emperor thanked Prince Andrew and bowed. Prince Andrew withdrew and was immediately surrounded by courtiers on all sides. Everywhere he saw friendly looks and heard friendly words. Yesterday's adjutant reproached him for not having stayed at the palace, and offered him his own house. The Minister of War came up and congratulated him on the Maria Theresa Order of the third grade, which the Emperor was conferring on him. The Empress's chamberlain invited him to see her Majesty. The archduchess also wished to see him. He did not know whom to answer, and for a few seconds collected his thoughts. Then the Russian ambassador took him by the shoulder, led him to the window, and began to talk to him.

Contrary to Bilibin's forecast the news he had brought was joyfully received. A thanksgiving service was arranged, Kutuzov was awarded the Grand Cross of Maria Theresa, and the whole army received rewards. Bolkonsky was invited everywhere, and had to spend the whole morning calling on the principal Austrian dignitaries. Between four and five in the afternoon, having made all his calls, he was returning to Bilibin's house thinking out a letter to his father about the battle and his visit to Brünn. At the door he found a vehicle half full of luggage. Franz, Bilibin's man, was dragging a portmanteau with some difficulty out of the front door.

Before returning to Bilibin's Prince Andrew had gone to a book-shop to provide himself with some books for the campaign, and had spent some time in the shop.

'What is it?' he asked.

'Oh, your Excellency!' said Franz, with difficulty rolling the portmanteau into the vehicle, 'we are to move on still farther. The scoundrel is again at our heels!'

'Eh? What?' asked Prince Andrew.

Bilibin came out to meet him. His usually calm face showed excitement.

'There now! Confess that this is delightful,' said he. 'This affair of the Thabor Bridge, at Vienna ... They have crossed without striking a blow!'

Prince Andrew could not understand.

'But where do you come from not to know what every coachman in the town knows?'

'I come from the archduchess's. I heard nothing there.'

'And you didn't see that everybody is packing up?'

'I did not ... What is it all about?' inquired Prince Andrew impatiently.

'What's it all about? Why, the French have crossed the bridge that Auersperg was defending, and the bridge was not blown up: so Murat is now rushing along the road to Brünn and will be here in a day or two.'

'What? Here? But why did they not blow up the bridge, if it was mined?'

'That is what I ask you. No one, not even Bonaparte, knows why.'

Bolkonsky shrugged his shoulders.

'But if the bridge is crossed it means that the army too is lost! It will be cut off,' said he.

'That's just it,' answered Bilibin. 'Listen! The French entered Vienna as I told you. Very well. Next day, which was yesterday, those gentlemen, *messieurs les maréchaux*, Murat, Lannes, and Belliard, mount and ride to the bridge. (Observe that all three are Gascons.) "Gentlemen," says one of them, "you know the Thabor Bridge is mined and doubly mined and that there are menacing fortifications at its head and an army of fifteen thousand men has been ordered to blow up the bridge and not let us cross? But it will please our sovereign the Emperor Napoleon if we take this bridge, so let us three go and take it!" "Yes, let's!" say the others. And off they go and take the bridge, cross it, and now with their whole army are on this side of the Danube, marching on us, you, and your lines of communication.'

'Stop jesting,' said Prince Andrew sadly and seriously. This news grieved him and yet he was pleased.

As soon as he learned that the Russian army was in such a hopeless situation it occurred to him that it was he who was destined to lead it out of this position; that here was the Toulon that would lift him from the ranks* of obscure officers and offer him the first step to fame! Listening to Bilibin he was already imagining how on reaching the army he would give an opinion . at the war council which would be the only one that could save the army, and how he alone would be entrusted with the execution of the plan.

'Stop this jesting,' he said.

'I am not jesting,' Bilibin went on. 'Nothing is truer or sadder. These gentlemen ride onto the bridge alone and wave white handkerchiefs; they assure the officer on duty that they, the marshals, are on their way to negotiate with Prince Auersperg. He lets them enter the *tête-de-pont*. They spin him a thousand gasconades, saying that the war is over, that the Emperor Francis is arranging a meeting with Bonaparte, that they desire to see Prince Auersperg, and so on. The officer sends for Auersperg; these gentlemen embrace the officers, crack jokes, sit on the cannon, and meanwhile a French battalion gets to the bridge unobserved, flings the bags of incendiary material into the water, and approaches the *tête-de-pont*. At length appears the lieutenant-general, our dear Prince Auersperg von Mautern himself. 'Dearest foe! Flower of the Austrian army, hero of the Turkish wars! Hostilities are ended, we can shake one another's hand ... The Emperor Napoleon burns with impatience to make Prince Auersperg's acquaintance.' In a word those gentlemen, Gascons indeed, so bewildered him with fine words, and he is so flattered by his rapidly established intimacy with the French marshals, and so dazzled by the sight of Murat's mantle and ostrich plumes, *qu'il n'y voit que du feu, et oublie celui qu'il devait faire, faire sur l'ennemi!*' In spite of the animation of his speech Bilibin did not forget to pause after this *mot* to give time for its due appreciation. 'The French battalion rushes to the bridge-head, spikes the guns, and the bridge is taken! But what is best of all,' he went on, his excitement subsiding under the delightful interest of his own story, 'is that the sergeant in charge of the cannon which was to give the signal to fire the mines and blow up the bridge, this sergeant seeing that the French troops were running onto the bridge, was about to fire, but Lannes stayed his hand. The sergeant, who was evidently wiser than his general, goes up to Auersperg and says: "Prince, you are being deceived, here are the French!" Murat, seeing that all is lost if the sergeant is allowed to speak, turns to Auersperg with feigned astonishment (he is a true Gascon) and says: "I don't recognize the world-famous Austrian discipline, if you allow a subordinate to address you like that!" It was a stroke of genius. Prince Auersperg feels

167

his dignity at stake and orders the sergeant to be arrested. Come, you must own that this affair of the Thabor Bridge is delightful! It is not exactly stupidity, nor rascality ...'

'It may be treachery,' said Prince Andrew, vividly imagining the grey overcoats, wounds, the smoke of gunpowder, the sounds of firing, and the glory that awaited him.

'Not that either. That puts the court in too bad a light,' replied Bilibin. 'It's not treachery nor rascality not stupidity: it is just as at Ulm ... it is ...' – he seemed to be trying to find the right expression. '*C'est ... c'est du Mack. Nous sommes mackés,*' he concluded, feeling that he had produced a good epigram, a fresh one that would be repeated. His hitherto puckered brow became smooth as a sign of pleasure, and with a slight smile he began to examine his nails.

'Where are you off to?' he said suddenly to Prince Andrew who had risen and was going towards his room.

'I am going away.'

'Where to?'

'To the army.'

'But you meant to stay another two days?'

'But now I am off at once.'

And Prince Andrew after giving directions about his departure went to his room.

'Do you know, *mon cher,*' said Bilibin following him, 'I have been thinking about you. Why are you going?'

And in proof of the conclusiveness of his opinion all the wrinkles vanished from his face.

Prince Andrew looked inquiringly at him and gave no reply.

'Why are you going? I know you think it your duty to gallop back to the army now that it is in danger. I understand that. *Mon cher,* it is heroism!'

'Not at all,' said Prince Andrew.

'But as you are a philosopher, be a consistent one, look at the other side of the question and you will see that your duty, on the contrary, is to take care of yourself. Leave it to those who are no longer fit for anything else. ... You have not been ordered to return and have not been dismissed from here; therefore you can stay and go with us wherever our ill-luck takes us. They say we are going to Olmütz, and Olmütz is a very decent town. You and I will travel comfortably in my calèche.'

'Do stop joking, Bilibin,' cried Bolkonsky.

'I am speaking sincerely as a friend! Consider! Where and why are you going, when you might remain here? You are faced by one of two things,' and the skin over his left temple puckered, 'either you will not reach your regiment before peace is concluded, or you will share defeat and disgrace with Kutuzov's whole army.'

And Bilibin unwrinkled his temple, feeling that the dilemma was insoluble.

'I cannot argue about it,' replied Prince Andrew coldly, but he thought: 'I am going to save the army.'

'My dear fellow, you are a hero!' said Bilibin.

## 13

THAT same night, having taken leave of the Minister of War, Bolkonsky set off to rejoin the army, not knowing where he would find it and fearing to be captured by the French on the way to Krems.

In Brünn everybody attached to the court was packing up, and the heavy baggage was already being dispatched to Olmütz. Near Hetzelsdorf Prince Andrew struck the high road along which the Russian army was moving with great haste and in the greatest disorder. The road was so obstructed with carts that it was impossible to get by in a carriage. Prince Andrew took a horse and a Cossack from a Cossack commander, and hungry and weary, making his way past the baggage-wagons, rode in search of the commander-in-chief and of his own luggage. Very sinister reports of the position of the army reached him as he went along, and the appearance of the troops in their disorderly flight confirmed these rumours.

'Cette armée russe que l'or de l'Angleterre a transportée des extrémités de l'univers, nous allons lui faire éprouver le même sort – (le sort de l'armée d'Ulm).' He remembered these words in Bonaparte's address to his army at the beginning of the campaign, and they awoke in him astonishment at the genius of his hero, a feeling of wounded pride, and a hope of glory. 'And should there be nothing left but to die?' he thought. 'Well, if need be, I shall do it no worse than others.'

He looked with disdain at the endless confused mass of detachments, carts, guns, artillery, and again baggage-wagons and vehicles of all kinds, overtaking one another and blocking the muddy road, three and sometimes four abreast. From all sides, behind and before, as far as ear could reach, there was the rattle of wheels, the creaking of carts and gun-carriages, the tramp of horses, the crack of whips, shouts, the urging of horses, and the swearing of soldiers, orderlies and officers. All along the sides of the road fallen horses were to be seen, some flayed, some not, and broken-down carts beside which solitary soldiers sat waiting for something, and again soldiers straggling from their companies, crowds of whom set off to the neighbouring villages, or returned from them dragging sheep, fowls, hay, and bulging sacks. At each ascent or descent of the road the crowds were yet denser and the din of shouting more incessant. Soldiers floundering knee-deep in mud pushed the guns and wagons themselves. Whips cracked, hoofs slipped, traces broke, and lungs were strained with shouting. The officers directing the march rode backward and forward between the carts. Their voices were but feebly heard amid the uproar and one saw by their faces that they despaired of the possibility of checking this disorder.

'Here is our dear Orthodox Russian army,' thought Bolkonsky, recalling Bilibin's words.

Wishing to find out where the commander-in-chief was, he rode up to a convoy. Directly opposite to him came a strange one-horse vehicle, evidently rigged up by soldiers out of any available materials and looking like something between a cart, a cabriolet, and a calèche. A soldier was driving, and a woman enveloped in shawls sat behind the apron under the leather hood of the vehicle. Prince Andrew rode up and was just putting his question to a soldier when his attention was diverted by the desperate shrieks of the woman in the vehicle. An officer in charge of transport was beating the soldier who was driving the woman's vehicle for trying to get ahead of others, and the strokes of his whip fell on the apron of the equipage. The woman screamed piercingly. Seeing Prince Andrew she leaned out from behind the apron, and waving her thin arms from under the woollen shawl, cried:

'Mr Aide-de-camp! Mr Aide-de-camp!...For heaven's sake... Protect me! What will become of us? I am the wife of the doctor of the Seventh Chasseurs...They won't let us pass, we are left behind and have lost our people...'

'I'll flatten you into a pancake!' shouted the angry officer to the soldier. 'Turn back with your slut!'

'Mr Aide-de-camp! Help me!...What does it all mean?' screamed the doctor's wife.

'Kindly let this cart pass. Don't you see it's a woman?' said Prince Andrew riding up to the officer.

The officer glanced at him, and without replying turned again to the soldier. 'I'll teach you to push on!...Back!'

'Let them pass, I tell you!' repeated Prince Andrew, compressing his lips.

'And who are you?' cried the officer, turning on him with tipsy rage, 'who are *you?* Are you in command here? Eh? I am commander here, not you! Go back or I'll flatten you into a pancake,' repeated he. This expression evidently pleased him.

'That was a nice snub for the little aide-de-camp,' came a voice from behind.

Prince Andrew saw that the officer was in that state of senseless tipsy rage when a man does not know what he is saying. He saw that his championship of the doctor's wife in her queer trap might expose him to what he dreaded more than anything in the world – to ridicule; but his instinct urged him on. Before the officer finished his sentence Prince Andrew, his face distorted with fury, rode up to him and raised his riding-whip.

'Kind ... ly let – them – pass!'

The officer flourished his arm and hastily rode away.

'It's all the fault of these fellows on the staff that there's this disorder,' he muttered. 'Do as you like.'

Prince Andrew without lifting his eyes rode hastily away from the doctor's wife, who was calling him her deliverer, and recalling with a sense of disgust the minutest details of this humiliating scene he galloped on to the village where he was told that the commander-in-chief was.

On reaching the village he dismounted and went to the nearest house, intending to rest if but for a moment, eat something, and try to sort out the stinging and tormenting thoughts that confused his mind. 'This is a mob of scoundrels and not an army,' he was thinking as he went up to the window of the first house, when a familiar voice called him by name.

He turned round. Nesvitsky's handsome face looked out of the little window. Nesvitsky, moving his moist lips as he chewed something, and flourishing his arm, called him to enter.

'Bolkonsky! Bolkonsky! ... Don't you hear? Eh? Come quick ...' he shouted.

Entering the house, Prince Andrew saw Nesvitsky and another adjutant having something to eat. They hastily turned round to him asking if he had any news. On their familiar faces he read agitation and alarm. This was particularly noticeable on Nesvitsky's usually laughing countenance.

'Where is the commander-in-chief?' asked Bolkonsky.

'Here, in that house,' answered the adjutant.

'Well, is it true that it's peace and capitulation?' asked Nesvitsky.

'I was going to ask you. I know nothing except that it was all I could do to get here.'

'And we, my dear boy! It's terrible! I was wrong to laugh at

171

Mack, we're getting it still worse,' said Nesvitsky. 'But sit down and have something to eat.'

'You won't be able to find either your baggage or anything else now, Prince. And God only knows where your man Peter is,' said the other adjutant.

'Where are head-quarters?'

'We are to spend the night in Znaim.'

'Well, I have got all I need into packs for two horses,' said Nesvitsky. 'They've made up splendid packs for me – fit to cross the Bohemian mountains with. It's a bad look-out, old fellow! But what's the matter with you? You must be ill to shiver like that,' he added, noticing that Prince Andrew winced as at an electric shock.

'It's nothing,' replied Prince Andrew.

He had just remembered his recent encounter with the doctor's wife and the convoy officer.

'What is the commander-in-chief doing here?' he asked.

'I can't make out at all,' said Nesvitsky.

'Well, all I can make out is that everything is abominable, abominable, quite abominable!' said Prince Andrew, and he went off to the house where the commander-in-chief was.

Passing by Kutuzov's carriage and the exhausted saddle-horses of his suite, with their Cossacks who were talking loudly together, Prince Andrew entered the passage. Kutuzov himself, he was told, was in the house with Prince Bagration and Weyrother. Weyrother was the Austrian general who had succeeded Schmidt. In the passage little Kozlovsky was squatting on his heels in front of a clerk. The clerk, with cuffs turned up, was hastily writing at a tub turned bottom upwards. Kozlovsky's face looked worn – he too had evidently not slept all night. He glanced at Prince Andrew and did not even nod to him.

'Second line . . . have you written it?' he continued dictating to the clerk. 'The Kiev Grenadiers, Podolian . . .'

'One can't write so fast, your honour,' said the clerk, glancing angrily and disrespectfully at Kozlovsky.

Through the door came the sounds of Kutuzov's voice, excited and dissatisfied, interrupted by another, an unfamiliar voice. From the sound of these voices, the inattentive way Kozlovsky looked at him, the disrespectful manner of the exhausted clerk, the fact that the clerk and Kozlovsky were squatting on the floor by a tub so near to the commander-in-chief, and from the noisy laughter of the Cossacks holding the horses near the window, Prince Andrew felt that something important and disastrous was about to happen.

He turned to Kozlovsky with urgent questions.

'Immediately, Prince,' said Kozlovsky. 'Dispositions for Bagration.'

'What about capitulation?'

'Nothing of the sort. Orders are issued for a battle.'

Prince Andrew moved towards the door from whence voices were heard. Just as he was going to open it the sounds ceased, the door opened, and Kutuzov with his eagle nose and puffy face appeared in the doorway. Prince Andrew stood right in front of Kutuzov but the expression of the commander-in-chief's one sound eye showed him to be so preoccupied with thoughts and anxieties as to be oblivious of his presence. He looked straight at his adjutant's face without recognizing him.

'Well, have you finished?' said he to Kozlovsky.

'One moment, your Excellency.'

Bagration, a gaunt middle-aged man of medium height with a firm, impassive face of oriental type, came out after the commander-in-chief.

'I have the honour to present myself,' repeated Prince Andrew rather loudly, handing Kutuzov an envelope.

'Ah, from Vienna? Very good. Later, later!'

Kutuzov went out into the porch with Bagration.

'Well, good-bye, Prince,' said he to Bagration. 'My blessing, and may Christ be with you in your great endeavour!'

His face suddenly softened and tears came into his eyes. With his left hand he drew Bagration towards him, and with his right, on which he wore a ring, he made the sign of the cross over him with a gesture evidently habitual, offering his puffy cheek, but Bagration kissed him on the neck instead.

'Christ be with you!' Kutuzov repeated and went towards his carriage. 'Get in with me,' said he to Bolkonsky.

'Your Excellency, I should like to be of use here. Allow me to remain with Prince Bagration's detachment.'

'Get in,' said Kutuzov, and noticing that Bolkonsky still delayed, he added: 'I need good officers myself, need them myself!'

They got into the carriage and drove for a few minutes in silence.

'There is still much, much before us,' he said, as if with an old man's penetration he understood all that was passing in Bolkonsky's mind. 'If a tenth part of his detachment returns I shall thank God,' he added as if speaking to himself.

Prince Andrew glanced at Kutuzov's face only a foot distant from him and involuntarily noticed the carefully washed seams of the scar near his temple, where an Ismail bullet had pierced his skull, and the empty eye-socket. 'Yes, he has a right to speak so calmly of those men's death,' thought Bolkonsky.

'That is why I beg to be sent to that detachment,' he said.

Kutuzov did not reply. He seemed to have forgotten what he had been saying, and sat plunged in thought. Five minutes later, gently swaying on the soft springs of the carriage, he turned to Prince Andrew. There was not a trace of agitation on his face. With delicate irony he questioned Prince Andrew about the details of his interview with the Emperor, about the remarks he had heard at court concerning the Krems affair, and about some ladies they both knew.

## 14

ON November 1st Kutuzov had received through a spy news that the army he commanded was in an almost hopeless position. The spy reported that the French, after crossing the bridge at Vienna, were advancing in immense force upon Kutuzov's line of communication with the troops that were arriving from Russia. If Kutuzov decided to remain at Krems, Napoleon's army of one hundred and fifty thousand men would cut him off completely and surround his exhausted army of forty thousand, and he would find himself in the position of Mack at Ulm. If Kutuzov decided to abandon the road connecting him with the troops arriving from Russia, he would have to march with no road into unknown parts of the Bohemian mountains, defending himself against superior forces of the enemy and abandoning all hopes of a junction with Buxhöwden. If Kutuzov decided to retreat along the road from Krems to Olmütz, to unite with the troops arriving from Russia, he risked being forestalled on that road by the French who had crossed the Vienna bridge, and encumbered by his baggage and transport, having to accept battle on the march against an enemy three times as strong, who would hem him in from two sides.

Kutuzov chose this latter course.

The French, the spy reported, having crossed the Vienna bridge were advancing by forced marches towards Znaim, which lay a hundred versts off on the line of Kutuzov's retreat. If he reached Znaim before the French, there would be great hope of saving the army; to let the French forestall him at Znaim meant the exposure of his whole army to a disgrace such as that of Ulm, or to utter destruction. But to forestall the French with his whole army was impossible. The road for the French from Vienna to Znaim was shorter and better than the road for the Russians from Krems to Znaim.

The night he received the news, Kutuzov sent Bagration's vanguard, four thousand strong, to the right across the hills from the Krems–Znaim to the Vienna–Znaim road. Bagration was to make this march without resting and to halt facing Vienna with Znaim to his rear, and if he succeeded in forestalling the French he was to delay them as long as possible. Kutuzov himself with all his transport took the road to Znaim.

Marching thirty miles that stormy night across roadless hills, with his hungry, ill-shod soldiers, and losing a third of his men as stragglers by the way, Bagration came out on the Vienna–Znaim road at Hollabrünn a few hours ahead of the French who were approaching Hollabrünn from Vienna. Kutuzov with his transport had still to march for some days before he could reach Znaim. Hence Bagration with his four thousand hungry exhausted men, would have to detain for days the whole enemy army that came upon him at Hollabrünn, which was clearly impossible. But a freak of fate made the impossible possible. The success of the trick that had placed the Vienna bridge in the hands of the French without a fight, led Murat to try to deceive Kutuzov in a similar way. Meeting Bagration's weak detachment on the Znaim road he supposed it to be Kutuzov's whole army. To be able to crush it absolutely he awaited the arrival of the rest of the troops who were on their way from Vienna, and with this object offered a three days' truce on condition that both armies should remain in position without moving. Murat declared that negotiations for peace were already proceeding, and that he therefore offered this truce to avoid unnecessary bloodshed. Count Nostitz, the Austrian general occupying the advanced posts, believed Murat's emissary and retired, leaving Bagration's division exposed. Another emissary rode to the Russian line to announce the peace negotiations and to offer the Russian army the three days' truce. Bagration replied that he was not authorized either to accept or refuse a truce, and sent his adjutant to Kutuzov to report the offer he had received.

A truce was Kutuzov's sole chance of gaining time, giving Bagration's exhausted troops some rest, and letting the transport and heavy convoys (whose movements were concealed from the French) advance if but one stage nearer Znaim. The offer of a truce gave the only, and a quite unexpected, chance of saving the army. On receiving the news he immediately dispatched Adjutant-General Wintzingerode, who was in attendance on him, to the enemy camp. Wintzingerode was not merely to agree to the truce but also to offer terms of capitulation, and meanwhile Kutuzov sent his adjutants back to hasten to the utmost the movements of the baggage-trains of the entire army along the Krems–Znaim road. Bagration's exhausted and hungry detachment which alone covered this movement of the transport and of the whole army, had to remain stationary in face of an enemy eight times as strong as itself.

Kutuzov's expectations that the proposals of capitulation (which were in no way binding) might give time for part of the transport to pass, and also that Murat's mistake would very soon be discovered proved correct. As soon as Bonaparte (who was at Schönbrunn, sixteen miles from Hollabrünn) received Murat's despatch with the proposal of a truce and a capitulation, he detected a ruse and wrote the following letter to Murat:

> Schönbrunn, 25th Brumaire, 1805,
> at eight o'clock in the morning.

To Prince Murat,

I cannot find words to express to you my displeasure. You command only my advance-guard, and have no right to arrange an armistice without my order. You are causing me to lose the fruits of a campaign. Break the armistice immediately and march on the enemy. Inform him that the general who signed that capitulation had no right to do so, and that no one but the Emperor of Russia has that right.

If however the Emperor of Russia ratifies that convention, I will ratify it; but it is only a trick. March on, destroy the Russian army... You are in a position to seize its baggage and artillery.

The Russian Emperor's aide-de-camp is an impostor. Officers are nothing when they have no powers; this one had none... The Austrians let themselves be tricked at the crossing of the Vienna bridge, you are letting yourself be tricked by an aide-de-camp of the Emperor.

> Napoleon.*

Bonaparte's adjutant rode full gallop with this menacing letter to Murat. Bonaparte himself, not trusting to his generals, moved with all the Guards to the field of battle, afraid of letting a ready victim escape, and Bagration's four thousand men merrily lighted camp fires, dried and warmed themselves, cooked their porridge for the first time for three days, and not one of them knew or imagined what was in store for him.

15

BETWEEN three and four o'clock in the afternoon Prince Andrew, who had persisted in his request to Kutuzov, arrived at Grunth and reported himself to Bagration. Bonaparte's adjutant had not yet reached Murat's detachment and the battle had not yet begun. In Bagration's detachment no one knew anything of the general position of affairs. They talked of peace but did not believe in its possibility; others talked of a battle but also disbelieved in the nearness of an engagement. Bagration, knowing Bolkonsky to be a favourite and trusted adjutant, received him with distinction and special marks of favour, explaining to him that there would probably be an engagement that day or the next, and giving him full liberty to remain with him during the battle or to join the rear-guard and have an eye on the order of retreat, 'which is also very important'.

'However there will hardly be an engagement to-day,' said Bagration as if to reassure Prince Andrew.

'If he is one of the ordinary little staff-dandies sent to earn a medal, he can get his reward just as well in the rearguard, but if he wishes to stay with me, let him . . . he'll be of use here if he's a brave officer,' thought Bagration. Prince Andrew, without replying, asked the prince's permission to ride round the position to see the disposition of the forces, so as to know his bearings should he be sent to execute an order. The officer on duty, a handsome, elegantly dressed man with a diamond ring on his forefinger, who was fond of speaking French though he spoke it badly, offered to conduct Prince Andrew.

On all sides they saw rain-soaked officers with dejected faces who seemed to be seeking something, and soldiers dragging doors, benches, and fencing, from the village.

'There now, Prince! We can't stop those fellows,' said the staff-officer pointing to the soldiers. 'The officers don't keep them in hand. And there,' he pointed to a sutler's tent, 'they crowd in and sit. This morning I turned them all out and now look, it's full again. I must go there, Prince, and scare them a bit. It won't take a moment.'

'Yes, let's go in and I will get myself a roll and some cheese,' said Prince Andrew who had not yet had time to eat anything.

'Why didn't you mention it, Prince? I would have offered you something.'

They dismounted and entered the tent. Several officers, with flushed and weary faces, were sitting at the table eating and drinking.

'Now what does this mean, gentlemen?' said the staff-officer, in the reproachful tone of a man who has repeated the same thing more than once. 'You know it won't do to leave your posts like this. The prince gave orders that no one should leave his post. Now you, Captain,' and he turned to a thin, dirty little artillery officer who without his boots (he had given them to the canteen keeper to dry) in only his stockings, rose when they entered, smiling not altogether comfortably.

'Well, aren't you ashamed of yourself, Captain Tushin?' he

continued. 'One would think that as an artillery officer you would set a good example, yet here you are without your boots! The alarm will be sounded and you'll be in a pretty position without your boots!' (The staff-officer smiled.) 'Kindly return to your posts, gentlemen, all of you, all!' he added in a tone of command.

Prince Andrew smiled involuntarily as he looked at the artillery officer Tushin, who silent and smiling, shifting from one stockinged foot to the other, glanced inquiringly with his large, intelligent, kindly eyes from Prince Andrew to the staff-officer.

'The soldiers say it feels easier without boots,' said Captain Tushin smiling shyly in his uncomfortable position, evidently wishing to adopt a jocular tone. But before he had finished he felt that his jest was unacceptable and had not come off. He grew confused.

'Kindly return to your posts,' said the staff-officer trying to preserve his gravity.

Prince Andrew glanced again at the artillery officer's small figure. There was something peculiar about it, quite unsoldierly, rather comic, but extremely attractive.

The staff-officer and Prince Andrew mounted their horses and rode on.

Having ridden beyond the village, continually meeting and over-taking soldiers and officers of various regiments, they saw on their left some entrenchments being thrown up, the freshly-dug clay of which showed up red. Several battalions of soldiers, in their shirt-sleeves despite the cold wind, swarmed in these earthworks like a ghost of white ants; spadeful of red clay were continually being thrown up from behind the bank by unseen hands. Prince Andrew and the officer rode up, looked at the entrenchment, and went on again. Just behind it they came upon some dozens of soldiers, continually replaced by others, who ran from the entrenchment. They had to hold their noses and put their horses to a trot to escape from the poisoned atmosphere of these latrines.

'Voilà l'agrément des camps, monsieur le prince,' said the staff-officer.

They rode up the opposite hill. From there the French could already be seen. Prince Andrew stopped and began examining the position.

'That's our battery,' said the staff-officer indicating the highest point. 'It's in charge of the queer fellow we saw without his boots. You can see everything from there; let's go there, Prince.'

'Thank you very much, I will go on alone,' said Prince Andrew, wishing to rid himself of this staff-officer's company, 'please don't trouble yourself further.'

The staff-officer remained behind and Prince Andrew rode on alone. The farther forward and nearer the enemy he went, the more orderly and cheerful were the troops. The greatest disorder and depression had been in the baggage-train he had passed that morning on the Znaim road seven miles away from the French. At Grunth also some apprehension and alarm could be felt, but the nearer Prince Andrew came to the French lines the more confident was the appearance of our troops. The soldiers in their greatcoats were ranged in lines, the sergeant-majors and company officers were counting the men, poking the last man in each section in the ribs and telling him to hold his hand up. Soldiers scattered over the whole place were dragging logs and brushwood and were building shelters with merry chatter and laughter; around the fires sat others, dressed and undressed, drying their shirts and leg-bands or mending boots or overcoats and crowding round the boilers and porridge-cookers. In one company dinner was ready and the soldiers were gazing eagerly at the steaming boiler, waiting till the sample, which a quartermaster-sergeant was carrying in a wooden bowl to an officer who sat on a log before his shelter, had been tasted.

Another company, a lucky one for not all the companies had vodka, crowded round a pock-marked, broad-shouldered sergeant-major who, tilting a keg, filled one after another the canteen-lids held out to him. The soldiers lifted the canteen-lids to their lips with reverential faces, emptied them rolling the vodka in their mouths, and walked away from the sergeant-major with brightened expressions, licking their lips and wiping them on the sleeves of their greatcoats. All their faces were as serene as if all this were happening at home awaiting peaceful encampment, and not within sight of the enemy before an action in which at least half of them would be left on the field. After passing a chasseur regiment and in the lines of the Kiev grenadiers – fine fellows busy with similar peaceful affairs – near the shelter of the regimental commander, higher than and different from the others, Prince Andrew came out in front of a platoon of grenadiers before whom lay a naked man. Two soldiers held him while two others were flourishing their switches and striking him regularly on his bare back. The man shrieked unnaturally. A stout major was pacing up and down the line, and regardless of the screams kept repeating:

'It's a shame for a soldier to steal; a soldier must be honest, honourable, and brave, but if he robs his fellows there is no honour in him, he's a scoundrel. Go on! Go on!'

So the swishing sounds of the strokes, and the desperate but unnatural screams, continued.

'Go on, go on!' said the major.

A young officer with a bewildered and pained expression on his face stepped away from the man and looked round inquiringly at the adjutant as he rode by.

Prince Andrew, having reached the front line, rode along it. Our front line and that of the enemy were far apart on the right and left flanks, but in the centre where the men with a flag of truce had passed that morning, the lines were so near together that the men could see one another's faces and speak to one another. Besides the soldiers who formed the picket line on either side, there were many curious onlookers who, jesting and laughing, stared at their strange foreign enemies.

Since early morning – despite an injunction not to approach the picket line – the officers had been unable to keep sightseers away. The soldiers forming the picket line, like showmen exhibiting a curiosity, no longer looked at the French but paid attention to the sightseers and grew weary waiting to be relieved. Prince Andrew halted to have a look at the French.

'Look! Look there!' one soldier was saying to another, pointing to a Russian musketeer who had gone up to the picket line with an officer and was rapidly and excitedly talking to a French grenadier. 'Hark to him jabbering! Fine, isn't it? It's all the Frenchy can do to keep up with him. There now, Sidorov!'

'Wait a bit and listen. It's fine!' answered Sidorov, who was considered an adept at French.

The soldier to whom the laughers referred was Dolokhov. Prince Andrew recognized him and stopped to listen to what he was saying. Dolokhov had come from the left flank where their regiment was stationed, with his captain.

'Now then, go on, go on!' incited the officer, bending forward and trying not to lose a word of the speech which was incomprehensible to him. 'More, please: more! What's he saying?'

Dolokhov did not answer the captain; he had been drawn into a hot dispute with the French grenadier. They were naturally talking about the campaign. The Frenchman, confusing the Austrians with the Russians, was trying to prove that the Russians had surrendered and had fled all the way from Ulm, while Dolokhov maintained that the Russians had not surrendered but had beaten the French.

'We have orders to drive you off here, and we shall drive you off,' said Dolokhov.

'Only take care you and your Cossacks are not all captured!' said the French grenadier.

The French onlookers and listeners laughed.

'We'll make you dance as we did under Suvorov...(*on vous fera danser*),' said Dolokhov.

'*Qu'est-ce qu'il chante?* (What's he singing about?)' asked a Frenchman.

'It's ancient history,' said another, guessing that it referred to a former war. 'The Emperor will teach your Suvara as he has taught the others...'

'Bonaparte...' began Dolokhov, but the Frenchman interrupted him.

'Not Bonaparte. He is the Emperor! *Sacré nom*...!' cried he angrily.

'The devil skin your Emperor.'

And Dolokhov swore at him in coarse soldier's Russian and shouldering his musket walked away.

'Let us go, Ivan Lukich,' he said to the captain.

'Ah, that's the way to talk French,' said the picket soldiers. 'Now, Sidorov, you have a try!'

Sidorov, turning to the French, winked, and began to jabber meaningless sounds very fast: '*Kari, mala, tafa, safi, muter, Kaská,*' he said, trying to give an expressive intonation to his voice.

'Ho! ho! ho! Ha! ha! ha! ha! Ouh! ouh!' came peals of such healthy and good-humoured laughter from the soldiers that it infected the French involuntarily, so much so that the only thing left to do seemed to be to unload the muskets, explode the ammunition, and all return home as quickly as possible.

But the guns remained loaded, the loop-holes in block-houses and entrenchments looked out just as menacingly, and the unlimbered cannon confronted one another as before.


16


HAVING ridden round the whole line from right flank to left, Prince Andrew made his way up to the battery from which the staff-officer had told him the whole field could be seen. Here he dismounted, and stopped beside the farthest of the four unlimbered cannon. Before the guns an artillery sentry was pacing up and down; he stood at attention when the officer arrived, but at a sign resumed his measured, monotonous pacing. Behind the guns were their limbers, and still farther back picket-ropes and artillerymen's bonfires. To the left, not far from the farthest cannon, was a small newly-constructed wattle-shed from which came the sound of officers' voices in eager conversation.

It was true that a view over nearly the whole Russian position and the greater part of the enemy's opened out from this battery. Just facing it, on the crest of the opposite hill, the village of Schön Graben could be seen, and in three places to left and right the French troops amid the smoke of their camp fires, the greater part of whom were evidently in the village itself and behind the hill. To the left from that village, amid the smoke, was something resembling a battery, but it was impossible to see it clearly with the naked eye. Our right flank was posted on a rather steep incline which dominated the French position. Our infantry were stationed there, and at the farthest point the dragoons. In the centre, where Tushin's battery stood and from which Prince Andrew was surveying the position, was the easiest and most direct descent and ascent to the brook separating us from Schön Graben. On the left our troops were close to a copse, in which smoked the bonfires of our infantry who were felling wood. The French line was wider than ours, and it was plain that they could easily outflank us on both sides. Behind our position was a steep and deep dip, making it difficult for artillery and cavalry to retire. Prince Andrew took out his notebook, and leaning on the cannon, sketched a plan of the position. He made some notes on two points, intending to mention them to Bagration. His idea was, first to concentrate all the artillery in the centre, and secondly, to withdraw the cavalry to the other side of the dip. Prince Andrew, being always near the commander-in-chief, closely following the mass movements and general orders, and constantly studying historical accounts of battles, involuntarily pictured to himself the course of events in the forthcoming action in broad outline. He imagined only important possibilities: 'If the enemy attacks the right flank,' he said to himself, 'the Kiev grenadiers and the Podolsk chasseurs must hold their position till reserves from the centre come up. In that case the dragoons could successfully make a flank counter-attack. If they attack our centre we, having the centre battery on this high ground, shall withdraw the left flank under its cover, and retreat to the dip by echelons.' So he reasoned . . . All the time he had been beside the gun he had heard the voices of the officers distinctly, but as often happens had not understood a word of what they were saying. Suddenly however he was struck by a voice coming from the shed, and its tone was so sincere that he could not but listen.

'No, friend,' said a pleasant and as it seemed to Prince Andrew a familiar voice, 'what I say is that if it were possible to know what is beyond death, none of us would be afraid of it. That's so, friend.'

Another, a younger voice, interrupted him:

'Afraid or not, you can't escape it anyhow.'

'All the same, one is afraid! Oh, you clever people,' said a third manly voice interrupting them both. 'Of course you artillerymen are very wise, because you can take everything along with you – vodka and snacks.'

And the owner of the manly voice, evidently an infantry officer, laughed.

'Yes, one is afraid,' continued the first speaker, he of the familiar voice. 'One is afraid of the unknown, that's what it is. Whatever we may say about the soul going to the sky ... we know there is no sky but only an atmosphere.'

The manly voice again interrupted the artillery officer.

'Well, stand us some of your herb-vodka, Tushin,' it said.

'Why,' thought Prince Andrew, 'that's the captain who stood up in the sutler's hut without his boots.' He recognized the agreeable philosophizing voice with pleasure.

'Some herb-vodka? Certainly!' said Tushin, '– but still, to conceive a future life ...'

He did not finish. Just then there was a whistle in the air; nearer and nearer, faster and louder, louder and faster, a cannon-ball, as if it had not finished saying what was necessary, thudded into the ground near the shed with superhuman force, throwing up a mass of earth. The ground seemed to groan at the terrible impact.

And immediately Tushin, with a short pipe in the corner of his mouth and his kind intelligent face rather pale, rushed out of the shed followed by the owner of the manly voice, a dashing infantry officer who hurried off to his company, buttoning up his coat as he ran.

17

MOUNTING his horse again Prince Andrew lingered with the battery, looking at the puff from the gun that had sent the ball. His eyes ran rapidly over the wide space, but he only saw that the hitherto motionless masses of the French now swayed, and that there really was a battery to their left. The smoke above it had not yet dispersed. Two mounted Frenchmen, probably adjutants, were galloping up the hill. A small but distinctly visible enemy column was moving down the hill, probably to strengthen the front line. The smoke of the first shot had not yet dispersed before another puff appeared, followed by a report. The battle had begun! Prince Andrew turned his horse and galloped back to Grunth to find Prince Bagration. He heard the cannonade behind him growing louder and more frequent. Evidently our guns had begun to reply.

From the bottom of the slope, where the parleys had taken place, came the report of musketry.

Lemarrois had just arrived at a gallop with Bonaparte's stern letter, and Murat, humiliated and anxious to expiate his fault, had at once moved his forces to attack the centre and outflank both the Russian wings, hoping before evening and before the arrival of the Emperor to crush the contemptible detachment that stood before him.

'It has begun. Here it is!' thought Prince Andrew, feeling the blood rush to his heart. 'But where and how will my Toulon* present itself?'

Passing between the companies that had been eating porridge and drinking vodka a quarter of an hour before he saw everywhere the same rapid movement of soldiers forming ranks and getting their muskets ready, and on all their faces he recognized the same eagerness that filled his heart. 'It has begun! Here it is, dreadful but enjoyable!' was what the face of each soldier and each officer seemed to say.

Before he had reached the embankments that were being thrown up, he saw, in the light of the dull autumn evening, mounted men coming towards him. The foremost, wearing a Cossack cloak and lambskin cap and riding a white horse, was Prince Bagration. Prince Andrew stopped, waiting for him to come up; Prince Bagration reined in his horse and recognizing Prince Andrew nodded to him. He still looked ahead while Prince Andrew told him what he had seen.

The feeling, 'It has begun! Here it is!' was seen even on Prince Bagration's hard brown face with its half-closed dull sleepy eyes. Prince Andrew gazed with anxious curiosity at that impassive face and wished he could tell what, if anything, this man was thinking and feeling at that moment. 'Is there anything at all behind that impassive face?' Prince Andrew asked himself as he looked. Prince Bagration bent his head in sign of agreement with what Prince Andrew told him, and said, 'Very good!' in a tone that seemed to imply that everything that took place and was reported to him was exactly what he had foreseen. Prince Andrew, out of breath with his rapid ride, spoke quickly. Prince Bagration, uttering his words with an oriental accent,* spoke particularly slowly, as if to impress the fact that there was no need to hurry. However he put his horse to a trot in the direction of Tushin's battery. Prince Andrew followed with the suite. Behind Prince Bagration rode an officer of the suite, the prince's personal adjutant, Zherkov, an orderly officer, the staff-officer on duty, riding a fine bob-tailed horse, and a civilian – an accountant who had asked permission to

184

be present at the battle out of curiosity. The accountant, a stout full-faced man, looked around him with a naïve smile of satisfaction and presented a strange appearance among the hussars, Cossacks and adjutants, in his camlet coat as he jolted on his horse with a convoy-officer's saddle.

'He wants to see a battle,' said Zherkov to Bolkonsky, pointing to the accountant, 'but he feels a pain in the pit of his stomach already.'

'Oh, leave off!' said the accountant with a beaming but rather cunning smile, as if flattered at being made the subject of Zherkov's joke, and purposely trying to appear stupider than he really was.

'It is very strange, *mon Monsieur Prince*,' said the staff-officer. (He remembered that in French there is some peculiar way of addressing a prince, but could not get it quite right.)

By this time they were all approaching Tushin's battery, and a ball struck the ground in front of them.

'What's that that has fallen?' asked the accountant with a naïve smile.

'A French pancake,' answered Zherkov.

'So that's what they hit with?' asked the accountant. 'How awful!'

He seemed to swell with satisfaction. He had hardly finished when they again heard an unexpectedly violent whistling which suddenly ended with a thud into something soft... f-f-flop! and a Cossack, riding a little to their right and behind the accountant, crashed to earth with his horse. Zherkov and the staff-officer bent over their saddles and turned their horses away. The accountant stopped facing the Cossack and examined him with attentive curiosity. The Cossack was dead, but the horse still struggled.

Prince Bagration screwed up his eyes, looked round, and seeing the cause of the confusion, turned away with indifference, as if to say, 'Is it worth while noticing trifles?' He reined in his horse with the ease of a skilful rider, and slightly bending over, disengaged his sabre which had caught in his cloak. It was an old-fashioned sabre of a kind no longer in general use. Prince Andrew remembered the story of Suvorov giving his sabre to Bagration in Italy, and the recollection was particularly pleasant at that moment. They had reached the battery at which Prince Andrew had been when he examined the battlefield.

'Whose company?' asked Prince Bagration of an artilleryman standing by the ammunition-wagon.

He asked, 'Whose company?' but he really meant, 'Are you frightened here?' and the artilleryman understood him.

'Captain Tushin's, your Excellency!' shouted the red-haired, freckled gunner in a merry voice, standing to attention.

'Yes, yes,' muttered Bagration as if considering something, and he rode past the limbers to the farthest cannon.

As he approached, a ringing shot issued from it deafening him and his suite, and in the smoke that suddenly surrounded the gun they could see the gunners who had seized it straining to roll it quickly back to its former position. A huge broad-shouldered gunner, Number One, holding a mop, his legs far apart, sprang to the wheel; while Number Two with a trembling hand placed a charge in the cannon's mouth. The short round-shouldered Captain Tushin, stumbling over the trail of the gun-carriage, moved forward, and not noticing the general, looked out shading his eyes with his small hand.

'Lift it two lines more and it will be just right,' cried he in a feeble voice to which he tried to impart a dashing note, ill suited to his weak figure. 'Number Two!' he squeaked. 'Fire Medvedev!'

Bagration called to him, and Tushin, raising three fingers to his cap, with a bashful and awkward gesture not at all like a military salute but like a priest's benediction, approached the general. Though Tushin's guns had been intended to cannonade the valley, he was firing incendiary balls at the village of Schön Graben visible just opposite, in front of which large masses of French were advancing.

No one had given Tushin orders where and at what to fire, but after consulting his sergeant-major Zakharchenko for whom he had great respect, he had decided that it would be a good thing to set fire to the village. 'Very good!' said Bagration in reply to the officer's report, and began deliberately to examine the whole battle-field extended before him. The French had advanced nearest on our right. Below the height on which the Kiev regiment was stationed, in the hollow where the rivulet flowed, the soul-stirring rolling and crackling of musketry was heard, and much farther to the right, beyond the dragoons, the officer of the suite pointed out to Bagration a French column that was outflanking us. To the left the horizon was bounded by the adjacent wood. Prince Bagration ordered two battalions from the centre to be sent to reinforce the right flank. The officers of the suite ventured to remark to the prince that if these battalions went away, the guns would remain without support. Prince Bagration turned to the officer and with his dull eyes looked at him in silence. It seemed to Prince Andrew that the officer's remark was just and that really no answer could be made to it. But at that moment an adjutant galloped up with a message from the commander of the regiment in the hollow and news that immense masses of the French were coming down upon them, and that his regiment was in disorder and was retreating upon the Kiev grenadiers. Prince Bagration bowed his head in sign of assent and approval. He rode off at a walk to the right and sent an adjutant to the dragoons with orders to attack the French. But this adjutant returned half-an-hour later with the news that the commander of the dragoons had already retreated beyond the dip in the ground, as a heavy fire had been opened on him and he was losing men uselessly, and so had hastened to throw some sharpshooters into the wood.

'Very good!' said Bagration.

As he was leaving the battery, firing was heard on the left also, and as it was too far to the left flank for him to have time to go there himself, Prince Bagration sent Zherkov to tell the general in command (the one who had paraded his regiment before Kutuzov at Braunau) that he must retreat as quickly as possible behind the hollow in the rear, as the right flank would probably not be able to withstand the enemy's attack very long. About Tushin and the battalion that had been in support of his battery, all was forgotten. Prince Andrew listened attentively to Bagration's colloquies with the commanding officers and the orders he gave them, and to his surprise found that no orders were really given but that Prince Bagration tried to make it appear that everything done by necessity, by accident, or by the will of subordinate commanders, was done, if not by his direct command at least in accord with his intentions. Prince Andrew noticed however that though what happened was due to chance and was independent of the commander's will, owing to the tact Bagration showed, his presence was very valuable. Officers who approached him with disturbed countenances became calm; soldiers and officers greeted him gaily, grew more cheerful in his presence, and were evidently anxious to display their courage before him.

18

PRINCE BAGRATION, having reached the highest point of our right flank, began riding downhill to where the roll of musketry was heard but where on account of the smoke nothing could be seen. The nearer they got to the hollow the less they could see but the more they felt the nearness of the actual battlefield. They began to meet wounded men. One with a bleeding head and no cap was being dragged along by two soldiers who supported him under the arms. There was a gurgle in his throat and he was spitting blood. A bullet had evidently hit him in the throat or mouth. Another was walking sturdily by himself but without his musket, groaning aloud and swinging his arm which had just been hurt, while blood from it was streaming over his greatcoat as from a bottle. He had that moment been wounded and his face showed fear rather than suffering. Crossing a road they descended a steep incline and saw several men lying on the ground, they also met a crowd of soldiers some of whom were unwounded. The soldiers were ascending the hill breathing heavily, and despite the general's presence were talking loudly and gesticulating. In front of them rows of grey cloaks were already visible through the smoke, and an officer catching sight of Bagration rushed shouting after the crowd of retreating soldiers, ordering them back. Bagration rode up to the ranks along which shots crackled now here and now there, drowning the sound of voices and the shouts of command. The whole air reeked with smoke. The excited faces of the soldiers were blackened with it. Some were using their ramrods, others putting powder on the touch-pans or taking charges from their pouches, while others were firing, though who they were firing at could not be seen for the smoke which there was no wind to carry away. A pleasant humming and whistling of bullets was often heard. 'What is this?' thought Prince Andrew approaching the crowd of soldiers. 'It can't be an attack for they are not moving; it can't be a square – for they are not drawn up for that.'

The commander of the regiment, a thin, feeble-looking old man with a pleasant smile – his eyelids drooping more than half over his old eyes giving him a mild expression, rode up to Bagration and welcomed him as a host welcomes an honoured guest. He reported that his regiment had been attacked by French cavalry and that, though the attack had been repulsed, he had lost more than half his men. He said the attack had been repulsed, employing this military term to describe what had occurred to his regiment, but in reality he did not himself know what had happened during that half-hour to the troops entrusted to him, and could not say with certainty whether the attack had been repulsed or his regiment had been broken up. All he knew was that at the commencement of the action balls and shells began flying all over his regiment and hitting men, and that afterwards someone had shouted 'Cavalry!' and our men had begun firing. They were still firing, not at the cavalry which had disappeared, but at French infantry who had come into the hollow and were firing at our men. Prince Bagration bowed his head as a sign that this was exactly what he had desired and expected. Turning to his adjutant he ordered him to bring down the two battalions of the Sixth Chasseurs whom they had just passed. Prince Andrew was struck by the changed expression on Prince Bagration's face at this moment. It expressed the concentrated and happy resolution you see on the face of a man who on a hot day takes a final run before plunging into the water. The dull sleepy expression was no longer there, nor the affectation of profound thought. The round, steady, hawk's eyes looked before him eagerly and rather disdainfully, not resting on anything although his movements were still slow and measured.

The commander of the regiment turned to Prince Bagration entreating him to go back as it was too dangerous to remain where they were. 'Please, your Excellency, for God's sake!' he kept saying, glancing for support at an officer of the suite who turned away from him. 'There, you see!' and he drew attention to the bullets whistling, singing and hissing continually around them. He spoke in the tone of entreaty and reproach that a carpenter uses to a gentleman who has picked up an axe: 'We are used to it, but you, sir, will blister your hands.' He spoke as if those bullets could not kill him, and his half-closed eyes gave still more persuasiveness to his words. The staff-officer joined in the colonel's appeals, but Bagration did not reply; he only gave an order to cease firing and re-form, so as to give room for the two approaching battalions. While he was speaking the curtain of smoke that had concealed the hollow, driven by a rising wind, began to move from right to left, as if drawn by an invisible hand, and the hill opposite with the French moving about on it opened out before them. All eyes fastened involuntarily on this French column advancing against them and winding down over the uneven ground. One could already see the soldiers' shaggy caps, distinguish the officers from the men, and see the standard flapping against its staff.

'They march splendidly,' remarked someone in Bagration's suite.

The head of the column had already descended into the hollow. The clash would take place on this side of it . . .

The remains of our regiment which had been in action rapidly formed up and moved to the right; from behind it, dispersing the laggards, came two battalions of the Sixth Chasseurs in fine order. Before they had reached Bagration the weighty tread of the mass of men marching in step could be heard. On their left flank, nearest to Bagration, marched a company commander, a fine round-faced man with a stupid and happy expression – the same man who had rushed out of the wattle-shed. At that moment he was clearly thinking of nothing but how dashing a fellow he would appear as he passed the commander.

With the self-satisfaction of a man on parade, he stepped lightly with his muscular legs as if sailing along, stretching himself to his full height without the smallest effort, his ease contrasting with the heavy tread of the soldiers who were keeping step with him. He carried close to his leg a narrow unsheathed sword (small, curved, and not like a real weapon) and looked now at the superior officers and now back at his men without losing step, his whole powerful body turning flexibly. It was as if all the powers of his soul were concentrated on passing the commander in the best possible manner, and feeling that he was doing it well, he was happy. 'Left ... left ... left ...' he seemed to repeat to himself at each alternate step; and in time to this with stern but varied faces, the wall of soldiers burdened with knapsacks and muskets, marched in step, and each one of these hundreds of soldiers seemed to be repeating to himself at each alternate step, 'Left ... left ... left ...' A fat major skirted a bush, puffing and falling out of step; a soldier who had fallen behind, his face showing alarm at his defection, ran at a trot, panting, to catch up with his company. A cannon-ball cleaving the air flew over the heads of Bagration and his suite and fell into the column to the measure of 'Left ... left!' 'Close up!' came the company commander's voice in jaunty tones. The soldiers passed in a semi-circle round something where the ball had fallen, and an old trooper on the flank, a non-commissioned officer, who had stopped beside the dead men, ran to catch up his line and falling into step with a hop, looked back angrily, and through the ominous silence and the regular tramp of feet beating the ground in unison, one seemed to hear left ... left ... left.

'Well done, lads!' said Prince Bagration.

'Glad to do our best, your Ex'len-lency!' came a confused shout from the ranks. A morose soldier marching on the left turned his eyes on Bagration as he shouted, with an expression that seemed to say: 'We know that ourselves!' Another, without looking round, as though fearing to relax, shouted with his mouth wide open and passed on.

The order was given to halt and down knapsacks.

Bagration rode round the ranks that had marched past him and dismounted. He gave the reins to a Cossack, took off and handed over his felt coat, stretched his legs, and set his cap straight. The head of the French column, with its officers leading, appeared from below the hill.

'Forward, with God!' said Bagration in a resolute sonorous voice, turning for a moment to the front line, and, slightly swinging his arms, he went forward uneasily over the rough field with the awkward gait of a cavalryman. Prince Andrew felt that an invisible power was leading him forward, and experienced great happiness.

The French were already near. Prince Andrew walking beside

Bagration, could clearly distinguish their bandoliers, red epaulettes, and even their faces. (He distinctly saw an old French officer, who with gaitered legs and turned-out toes climbed the hill with difficulty.) Prince Bagration gave no further orders and silently continued to walk on in front of the ranks. Suddenly one shot after another rang out from among the French, smoke appeared all along their uneven ranks, and musket shots sounded. Several of our men fell, among them the round-faced officer who had marched so gaily and complacently. But at the moment the first report was heard, Bagration looked round and shouted 'Hurrah!'

'Hurrah – ah! – ah!' rang a long-drawn shout from our ranks, and passing Bagration and racing one another, they rushed in an irregular but joyous and eager crowd down the hill at their disordered foe.*

## 19

THE attack of the Sixth Chasseurs secured the retreat of our right flank. In the centre Tushin's forgotten battery, which had managed to set fire to the Schön Graben village, delayed the French advance. The French were putting out the fire which the wind was spreading, and thus gave us time to retreat. The retirement of the centre to the other side of the dip in the ground at the rear was hurried and noisy, but the different companies did not get mixed. But our left – which consisted of the Azov and Podolsk infantry and the Pavlograd hussars – was simultaneously attacked and outflanked by superior French forces under Lannes, and was thrown into confusion. Bagration had sent Zherkov to the general commanding that left flank with orders to retreat immediately.

Zherkov, not removing his hand from his cap, turned his horse about and galloped off. But no sooner had he left Bagration than his courage failed him. He was seized by panic and could not go where it was dangerous.

Having reached the left bank, instead of going to the front where the firing was, he began to look for the general and his staff where they could not possibly be, and so did not deliver the order.

The command of the left flank belonged by seniority to the commander of the regiment Kutuzov had reviewed at Braunau and in which Dolokhov was serving as a private. But the command of the extreme left flank had been assigned to the commander of the Pavlograd regiment in which Rostov was serving, and a misunderstanding arose. The two commanders were much exasperated with one another and long after the action had begun on the right flank and the French were already advancing, were engaged in discussion, with the sole object of offending one another. But the regiments, both cavalry and infantry, were by no means ready for the impending action. From privates to general they were not expecting a battle and were engaged in peaceful occupations, the cavalry feeding their horses and the infantry collecting wood.

'He higher iss dan I in rank,' said the German colonel of the hussars, flushing and addressing an adjutant who had ridden up, 'so let him do vhat he vill, but I cannot sacrifice my hussars ... Bugler, sount ze retreat!'

But haste was becoming imperative. Cannon and musketry mingling together, thundered on the right and in the centre, while the capotes of Lannes's sharpshooters were already seen crossing the mill-dam and forming up within twice the range of a musket-shot. The general in command of the infantry went towards his horse with jerky steps, and having mounted drew himself up very straight and tall and rode to the Pavlograd commander. The commanders met with polite bows but with secret malevolence in their hearts.

'Once again, Colonel,' said the general, 'I can't leave half my men in the wood. I *beg* of you, I *beg* of you,' he repeated, 'to occupy the *position* and prepare for an attack.'

'I peg of you yourself not to mix in vot is not your pusiness!' suddenly replied the irate colonel. 'If you vere in the cavalry ...'

'I am not in the cavalry, Colonel, but I am a Russian general and if you are not aware of the fact ...'

'Quite avare, your Excellency,' suddenly shouted the colonel, touching his horse and turning purple in the face. 'Vill you be so goot to come to ze front and see dat zis position iss no goot? I don't vish to desstroy my men for your pleasure!'

'You forget yourself, Colonel. I am not considering my own pleasure and I won't allow it to be said!'

Taking the colonel's outburst as a challenge to his courage, the general expanded his chest and rode, frowning, beside him to the front line, as if their differences would be settled there amongst the bullets. They reached the front, several bullets sped over them, and they halted in silence. There was nothing fresh to be seen from the line, for from where they had been before it had been evident that it was impossible for cavalry to act among the bushes and broken ground, as well as that the French were outflanking our left. The general and colonel looked sternly and significantly at one another like two fighting-cocks preparing for battle, each vainly trying to detect signs of cowardice in the other. Both passed the examination successfully. As there was nothing to be said, and neither wished to give occasion for it to be alleged that he had been the first to leave the range of fire, they would have remained there for a long time testing each other's courage, had it not been that just then they heard the rattle of musketry and a muffled shout almost behind them in the wood. The French had attacked the men collecting wood in the copse. It was no longer possible for the hussars to retreat with the infantry. They were cut off from the line of retreat on the left by the French. However inconvenient the position, it was now necessary to attack in order to cut a way through for themselves.

The squadron in which Rostov was serving had scarcely time to mount before it was halted facing the enemy. Again, as at the Enns bridge, there was nothing between the squadron and the enemy, and again that terrible dividing line of uncertainty and fear – resembling the line separating the living from the dead – lay between them. All were conscious of this unseen line, and the question whether they would cross it or not, and how they would cross it, agitated them all.

The colonel rode to the front, angrily gave some reply to questions put to him by the officers, and like a man desperately insisting on having his own way, gave an order. No one said anything definite, but the rumour of an attack spread through the squadron. The command to form up rang out and the sabres whizzed as they were drawn from their scabbards. Still no one moved. The troops of the left flank, infantry and hussars alike, felt that the commander did not himself know what to do, and this irresolution communicated itself to the men.

'If only they would be quick!' thought Rostov, feeling that at last the time had come to experience the joy of an attack of which he had so often heard from his fellow hussars.

'Fo'ward, with God, lads!' rang out Denisov's voice. 'At a twot, fo'ward!'

The horses' croups began to sway in the front line. Rook pulled at the reins and started of his own accord.

Before him on the right Rostov saw the front lines of his hussars, and still farther ahead a dark line, which he could not see distinctly but took to be the enemy. Shots could be heard, but some way off.

'Faster!' came the word of command, and Rostov felt Rook's flanks drooping as he broke into a gallop.

Rostov anticipated his horse's movements and became more and more elated. He had noticed a solitary tree ahead of him. This tree had been in the middle of the line that had seemed so terrible – and now he had crossed that line, and not only was there nothing terrible, but everything was becoming more and more happy and animated. 'Oh, how I will slash at him!' thought Rostov, gripping the hilt of his sabre.

'Hurr-a-a-a-ah!' came a roar of voices. 'Let anyone come my way now,' thought Rostov driving his spurs into Rook and letting him go at full gallop so that he outstripped the others. Ahead the enemy was already visible. Suddenly something like a birch-broom seemed to sweep over the squadron. Rostov raised his sabre ready to strike, but at that instant the trooper Nikitenko who was gallop-ing ahead, shot away from him, and Rostov felt as in a dream that he continued to be carried forward with unnatural speed but yet stayed on the same spot. From behind him Bondarchuk, an hussar he knew, jolted against him and looked at him angrily. Bondarchuk's horse swerved and galloped past.

'How is it I am not moving? I have fallen, I am killed!' Rostov asked and answered at the same instant. He was alone in the middle of a field. Instead of the moving horses and hussars' backs, he saw nothing before him but the motionless earth and the stubble around him. There was warm blood under his arm. 'No, I am wounded and the horse is killed.' Rook tried to rise on his forelegs but fell back, pinning his rider's leg. Blood was flowing from his head, he struggled but could not rise. Rostov also tried to rise but fell back, his sabretache having become entangled in the saddle. Where our men were, and where the French, he did not know. There was no one near.

Having disentangled his leg, he rose. 'Where, on which side, was now the line that had so sharply divided the two armies?' he asked himself and could not answer. 'Can something bad have happened to me?' he wondered as he got up; and at that moment he felt that something superfluous was hanging on his benumbed left arm. The wrist felt as if it were not his. He examined his hand carefully, vainly trying to find blood on it. 'Ah, here are people coming,' he thought joyfully, seeing some men running towards him. 'They will help me!' In front came a man wearing a strange shako and a blue cloak, swarthy, sunburnt, and with a hooked nose. Then came two more, and many more running behind. One of them said something strange, not in Russian. In among the hindmost of these men wearing similar shakos was a Russian hussar. He was being held by the arms, and his horse was being led behind him.

'It must be one of ours, a prisoner. Yes. Can it be that they will take me too? Who are these men?' thought Rostov scarcely believing his eyes. 'Can they be French?' He looked at the approach-ing Frenchmen, and though but a moment before he had been galloping to get at them and hack them to pieces, their proximity now seemed so awful that he could not believe his eyes. 'Who are they? Why are they running? Can they be coming at me? And why? To kill me? *Me* whom everyone is so fond of?' He remembered his mother's love for him, and his family's, and his friends', and the enemy's intention to kill him seemed impossible. 'But perhaps they may do it!' For more than ten seconds he stood not moving from the spot or realizing the situation. The foremost Frenchman, the one with the hooked nose, was already so close that the expression of his face could be seen. And the excited, alien face of that man, his bayonet hanging down, holding his breath, and running so lightly, frightened Rostov. He seized his pistol, and instead of firing it flung it at the Frenchman and ran with all his might towards the bushes. He did not now run with the feeling of doubt and conflict with which he had trodden the Enns bridge, but with the feeling of a hare fleeing from the hounds. One single sentiment, that of fear for his young and happy life, possessed his whole being. Rapidly leaping the furrows he fled across the field with the impetuosity he used to show at catchplay, now and then turning his good-natured, pale, young face to look back. A shudder of terror went through him: 'No, better not look,' he thought, but having reached the bushes he glanced round once more. The French had fallen behind, and just as he looked round the first man changed his run to a walk, and turning, shouted something loudly to a comrade farther back. Rostov paused. 'No, there's some mistake,' thought he. 'They can't have wanted to kill me.' But at the same time his left arm felt as heavy as if a five-stone weight were tied to it. He could run no more. The Frenchman also stopped and took aim. Rostov closed his eyes and stooped down. One bullet and then another whistled past him. He mustered his last remaining strength, took hold of his left hand with his right and reached the bushes. Behind these were some Russian sharpshooters.

## 20

THE infantry regiments that had been caught unawares in the outskirts of the wood ran out of it, the different companies getting mixed, and retreated as a disorderly crowd. One soldier in his fear uttered the senseless cry, 'Cut off!' that is so terrible in battle, and that word infected the whole crowd with a feeling of panic.

'Surrounded! Cut off! We're lost!' shouted the fugitives.

The moment he heard the firing and the cry from behind, the general realized that something dreadful had happened to his regiment, and the thought that he, an exemplary officer of many years' service who had never been to blame, might be held responsible at head-quarters for negligence or inefficiency, so staggered him that forgetting the recalcitrant cavalry colonel, his own dignity as a general, and above all quite forgetting the danger and all regard for self-preservation, he clutched the pommel of his saddle and spurring his horse galloped to the regiment under a hail of bullets which fell around, but fortunately missed him. His one desire was to know what was happening and at any cost correct, or remedy, the mistake if he had made one, so that he, an exemplary officer of twenty-two years' service who had never been censured, should not be held to blame.

Having galloped safely through the French, he reached a field behind the copse across which our men, regardless of orders, were running, and descending the valley. That moment of moral hesitation which decides the fate of battles had arrived. Would this disorderly crowd of soldiers attend to the voice of their commander, or would they, disregarding him, continue their flight? Despite his desperate shouts that used to seem so terrible to the soldiers, despite his furious purple countenance distorted out of all likeness to his former self, and the flourishing of his sabre, the soldiers all continued to run, talking, firing into the air and disobeying orders. The moral hesitation which decides the fate of battles was evidently culminating in a panic.

The general had a fit of coughing as a result of shouting and of the powder-smoke, and stopped in despair. Everything seemed lost. But at that moment the French who were attacking, suddenly and without any apparent reason, ran back and disappeared from the outskirts, and Russian sharpshooters showed themselves in the copse. It was Timokhin's company, which alone had maintained its order in the wood, and having lain in ambush in a ditch now attacked the French unexpectedly. Timokhin armed only with a sword, had rushed at the enemy with such a desperate cry and such mad drunken determination, that taken by surprise the French had thrown down their muskets and run. Dolokhov, running beside Timokhin, killed a Frenchman at close quarters and was the first to seize the surrendering French officer by his collar. Our fugitives returned, the battalions re-formed, and the French who had nearly cut our left flank in half, were for the moment repulsed. Our reserve units were able to join up, and the fight was at an end. The regimental commander and Major Ekonomov had stopped beside a bridge letting the retreating companies pass by them, when a soldier came up and took hold of the commander's stirrup almost leaning against him. The man was wearing a bluish coat of broadcloth, he had no knapsack or cap, his head was bandaged, and over his shoulder a French munition pouch was slung. He had an officer's sword in his hand. The soldier was pale, his blue eyes looked impudently into the commander's face, and his lips were smiling. Though the commander was occupied in giving instructions to Major Ekonomov, he could not help taking notice of the soldier.

'Your Excellency, here are two trophies,' said Dolokhov, pointing to the French sword and pouch. 'I have taken an officer prisoner. I stopped the company.' Dolokhov breathed heavily from weariness and spoke in abrupt sentences. 'The whole company can bear witness. I beg you will remember this, your Excellency!'

'All right, all right,' replied the commander, and turned to Major Ekonomov.

But Dolokhov did not go away; he untied the handkerchief around his head, pulled it off, and showed the blood congealed on his hair.

'A bayonet wound. I remained at the front. Remember, your Excellency!'

\*

Tushin's battery had been forgotten and only at the very end of the action did Prince Bagration, still hearing the cannonade in the centre, send his orderly staff-officer and later Prince Andrew also, 'to order the battery to retire as quickly as possible. When the supports attached to Tushin's battery had been moved away in the middle of the action by someone's order, the battery had continued firing and was only not captured by the French because the enemy could not surmise that anyone could have the effrontery to continue firing from four quite undefended guns. On the contrary, the energetic action of that battery led the French to suppose that here – in the centre – the main Russian forces were concentrated. Twice they had attempted to attack this point, but on each occasion had been driven back by grapeshot from the four isolated guns on the hillock.

Soon after Prince Bagration had left him, Tushin had succeeded in setting fire to Schön Graben.

'Look at them scurrying! It's burning! Just see the smoke! Fine! Grand! Look at the smoke, the smoke!' exclaimed the artillerymen, brightening up.

All the guns without waiting for orders, were being fired in the direction of the conflagration. As if urging each other on the soldiers cried at each shot: 'Fine! That's good! Look at it . . . Grand!' The fire, fanned by the breeze, was rapidly spreading. The French columns that had advanced beyond the village went back, but as though in revenge for this failure, the enemy placed ten guns to the right of the village and began firing them at Tushin's battery.

In their childlike glee, aroused by the fire and their luck in successfully cannonading the French, our artillerymen only noticed this battery when two balls, and then four more, fell among our guns, one knocking over two horses and another tearing off a munition-wagon driver's leg. Their spirits once roused were however not diminished, but only changed character. The horses were replaced by others from a reserve gun-carriage, the wounded were carried away, and the four guns were turned against the ten-gun battery. Tushin's companion officer had been killed at the beginning of the engagement and within an hour seventeen of the forty men of the guns' crews had been disabled, but the artillerymen were still as merry and lively as ever. Twice they noticed the French appearing below them, and then they fired grape-shot at them.

Little Tushin, moving feebly and awkwardly, kept telling his orderly to 'refill my pipe for that one!' and then, scattering sparks from it, ran forward shading his eyes with his small hand to look at the French.

'Smack at 'em, lads!' he kept saying, seizing the guns by the wheels and working the screws himself.

Amid the smoke, deafened by the incessant reports which always made him jump, Tushin, not taking his pipe from his mouth, ran from gun to gun, now aiming, now counting the charges, now giving orders about replacing dead or wounded horses and harnessing fresh ones, and shouting in his feeble voice, so high-pitched and irresolute. His face grew more and more animated. Only when a man was killed or wounded did he frown and turn away from the sight, shouting angrily at the men who, as is always the case, hesitated about lifting the injured or dead. The soldiers, for the most part handsome fellows and, as is always the case in an artillery company, a head and shoulders taller and twice as broad as their officer – all looked at their commander like children in an embarrassing situation, and the expression on his face was invariably reflected on theirs.

Owing to the terrible uproar and the necessity for concentration and activity, Tushin did not experience the slightest unpleasant sense of fear, and the thought that he might be killed or badly wounded never occurred to him. On the contrary he became more and more elated. It seemed to him that it was a very long time ago, almost a day, since he had first seen the enemy and fired the first shot, and that the corner of the field he stood on was well known and familiar ground. Though he thought of everything, considered everything, and did everything the best of officers could do in his position, he was in a state akin to feverish delirium or drunkenness.

From the deafening sounds of his own guns around him, the whistle and thud of the enemy's cannon-balls, from the flushed and perspiring faces of the crews bustling round the guns, from the sight of the blood of men and horses, from the little puffs of smoke on the enemy's side (always followed by a ball flying past and striking the earth, a man, a gun, or a horse), from the sight of all these things a fantastic world of his own had taken possession of his brain and at that moment afforded him pleasure. The enemy's guns were in his fancy not guns but pipes from which occasional puffs were blown by an invisible smoker.

'There ... he's puffing again,' muttered Tushin to himself as a small cloud rose from the hill and was borne in a streak to the left by the wind. 'Now look out for the ball ... we'll throw it back.'

'What do you want, your honour?' asked an artilleryman standing close by, who heard him muttering.

'Nothing ... only a shell ...' he answered.

'Come along, our Matvevna!' he said to himself. 'Matvevna' (daughter of Matthew) was the name his fancy gave to the farthest gun of the battery, which was large and of an old pattern. The French swarming round their guns seemed to him like ants. In that world the handsome drunkard, Number One of the second gun's crew, was 'uncle'; Tushin looked at him more often than at anyone else, and took delight in his every movement. The sound of musketry at the foot of the hill, now diminishing now increasing, seemed like someone's breathing. He listened intently to the ebb and flow of these sounds.

'Ah! Breathing again, breathing!' he muttered to himself.

He imagined himself as an enormously tall, powerful man who was throwing cannon-balls at the French with both hands.

'Now then, Matvevna, dear old lady, don't let me down!' he was saying as he moved from the gun, when a strange, unfamiliar voice called above his head: 'Captain Tushin! Captain!'

Tushin turned round in dismay. It was the staff-officer who had turned him out of the booth at Grunth. He was shouting in a gasping voice:

'Are you mad? You have twice been ordered to retreat, and you ...'

'Why are they down on me?' thought Tushin, looking in alarm at his superior.

'I ... don't ...' he muttered, holding up two fingers to his cap. 'I ...'

But the staff-officer did not finish what he wanted to say. A cannon-ball flying close to him caused him to duck and bend over his horse. He paused, and just as he was about to say something more another ball stopped him. He turned his horse and galloped off.

'Retire! All to retire!' he shouted from a distance.

The soldiers laughed. A moment later an adjutant arrived with the same order.

It was Prince Andrew. The first thing he saw on riding up to the space where Tushin's guns were stationed was an unharnessed horse with a broken leg, that lay screaming piteously beside the harnessed horses. Blood was gushing from its leg as from a spring. Among the limbers lay several dead men. One ball after another passed over as he approached and he felt a nervous shudder run down his spine. But the mere thought of being afraid roused him again. 'I cannot be afraid,' thought he, and dismounted slowly among the guns. He delivered the order and did not leave the battery. He decided to have the guns removed from their positions and withdrawn in his presence. Together with Tushin, stepping across the bodies and under a terrible fire from the French, he attended to the removal of the guns.

'A staff-officer was here a minute ago but skipped off,' said an artilleryman to Prince Andrew. 'Not like your honour!'

Prince Andrew said nothing to Tushin. They were both so busy as to seem not to notice one another. When, having limbered up the only two cannon that remained uninjured out of the four, they began moving down the hill (one shattered gun and one unicorn* were left behind), Prince Andrew rode up to Tushin.

'Well, till we meet again ...' he said, holding out his hand to Tushin.

'Good-bye, my dear fellow,' said Tushin. 'Dear soul! Good-bye, my dear fellow!' and for some unknown reason tears suddenly filled his eyes.

21

THE wind had fallen and black clouds, merging with the powder-smoke, hung low over the field of battle on the horizon. It was growing dark and the glow of two conflagrations was the more conspicuous. The cannonade was dying down, but the rattle of musketry behind and on the right sounded oftener and nearer. As soon as Tushin with his guns, continually driving round or coming upon wounded men, was out of range of fire and had descended into the dip, he was met by some of the staff, among them the staff-officer and Zherkov, who had been twice sent to Tushin's battery but had never reached it. Interrupting one another they all gave, and transmitted, orders as to how to proceed, reprimanding and reproaching him. Tushin gave no orders, and silently – fearing to speak because at every word he felt ready to weep without knowing why – rode behind on his artillery nag. Though the orders were to abandon the wounded, many of them dragged themselves after the troops and begged for seats on the gun-carriages. The jaunty infantry officer who just before the battle had rushed out of Tushin's wattle-shed, was laid, with a bullet in his stomach, on Matvevna's carriage. At the foot of the hill a pale hussar cadet supporting one hand with the other, came up to Tushin and asked for a seat.

'Captain, for God's sake! I've hurt my arm,' he said timidly. 'For God's sake . . . I can't walk. For God's sake!'

It was plain that this cadet had already repeatedly asked for a lift and been refused. He asked in a hesitating, piteous voice.

'Tell them to give me a seat, for God's sake!'

'Give him a seat,' said Tushin. 'Lay a cloak for him to sit on, lad,' he said, addressing his favourite soldier. 'And where is the wounded officer?'

'He has been set down. He died,' replied someone.

'Help him up. Sit down, dear fellow, sit down! Spread out the cloak, Antonov.'

The cadet was Rostov. With one hand he supported the other; he was pale and his jaw trembled, shivering feverishly. He was placed on 'Matvevna', the gun from which they had removed the dead officer. The cloak they spread under him was wet with blood which stained his breeches and arm.

'What, are you wounded, my lad?' said Tushin, approaching the gun on which Rostov sat.

'No, it's a sprain.'

Then what is this blood on the gun-carriage?' inquired Tushin.

'It was the officer, your honour, stained it,' answered the artilleryman, wiping away the blood with his coat-sleeve as if apologizing for the state of his gun.

It was all that they could do to get the guns up the rise, aided by the infantry, and having reached the village of Guntersdorf they halted. It had grown so dark that one could not distinguish the uniforms ten paces off, and the firing had begun to subside. Suddenly, nearby on the right, shouting and firing were again heard. Flashes of shots gleamed in the darkness. This was the last

French attack, and was met by soldiers who had sheltered in the village houses. They all rushed out of the village again, but Tushin's guns could not move, and the artillerymen, Tushin, and the cadet, exchanged silent glances as they awaited their fate. The firing died down, and soldiers talking eagerly streamed out of a side-street.

'Not hurt, Petrov?' asked one.

'We've given it 'em hot, mate! They won't make another push now,' said another.

'You couldn't see a thing. How they shot at their own fellows! Nothing could be seen. Pitch dark, brother! Isn't there something to drink?'

The French had been repulsed for the last time. And again and again in the complete darkness Tushin's guns moved forward, surrounded by the humming infantry as by a frame.

In the darkness it seemed as though a gloomy unseen river was flowing always in one direction, humming with whispers and talk and the sound of hoofs and wheels. Amid the general rumble the groans and voices of the wounded were more distinctly heard than any other sound in the darkness of the night. The gloom that enveloped the army was filled with their groans, which seemed to melt into one with the darkness of the night. After a while the moving mass became agitated, someone rode past on a white horse followed by his suite, and said something in passing: 'What did he say? Where to, now? Halt, is it? Did he thank us?' came eager questions from all sides. The whole moving mass began pressing closer together and a report spread that they were ordered to halt: evidently those in front had halted. All remained where they were in the middle of the muddy road.

Fires were lighted and the talk became more audible. Captain Tushin, having given orders to his company, sent a soldier to find a dressing station or a doctor for the cadet, and sat down by a bonfire the soldiers had kindled on the road. Rostov, too, dragged himself to the fire. From pain, cold and damp, a feverish shivering shook his whole body. Drowsiness was irresistibly mastering him, but he was kept awake by an excruciating pain in his arm for which he could find no satisfactory position. He kept closing his eyes and then again looking at the fire, which seemed to him dazzling red, and at the feeble round-shouldered figure of Tushin who was sitting cross-legged like a Turk beside him. Tushin's large kind intelligent eyes were fixed with sympathy and commiseration on Rostov, who saw that Tushin with his whole heart wished to help him but could not.

From all sides were heard the footsteps and talk of the infantry, who were walking, driving past, and settling down all around. The sound of voices, the tramping feet, the horses' hoofs moving in the mud, the crackling of wood fires near and afar, merged into one tremulous rumble.

It was no longer as before, a dark unseen river flowing through the gloom, but a dark sea swelling and gradually subsiding after a storm. Rostov looked at and listened listlessly to what passed before and around him. An infantryman came to the fire, squatted on his heels, held his hands to the blaze, and turned away his face.

'You don't mind, your honour?' he asked Tushin. 'I've lost my company, your honour. I don't know where ... such bad luck!'

With the soldier an infantry officer with a bandaged cheek came up to the bonfire, and addressing Tushin asked him to have the guns moved a trifle to let a wagon go past. After he had gone two soldiers rushed to the camp fire. They were quarrelling and fighting desperately, each trying to snatch from the other a boot they were both holding on to.

'You picked it up? ... I dare say! You're very smart!' one of them shouted hoarsely.

Then a thin pale soldier, his neck bandaged with a blood-stained leg-band, came up and in angry tones asked the artillerymen for water.

'Must one die like a dog?' said he.

Tushin told them to give the man some water. Then a cheerful soldier ran up begging a little fire for the infantry.

'A nice little hot torch for the infantry! Good luck to you, fellow countrymen. Thanks for the fire – we'll return it with interest,' said he carrying away into the darkness a glowing stick.

Next came four soldiers carrying something heavy on a cloak, and passed by the fire. One of them stumbled.

'Who the devil has put logs on the road?' snarled he.

'He's dead – why carry him?' said another.

'Shut up!'

And they disappeared into the darkness with their load.

'Still aching?' Tushin asked Rostov in a whisper.

'Yes.'

'Your honour, you're wanted by the general. He is in the hut here,' said a gunner, coming up to Tushin.

'Coming, friend.'

Tushin rose and buttoning his greatcoat and pulling it straight, walked away from the fire.

Not far from the artillery camp-fire, in a hut that had been prepared for him, Prince Bagration sat at dinner, talking with some commanding officers who had gathered at his quarters. The little old man with the half-closed eyes was there, greedily gnawing a mutton-bone, and the general who had served blamelessly for twenty-two years, flushed by a glass of vodka and the dinner; and the staff-officer with the signet-ring, and Zherkov uneasily glancing at them all, and Prince Andrew, pale, with compressed lips and feverishly glittering eyes.

In a corner of the hut stood a standard captured from the French, and the accountant with the naïve face was feeling its texture, shaking his head in perplexity – perhaps because the banner really interested him, perhaps because it was hard for him, hungry as he was, to look on at a dinner where there was no place for him. In the next hut there was a French colonel who had been taken prisoner by our dragoons. Our officers were flocking in to look at him. Prince Bagration was thanking the individual commanders and inquiring into details of the action and our losses. The general whose regiment had been inspected at Braunau was informing the prince that as soon as the action began he had withdrawn from the wood, mustered the men who were wood-cutting, and allowing the French to pass him had made a bayonet charge with two battalions and had broken up the French troops.

'When I saw, your Excellency, that their first battalion was disorganized, I stopped in the road and thought: "I'll let them come on and will meet them with the fire of the whole battalion" – and that's what I did.'

The general had so wished to do this, and was so sorry he had not managed to do it, that it seemed to him as if it had really happened. Perhaps it might really have been so? Could one possibly make out amid all that confusion, what did or did not happen?

'By the way, your Excellency, I should inform you,' he continued – remembering Dolokhov's conversation with Kutuzov, and his last interview with the gentleman-ranker – 'that Private Dolokhov, who was reduced to the ranks, took a French officer prisoner in my presence and particularly distinguished himself.'

'I saw the Pavlograd hussars attack there, your Excellency,' chimed in Zherkov, looking uneasily around. He had not seen the hussars all that day, but had heard about them from an infantry officer. 'They broke up two squares, your Excellency.'

Several of those present smiled at Zherkov's words expecting one of his usual jokes, but noticing that what he was saying redounded to the glory of our arms and of the day's work, they assumed a serious expression, though many of them knew that what he was saying was a lie devoid of any foundation. Prince Bagration turned to the old colonel:

'Gentlemen, I thank you all; all arms have behaved heroically: infantry, cavalry, and artillery. How was it that two guns were abandoned in the centre?' he inquired, searching with his eyes for someone. (Prince Bagration did not ask about the guns on the left flank; he knew that all the guns there had been abandoned at the very beginning of the action.) 'I think I sent you?' he added turning to the staff-officer on duty.

'One was damaged,' answered the staff-officer, 'and the other I can't understand. I was there all the time giving orders, and had only just left ... It is true it was hot there,' he added modestly.

Someone mentioned that Captain Tushin was bivouacking close to the village and had already been sent for.

'Oh, but you were there?' said Prince Bagration, addressing Prince Andrew.

'Of course, we only just missed one another,' said the staff-officer, with a smile to Bolkonsky.

'I had not the pleasure of seeing you,' said Prince Andrew coldly and abruptly.

All were silent. Tushin appeared at the threshold and made his way timidly from behind the backs of the generals. As he stepped past the generals in the crowded hut, feeling embarrassed as he always was by the sight of his superiors, he did not notice the staff of the banner and stumbled over it. Several of those present laughed.

'How is it a gun was abandoned?' asked Bagration, frowning, not so much at the captain as at those who were laughing, among whom Zherkov laughed loudest.

Only now, when he was confronted by the stern authorities, did his guilt and the disgrace of having lost two guns and yet remaining alive, present themselves to Tushin in all their horror. He had been so excited that he had not thought about it until that moment. The officers' laughter confused him still more. He stood before Bagration with his lower jaw trembling, and was hardly able to mutter:

'I don't know ... your Excellency ... I had no men ... your Excellency.'

'You might have taken some from the covering troops.'

Tushin did not say that there were no covering troops though that was perfectly true. He was afraid of getting some other officer into trouble, and silently fixed his eyes on Bagration as a schoolboy who has blundered looks at an examiner.

The silence lasted some time. Prince Bagration, apparently not wishing to be severe, found nothing to say, the others did not venture to intervene. Prince Andrew looked at Tushin from under his brows and his fingers twitched nervously.

'Your Excellency!' Prince Andrew broke the silence with his abrupt voice, 'you were pleased to send me to Captain Tushin's battery. I went there and found two-thirds of the men and horses knocked out, two guns smashed, and no supports at all.'

Prince Bagration and Tushin looked with equal intentness at Bolkonsky who spoke with suppressed agitation.

'And if your Excellency will allow me to express my opinion,' he continued, 'we owe to-day's success chiefly to the action of that battery and the heroic endurance of Captain Tushin and his company,' and without awaiting a reply, Prince Andrew rose and left the table.

Prince Bagration looked at Tushin, evidently reluctant to show distrust in Bolkonsky's emphatic opinion yet not feeling able fully to credit it, bent his head, and told Tushin that he could go. Prince Andrew went out with him.

'Thank you; you saved me, my dear fellow!' said Tushin.

Prince Andrew gave him a look, but said nothing and went away. He felt sad and depressed. It was all so strange, so unlike what he had hoped.

*

'Who are they? Why are they here? What do they want? And when will this all end?' thought Rostov looking at the changing shadows before him. The pain in his arm became more and more intense. Irresistible drowsiness overpowered him, red rings danced before his eyes, and the impression of those voices and faces and a sense of loneliness merged with the physical pain. It was they, these soldiers – wounded and unwounded – it was they who were crushing, weighing down and twisting the sinews and scorching the flesh of his sprained arm and shoulder. To rid himself of them he closed his eyes.

For a moment he dozed, but in that short interval innumerable things appeared to him in a dream: his mother and her large white hand, Sonya's thin little shoulders, Natasha's eyes and laughter, Denisov with his voice and moustache, and Telyanin, and all that affair with Telyanin and Bogdanich. That affair was the same thing as this soldier with the harsh voice, and it was that affair and this soldier that were so agonizingly, incessantly, pulling and pressing his arm and always dragging it in one direction. He tried to get away from them, but they would not for an instant let his shoulder move a hair's breadth. It would not ache – it would be well – if only they did not pull it, but it was impossible to get rid of them.

He opened his eyes and looked up. The black canopy of night

hung less than a yard above the glow of the charcoal. Flakes of falling snow were fluttering in that light. Tushin had not returned, the doctor had not come. He was alone now except for a soldier who was sitting naked at the other side of the fire warming his thin yellow body.

'Nobody wants me!' thought Rostov. 'There is no one to help me or pity me. Yet I was once at home, strong, happy, and loved.' He sighed, and doing so groaned involuntarily.

'Eh, is anything hurting you?' asked the soldier, shaking his shirt out over the fire, and not waiting for an answer he gave a grunt and added: 'What a lot of men have been crippled to-day – frightful!'

Rostov did not listen to the soldier. He looked at the snowflakes fluttering above the fire, and remembered a Russian winter at his warm bright home, his fluffy fur coat, his quickly-gliding sledge, his healthy body, and all the affection and care of his family. 'And why did I come here?' he wondered.

Next day the French did not renew their attack, and the remnant of Bagration's detachment was reunited to Kutuzov's army.


END OF PART TWO

# PART THREE

## 1

PRINCE VASILI was not a man who deliberately thought out his plans. Still less did he think of injuring anyone for his own advantage. He was merely a man of the world who had got on and to whom getting on had become a habit. Schemes and devices for which he never rightly accounted to himself, but which formed the whole interest of his life, were constantly shaping themselves in his mind, arising from the circumstances and persons he met. Of these plans he had not merely one or two in his head but dozens, some only beginning to form themselves, some approaching achievement, and some in course of disintegration. He did not, for instance, say to himself: 'This man now has influence, I must gain his confidence and friendship and through him obtain a special grant.' Nor did he say to himself: 'Pierre is a rich man, I must entice him to marry my daughter and lend me the forty thousand rubles I need.' But when he came across a man of position his instinct immediately told him that this man could be useful, and without any premeditation Prince Vasili took the first opportunity to gain his confidence, flatter him, become intimate with him, and finally make his request.

He had Pierre at hand in Moscow and procured for him an appointment as Gentleman of the Bed-chamber, which at that time conferred the status of Councillor of State,* and insisted on the young man accompanying him to Petersburg and staying at his house. With apparent absent-mindedness, yet with unhesitating assurance that he was doing the right thing, Prince Vasili did everything to get Pierre to marry his daughter. Had he thought out his plans beforehand he could not have been so natural and shown such unaffected familiarity in intercourse with everybody, both above and below him in social standing. Something always drew him towards those richer and more powerful than himself and he had rare skill in seizing the most opportune moment for making use of people.

Pierre on unexpectedly becoming Count Bezukhov and a rich man, felt himself after his recent loneliness and freedom from cares, so beset and preoccupied that only in bed was he able to be by himself. He had to sign papers, to present himself at government offices the function of which was not clear to him, to question his chief steward, to visit his estate near Moscow, and to receive many people who formerly did not even wish to know of his existence but would now have been offended and grieved had he chosen not to see them. These different people – business men, relations, and acquaintances alike – were all disposed to treat the young heir in the most friendly and flattering manner: they were all evidently firmly convinced of Pierre's noble qualities. He was always hearing such words as: 'With your remarkable kindness,' or, 'With your excellent heart,' 'You are yourself so honourable, Count,' or, 'Were he as clever as you,' and so on, till he began sincerely to believe in his own exceptional kindness and extraordinary intelligence, the more so as in the depth of his heart it had always seemed to him that he really was very kind and intelligent. Even people who had formerly been spiteful towards him and evidently unfriendly now became gentle and affectionate. The angry eldest princess with the long waist and hair plastered down like a doll's, had come into Pierre's room after the funeral. With drooping eyes and frequent blushes she told him she was very sorry about their past misunderstandings and did not now feel she had a right to ask him for anything, except only for permission, after the blow she had received, to remain for a few weeks longer in the house she so loved and where she had sacrificed so much. She could not refrain from weeping at these words. Touched that this statuesque princess could so change, Pierre took her hand and begged her forgiveness, without knowing what for. From that day the eldest princess quite changed towards Pierre and began knitting a striped scarf for him.

'Do this for my sake, *mon cher*; after all, she had to put up with a great deal from the deceased,' said Prince Vasili to him, handing him a deed to sign for the princess's benefit.

Prince Vasili had come to the conclusion that it was necessary to throw this bone – a bill for thirty thousand rubles – to the poor princess, that it might not occur to her to speak of his share in the affair of the inlaid portfolio. Pierre signed the deed, and after that the princess grew still kinder. The younger sisters also became affectionate to him, especially the youngest, the pretty one with the mole, who often made him feel confused by her smiles and her own confusion when meeting him.

It seemed so natural to Pierre that everyone should like him, and it would have seemed so unnatural had anyone disliked him, that he could not but believe in the sincerity of those around him.

Besides he had no time to ask himself whether these people were sincere or not. He was always busy and always felt in a state of mild and cheerful intoxication. He felt as though he were the centre of some important and general movement; that something was constantly expected of him, that if he did not do it he would grieve and disappoint many people, but if he did this and that, all would be well; and he did what was demanded of him, but still that happy result always remained in the future.

More than anyone else Prince Vasili took possession of Pierre's affairs and of Pierre himself in those early days. From the death of Count Bezukhov he did not let go his hold of the lad. He had the air of a man oppressed by business, weary and suffering, who yet would not, for pity's sake, leave this helpless youth who after all was the son of his old friend and the possessor of such enormous wealth, to the caprice of fate and the designs of rogues. During the few days he spent in Moscow after the death of Count Bezukhov, he would call Pierre, or go to him himself, and tell him what ought to be done in a tone of weariness and assurance, as if he were adding every time: 'You know I am overwhelmed with business and it is purely out of charity that I trouble myself about you, and you also know quite well that what I propose is the only thing possible.'

'Well, my dear fellow, to-morrow we are off at last,' said Prince Vasili one day, closing his eyes and fingering Pierre's elbow, speaking as if he were saying something which had long since been agreed upon and could not now be altered. 'We start to-morrow and I'm giving you a place in my carriage. I am very glad. All our important business here is now settled, and I ought to have been off long ago. Here is something I have received from the chancellor. I asked him for you, and you have been entered in the diplomatic corps and made a Gentleman of the Bed-chamber. The diplomatic career now lies open before you.'

Notwithstanding the tone of wearied assurance with which these words were pronounced, Pierre, who had so long been considering his career, wished to make some suggestion. But Prince Vasili interrupted him in the special deep cooing tone, precluding the possibility of interrupting his speech, which he used in extreme cases when special persuasion was needed.

'*Mais, mon cher*, I did this for my own sake, to satisfy my conscience, and there is nothing to thank me for. No one has ever complained yet of being too much loved; and besides, you are free, you could throw it up to-morrow. But you will see everything for yourself when you get to Petersburg. It is high time for you to get away from these terrible recollections.' Prince Vasili sighed.

'Yes, yes, my boy. And my valet can go in your carriage. Ah! I was nearly forgetting,' he added. 'You know, *mon cher*, your father and I had some accounts to settle, so I have received what was due from the Ryazan estate and will keep it; you won't require it. We'll go into the accounts later.'

By 'what was due from the Ryazan estate' Prince Vasili meant several thousand rubles quit-rent received from Pierre's peasants, which the prince had retained for himself.

In Petersburg as in Moscow, Pierre found the same atmosphere of gentleness and affection. He could not refuse the post, or rather the rank (for he did nothing), that Prince Vasili had procured for him, and acquaintances, invitations, and social occupations were so numerous that even more than in Moscow he felt a sense of bewilderment, bustle, and continual expectation of some good, always in front of him but never attained.

Of his former bachelor acquaintances many were no longer in Petersburg. The Guards had gone to the front; Dolokhov had been reduced to the ranks; Anatole was in the army somewhere in the provinces; Prince Andrew was abroad; so Pierre had not the opportunity to spend his nights as he used to like to spend them, or to open his mind by intimate talks with a friend older than himself and whom he respected. His whole time was taken up with dinners and balls, and was spent chiefly at Prince Vasili's house in the company of the stout princess, his wife, and his beautiful daughter Hélène.

Like the others, Anna Pavlovna Scherer showed Pierre the change of attitude towards him that had taken place in society.

Formerly in Anna Pavlovna's presence Pierre had always felt that what he was saying was out of place, tactless and unsuitable, that remarks which seemed to him clever while they formed in his mind became foolish as soon as he uttered them, while on the contrary Hippolyte's stupidest remarks came out clever and apt. Now everything Pierre said was *charmant*. Even if Anna Pavlovna did not say so he could see that she wished to, and only refrained out of regard for his modesty.

In the beginning of the winter of 1805–6 Pierre received one of Anna Pavlovna's usual notes with an invitation to which was added: 'You will find the beautiful Hélène here, whom it is always delightful to see.'

When he read that sentence Pierre felt for the first time that some link which other people recognized, had grown up between himself and Hélène, and that thought both alarmed him, as if some obligation were being imposed on him which he could not fulfil, and pleased him as an entertaining supposition.

Anna Pavlovna's 'At home' was like the former one, only the novelty she offered her guests this time was not Mortemart, but a diplomatist fresh from Berlin with the very latest details of the Emperor Alexander's visit to Potsdam, and of how the two august friends had pledged themselves in an indissoluble alliance to uphold the cause of justice against the enemy of the human race. Anna Pavlovna received Pierre with a shade of melancholy, evidently relating to the young man's recent loss by the death of Count Bezukhov (everyone constantly considered it a duty to assure Pierre that he was greatly afflicted by the death of the father he had hardly known), and her melancholy was just like the august melancholy she showed at the mention of her most august Majesty the Empress Marya Fëdorovna. Pierre felt flattered by this. Anna Pavlovna arranged the different groups in her drawing-room with her habitual skill. The large group, in which were Prince Vasili and the generals, had the benefit of the diplomat. Another group was at the tea table. Pierre wished to join the former, but Anna Pavlovna – who was in the excited condition of a commander on a battlefield to whom thousands of new and brilliant ideas occur which there is hardly time to put in action – seeing Pierre touched his sleeve with her finger, saying:

'Wait a bit, I have something in view for you this evening.' (She glanced at Hélène and smiled at her.) 'My dear Hélène, be charitable to my poor aunt who adores you. Go and keep her company for ten minutes. And that it may not be too dull, here is the dear Count who will not refuse to accompany you.'

The beauty went to the aunt, but Anna Pavlovna detained Pierre, looking as if she had to give some final necessary instructions.

'Isn't she exquisite?' she said to Pierre, pointing to the stately beauty as she glided away. 'And how she carries herself! For so young a girl, such tact, such masterly perfection of manner! It comes from her heart. Happy the man who wins her! With her the least worldly of men would occupy a most brilliant position in society. Don't you think so? I only wanted to know your opinion,' and Anna Pavlovna let Pierre go.

Pierre in reply sincerely agreed with her as to Hélène's perfection of manner. If he ever thought of Hélène it was just of her beauty and her remarkable skill in appearing silently dignified in society.

The old aunt received the two young people in her corner, but seemed desirous of hiding her adoration for Hélène and inclined rather to show her fear of Anna Pavlovna. She looked at her niece as if inquiring what she was to do with these people. On leaving them Anna Pavlovna again touched Pierre's sleeve, saying: 'I hope you won't say that it is dull in my house again,' and she glanced at Hélène.

Hélène smiled, with a look implying that she did not admit the possibility of anyone seeing her without being enchanted. The aunt coughed, swallowed, and said in French that she was very pleased to see Hélène, then she turned to Pierre with the same words of welcome and the same look. In the middle of a dull and halting conversation Hélène turned to Pierre with the beautiful bright smile she gave everyone. Pierre was so used to that smile, and it had so little meaning for him, that he paid no attention to it. The aunt was just speaking of a collection of snuff-boxes that had belonged to Pierre's father, Count Bezukhov, and showed them her own box. Princess Hélène asked to see the portrait of the aunt's husband on the box-lid.

That is probably the work of Vinesse,' said Pierre, mentioning a celebrated miniaturist, and he leant over the table to take the snuff-box while trying to hear what was being said at the other table.

He half rose, meaning to go round, but the aunt handed him the snuff-box, passing it across Hélène's back. Hélène stooped forward to make room, and looked round with a smile. She was, as always at evening parties, wearing a dress such as was then fashionable, cut very low at front and back. Her bust, which had always seemed like marble to Pierre, was so close to him that his short-sighted eyes could not but perceive the living charm of her neck and shoulders, so near to his lips that he need only have bent his head a little to have touched them. He was conscious of the warmth of her body, the scent of perfume, and the creaking of her corset as she moved. He did not see her marble beauty forming a complete whole with her dress, but all the charm of her body only covered by her garments. And having once seen this he could not help being aware of it, just as we cannot renew an illusion we have once seen through.

'So you have never before noticed how beautiful I am?' Hélène seemed to say. 'You had not noticed that I am a woman? Yes, I am a woman who may belong to anyone – to you too,' said her glance. And at that moment Pierre felt that Hélène not only could, but must, be his wife, and that it could not be otherwise.

He knew this at that moment as surely as if he had been standing at the altar with her. How and when this would be he did not know, he did not even know if it would be a good thing (he even felt, he knew not why, that it would be a bad thing) but he knew it would happen.

Pierre dropped his eyes, lifted them again, and wished once more to see her as a distant beauty far removed from him, as he had seen her every day until then, but he could no longer do it. He could not, any more than a man who has been looking at a tuft of steppe grass through the mist and taking it for a tree, can again take it for a tree after he has once recognized it to be a tuft of grass. She was terribly close to him. She already had power over him, and between them there was no longer any barrier, except the barrier of his own will.

'Well, I will leave you in your little corner,' came Anna Pavlovna's voice, 'I see you are all right there.'

And Pierre, anxiously trying to remember whether he had done anything reprehensible, looked round with a blush. It seemed to him that everyone knew what had happened to him as he knew it himself.

A little later when he went up to the large circle, Anna Pavlovna said to him: 'I hear you are refitting your Petersburg house?'

This was true. The architect had told him it was necessary, and Pierre, without knowing why, was having his enormous Petersburg house done up.

'That's a good thing, but don't move from Prince Vasili's. It is good to have a friend like the prince,' she said smiling at Prince Vasili. 'I know something about that. Don't I? And you are still so young. You need advice. Don't be angry with me for exercising an old woman's privilege.'

She paused as women always do, expecting something after they have mentioned their age. 'If you marry it will be a different thing,' she continued, uniting them both in one glance. Pierre did not look at Hélène nor she at him. But she was just as terribly close to him. He muttered something, and coloured.

When he got home he could not sleep for a long time for thinking of what had happened. What had happened? Nothing. He had merely understood that the woman he had known as a child, of whom when her beauty was mentioned he had said absent-mindedly: 'Yes, she's good-looking,' he had understood that this woman might belong to him.

'But she's stupid. I have myself said she is stupid,' he thought. 'There is something nasty, something wrong, in the feeling she excites in me. I have been told that her brother Anatole was in love with her and she with him, that there was quite a scandal and that that's why he was sent away. Hippolyte is her brother . . . Prince Vasili is her father . . . It's bad . . .' he reflected, but while he was thinking this (the reflection was still incomplete) he caught himself smiling and was conscious that another line of thought had sprung up, and while thinking of her worthlessness he was also dreaming of how she would be his wife, how she would love him and become quite different, and how all he had thought and heard of her might be false. And he again saw her not as the daughter of Prince Vasili, but visualized her whole body only veiled by its grey dress. 'But no! Why did this thought never occur to me before?' and again he told himself that it was impossible, that there would be something unnatural, and as it seemed to him dishonourable, in this marriage. He recalled her former words and looks and the words and looks of those who had seen them together. He recalled Anna Pavlovna's words and looks when she spoke to him about his house, recalled thousands of such hints from Prince Vasili and others, and was seized by terror lest he had already in some way bound himself to do something that was evidently wrong, and that he ought not to do. But at the very time he was expressing this conviction to himself, in another part of his mind her image rose in all its womanly beauty.

2

In November 1805 Prince Vasili had to go on a tour of inspection in four different provinces. He had arranged this for himself so as to visit his neglected estates at the same time, and pick up his son Anatole where his regiment was stationed, and take him to visit Prince Nicholas Bolkonsky in order to arrange a match for him with the daughter of that rich old man. But before leaving home and undertaking these new affairs, Prince Vasili had to settle matters with Pierre, who it is true had latterly spent whole days at home, that is in Prince Vasili's house where he was staying, and had been absurd, excited, and foolish in Hélène's presence (as a lover should be) but had not yet proposed to her.

'This is all very fine, but things must be settled,' said Prince Vasili to himself with a sorrowful sigh one morning, feeling that Pierre who was under such obligations to him ('But never mind that') was not behaving very well in this matter. 'Youth, frivolity ... well, God be with him,' thought he, relishing his own goodness of heart, 'but it must be brought to a head. The day after to-morrow will be Lëlya's* nameday. I will invite two or three people, and if he does not understand what he ought to do, then it will be my affair – yes, my affair. I am her father.'

Six weeks after Anna Pavlovna's 'At home' and after the sleepless night when he had decided that to marry Hélène would be a calamity and that he ought to avoid her and go away, Pierre, despite that decision, had not left Prince Vasili's and felt with terror that in people's eyes he was every day more and more connected with her, that it was impossible for him to return to his former conception of her, that he could not break away from her, and that though it would be a terrible thing he would have to unite his fate with hers. He might perhaps have been able to free himself but that Prince Vasili (who had rarely before given receptions) now hardly let a day go by without having an evening party at which Pierre had to be present unless he wished to spoil the general pleasure and disappoint everyone's expectation. Prince Vasili in the rare moments when he was at home, would take Pierre's hand in passing and draw it downwards, or absent-mindedly hold out his wrinkled, clean-shaven cheek for Pierre to kiss, and would say: 'Till to-morrow,' or, 'Be in to dinner or I shall not see you,' or, 'I am staying in for your sake,' and so on. And though Prince Vasili when he stayed in (as he said) for Pierre's sake, hardly exchanged a couple of words with him, Pierre felt unable to disappoint him. Every day he said to himself one and the same thing: 'It is time I understood her and made up my mind what she really is. Was I mistaken before, or am I mistaken now? No, she is not stupid, she is an excellent girl,' he sometimes said to himself, 'she never makes a mistake, never says anything stupid. She says little, but what she does say is always clear and simple, so she is not stupid. She never was abashed and is not abashed now, so she cannot be a bad woman!' He had often begun to make reflections or think aloud in her company, and she had always answered him either by a brief but appropriate remark – showing that it did not interest her – or by a silent look and smile which more palpably than anything else showed Pierre her superiority. She was right in regarding all arguments as nonsense in comparison with that smile.

She always addressed him with a radiantly confiding smile meant for him alone, in which there was something more significant than in the general smile that usually brightened her face. Pierre knew that everyone was waiting for him to say a word and cross a certain line, and he knew that sooner or later he would step across it, but an incomprehensible terror seized him at the thought of that dreadful step. A thousand times during that month and a half while he felt himself drawn nearer and nearer to that dreadful abyss, Pierre said to himself: 'What am I doing? I need resolution. Can it be that I have none?'

He wished to take a decision, but felt with dismay that in this matter he lacked that strength of will which he had known in himself and really possessed. Pierre was one of those who are only strong when they feel themselves quite innocent, and since that day when he was overpowered by a feeling of desire while stooping over the snuff-box at Anna Pavlovna's, an unacknowledged sense of the guilt of that desire paralysed his will.

On Hélène's nameday a small party of just their own people – as his wife said – met for supper at Prince Vasili's. All these friends and relations had been given to understand that the fate of the young girl would be decided that evening. The visitors were seated at supper. Princess Kuragina, a portly imposing woman who had once been handsome, was sitting at the head of the table. On either side of her sat the more important guests – an old general and his wife, and Anna Pavlovna Scherer. At the other end sat the younger and less important guests, and there too sat the members of the family, and Pierre and Hélène side by side. Prince Vasili was not having any supper: he went round the table in a merry mood sitting down now by one now by another of the guests. To each of them he made some careless and agreeable remark except to Pierre and Hélène, whose presence he seemed not to notice. He enlivened the whole party. The wax candles burned brightly, the silver and crystal gleamed, so did the ladies, *toilettes* and the gold and silver of the men's epaulettes; servants in scarlet liveries moved round the table, and the clatter of plates, knives, and glasses, mingled with the animated hum of several conversations. At one end of the table an old chamberlain was heard assuring an old baroness that he loved her passionately at which she laughed; at the other could be heard the story of the misfortunes of some Mary Viktorovna or other. At the centre of the table Prince Vasili attracted everybody's attention. With a facetious smile on his face he was telling the ladies about last Wednesday's meeting of the Imperial Council, at which Sergey Kuzmich Vyazmitinov, the new military governor-general of Petersburg, had received and read the then famous rescript of the Emperor Alexander from the army to Sergey Kuzmich, in which the Emperor said that he was receiving from all sides declarations of the people's loyalty, that the declaration from Petersburg gave him particular pleasure, and that he was proud to be at the head of such a nation and would endeavour to be worthy of it. This rescript began with the words: 'Sergey Kuzmich, From all sides reports reach me,' etc.

'Well, and so he never got farther than: "Sergey Kuzmich"?' asked one of the ladies.

'Exactly, not a hair's breadth farther,' answered Prince Vasili laughing, '"Sergey Kuzmich … From all sides … From all sides … Sergey Kuzmich …" Poor Vyazmitinov could not get any farther. He began the rescript again and again but as soon as he uttered *"Sergey"* he sobbed, *"Kuz-mi-ch"* tears, and *"From all sides"* was smothered in sobs, and he could get no farther. And again his handkerchief, and again: *"Sergey Kuzmich, From all sides,"* . . . and tears, till at last somebody else was asked to read it.'

'Kuzmich . . . From all sides . . . and then tears,' someone repeated laughing.

'Don't be unkind,' cried Anna Pavlovna from her end of the table, holding up a threatening finger. 'He is such a worthy and excellent man, our dear Vyazmitinov . . .'

Everybody laughed a great deal. At the head of the table, where the honoured guests sat, everyone seemed to be in high spirits and under the influence of a variety of exciting sensations. Only Pierre and Hélène sat silently side by side almost at the bottom of the table, a suppressed smile brightening both their faces, a smile that had nothing to do with Sergey Kuzmich – a smile of bashfulness at their own feelings. But much as all the rest laughed, talked, and joked, much as they enjoyed their Rhine wine, *sauté*, and ices, and however they avoided looking at the young couple, and heedless and unobservant as they seemed of them, one could feel by the occasional glances they gave that the story about Sergey Kuzmich, the laughter and the food, were all a pretence, and that the whole attention of that company was directed to – Pierre and Hélène. Prince Vasili mimicked the sobbing of Sergey Kuzmich and at the same time his eyes glanced towards his daughter, and while he laughed the expression on his face clearly said: 'Yes . . . it's getting on, it will all be settled to-day.' Anna Pavlovna threatened him on behalf of 'our dear Vyazmitinov', and in her eyes, which for an instant glanced at Pierre, Prince Vasili read a congratulation on his future son-in-law and on his daughter's happiness. The old princess sighed sadly as she offered some wine to the old lady next to her and glanced angrily at her daughter, and her sigh seemed to say: 'Yes, there's nothing left for you and me but to sip sweet wine, my dear, now that the time has come for these young ones to be thus boldly, provocatively happy.' 'And what nonsense all this is that I am saying!' thought a diplomatist, glancing at the happy faces of the lovers. 'That's happiness!'

Into the insignificant, trifling, and artificial interests uniting that society, had entered the simple feeling of the attraction of a healthy and handsome young man and woman for one another. And this human feeling dominated everything else and soared above all their affected chatter. Jests fell flat, news was not interesting, and the animation was evidently forced. Not only the guests but even the footmen waiting at table seemed to feel this, and they forgot their duties as they looked at the beautiful Hélène with her radiant face and at the red, broad, and happy though uneasy face of Pierre. It seemed as if the very light of the candles was focused on those two happy faces alone.

Pierre felt that he was the centre of it all, and this both pleased and embarrassed him. He was like a man entirely absorbed in some occupation. He did not see, hear, or understand anything clearly. Only now and then detached ideas and impressions from the world of reality shot unexpectedly through his mind.

'So it is all finished!' he thought, 'And how has it all happened? How quickly! Now I know that not because of her alone, nor of myself alone, but because of everyone, it must inevitably come about. They are all expecting it, they are so sure that it will happen that I cannot, I cannot, disappoint them. But how will it be? I do not know, but it will certainly happen!' thought Pierre, glancing at those dazzling shoulders close to his eyes.

Or he would suddenly feel ashamed of he knew not what. He felt it awkward to attract everyone's attention and to be considered a lucky man and, with his plain face, to be looked on as a sort of Paris possessed of a Helen. 'But no doubt it always is and must be so!' he consoled himself. 'And besides, what have I done to bring it about? How did it begin? I travelled from Moscow with Prince Vasili. Then there was nothing. So why should I not stay at his house? Then I played cards with her and picked up her reticule and drove out with her. How did it begin, when did it all come about?' And here he was sitting by her side as her betrothed, seeing, hearing, feeling her nearness, her breathing, her movements, her beauty. Then it would suddenly seem to him that it was not she but he who was so unusually beautiful, and that that was why they all looked so at him, and flattered by this general admiration he would expand his chest, raise his head, and rejoice at his good fortune. Suddenly he heard a familiar voice repeating something to him a second time. But Pierre was so absorbed that he did not understand what was said.

'I am asking you when you last heard from Bolkonsky,' repeated Prince Vasili a third time. 'How absent-minded you are, my dear fellow.'

Prince Vasili smiled, and Pierre noticed that everyone was smiling at him and Hélène. 'Well what of it, if you all know it?' thought Pierre. 'What of it? It's the truth!' and he himself smiled his gentle childlike smile, and Hélène smiled too.

'When did you get the letter? Was it from Olmütz?' repeated Prince Vasili, who pretended to want to know this in order to settle a dispute.

'How can one talk or think of such trifles?' thought Pierre.

'Yes, from Olmütz,' he answered with a sigh.

After supper Pierre with his partner followed the others into the drawing-room. The guests began to disperse, some without taking leave of Hélène. Some as if unwilling to distract her from an important occupation, came up to her for a moment and made haste to go away, refusing to let her see them off. The diplomatist preserved a mournful silence as he left the drawing-room. He pictured the vanity of his diplomatic career in comparison with Pierre's happiness. The old general grumbled at his wife when she asked how his leg was. 'Oh, the old fool,' he thought. 'That Princess Hélène will be beautiful still when she's fifty.'

'I think I may congratulate you,' whispered Anna Pavlovna to the old princess, kissing her soundly. 'If I hadn't this headache I'd have stayed longer.'

The old princess did not reply, she was tormented by jealousy of her daughter's happiness.

While the guests were taking their leave Pierre remained for a long time alone with Hélène in the little drawing-room where they were sitting. He had often before, during the last six weeks, remained alone with her, but had never spoken to her of love. Now he felt that it was inevitable, but he could not make up his mind to take the final step. He felt ashamed; he felt that he was occupying someone else's place here beside Hélène. 'This happiness is not for you,' some inner voice whispered to him. 'This happiness is for those who have not in them what there is in you.'

But as he had to say something, he began by asking her whether she was satisfied with the party. She replied in her usual simple manner that this name-day of hers had been one of the pleasantest she had ever had.

Some of the nearest relatives had not yet left. They were sitting in the large drawing-room. Prince Vasili came up to Pierre with languid footsteps. Pierre rose, and said it was getting late. Prince Vasili gave him a look of stern inquiry, as though what Pierre had just said was so strange that one could not take it in. But then the expression of severity changed and he drew Pierre's hand downwards, made him sit down, and smiled affectionately.

'Well, Lëlya?' he asked, turning instantly to his daughter and addressing her with the careless tone of habitual tenderness natural to parents who have petted their children from babyhood, but which Prince Vasili had only acquired by imitating other parents.

And he again turned to Pierre.

'Sergey Kuzmich – from all sides—,' he said unbuttoning the top button of his waistcoat.

Pierre smiled, but his smile showed that he knew it was not the story about Sergey Kuzmich that interested Prince Vasili just then, and Prince Vasili saw that Pierre knew this. He suddenly muttered something and went away. It seemed to Pierre that even the prince was disconcerted. The sight of the discomposure of that old man of the world touched Pierre: he looked at Hélène and she too seemed disconcerted, and her look seemed to say: 'Well, it is your own fault.'

'The step must be taken but I cannot, I cannot!' thought Pierre, and he again began speaking about indifferent matters, about Sergey Kuzmich, asking what the point of the story was as he had not heard it properly. Hélène answered with a smile that she too had missed it.

When Prince Vasili returned to the drawing-room the princess, his wife, was talking in low tones to the elderly lady about Pierre.

'Of course it is a very brilliant match, but happiness, my dear . . .'

'Marriages are made in heaven,' replied the elderly lady.

Prince Vasili passed by, seeming not to hear the ladies, and sat down on a sofa in a far corner of the room. He closed his eyes and seemed to be dozing. His head sank forward and then he roused himself.

'Aline,' he said to his wife, 'go and see what they are about.'

The princess went up to the door, passed by it with a dignified and indifferent air and glanced into the little drawing-room. Pierre and Hélène still sat talking just as before.

'Still the same,' she said to her husband.

Prince Vasili frowned, twisting his mouth, his cheeks quivered and his face assumed the coarse unpleasant expression peculiar to him. Shaking himself, he rose, threw back his head and with resolute steps went past the ladies into the little drawing-room. With quick steps he went joyfully up to Pierre. His face was so unusually triumphant that Pierre rose in alarm on seeing it.

'Thank God!' said Prince Vasili. 'My wife has told me everything!' – (He put one arm around Pierre and the other around his daughter.) – 'My dear boy . . . Lëlya . . . I am very pleased.' (His voice trembled.) 'I loved your father . . . and she will make you a good wife . . . God bless you! . . .'

He embraced his daughter, and then again Pierre, and kissed him with his malodorous mouth. Tears actually moistened his cheeks.

'Princess, come here!' he shouted.

The old princess came in, and also wept. The elderly lady was using her handkerchief too. Pierre was kissed, and he kissed the beautiful Hélène's hand several times. After a while they were left alone again.

'All this had to be and could not be otherwise,' thought Pierre, 'so it is useless to ask whether it is good or bad. It is good because it's definite and one is rid of the old tormenting doubt.' Pierre held the hand of his betrothed in silence, looking at her beautiful bosom as it rose and fell.

'Hélène!' he said aloud and paused.

'Something special is always said in such cases,' he thought, but could not remember what it was that people say. He looked at her face. She drew nearer to him. Her face flushed.

'Oh, take those off . . . those . . .' she said pointing to his spectacles.

Pierre took them off, and his eyes besides the strange look eyes have from which spectacles have just been removed, had also a frightened and inquiring look. He was about to stoop over her hand and kiss it, but with a rapid, almost brutal movement of her head she intercepted his lips and met them with her own. Her face struck Pierre by its altered, unpleasantly excited expression.

'It is too late now, it's done; besides I love her,' thought Pierre.

'*Je vous aime!*' he said, remembering what has to be said at such moments: but his words sounded so weak that he felt ashamed of himself.

Six weeks later he was married, and settled in Count Bezukhov's large newly-furnished, Petersburg house, the happy possessor, as people said, of a wife who was a celebrated beauty, and of millions of money.

3

OLD Prince Nicholas Bolkonsky received a letter from Prince Vasili in November 1805 announcing that he and his son would be paying him a visit. 'I am starting on a journey of inspection, and of course I shall think nothing of an extra seventy miles to come and see you at the same time, my honoured benefactor,' wrote Prince Vasili. 'My son Anatole is accompanying me on his way to the army, so I hope you will allow him personally to express the deep respect that, emulating his father, he feels for you.'

'It seems there will be no need to bring Mary out, suitors are coming to us of their own accord,' incautiously remarked the little princess on hearing the news.

Prince Nicholas frowned, but said nothing.

A fortnight after the letter Prince Vasili's servants came one evening in advance of him, and he and his son arrived next day.

Old Bolkonsky had always had a poor opinion of Prince Vasili's character, but more so recently, since in the new reigns of Paul and Alexander Prince Vasili had risen to high position and honours. And now from the hints contained in his letter and given by the little princess, he saw which way the wind was blowing, and his low opinion changed into a feeling of contemptuous ill will. He snorted whenever he mentioned him. On the day of Prince Vasili's arrival Prince Bolkonsky was particularly discontented and out of temper. Whether he was in a bad temper because Prince Vasili was coming, or whether his being in a bad temper made him specially annoyed at Prince Vasili's visit, he was in a bad temper, and in the morning Tikhon had already advised the architect not to go to the prince with his report.

'Do you hear how he's walking?' said Tikhon, drawing the architect's attention to the sound of the prince's footsteps. 'Stepping flat on his heels – we know what that means . . .'

However, at nine o'clock the prince, in his velvet coat with a sable collar and cap, went out for his usual walk. It had snowed the day before and the path to the hot-house, along which the prince was in the habit of walking, had been swept: the marks of the broom were still visible in the snow and a shovel had been left sticking in one of the soft snow banks that bordered both sides of the path. The prince went through the conservatories, the serfs' quarters, and the out-buildings, frowning and silent.

'Can a sledge pass?' he asked his overseer, a venerable man resembling his master in manners and looks, who was accompanying him back to the house.

'The snow is deep. I am having the avenue swept, your honour.'

The prince bowed his head and went up to the porch. 'God be thanked,' thought the overseer, 'the storm has blown over!'

'It would have been hard to drive up, your honour,' he added. 'I heard, your honour, that a minister is coming to visit your honour.'

The prince turned round to the overseer and fixed his eyes on him frowning.

'What? A minister? What minister? Who gave orders?' he said in his shrill harsh voice. 'The road is not swept for the princess, my daughter, but for a minister! For me there are no ministers!'

'Your honour, I thought . . .'

'You thought!' shouted the prince, his words coming more and more rapidly and indistinctly. 'You thought! . . . Rascals! Blackguards! . . . I'll teach you to think!' and lifting his stick he swung it and would have hit Alpatych, the overseer, had not the latter instinctively avoided the blow. 'Thought ... Blackguards ...' shouted the prince rapidly.

But although Alpatych, frightened at his own temerity in avoiding the stroke, came up to the prince bowing his bald head resignedly before him, or perhaps for that very reason, the prince, though he continued to shout: 'Blackguards! ... Throw the snow back on the road!' did not lift his stick again but hurried into the house.

Before dinner Princess Mary and Mademoiselle Bourienne, who knew that the prince was in a bad humour, stood awaiting him; Mademoiselle Bourienne with a radiant face that said: 'I know nothing, I am the same as usual,' and Princess Mary, pale, frightened and with downcast eyes. What she found hardest to bear was to know that on such occasions she ought to behave like Mademoiselle Bourienne, but could not. She thought: 'If I seem not to notice he will think that I do not sympathize with him; if I seem sad and out of spirits myself, he will say (as he has done before) that I'm in the dumps.'

The prince looked at his daughter's frightened face and snorted.

'Fool ... or dummy!' he muttered.

'And the other one is not here. They've been telling tales,' he thought – referring to the little princess who was not in the dining-room.

'Where is the princess?' he asked. 'Hiding?'

'She is not very well,' answered Mademoiselle Bourienne with a bright smile, 'she won't come down. It is natural in her state.'

'Hm! Hm!' muttered the prince sitting down.

His plate seemed to him not quite clean, and pointing to a spot he flung it away. Tikhon caught it and handed it to a footman. The little princess was not unwell, but had such an overpowering fear of the prince that, hearing he was in a bad humour, she had decided not to appear.

'I am afraid for the baby,' she said to Mademoiselle Bourienne: 'Heaven knows what a fright might do.'

In general at Bald Hills the little princess lived in constant fear, and with a sense of antipathy to the old prince which she did not realize because the fear was so much the stronger feeling. The prince reciprocated this antipathy, but it was overpowered by his contempt for her. When the little princess had grown accustomed to life at Bald Hills, she took a special fancy to Mademoiselle Bourienne, spent whole days with her, asked her to sleep in her room, and often talked with her about the old prince and criticized him.

'So we are to have visitors, *mon prince?*' remarked Mademoiselle Bourienne, unfolding her white napkin with her rosy fingers. 'His Excellency Prince Vasili Kuragin and his son, I understand?' she said inquiringly.

'Hm! – his Excellency is a puppy ... I got him his appointment in the service,' said the prince disdainfully. 'Why his son is coming I don't understand. Perhaps Princess Elizabeth and Princess Mary know. I don't know why he brings his son here. I don't want him.' (He looked at his blushing daughter.) 'Are you unwell to-day? Eh? Afraid of the "minister" as that idiot Alpatych called him this morning?'

'No, *mon père.*'

Though Mademoiselle Bourienne had been so unsuccessful in her choice of a subject she did not stop talking, but chattered about the conservatories, and the beauty of a flower that had just opened, and after the soup the prince became more genial.

After dinner he went to see his daughter-in-law. The little princess was sitting at a small table chattering with Masha, her maid. She grew pale on seeing her father-in-law.

She was much altered. She was now plain rather than pretty. Her cheeks had sunk, her lip was drawn up, and her eyes drawn down.

'Yes, I feel a kind of oppression,' she said in reply to the prince's question as to how she felt.

'Do you want anything?'

'No, *merci, mon père.*'

'Well, all right, all right.'

He left the room and went to the waiting-room, where Alpatych stood with bowed head.

'Has the snow been shovelled back?'

'Yes, your Excellency. Forgive me for heaven's sake ... It was only my stupidity.'

'All right, all right,' interrupted the prince, and laughing in his unnatural way he stretched out his hand for Alpatych to kiss and then proceeded to his study.

Prince Vasili arrived that evening. He was met in the avenue by coachmen and footmen, who with loud shouts dragged his sledges up to one of the lodges over the road purposely laden with snow.

Prince Vasili and Anatole had separate rooms assigned to them.

Anatole having taken off his overcoat, sat with arms akimbo before a table on a corner of which he smilingly and absent-mindedly fixed his large and handsome eyes. He regarded his whole life as a continual round of amusement which someone for some reason had to provide for him. And he looked on this visit to a churlish old man and a rich and ugly heiress in the same way. All this might, he thought, turn out very well and amusingly. 'And why not marry her if she really has so much money? That never does any harm,' thought Anatole.

He shaved and scented himself with the care and elegance which had become habitual to him, and his handsome head held high, entered his father's room with the good-humoured and victorious air natural to him. Prince Vasili's two valets were busy dressing him, and he looked round with much animation and cheerfully nodded to his son as the latter entered, as if to say: 'Yes, that's how I want you to look.'

'I say, father, joking apart, is she very hideous?' Anatole asked, as if continuing a conversation the subject of which had often been mentioned during the journey.

'Enough! What nonsense! Above all, try to be respectful and cautious with the old prince.'

'If he starts a row I'll go away,' said Prince Anatole. 'I can't bear those old men! Eh?'

'Remember, for you everything depends on this.'

In the meantime not only was it known in the maidservants' rooms that the minister and his son had arrived, but the appearance of both had been minutely described. Princess Mary was sitting alone in her room vainly trying to master her agitation.

'Why did they write, why did Lise tell me about it? It can never happen!' she said looking at herself in the glass. 'How shall I enter the drawing-room? Even if I like him I can't now be myself with him.' The mere thought of her father's look filled her with terror. The little princess and Mademoiselle Bourienne had already received from Masha, the lady's maid, the necessary report of how handsome the minister's son was, with his rosy cheeks and dark eyebrows, and with what difficulty the father had dragged his legs upstairs while the son had followed him like an eagle, three steps at a time. Having received this information the little princess and Mademoiselle Bourienne, whose chattering voices had reached her from the corridor, went into Princess Mary's room.

'You know they've come, Marie?' said the little princess, waddling in, and sinking heavily into an arm-chair.

She was no longer in the loose gown she generally wore in the morning, but had on one of her best dresses. Her hair was carefully done and her face was animated, which, however, did not conceal its sunken and faded outlines. Dressed as she used to be in Petersburg society, it was still more noticeable how much plainer she had become. Some unobtrusive touch had been added to Mademoiselle

Bourienne's toilette which rendered her fresh and pretty face yet more attractive.

'What! Are you going to remain as you are, dear princess?' she began. 'They'll be announcing that the gentlemen are in the drawing-room and we shall have to go down, and you have not smartened yourself up at all!'

The little princess got up, rang for the maid, and hurriedly and merrily began to devise and carry out a plan of how Princess Mary should be dressed. Princess Mary's self-esteem was wounded by the fact that the arrival of a suitor agitated her, and still more so by both her companions not having the least conception that it could be otherwise. To tell them that she felt ashamed for herself and for them would be to betray her agitation, while to decline their offers to dress her would prolong their banter and insistence. She flushed, her beautiful eyes grew dim, red blotches came on her face and it took on the unattractive martyr-like expression it so often wore, as she submitted herself to Mademoiselle Bourienne and Lise. Both these women *quite sincerely* tried to make her look pretty. She was so plain that neither of them could think of her as a rival, so they began dressing her with perfect sincerity, and with the naïve and firm conviction women have that dress can make a face pretty.

'No really, my dear, this dress is not pretty,' said Lise, looking sideways at Princess Mary from a little distance. 'You have a maroon dress, have it fetched. Really! You know the fate of your whole life may be at stake. But this one is too light, it's not becoming!'

It was not the dress, but the face and whole figure of Princess Mary that was not pretty, but neither Mademoiselle Bourienne nor the little princess felt this, they still thought that if a blue ribbon were placed in the hair, the hair combed up, and the blue scarf arranged lower on the best maroon dress, and so on, all would be well. They forgot that the frightened face and the figure could not be altered, and that however they might change the setting and adornment of that face it would still remain piteous and plain. After two or three changes to which Princess Mary meekly submitted, just as her hair had been arranged on the top of her head (a style that quite altered and spoilt her looks) and she had put on a maroon dress with a pale-blue scarf, the little princess walked twice round her, now adjusting a fold of the dress with her little hand, now arranging the scarf and looking at her with her head bent first on one side and then on the other.

'No, it will not do,' she said decidedly, clasping her hands. 'No, Mary, really this dress does not suit you. I prefer you in your little grey everyday dress. Now please, do it for my sake. Katie,' she said to the maid, 'bring the princess her grey dress, and you'll see, Mademoiselle Bourienne, how I shall arrange it,' she added, smiling with a foretaste of artistic pleasure.

But when Katie brought the required dress Princess Mary remained sitting motionless before the glass looking at her face, and saw in the mirror her eyes full of tears and her mouth quivering, ready to burst into sobs.

'Come, dear princess,' said Mademoiselle Bourienne, 'just one more little effort.'

The little princess, taking the dress from the maid, came up to Princess Mary.

'Well, now we'll arrange something quite simple and becoming,' she said.

The three voices, hers, Mademoiselle Bourienne's, and Katie's who was laughing at something, mingled in a merry sound like the chirping of birds.

'No, leave me alone,' said Princess Mary.

Her voice sounded so serious and so sad that the chirping of the birds was silenced at once. They looked at the beautiful, large, thoughtful eyes full of tears and of thoughts, gazing shiningly and imploringly at them, and understood that it was useless and even cruel to insist.

'At least, change your coiffure,' said the little princess. 'Didn't I tell you,' she went on, turning reproachfully to Mademoiselle Bourienne, 'Mary's is a face which such a coiffure does not suit in the least. Not in the least! Please change it.'

'Leave me alone, please leave me alone! It is all quite the same to me,' answered a voice struggling with tears.

Mademoiselle Bourienne and the little princess had to own to themselves that Princess Mary in this guise looked very plain, worse than usual, but it was too late. She was looking at them with an expression they both knew, an expression thoughtful and sad. This expression in Princess Mary did not frighten them (she never inspired fear in anyone) but they knew that when it appeared on her face she became mute and was not to be shaken in her determination.

'You will change it, won't you?' said Lise. And as Princess Mary gave no answer she left the room.

Princess Mary was left alone. She did not comply with Lise's request, she not only left her hair as it was but did not even look in her glass. Letting her arms fall helplessly she sat with downcast eyes and pondered. A husband, a man, a strong dominant and strangely attractive being rose in her imagination, and carried her into a totally different happy world of his own. She fancied a child, *her own* – such as she had seen the day before in the arms of her nurse's daughter – at her own breast, the husband standing by and gazing tenderly at her and the child. 'But no, it is impossible, I am too ugly,' she thought.

'Please come to tea. The prince will be out in a moment,' came the maid's voice at the door.

She roused herself, and felt appalled at what she had been thinking, and before going down she went into the room where the icons hung and, her eyes fixed on the dark face of a large icon of the Saviour lit up by a lamp, she stood before it with folded hands for a few moments. A painful doubt filled her soul. Could the joy of love, of earthly love for a man, be for her? In her thoughts of marriage Princess Mary dreamed of happiness and of children, but her strongest most deeply-hidden longing was for earthly love. The more she tried to hide this feeling from others and even from herself, the stronger it grew. 'O God,' she said, 'how am I to stifle in my heart these temptations of the devil? How am I to renounce for ever these vile fancies, so as peacefully to fulfil Thy will?' And scarcely had she put that question than God gave her the answer in her own heart. 'Desire nothing for thyself, seek nothing, be not anxious or envious. Man's future and thy own fate must remain hidden from thee, but live so that thou mayest be ready for anything. If it be God's will to prove thee in the duties of marriage, be ready to fulfil His will.' With this consoling thought (but yet with a hope for the fulfilment of her forbidden earthly longing) Princess Mary sighed, and having crossed herself went down, thinking neither of her gown and coiffure nor of how she would go in nor of what she would say. What could all that matter in comparison with the will of God, without Whose care not a hair of man's head can fall?

4

When Princess Mary came down, Prince Vasili and his son were already in the drawing-room talking to the little princess and Mademoiselle Bourienne. When she entered with her heavy step, treading on her heels, the gentlemen and Mademoiselle Bourienne rose and the little princess, indicating her to the gentlemen, said: '*Voilà Marie!*' Princess Mary saw them all and saw them in detail. She saw Prince Vasili's face, serious for an instant at the sight of her, but immediately smiling again, and the little princess curiously noting the impression 'Marie' produced on the visitors.

And she saw Mademoiselle Bourienne with her ribbon and pretty face and her unusually animated look which was fixed on *him*, but *him* she could not see, she only saw something large, brilliant and handsome moving towards her as she entered the room. Prince Vasili approached first, and she kissed the bold forehead that bent over her hand and answered his question by saying that, on the contrary, she remembered him quite well. Then Anatole came up to her. She still could not see him. She only felt a soft hand taking hers firmly, and she touched with her lips a white forehead over which was beautiful light-brown hair smelling of pomade. When she looked up at him she was struck by his beauty. Anatole stood with his right thumb under a button of his uniform, his chest expanded and his back drawn in, slightly swinging one foot and, with his head a little bent, looked with beaming face at the princess without speaking and evidently not thinking about her at all. Anatole was not quick-witted, not ready or eloquent in conversation, but he had the faculty, so invaluable in society, of composure and imperturbable self-possession. If a man lacking in self-confidence remains dumb on a first introduction and betrays a consciousness of the impropriety of such silence and an anxiety to find something to say, the effect is bad. But Anatole was dumb, swung his foot, and smilingly examined the princess's hair. It was evident that he could be silent in this way for a very long time. 'If anyone finds this silence inconvenient, let him talk, but I don't want to,' he seemed to say. Besides this, in his behaviour to women Anatole had a manner which particularly inspired in them curiosity, awe, and even love – a supercilious consciousness of his own superiority. It was as if he said to them: 'I know you, I know you, but why should I bother about you? You'd be only too glad, of course.' Perhaps he did not really think this when he met women – even probably he did not, for in general he thought very little – but his looks and manner gave that impression. The princess felt this, and as if wishing to show him that she did not even dare expect to interest him, she turned to his father. The conversation was general and animated, thanks to Princess Lise's voice and little downy lip that lifted over her white teeth. She met Prince Vasili with that playful manner often employed by lively chatty people, and consisting in the assumption that between the person they so address and themselves there are some semi-private long-established jokes and amusing reminiscences, though no such reminiscences really exist – just as none existed in this case. Prince Vasili readily adopted her tone and the little princess also drew Anatole, whom she hardly knew, into these amusing recollections of things that had never occurred. Mademoiselle Bourienne also shared them and even Princess Mary felt herself pleasantly made to share in these merry reminiscences.

'Here at least we shall have the benefit of your company all to ourselves, dear Prince,' said the little princess (of course in French) to Prince Vasili. 'It's not as at Annette's receptions where you always ran away; you remember *cette chère Annette*!'

'Ah, but you won't talk politics to me like Annette!'

'And our little tea-table?'

'Oh, yes!'

'Why is it you were never at Annette's?' the little princess asked Anatole. 'Ah, I know, I know,' she said with a sly glance, 'your brother Hippolyte told me about your goings on. Oh!' and she shook her finger at him, 'I have even heard of your doings in Paris!'

'And didn't Hippolyte tell you?' asked Prince Vasili, turning to his son and seizing the little princess's arm as if she would have run away and he had just managed to catch her, 'didn't he tell you how he himself was pining for the dear princess, and how she showed him the door? Oh, she is a pearl among women, Princess,' he added, turning to Princess Mary.

When Paris was mentioned, Mademoiselle Bourienne for her part seized the opportunity of joining in the general current of recollections.

She took the liberty of inquiring whether it was long since Anatole had left Paris and how he had liked that city. Anatole answered the Frenchwoman very readily, and looking at her with a smile talked to her about her native land. When he saw the pretty little Bourienne, Anatole came to the conclusion that he would not find Bald Hills dull either. 'Not at all bad!' he thought, examining her, 'not at all bad, that little companion! I hope she will bring her along with her when we're married, *la petite est gentille*.'

The old prince dressed leisurely in his study, frowning and considering what he was to do. The coming of these visitors annoyed him. 'What are Prince Vasili and that son of his to me? Prince Vasili is a shallow braggart and his son, no doubt, is a fine specimen,' he grumbled to himself. What angered him was that the coming of these visitors revived in his mind an unsettled question he always tried to stifle, one about which he always deceived himself. The question was whether he could ever bring himself to part from his daughter and give her to a husband. The prince never directly asked himself that question, knowing beforehand that he would have to answer it justly, and justice clashed not only with his feelings but with the very possibility of life. Life without Princess Mary, little as he seemed to value her, was unthinkable to him. 'And why should she marry?' he thought. 'To be unhappy for certain. There's Lise, married to Andrew – a better husband one would think could hardly be found nowadays – but is she contented with her lot? And who would marry Marie for love? Plain and awkward! They'll take her for her connexions and wealth. Are there no women living unmarried, and even the happier for it?' So thought Prince Bolkonsky while dressing, and yet the question he was always putting off demanded an immediate answer. Prince Vasili had brought his son with the evident intention of proposing, and to-day or to-morrow he would probably ask for an answer. His birth and position in society were not bad. 'Well, I've nothing against it,' the prince said to himself, 'but he must be worthy of her. And that is what we shall see.'

'That is what we shall see! That is what we shall see!' he added aloud.

He entered the drawing-room with his usual alert step, glancing rapidly round the company. He noticed the change in the little princess's dress, Mademoiselle Bourienne's ribbon, Princess Mary's unbecoming coiffure, Mademoiselle Bourienne's and Anatole's smiles, and the loneliness of his daughter amid the general conversation. 'Got herself up like a fool!' he thought, looking irritably at her. 'She is shameless, and he ignores her!'

He went straight up to Prince Vasili.

'Well! How d'ye do? How d'ye do? Glad to see you!'

'Friendship laughs at distance,' began Prince Vasili in his usual rapid, self-confident, familiar tone. 'Here is my second son; please love and befriend him.'

Prince Bolkonsky surveyed Anatole.

'Fine young fellow! Fine young fellow!' he said. 'Well, come and kiss me,' and he offered his cheek.

Anatole kissed the old man, and looked at him with curiosity and perfect composure, waiting for a display of the eccentricities his father had told him to expect.

Prince Bolkonsky sat down in his usual place in the corner of the sofa, and drawing up an arm-chair for Prince Vasili pointed to it and began questioning him about political affairs and news. He seemed to listen attentively to what Prince Vasili said, but kept glancing at Princess Mary.

'And so they are writing from Potsdam already?' he said, repeating Prince Vasili's last words. Then rising he suddenly went up to his daughter.

'Is it for visitors you've got yourself up like that, eh?' said he. 'Fine, very fine! You have done up your hair in this new way for the visitors, and before the visitors I tell you that in future you are never to dare to change your way of dress without my consent.'

'It was my fault, *mon père*,' interceded the little princess with a blush.

'*You* must do as you please,' said Prince Bolkonsky, bowing to his daughter-in-law, 'but she need not make a guy of herself, she's plain enough as it is.'

And he sat down again, paying no more attention to his daughter who was reduced to tears.

'On the contrary that coiffure suits the princess very well,' said Prince Vasili.

'Now you, young Prince, what's your name?' said Prince Bolkonsky turning to Anatole, 'come here, let us talk and get acquainted.'

'Now the fun begins,' thought Anatole, sitting down with a smile beside the old prince.

'Well, my dear boy, I hear you've been educated abroad, not taught to read and write by the deacon like your father and me. Now tell me, my dear boy, are you serving in the Horse Guards?' asked the old man, scrutinizing Anatole closely and intently.

'No, I have been transferred to the line,' said Anatole hardly able to restrain his laughter.

'Ah! That's a good thing. So, my dear boy, you wish to serve the Tsar and the country? It is war time. Such a fine fellow must serve. Well, are you off to the front?'

'No, Prince, our regiment has gone to the front, but I am attached . . . what is it I am attached to, papa?' said Anatole, turning to his father with a laugh.

'A splendid soldier, splendid! "What am I attached to!" Ha, ha, ha!' laughed Prince Bolkonsky, and Anatole laughed still louder. Suddenly Prince Bolkonsky frowned.

'You may go,' he said to Anatole.

Anatole returned smiling to the ladies.

'And so you've had him educated abroad, Prince Vasili, haven't you?' said the old prince to Prince Vasili.

'I have done my best for him, and I can assure you the education there is much better than ours.'

'Yes, everything is different nowadays, everything is changed. The lad's a fine fellow, a fine fellow! Well, come with me now.' He took Prince Vasili's arm and led him to his study. As soon as they were alone together Prince Vasili announced his hopes and wishes to the old prince.

'Well, do you think I shall prevent her, that I can't part from

234

her?' said the old prince angrily. 'What an idea! I'm ready for it to-morrow! Only let me tell you, I want to know my son-in-law better. You know my principles – everything above-board! I will ask her to-morrow in your presence; if she is willing, then he can stay on. He can stay and I'll see.' The old prince snorted. 'Let her marry, it's all the same to me!' he screamed in the same piercing tone as when parting from his son.

'I will tell you frankly,' said Prince Vasili in the tone of a crafty man convinced of the futility of being cunning with so keen-sighted a companion. 'You know, you see right through people. Anatole is no genius, but he is an honest, good-hearted lad; an excellent son or kinsman.'

'All right, all right, we'll see!'

As always happens when women lead lonely lives for any length of time without male society, on Anatole's appearance all the three women of Prince Bolkonsky's household felt that their life had not been real till then. Their powers of reasoning, feeling, and observing, immediately increased tenfold, and their life, which seemed to have been passed in darkness, was suddenly lit up by a new brightness full of significance.

Princess Mary grew quite unconscious of her face and coiffure. The handsome open face of the man who might perhaps be her husband absorbed all her attention. He seemed to her kind, brave, determined, manly, and magnanimous. She felt convinced of that. Thousands of dreams of a future family life continually rose in her imagination. She drove them away and tried to conceal them.

'But am I not too cold with him?' thought the princess. 'I try to be reserved because in the depth of my soul I feel too near to him already, but then he cannot know what I think of him and may imagine that I do not like him.'

And Princess Mary tried, but could not manage, to be cordial to her new guest. 'Poor girl, she's devilish ugly!' thought Anatole.

Mademoiselle Bourienne, also roused to great excitement by Anatole's arrival, thought in another way. Of course she, a handsome young woman without any definite position, without relations or even a country, did not intend to devote her life to serving Prince Bolkonsky, to reading aloud to him and being friends with Princess Mary. Mademoiselle Bourienne had long been waiting for a Russian prince who, able to appreciate at a glance her superiority to the plain, badly dressed, ungainly Russian princesses, would fall in love with her and carry her off; and here at last was the Russian prince. Mademoiselle Bourienne knew a story, heard from her aunt but finished in her own way, which she liked to repeat to herself. It was the story of a girl who had been seduced, and to whom her poor mother (*sa pauvre mère*) appeared, and reproached her for yielding to a man without being married. Mademoiselle Bourienne was often touched to tears as in imagination she told this story to *him*, her seducer. And now *he*, a real Russian prince, had appeared. He would carry her away and then *sa pauvre mère* would appear and he would marry her. So her future shaped itself in Mademoiselle Bourienne's head at the very time she was talking to Anatole about Paris. It was not calculation that guided her (she did not even for a moment consider what she should do) but all this had long been familiar to her, and now that Anatole had appeared it just grouped itself around him and she wished and tried to please him as much as possible.

The little princess, like an old war-horse that hears the trumpet, unconsciously and quite forgetting her condition prepared for the familiar gallop of coquetry, without any ulterior motive or any struggle but with naïve and light-hearted gaiety.

Although in female society Anatole usually assumed the role of a man tired of being run after by women, his vanity was flattered by the spectacle of his power over these three women. Besides that he was beginning to feel for the pretty and provocative Mademoiselle Bourienne that passionate animal feeling which was apt to master him with great suddenness and prompt him to the coarsest and most reckless actions.

After tea the company went into the sitting-room and Princess Mary was asked to play on the clavichord. Anatole laughing and in high spirits, came and leaned on his elbow, facing her and beside Mademoiselle Bourienne. Princess Mary felt his look with a painfully joyous emotion. Her favourite sonata bore her into a most intimately poetic world, and the look she felt upon her made that world still more poetic. But Anatole's expression, though his eyes were fixed on her, referred not to her but to the movements of Mademoiselle Bourienne's little foot, which he was then touching with his own under the clavichord. Mademoiselle Bourienne was also looking at Princess Mary, and in her lovely eyes there was a look of fearful joy and hope that was also new to the princess.

'How she loves me!' thought Princess Mary. 'How happy I am now, and how happy I may be with such a friend and such a husband! Husband? Can it be possible?' she thought, not daring to look at his face, but still feeling his eyes gazing at her.

In the evening after supper when all were about to retire, Anatole kissed Princess Mary's hand. She did not know how she found the courage, but she looked straight into his handsome face as it came near to her short-sighted eyes. Turning from Princess

Mary he went up and kissed Mademoiselle Bourienne's hand. (This was not etiquette, but then he did everything so simply and with such assurance!) Mademoiselle Bourienne flushed, and gave the princess a frightened look.

'What delicacy!' thought the princess. 'Is it possible that Amélie' (Mademoiselle Bourienne) 'thinks I could be jealous of her, and not value her pure affection and devotion to me?' She went up to her and kissed her warmly. Anatole went up to kiss the little princess's hand.

'No! No! No! When your father writes to tell me that you are behaving well I will give you my hand to kiss. Not till then!' she said. And smilingly raising a finger at him she left the room.

5

THEY all separated, but except Anatole who fell asleep as soon as he got into bed, all kept awake a long time that night.

'Is he really to be my husband, this stranger who is so kind – yes, kind, that is the chief thing,' thought Princess Mary, and fear, which she had seldom experienced, came upon her. She feared to look round, it seemed to her that someone was there standing behind the screen in the dark corner. And this someone was *he* – the devil – and *he* was also this man with the white forehead, black eyebrows, and red lips.

She rang for her maid, and asked her to sleep in her room.

Mademoiselle Bourienne walked up and down the conservatory for a long time that evening vainly expecting someone, now smiling at someone, now working herself up to tears with the imaginary words of her *pauvre mère* rebuking her for her fall.

The little princess grumbled to her maid that her bed was badly made. She could not lie either on her face or on her side. Every position was awkward and uncomfortable, and her burden oppressed her now more than ever because Anatole's presence had vividly recalled to her the time when she was not like that, and when everything was light and gay. She sat in an arm-chair in her dressing jacket and night-cap, and Katie, sleepy and dishevelled, beat and turned the heavy feather-bed for the third time, muttering to herself.

'I told you it was all lumps and holes!' the little princess repeated. 'I should be glad enough to fall asleep, so it's not my fault!' and her voice quivered like that of a child about to cry.

The old prince did not sleep either. Tikhon, half asleep, heard him pacing angrily about and snorting. The old prince felt as though he had been insulted through his daughter. The insult was the more pointed because it concerned not himself but another, his daughter, whom he loved more than himself. He kept telling himself that he would consider the whole matter and decide what was right and how he should act, but instead of that he only excited himself more and more.

'The first man that turns up – she forgets her father and everything else, runs upstairs and does up her hair and wags her tail and is unlike herself! Glad to throw her father over! And she knew I should notice it. Frr . . . frr . . . frr . . . ! And don't I see that that idiot had eyes only for Bourienne – I shall have to get rid of her. And how is it she has not pride enough to see it? If she has no pride for herself she might at least have some for my sake! She must be shown that the blockhead thinks nothing of her and looks only at Bourienne. No, she has no pride . . . but I'll let her see . . .'

The old prince knew that if he told his daughter she was making a mistake, and that Anatole meant to flirt with Mademoiselle Bourienne, Princess Mary's self-esteem would be wounded and his point (not to be parted from her) would be gained, so pacifying himself with this thought he called Tikhon and began to undress.

'What devil brought them here?' thought he while Tikhon was putting the night-shirt over his dried-up old body and grey-haired chest. 'I never invited them. They came to disturb my life – and there is not much of it left.'

'Devil take 'em!' he muttered, while his head was still covered by the shirt.

Tikhon knew his master's habit of sometimes thinking aloud, and therefore met with unaltered looks the angrily inquisitive expression of the face that emerged from the shirt.

'Gone to bed?' asked the prince.

Tikhon, like all good valets, instinctively knew the direction of his master's thoughts. He guessed that the question referred to Prince Vasili and his son.

'They have gone to bed and put out their lights, your Excellency.'

'No good . . . no good . . .' said the prince rapidly, and thrusting his feet into his slippers and his arms into the sleeves of his dressing-gown, he went to the couch on which he slept.

Though no words had passed between Anatole and Mademoiselle Bourienne they quite understood one another as to the first part of their romance, up to the appearance of the *pauvre mère*; they understood that they had much to say to one another in private and so they had been seeking an opportunity since morning to meet one another alone. When Princess Mary went to her father's room at the usual hour, Mademoiselle Bourienne and Anatole met in the conservatory.

Princess Mary went to the door of the study with special trepidation. It seemed to her that not only did everybody know that her fate would be decided that day, but that they also knew what she thought about it. She read this in Tikhon's face and in that of Prince Vasili's valet who made her a low bow when she met him in the corridor carrying hot water.

The old prince was very affectionate and careful in his treatment of his daughter that morning. Princess Mary well knew this painstaking expression of her father's. His face wore that expression when his dry hands clenched with vexation at her not understanding a sum in arithmetic, when rising from his chair he would walk away from her repeating in a low voice the same words several times over.

He came to the point at once, treating her ceremoniously.

'I have had a proposition made me concerning you,' he said with an unnatural smile. 'I expect you have guessed that Prince Vasili has not come and brought his pupil with him' (for some reason Prince Bolkonsky referred to Anatole as a 'pupil') 'for the sake of my beautiful eyes. Last night a proposition was made me on your account and, as you know my principles, I refer it to you.'

'How am I to understand you, *mon père?*' said the princess, growing pale and then blushing.

'How understand me!' cried her father angrily. 'Prince Vasili finds you to his taste as a daughter-in-law and makes a proposal to you on his pupil's behalf. That's how it's to be understood! "How understand it"! . . . And I ask you!'

'I do not know what you think, father,' whispered the princess.

'I? I? What of me? Leave me out of the question. I'm not going to get married. What about *you?* That's what I want to know.'

The princess saw that her father regarded the matter with disapproval, but at that moment the thought occurred to her that her fate would be decided now or never. She lowered her eyes so as not to see the gaze under which she felt that she could not think but would be only able to submit from habit, and she said:

'I wish only to do your will, but if I had to express my own desire . . .' She had no time to finish. The old prince interrupted her.

'That's admirable!' he shouted. 'He will take you with your

dowry and take Mademoisella Bourienne into the bargain. She'll be the wife, while you . . .'

The prince stopped. He saw the effect these words had produced on his daughter. She lowered her head and was ready to burst into tears.

'Now then, now then, I'm only joking!' he said. 'Remember this, Princess, I hold to the principle that a maiden has a full right to choose. I give you freedom. Only remember that your life's happiness depends on your decision. Never mind me!'

'But I do not know, father!'

'There's no need to talk! He receives his orders and will marry you or anybody; but you are free to choose . . . Go to your room, think it over, and come back in an hour and tell me in his presence: yes, or no, I know you will pray over it. Well, pray if you like, but you had better *think* it over. Go! Yes or no, yes or no, yes or no!' he still shouted, when the princess, as if lost in a fog, had already staggered out of the study.

Her fate was decided and happily decided. But what her father had said about Mademoiselle Bourienne was dreadful. It was untrue to be sure, but still it was terrible, and she could not help thinking of it. She was going straight on through the conservatory, neither seeing nor hearing anything, when suddenly the well-known whispering of Mademoiselle Bourienne aroused her. She raised her eyes, and two steps away saw Anatole embracing the Frenchwoman and whispering something to her. With a horrified expression on his handsome face Anatole looked at Princess Mary, but did not at once take his arm from the waist of Mademoiselle Bourienne who had not yet seen her.

'Who's that? Why? Wait a moment!' Anatole's face seemed to say. Princess Mary looked at them in silence. She could not understand it. At last Mademoiselle Bourienne gave a scream and ran away. Anatole bowed to Princess Mary with a gay smile, as if inviting her to join in a laugh at this strange incident, and then shrugging his shoulders went to the door that led to his own apartments.

An hour later Tikhon came to call Princess Mary to the old prince; he added that Prince Vasili was also there. When Tikhon came over to her, Princess Mary was sitting on the sofa in her room holding the weeping Mademoiselle Bourienne in her arms and gently stroking her hair. The princess's beautiful eyes with all their former calm radiance were looking with tender affection and pity at Mademoiselle Bourienne's pretty face.

'No, Princess, I have lost your affection for ever!' said Mademoiselle Bourienne.

'Why? I love you more than ever,' said Princess Mary, 'and I will try to do all I can for your happiness.'

'But you despise me. You who are so pure can never understand being so carried away by passion. Oh, only my poor mother...'

'I quite understand,' answered Princess Mary with a sad smile. 'Calm yourself, my dear. I will go to my father,' she said, and went out.

Prince Vasili, with one leg thrown high over the other and a snuff-box in his hand, was sitting there with a smile of deep emotion on his face, as if stirred to his heart's core and himself regretting and laughing at his own sensibility, when Princess Mary entered. He hurriedly took a pinch of snuff.

'Ah, my dear, my dear!' he began, rising and taking her by both hands. Then, sighing, he added: 'My son's fate is in your hands. Decide, my dear, good, gentle Marie, whom I have always loved as a daughter!'

He drew back, and a real tear appeared in his eye.

'Fr... fr...' snorted Prince Bolkonsky. 'The prince is making a proposition to you in his pupil's – I mean his son's – name. Do you wish, or not, to be Prince Anatole Kuragin's wife? Reply: yes or no,' he shouted, 'and then I shall reserve the right to state my opinion also. Yes, my opinion, and only my opinion,' added Prince Bolkonsky, turning to Prince Vasili and answering his imploring look. 'Yes, or no?'

'My desire is never to leave you, father, never to separate my life from yours. I don't wish to marry,' she answered positively, glancing at Prince Vasili and at her father with her beautiful eyes.

'Humbug! Nonsense! Humbug, humbug, humbug!' cried Prince Bolkonsky, frowning, and taking his daughter's hand he did not kiss her, but only, bending his forehead to hers, just touched it, and pressed her hand so that she winced and uttered a cry.

Prince Vasili rose.

'My dear, I must tell you that this is a moment I shall never, never forget. But, my dear, will you not give us a little hope of touching this heart, so kind and generous? Say "perhaps"... The future is so long. Say "perhaps".'

'Prince, what I have said is all there is in my heart. I thank you for the honour, but I shall never be your son's wife.'

'Well, so that's finished, my dear fellow! I am very glad to have seen you. Very glad! Go back to your rooms, Princess. Go!' said the old prince. 'Very, very glad to have seen you,' repeated he, embracing Prince Vasili.

'My vocation is a different one,' thought Princess Mary. 'My vocation is to be happy with another kind of happiness, the happiness of love and self-sacrifice. And cost what it may, I will arrange poor Amélie's happiness, she loves him so passionately, and so passionately repents. I will do all I can to arrange the match between them. If he is not rich I will give her the means; I will ask my father and Andrew. I shall be so happy when she is his wife. She is so unfortunate, a stranger, alone, helpless! And, oh God, how passionately she must love him if she could so far forget herself! Perhaps I might have done the same!...' thought Princess Mary.

## 6

It was long since the Rostovs had news of Nicholas. Not till mid-winter was the count at last handed a letter addressed in his son's handwriting. On receiving it he ran on tiptoe to his study in alarm and haste trying to escape notice, closed the door and began to read the letter.

Anna Mikhaylovna, who always knew everything that passed in the house, on hearing of the arrival of the letter went softly into the room and found the count with it in his hand sobbing and laughing at the same time.

Anna Mikhaylovna though her circumstances had improved was still living with the Rostovs.

'My dear friend?' said she in a tone of pathetic inquiry, prepared to sympathize in any way.

The count sobbed yet more.

'Nikolenka...a letter...wa...a...s...wounded...my darling boy...the countess...promoted to be an officer...thank God...How tell the little countess!'

Anna Mikhaylovna sat down beside him, with her own handkerchief wiped the tears from his eyes and from the letter, then having dried her own eyes she comforted the count, and decided that at dinner and till tea-time she would prepare the countess, and after tea with God's help would inform her.

At dinner Anna Mikhaylovna talked the whole time about the war news and about Nikolenka, twice asked when the last letter had been received from him, though she knew that already, and remarked that they might very likely be getting a letter from him that day. Each time that these hints began to make the countess anxious and she glanced uneasily at the count and at Anna Mikhaylovna, the latter very adroitly turned the conversation to insignificant matters. Natasha, who of the whole family was the most gifted with a capacity to feel any shades of intonation, look, and expression, pricked up her ears from the beginning of the meal, and was certain that there was some secret between her father and Anna Mikhaylovna, that it had something to do with her brother, and that Anna Mikhaylovna was preparing them for it. Bold as she was, Natasha, who knew how sensitive her mother was to anything relating to Nikolenka, did not venture to ask any questions at dinner, but she was too excited to eat anything and kept wriggling about on her chair regardless of her governess's remarks. After dinner she rushed headlong after Anna Mikhaylovna, and dashing at her, flung herself on her neck as soon as she overtook her in the sitting-room.

'Auntie darling, do tell me what it is!'

'Nothing, my dear.'

'No, dearest, sweet one, honey, I won't give up – I know you know something.'

Anna Mikhaylovna shook her head.

'You are a little sly-boots,' she said.

'A letter from Nikolenka! I'm sure of it!' exclaimed Natasha, reading confirmation in Anna Mikhaylovna's face.

'But for God's sake be careful, you know how it may affect your mamma.'

'I will, I will, only tell me! You won't? Then I will go and tell at once.'

Anna Mikhaylovna in a few words told her the contents of the letter, on condition that she should tell no one.

'No, on my true word of honour,' said Natasha crossing herself, 'I won't tell anyone!' and she ran off at once to Sonya.

'Nikolenka ... wounded ... a letter,' she announced in gleeful triumph.

'*Nicholas!*' was all Sonya said, instantly turning white.

Natasha seeing the impression the news of her brother's wound produced on Sonya, felt for the first time the sorrowful side of the news.

She rushed to Sonya, hugged her, and began to cry.

'A little wound, but he has been made an officer; he is well now, he wrote himself,' said she through her tears.

'There now! It's true that all you women are cry-babies,' remarked Petya, pacing the room with large, resolute strides. 'Now I'm very glad, very glad indeed, that my brother has distinguished himself so. You are all blubberers and understand nothing.'

Natasha smiled through her tears.

'You haven't read the letter?' asked Sonya.

'No, but she said that it was all over and that he's now an officer.'

'Thank God!' said Sonya, crossing herself. 'But perhaps she deceived you. Let us go to Mamma.'

Petya paced the room in silence for a time.

'If I'd been in Nikolenka's place I would have killed even more of those Frenchmen,' he said. 'What nasty brutes they are! I'd have killed so many that there'd have been a heap of them.'

'Hold your tongue, Petya, what a goose you are!'

'I'm not a goose, but they are who cry about trifles,' said Petya.

'Do you remember him?' Natasha suddenly asked, after a moment's silence.

Sonya smiled.

'Do I remember Nicholas?'

'No, Sonya, but do you remember so that you remember him perfectly, remember everything?' said Natasha with an expressive gesture, evidently wishing to give her words a very definite meaning. 'I remember Nikolenka too, I remember him well,' she said. 'But I don't remember Boris. I don't remember him a bit.'

'What! You don't remember Boris?' asked Sonya in surprise.

'It's not that I don't remember – I know what he is like, but not as I remember Nikolenka. Him – I just shut my eyes and remember, but Boris . . . No!' (She shut her eyes.) 'No! there's nothing at all.'

'Oh, Natasha!' said Sonya, looking ecstatically and earnestly at her friend as if she did not consider her worthy to hear what she meant to say, and as if she were saying it to someone else with whom joking was out of the question, 'I am in love with your brother once for all, and whatever may happen to him or to me I shall never cease to love him as long as I live.'

Natasha looked at Sonya with wondering and inquisitive eyes, and said nothing. She felt that Sonya was speaking the truth, that there was love such as Sonya was speaking of. But Natasha had not yet felt anything like it. She believed it could be, but did not understand it.

'Shall you write to him?' she asked.

Sonya became thoughtful. The question of how to write to Nicholas, and whether she ought to write, tormented her. Now that he was already an officer and a wounded hero would it be right to remind him of herself and, as it might seem, of the obligations to her he had taken on himself?

'I don't know. I think if he writes, I will write too,' she said blushing.

'And you won't feel ashamed to write to him?'

Sonya smiled.

'No.'

'And I should be ashamed to write to Boris. I'm not going to.'

'Why should you be ashamed?'

'Well, I don't know. It's awkward, and would make me ashamed.'

'And I know why she'd be ashamed,' said Petya, offended by Natasha's previous remark. 'It's because she was in love with that fat one in spectacles' (that was how Petya described his namesake, the new Count Bezukhov), 'and now she's in love with that singer' (he meant Natasha's Italian singing-master), 'that's why she's ashamed!'

'Petya, you're a stupid!' said Natasha.

'Not more stupid than you, madam,' said the nine-year-old Petya, with the air of an old brigadier.

The countess had been prepared by Anna Mikhaylovna's hints at dinner. On retiring to her own room, she sat in an arm-chair, her eyes fixed on a miniature portrait of her son on the lid of a snuff-box, while the tears kept coming into her eyes. Anna Mikhaylovna, with the letter, came on tiptoe to the countess's door and paused.

'Don't come in,' she said to the old count who was following her. 'Come later.' And she went in, closing the door behind her.

The count put his ear to the keyhole and listened.

At first he heard the sound of indifferent voices, then Anna Mikhaylovna's voice alone in a long speech, then a cry, then silence, then both voices together with glad intonations, and then footsteps. Anna Mikhaylovna opened the door. Her face wore the proud expression of a surgeon who has just performed a difficult operation, and admits the public to appreciate his skill.

'It is done!' she said to the count, pointing triumphantly to the countess, who sat holding in one hand the snuff-box with its portrait and in the other the letter, and pressing them alternately to her lips.

When she saw the count she stretched out her arms to him, embraced his bald head, over which she again looked at the letter and the portrait, and in order to press them again to her lips she lightly pushed away the bald head. Vera, Natasha, Sonya, and Petya now entered the room, and the reading of the letter began. After a brief description of the campaign and the two battles in which he had taken part, and his promotion, Nicholas said that he kissed his father's and mother's hands asking for their blessing, and that he kissed Vera, Natasha, and Petya. Besides that he sent greetings to Monsieur Schelling, Madame Schoss, and his old nurse, and asked them to kiss for him 'dear Sonya, whom he loved and thought of just the same as ever'. When she heard this, Sonya blushed so that tears came into her eyes, and unable to bear the looks turned upon her, ran away into the dancing hall, whirled round it at full speed with her dress puffed out like a balloon, and flushed and smiling, plumped down on the floor. The countess was crying.

'Why are you crying, Mamma?' asked Vera. 'From all he says one should be glad and not cry.'

This was quite true, but the count, the countess, and Natasha, looked at her reproachfully. 'And who is it she takes after?' thought the countess.

Nicholas's letter was read over hundreds of times, and those who were considered worthy to hear it had to come to the countess, for she did not let it out of her hands. The tutors came, and the nurses, and Dmitri, and several acquaintances, and the countess re-read the letter each time with fresh pleasure and each time discovered in it fresh proofs of Nikolenka's virtues. How strange, how extraordinary, how joyful it seemed, that her son, the scarcely perceptible motion of whose tiny limbs she had felt twenty years ago within her, that son about whom she used to have quarrels with the too-indulgent count, that son who had first learnt to say 'pear' and then 'granny', that this son should now be away in a foreign land amid strange surroundings, a manly warrior doing some kind of man's work of his own without help or guidance. The universal experience of ages, showing that children do grow imperceptibly from the cradle to manhood, did not exist for the countess. Her son's growth towards manhood at each of its stages had seemed as extraordinary to her as if there had never existed the millions of human beings who grew up in the same way. As twenty years before it seemed impossible that the little creature who lived somewhere under her heart would ever cry, suck her breast, and begin to speak, so now she could not believe that that little creature could be this strong, brave man, this model son and officer, that judging by this letter, he now was.

'What a *style*! How charmingly he describes!' said she, reading the descriptive part of the letter. 'And what a soul! Not a word about himself... Not a word! About some Denisov or other, though he himself I dare say is braver than any of them! He says nothing about his sufferings. What a heart! How like him it is! And how he has remembered everybody! Not forgetting anyone. I always said when he was only so high – I always said...'

For more than a week preparations were being made, rough drafts of letters to Nicholas from all the household were written and copied out, while under the supervision of the countess and the solicitude of the count, money and all things necessary for the uniform and equipment of the newly commissioned officer were collected. Anna Mikhaylovna, practical woman that she was, had even managed by favour with the army authorities to secure advantageous means of communication for herself and her son. She had opportunities of sending her letters to the Grand Duke Constantine Pavlovich who commanded the Guards. The Rostovs supposed that *The Russian Guards, Abroad*, was a quite definite address, and that if a letter reached the Grand Duke in command of the Guards there was no reason why it should not reach the Pavlograd regiment, which was presumably somewhere in the same neighbourhood. And so it was decided to send the letters and money by the Grand Duke's courier to Boris, and Boris was to forward them to Nicholas. The letters were from the old count, the countess, Petya, Vera, Natasha and Sonya, and finally there were six thousand rubles for his outfit and various other things the old count sent to his son.

## 7

On the 12th of November Kutuzov's active army, in camp before Olmütz, was preparing to be reviewed next day by the two Emperors – the Russian and the Austrian. The Guards, just arrived from Russia, spent the night ten miles from Olmütz, and next morning were to come straight to the review, reaching the field at Olmütz by ten o'clock.

That day Nicholas Rostov received a letter from Boris telling him that the Ismaylov* regiment was quartered for the night ten miles from Olmütz, and that he wanted to see him as he had a letter and money for him. Rostov was particularly in need of money now that the troops, after their active service, were stationed near Olmütz and the camp swarmed with well-provisioned sutlers and Austrian Jews offering all sorts of tempting wares. The Pavlograds held feast after feast celebrating awards they had received for the campaign, and made expeditions to Olmütz to visit a certain Caroline the Hungarian, who had recently opened a restaurant there with girls as waitresses. Rostov who had just celebrated his promotion to a cornetcy and bought Denisov's horse, Bedouin, was in debt all round, to his comrades and the sutlers. On receiving Boris's letter he rode with a fellow-officer to Olmütz, dined there, drank a bottle of wine, and then set off alone to the Guards' camp to find his old playmate. Rostov had not yet had time to get his uniform. He had on a shabby cadet jacket decorated with a soldier's cross, equally shabby cadet's riding breeches lined with worn leather, and an officer's sabre with a sword-knot. The Don horse he was riding was one he had bought from a Cossack during the campaign, and he wore a crumpled hussar cap stuck jauntily back on one side of his head. As he rode up to the camp he thought how he would impress Boris and all his comrades of the Guards by his appearance – that of a fighting hussar who had been under fire.

The Guards had made their whole march as if on a pleasure trip, parading their cleanliness and discipline. They had come by easy stages, their knapsacks conveyed on carts, and the Austrian authorities had provided excellent dinners for the officers at every halting-place. The regiments had entered and left the towns with their bands playing, and by the Grand Duke's orders the men had marched all the way in step (a practice on which the Guards prided themselves), the officers on foot and at their proper posts. Boris had been quartered, and had marched all the way, with Berg who was already in command of a company. Berg, who had obtained his captaincy during the campaign, had gained the confidence of his superiors by his promptitude and accuracy and had arranged his money matters very satisfactorily. Boris during the campaign had made the acquaintance of many persons who might prove useful to him, and by a letter of recommendation he had brought from Pierre, had become acquainted with Prince Andrew Bolkonsky through whom he hoped to obtain a post on the commander-in-chief's staff. Berg and Boris having rested after yesterday's march, were sitting, clean and neatly dressed at a round table in the clean quarters allotted to them, playing chess. Berg held a smoking pipe between his knees. Boris in the accurate way characteristic of him was building a little pyramid of chessmen with his delicate white fingers while awaiting Berg's move, and watched his opponent's face, evidently thinking about the game, as he always thought only of whatever he was engaged on.

'Well, how are you going to get out of that?' he remarked.

'We'll try to,' replied Berg, touching a pawn and then removing his hand.

At that moment the door opened.

'Here he is at last!' shouted Rostov. 'And Berg too! Oh, you *petisenfans, allay cushay dormir!*' he exclaimed, imitating his Russian nurse's French, at which he and Boris used to laugh long ago.

'Dear me, how you have changed!'

Boris rose to meet Rostov, but in doing so did not omit to steady and replace some chessmen that were falling. He was about to embrace his friend but Nicholas avoided him. With that peculiar feeling of youth, that dread of beaten tracks, and wish to express itself in a manner different from that of its elders which

248

is often insincere, Nicholas wished to do something special on meeting his friend. He wanted to pinch him, push him, do anything but kiss him – a thing everybody did. But notwithstanding this, Boris embraced him in a quiet friendly way and kissed him three times.

They had not met for nearly half a year and, being at the age when young men take their first steps on life's road, each saw immense changes in the other, quite a new reflection of the society in which they had taken those first steps. Both had changed greatly since they last met and both were in a hurry to show the changes that had taken place in them.

'Oh, you damned dandies! Clean and fresh as if you'd been to a fête, not like us sinners of the line,' cried Rostov, with martial swagger and with baritone notes in his voice new to Boris, pointing to his own mud-bespattered breeches. The German landlady, hearing Rostov's loud voice, popped her head in at the door.

'Eh, is she pretty?' he asked with a wink.

'Why do you shout so? You'll frighten them!' said Boris. 'I did not expect you to-day,' he added. 'I only sent you the note yesterday by Bolkonsky – an adjutant of Kutuzov's, who's a friend of mine. I did not think he would get it to you so quickly . . . Well, how are you? Been under fire already?' asked Boris.

Without answering, Rostov shook the soldier's Cross of St George fastened to the cording of his uniform, and indicating his bandaged arm, glanced at Berg with a smile.

'As you see,' he said.

'Indeed? Yes, yes!' said Boris with a smile. 'And we too have had a splendid march. You know of course that his Imperial Highness rode with our regiment all the time, so that we had every comfort and every advantage. What receptions we had in Poland! What dinners and balls! I can't tell you. And the Tsarevich was very gracious to all our officers.'

And the two friends told each other of their doings, the one of his hussar revels, and life in the fighting line, the other of the pleasures and advantages of service under members of the Imperial family.

'Oh, you Guards!' said Rostov. 'I say, send for some wine.'

Boris made a grimace.

'If you really want it,' said he.

He went to his bed, drew a purse from under the clean pillow, and sent for wine.

'Yes, and I have some money and a letter to give you,' he added.

Rostov took the letter, and throwing the money on the sofa put both arms on the table and began to read. After reading a few lines he glanced angrily at Berg, then, meeting his eyes, hid his face behind the letter.

'Well, they've sent you a tidy sum,' said Berg, eyeing the heavy purse that sank into the sofa. 'As for us, Count, we get along on our pay. I can tell you for myself . . .'

'I say Berg, my dear fellow,' said Rostov, 'when you get a letter from home and meet one of your own people whom you want to talk everything over with, and I happen to be there, I'll go at once, to be out of your way! Do go somewhere, anywhere . . . to the devil!' he exclaimed, and immediately seizing him by the shoulder and looking amiably into his face, evidently wishing to soften the rudeness of his words, he added, 'Don't be hurt, my dear fellow; you know I speak from my heart as to an old acquaintance.'

'Oh, don't mention it, Count! I quite understand,' said Berg, getting up and speaking in a muffled and guttural voice.

'Go across to our hosts: they invited you,' added Boris.

Berg put on the cleanest of coats, without a spot or speck of dust, stood before a looking-glass and brushed the hair on his temples upwards, in the way affected by the Emperor Alexander, and having assured himself from the way Rostov looked at it that his coat had been noticed, left the room with a pleasant smile.

'Oh dear, what a beast I am!' muttered Rostov, as he read the letter.

'Why?'

'Oh, what a pig I am, not once to have written, and to have given them such a fright! Oh, what a pig I am!' he repeated, flushing suddenly. 'Well, have you sent Gabriel for some wine? All right, let's have some!'

In the letter from his parents was enclosed a letter of recommendation to Bagration which the old countess at Anna Mikhaylovna's advice had obtained through an acquaintance and sent to her son, asking him to take it to its destination and make use of it.

'What nonsense! Much I need it!' said Rostov, throwing the letter under the table.

'Why have you thrown that away?' asked Boris.

'It is some letter of recommendation . . . what the devil do I want it for!'

'Why "What the devil"?' said Boris, picking it up and reading the address. 'This letter would be of great use to you.'

'I want nothing, and I won't be anyone's adjutant.'

'Why not?' inquired Boris.

'It's a lackey's job!'

'You are still the same dreamer, I see,' remarked Boris, shaking his head.

'And you're still the same diplomatist! But that's not the point. ... Come, how are you?' asked Rostov.

'Well, as you see. So far everything's all right, but I confess I should much like to be an adjutant and not remain at the front.'

'Why?'

'Because when once a man starts on military service he should try to make as successful a career of it as possible.'

'Oh, that's it!' said Rostov, evidently thinking of something else.

He looked intently and inquiringly into his friend's eyes, evidently trying in vain to find the answer to some question.

Old Gabriel brought in the wine.

'Shouldn't we now send for Berg?' asked Boris. 'He would drink with you. I can't.'

'Well, send for him ... and how do you get on with that German?' said Rostov with a contemptuous smile.

'He is a very, very nice, honest, and pleasant fellow,' answered Boris.

Again Rostov looked intently into Boris's eyes and sighed. Berg returned, and over the bottle of wine conversation between the three officers grew animated. The Guardsmen told Rostov of their march and how they had been made much of in Russia, Poland, and abroad. They spoke of the sayings and doings of their commander, the Grand Duke, and told stories of his kindness and irascibility. Berg as usual kept silent when the subject did not relate to himself, but in connexion with the stories of the Grand Duke's quick temper he related with gusto how in Galicia he had managed to deal with the Grand Duke when the latter made a tour of the regiments and was annoyed at the irregularity of a movement. With a pleasant smile Berg related how the Grand Duke had ridden up to him in a violent passion shouting: 'Arnauts!'* (Arnauts was the Tsarevich's favourite expression when he was in a rage) and called for the company commander.

'Would you believe it, Count, I was not at all alarmed, because I knew I was right. Without boasting, you know, I may say that I know the Army Orders by heart and know the Regulations as well as I do the Lord's Prayer. So, Count, there never is any negligence in my company, and so my conscience was at ease. I came forward ...' (Berg stood up and showed how he presented himself, with his hand to his cap, and really it would have been difficult for a face to express greater respect and self-complacency than his did.) 'Well he stormed at me, as the saying is, stormed and stormed and stormed! It was not a matter of life but rather of death, as the saying is. "Albanians!" and "devils!" and "To Siberia!"' said Berg with a sagacious smile. 'I knew I was in the right so I kept silent; was not that best, Count? ... "Hey, are you dumb?" he shouted. Still I remained silent. And what do you think, Count? The next day it was not even mentioned in the Orders of the Day! That's what keeping one's head means. That's the way, Count,' said Berg, lighting his pipe and emitting rings of smoke.

'Yes, that was fine,' said Rostov smiling.

But Boris noticed that he was preparing to make fun of Berg, and skilfully changed the subject. He asked him to tell them how and where he got his wound. This pleased Rostov and he began talking about it, and as he went on became more and more animated. He told them of his Schön Graben affair just as those who have taken part in a battle generally do describe it, that is, as they would like it to have been, as they have heard it described by others, and as sounds well, but not at all as it really was. Rostov was a truthful young man and would on no account have told a deliberate lie. He began his story meaning to tell everything just as it happened, but imperceptibly, involuntarily, and inevitably he lapsed into falsehood. If he had told the truth to his hearers – who like himself had often heard stories of attacks and had formed a definite idea of what an attack was and were expecting to hear just such a story – they would either not have believed him or, still worse, would have thought that Rostov was himself to blame since what generally happens to the narrators of cavalry attacks had not happened to him. He could not tell them simply that everyone went at a trot, and that he fell off his horse and sprained his arm and then ran as hard as he could from a Frenchman into the wood. Besides, to tell everything as it really happened it would have been necessary to make an effort of will to tell only what happened. It is very difficult to tell the truth, and young people are rarely capable of it. His hearers expected a story of how beside himself and all aflame with excitement, he had flown like a storm at the square, cut his way in, slashed right and left, how his sabre had tasted flesh, and he had fallen exhausted, and so on. And so he told them all that.

In the middle of his story, just as he was saying: 'You cannot imagine what a strange frenzy one experiences during an attack,' Prince Andrew, whom Boris was expecting, entered the room. Prince Andrew, who liked to help young men, was flattered by being asked for his assistance, and being well-disposed towards

Boris who had managed to please him the day before, he wished to do what the young man wanted. Having been sent with papers from Kutuzov to the Tsarevich he looked in on Boris hoping to find him alone. When he came in and saw an hussar of the line recounting his military exploits (Prince Andrew could not endure that sort of man) he gave Boris a pleasant smile, frowned as with half-closed eyes he looked at Rostov, bowed slightly and wearily, and sat down languidly on the sofa: he felt it unpleasant to have dropped in on bad company. Rostov flushed up on noticing this, but he did not care, this was a mere stranger. Glancing however at Boris he saw that he too seemed ashamed of the hussar of the line.

In spite of Prince Andrew's disagreeable, ironical tone, in spite of the contempt with which Rostov from his fighting army point of view regarded all these little adjutants on the staff, of whom the newcomer was evidently one, Rostov felt confused, blushed, and became silent. Boris inquired what news there might be on the staff, and what, without indiscretion, one might ask about our plans.

'We shall probably advance,' replied Bolkonsky, evidently reluctant to say more in the presence of a stranger.

Berg took the opportunity to ask, with great politeness, whether, as was rumoured, the allowance of forage-money to captains of companies would be doubled. To this Prince Andrew answered with a smile that he could give no opinion on such an important government order, and Berg laughed gaily.

'As to your business,' Prince Andrew continued, addressing Boris, 'we will talk of it later' (and he looked round at Rostov). 'Come to me after the review and we will do what is possible.'

And having glanced round the room Prince Andrew turned to Rostov, whose state of unconquerable childish embarrassment now changing to anger he did not condescend to notice, and said: 'I think you were talking of the Schön Graben affair? Were you there?'

'I was there,' said Rostov angrily as if intending to insult the aide-de-camp.

Bolkonsky noticed the hussar's state of mind, and it amused him. With a slightly contemptuous smile he said:

'Yes, there are many stories now told about that affair!'

'Yes, stories!' repeated Rostov loudly, looking with eyes suddenly grown furious, now at Boris, now at Bolkonsky. 'Yes, many stories! But our stories are the stories of men who have been under the enemy's fire! Our stories have some weight, not like the stories of those fellows on the staff who get rewards without doing anything!'

'Of whom you imagine me to be one?' said Prince Andrew with a quiet and particularly amiable smile.

A strange feeling of exasperation and yet of respect for this man's self-possession mingled at that moment in Rostov's soul.

'I am not talking about you,' he said, 'I don't know you and frankly I don't want to. I am speaking of the staff in general.'

'And I will tell you this,' Prince Andrew interrupted in a tone of quiet authority, 'you wish to insult me, and I am ready to agree with you that it would be very easy to do so if you haven't sufficient self-respect, but admit that the time and place are very badly chosen. In a day or two we shall all have to take part in a greater and more serious duel, and besides, Drubetskoy, who says he is an old friend of yours, is not at all to blame that my face has the misfortune to displease you. However,' he added rising, 'you know my name and where to find me, but don't forget that I do not regard either myself or you as having been at all insulted, and as a man older than you, my advice is to let the matter drop. Well then, on Friday after the review I shall expect you, Drubetskoy. *Au revoir!*' exclaimed Prince Andrew and with a bow to them both he went out.

Only when Prince Andrew was gone did Rostov think of what he ought to have said. And he was still more angry at having omitted to say it. He ordered his horse at once, and coldly taking leave of Boris, rode home. Should he go to head-quarters next day and challenge that affected adjutant, or really let the matter drop, was the question that worried him all the way. He thought angrily of the pleasure he would have at seeing the fright of that small and frail but proud man when covered by his pistol, and then he felt with surprise that of all the men he knew there was none he would so much like to have for a friend as that very adjutant whom he so hated.

8

THE day after Rostov had been to see Boris, a review was held of the Austrian and Russian troops, both those freshly arrived from Russia and those who had been campaigning under Kutuzov. The two Emperors, the Russian with his heir the Tsarevich, and the Austrian with the Archduke, inspected the Allied army of eighty thousand men.

From early morning the smart clean troops were on the move, forming up on the field before the fortress. Now thousands of feet and bayonets moved and halted at the officer's command, turned with banners flying, formed up at intervals, and wheeled round other similar masses of infantry in different uniforms; now was heard the rhythmic beat of hoofs and the jingling of showy cavalry in blue, red, and green braided uniforms, with smartly dressed bandsmen in front mounted on black, roan, or grey horses; then again, spreading out with the brazen clatter of the polished shining cannon that quivered on the gun-carriages and with the smell of linstocks, came the artillery which crawled between the infantry and cavalry and took up its appointed position. Not only the generals in full parade uniforms, with their thin or thick waists drawn in to the utmost, their red necks squeezed into their stiff collars, and wearing scarves and all their decorations, not only the elegant, pomaded officers, but every soldier with his freshly washed and shaven face and his weapons clean and polished to the utmost, and every horse groomed till its coat shone like satin and every hair of its wetted mane lay smooth – felt that no small matter was happening, but an important and solemn affair. Every general and every soldier was conscious of his own insignificance, aware of being but a drop in that ocean of men, and yet at the same time was conscious of his strength as a part of that enormous whole.

From early morning strenuous activities and efforts had begun and by ten o'clock all had been brought into due order. The ranks were drawn up on the vast field. The whole army was extended in three lines: the cavalry in front, behind it the artillery, and behind that again the infantry.

A space like a street was left between each two lines of troops. The three parts of that army were sharply distinguished: Kutuzov's fighting army (with the Pavlograds on the right flank of the front); those recently arrived from Russia, both Guards and regiments of the line; and the Austrian troops. But they all stood in the same lines, under one command, and in a like order.

Like wind over leaves ran an excited whisper: 'They're coming! They're coming!' Alarmed voices were heard, and a stir of final preparation swept over all the troops.

From the direction of Olmütz in front of them, a group was seen approaching. And at that moment, though the day was still, a light gust of wind blowing over the army slightly stirred the streamers on the lances and the unfolded standards fluttered against their staffs. It looked as if by that slight motion the army itself was expressing its joy at the approach of the Emperors. One voice was heard shouting: 'Eyes front!' Then, like the crowing of cocks at sunrise, this was repeated by others from various sides and all became silent.

In the deathlike stillness only the tramp of horses was heard.

This was the Emperors' suites. The Emperors rode up to the flank, and the trumpets of the first cavalry regiment played the general march. It seemed as though not the trumpeters were playing, but as if the army itself, rejoicing at the Emperor's approach, had naturally burst into music. Amid these sounds, only the youthful kindly voice of the Emperor Alexander was clearly heard. He gave the words of greeting, and the first regiment roared 'hurrah!' so deafeningly, continuously, and joyfully, that the men themselves were awed by their multitude and the immensity of the power they constituted.

Rostov standing in the front lines of Kutuzov's army which the Tsar approached first, experienced the same feeling as every other man in that army: a feeling of self-forgetfulness, a proud consciousness of might, and a passionate attraction to him who was the cause of this triumph.

He felt that at a single word from that man all this vast mass (and he himself an insignificant atom in it) would go through fire and water, commit crime, die, or perform deeds of highest heroism, and so he could not but tremble and his heart stand still at the imminence of that word.

'Hurrah! Hurrah! Hurrah!' thundered from all sides, one regiment after another greeting the Tsar with the strains of the march, and then 'hurrah!' ... Then the general march, and again 'hurrah! hurrah!' growing ever stronger, and fuller, and merging into a deafening roar.

Till the Tsar reached it, each regiment in its silence and immobility seemed like a lifeless body, but as soon as he came up it became alive, its thunder joining the roar of the whole line along which he had already passed. Through the terrible and deafening roar of those voices, amid the square masses of troops standing motionless as if turned to stone, hundreds of riders composing the suites moved carelessly but symmetrically and above all freely, and in front of them two men – the Emperors. Upon them the undivided, tensely passionate attention of that whole mass of men was concentrated.

The handsome young Emperor Alexander, in the uniform of the Horse Guards, wearing a cocked hat with its peaks front and back, with his pleasant face and resonant though not loud voice, attracted everyone's attention.

Rostov was not far from the trumpeters, and with his keen sight had recognized the Tsar and watched his approach. When he was within twenty paces, and Nicholas could clearly distinguish every detail of his handsome, happy young face, he experienced a feeling of tenderness and ecstasy such as he had never before known. Every trait and every movement of the Tsar's seemed to him enchanting.

Stopping in front of the Pavlograds, the Tsar said something in French to the Austrian Emperor and smiled.

Seeing that smile Rostov involuntarily smiled himself and felt a still stronger flow of love for his sovereign. He longed to show that love in some way, and knowing that this was impossible was ready to cry. The Tsar called the colonel of the regiment and said a few words to him.

'Oh God, what would happen to me if the Emperor spoke to me?' thought Rostov. 'I should die of happiness!'

The Tsar addressed the officers also: 'I thank you all, gentlemen, I thank you with my whole heart.' To Rostov every word sounded like a voice from heaven. How gladly would he have died at once for his Tsar!

'You have earned the St George's standards and will be worthy of them.'

'Oh, to die, to die for him!' thought Rostov.

The Tsar said something more which Rostov did not hear, and the soldiers, straining their lungs, shouted 'hurrah!'

Rostov too, bending over his saddle, shouted 'hurrah!' with all his might, feeling that he would like to injure himself by that shout, if only to express his rapture fully.

The Tsar stopped a few minutes in front of the hussars as if undecided.

'How can the Emperor be undecided?' thought Rostov, but then even this indecision appeared to him majestic and enchanting, like everything else the Tsar did.

That hesitation lasted only an instant. The Tsar's foot, in the narrow pointed boot then fashionable, touched the groin of the bob-tailed bay mare he rode, his hand in a white glove gathered up the reins, and he moved off accompanied by an irregularly swaying sea of aides-de-camp. Farther and farther he rode away, stopping at the other regiments, till at last only his white plumes were visible to Rostov from amid the suites that surrounded the Emperors.

Among the gentlemen of the suite Rostov noticed Bolkonsky, sitting his horse indolently and carelessly. Rostov recalled their quarrel of yesterday and the question presented itself whether he ought or ought not to challenge Bolkonsky. 'Of course not!' he now thought. 'Is it worth thinking or speaking of it at such a moment? At a time of such love, such rapture, and such self-sacrifice, what do any of our quarrels and affronts matter? I love and forgive everybody now.'

When the Emperor had passed nearly all the regiments, the troops began a ceremonial march past him, and Rostov on Bedouin, recently purchased from Denisov, rode past too, at the rear of his squadron – that is, alone and in full view of the Emperor.

Before he reached him, Rostov, who was a splendid horseman, spurred Bedouin twice and successfully put him to the showy trot in which the animal went when excited. Bending his foaming muzzle to his chest, his tail extended, Bedouin, as if also conscious of the Emperor's eye upon him, passed splendidly, lifting his feet with a high and graceful action as if flying through the air without touching the ground.

Rostov himself, his legs well back and his stomach drawn in and feeling himself one with his horse, rode past the Emperor with a frowning but blissful face 'like a vewy devil', as Denisov expressed it.

'Fine fellows, the Pavlograds!' remarked the Emperor.

'My God, how happy I should be if he ordered me to leap into the fire this instant!' thought Rostov.

When the review was over the newly arrived officers, and also Kutuzov's, collected in groups and began to talk about the awards, about the Austrians and their uniforms, about their lines, about Bonaparte, and how badly the latter would fare now, especially if the Essen corps arrived and Prussia took our side.

But the talk in every group was chiefly about the Emperor Alexander. His every word and movement was described with ecstasy.

They all had but one wish: to advance as soon as possible against the enemy under the Emperor's command. Commanded by the Emperor himself they could not fail to vanquish anyone, be it whom it might: so thought Rostov and most of the officers after the review.

All were then more confident of victory than the winning of two battles would have made them.

9

THE day after the review, Boris in his best uniform and with his comrade Berg's best wishes for success, rode to Olmütz to see Bolkonsky, wishing to profit by his friendliness and obtain for himself the best post he could – preferably that of adjutant to some important personage, a position in the army which seemed to him most attractive. 'It is all very well for Rostov whose father sends him ten thousand rubles at a time, to talk about not wishing to cringe to anybody and not be anyone's lackey, but I who have nothing but my brains, have to make a career, and must not miss opportunities but must avail myself of them!' he reflected.

He did not find Prince Andrew in Olmütz that day, but the appearance of the town where the head-quarters and the diplomatic corps were stationed, and the two Emperors were living with their suites, households, and courts, only strengthened his desire to belong to that higher world.

He knew no one, and despite his smart Guardsman's uniform, all these exalted personages passing in the streets in their elegant carriages with their plumes, ribbons, and medals, both courtiers and military men, seemed so immeasurably above him, an insignificant officer of the Guards, that they not only did not wish to, but simply could not be aware of his existence. At the quarters of the commander-in-chief, Kutuzov, where he inquired for Bolkonsky, all the adjutants and even the orderlies looked at him as if they wished to impress on him that a great many officers like him were always coming there and that everybody was heartily sick of them. In spite of this, or rather because of it, next day, November the 15th, after dinner he again went to Olmütz, and entering the house occupied by Kutuzov, asked for Bolkonsky. Prince Andrew was in and Boris was shown into a large hall probably formerly used for dancing, but in which five beds now stood, and furniture of various kinds: a table, chairs, and a clavichord. One adjutant, nearest the door, was sitting at the table in a Persian dressing-gown, writing. Another, the red stout Nesvitsky, lay on a bed with his arms under his head, laughing with an officer who had sat down beside him. A third was playing a Viennese waltz on the clavichord, while a fourth, lying on the clavichord, sang the tune. Bolkonsky was not there. None of these gentlemen changed his position on seeing Boris. The one who was writing, and whom Boris addressed, turned round crossly and told him Bolkonsky was on duty, and that he should go through the door on the left into the reception-room if he wished to see him. Boris thanked him and went to the reception-room, where he found some ten officers and generals.

When he entered, Prince Andrew, his eyes drooping contemptuously (with that peculiar expression of polite weariness which plainly says, 'if it were not my duty I would not talk to you for a moment'), was listening to an old Russian general with decorations, who stood very erect, almost on tiptoe, with a soldier's obsequious expression on his purple face, reporting something.

'Very well, then, be so good as to wait,' said Prince Andrew to the general in Russian, speaking with the French intonation he affected when he wished to speak contemptuously, and noticing Boris, Prince Andrew, paying no more heed to the general who ran after him imploring him to hear something more, nodded and turned to him with a cheerful smile.

At that moment Boris clearly realized what he had before surmised, that in the army, besides the subordination and discipline prescribed in the military code, which he and the others knew in the regiment, there was another, more important, subordination, which made this tight-laced, purple-faced general wait respectfully while Captain Prince Andrew for his own pleasure chose to chat with Lieutenant Drubetskoy. More than ever was Boris resolved to serve in future not according to the written code, but under this unwritten law. He felt now that merely by having been recommended to Prince Andrew he had already risen above the general who at the front had the power to annihilate him, a lieutenant of the Guards. Prince Andrew came up to him and took his hand.

'I am very sorry you did not find me in yesterday. I was fussing about with Germans all day. We went with Weyrother to survey the dispositions. When Germans start being accurate there's no end to it!'

Boris smiled, as if he understood what Prince Andrew was alluding to as something generally known. But it was the first time he had heard Weyrother's name, or even the term 'dispositions'.

'Well, my dear fellow, so you still want to be an adjutant? I have been thinking about you.'

'Yes, I was thinking' – for some reason Boris could not help blushing – 'of asking the commander-in-chief. He has had a letter from Prince Kuragin about me. I only wanted to ask because I fear the Guards won't be in action,' he added as if in apology.

'All right, all right. We'll talk it over,' replied Prince Andrew. 'Only let me report this gentleman's business, and I shall be at your disposal.'

While Prince Andrew went to report about the purple-faced general, that gentleman – evidently not sharing Boris's conception of the advantages of the unwritten code of subordination – looked so fixedly at the presumptuous lieutenant who had prevented his finishing what he had to say to the adjutant, that Boris felt uncomfortable. He turned away and waited impatiently for Prince Andrew's return from the commander-in-chief's room.

'You see, my dear fellow, I have been thinking about you,' said Prince Andrew when they had gone into the large room where the clavichord was. 'It's no use your going to the commander-in-chief. He would say a lot of pleasant things, ask you to dinner' ('that would not be bad as regards the unwritten code,' thought Boris), 'but nothing more would come of it. There will soon be a battalion of us aides-de-camp and adjutants! But this is what we'll do: I have a good friend, an adjutant-general and an excellent fellow, Prince Dolgorukov; and though you may not know it, the fact is that now Kutuzov with his staff and all of us count for nothing. Everything is now centred round the Emperor. So we will go to Dolgorukov; I have to go there anyhow, and I have already spoken to him about you. We shall see whether he cannot attach you to himself or find a place for you somewhere nearer the sun.'

Prince Andrew always became specially keen when he had to guide a young man and help him to worldly success. Under cover of obtaining help of this kind for another, which from pride he would never accept for himself, he kept in touch with the circle which confers success and which attracted him. He very readily took up Boris's cause and went with him to Dolgorukov.

It was late in the evening when they entered the palace at Olmütz occupied by the Emperors and their retinues.

That same day a council of war had been held in which all the members of the Hofkriegsrath and both Emperors took part. At that council, contrary to the views of the old generals Kutuzov and Prince Schwartzenberg, it had been decided to advance immediately and give battle to Bonaparte. The council of war was just over when Prince Andrew accompanied by Boris arrived at the palace to find Dolgorukov. Everyone at head-quarters was still under the spell of the day's council, at which the party of the young had triumphed. The voices of those who counselled delay and advised waiting for something else before advancing, had been so completely silenced and their arguments confuted by such conclusive evidence of the advantages of attacking, that what had been discussed at the council – the coming battle and the victory that would certainly result from it – no longer seemed to be in the future but in the past. All the advantages were on our side. Our enormous forces, undoubtedly superior to Napoleon's, were concentrated in one place, the troops inspired by the Emperor's presence were eager for action. The strategic position where the operations would take place was familiar in all its details to the Austrian General Weyrother: a lucky accident had ordained that the Austrian army should manœuvre the previous year on the very fields where the French had now to be fought; the adjacent locality was known and shown in every detail on the maps, and Bonaparte, evidently weakened, was undertaking nothing.

Dolgorukov, one of the warmest advocates of an attack, had just returned from the council, tired and exhausted but eager and proud of the victory that had been gained. Prince Andrew introduced his protégé, but Prince Dolgorukov politely and firmly pressing his hand said nothing to Boris, and evidently unable to suppress the thoughts which were uppermost in his mind at that moment, addressed Prince Andrew in French.

'Ah, my dear fellow, what a battle we have gained! God grant that the one that will result from it will be as victorious! However, my dear fellow,' he said abruptly and eagerly, 'I must confess to having been unjust to the Austrians and especially to Weyrother. What exactitude, what minuteness, what knowledge of the locality, what foresight for every eventuality, every possibility, even to the smallest detail! No, my dear fellow, no conditions better than our present ones could have been devised. This combination of Austrian precision with Russian valour – what more could be wished for?'

'So the attack is definitely resolved on?' asked Bolkonsky.

'And do you know, my dear fellow, it seems to me that Bonaparte has decidedly lost his bearings, you know that a letter was received from him to-day for the Emperor.' Dolgorukov smiled significantly.

'Is that so? And what does he say?' inquired Bolkonsky.

'What can he say? Tra-di-ri-di-ra and so on ... merely to gain time. I tell you he is in our hands, that's certain! But what was most amusing,' he continued, with a sudden, good-natured laugh, 'was that we could not think how to address the reply! If not as "Consul" and of course not as "Emperor", it seemed to me it should be to "General Bonaparte".'

'But between not recognizing him as Emperor and calling him General Bonaparte there is a difference,' remarked Bolkonsky.

'That's just it,' interrupted Dolgorukov quickly, laughing. 'You know Bilibin – he's a very clever fellow. He suggested addressing him as "Usurper and Enemy of Mankind".'

Dolgorukov laughed merrily.

'Only that?' said Bolkonsky.

'All the same it was Bilibin who found a suitable form for the address. He is a wise and clever fellow.'

'What was it?'

'To the Head of the French Government ... *Au chef du gouvernement français*,' said Dolgorukov with grave satisfaction. 'Good, wasn't it?'

'Yes, but he will dislike it extremely,' said Bolkonsky.

'Oh yes, very much! My brother knows him, he's dined with him – the present Emperor – more than once in Paris, and tells me he never met a more cunning or subtle diplomatist – you know, a combination of French adroitness and Italian play-acting! Do you know the tale about him and Count Markov? Count Markov was the only man who knew how to handle him. You know the story of the handkerchief? It is delightful!'

And the talkative Dolgorukov, turning now to Boris now to Prince Andrew, told how Bonaparte wishing to test Markov, our ambassador, purposely dropped a handkerchief in front of him and stood looking at Markov, probably expecting Markov to pick it up for him, and how Markov immediately dropped his own beside it and picked it up without touching Bonaparte's.

'Delightful!' said Bolkonsky. 'But I have come to you, Prince, as a petitioner on behalf of this young man. You see...' but before Prince Andrew could finish, an aide-de-camp came in to summon Dolgorukov to the Emperor.

'Oh, what a nuisance,' said Dolgorukov, getting up hurriedly and pressing the hands of Prince Andrew and Boris. 'You know I should be very glad to do all in my power both for you and for this dear young man.' Again he pressed the hand of the latter with an expression of good-natured, sincere, and animated levity. 'But you see... another time!'

Boris was excited by the thought of being so close to the higher powers as he felt himself to be at that moment. He was conscious that here he was in contact with the springs that set in motion the enormous movements of the mass of which in his regiment he felt himself a tiny, obedient, and insignificant atom. They followed Prince Dolgorukov out into the corridor, and met – coming out of the door of the Emperor's room by which Dolgorukov had entered – a short man in civilian clothes with a clever face and sharply projecting jaw which, without spoiling his face, gave him a peculiar vivacity and shiftiness of expression. This short man nodded to Dolgorukov as to an intimate friend, and stared at Prince Andrew with cool intensity, walking straight towards him and evidently expecting him to bow or to step out of his way. Prince Andrew did neither: a look of animosity appeared on his face and the other turned away and went down the side of the corridor.

'Who was that?' asked Boris.

'He is one of the most remarkable, but to me most unpleasant of men – the Minister of Foreign Affairs, Prince Adam Czartoryski ...It is such men as he who decide the fate of nations,' added Bolkonsky with a sigh he could not suppress, as they passed out of the palace.

Next day the army began its campaign, and up to the very battle of Austerlitz Boris was unable to see either Prince Andrew or Dolgorukov again, and remained for a while with the Ismaylov regiment.

AT dawn on the 16th of November Denisov's squadron, in which Nicholas Rostov served and which was in Prince Bagration's detachment, moved from the place where it had spent the night, advancing into action as arranged, and after going behind other columns for about a verst, was stopped on the high road. Rostov saw the Cossacks and then the first and second squadrons of hussars, and infantry battalions and artillery pass by and go forward, and then Generals Bagration and Dolgorukov ride past with their adjutants. All the fear before action which he had experienced as previously, all the inner struggle to conquer that fear, all his dreams of distinguishing himself as a true hussar in this battle, had been wasted. Their squadron remained in reserve and Nicholas Rostov spent that day in a dull and wretched mood. At nine in the morning he heard firing in front and shouts of *hurrah*, and saw wounded being brought back (there were not many of them), and at last he saw how a whole detachment of French cavalry was brought in, convoyed by a sótnya* of Cossacks. Evidently the affair was over, and though not big, had been a successful engagement. The men and officers returning spoke of a brilliant victory, of the occupation of the town of Wischau and the capture of a whole French squadron. The day was bright and sunny after a sharp night frost, and the cheerful glitter of that autumn day was in keeping with the news of victory which was conveyed not only by the tales of those who had taken part in it, but also by the joyful expression on the faces of soldiers, officers, generals, and adjutants, as they passed Rostov going or coming. And Nicholas, who had vainly suffered all the dread that precedes a battle and had spent that happy day in inactivity, was all the more depressed.

'Come here, Wostov. Let's dwink to dwown our gwief!' shouted Denisov, who had settled down by the roadside with a flask and some food.

The officers gathered round Denisov's canteen, eating and talking.

'There! They are bringing another!' cried one of the officers, indicating a captive French dragoon who was being brought in on foot by two Cossacks.

One of them was leading by the bridle a fine large French horse he had taken from the prisoner.

'Sell us that horse!' Denisov called out to the Cossacks.

'If you like, your honour!'

The officers got up and stood round the Cossacks and their prisoner. The French dragoon was a young Alsatian who spoke French with a German accent. He was breathless with agitation, his face was red, and when he heard some French spoken he at once began speaking to the officers, addressing first one, then another. He said he would not have been taken, it was not his fault but the corporal's who had sent him to seize some horse-cloths, though he had told him the Russians were there. And at every word he added: 'But don't hurry my little horse!' and stroked the animal. It was plain that he did not quite grasp where he was. Now he excused himself for having been taken prisoner, and now imagining himself before his own officers, insisted on his soldierly discipline and zeal in the service. He brought with him into our rearguard all the freshness of atmosphere of the French army, which was so alien to us.

The Cossacks sold the horse for two gold pieces, and Rostov, being the richest of the officers now that he had received his money, bought it.

'But don't hurt my little horse!' said the Alsatian good-naturedly to Rostov when the animal was handed over to the hussar.

Rostov smilingly reassured the dragoon and gave him money.

'Alley! Alley!' said the Cossack, touching the prisoner's arm to make him go on.

'The Emperor! The Emperor!' was suddenly heard among the hussars.

All began to run and bustle, and Rostov saw coming up the road behind him several riders with white plumes in their hats. In a moment everyone was in his place, waiting.

Rostov did not know or remember how he ran to his place and mounted. Instantly his regret at not having been in action and his dejected mood amid people of whom he was weary, had gone, instantly every thought of himself had vanished. He was filled with happiness at his nearness to the Emperor. He felt that this nearness by itself made up to him for the day he had lost. He was happy as a lover when the longed-for moment of meeting arrives. Not daring to look round and without looking round, he was ecstatically conscious of *his* approach. He felt it not only from the sound of the hoofs of the approaching cavalcade, but because as *he* drew near everything grew brighter, more joyful, more significant, and more festive around him. Nearer and nearer to Rostov came that sun shedding beams of mild and majestic light around, and already he felt himself enveloped in those beams, he heard *his* voice, that kindly, calm, and majestic voice, that was yet so simple! And as if in accord with Rostov's feeling, there was a deathly stillness amid which was heard the Emperor's voice.

'The Pavlograd hussars?' he inquired.

'The reserves, sire!' replied a voice, a very human one compared to that which had said: 'The Pavlograd hussars?'

The Emperor drew level with Rostov and halted. Alexander's face was even more beautiful than it had been three days before at the review. It shone with such gaiety and youth, such innocent youth, that it suggested the liveliness of a fourteen-year-old boy, and yet it was the face of the majestic Emperor. Casually, while surveying the squadron, the Emperor's eyes met Rostov's and rested on them for not more than two seconds. Whether or no the Emperor understood what was going on in Rostov's soul (it seemed to Rostov that he understood everything), at any rate his blue eyes gazed for about two seconds into Rostov's face. A gentle, mild light poured from them. Then all at once he raised his eyebrows, abruptly touched his horse with his left foot, and galloped on.

The young Emperor could not restrain his wish to be present at the battle and, in spite of the remonstrances of his courtiers, at twelve o'clock left the third column with which he had been, and galloped towards the vanguard. Before he came up with the hussars several adjutants met him with news of the successful result of the action.

This battle which consisted in the capture of a French squadron, was represented as a brilliant victory over the French, and so the Emperor and the whole army, especially while the smoke hung over the battlefield, believed that the French had been defeated and were retreating against their will. A few minutes after the Emperor had passed, the Pavlograd division was ordered to advance. In Wischau itself, a petty German town, Rostov saw the Emperor again. In the market-place where there had been some rather heavy firing before the Emperor's arrival, lay several killed and wounded soldiers whom there had not been time to move. The Emperor, surrounded by his suite of officers and courtiers, was riding a bob-tailed chestnut mare, a different one from that which he had ridden at the review, and bending to one side he gracefully held a gold lorgnette to his eyes and looked at a soldier who lay prone, with blood on his uncovered head. The wounded soldier was so dirty, coarse, and revolting, that his proximity to the Emperor shocked Rostov. Rostov saw how the Emperor's rather round shoulders shuddered as if a cold shiver had run down them, how his left foot began convulsively tapping the horse's side with the spur, and how the well-trained horse looked round unconcerned and did not stir. An adjutant, dismounting, lifted the soldier under the arms to place him on a stretcher that had been brought. The soldier groaned.

'Gently, gently! Can't you do it more gently?' said the Emperor, apparently suffering more than the dying soldier, and he rode away.

Rostov saw tears filling the Emperor's eyes and heard him, as he was riding away, say to Czartoryski:

'What a terrible thing war is: what a terrible thing! *Quelle terrible chose que la guerre!*'

The troops of the vanguard were stationed before Wischau within sight of the enemy's lines, which all day long had yielded ground to us at the least firing. The Emperor's gratitude was announced to the vanguard, rewards were promised and the men received a double ration of vodka. The camp-fires crackled and the soldiers' songs resounded even more merrily than on the previous night. Denisov celebrated his promotion to the rank of major, and Rostov, who had already drunk enough, at the end of the feast proposed the Emperor's health. 'Not "our Sovereign, the Emperor", as they say at official dinners,' said he, 'but the health of our Sovereign, that good, enchanting, and great man! Let us drink to his health and to the certain defeat of the French!'

'If we fought before,' he said, 'not letting the French pass, as at Schön Graben, what shall we not do now when *he* is at the front? We will all die for him gladly! Is it not so, gentlemen? Perhaps I am not saying it right, I have drunk a good deal – but that is how I feel, and so do you too! To the health of Alexander the First! Hurrah!'

'Hurrah!' rang the enthusiastic voices of the officers.

And the old cavalry captain Kirsten shouted enthusiastically and no less sincerely than the twenty-year-old Rostov.

When the officers had emptied and smashed their glasses, Kirsten filled others, and in shirt-sleeves and breeches went glass in hand to the soldiers' bonfires and with his long grey moustache, his white chest showing from under his open shirt, he stood in a majestic pose in the light of the camp-fire, waving his uplifted arm.

'Lads! here's to our Sovereign, the Emperor, and victory over our enemies! Hurrah!' he exclaimed in his dashing, old, hussar's baritone.

The hussars crowded round and responded heartily with loud shouts.

Late that night when all had separated, Denisov with his short hand patted his favourite, Rostov, on the shoulder.

'As there's no one to fall in love with on campaign, he's fallen in love with the Tsar,' he said.

'Denisov, don't make fun of it!' cried Rostov. 'It is such a lofty, beautiful feeling, such a . . .'

'I believe it, I believe it, fwiend, and I share and appwove . . .'

'No, you don't understand!'

And Rostov got up and went wandering among the camp-fires dreaming of what happiness it would be to die – not in saving the Emperor's life (he did not even dare to dream of that) but simply to die before his eyes. He really was in love with the Tsar and the glory of the Russian arms and the hope of future triumph. And he was not the only man to experience that feeling during those memorable days preceding the battle of Austerlitz; nine-tenths of the men in the Russian army were then in love, though less ecstatically, with their Tsar and the glory of the Russian arms.


11

THE next day the Emperor stopped at Wischau, and Villier, his physician, was repeatedly summoned to see him. At head-quarters and among the troops near by the news spread that the Emperor was unwell. He ate nothing and had slept badly that night, those around him reported. The cause of this indisposition was the strong impression made on his sensitive mind by the sight of the killed and wounded.

At daybreak on the 17th a French officer, who had come with a flag of truce demanding an audience with the Russian Emperor, was brought into Wischau from our outposts. This officer was Savary. The Emperor had only just fallen asleep and so Savary had to wait. At midday he was admitted to the Emperor, and an hour later he rode off with Prince Dolgorukov to the advanced post of the French army.

It was rumoured that Savary had been sent to propose to Alexander a meeting with Napoleon. To the joy and pride of the whole army a personal interview was refused, and instead of the Sovereign, Prince Dolgorukov, the victor at Wischau, was sent with Savary to negotiate with Napoleon, if contrary to expectation these negotiations were actuated by a real desire for peace.

Towards evening Dolgorukov came back, went straight to the Tsar, and remained alone with him for a long time.

On the 18th and 19th of November the army advanced two days' march, and the enemy's outposts after a brief interchange of shots retreated. In the highest army circles from midday on the 19th a great, excitedly bustling activity began which lasted till the morning of the 20th, when the memorable battle of Austerlitz was fought.

Till midday on the 19th the activity, the eager talk, running to and fro, and dispatching of adjutants, was confined to the Emperor's head-quarters. But on the afternoon of that day this activity reached Kutuzov's head-quarters and the staffs of the commanders of columns. By evening the adjutants had spread it to all ends and parts of the army, and in the night from the 19th to the 20th the whole eighty thousand allied troops rose from their bivouacs to the hum of voices, and the army swayed and started in one enormous mass six miles long.

The concentrated activity which had begun at the Emperor's head-quarters in the morning and had started the whole movement that followed, was like the first movement of the main wheel of a large tower-clock. One wheel slowly moved, another was set in motion, and a third, and wheels began to revolve faster and faster, levers and cogwheels to work, chimes to play, figures to pop out, and the hands to advance with regular motion as a result of all that activity.

Just as in the mechanism of a clock, so in the mechanism of the military machine, an impulse once given leads to the final result; and just as indifferently quiescent till the moment when motion is transmitted to them are the parts of the mechanism which the impulse has not yet reached. Wheels creak on their axles as the cogs engage one another and the revolving pulleys whirr with the rapidity of their movement, but a neighbouring wheel is as quiet and motionless as though it were prepared to remain so for a hundred years; but the moment comes when the lever catches it, and obeying the impulse that wheel begins to creak, and joins in the common motion the result and aim of which are beyond its ken.

Just as in a clock the result of the complicated motion of innumerable wheels and pulleys is merely a slow and regular movement of the hands which show the time, so the result of all the complicated human activities of 160,000 Russians and French – all their passions, desires, remorse, humiliations, sufferings, outbursts of pride, fear, and enthusiasm – was only the loss of the battle of Austerlitz, the so-called battle of the three Emperors – that is to say, a slow movement of the hand on the dial of human history.

Prince Andrew was on duty that day and in constant attendance on the commander-in-chief.

At six in the evening Kutuzov went to the Emperor's head-quarters and after staying but a short time with the Tsar went to see the grand marshal of the court, Count Tolstoy.

Bolkonsky took the opportunity to go in to get some details of the coming action from Dolgorukov. He felt that Kutuzov was upset and dissatisfied about something and that at head-quarters they were dissatisfied with him, and also that at the Emperor's head-quarters everyone adopted towards him the tone of men who knew something others did not know: he therefore wished to speak to Dolgorukov.

'Well, how d'you do, my dear fellow?' said Dolgorukov who was sitting at tea with Bilibin. 'The fête is for to-morrow. How is your old fellow? Out of sorts?'

'I won't say he is out of sorts, but I fancy he would like to be heard.'

'But they heard him at the council of war and will hear him when he talks sense, but to temporize and wait for something now when Bonaparte fears nothing so much as a general battle is impossible.'

'Yes, you have seen him?' said Prince Andrew. 'Well, what is Bonaparte like? How did he impress you?'

'Yes, I saw him, and am convinced that he fears nothing so much as a general engagement,' repeated Dolgorukov, evidently prizing this general conclusion which he had arrived at from his interview with Napoleon. 'If he weren't afraid of a battle why did he ask for that interview? Why negotiate, and above all why retreat, when to retreat is so contrary to his method of conducting war? Believe me he is afraid, afraid of a general battle. His hour has come! Mark my words!'

'But tell me, what is he like, eh?' said Prince Andrew again.

'He is a man in a grey overcoat, very anxious that I should call him "Your Majesty", but who to his chagrin got no title from me! That's the sort of man he is, and nothing more,' replied Dolgorukov, looking round at Bilibin with a smile.

'Despite my great respect for old Kutuzov,' he continued, 'we should be a nice set of fellows if we were to wait about and so give him a chance to escape, or to trick us, now that we certainly have him in our hands! No, we mustn't forget Suvorov and his rule – not to put yourself in a position to be attacked, but yourself to attack. Believe me in war the energy of young men often shows the way better than all the experience of old Cunctators.'

'But in what position are we going to attack him? I have been at the outposts to-day and it is impossible to say where his chief forces are situated,' said Prince Andrew.

He wished to explain to Dolgorukov a plan of attack he had himself formed.

'Oh, that is all the same,' Dolgorukov said quickly, and getting up he spread a map on the table. 'All eventualities have been foreseen. If he is standing before Brunn . . .'

And Prince Dolgorukov rapidly but indistinctly explained Weyrother's plan of a flanking movement.

Prince Andrew began to reply and to state his own plan, which might have been as good as Weyrother's but for the disadvantage that Weyrother's had already been approved. As soon as Prince Andrew began to demonstrate the defects of the latter and the merits of his own plan, Prince Dolgorukov ceased to listen to him and gazed absent-mindedly not at the map but at Prince Andrew's face.

'There will be a council of war at Kutuzov's to-night though; you can say all this there,' remarked Dolgorukov.

'I will do so,' said Prince Andrew, moving away from the map.

'Whatever are you bothering about, gentlemen?' said Bilibin, who till then had listened with an amused smile to their conversation and now was evidently ready with a joke. 'Whether to-morrow brings victory or defeat the glory of our Russian arms is secure. Except your Kutuzov there is not a single Russian in command of a column! The commanders are: Herr General Wimpfen, le Comte de Langeron, le Prince de Lichtenstein, le Prince de Hohenlohe, and finally Prishprish,* and so on like all those Polish names.'

'Be quiet, backbiter!' said Dolgorukov. 'It is not true; there are now two Russians, Miloradovich and Dokhturov, and there would be a third, Count Arakcheev, if his nerves were not too weak.'

'However, I think General Kutuzov has come out,' said Prince Andrew. 'I wish you good luck and success, gentlemen!' he added, and went out after shaking hands with Dolgorukov and Bilibin.

On the way home Prince Andrew could not refrain from asking Kutuzov, who was sitting silently beside him, what he thought of to-morrow's battle.

Kutuzov looked sternly at his adjutant and after a pause replied: 'I think the battle will be lost, and so I told Count Tolstoy and asked him to tell the Emperor. What do you think he replied? "My dear General, I am engaged with rice and cutlets, look after military matters yourself!" Yes . . . That was the answer I got!'

## 12

SHORTLY after nine o'clock that evening Weyrother drove with his plans to Kutuzov's quarters where the council of war was to be held. All the commanders of columns were summoned to the commander-in-chief's and with the exception of Prince Bagration, who declined to come, were all there at the appointed time.

Weyrother who was in full control of the proposed battle, by his eagerness and briskness presented a marked contrast to the dissatisfied and drowsy Kutuzov who reluctantly played the part of chairman and president of the council of war. Weyrother evidently felt himself to be at the head of a movement that had already become unrestrainable. He was like a horse running downhill harnessed to a heavy cart. Whether he was pulling it or being pushed by it he did not know, but rushed along at headlong speed with no time to consider what this movement might lead to. Weyrother had been twice that evening to the enemy's picket line to reconnoitre personally, and twice to the Emperors, Russian and Austrian, to report and explain, and to his head-quarters where he had dictated the disposition in German, and now much exhausted he arrived at Kutuzov's.

He was evidently so busy that he even forgot to be polite to the commander-in-chief. He interrupted him, talked rapidly and indistinctly without looking at the man he was addressing, and did not reply to questions put to him. He was bespattered with mud and had a pitiful, weary, and distracted air, though at the same time he was haughty and self-confident.

Kutuzov was occupying a nobleman's castle of modest dimensions near Ostralitz. In the large drawing-room which had become the commander-in-chief's office, were gathered Kutuzov himself, Weyrother, and the members of the council of war. They were drinking tea, and only awaited Prince Bagration to begin the council. At last Bagration's orderly came with the news that the prince could not attend. Prince Andrew came in to inform the commander-in-chief of this, and availing himself of permission previously given him by Kutuzov to be present at the council, he remained in the room.

'Since Prince Bagration is not coming we may begin,' said Weyrother, hurriedly rising from his seat and going up to the table on which an enormous map of the environs of Brunn was spread out.

Kutuzov, with his uniform unbuttoned so that his fat neck bulged over his collar as if escaping, was sitting almost asleep in a low chair with his podgy old hands resting symmetrically on its arms. At the sound of Weyrother's voice he opened his one eye with an effort.

'Yes, yes, if you please! It is already late,' said he, and nodding his head he let it droop and again closed his eye.

If at first the members of the council thought that Kutuzov was pretending to be asleep, the sounds his nose emitted during the reading that followed proved that the commander-in-chief at that moment was absorbed by a far more serious matter than a desire to show his contempt for the dispositions or anything else – he was engaged in satisfying the irresistible human need for sleep. He really was asleep. Weyrother, with the gesture of a man too busy to lose a moment, glanced at Kutuzov and having convinced himself that he was asleep, took up a paper and in a loud monotonous voice began to read out the dispositions for the impending battle, under a heading which he also read out:

'Dispositions for an attack on the enemy position behind Kobelnitz and Sokolnitz, 30th November* 1805.'

The dispositions were very complicated and difficult. They began as follows:

'As the enemy's left wing rests on wooded hills and his right extends along Kobelnitz and Sokolnitz behind the ponds that are there, while we on the other hand with our left wing by far outflank his right, it is advantageous to attack the enemy's latter wing especially if we occupy the villages of Sokolnitz and Kobelnitz, whereby we can both fall on his flank and pursue him over the plain between Schlappanitz and the Thuerassa forest, avoiding the defiles of Schlappanitz and Bellowitz which cover the enemy's front. For this object it is necessary that . . . The first column marches . . . The second column marches . . . The third column marches . . .' and so on, read Weyrother.

The generals seemed to listen reluctantly to the difficult dispositions. The tall fair-haired General Buxhöwden stood leaning his back against the wall, his eyes fixed on a burning candle, and seemed not to listen nor even to wish to be thought to listen. Exactly opposite Weyrother, with his glistening wide-open eyes fixed upon him and his moustache twisted upwards, sat the ruddy Miloradovich in a military pose, his elbows turned outwards, his hands on his knees, and his shoulders raised. He remained stubbornly silent, gazing at Weyrother's face, and only turned away his eyes when the Austrian chief-of-staff finished reading. Then Miloradovich looked round significantly at the other generals. But one could not tell from that significant look whether he agreed or disagreed and was satisfied or not with the arrangements. Next to Weyrother sat Count Langeron who, with a subtle smile that never left his typically southern French face during the whole time of the reading, gazed at his delicate fingers which rapidly twirled by its corners a gold snuff-box on which was a portrait. In the middle of one of the longest sentences he stopped the rotary motion of the snuff-box, raised his head, and with inimical politeness lurking in the corners of his thin lips, interrupted Weyrother wishing to say something. But the Austrian general continuing to read, frowned angrily and jerked his elbows, as if to say: 'You can tell me your views later, but now be so good as to look at the map and listen.' Langeron lifted his eyes with an expression of perplexity, turned round to Miloradovich as if seeking an explanation, but meeting the latter's impressive but meaningless gaze, drooped his eyes sadly and again took to twirling his snuff-box.

'A geography lesson!' he muttered as if to himself, but loud enough to be heard.

Przebyszewski, with respectful but dignified politeness, held his hand to his ear towards Weyrother with the air of a man absorbed in attention. Dohkturov, a little man, sat opposite Weyrother with an assiduous and modest mien, and stooping over the outspread map conscientiously studied the dispositions and the unfamiliar locality. He asked Weyrother several times to repeat words he had not clearly heard and the difficult names of villages. Weyrother complied and Dohkturov noted them down.

When the reading which lasted more than an hour was over, Langeron again brought his snuff-box to rest and, without looking at Weyrother or at anyone in particular, began to say how difficult it was to carry out such a plan in which the enemy's position was assumed to be known, whereas it was perhaps not known, since the enemy was in movement. Langeron's objections were valid but it was obvious that their chief aim was to show General Weyrother – who had read his dispositions with as much self-confidence as if he were addressing school-children – that he had to do not with fools but with men who could teach him something in military matters.

When the monotonous sound of Weyrother's voice ceased, Kutuzov opened his eye as a miller wakes up when the soporific drone of the mill-wheel is interrupted. He listened to what Langeron said, as if remarking, 'So you are still at that silly business!' quickly closed his eye again and let his head sink still lower.

Langeron, trying as virulently as possible to sting Weyrother's vanity as author of the military plan, argued that Bonaparte might easily attack instead of being attacked, and so render the whole of this plan perfectly worthless. Weyrother met all objections with a firm and contemptuous smile, evidently prepared beforehand to meet all objections be they what they might.

'If he could attack us he would have done so to-day,' said he.

'So you think he is powerless?' said Langeron.

'He has forty thousand men at most,' replied Weyrother with the smile of a doctor to whom an old wife wishes to explain the treatment of a case.

'In that case he is inviting his doom by awaiting our attack,' said Langeron with a subtly ironical smile, again glancing round for support to Miloradovich who was near him.

But Miloradovich was at that moment evidently thinking of anything rather than of what the generals were disputing about.

'*Ma foi!*' said he, 'to-morrow we shall see all that on the battlefield.'

Weyrother again gave that smile which seemed to say that to him it was strange and ridiculous to meet objections from Russian generals, and to have to prove to them what he had not merely convinced himself of, but had also convinced the sovereign Emperors of.

'The enemy has quenched his fires and a continual noise is heard from his camp,' said he. 'What does that mean? Either he is retreating, which is the only thing we need fear, or he is changing his position.' (He smiled ironically.) 'But even if he also took up a position in the Thuerassa, he merely saves us a great deal of trouble and all our arrangements to the minutest detail remain the same.'

'How is that? . . .' began Prince Andrew, who had for long been awaiting an opportunity to express his doubts.

Kutuzov here woke up, coughed heavily, and looked round at the generals.

'Gentlemen, the dispositions for to-morrow – or rather for to-day, for it is past midnight – cannot now be altered,' said he. 'You have heard them, and we shall all do our duty. But before a battle there is nothing more important . . .' he paused, 'than to have a good sleep.'

He moved as if to rise. The generals bowed and retired. It was past midnight. Prince Andrew went out.

The council of war, at which Prince Andrew had not been able to express his opinion as he had hoped to, left on him a vague and uneasy impression. Whether Dolgorukov and Weyrother, or Kutuzov, Langeron, and the others who did not approve of the plan of attack, were right – he did not know. 'But was it really not possible for Kutuzov to state his views plainly to the Emperor?

Is it possible that on account of court and personal considerations tens of thousands of lives, and my life, my life,' he thought, 'must be risked?'

'Yes, it is very likely that I shall be killed to-morrow,' he thought. And suddenly at this thought of death a whole series of most distant, most intimate, memories rose in his imagination: he remembered his last parting from his father and his wife; he remembered the days when he first loved her. He thought of her pregnancy and felt sorry for her and for himself, and in a nervously emotional and softened mood he went out of the hut in which he was billeted with Nesvitsky and began to walk up and down before it.

The night was foggy and through the fog the moonlight gleamed mysteriously. 'Yes, to-morrow, to-morrow!' he thought. 'To-morrow everything may be over for me! All these memories will be no more, none of them will have any meaning for me. To-morrow perhaps, even certainly, I have a presentiment that for the first time I shall have to show all I can do.' And his fancy pictured the battle, its loss, the concentration of fighting at one point, and the hesitation of all the commanders. And then that happy moment, that Toulon for which he had so long waited, presents itself to him at last. He firmly and clearly expresses his opinion to Kutuzov, to Weyrother, and to the Emperors. All are struck by the justness of his views but no one undertakes to carry them out, so he takes a regiment, a division – stipulates that no one is to interfere with his arrangements – leads his division to the decisive point, and gains the victory alone. 'But death and suffering?' suggested another voice. Prince Andrew however did not answer that voice and went on dreaming of his triumphs. The dispositions for the next battle are planned by him alone. Nominally he is only an adjutant on Kutuzov's staff, but he does everything alone. Kutuzov is removed and he is appointed ... 'Well and then?' asked the other voice. 'If before that you are not ten times wounded, killed, or betrayed, well ... what then? ...'* 'Well then,' Prince Andrew answered himself, 'I don't know what will happen and don't want to know, and can't, but if I want this – want glory, want to be known to men, want to be loved by them, it is not my fault that I want it and want nothing but that and live only for that. Yes, for that alone! I shall never tell anyone, but, oh God! what am I to do if I love nothing but fame and men's love? Death, wounds, the loss of family – I fear nothing. And precious and dear as many persons are to me – father, sister, wife – those dearest to me – yet dreadful and unnatural as it seems, I would give them all at once for a moment of glory, of triumph over men, of love from men I don't know and never shall know, for the love of these men here,' he thought, as he listened to voices in Kutuzov's courtyard. The voices were those of the orderlies who were packing up; one voice, probably a coachman's, was teasing Kutuzov's old cook whom Prince Andrew knew, and who was called Tit. He was saying, 'Tit, I say, Tit!'

'Well?' returned the old man.

'Go, Tit, thresh a bit!' said the wag.

'Oh, go to the devil!' called out a voice, drowned by the laughter of the orderlies and servants.

'All the same, I love and value nothing but triumph over them all, I value this mystic power and glory that is floating here above me in this mist!'

## 13

THAT same night Rostov was with a platoon on skirmishing duty in front of Bagration's detachment. His hussars were placed along the line in couples and he himself rode along the line trying to master the sleepiness that kept coming over him. An enormous space, with our army's camp fires dimly glowing in the fog, could be seen behind him, in front of him was misty darkness. Rostov could see nothing, peer as he would into that foggy distance: now something gleamed grey, now there was something black, now little lights seemed to glimmer where the enemy ought to be, now he fancied it was only something in his own eyes. His eyes kept closing, and in his fancy appeared – now the Emperor, now Denisov, and now Moscow memories – and he again hurriedly opened his eyes and saw close before him the head and ears of the horse he was riding, and sometimes when he came within six paces of them, the black figures of hussars, but in the distance was still the same misty darkness. 'Why not? . . . it might easily happen,' thought Rostov, 'that the Emperor will meet me and give me an order as he would to any other officer; he'll say: "Go and find out what's there." There are many stories of his getting to know an officer in just such a chance way and attaching him to himself! What if he gave me a place near him? Oh, how I would guard him, how I would tell him the truth, how I would unmask his deceivers!' And in order to realize vividly his love and devotion to the sovereign, Rostov pictured to himself an enemy or a deceitful German, whom he would not only kill with pleasure but whom he would slap in the face before the Emperor. Suddenly a distant shout aroused him. He started and opened his eyes.

'Where am I? Oh yes, in the skirmishing line . . . pass and

watchword – *shaft, Olmütz*. What a nuisance that our squadron will be in reserve to-morrow,' he thought. 'I'll ask leave to go to the front, this may be my only chance of seeing the Emperor. It won't be long now before I am off duty. I'll take another turn and when I get back I'll go to the general and ask him.' He readjusted himself in the saddle and touched up his horse to ride once more round his hussars. It seemed to him that it was getting lighter. To the left he saw a sloping descent lit up, and facing it a black knoll that seemed as steep as a wall. On this knoll there was a white patch that Rostov could not at all make out: was it a glade in the wood lit up by the moon, or some unmelted snow, or some white houses? He even thought something moved on that white spot. 'I expect it's snow . . . that spot . . . a spot – *une tache*,' he thought. 'There now . . . it's not a *tache* . . . Natasha . . . sister, black eyes . . . Na . . . tasha . . . (won't she be surprised when I tell her how I've seen the Emperor?) Natasha . . . take my *sabretache* . . .' – 'Keep to the right, your honour, there are bushes here,' came the voice of an hussar past whom Rostov was riding in the act of falling asleep. Rostov lifted his head that had sunk almost to his horse's mane and pulled up beside the hussar. He was succumbing to irresistible, youthful, childish drowsiness. 'But what was I thinking? I mustn't forget. How I shall speak to the Emperor? No, that's not it – that's to-morrow. Oh yes! Na-tasha . . . *sabretache* . . . sabre them . . . Whom? The hussars . . . Ah, the hussars with moustaches. Along the Tverskaya Street rode that hussar with moustaches . . . I thought about him too just opposite Guryev's house . . . Old Guryev . . . Oh, but Denisov's a fine fellow. But that's all nonsense. The chief thing is that the Emperor is here. How he looked at me and wished to say something, but dared not . . . No, it was I who dared not. But that's nonsense, the chief thing is not to forget the important thing I was thinking of. Yes, Na-tasha, *sabretache*, oh, yes, yes! That's right!' And his head once more sank to his horse's neck. All at once it seemed to him that he was being fired at. 'What? What? What? . . . Cut them down! What? . . .' said Rostov, waking up. At the moment he opened his eyes he heard in front of him, where the enemy was, the long-drawn shouts of thousands of voices. His horse and the horse of the hussar near him pricked their ears at these shouts. Over there, where the shouting came from, a fire flared up and went out again, then another, and all along the French line on the hill fires flared up and the shouting grew louder and louder. Rostov could hear the sound of French words but could not distinguish them. The din of many voices was too great; all he could hear was: 'ahahah!' and 'rrrr!'

'What's that? What do you make of it?' said Rostov to the hussar beside him. 'That must be the enemy's camp!'

The hussar did not reply.

'Why, don't you hear it?' Rostov asked again, after waiting for a reply.

'Who can tell, your honour?' replied the hussar reluctantly.

'From the direction it must be the enemy,' repeated Rostov.

'It may be him or it may be nothing,' muttered the hussar. 'It's dark . . . Steady!' he cried to his fidgeting horse.

Rostov's horse was also getting restive: it pawed the frozen ground, pricking its ears at the noise and looking at the lights. The shouting grew still louder and merged into a general roar that only an army of several thousand men could produce. The lights spread farther and farther, probably along the line of the French camp. Rostov no longer wanted to sleep. The gay triumphant shouting of the enemy army had a stimulating effect on him. '*Vive l'Empereur! l'Empereur!*' he now heard distinctly.

'They can't be far off, probably just beyond the stream,' he said to the hussar beside him.

The hussar only sighed without replying, and coughed angrily. The sound of horse's hoofs approaching at a trot along the line of hussars was heard, and out of the foggy darkness the figure of a sergeant of hussars suddenly appeared, looming huge as an elephant.

'Your honour, the generals!' said the sergeant, riding up to Rostov.

Rostov, still looking round towards the fires and the shouts, rode with the sergeant to meet some mounted men who were riding along the line. One was on a white horse. Prince Bagration and Prince Dolgorukov with their adjutants had come to witness the curious phenomenon of the lights and shouts in the enemy's camp. Rostov rode up to Bagration, reported to him, and then joined the adjutants listening to what the generals were saying.

'Believe me,' said Prince Dolgorukov, addressing Bagration, 'it is nothing but a trick! He has retreated and ordered the rearguards to kindle fires and make a noise to deceive us.'

'Hardly,' said Bagration. 'I saw them this evening on that knoll; if they had retreated they would have withdrawn from that too . . . Officer!' said Bagration to Rostov, 'are the enemy's skirmishers still there?'

'They were there this evening, but now I don't know, your Excellency. Shall I go with some of my hussars to see?' replied Rostov.

Bagration stopped, and before replying tried to see Rostov's face in the mist.

'Well, go and see,' he said, after a pause.

'Yes, sir.'

Rostov spurred his horse, called to Sergeant Fedchenko and two other hussars, told them to follow him, and trotted downhill in the direction from which the shouting came. He felt both frightened and pleased to be riding alone with three hussars into that mysterious and dangerous misty distance where no one had been before him. Bagration called to him from the hill not to go beyond the stream, but Rostov pretended not to hear him and did not stop but rode on and on, continually mistaking bushes for trees and gullies for men, and continually discovering his mistakes. Having descended the hill at a trot he no longer saw either our own or the enemy's fires, but heard the shouting of the French more loudly and distinctly. In the valley he saw before him something like a river, but when he reached it he found it was a road. Having come out onto the road he reined in his horse, hesitating whether to ride along it or cross it and ride over the black field up the hill-side. To keep to the road which gleamed white in the mist would have been safer because it would be easier to see people coming along it. 'Follow me!' said he, crossed the road, and began riding up the hill at a gallop towards the point where the French pickets had been standing that evening.

'Your honour, there he is!' cried one of the hussars behind him. And before Rostov had time to make out what the black thing was that had suddenly appeared in the fog, there was a flash followed by a report, and a bullet whizzing high up in the mist with a plaintive sound passed out of hearing. Another musket missed fire but flashed in the pan. Rostov turned his horse and galloped back. Four more reports followed at intervals, and the bullets passed somewhere in the fog singing in different tones. Rostov reined in his horse, whose spirits had risen like his own at the firing, and went back at a foot-pace. 'Well, some more! Some more!' a merry voice was saying in his soul. But no more shots came.

Only when approaching Bagration did Rostov let his horse gallop again, and with his hand at the salute rode up to the general.

Dolgorukov was still insisting that the French had retreated and had only lit fires to deceive us.

'What does that prove?' he was saying as Rostov rode up. 'They might retreat and leave the pickets.'

'It's plain they have not all gone yet, Prince,' said Bagration. 'Wait till to-morrow morning, we'll find out everything to-morrow.'

'The picket is still on the hill, your Excellency, just where it was in the evening,' reported Rostov, stooping forward with his hand at the salute and unable to repress the smile of delight induced by his ride and especially by the sound of the bullets.

'Very good, very good,' said Bagration. 'Thank you, officer.'

'Your Excellency,' said Rostov, 'may I ask a favour?'

'What is it?'

'To-morrow our squadron is to be in reserve. May I ask to be attached to the first squadron?'

'What's your name?'

'Count Rostov.'

'Oh, very well, you may stay in attendance on me.'

'Count Ilya Rostov's son?' asked Dolgorukov.

But Rostov did not reply.

'Then I may reckon on it, your Excellency?'

'I will give the order.'

'To-morrow very likely I may be sent with some message to the Emperor,' thought Rostov. 'Thank God!'

The fires and shouting in the enemy's army were occasioned by the fact that while Napoleon's proclamation was being read to the troops the Emperor himself rode round his bivouacs. The soldiers on seeing him lit wisps of straw and ran after him shouting, 'Vive l'Empereur!' Napoleon's proclamation was as follows:

Soldiers! The Russian army is advancing against you to avenge the Austrian army of Ulm. They are the same battalions you broke at Hollabrünn* and have pursued ever since to this place. The position we occupy is a strong one, and while they are marching to go round me on the right they will expose a flank to me. Soldiers! I will myself direct your battalions. I will keep out of fire if you with your habitual valour carry disorder and confusion into the enemy's ranks, but should victory be in doubt even for a moment, you will see your Emperor exposing himself to the first blows of the enemy, for there must be no doubt of victory, especially on this day when what is at stake is the honour of the French infantry, so necessary to the honour of our nation.

Do not break your ranks on the plea of removing the wounded! Let every man be fully imbued with the thought that we must defeat these hirelings of England, inspired by such hatred of our nation! This victory will conclude our campaign and we can return to winter quarters, where fresh French troops who are being raised in France will join us, and the peace I shall conclude will be worthy of my people, of you, and of myself.

Napoleon.

## 14

AT five in the morning it was still quite dark. The troops of the centre, the reserves, and Bagration's right flank, had not yet moved, but on the left flank the columns of infantry, cavalry, and artillery which were to be the first to descend the heights to attack the French right flank and drive it into the Bohemian mountains according to plan, were already up and astir. The smoke of the camp-fires, into which they were throwing everything superfluous, made the eyes smart! It was cold and dark. The officers were hurriedly drinking tea and breakfasting, the soldiers, munching biscuit and beating a tattoo with their feet to warm themselves, gathering round the fires throwing into the flames the remains of sheds, chairs, tables, wheels, tubs, and everything that they did not want or could not carry away with them. Austrian column-guides were moving in and out among the Russian troops and served as heralds of the advance. As soon as an Austrian officer showed himself near a commanding officer's quarters the regiment began to move: the soldiers ran from the fires, thrust their pipes into their boots, their bags into the carts, got their muskets ready, and formed rank. The officers buttoned up their coats, buckled on their swords and pouches, and moved along the ranks shouting. The train-drivers and orderlies harnessed and packed the wagons and tied on the loads. The adjutants and battalion and regimental commanders mounted, crossed themselves, gave final instructions, orders, and commissions to the baggage men who remained behind, and the monotonous tramp of thousands of feet resounded. The columns moved forward without knowing where, and unable from the masses around them, the smoke, and the increasing fog, to see either the place they were leaving or that to which they were going.

A soldier on the march is hemmed in and borne along by his regiment as much as a sailor is by his ship. However far he has walked, whatever strange, unknown, and dangerous places he reaches, just as a sailor is always surrounded by the same decks, masts, and rigging of his ship, so the soldier always has around him the same comrades, the same ranks, the same sergeant-major Ivan Mitrich, the same company dog Jack, and the same commanders. The sailor rarely cares to know the latitude in which his ship is sailing, but on the day of battle – heaven knows how and whence – a stern note of which all are conscious sounds in the moral atmosphere of an army, announcing the approach of something decisive and solemn, and awakening in the men an unusual curiosity. On the day of battle the soldiers excitedly try to get beyond the interests of their regiment, they listen intently, look about, and eagerly ask concerning what is going on around them.

The fog had grown so dense that though it was growing light they could not see ten paces ahead. Bushes looked like gigantic trees and level ground like cliffs and slopes. Anywhere, on any side, one might encounter an enemy invisible ten paces off. But the columns advanced for a long time, always in the same fog, descending and ascending hills, avoiding gardens and enclosures, going over new and unknown ground, and nowhere encountering the enemy. On the contrary, the soldiers became aware that in front, behind, and on all sides, other Russian columns were moving in the same direction. Every soldier felt glad to know that to the unknown place where he was going, many many more of our men were going too.

'There now, the Kurskies have also gone past,' was being said in the ranks.

'It's wonderful what a lot of our troops have gathered, lads! Last night I looked at the camp-fires and there was no end of them. A regular Moscow!'

Though none of the column commanders rode up to the ranks or talked to the men (the commanders, as we saw at the council of war, were out of humour and dissatisfied with the affair, and so did not extend themselves to cheer the men but merely carried out the orders), yet the troops marched gaily, as they always do when going into action, especially to an attack. But when they had marched for about an hour in the dense fog, the greater part of the men had to halt, and an unpleasant consciousness of some dislocation and blunder spread through the ranks. How such a consciousness is communicated is very difficult to define, but it certainly is communicated very surely, and flows rapidly, imperceptibly, and irresponsibly, as water does in a creek. Had the Russian army been alone without any allies, it might perhaps have been a long time before this consciousness of mismanagement became a general conviction, but as it was, the disorder was readily and naturally attributed to the stupid Germans, and everyone was convinced that a dangerous muddle had been occasioned by the sausage-eaters.

'Why have we stopped? Is the way blocked? Or have we already come up against the French?'

'No, one can't hear them. They'd be firing if we had.'

'They were in hurry enough to start us, and now here we stand in the middle of a field without rhyme or reason. It's all those damned Germans' muddling! What stupid devils!'

'Yes, I'd send them on in front, but no fear, they're crowding up behind. And now here we stand hungry.'

'I say, shall we soon be clear? They say the cavalry are blocking the way,' said an officer.

'Ah, those damned Germans! They don't know their own country!' said another.

'What division are you?' shouted an adjutant, riding up.

'The Eighteenth.'

'Then why are you here? You should have gone on long ago, now you won't get there till evening.'

'What stupid orders! They don't themselves know what they are doing!' said the officer and rode off.

Then a general rode past shouting something angrily, not in Russian.

'Tafa-lafa! But what he's jabbering no one can make out,' said a soldier, mimicking the general who had ridden away. 'I'd shoot them, the scoundrels!'

'We were ordered to be at the place before nine, but we haven't got halfway. Fine orders!' was being repeated on different sides.

And the feeling of energy with which the troops had started began to turn into vexation and anger at the stupid arrangements, and at the Germans.

The cause of the confusion was that while the Austrian cavalry was moving towards our left flank, the higher command found that our centre was too far separated from our right flank and the cavalry were all ordered to turn back to the right. Several thousand cavalry crossed in front of the infantry, who had to wait.

At the front an altercation occurred between an Austrian guide and a Russian general. The general shouted a demand that the cavalry should be halted, the Austrian argued that not he, but the higher command, was to blame. The troops meanwhile stood growing listless and dispirited. After an hour's delay they at last moved on, descending the hill. The fog that was dispersing on the hill lay still more densely below, where they were descending. In front in the fog a shot was heard and then another, at first irregularly at varying intervals – trata . . . tat – and then more and more regularly and rapidly, and the action at the Goldbach stream began.

Not expecting to come on the enemy down by the stream, and having stumbled on him in the fog, hearing no encouraging word from their commanders, and with a consciousness of being too late spreading through the ranks, and above all being unable to see anything in front or around them in the thick fog, the Russians exchanged shots with the enemy lazily, and advanced and again halted, receiving no timely orders from the officers or adjutants who wandered about in the fog in those unknown surroundings unable to find their own regiments. In this way the action began for the first, second, and third columns, which had gone down into the valley. The fourth column, with which Kutuzov was, stood on the Pratzen heights.

Below, where the fight was beginning, there was still thick fog; on the higher ground it was clearing, but nothing could be seen of what was going on in front. Whether all the enemy forces were, as we supposed, six miles away, or whether they were near by in that sea of mist, no one knew till after eight o'clock.

It was nine o'clock in the morning. The fog lay unbroken like a sea down below, but higher up at the village of Schlappanitz where Napoleon stood with his marshals around him, it was quite light. Above him was a clear blue sky, and the sun's vast orb quivered like a huge, hollow, crimson float on the surface of that milky sea of mist. The whole French army, and even Napoleon himself with his staff, were not on the far side of the streams and hollows of Sokolnitz and Schlappanitz beyond which we intended to take up our position and begin the action, but were on this side, so close to our own forces that Napoleon with the naked eye could distinguish a mounted man from one on foot. Napoleon, in the blue cloak which he had worn on his Italian campaign, sat on his small grey Arab horse a little in front of his marshals. He gazed silently at the hills which seemed to rise out of the sea of mist and on which the Russian troops were moving in the distance, and he listened to the sounds of firing in the valley. Not a single muscle of his face – which in those days was still thin – moved. His gleaming eyes were fixed intently on one spot. His predictions were being justified. Part of the Russian force had already descended into the valley towards the ponds and lakes, and part were leaving these Pratzen heights which he intended to attack and regarded as the key to the position. He saw over the mist that in a hollow between two hills near the village of Pratzen, the Russian columns, their bayonets glittering, were moving continuously in one direction towards the valley and disappearing one after another into the mist. From information he had received the evening before, from the sound of wheels and footsteps heard by the outposts during the night, by the disorderly movement of the Russian columns, and from all indications, he saw clearly that the allies believed him to be far away in front of them, and that the columns moving near Pratzen constituted the centre of the Russian army, and that centre was already sufficiently weakened to be successfully attacked. But still he did not begin the engagement.

To-day was a great day for him – the anniversary of his coronation. Before dawn he had slept for a few hours, and refreshed, vigorous, and in good spirits, he mounted his horse and rode out into the field in that happy mood in which everything seems possible and everything succeeds. He sat motionless, looking at the heights visible above the mist, and his cold face wore that special look of confident, self-complacent happiness that one sees on the face of a boy happily in love. The marshals stood behind him not venturing to distract his attention. He looked now at the Pratzen heights, now at the sun floating up out of the mist.

When the sun had entirely emerged from the fog, and fields and mist were aglow with dazzling light – as if he had only awaited this to begin the action – he drew the glove from his shapely white hand, made a sign with it to the marshals, and ordered the action to begin. The marshals, accompanied by adjutants, galloped off in different directions, and a few minutes later the chief forces of the French army moved rapidly towards those Pratzen heights which were being more and more denuded by Russian troops moving down the valley to their left.

15

AT eight o'clock Kutuzov rode to Pratzen at the head of the fourth column, Miloradovich's, the one that was to take the place of Przebyszewski's and Langeron's columns which had already gone down into the valley. He greeted the men of the foremost regiment and gave them the order to march, thereby indicating that he intended to lead that column himself. When he had reached the village of Pratzen he halted. Prince Andrew was behind, among the immense number forming the commander-in-chief's suite. He was in a state of suppressed excitement and irritation, though controlledly calm as a man is at the approach of a long-awaited moment. He was firmly convinced that this was the day of his Toulon, or his bridge of Arcole. How it would come about he did not know, but he felt sure it would do so. The locality and the position of our troops were known to him as far as they could be known to anyone in our army. His own strategic plan, which obviously could not now be carried out, was forgotten. Now, entering into Weyrother's plan, Prince Andrew considered possible contingencies and formed new projects such as might call for his rapidity of perception and decision.

To the left down below in the mist, the musketry fire of unseen forces could be heard. It was there Prince Andrew thought the fight would concentrate. 'There we shall encounter difficulties, and there,' thought he, 'I shall be sent with a brigade or division, and there, standard in hand, I shall go forward and break whatever is in front of me.'

He could not look calmly at the standards of the passing battalions. Seeing them he kept thinking, 'That may be the very standard with which I shall lead the army.'

In the morning all that was left of the night-mist on the heights was a hoar frost now turning to dew, but in the valleys it still lay like a milk-white sea. Nothing was visible in the valley to the left into which our troops had descended and from whence came the sounds of firing. Above the heights was the dark clear sky, and to the right the vast orb of the sun. In front, far off on the farther shore of that sea of mist some wooded hills were discernible, and it was there the enemy probably was, for something could be descried. On the right the Guards were entering the misty region with a sound of hoofs and wheels and now and then a gleam of bayonets; to the left beyond the village similar masses of cavalry came up and disappeared in the sea of mist. In front and behind moved infantry. The commander-in-chief was standing at the end of the village letting the troops pass by him. That morning Kutuzov seemed worn and irritable. The infantry passing before him came to a halt without any command being given, apparently obstructed by something in front.

'Do order them to form into battalion columns and go round the village!' he said angrily to a general who had ridden up. 'Don't you understand, your Excellency, my dear sir, that you must not defile through narrow village streets when we are marching against the enemy?'

'I intended to re-form them beyond the village, your Excellency,' answered the general.

Kutuzov laughed bitterly.

'You'll make a fine thing of it, deploying in sight of the enemy! Very fine!'

'The enemy is still far away, your Excellency. According to the dispositions...'

'The dispositions!' exclaimed Kutuzov bitterly. 'Who told you that? ...Kindly do as you are ordered.'

'Yes, sir.'

'My dear fellow,' Nesvitsky whispered to Prince Andrew, 'the old man is as surly as a dog.'

An Austrian officer in a white uniform with green plumes in

his hat galloped up to Kutuzov and asked in the Emperor's name, Had the fourth column advanced into action?

Kutuzov turned round without answering and his eye happened to fall upon Prince Andrew, who was beside him, Seeing him, Kutuzov's malevolent and caustic expression softened, as if admitting that what was being done was not his adjutant's fault, and still not answering the Austrian adjutant, he addressed Bolkonsky.

'Go, my dear fellow, and see whether the third division has passed the village. Tell it to stop and await my orders.'

Hardly had Prince Andrew started than he stopped him.

'And ask whether sharpshooters have been posted,' he added. 'What are they doing? What are they doing?' he murmured to himself, still not replying to the Austrian.

Prince Andrew galloped off to execute the order.

Overtaking the battalions that continued to advance, he stopped the third division and convinced himself that there really were no sharpshooters in front of our columns. The colonel at the head of the regiment was much surprised at the commander-in-chief's order to throw out skirmishers. He had felt perfectly sure that there were other troops in front of him and that the enemy must be at least six miles away. There was really nothing to be seen in front except a barren descent hidden by dense mist. Having given orders in the commander-in-chief's name to rectify this omission, Prince Andrew galloped back. Kutuzov, still in the same place, his stout body resting heavily in the saddle with the lassitude of age, sat yawning wearily with closed eyes. The troops were no longer moving, but stood with the butts of their muskets on the ground.

'All right, all right!' he said to Prince Andrew, and turned to a general who watch in hand was saying it was time they started as all the left flank columns had already descended.

'Plenty of time, your Excellency,' muttered Kutuzov in the midst of a yawn. 'Plenty of time,' he repeated.

Just then at a distance behind Kutuzov was heard the sound of regiments saluting, and this sound rapidly came nearer along the whole extended line of the advancing Russian columns. Evidently the person they were greeting was riding quickly. When the soldiers of the regiment in front of which Kutuzov was standing began to shout, he rode a little to one side and looked round with a frown. Along the road from Pratzen galloped what looked like a squadron of horsemen in various uniforms. Two of them rode side by side in front, at full gallop. One in a black uniform with white plumes in his hat rode a bob-tailed chestnut horse, the other who was in a white uniform, rode a black one. These were the two Emperors followed by their suites. Kutuzov, affecting the manners of an old soldier at the front, gave the command 'Attention!' and rode up to the Emperors with a salute. His whole appearance and manner was suddenly transformed. He put on the air of a subordinate who obeys without reasoning. With an affectation of respect which evidently struck Alexander unpleasantly, he rode up and saluted.

This unpleasant impression merely flitted over the young and happy face of the Emperor like a cloud of haze across a clear sky, and vanished. After his illness he looked rather thinner that day than on the field of Olmütz where Bolkonsky had seen him for the first time abroad, but there was still the same bewitching combination of majesty and mildness in his fine grey eyes, and on his delicate lips the same capacity for varying expression and the same prevalent appearance of good-hearted innocent youth.

At the Olmütz review he had seemed more majestic, here he seemed brighter and more energetic. He was slightly flushed after galloping two miles, and reining in his horse he sighed restfully and looked round at the faces of his suite, young and animated as his own. Czartoryski, Novosiltsev, Prince Volkonsky, Strogonov and the others, all richly dressed gay young men on splendid, well-groomed, fresh, only slightly heated horses, exchanging remarks and smiling, had stopped behind the Emperor. The Emperor Francis, a rosy long-faced young man, sat very erect on his handsome black horse looking about him in a leisurely and preoccupied manner. He beckoned to one of his white adjutants and asked some question – 'Most likely he is asking at what o'clock they started,' thought Prince Andrew, watching his old acquaintance with a smile he could not repress as he recalled his reception at Brünn. In the Emperors' suite were the picked young orderly officers of the Guard and line regiments, Russian and Austrian. Among them were grooms leading the Tsar's beautiful relay horses covered with embroidered cloths.

As when a window is opened a whiff of fresh air from the fields enters a stuffy room, so a whiff of youthfulness, energy, and confidence of success reached Kutuzov's cheerless staff with the galloping advent of all these brilliant young men.

'Why aren't you beginning, Michael Ilarinovich?'* said the Emperor Alexander hurriedly to Kutuzov, glancing courteously at the same time at the Emperor Francis.

'I am waiting, your Majesty,' answered Kutuzov, bending forward respectfully.

The Emperor, frowning slightly, bent his ear forward as if he had not quite heard.

'Waiting, your Majesty,' repeated Kutuzov. (Prince Andrew noted that Kutuzov's upper lip twitched unnaturally as he said the word 'waiting'). 'Not all the columns have formed up yet, your Majesty.'

The Tsar heard but obviously did not like the reply; he shrugged his rather round shoulders and glanced at Novosiltsev who was near him, as if complaining of Kutuzov.

'You know, Michael Ilarionovich, we are not on the Empress's Field where a parade does not begin till all the troops are assembled,' said the Tsar with another glance at the Emperor Francis, as if inviting him if not to join in at least to listen to what he was saying. But the Emperor Francis continued to look about him and did not listen.

'That is just why I do not begin, sire,' said Kutuzov in a resounding voice, apparently to preclude the possibility of not being heard, and again something in his face twitched – 'That is just why I do not begin, sire, because we are not on parade and not on the Empress's Field,' said he clearly and distinctly.

In the Emperor's suite all exchanged rapid looks that expressed dissatisfaction and reproach. 'Old though he may be, he should not, he certainly should not, speak like that,' their glances seemed to say.

The Tsar looked intently and observantly into Kutuzov's eye waiting to hear whether he would say anything more. But Kutuzov, with respectfully bowed head, seemed also to be waiting. The silence lasted for about a minute.

'However, if you command it, your Majesty,' said Kutuzov, lifting his head and again assuming his former tone of a dull, unreasoning, but submissive general.

He touched his horse and having called Miloradovich, the commander of the column, gave him the order to advance.

The troops again began to move, and two battalions of the Novgorod and one of the Apsheron regiment went forward past the Emperor.

As this Apsheron battalion marched by, the red-faced Miloradovich, without his greatcoat, with his Orders on his breast and an enormous tuft of plumes in his cocked hat worn on one side with its corners front and back, galloped strenuously forward, and with a dashing salute reined in his horse before the Emperor.

'God be with you, general!' said the Emperor.

'*Ma foi, sire, nous ferons ce qui sera dans notre possibilité, sire,*' he answered gaily, raising nevertheless ironic smiles among the gentlemen of the Tsar's suite by his poor French.

Miloradovich wheeled his horse sharply and stationed himself a little behind the Emperor. The Apsheron men, excited by the

Tsar's presence, passed in step before the Emperors and their suites at a bold brisk pace.

'Lads!' shouted Miloradovich in a loud self-confident and cheery voice, obviously so elated by the sound of firing, by the prospect of battle, and by the sight of the gallant Apsherons, his comrades in Suvorov's time, now passing so gallantly before the Emperors, that he forgot the sovereigns' presence. 'Lads, it's not the first village you've had to take,' cried he.

'Glad to do our best!' shouted the soldiers.

The Emperor's horse started at the sudden cry. This horse that had carried the sovereign at reviews in Russia bore him also here on the field of Austerlitz, enduring the heedless blows of his left foot and pricking its ears at the sound of shots just as it had done on the Empress's Field, not understanding the significance of the firing, nor of the nearness of the Emperor Francis's black cob, nor of all that was being said, thought, and felt that day by its rider.

The Emperor turned with a smile to one of his followers and made a remark to him, pointing to the gallant Apsherons.

16

KUTUZOV accompanied by his adjutants rode at a walking pace behind the carabineers.

When he had gone less than half a mile in the rear of the column he stopped at a solitary, deserted house that had probably once been an inn, where two roads parted. Both of them led downhill and troops were marching along both.

The fog had begun to clear and enemy troops were already dimly visible about a mile and a half off on the opposite heights. Down below, on the left, the firing became more distinct. Kutuzov had stopped and was speaking to an Austrian general. Prince Andrew, who was a little behind and looking at them, turned to an adjutant to ask him for a field-glass.

'Look, look!' said this adjutant, looking not at the troops in the distance, but down the hill before him. 'It's the French!'

The two generals and the adjutant took hold of the field-glass, trying to snatch it from one another. The expression on all their faces suddenly changed to one of horror. The French were supposed to be a mile and a half away, but had suddenly and unexpectedly appeared just in front of us.

'It's the enemy? ... No! ... Yes, see it is! ... for certain ... But how is that?' said different voices.

With the naked eye Prince Andrew saw below them to the right, not more than five hundred paces from where Kutuzov was standing, a dense French column coming up to meet the Apsherons.

'Here it is! The decisive moment has arrived. My turn has come,' thought Prince Andrew, and striking his horse he rode up to Kutuzov.

'The Apsherons must be stopped, your Excellency,' cried he. But at that very instant a cloud of smoke spread all round, firing was heard quite close at hand and a voice of naïve terror barely two steps from Prince Andrew, shouted, 'Brothers! All's lost!' And at this voice, as if at a command, everyone began to run.

Confused and ever-increasing crowds were running back to where five minutes before the troops had passed the Emperors. Not only would it have been difficult to stop that crowd, it was even impossible not to be carried back with it oneself. Bolkonsky only tried not to lose touch with it, and looked around bewildered and unable to grasp what was happening in front of him. Nesvitsky with an angry face, red and unlike himself, was shouting to Kutuzov that if he did not ride away at once he would certainly be taken prisoner. Kutuzov remained in the same place, and without answering drew out a handkerchief. Blood was flowing from his cheek. Prince Andrew forced his way to him.

'You are wounded?' he asked, hardly able to master the trembling of his lower jaw.

'The wound is not here, it is there!' said Kutuzov, pressing the handkerchief to his wounded cheek and pointing to the fleeing soldiers. 'Stop them!' he shouted, and at the same moment, probably realizing that it was impossible to stop them, spurred his horse and rode to the right.

A fresh wave of the flying mob caught him and bore him back with it.

The troops were running in such a dense mass that once surrounded by them it was difficult to get out again. One was shouting 'Get on! Why are you hindering us?' Another in the same place turned round and fired in the air; a third was striking the horse Kutuzov himself rode. Having by a great effort got away to the left from that flood of men, Kutuzov, with his suite diminished by more than half, rode towards a sound of artillery fire near by. Having forced his way out of the crowd of fugitives, Prince Andrew, trying to keep near Kutuzov, saw on the slope of the hill amid the smoke a Russian battery that was still firing and Frenchmen running towards it. Higher up stood some Russian infantry, neither moving forward to protect the battery nor backward with the fleeing crowd. A mounted general separated himself from the infantry and approached Kutuzov. Of Kutuzov's suite only four remained. They were all pale and exchanged looks in silence.

'Stop those wretches!' gasped Kutuzov to the regimental commander, pointing to the flying soldiers; but at that instant, as if to punish him for those words, bullets flew hissing across the regiment and across Kutuzov's suite like a flock of little birds. The French had attacked the battery, and seeing Kutuzov, were firing at him. After this volley the regimental commander clutched at his leg; several soldiers fell, and a second lieutenant who was holding the flag let it fall from his hands. It swayed and fell, but caught on the muskets of the nearest soldiers. The soldiers started firing without orders.

'Oh! Oh! Oh!' groaned Kutuzov despairingly and looked around ... 'Bolkonsky!' he whispered, his voice trembling from a consciousness of the feebleness of age, 'Bolkonsky!' he whispered pointing to the disordered battalion and at the enemy, 'What's that?'

But before he had finished speaking, Prince Andrew, feeling tears of shame and anger choking him, had already leapt from his horse and run to the standard.

'Forward, lads!' he shouted in a voice piercing as a child's.

'Here it is!' thought he, seizing the staff of the standard and hearing with pleasure the whistle of bullets evidently aimed at him. Several soldiers fell.

'Hurrah!' shouted Prince Andrew, and scarcely able to hold up the heavy standard, he ran forward with full confidence that the whole battalion would follow him.

And really he only ran a few steps alone. One soldier moved and then another and soon the whole battalion ran forward shouting 'hurrah!' and overtook him. A sergeant of the battalion ran up and took the flag that was swaying from its weight in Prince Andrew's hands, but he was immediately killed. Prince Andrew again seized the standard, and dragging it by the staff ran on with the battalion. In front he saw our artillerymen, some of whom were fighting, while others having abandoned their guns were running towards him. He also saw French infantry soldiers who were seizing the artillery horses and turning the guns round. Prince Andrew and the battalion were already within twenty paces of the cannon. He heard the whistle of bullets above him unceasingly and to right and left of him soldiers continually groaned and dropped. But he did not look at them: he looked only at what was going on in front of him – at the battery. He now saw clearly the figure of a red-haired gunner with his shako

knocked awry, pulling one end of a mop while a French soldier
tugged at the other. He could distinctly see the distraught yet
angry expression on the faces of these two men, who evidently
did not realize what they were doing.

'What are they about?' thought Prince Andrew as he gazed
at them. 'Why doesn't the red-haired gunner run away as he is
unarmed? Why doesn't the Frenchman stab him? He will not get
away before the Frenchman remembers his bayonet and stabs
him...'

And really another French soldier, trailing his musket, ran up
to the struggling men and the fate of the red-haired gunner who
had triumphantly secured the mop and still did not realize what
awaited him, was about to be decided. But Prince Andrew did not
see how it ended. It seemed to him as though one of the soldiers
near him hit him on the head with the full swing of a bludgeon.
It hurt a little, but the worst of it was that the pain distracted
him and prevented his seeing what he had been looking at.

'What's this? Am I falling? My legs are giving way,' thought
he, and fell on his back. He opened his eyes, hoping to see how
the struggle of the Frenchmen with the gunners ended, whether
the red-haired gunner had been killed or not, and whether the
cannon had been captured or saved. But he saw nothing. Above him
there was now nothing but the sky – the lofty sky, not clear yet
still immeasurably lofty, with grey clouds gliding slowly across it.
'How quiet, peaceful, and solemn, not at all as I ran,' thought
Prince Andrew '– not as we ran, shouting and fighting, not at
all as the gunner and the Frenchman with frightened and angry
faces struggled for the mop: how differently do those clouds glide
across that lofty infinite sky! How was it I did not see that lofty
sky before? And how happy I am to have found it at last! Yes!
All is vanity, all falsehood, except that infinite sky. There is
nothing, nothing, but that. But even it does not exist, there is
nothing but quiet and peace. Thank God!...'

17

On our right flank commanded by Bagration, at nine o'clock the
battle had not yet begun. Not wishing to agree to Dolgorukov's
demand to commence the action, and wishing to avert responsibility
from himself, Prince Bagration proposed to Dolgorukov to send
to inquire of the commander-in-chief. Bagration knew that as the
distance between the two flanks was more than six miles, even if
the messenger were not killed (which he very likely would be),

and found the commander-in-chief (which would be very difficult), he would not be able to get back before evening.

Bagration cast his large, expressionless, sleepy eyes round his suite, and the boyish face of Rostov, breathless with excitement and hope, was the first to catch his eye. He sent him.

'And if I should meet his Majesty before I meet the commander-in-chief, your Excellency?' said Rostov, with his hand to his cap.

'You can give the message to his Majesty,' said Dolgorukov, hurriedly interrupting Bagration.

On being relieved from picket duty Rostov had managed to get a few hours' sleep before morning, and felt cheerful, bold, and resolute, with elasticity of movement, faith in his good fortune, and generally in that state of mind which makes everything seem possible, pleasant and easy.

All his wishes were being fulfilled that morning: there was to be a general engagement in which he was taking part, more than that, he was orderly to the bravest general, and still more, he was going with a message to Kutuzov, perhaps even to the sovereign himself. The morning was bright, he had a good horse under him, and his heart was full of joy and happiness. On receiving the order he gave his horse the rein and galloped along the line. At first he rode along the line of Bagration's troops, which had not yet advanced into action but were standing motionless; then he came to the region occupied by Uvarov's cavalry and here he noticed a stir and signs of preparation for battle; having passed Uvarov's cavalry he clearly heard the sound of cannon and musketry ahead of him. The firing grew louder and louder.

In the fresh morning air were now heard, not two or three musket shots at irregular intervals as before, followed by one or two cannon shots, but a roll of volleys of musketry from the slopes of the hill before Pratzen, interrupted by such frequent reports of cannon that sometimes several of them were not separated from one another but merged into a general roar.

He could see puffs of musketry smoke that seemed to chase one another down the hillsides, and clouds of cannon smoke rolling, spreading, and mingling with one another. He could also, by the gleam of bayonets visible through the smoke, make out moving masses of infantry and narrow lines of artillery with green caissons.

Rostov stopped his horse for a moment on a hillock to see what was going on, but strain his attention as he would he could not understand or make out anything of what was happening: there in the smoke men of some sort were moving about, and in front and behind moved lines of troops; but why, whither, and who they were, it was impossible to make out. These sights and sounds had no depressing or intimidating effect on him, on the contrary they stimulated his energy and determination.

'Go on! Go on! Give it them!' he mentally exclaimed at these sounds, and again proceeded to gallop along the line, penetrating farther and farther into the region where the army was already in action.

'How it will be there I don't know, but all will be well!' thought Rostov.

After passing some Austrian troops he noticed that the next part of the line (the Guards) was already in action.

'So much the better! I shall see it close,' he thought.

He was riding almost along the front line. A handful of men came galloping towards him. They were our Uhlans who with disordered ranks were returning from the attack. Rostov got out of their way, involuntarily noticed that one of them was bleeding, and galloped on.

'That is no business of mine,' he thought. He had not ridden many hundred yards after that before he saw to his left, across the whole width of the field, an enormous mass of cavalry in brilliant white uniforms, mounted on black horses, trotting straight towards him and across his path. Rostov put his horse to full gallop to get out of the way of these men, and he would have got clear had they continued at the same speed, but they kept increasing their pace, so that some of the horses were already galloping. Rostov heard the thud of their hoofs and the jingle of their weapons and saw their horses, their figures, and even their faces, more and more distinctly. They were our Horse Guards, advancing to attack the French cavalry that was coming to meet them.

The Horse Guards were galloping, but still holding in their horses. Rostov could already see their faces and heard the command: 'Charge!' shouted by an officer who was urging his thoroughbred to full speed. Rostov fearing to be crushed or swept into the attack on the French, galloped along the front as hard as his horse could go, but still was not in time to avoid them.

The last of the Horse Guards, a huge pock-marked fellow, frowned angrily on seeing Rostov before him, with whom he would inevitably collide. This Guardsman would certainly have bowled Rostov and his Bedouin over (Rostov felt himself quite tiny and weak compared to these gigantic men and horses) had it not occurred to Rostov to flourish his whip before the eyes of the Guardsman's horse. The heavy black horse, sixteen hands high, shied, throwing back its ears; but the pock-marked Guardsman drove his huge spurs in violently, and the horse flourishing its tail and extending its neck, galloped on yet faster. Hardly had the Horse Guards passed Rostov before he heard them shout, 'Hurrah!' and looking back saw that their foremost ranks were mixed up with some foreign cavalry with red epaulettes, probably French. He could see nothing more, for immediately afterwards cannon began firing from somewhere and smoke enveloped everything.

At that moment, as the Horse Guards having passed him disappeared in the smoke. Rostov hesitated whether to gallop after them or to go where he was sent. This was the brilliant charge of the Horse Guards that amazed the French themselves. Rostov was horrified to hear later that of all that mass of huge and handsome men, of all those brilliant, rich youths, officers and cadets, who had galloped past him on their thousand-ruble horses, only eighteen were left after the charge.

'Why should I envy them? My chance is not lost, and maybe I shall see the Emperor immediately!' thought Rostov and galloped on.

When he came level with the Foot Guards he noticed that about them and around them cannon-balls were flying, of which he was aware not so much because he heard their sound as because he saw uneasiness on the soldiers' faces, and unnatural warlike solemnity on those of the officers.

Passing behind one of the lines of a regiment of Foot Guards he heard a voice calling him by name.

'Rostov!'

'What?' he answered, not recognizing Boris.

'I say, we've been in the front line! Our regiment attacked!' said Boris with the happy smile seen on the faces of young men who have been under fire for the first time.

Rostov stopped.

'Have you?' he said. 'Well, how did it go?'

'We drove them back!' said Boris with animation, growing talkative. 'Can you imagine it?' and he began describing how the Guards having taken up their position and seeing troops before them, thought they were Austrians, and all at once discovered from the cannon-balls discharged by those troops, that they were themselves in the front line and had unexpectedly to go into action. Rostov without hearing Boris to the end spurred his horse.

'Where are you off to?' asked Boris.

'With a message to his Majesty.'

'There he is!' said Boris, thinking Rostov had said 'his Highness' and pointing to the Grand Duke who with his high shoulders and frowning brows stood a hundred paces away from them in his helmet and horse guards' jacket, shouting something to a pale, white-uniformed Austrian officer.

'But that's the Grand Duke, and I want the commander-in-chief or the Emperor,' said Rostov, and was about to spur his horse.

'Count! Count!' shouted Berg who ran up from the other side as eager as Boris. 'Count! I am wounded in my right hand' (and he showed his bleeding hand with a handkerchief tied round it) 'and I remained at the front. I held my sword in my left hand, Count. All our family – the von Bergs – have been knights!'

He said something more, but Rostov did not wait to hear it and rode away.

Having passed the Guards and traversed an empty space, Rostov to avoid again getting in front of the first line as he had done when the Horse Guards charged, followed the line of reserves, going far round the place where the hottest musket-fire and cannonade was heard. Suddenly he heard musket-fire quite close in front of him and behind our troops, where he could never have expected the enemy to be.

'What can it be?' he thought. 'The enemy in the rear of our army? Impossible!' And suddenly he was seized by a panic of fear for himself and for the issue of the whole battle. 'But be that what it may,' he reflected, 'there is no riding round it now. I must look for the commander-in-chief here, and if all is lost it is for me to perish with the rest.'

The foreboding of evil that had suddenly come over Rostov was more and more confirmed the farther he rode into the region behind the village of Pratzen, which was full of troops of all kinds.

'What does it mean? What is it? Whom are they firing at? Who is firing?' Rostov kept asking as he came up to Russian and Austrian soldiers running in confused crowds across his path.

'The devil knows! They've killed everybody! It's all up now!' he was told in Russian, German, and Czech, by the crowd of fugitives who understood what was happening as little as he did.

'Kill the Germans!' shouted one.

'May the devil take them – the traitors!'

'*Zum Henker diese Russen!*' muttered a German.

Several wounded men passed along the road, and words of abuse, screams, and groans mingled in a general hubbub, then the firing died down. Rostov learnt later that Russian and Austrian soldiers had been firing at one another.

'My God! What does it all mean?' thought he. 'And here, where at any moment the Emperor may see them ... But no, these must be only a handful of scoundrels. It will soon be over, it can't be *that*, it can't be! Only to get past them quicker, quicker!'

The idea of defeat and flight could not enter Rostov's head. Though he saw French cannon and French troops on the Pratzen heights just where he had been ordered to look for the commander-in-chief, he could not, did not wish, to believe *that*.

## 18

ROSTOV had been ordered to look for Kutuzov and the Emperor near the village of Pratzen. But neither they nor a single commanding officer was there, only disorganized crowds of troops of various kinds. He urged on his already weary horse to get quickly past these crowds, but the farther he went the more disorganized they were. The high road on which he had come out was thronged with calèches, carriages of all sorts, and Russian and Austrian soldiers of all arms, some wounded and some not. This whole mass droned and jostled in confusion under the dismal influence of cannon-balls flying from the French batteries stationed on the Pratzen heights.

'Where is the Emperor? Where is Kutuzov?' Rostov kept asking everyone he could stop, but got no answer from anyone.

At last seizing a soldier by his collar he forced him to answer.

'Eh, brother! They've all bolted long ago!' said the soldier, laughing for some reason and shaking himself free.

Having left that soldier who was evidently drunk, Rostov stopped the horse of a batman or groom of some important personage and began to question him. The man announced that the Tsar had been driven in a carriage at full speed about an hour before along that very road and that he was dangerously wounded.

'It can't be!' said Rostov. 'It must have been someone else.'

'I saw him myself,' replied the man with a self-confident smile of derision. 'I ought to know the Emperor by now, after the times I've seen him in Petersburg. I saw him just as I see you . . . There he sat in the carriage as pale as anything. How they made the four black horses fly! Gracious me, they did rattle past! It's time I knew the imperial horses and Ilya Ivanych. I don't think Ilya drives anyone except the Tsar!'

Rostov let go of the horse and was about to ride on, when a wounded officer passing by addressed him:

'Who is it you want?' he asked. 'The commander-in-chief? He was killed by a cannon-ball – struck in the breast before our regiment.'

'Not killed – wounded!' another officer corrected him.

'Who? Kutuzov?' asked Rostov.

'Not Kutuzov, but what's his name – well, never mind ... there are not many left alive. Go that way, to that village, all the commanders are there,' said the officer, pointing to the village of Hosjeradek, and he walked on.

Rostov rode on at a foot pace not knowing why nor to whom he was now going. The Emperor was wounded, the battle lost. It was impossible to doubt it now. Rostov rode in the direction pointed out to him, in which he saw turrets and a church. What need to hurry? What was he now to say to the Tsar or to Kutuzov, even if they were alive and unwounded?

'Take this road, your honour, that way you will be killed at once!' a soldier shouted to him. 'They'd kill you there!'

'Oh, what are you talking about?' said another. 'Where is he to go? That way is nearer.'

Rostov considered, and then went in the direction where they said he would be killed.

'It's all the same now. If the Emperor is wounded, am I to try to save myself?' he thought. He rode on to the region where the greatest number of men had perished in fleeing from Pratzen. The French had not yet occupied that region, and the Russians – the uninjured and slightly wounded – had left it long ago. All about the field, like heaps of manure on well-kept plough-land, lay from ten to fifteen dead and wounded to each couple of acres. The wounded crept together in twos and threes and one could hear their distressing screams and groans, sometimes feigned – or so it seemed to Rostov. He put his horse to a trot to avoid seeing all these suffering men, and he felt afraid – not for his life, but for the courage he needed and which he knew would not stand the sight of these unfortunates.

The French, who had ceased firing at this field strewn with dead and wounded where there was no one left to fire at, on seeing an adjutant riding over it trained a gun on him and fired several shots. The sensation of those terrible whistling sounds and of the corpses around him merged in Rostov's mind into a single feeling of terror and pity for himself. He remembered his mother's last letter. 'What would she feel,' thought he, 'if she saw me here now on this field with the cannon aimed at me?'

In the village of Hosjeradek there were Russian troops retiring from the field of battle, who though still in some confusion were less disordered. The French cannon did not reach there and the musketry fire sounded far away. Here everyone clearly saw and said that the battle was lost. No one whom Rostov asked could tell him where the Emperor or Kutuzov was. Some said the report that the Emperor was wounded was correct, others that it was not, and explained the false rumour that had spread by the fact that the Emperor's carriage had really galloped from the field of battle with the pale and terrified Ober-Hofmarschal Count Tolstoy, who had ridden out to the battlefield with others in the Emperor's suite. One officer told Rostov that he had seen someone from head-quarters behind the village to the left, and thither Rostov rode, not hoping to find anyone but merely to ease his conscience. When he had ridden about two miles and had passed the last of the Russian troops, he saw, near a kitchen-garden with a ditch round it, two men on horseback facing the ditch. One with a white plume in his hat seemed familiar to Rostov; the other on a beautiful chestnut horse (which Rostov fancied he had seen before) rode up to the ditch, struck his horse with his spurs, and giving it the rein leaped lightly over. Only a little earth crumbled from the bank under the horse's hind hoofs. Turning the horse sharply, he again jumped the ditch, and deferentially addressed the horseman with the white plumes, evidently suggesting that he should do the same. The rider, whose figure seemed familiar to Rostov and involuntarily riveted his attention, made a gesture of refusal with his head and hand and by that gesture Rostov instantly recognized his lamented and adored monarch.

'But it can't be he, alone in the midst of this empty field!' thought Rostov. At that moment Alexander turned his head and Rostov saw the beloved features that were so deeply engraved on his memory. The Emperor was pale, his cheeks sunken and his eyes hollow, but the charm, the mildness of his features, was all the greater. Rostov was happy in the assurance that the rumours about the Emperor being wounded were false. He was happy to be seeing him. He knew that he might, and even ought, to go straight to him and give the message Dolgorukov had ordered him to deliver.

But as a youth in love trembles, is unnerved, and dares not utter the thoughts he has dreamt of for nights, but looks around for help or a chance of delay and flight when the longed-for moment comes and he is alone with *her*, so Rostov, now that he had attained what he had longed for more than anything else in the world, did not know how to approach the Emperor, and a thousand reasons occurred to him why it would be inconvenient, unseemly, and impossible to do so.

'What! It is as if I were glad of a chance to take advantage of his being alone and despondent! A strange face may seem un-pleasant or painful to him at this moment of sorrow; besides, what can I say to him now, when my heart fails me and my mouth feels dry at the mere sight of him?' Not one of the innumerable speeches addressed to the Emperor that he had composed in his imagination could he now recall. Those speeches were intended for quite other conditions, they were for the most part to be spoken at a moment of victory and triumph, generally when he was dying of wounds and the sovereign had thanked him for heroic deeds, and while dying he expressed the love his actions had proved.

'Besides how can I ask the Emperor for his instructions for the right flank now that it is nearly four o'clock and the battle is lost? No, certainly I must not approach him, I must not intrude on his reflections. Better die a thousand times than risk receiving an unkind look or bad opinion from him,' Rostov decided, and sorrowfully and with a heart full of despair he rode away, continually looking back at the Tsar, who still remained in the same attitude of indecision.

While Rostov was thus arguing with himself and riding sadly away, Captain von Toll chanced to ride to the same spot, and seeing the Emperor at once rode up to him, offered his services, and assisted him to cross the ditch on foot. The Emperor, wishing to rest and feeling unwell, sat down under an apple-tree and von Toll remained beside him. Rostov from a distance saw with envy and remorse how von Toll spoke long and warmly to the Emperor and how the Emperor, evidently weeping, covered his eyes with his hand and pressed von Toll's hand.

'And I might have been in his place!' thought Rostov, and hardly restraining his tears of pity for the Emperor, he rode on in utter despair, not knowing where to or why he was now riding.

His despair was all the greater from feeling that his own weakness was the cause of his grief.

He might . . . not only might but should, have gone up to the sovereign. It was a unique chance to show his devotion to the Emperor and he had not made use of it . . . 'What have I done?' thought he. And he turned round and galloped back to the place where he had seen the Emperor, but there was no one beyond the ditch now. Only some carts and carriages were passing by. From one of the drivers he learnt that Kutuzov's staff were not far off, in the village the vehicles were going to. Rostov followed them. In front of him walked Kutuzov's groom leading horses in horse-cloths. Then came a cart, and behind that walked an old, bandy-legged domestic serf in a peaked cap and sheepskin coat.

'Tit! I say, Tit!' said the groom.

'What?' answered the old man absent-mindedly.

'Go Tit! Thresh a bit!'

'Oh, you fool!' said the old man, spitting angrily. Some time passed in silence, and then the same joke was repeated.

Before five in the evening the battle had been lost at all points. More than a hundred cannon were already in the hands of the French.

Przebyszewski and his corps had laid down their arms. Other columns after losing half their men were retreating in disorderly confused masses.

The remains of Langeron's and Dokhturov's mingled forces were crowding around the dams and banks of the ponds near the village of Augesd.

After five o'clock it was only at the Augesd dam that a hot cannonade (delivered by the French alone) was still to be heard from numerous batteries ranged on the slopes of the Pratzen heights, directed at our retreating forces.

In the rearguard Dokhturov and others, rallying some battalions, kept up a musketry fire at the French cavalry that was pursuing our troops. It was growing dusk. On the narrow Augesd dam where for so many years the old miller had been accustomed to sit in his tasselled cap peacefully angling, while his grandson, with shirtsleeves rolled up, handled the floundering silvery fish in the watering-can, on that dam over which for so many years Moravians in shaggy caps and blue jackets had peacefully driven their two-horse carts loaded with wheat and had returned dusty with flour whitening their carts – on that narrow dam amid the wagons and the cannon, under the horse's hoofs and between the wagon wheels, men disfigured by fear of death now crowded together, crushing one another, dying, stepping over the dying and killing one another, only to move on a few steps and be killed themselves in the same way.

Every ten seconds a cannon-ball flew compressing the air around, or a shell burst in the midst of that dense throng, killing some and splashing with blood those near them.

Dolokhov – now an officer – wounded in the arm, and on foot, with the regimental commander on horseback and some ten men of his company, represented all that was left of that whole regiment. Impelled by the crowd they had got wedged in at the approach to the dam and, jammed in on all sides, had stopped because a horse in front had fallen under a cannon and the crowd were dragging it out. A cannon-ball killed someone behind them, another fell in front and splashed Dolokhov with blood. The crowd, pushing forward desperately, squeezed together, moved a few steps, and again stopped.

'Move on a hundred yards and we are certainly saved, remain here another two minutes and it is certain death,' thought each one.

Dolokhov who was in the midst of the crowd forced his way to the edge of the dam, throwing two soldiers off their feet, and ran onto the slippery ice that covered the mill-pool.

'Turn this way!' he shouted, jumping over the ice which creaked under him; 'turn this way!' he shouted to those with the gun. 'It bears! . . .'

The ice bore him but it swayed and creaked, and it was plain that it would give way not only under a cannon or a crowd, but very soon even under his weight alone. The men looked at him and pressed to the bank, hesitating to step onto the ice. The general on horseback at the entrance to the dam, raised his hand and opened his mouth to address Dolokhov. Suddenly a cannon-ball hissed so low above the crowd that everyone ducked. It flopped into something moist, and the general fell from his horse in a pool of blood. Nobody gave him a look or thought of raising him.

'Get onto the ice, over the ice! Go on! Turn! Don't you hear? Go on!' innumerable voices suddenly shouted after the ball had struck the general, the men themselves not knowing what, or why, they were shouting.

One of the hindmost guns that was going onto the dam turned off onto the ice. Crowds of soldiers from the dam began running onto the frozen pond. The ice gave way under one of the foremost soldiers, and one leg slipped into the water. He tried to right himself but fell in up to his waist. The nearest soldiers shrank back, the gun-driver stopped his horse, but from behind still came the shouts: 'Onto the ice, why do you stop? Go on! Go on!' And cries of horror were heard in the crowd. The soldiers near the gun waved their arms and beat the horses to make them turn and move on. The horses moved off the bank. The ice, that had held under those on foot, collapsed in a great mass, and some forty men who were on it dashed, some forwards and some back, drowning one another.

Still the cannon-balls continued regularly to whistle and flop onto the ice and into the water, and oftenest of all among the crowd that covered the dam, the pond, and the bank.

19

On the Pratzen heights, where he had fallen with the flagstaff in his hand, lay Prince Andrew Bolkonsky bleeding profusely and unconsciously uttering a gentle, piteous, and childlike moan.

Towards evening he ceased moaning and became quite still. He did not know how long his unconsciousness lasted. Suddenly he again felt that he was alive and suffering from a burning, lacerating pain in his head.

'Where is it, that lofty sky that I did not know till now, but saw to-day?' was his first thought. 'And I did not know this suffering either,' he thought. 'Yes, I did not know anything, anything at all till now. But where am I?'

He listened, and heard the sound of approaching horses, and voices speaking French. He opened his eyes. Above him again was the same lofty sky with clouds that had risen and were floating still higher, and between them gleamed blue infinity. He did not turn his head and did not see those who, judging by the sound of hoofs and voices, had ridden up and stopped near him.

It was Napoleon accompanied by two aides-de-camp. Bonaparte riding over the battlefield had given final orders to strengthen the batteries firing at the Augesd dam, and was looking at the killed and wounded left on the field.

'Fine men!' remarked Napoleon, looking at a dead Russian grenadier who with his face buried in the ground and a blackened nape, lay on his stomach with an already stiffened arm flung wide.

'The ammunition for the guns in position is exhausted, your Majesty,' said an adjutant who had come from the batteries that were firing at Augesd.

'Have some brought from the reserve,' said Napoleon, and having gone on a few steps he stopped before Prince Andrew, who lay on his back with the flagstaff that had been dropped beside him. (The flag had already been taken by the French as a trophy.)

'That's a fine death!' said Napoleon as he gazed at Bolkonsky.

Prince Andrew understood that this was said of him, and that it was Napoleon who said it. He heard the speaker addressed as *Sire*. But he heard the words as he might have heard the buzzing of a fly. Not only did they not interest him, but he took no notice of them and at once forgot them. His head was burning, he felt himself bleeding to death, and he saw above him the remote, lofty, and everlasting sky. He knew it was Napoleon – his hero – but at that moment Napoleon seemed to him such a small insignificant creature compared with what was passing now between himself and that lofty infinite sky with the clouds flying over it. At that moment it meant nothing to him who might be standing over him, or what was said of him; he was only glad that people were standing near him, and only wished that they would help him and bring him back to life, which seemed to him so beautiful now that he had to-day learned to understand it so differently. He collected all his strength, to stir and utter a sound. He feebly moved his leg, and uttered a weak sickly groan which aroused his own pity.

'Ah! He is alive,' said Napoleon. 'Lift this young man up and carry him to the dressing-station.'

Having said this, Napoleon rode on to meet Marshal Lannes, who, hat in hand, rode up smiling to the Emperor to congratulate him on the victory.

Prince Andrew remembered nothing more: he lost consciousness from the terrible pain of being lifted onto the stretcher, the jolting while being moved, and the probing of his wound at the dressing-station. He did not regain consciousness till late in the day, when with other wounded and captured Russian officers he was carried to the hospital. During this transfer he felt a little stronger and was to look about him and even speak.

The first words he heard on coming to his senses were those of a French convoy officer, who said rapidly:

'We must halt here: the Emperor will pass here immediately; it will please him to see these gentlemen prisoners.'

'There are so many prisoners to-day, nearly the whole Russian army, that he is probably tired of them,' said another officer.

'All the same! They say this one is the commander of all the Emperor Alexander's Guards,' said the first one, indicating a Russian officer in the white uniform of the Horse Guards.

Bolkonsky recognized Prince Repnin whom he had met in Petersburg society. Beside him stood a lad of nineteen, also a wounded officer of the Horse Guards.

Bonaparte, having come up at a gallop, stopped his horse.

'Which is the senior?' he asked, on seeing the prisoners.

They named the colonel, Prince Repnin.

'You are the commander of the Emperor Alexander's regiment of Horse Guards?' asked Napoleon.

'I commanded a squadron,' replied Repnin.

'Your regiment fulfilled its duty honourably,' said Napoleon.

'The praise of a great commander is a soldier's highest reward,' said Repnin.

'I bestow it with pleasure,' said Napoleon. 'And who is that young man beside you?'

Prince Repnin named Lieutenant Sukhtelen.

After looking at him Napoleon smiled.

'He's very young to come to meddle with us.'

'Youth is no hindrance to courage,' muttered Sukhtelen in a failing voice.

'A splendid reply!' said Napoleon. 'Young man, you will go far!'

Prince Andrew, who had also been brought forward before the

Emperor's eyes to complete the show of prisoners, could not fail to attract his attention. Napoleon apparently remembered seeing him on the battlefield, and addressing him, again used the epithet 'young man' that was connected in his memory with Prince Andrew.

'Well, and you, young man,' said he. 'How do you feel, *mon brave?*'

Though five minutes before Prince Andrew had been able to say a few words to the soldiers who were carrying him, now with his eyes fixed straight on Napoleon, he was silent ... So insignificant at that moment seemed to him all the interests that engrossed Napoleon, so mean did his hero himself with his paltry vanity and joy in victory appear, compared to the lofty, equitable, and kindly sky which he had seen and understood, that he could not answer him.

Everything seemed so futile and insignificant in comparison with the stern and solemn train of thought that weakness from loss of blood, suffering, and the nearness of death, aroused in him. Looking into Napoleon's eyes Prince Andrew thought of the insignificance of greatness, the unimportance of life which no one could understand, and the still greater unimportance of death, the meaning of which no one alive could understand or explain.

The Emperor without waiting for an answer turned away, and said to one of the officers as he went:

'Have these gentlemen attended to and taken to my bivouac; let my doctor Larrey examine their wounds. Au *revoir*, Prince Repnin!' and he spurred his horse and galloped away.

His face shone with self-satisfaction and pleasure.

The soldiers who had carried Prince Andrew had noticed and taken the little gold icon Princess Mary had hung round her brother's neck, but seeing the favour the Emperor showed the prisoners, they now hastened to return the holy image.

Prince Andrew did not see how and by whom it was replaced, but the little icon with its thin gold chain suddenly appeared upon his chest outside his uniform.

'It would be good,' thought Prince Andrew, glancing at the icon his sister had hung round his neck with such emotion and reverence, 'it would be good if everything were as clear and simple as it seems to Mary. How good it would be to know where to seek for help in this life, and what to expect after it beyond the grave! How happy and calm I should be if I could now say: "Lord, have mercy on me!" ... but to whom should I say that? Either to a Power indefinable, incomprehensible, which I not only cannot address but which I cannot even express in words – the Great All or Nothing –' said he to himself, 'or to that God who has been sewn into this amulet by Mary! There is nothing certain, nothing at all except the unimportance of everything I understand, and the greatness of something incomprehensible but all-important.'

The stretchers moved on. At every jolt he again felt unendurable pain; his feverishness increased and he grew delirious. Visions of his father, wife, sister, and future son, and the tenderness he had felt the night before the battle, the figure of the insignificant little Napoleon, and above all this the lofty sky, formed the chief subjects of his delirious fancies.

The quiet home life and peaceful happiness of Bald Hills presented itself to him. He was already enjoying that happiness when that little Napoleon had suddenly appeared with his unsympathizing look of short-sighted delight at the misery of others, and doubts and torments had followed, and only the heavens promised peace. Towards morning all these dreams melted and merged into the chaos and darkness of unconsciousness and oblivion, which in the opinion of Napoleon's doctor, Larrey, was much more likely to end in death than in convalescence.

'He is a nervous, bilious subject,' said Larrey, 'and will not recover.'

And Prince Andrew, with others fatally wounded, was left to the care of the inhabitants of the district.


END OF BOOK ONE

# WAR AND PEACE

*

## BOOK TWO

# PART ONE

## 1

EARLY in the year 1806 Nicholas Rostov returned home on leave. Denisov was going home to Voronezh and Rostov persuaded him to travel with him as far as Moscow and to stay with him there. Meeting a comrade at the last post-station but one before Moscow, Denisov had drunk three bottles of wine with him, and despite the jolting ruts across the snow-covered road, did not once wake up, on the way to Moscow, but lay at the bottom of the sledge beside Rostov, who grew more and more impatient the nearer they got to Moscow.

'How much longer? How much longer? Oh, these insufferable streets, shops, bakers' signboards, street lamps and sledges!' thought Rostov when their leave-permits had been passed at the town gate, and they had entered Moscow.

'Denisov! We're here! He's asleep,' he added, leaning forward with his whole body as if in that position he hoped to hasten the speed of the sledge.

Denisov gave no answer.

'There's the corner at the cross-roads, where the cabman Zakhar has his stand, and there's Zakhar himself and still the same horse! And here's the little shop where we used to buy gingerbread! Can't you hurry up? Now then!'

'Which house is it?' asked the driver.

'Why that one, right at the end, the big one. Don't you see? That's our house,' said Rostov. 'Of course it's our house! Denisov, Denisov! We're almost there!'

Denisov raised his head, coughed, and made no answer.

'Dmitri,' said Rostov to his valet on the box, 'those lights are in our house, aren't they?'

'Yes, sir, and there's a light in your father's study.'

'Then they've not gone to bed yet? What do you think? Mind now, don't forget to put out my new coat,' added Rostov, fingering his new moustache. 'Now then, get on,' he shouted to the driver. 'Do wake up, Vaska,' he went on, turning to Denisov, whose head was again nodding. 'Come, get on! You shall have three rubles

311

for vodka – get on!' Rostov shouted, when the sledge was only three houses from his door. It seemed to him the horses were not moving at all. At last the sledge bore to the right, drew up at an entrance, and Rostov saw overhead the old familiar cornice with a bit of plaster broken off, the porch, and the post by the side of the pavement. He sprang out before the sledge stopped, and ran into the hall. The house stood cold and silent, as if quite regardless of who had come to it. There was no one in the hall. 'Oh God! Is everyone all right?' he thought, stopping for a moment with a sinking heart and then immediately starting to run along the hall and up the warped steps of the familiar staircase. The well-known old door-handle, which always angered the countess when it was not properly cleaned, turned as loosely as ever. A solitary tallow candle burnt in the ante-room.

Old Michael was asleep on the chest. Prokofy, the footman, who was so strong that he could lift the back of the carriage from behind, sat plaiting slippers out of cloth selvedges. He looked up at the opening door and his expression of sleepy indifference suddenly changed to one of delighted amazement.

'Gracious heavens! The young Count!' he cried, recognizing his young master. 'Can it be? My treasure!' and Prokofy, trembling with excitement rushed towards the drawing-room door, probably in order to announce him, but changing his mind came back and stooped to kiss the young man's shoulder.

'All well?' asked Rostov, drawing away his arm.

'Yes, God be thanked! Yes! They've just finished supper. Let me have a look at you, your Excellency.'

'Is everything quite all right?'

'The Lord be thanked, yes!'

Rostov, who had completely forgotten Denisov, not wishing any one to forestall him, threw off his fur coat and ran on tiptoe through the large dark ball-room. All was the same: there were the same old card-tables and the same chandelier with a cover over it; but someone had already seen the young master, and before he had reached the drawing-room something flew out from a side door like a tornado and began hugging and kissing him. Another and yet another creature of the same kind sprang from a second door and a third; more hugging, more kissing, more outcries, and tears of joy. He could not distinguish which was papa, which Natasha, and which Petya. Everyone shouted, talked, and kissed him at the same time. Only his mother was not there, he noticed that.

'And I did not know ... Nicholas ... My darling ... !'

'Here he is ... our own ... Kolya, dear fellow ... How he has changed! ... Where are the candles? ... Tea! ...'

'And me, kiss me!'

'Dearest . . . and me!'

Sonya, Natasha, Petya, Anna Mikhaylovna, Vera, and the old count were all hugging him, and the serfs, men and maids, flocked into the room, exclaiming and oh-ing and ah-ing.

Petya, clinging to his legs, kept shouting, 'And me too!'

Natasha, after she had pulled him down towards her and covered his face with kisses, holding him tight by the skirt of his coat, sprang away and pranced up and down in one place like a goat, and shrieked piercingly.

All around were loving eyes glistening with tears of joy, and all around were lips seeking a kiss.

Sonya too, all rosy red, clung to his arm and, radiant with bliss, looked eagerly towards his eyes, waiting for the look for which she longed. Sonya now was sixteen and she was very pretty, especially at this moment of happy rapturous excitement. She gazed at him, not taking her eyes off him, and smiling and holding her breath. He gave her a grateful look, but was still expectant and looking for someone. The old countess had not yet come. But now steps were heard at the door, steps so rapid that they could hardly be his mother's.

Yet it was she, dressed in a new gown which he did not know, made since he had left. All the others let him go, and he ran to her. When they met she fell on his breast, sobbing. She could not lift her face, but only pressed it to the cold braiding of his hussar's jacket. Denisov, who had come into the room unnoticed by anyone, stood there and wiped his eyes at the sight.

'Vasili Denisov, your son's friend,' he said, introducing himself to the count who was looking inquiringly at him.

'You are most welcome! I know, I know,' said the count, kissing and embracing Denisov. 'Nicholas wrote us . . . Natasha, Vera, look! Here is Denisov!'

The same happy rapturous faces turned to the shaggy figure of Denisov.

'Darling Denisov!' screamed Natasha beside herself with rapture, springing to him, putting her arms round him, and kissing him. This escapade made everybody feel confused. Denisov blushed too, but smiled, and taking Natasha's hand kissed it.

Denisov was shown to the room prepared for him, and the Rostovs all gathered round Nicholas in the sitting-room.

The old countess, not letting go of his hand and kissing it every moment, sat beside him: the rest, crowding round him, watched every movement, word, or look of his, never taking their blissfully adoring eyes off him. His brother and sisters struggled for the places nearest to him, and disputed with one another who should bring him his tea, handkerchief, and pipe.

Rostov was very happy in the love they showed him; but the first moment of meeting had been so beatific that his present joy seemed insufficient, and he kept expecting something more, more, and yet more.

Next morning, after the fatigues of their journey, the travellers slept till ten o'clock.

In the room next their bedroom there was a confusion of sabres, satchels, sabretaches, open portmanteaus, and dirty boots. Two freshly cleaned pairs with spurs had just been placed by the wall. The servants were bringing in jugs and basins, hot water for shaving, and their well-brushed clothes. There was a masculine odour and a smell of tobacco.

'Hallo, Gwishka – my pipe!' came Vasili Denisov's husky voice. 'Wostov, get up!'

Rostov, rubbing his eyes that seemed glued together, raised his dishevelled head from the hot pillow.

'Why, is it late?'

'Late! It's nearly ten o'clock,' answered Natasha's voice. A rustle of starched petticoats and the whispering and laughter of girls' voices came from the adjoining room. The door was opened a crack, and there was a glimpse of something blue, of ribbons, black hair and merry faces. It was Natasha, Sonya, and Petya, who had come to see whether they were getting up.

'Nicholas! Get up!' Natasha's voice was again heard at the door. 'Directly!'

Meanwhile Petya having found and seized the sabres in the outer room, with the delight boys feel at the sight of a military elder brother, and forgetting that it was unbecoming for the girls to see men undressed, opened the bedroom door.

'Is this your sabre?' he shouted.

The girls sprang aside. Denisov hid his hairy legs under the blanket, looking with a scared face at his comrade for help. The door having let Petya in, closed again. A sound of laughter came from behind it.

'Nicholas! Come out in your dressing-gown!' said Natasha's voice.

'Is this your sabre?' asked Petya, 'Or is it yours?' he said, addressing the black-moustached Denisov with servile deference.

Rostov hurriedly put something on his feet, drew on his dressing-gown, and went out. Natasha had put on one spurred boot and was just getting her foot into the other. Sonya when he came in was twirling round and was about to expand her dress into a balloon and sit down. They were dressed alike in new pale-blue frocks, and were both fresh, rosy, and bright. Sonya ran away, but Natasha, taking her brother's arm, led him into the sitting-room, where they began talking. They hardly gave one another time to ask questions and give replies concerning a thousand little matters which could not interest anyone but themselves. Natasha laughed at every word he said or that she said herself, not because what they were saying was amusing, but because she felt happy and was unable to control her joy which expressed itself by laughter.

'Oh, how nice, how splendid!' she said to everything.

Rostov felt that under the influence of the warm rays of love, that childlike smile which had not once appeared on his face since he left home, now for the first time after eighteen months again brightened his soul and his face.

'No, but listen,' she said, 'now you are quite a man, aren't you? I'm awfully glad you're my brother.' She touched his moustache. 'I want to know what you men are like. Are you the same as we? No?'

'Why did Sonya run away?' asked Rostov.

'Ah, yes! That's a whole long story! How are you going to speak to her – Thou or you?'

'As may happen,' said Rostov.

'No, call her you, please! I'll tell you all about it some other time. No, I'll tell you now. You know Sonya's my dearest friend. Such a friend that I burnt my arm for her sake. Look here!'

She pulled up her muslin sleeve and showed him a red scar on her long, slender, delicate arm, high above the elbow on the part that is covered even by a ball-dress.

'I burnt this to prove my love for her. I just heated a ruler in the fire and pressed it there!'

Sitting on the sofa with the little cushions on its arms, in what used to be his old schoolroom, and looking into Natasha's wildly bright eyes, Rostov re-entered that world of home and childhood which had no meaning for anyone else, but gave him some of the best joys of his life; and the burning of an arm with a ruler as a proof of love did not seem to him senseless, he understood and was not surprised at it.

'Well, and is that all?' he asked.

'We are such friends, such friends! All that ruler business was just nonsense, but we are friends for ever. She if she loves anyone, does it for life, but I don't understand that, I forget quickly.'

'Well, what then?'

'Well, she loves me and you like that.'

Natasha suddenly flushed.

'Why, you remember before you went away? ... Well, she says you are to forget all that ... She says: "I shall love him always, but let him be free." Isn't that lovely and noble! Yes, very noble? Isn't it?' asked Natasha so seriously and excitedly that it was evident that what she was now saying she had talked of before with tears.

Rostov became thoughtful.

'I never go back on my word,' he said. 'Besides, Sonya is so charming that only a fool would renounce such happiness.'

'No, no!' cried Natasha, 'she and I have already talked it over. We knew you'd say so. But it won't do, because you see, if you say that – if you consider yourself bound by your promise – it will seem as if she had not meant it seriously. It makes it as if you were marrying her because you must, and that wouldn't do at all.'

Rostov saw that it had been well considered by them. Sonya had already struck him by her beauty on the preceding day. To-day, when he had caught a glimpse of her, she seemed still more lovely. She was a charming girl of sixteen, evidently passionately in love with him (he did not doubt that for an instant). Why should he not love her now, and even marry her, Rostov thought, but just now there were so many other pleasures and interests before him! 'Yes, they have taken a wise decision,' he thought. 'I must remain free.'

'Well then, that's excellent,' said he. 'We'll talk it over later on. Oh, how glad I am to have you!'

'Well, and are you still true to Boris?' he continued.

'Oh, what nonsense!' cried Natasha laughing. 'I don't think about him or anyone else, and I don't want anything of the kind.'

'Dear me! Then what are you up to now?'

'Now?' repeated Natasha, and a happy smile lit up her face. 'Have you seen Duport?'

'No.'

'Not seen Duport – the famous dancer? Well then, you won't understand. That's what I'm up to.'

Curving her arms, Natasha held out her skirt as dancers do, ran back a few steps, turned, cut a caper, brought her little feet sharply together, and made some steps on the very tips of her toes.

'See, I'm standing! See!' she said, but could not maintain herself on her toes any longer. 'So that's what I'm up to! I'll never marry anyone, but will be a dancer. Only don't tell anyone.'

Rostov laughed so loud and merrily that Denisov in the bedroom felt envious and Natasha could not help joining in.

'No, but don't you think it's nice?' she kept repeating.

'Nice! And so you no longer wish to marry Boris?'

Natasha flared up. 'I don't want to marry anyone. And I'll tell him so when I see him!'

'Dear me!' said Rostov.

'But that's all rubbish,' Natasha chattered on. 'And is Denisov nice?' she asked.

'Yes, indeed!'

'Oh, well then, good-bye: go and dress. Is he very terrible, Denisov?'

'Why terrible?' asked Nicholas. 'No, Vaska is a splendid fellow.'

'You call him Vaska? That's funny! And is he very nice?'

'Very.'

'Well then, be quick. We'll all have breakfast together.'

And Natasha rose and went out of the room on tiptoe like a ballet dancer, but smiling as only happy girls of fifteen can smile. When Rostov met Sonya in the drawing-room he reddened. He did not know how to behave with her. The evening before, in the first happy moment of meeting, they had kissed each other, but to-day they felt it could not be done; he felt that everybody, including his mother and sisters, was looking inquiringly at him and watching to see how he would behave with her. He kissed her hand and addressed her not as *thou* but as *you* – Sonya. But their eyes met and said *thou*, and exchanged tender kisses. Her looks asked him to forgive her for having dared, by Natasha's intermediacy, to remind him of his promise, and then thanked him for his love. His looks thanked her for offering him his freedom, and told her that one way or other he would never cease to love her, for that would be impossible.

'How strange it is,' said Vera, selecting a moment when all were silent, 'that Sonya and Nicholas now say *you* to one another and meet like strangers.'

Vera's remark was correct as her remarks always were, but like most of her observations it made everyone feel uncomfortable, not only Sonya, Nicholas, and Natasha, but even the old countess, who – dreading this love affair which might hinder Nicholas from making a brilliant match – blushed like a girl.

Denisov to Rostov's surprise appeared in the drawing-room with pomaded hair, perfumed, and in a new uniform, looking just as smart as he made himself when going into battle, and he was more amiable to the ladies and gentlemen than Rostov had ever expected to see him.

## 2

ON his return to Moscow from the army Nicholas Rostov was welcomed by his home circle as the best of sons, a hero, and their darling Nikolenka, by his relations as a charming, attractive, and polite young man, by his acquaintances as a handsome lieutenant of hussars, a good dancer, and one of the best matches in the city.

The Rostovs knew everybody in Moscow. The old count had money enough that year, as all his estates had been re-mortgaged, and so Nicholas, acquiring a trotter of his own, very stylish riding-breeches of the latest cut, such as no one else yet had in Moscow, and boots of the latest fashion with extremely pointed toes and small silver spurs, passed his time very gaily. After a short period of adapting himself to the old conditions of life, Nicholas found it very pleasant to be at home again. He felt that he had grown up and matured very much. His despair at failing in a Scripture examination, his borrowing money from Gavril to pay a sledge-driver, his kissing Sonya on the sly – he now recalled all this as childishness he had left immeasurably behind. Now he was a lieutenant of hussars, in a jacket laced with silver, and wearing the cross of St George awarded to soldiers for bravery in action, and in the company of well-known, elderly and respected racing-men was training a trotter of his own for a race. He knew a lady on one of the boulevards whom he visited of an evening. He led the mazurka at the Arkharovs' ball, talked about the war with Field-Marshal Kamensky, visited the English Club,* and was on intimate terms with a colonel of forty to whom Denisov had introduced him.

His passion for the Emperor had cooled somewhat in Moscow. But still, as he did not see him and had no opportunity of seeing him, he often spoke about him and about his love for him, letting it be understood that he had not told all and that there was something in his feelings for the Emperor not everyone could understand, and with his whole soul he shared the adoration then common in Moscow for the Emperor, who was spoken of as the 'angel incarnate'.

During Rostov's short stay in Moscow before rejoining the army he did not draw closer to Sonya, but rather drifted away from her. She was very pretty and sweet, and evidently deeply in love with him, but he was at the period of youth when there seems so much to do that there is *no time* for that sort of thing and a young man fears to bind himself, and prizes his freedom which he needs for so many other things. When he thought of Sonya during this stay in

Moscow he said to himself, 'Ah, there will be, and there are, many more such girls somewhere whom I do not yet know. There will be time enough to think about love when I want to, but now I have no time.' Besides it seemed to him that the society of women was rather derogatory to his manhood. He went to balls and into ladies' society with an affectation of doing so against his will. The races, the English Club, sprees with Denisov and visits to a certain house – that was another matter and quite the thing for a dashing young hussar!

At the beginning of March old Count Ilya Rostov was very busy arranging a dinner in honour of Prince Bagration at the English Club.

The count walked up and down the hall in his dressing-gown, giving orders to the club steward and to the famous Feoktist, the club's head cook, about asparagus, fresh cucumbers, strawberries, veal, and fish for this dinner. The count had been a member and on the committee of the club from the day it was founded. To him the club entrusted the arrangement of the festival in honour of Bagration, for few men knew so well how to arrange a feast on an open-handed, hospitable scale, and still fewer men would be so well able and willing to make up out of their own resources what might be needed for the success of the fête. The club cook and the steward listened to the count's orders with pleased faces, for they knew that under no other management could they so easily extract a good profit for themselves from a dinner costing several thousand rubles.

'Well then, mind and have cocks' combs in the turtle soup, you know!'

'Shall we have three cold dishes then?' asked the cook.

The count considered.

'We can't have less – yes, three . . . the mayonnaise, that's one,' said he, bending down a finger.

'Then am I to order those large sterlets?' asked the steward.

'Yes, it can't be helped if they won't take less. Ah, dear me! I was forgetting. We must have another entrée. Ah, goodness gracious!' he clutched at his head. 'Who is going to get me the flowers? Dmitri! Eh, Dmitri! Gallop off to our Moscow estate,' he said to the factotum who appeared at his call. 'Hurry off and tell Maksim, the gardener, to set the serfs to work. Say that everything out of the hothouses must be brought here well wrapped up in felt. I must have two hundred pots here on Friday.'

Having given several more orders he was about to go to his 'little Countess' to have a rest, but remembering something else of importance, he returned again, called back the cook and the club steward, and again began giving orders. A light footstep and the clinking of spurs were heard at the door, and the young count, handsome, rosy, with a dark little moustache, evidently rested and made sleeker by his easy life in Moscow, entered the room.

'Ah, my boy, my head's in a whirl!' said the old man with a smile as if he felt a little confused before his son. 'Now if you would only help a bit! I must have singers too. I shall have my own orchestra, but shouldn't we get the gipsy singers as well? You military men like that sort of thing.'

'Really, papa, I believe Prince Bagration worried himself less before the battle of Schön Graben than you do now,' said his son with a smile.

The old count pretended to be angry.

'Yes, you talk, but try it yourself!'

And the count turned to the cook, who with a shrewd and respectful expression, looked observantly and sympathetically at the father and son.

'What have the young people come to nowadays, eh, Feoktist?' said he ' – laughing at us old fellows!'

'That's so, your Excellency, all they have to do is to eat a good dinner, but providing it and serving it all up, that's not their business!'

'That's it, that's it!' exclaimed the count, and gaily seizing his son by both hands he cried, 'Now I've got you, so take the sledge and pair at once, and go to Bezukhov's, and tell him "Count Ilya has sent you to ask for strawberries and fresh pineapples." We can't get them from anyone else. He's not there himself, so you'll have to go in and ask the princesses; and from there go on to the Rasgulyay – the coachman Ipatka knows – and look up the gipsy Ilyushka, the one who danced at Count Orlov's, you remember, in a white Cossack coat, and bring him along to me.'

'And am I to bring the gipsy girls along with him?' asked Nicholas laughing. 'Dear, dear!' ...

At that moment, with noiseless footsteps and with the business-like, preoccupied, yet meekly Christian look which never left her face, Anna Mikhaylovna entered the hall. Though she came upon the count in his dressing-gown every day, he invariably became confused and begged her to excuse his costume.

'No matter at all, my dear Count,' she said, meekly closing her eyes. 'But I'll go to Bezukhov's myself. Pierre has arrived, and now we shall get anything we want from his hothouses. I have to see him in any case. He has forwarded me a letter from Boris. Thank God, Boris is now on the staff.'

The count was delighted at Anna Mikhaylovna's taking upon

herself one of his commissions, and ordered the small closed carriage for her.

'Tell Bezukhov to come. I'll put his name down. Is his wife with him?' he asked.

Anna Mikhaylovna turned up her eyes, and profound sadness was depicted on her face.

'Ah, dear friend, he is very unfortunate,' she said. 'If what we hear is true, it is dreadful. How little we dreamed of such a thing when we were rejoicing at his happiness! And such a lofty angelic soul as young Bezukhov! Yes, I pity him from my heart, and shall try to give him what consolation I can.'

'Wh-what is the matter?' asked both the young and old Rostov.

Anna Mikhaylovna sighed deeply.

'Dolokhov, Mary Ivanovna's son,' she said in a mysterious whisper, 'has compromised her completely, they say. Pierre took him up, invited him to his house in Petersburg, and now ... she has come here and that dare-devil after her!' said Anna Mikhaylovna, wishing to show her sympathy for Pierre, but by involuntary intonations and a half-smile betraying her sympathy for the dare-devil', as she called Dolokhov. 'They say Pierre is quite broken by his misfortune.'

'Dear, dear! But still tell him to come to the Club – it will all blow over. It will be a tremendous banquet.'

Next day, the 3rd of March, soon after one o'clock, two hundred and fifty members of the English Club and fifty guests were awaiting the guest of honour and hero of the Austrian campaign, Prince Bagration, to dinner.

On the first arrival of the news of the battle of Austerlitz, Moscow had been bewildered. At that time the Russians were so used to victories that on receiving news of a defeat some would simply not believe it, while others sought some extraordinary explanation of so strange an event. In the English Club where all who were distinguished, important, and well-informed, foregathered, when the news began to arrive in December nothing was said about the war and the last battle, as though all were in a conspiracy of silence. The men who set the tone in conversation* – Count Rostopchin, Prince Yuri Dolgorukov, Valuev, Count Markov and Prince Vyazemsky – did not show themselves at the Club but met in private houses in intimate circles, and the Moscovites who took their opinions from others – Ilya Rostov among them – remained for a while without any definite opinion on the subject of the war, and without leaders. The Moscovites felt that something was wrong, and that to discuss the bad news was difficult, and so it was best to be silent. But after a while, just as a jury comes out of its room, the bigwigs who guided the Club's opinion reappeared, and everybody began speaking clearly and definitely. Reasons were found for the incredible, unheard-of, and impossible event of a Russian defeat, everything became clear, and in all corners of Moscow the same things began to be said. These reasons were the treachery of the Austrians, a defective commissariat, the treachery of the Pole Przebyszewski and of the Frenchman Langeron, Kutuzov's incapacity, and (it was whispered) the youth and inexperience of the sovereign, who had trusted worthless and insignificant people. But the army, the Russian army, everyone declared was extraordinary, and had achieved miracles of valour. The soldiers, officers, and generals were heroes. But the hero of heroes was Prince Bagration, distinguished by his Schön Graben affair and by the retreat from Austerlitz, where he alone had withdrawn his column unbroken, and had all day beaten back an enemy force twice as numerous as his own. What also conduced to Bagration being selected as Moscow's hero was the fact that he had no connexions in the city and was a stranger there. In his person honour was shown to a simple fighting Russian soldier without connexions and intrigues, and to one who was associated by memories of the Italian campaign with the name of Suvorov. Moreover paying such honour to Bagration was the best way of expressing disapproval and dislike of Kutuzov.

'Had there been no Bagration it would have been necessary to invent him,' said the wit Shinshin, parodying the words of Voltaire. Kutuzov no one spoke of, except some who abused him in whispers, calling him a court-weathercock and an old satyr.

All Moscow repeated Prince Dolgorukov's saying: 'If you go on modelling and modelling you must get smeared with clay,' suggesting consolation for our defeat by the memory of former victories; and the words of Rostopchin, that French soldiers have to be incited to battle by high-falutin' words, and Germans by logical arguments to show them that it is more dangerous to run away than to advance, but that Russian soldiers only need to be restrained and held back! On all sides new and fresh anecdotes were heard of individual examples of heroism shown by our officers and men at Austerlitz. One had saved a standard, another had killed five Frenchmen, a third had loaded five cannon single-handed. Berg was mentioned by those who did not know him, as having when wounded in the right hand, taken his sword in the left, and gone forward. Of Bolkonsky nothing was said, and only those who knew him intimately regretted that he had died so young, leaving a pregnant wife with his eccentric father.

## 3

ON that 3rd of March all the rooms in the English Club were filled with a hum of conversation, like the hum of bees swarming in spring-time. The members and guests of the club wandered hither and thither, sat, stood, met, and separated, some in uniform and some in evening dress and a few here and there with powdered hair and in Russian *kaftáns*. Powdered footmen in livery with buckled shoes and smart stockings stood at every door anxiously noting visitors' every movement in order to offer their services. Most of those present were elderly respected men with broad self-confident faces, fat fingers, and resolute gestures and voices. This class of guests and members sat in certain habitual places and met in certain habitual groups. A minority of those present were casual guests – chiefly young men, among whom were Denisov, Rostov and Dolokhov – who was now again an officer in the Semënov regiment. The faces of these young people, especially those who were military men, bore that expression of condescending respect for their elders which seems to say to the older generation, 'We are prepared to respect and honour you, but all the same remember that the future belongs to us.'

Nesvitsky was there as an old member of the club. Pierre, who at his wife's command had let his hair grow and abandoned his spectacles, went about the rooms fashionably dressed but looking sad and dull. Here as elsewhere he was surrounded by an atmosphere of subservience to his wealth, and being in the habit of lording it over these people he treated them with absent-minded contempt.

By his age he should have belonged to the younger men, but by his wealth and connexions he belonged to the groups of old and honoured guests, and so he went from one group to another. Some of the most important old men were the centre of groups which even strangers approached respectfully to hear the voices of well-known men. The largest circles formed round Count Rostopchin, Valuev, and Naryshkin. Rostopchin was describing how the Russians had been overwhelmed by flying Austrians and had had to force their way through them with bayonets.

Valuev was confidentially telling that Uvarov had been sent from Petersburg to ascertain what Moscow was thinking about Austerlitz.

In a third circle Naryshkin was speaking of the meeting of the Austrian Council of War at which Suvorov crowed like a cock in reply to the nonsense talked by the Austrian generals. Shinshin, standing close by, tried to make a joke, saying that Kutuzov had evidently failed to learn from Suvorov even so simple a thing as the art of crowing like a cock, but the elder members glanced severely at the wit, making him feel that in that place and on that day it was improper to speak so of Kutuzov.

Count Ilya Rostov, hurried and preoccupied, went about in his soft boots between the dining and drawing-rooms hastily greeting the important and unimportant, all of whom he knew, as if they were all equals, while his eyes occasionally sought out his fine well-set-up young son, resting on him and winking joyfully at him. Young Rostov stood at a window with Dolokhov, whose acquaintance he had lately made and highly valued. The old count came up to them and pressed Dolokhov's hand.

'Please come and visit us . . . you know my brave boy . . . been together out there . . . both playing the hero . . . Ah, Vasili Ignato-vich . . . How d'ye do, old fellow?' he said, turning to an old man who was passing, but before he had finished his greeting there was a general stir, and a footman who had run in announced with a frightened face: 'He's arrived!'

Bells rang, the stewards rushed forward, and – like rye shaken together in a shovel – the guests who had been scattered about in different rooms came together and crowded in the large drawing-room by the door of the ball-room.

Bagration appeared in the doorway of the ante-room without hat or sword, which in accord with the Club custom he had given up to the hall-porter. He had no lambskin cap on his head, nor had he a loaded whip over his shoulder, as when Rostov had seen him on the eve of the battle of Austerlitz, but wore a tight new uniform with Russian and foreign Orders, and the Star of St George on his left breast. Evidently just before coming to the dinner he had had his hair and whiskers trimmed, which changed his appearance for the worse. There was something naïvely festive in his air, which in conjunction with his firm and virile features gave him a rather comical expression. Bekleshëv and Theodore Uvarov who had arrived with him, paused at the doorway to allow him, as the guest of honour, to enter first. Bagration was embarrassed, not wishing to avail himself of their courtesy, and this caused some delay at the doors, but after all he did at last enter first. He walked shyly and awkwardly over the parquet floor of the reception-room not knowing what to do with his hands; he was more accustomed to walk over a ploughed field under fire, as he had done at the head of the Kursk regiment at Schön Graben – and he would have found that easier. The committee-men met him at the first door and expressing their delight at seeing such a highly honoured guest, took possession of him as it were, without waiting for his reply, surrounded him, and led him to the drawing-room. It was at first impossible to enter the drawing-room door for the crowd of members and guests jostling one another and trying to get a good look at Bagration over each other's shoulders, as if he were some rare animal. Count Ilya Rostov, laughing and repeating the words, 'Make way, dear boy! Make way, make way!' pushed through the crowd more energetically than anyone, led the guests into the drawing-room, and seated them on the centre sofa. The bigwigs, the most respected members of the Club, beset the new arrivals. Count Ilya again thrusting his way through the crowd, went out of the drawing-room, and reappeared a minute later with another committee-man, carrying a large silver salver which he presented to Prince Bagration. On the salver lay some verses composed and printed in the hero's honour. Bagration on seeing the salver glanced around in dismay, as though seeking help. But all eyes demanded that he should submit. Feeling himself in their power, he resolutely took the salver with both hands and looked sternly and reproach-fully at the count who had presented it to him. Someone obligingly took the dish from Bagration (or he would, it seemed, have held it till evening and have gone in to dinner with it) and drew his attention to the verses. 'Well, I will read them, then!' Bagration seemed to say, and fixing his weary eyes on the paper, began to read them with a fixed and serious expression. But the author himself took the verses and began reading them aloud. Bagration bowed his head and listened:*

> Bring glory then to Alexander's reign
> And on the throne our Titus shield.
> A dreaded foe be thou, kind-hearted as a man,
> A Rhipheus at home, a Caesar in the field!
>
> E'en fortunate Napoleon
> Knows by experience, now, Bagration,
> And dare not Herculean Russians trouble....

But before he had finished reading, a stentorian major-domo announced that dinner was ready. The door opened, and from the dining-room came the resounding strains of the Polonaise:

> Conquest's joyful thunder waken,
> Triumph, valiant Russians, now!...

and Count Rostov, glancing angrily at the author who went on reading his verses, bowed to Bagration. Everyone rose, feeling that dinner was more important than verses, and Bagration, again preceding all the rest, went in to dinner. He was seated in the place of honour between two Alexanders – Beklesḧev and Naryshkin – which was a significant allusion to the name of the sovereign. Three hundred persons took their seats in the dining-room, according to their rank and importance: the more important nearer to the honoured guest, as naturally as water flows deepest where the land lies lowest.

Just before dinner Count Ilya Rostov presented his son to Bagration, who recognized him and said a few words to him, disjointed and awkward, as were all the words he spoke that day, and Count Ilya looked joyfully and proudly around while Bagration spoke to his son.

Nicholas Rostov, with Denisov and his new acquaintance Dolokhov, sat almost at the middle of the table. Facing them sat Pierre beside Prince Nesvitsky. Count Ilya Rostov with the other members of the committee sat facing Bagration, and as the very personification of Moscow hospitality did the honours to the Prince.

His efforts had not been in vain. The dinner, both the lenten and the other fare, was splendid, yet he could not feel quite at ease till the end of the meal. He winked at the butler, whispered directions to the footmen, and awaited each expected dish with some anxiety. Everything was excellent. With the second course, a gigantic sterlet (at sight of which Ilya Rostov blushed with self-conscious pleasure), the footmen began popping corks and filling the champagne glasses. After the fish, which made a certain sensation, the count exchanged glances with the other committee-men. 'There will be many toasts, it's time to begin,' he whispered, and taking up his glass he rose. All were silent, waiting for what he would say.

'To the health of our Sovereign, the Emperor!' he cried, and at the same moment his kindly eyes grew moist with tears of joy and enthusiasm. The band immediately struck up 'Conquest's joyful thunder waken . . .' All rose and cried 'hurrah!' Bagration also rose, and shouted 'hurrah!' in exactly the same voice in which he had shouted it on the field at Schön Graben. Young Rostov's ecstatic voice could be heard above the three hundred others. He nearly wept. 'To the health of our Sovereign, the Emperor!' he roared, 'hurrah!' and emptying his glass at one gulp he dashed it to the floor. Many followed his example, and the loud shouting continued for a long time. When the voices subsided, the footmen cleared away the broken glass and everybody sat down again, smiling at the noise they had made and exchanging remarks. The old count rose once more, glanced at a note lying beside his plate, and proposed a toast, 'To the health of the hero of our last campaign, Prince Peter Ivanovich Bagration!', and again his blue eyes grew moist. 'Hurrah!' cried the three hundred voices again, but instead

of the band a choir began singing a cantata composed by Paul
Ivanovich Kutuzov:*

> Russians! O'er all barriers on!
> Courage conquest guarantees;
> Have we not Bagration?
> He brings foemen to their knees, ... &c.

As soon as the singing was over, another and another toast was
proposed and Count Ilya Rostov became more and more moved,
more glass was smashed and the shouting grew louder. They drank
to Bekleshëv, Naryshkin, Uvarov, Dolgorukov, Apraksin, Valuev,
to the committee, to all the Club members and to all the Club
guests, and finally to Count Ilya Rostov separately, as the organizer
of the banquet. At that toast the count took out his handkerchief
and, covering his face, wept outright.

4

PIERRE sat opposite Dolokhov and Nicholas Rostov. As usual he
ate and drank much and eagerly. But those who knew him intimately noticed that some great change had come over him that
day. He was silent all through dinner and looked about, blinking
and scowling, or with fixed eyes and a look of complete absent-
mindedness kept rubbing the bridge of his nose. His face was
depressed and gloomy. He seemed to see and hear nothing of what
was going on around him and to be absorbed by some depressing
and unsolved problem.

The unsolved problem that tormented him was caused by hints
given by the princess, his cousin, at Moscow, concerning Dolokhov's
intimacy with his wife, and by an anonymous letter he had received
that morning, which in the mean jocular way common to anonymous letters said that he saw badly through his spectacles, but that
his wife's connexion with Dolokhov was a secret to no one but
himself. Pierre absolutely disbelieved both the princess's hints and
the letter, but he feared now to look at Dolokhov, who was sitting
opposite him. Every time he chanced to meet Dolokhov's handsome
insolent eyes, Pierre felt something terrible and monstrous rising
in his soul and turned quickly away. Involuntarily recalling his
wife's past and her relations with Dolokhov, Pierre saw clearly
that what was said in the letter might be true, or might at least
seem to be true had it not referred to *his wife*. He involuntarily
remembered how Dolokhov who had fully recovered his former
position after the campaign, had returned to Petersburg and come

to him. Availing himself of his friendly relations with Pierre as a boon companion, Dolokhov had come straight to his house, and Pierre had put him up and lent him money. Pierre recalled how Hélène had smilingly expressed disapproval of Dolokhov's living at their house, and how cynically Dolokhov had praised his wife's beauty to him and from that time till they came to Moscow had not left them for a day.

'Yes, he is very handsome,' thought Pierre, 'and I know him. It would be particularly pleasant to him to dishonour my name and ridicule me, just because I have exerted myself on his behalf, befriended him and helped him. I know and understand what a spice that would add to the pleasure of deceiving me, if it really were true. Yes, if it were true, but I do not believe it. I have no right to, and can't believe it.' He remembered the expression Dolokhov's face assumed in his moments of cruelty, as when tying the policeman to the bear and dropping them into the water, or when he challenged a man to a duel without any reason, or shot a postboy's horse with a pistol. That expression was often on Dolokhov's face when looking at him. 'Yes, he is a bully,' thought Pierre, 'to kill a man means nothing to him. It must seem to him that everyone is afraid of him, and that must please him. He must think that I, too, am afraid of him – and in fact I am afraid of him,' he thought, and again he felt something terrible and monstrous rising in his soul. Dolokhov, Denisov, and Rostov, were now sitting opposite Pierre and seemed very gay. Rostov was talking merrily to his two friends, one of whom was a dashing hussar and the other a notorious duellist and rake, and every now and then he glanced ironically at Pierre whose preoccupied, absent-minded, and massive figure was a very noticeable one at the dinner. Rostov looked inimically at Pierre, first because Pierre appeared to his hussar eyes as a rich civilian, the husband of a beauty, and in a word – an old woman, and secondly because Pierre in his preoccupation and absent-mindedness had not recognized Rostov and had not responded to his greeting. When the Emperor's health was drunk Pierre, lost in thought, did not rise or lift his glass.

'What are you about?' shouted Rostov looking at him in an ecstasy of exasperation. 'Don't you hear it's his Majesty the Emperor's health?'

Pierre sighed, rose submissively, emptied his glass, and waiting till all were seated again turned with his kindly smile to Rostov.

'Why, I didn't recognize you!' he said. But Rostov was otherwise engaged; he was shouting 'hurrah!'

'Why don't you renew the acquaintance?' said Dolokhov to Rostov.

'Confound him, he's a fool!' said Rostov.

'One should make up to the husbands of pretty women,' said Denisov.

Pierre did not catch what they were saying, but knew they were talking about him. He reddened and turned away.

'Well, now to the health of handsome women!' said Dolokhov, and with a serious expression, but with a smile lurking at the corners of his mouth, he turned with his glass to Pierre.

'Here's to the health of lovely women, Peterkin – and their lovers!' he added.

Pierre with downcast eyes drank out of his glass without looking at Dolokhov or answering him. The footman, who was distributing leaflets with Kutuzov's cantata, laid one before Pierre as one of the principal guests. He was just going to take it when Dolokhov, leaning across, snatched it from his hand and began reading it. Pierre looked at Dolokhov and his eyes dropped, the something terrible and monstrous that had tormented him all dinner-time rose and took possession of him. He leaned his whole massive body across the table.

'How dare you take it?' he shouted.

Hearing that cry and seeing to whom it was addressed, Nesvitsky and the neighbour on his right quickly turned in alarm to Bezukhov.

'Don't! Don't! What are you about?' whispered their frightened voices.

Dolokhov looked at Pierre with clear mirthful cruel eyes, and that smile of his which seemed to say, 'Ah! This is what I like!'

'You shan't have it!' he said distinctly.

Pale, with quivering lips, Pierre snatched the copy.

'You . . . ! you . . . scoundrel! I challenge you!' he ejaculated, and pushing back his chair he rose from the table.

At the very instant he did this and uttered those words Pierre felt that the question of his wife's guilt which had been tormenting him the whole day, was finally and indubitably answered in the affirmative. He hated her and was for ever sundered from her. Despite Denisov's request that he would take no part in the matter, Rostov agreed to be Dolokhov's second, and after dinner he discussed the arrangements for the duel with Nesvitsky, Bezukhov's second. Pierre went home, but Rostov with Dolokhov and Denisov stayed on at the club till late, listening to the gipsies and other singers.

'Well, then, till to-morrow at Sokolniki,' said Dolokhov as he took leave of Rostov in the club porch.

'And do you feel quite calm?' Rostov asked.

Dolokhov paused.

'Well, you see, I'll tell you the whole secret of duelling in two words. If you are going to fight a duel, and you make a will and write affectionate letters to your parents, and if you think you may be killed, you are a fool and are lost for certain. But go with the firm intention of killing your man as quickly and surely as possible, and then all will be right, as our bear-huntsman at Kostroma used to tell me. "Everyone fears a bear," he says, "but when you see one your fear's all gone, and your only thought is not to let him get away!" And that's how it is with me. A *demain, mon cher.*'

Next day at eight in the morning Pierre and Nesvitsky drove to the Sokolniki forest and found Dolokhov, Denisov and Rostov already there. Pierre had the air of a man preoccupied with considerations which had no connexion with the matter in hand. His haggard face was yellow. He had evidently not slept that night. He looked about distractedly and screwed up his eyes as if dazzled by the sun. He was entirely absorbed by two considerations: his wife's guilt, of which after his sleepless night he had not the slightest doubt, and the guiltlessness of Dolokhov, who had no reason to preserve the honour of a man who was nothing to him . . . 'I should perhaps have done the same in his place,' thought Pierre. 'It's even certain that I should have done the same, then why this duel, this murder? Either I shall kill him, or he will hit me in the head, or elbow, or knee. Can't I go away from here, run away, bury myself somewhere?' passed through his mind. But just at moments when such thoughts occurred to him, he would ask in a particularly calm and absent-minded way, which inspired the respect of the onlookers, 'Will it be long? Are things ready?'

When all was ready, the sabres struck in the snow to mark the barriers, and the pistols loaded, Nesvitsky went up to Pierre.

'I should not be doing my duty, Count,' he said in timid tones, 'and should not justify your confidence and the honour you have done me in choosing me for your second, if at this grave, this very grave, moment I did not tell you the whole truth. I think there is no sufficient ground for this affair, or for blood to be shed over it. . . . You were not right, not quite in the right, you were impetuous . . .'

'Oh yes, it is horribly stupid,' said Pierre.

'Then allow me to express your regrets, and I am sure your opponent will accept them,' said Nesvitsky (who like the others concerned in the affair, and like everyone in similar cases, did not yet believe that the affair had come to an actual duel). 'You know, Count, it is much more honourable to admit one's mistake than to let matters become irreparable. There was no insult on either side. Allow me to convey . . .'

'No! What is there to talk about?' said Pierre. 'It's all the same . . . Is everything ready?' he added. 'Only tell me where to go and where to shoot,' he said with an unnaturally gentle smile.

He took the pistol in his hand and began asking about the working of the trigger, as he had not before held a pistol in his hand – a fact he did not wish to confess.

'Oh yes, like that, I know, I only forgot,' said he.

'No apologies, none whatever,' said Dolokhov to Denisov (who on his side had been attempting a reconciliation) and he also went up to the appointed place.

The spot chosen for the duel was some eighty paces from the road where the sledges had been left, in a small clearing in the pine forest covered with melting snow, the frost having begun to break up during the last few days. The antagonists stood forty paces apart at the farther edge of the clearing. The seconds, measuring the paces, left tracks in the deep wet snow between the place where they had been standing and Nesvitsky's and Dolokhov's sabres, which were stuck into the ground ten paces apart to mark the barrier. It was thawing and misty, at forty paces' distance nothing could be seen. For three minutes all had been ready, but they still delayed and all were silent.

5

'WELL, begin!' said Dolokhov.

'All right,' said Pierre still smiling in the same way.

A feeling of dread was in the air. It was evident that the affair so lightly begun could no longer be averted but was taking its course independently of men's will. Denisov first went to the barrier and announced:

'As the adve'sawies have wefused a weconciliation, please pwoceed. Take your pistols, and at the word *thwee* begin to advance.'

'O-ne! T-wo! Thwee!' he shouted angrily and stepped aside.

The combatants advanced along the trodden tracks, nearer and nearer to one another, beginning to see one another through the mist. They had the right to fire when they liked as they approached the barrier. Dolokhov walked slowly without raising his pistol, looking intently with his bright sparkling blue eyes into his antagonist's face. His mouth wore its usual semblance of a smile.

'So I can fire when I like!' said Pierre, and at the word 'three' he went quickly forward missing the trodden path and stepping into the deep snow. He held the pistol in his right hand at arm's length, apparently afraid of shooting himself with it. His left hand he held carefully back, because he wished to support his right hand with it and knew he must not do so. Having advanced six paces and strayed off the track into the snow, Pierre looked down at his feet, then quickly glanced at Dolokhov and bending his finger as he had been shown, fired. Not at all expecting so loud a report, Pierre shuddered at the sound, and then smiling at his own sensations, stood still. The smoke, rendered denser by the mist, prevented him from seeing anything for an instant, but there was no second report as he had expected. He only heard Dolokhov's hurried steps, and his figure came in view through the smoke. He was pressing one hand to his left side, while the other clutched his drooping pistol. His face was pale. Rostov ran towards him and said something.

'No-o-o!' muttered Dolokhov through his teeth, 'no, it's not over.' And after stumbling a few staggering steps right up to the sabre, he sank on the snow beside it. His left hand was bloody; he wiped it on his coat and supported himself with it. His frowning face was pallid and quivered.

'Plea . . .' began Dolokhov, but could not at first pronounce the word.

'Please,' he uttered with an effort.

Pierre hardly restraining his sobs, began running towards Dolokhov and was about to cross the space between the barriers, when Dolokhov cried:

'To your barrier!' and Pierre, grasping what was meant, stopped by his sabre. Only ten paces divided them. Dolokhov lowered his head to the snow, greedily bit at it, again raised his head, adjusted himself, drew in his legs and sat up, seeking a firm centre of gravity. He sucked and swallowed the cold snow, his lips quivered, but his eyes, still smiling, glittered with effort and exasperation as he mustered his remaining strength. He raised his pistol and aimed.

'Sideways! Cover yourself with your pistol!' ejaculated Nesvitsky.

'Cover yourself!' even Denisov cried to his adversary.

Pierre with a gentle smile of pity and remorse, his arms and legs helplessly spread out, stood with his broad chest directly facing Dolokhov and looked sorrowfully at him. Denisov, Rostov, and Nesvitsky closed their eyes. At the same instant they heard a report and Dolokhov's angry cry.

'Missed!' shouted Dolokhov, and he lay helplessly face downwards on the snow.

Pierre clutched his temples, and turning round went into the forest, trampling through the deep snow, and muttering incoherent words:

'Folly . . . folly! Death . . . lies . . .' he repeated, puckering his face. Nesvitsky stopped him and took him home.

Rostov and Denisov drove away with the wounded Dolokhov.

The latter lay silent in the sledge with closed eyes, and did not answer a word to the questions addressed to him. But on entering Moscow he suddenly came to, and lifting his head with an effort, took Rostov, who was sitting beside him, by the hand. Rostov was struck by the totally altered and unexpectedly rapturous and tender expression on Dolokhov's face.

'Well? How do you feel?' he asked.

'Bad! But it's not that, my friend –' said Dolokhov with a gasping voice. 'Where are we? In Moscow, I know. I don't matter, but I have killed her, killed . . . She won't get over it! She won't survive . . .'

'Who?' asked Rostov.

'My mother! My mother, my angel, my adored angel-mother,' and Dolokhov pressed Rostov's hand and burst into tears.

When he had become a little quieter he explained to Rostov that he was living with his mother, who if she saw him dying would not survive it. He implored Rostov to go on and prepare her.

Rostov went on ahead to do what was asked, and to his great surprise learned that Dolokhov the brawler, Dolokhov the bully, lived in Moscow with an old mother and a hunchback sister, and was the most affectionate of sons and brothers.

6

PIERRE had of late rarely seen his wife alone. Both in Petersburg and in Moscow their house was always full of visitors. The night after the duel he did not go to his bedroom, but as he often did, remained in his father's room, that huge room in which Count Bezukhov had died.

He lay down on the sofa meaning to fall asleep and forget all that had happened to him, but could not do so. Such a storm of feelings, thoughts, and memories suddenly arose within him, that he could not fall asleep, nor even remain in one place, but had to jump up and pace the room with rapid steps. Now he seemed to see her in the early days of their marriage, with bare shoulders and a languid, passionate look on her face, and then immediately he saw beside her Dolokhov's handsome, insolent, hard and mocking face as he had seen it at the banquet, and then that same face pale, quivering, and suffering as it had been when he reeled and sank on the snow.

'What has happened?' he asked himself. 'I have killed her *lover*, yes, killed my wife's lover. Yes, that was it! And why? How did I come to do it?' – 'Because you married her,' answered an inner voice.

'But in what was I to blame?' he asked. 'In marrying her without loving her; in deceiving yourself and her.' And he vividly recalled that moment after supper at Prince Vasili's, when he spoke those words he had found so difficult to utter. 'I love you.' 'It all comes from that! Even then I felt it,' he thought. 'I felt then that it was not so, that I had no right to do it. And so it turns out.'

He remembered his honeymoon, and blushed at the recollection. Particularly vivid, humiliating, and shameful was the recollection of how one day soon after his marriage he came out of the bedroom into his study a little before noon in his silk dressing-gown, and found his head-steward there, who, bowing respectfully, looked into his face and at his dressing-gown, and smiled slightly, as if expressing respectful understanding of his employer's happiness.

'But how often I have felt proud of her, proud of her majestic beauty and social tact,' thought he; 'been proud of my house, in which she received all Petersburg, proud of her unapproachability and beauty. So this is what I was proud of! I then thought that I did not understand her. How often when considering her character I have told myself that I was to blame for not understanding her, for not understanding that constant composure and complacency and lack of all interests or desires, and the whole secret lies in the terrible truth that she is a depraved woman. Now I have spoken that terrible word to myself all has become clear.

'Anatole used to come to borrow money from her* and used to kiss her naked shoulders. She did not give him the money but let herself be kissed. Her father in jest tried to rouse her jealousy, and she replied with a calm smile that she was not so stupid as to be jealous: "Let him do what he pleases," she used to say of me. One day I asked her if she felt any symptoms of pregnancy. She laughed contemptuously and said she was not a fool to want to have children, and that she was not going to have any children by *me*.'

Then he recalled the coarseness and bluntness of her thoughts and the vulgarity of the expressions that were natural to her, though she had been brought up in the most aristocratic circles. 'I'm not such a fool...Just you try it on...*Allez-vous promener*,' she used to say. Often seeing the success she had with young and old men and women Pierre could not understand why he did not love her.

'Yes, I never loved her,' said he to himself; 'I knew she was a depraved woman,' he repeated, 'but dared not admit it to myself. And now there's Dolokhov sitting in the snow with a forced smile and perhaps dying, while meeting my remorse with some forced bravado!'

Pierre was one of those people who, in spite of an appearance of what is called weak character, do not seek a confidant in their troubles. He digested his sufferings alone.

'It is all, all her fault,' he said to himself; 'but what of that? Why did I bind myself to her? Why did I say "*Je vous aime*" to her, which was a lie, and worse than a lie? I am guilty and must endure ... what? A slur on my name? A misfortune for life? Oh, that's nonsense,' he thought. 'The slur on my name and honour – that's all apart from myself.'

'Louis XVI was executed because they said he was dishonourable and a criminal,' came into Pierre's head, 'and from their point of view they were right, as were those too who canonised him and died a martyr's death for his sake. Then Robespierre was beheaded for being a despot. Who is right and who is wrong? No one! But if you are alive – live: to-morrow you'll die as I might have died an hour ago. And is it worth tormenting oneself, when one has only a moment of life in comparison with eternity?'

But at the moment when he imagined himself calmed by such reflections, *she* suddenly came into his mind as she was at the moments when he had most strongly expressed his insincere love for her, and he felt the blood rush to his heart and had again to get up and move about and break and tear whatever came to his hand. 'Why did I tell her that "*Je vous aime*"?' he kept repeating to himself. And when he had said it for the tenth time, Moliere's words: *Mais que diable alloit-il faire dans cette galère** occurred to him, and he began to laugh at himself.

In the night he called his valet and told him to pack up to go to Petersburg. He could not imagine how he could speak to her now. He resolved to go away next day and leave a letter informing her of his intention to part from her for ever.

Next morning when the valet came into the room with his coffee, Pierre was lying asleep on the ottoman with an open book in his hand.

He woke up and looked round for awhile with a startled expression, unable to realize where he was.

'The countess told me to inquire whether your Excellency was at home,' said the valet.

But before Pierre could decide what answer he would send, the countess herself in a white satin dressing-gown embroidered with silver and with simply dressed hair (two immense plaits twice round her lovely head like a coronet) entered the room, calm and majestic, except that there was a wrathful wrinkle on her rather prominent marble brow. With her imperturbable calm she did not begin to speak in front of the valet. She knew of the duel and had come to speak about it. She waited till the valet had set down the coffee things and left the room. Pierre looked at her timidly over his spectacles, and like a hare surrounded by hounds who lays back her ears and continues to crouch motionless before her enemies he tried to continue reading. But feeling this to be senseless and impossible, he again glanced timidly at her. She did not sit down but looked at him with a contemptuous smile, waiting for the valet to go.

'Well, what's this now? What have you been up to now, I should like to know?' she asked sternly.

'I? What have I...?' stammered Pierre.

'So it seems you're a hero, eh? Come now, what was this duel about? What is it meant to prove? What? I ask you.'

Pierre turned over heavily on the ottoman and opened his mouth, but could not reply.

'If you won't answer, I'll tell you...' Hélène went on. 'You believe everything you're told. You were told...' Hélène laughed, 'that Dolokhov was my lover,' she said in French with her coarse plainness of speech, uttering the word *amant* as casually as any other word, 'and you believed it! Well, what have you proved? What does this duel prove? That you're a fool, *que vous êtes un sot*, but everybody knew that. What will be the result? That I shall be the laughing-stock of all Moscow, that everyone will say that you, drunk and not knowing what you were about, challenged a man you are jealous of without cause.' Hélène raised her voice and became more and more excited, 'a man who's a better man than you in every way...'

'Hm...Hm...!' growled Pierre, frowning without looking at her, and not moving a muscle.

'And how could you believe he was my lover? Why? Because I like his company? If you were cleverer and more agreeable, I should prefer yours.'

'Don't speak to me...I beg you,' muttered Pierre hoarsely.

'Why shouldn't I speak? I can speak as I like, and I tell you plainly that there are not many wives with husbands such as you who would not have taken lovers (*des amants*), but I have not done so,' said she.

Pierre wished to say something, looked at her with eyes whose strange expression she did not understand, and lay down again. He was suffering physically at that moment, there was a weight on his chest and he could not breathe. He knew that he must do something to put an end to this suffering, but what he wanted to do was too terrible.

'We had better separate,' he muttered in a broken voice.

'Separate? Very well, but only if you give me a fortune,' said Hélène. 'Separate! That's a thing to frighten me with!'

Pierre leaped up from the sofa and rushed staggering towards her.

'I'll kill you!' he shouted, and seizing the marble top of a table with a strength he had never before felt, he made a step towards her brandishing the slab.

Hélène's face became terrible, she shrieked and sprang aside. His father's nature showed itself in Pierre. He felt the fascination and delight of frenzy. He flung down the slab, broke it, and swooping down on her with outstretched hands shouted, 'Get out!' in such a terrible voice that the whole house heard it with horror. God knows what he would have done at that moment had Hélène not fled from the room.

*

A week later Pierre gave his wife full power to control all his estates in Great Russia, which formed the larger part of his property, and left for Petersburg alone.

7

Two months had elapsed since the news of the battle of Austerlitz and the loss of Prince Andrew had reached Bald Hills, and in spite of the letters sent through the embassy and all the searches made, his body had not been found nor was he on the list of prisoners. What was worst of all for his relations was the fact that there was still a possibility of his having been picked up on the battlefield by the people of the place and that he might now be lying, recovering or dying, alone among strangers and unable to send news of himself. The gazettes from which the old prince first heard of the defeat at Austerlitz stated, as usual very briefly and vaguely, that after brilliant engagements the Russians had had to retreat and had made their withdrawal in perfect order. The old prince understood from this official report that our army had been defeated. A week after the gazette report of the battle of Austerlitz came a letter from Kutuzov informing the prince of the fate that had befallen his son.

'Your son,' wrote Kutuzov, 'fell before my eyes, a standard in his hand and at the head of a regiment – he fell as a hero, worthy of his father and his fatherland. To the great regret of myself and of the whole army it is still uncertain whether he is alive or not. I comfort myself and you with the hope that your son is alive, for otherwise he would have been mentioned among the officers found on the field of battle, a list of whom has been sent me under flag of truce.'

After receiving this news late in the evening, when he was alone in his study, the old prince went for his walk as usual next morning, but he was silent with his steward, the gardener, and the architect, and though he looked very grim he said nothing to anyone.

When Princess Mary went to him at the usual hour he was working at his lathe and, as usual, did not look round at her.

'Ah, Princess Mary!' he said suddenly in an unnatural voice, throwing down his chisel. (The wheel continued to revolve by its own impetus, and Princess Mary long remembered the dying creak of that wheel which merged in her memory with what followed.)

She approached him, saw his face, and something gave way within her. Her eyes grew dim. By the expression of her father's face, not sad, not crushed, but angry and working unnaturally, she saw that hanging over her and about to crush her was some terrible misfortune, the worst in life, one she had not yet experienced, irreparable and incomprehensible – the death of one she loved.

'Father! Andrew!' – said the ungraceful, awkward princess with such an indescribable charm of sorrow and self-forgetfulness that her father could not bear her look but turned away with a sob.

'Bad news! He's not among the prisoners nor among the killed! Kutuzov writes . . .' and he screamed as piercingly as if he wished to drive the princess away by that scream . . . 'Killed!'

The princess did not fall down or faint. She was already pale, but on hearing these words her face changed and something brightened in her beautiful radiant eyes. It was as if joy – a supreme joy apart from the joys and sorrows of this world – overflowed the great grief within her. She forgot all fear of her father, went up to him, took his hand, and drawing him down put her arm round his thin scraggy neck.

'Father,' she said, 'do not turn away from me, let us weep together.'

'Scoundrels! Blackguards!' shrieked the old man, turning his face away from her. 'Destroying the army, destroying the men! And why? Go, go and tell Lise.'

The princess sank helplessly into an arm-chair beside her father and wept. She saw her brother now as he had been at the moment when he took leave of her and of Lise, his look tender yet proud. She saw him tender and amused as he was when he put on the little icon. 'Did he believe? Had he repented of his unbelief? Was he now there? There in the realms of eternal peace and blessedness?' she thought.

'Father, tell me how it happened,' she asked through her tears.

'Go! Go! Killed in battle, where the best of Russian men and Russia's glory were led to destruction. Go, Princess Mary. Go and tell Lise. I will follow.'

When Princess Mary returned from her father, the little princess sat working, and looked up with that curious expression of inner, happy calm peculiar to pregnant women. It was evident that her eyes did not see Princess Mary but were looking within . . . into herself . . . at something joyful and mysterious taking place within her.

'Mary,' she said, moving away from the embroidery-frame and lying back, 'give me your hand.' She took her sister-in-law's hand and held it below her waist.

Her eyes were smiling expectantly, her downy lip rose, and remained lifted in child-like happiness.

Princess Mary knelt down before her and hid her face in the folds of her sister-in-law's dress.

'There, there! Do you feel it? I feel so strange. And do you know, Mary, I am going to love him very much,' said Lise, looking with bright and happy eyes at her sister-in-law.

Princess Mary could not lift her head, she was weeping.

'What is the matter, Mary?'

'Nothing . . . only I feel sad . . . sad about Andrew,' she said, wiping away her tears on her sister-in-law's knee.

Several times in the course of the morning Princess Mary began trying to prepare her sister-in-law, and every time began to cry. Unobservant as was the little princess, these tears, the cause of which she did not understand, agitated her. She said nothing but looked about uneasily as if in search of something. Before dinner the old prince, of whom she was always afraid, came into her room with a peculiarly restless and malign expression, and went out again without saying a word. She looked at Princess Mary, then sat thinking for awhile with that expression of attention to something within her that is only seen in pregnant women, and suddenly began to cry.

'Has anything come from Andrew?' she asked.

'No, you know it's too soon for news. But my father is anxious and I feel afraid.'

'So there's nothing?'

'Nothing,' answered Princess Mary, looking firmly with her radiant eyes at her sister-in-law.

She had determined not to tell her, and persuaded her father to hide the terrible news from her till after her confinement, which was expected within a few days. Princess Mary and the old prince each bore and hid their grief in their own way. The old prince would not cherish any hope; he made up his mind that Prince Andrew had been killed, and though he sent an official to Austria to seek for traces of his son, he ordered a monument from Moscow which he intended to erect in his own garden to his memory, and he told everybody that his son had been killed. He tried not to change his former way of life, but his strength failed him. He walked less, ate less, slept less, and became weaker every day. Princess Mary hoped. She prayed for her brother as living, and was always awaiting news of his return.

8

'DEAREST,' said the little princess after breakfast on the morning of the 19th of March, and her downy little lip rose from old habit, but as sorrow was manifest in every smile, the sound of every word, and even every footstep in that house since the terrible news had come, so now the smile of the little princess – influenced by the general mood though without knowing its cause – was such as to remind one still more of the general sorrow.

'Dearest, I'm afraid this morning's fruschtique* – as Foka the cook calls it – has disagreed with me.'

'What is the matter with you, my darling? You look pale. Oh, you are very pale!' said Princess Mary in alarm, running with her soft, ponderous steps up to her sister-in-law.

'Your Excellency, should not Mary Bogdanovna be sent for?' said one of the maids who was present. (Mary Bogdanovna was a midwife from the neighbouring town who had been at Bald Hills for the last fortnight.)

'Oh yes,' assented Princess Mary, 'perhaps that's it. I'll go. Courage, my angel.' She kissed Lise and was about to leave the room.

'Oh, no, no!' And besides the pallor and the physical suffering on the little princess's face, an expression of childish fear of inevitable pain showed itself.

340

'No, it's only indigestion...! Say it's only indigestion, say so, Mary! Say...' And the little princess began to cry capriciously like a suffering child, and to wring her little hands even with some affectation. Princess Mary ran out of the room to fetch Mary Bogdanovna.

'*Mon Dieu! Mon Dieu!* Oh!' she heard as she left the room.

The midwife was already on her way to meet her, rubbing her small plump white hands with an air of calm importance.

'Mary Bogdanovna, I think it's beginning!' said Princess Mary looking at the midwife with wide-open eyes of alarm.

'Well, the Lord be thanked, Princess,' said Mary Bogdanovna, not hastening her steps. 'You young ladies should not know anything about it.'

'But how is it the doctor from Moscow is not here yet?' said the princess. (In accordance with Lise's and Prince Andrew's wishes they had sent in good time to Moscow for a doctor and were expecting him at any moment.)

'No matter, Princess, don't be alarmed,' said Mary Bogdanovna. 'We'll manage very well without a doctor.'

Five minutes later Princess Mary from her room heard something heavy being carried by. She looked out. The menservants were carrying the large leather sofa from Prince Andrew's study into the bedroom. On their faces was a quiet and solemn look.

Princess Mary sat alone in her room listening to the sounds in the house, now and then opening her door when someone passed and watching what was going on in the passage. Some women passing with quiet steps in and out of the bedroom glanced at the princess and turned away. She did not venture to ask any questions, and shut the door again, now sitting down in her easy chair, now taking her prayer book, now kneeling before the icon-stand. To her surprise and distress she found that her prayers did not calm her excitement. Suddenly her door opened softly and her old nurse, Praskovya Savishna, who hardly ever came to that room, as the old prince had forbidden it, appeared on the threshold with a shawl round her head.

'I've come to sit with you a bit, Masha,' said the nurse, 'and here I've brought the prince's wedding candles to light before his saint, my angel,' she said with a sigh.

'Oh, nurse, I'm so glad!'

'God is merciful, birdie.'

The nurse lit the gilt candles before the icons and sat down by the door with her knitting. Princess Mary took a book and began reading. Only when footsteps or voices were heard did they look at one another, the princess anxious and inquiring, the nurse encouraging. Everyone in the house was dominated by the same feeling that Princess Mary experienced as she sat in her room. But owing to the superstition that the fewer the people who know of it the less a woman in travail suffers, everyone tried to pretend not to know; no one spoke of it, but apart from the ordinary staid and respectful good manners habitual in the prince's household, a common anxiety, a softening of the heart, and a consciousness that something great and mysterious was being accomplished at that moment, made itself felt.

There was no laughter in the maids' large hall. In the men-servants' hall all sat waiting, silently and alert. In the outlying serfs' quarters torches and candles were burning and no one slept. The old prince, stepping on his heels, paced up and down his study and sent Tikhon to ask Mary Bogdanovna what news? – 'Say only that "the prince told me to ask", and come and tell me her answer.'

'Inform the prince that labour has begun,' said Mary Bogdanovna, giving the messenger a significant look.

Tikhon went and told the prince.

'Very good!' said the prince closing the door behind him, and Tikhon did not hear the slightest sound from the study after that.

After a while he re-entered it as if to snuff the candles, and seeing that the prince was lying on the sofa, looked at him, noticed his perturbed face, shook his head, and going up to him, silently kissed him on the shoulder and left the room without snuffing the candles or saying why he had entered. The most solemn mystery in the world continued its course. Evening passed, night came, and the feeling of suspense and softening of heart in the presence of the unfathomable did not lessen but increased. No one slept.

*

It was one of those March nights when winter seems to wish to resume its sway, and scatters its last snows and storms with desperate fury. A relay of horses had been sent up the high road to meet the German doctor from Moscow who was expected every moment, and men on horseback with lanterns were sent to the cross-roads to guide him over the country road with its hollows and snow-covered pools of water.

Princess Mary had long since put aside her book: she sat silent, her luminous eyes fixed on her nurse's wrinkled face (every line of which she knew so well), on the lock of grey hair that escaped from under the kerchief, and the loose skin that hung under her chin.

Nurse Savishna, knitting in hand, was telling in low tones, scarcely hearing or understanding her own words, what she had told hundreds of times before: how the late princess had given birth to Princess Mary in Kishenëv with only a Moldavian peasant woman to help instead of a midwife.

'God is merciful, doctors are never needed,' she said.

Suddenly a gust of wind beat violently against the casement of the window, from which the double frame had been removed (by order of the prince, one window frame was removed in each room as soon as the larks returned), and forcing open a loosely closed latch, set the damask curtain flapping and blew out the candle with its chill, snowy draught. Princess Mary shuddered; her nurse, putting down the stockings she was knitting, went to the window and leaning out tried to catch the open casement. The cold wind flapped the ends of her kerchief and her loose locks of grey hair.

'Princess, my dear, there's someone driving up the avenue!' she said, holding the casement and not closing it. 'With lanterns. Most likely the doctor.'

'Oh, my God! thank God!' said Princess Mary. 'I must go and meet him, he does not know Russian.'

Princess Mary threw a shawl over her head and ran to meet the newcomer. As she was crossing the ante-room she saw through the window a carriage with lanterns standing at the entrance. She went out on the stairs. On a banister-post stood a tallow candle which guttered in the draught. On the landing below, Philip, the footman, stood looking scared and holding another candle. Still lower, beyond the turn of the staircase, one could hear the footstep of someone in thick felt boots, and a voice that seemed familiar to Princess Mary was saying something.

'Thank God!' said the voice. 'And father?'

'Gone to bed,' replied the voice of Demyan the house-steward, who was downstairs.

Then the voice said something more, Demyan replied, and the steps in the felt boots approached the unseen bend of the staircase more rapidly.

'It's Andrew!' thought Princess Mary. 'No it can't be, that would be too extraordinary,' and at the very moment she thought this, the face and figure of Prince Andrew, in a fur cloak the deep collar of which was covered with snow, appeared on the landing where the footman stood with the candle. Yes, it was he, pale, thin, with a changed and strangely softened but agitated expression on his face. He came up the stairs and embraced his sister.

'You did not get my letter?' he asked, and not waiting for a reply – which he would not have received, for the princess was unable to speak – he turned back, rapidly mounted the stairs again

343

with the doctor who had entered the hall after him (they had met at the last post-station) and again embraced his sister.

'What a strange fate, Masha darling!' And having taken off his cloak and felt boots, he went to the little princess's apartment.

9

THE little princess lay supported by pillows, with a white cap on her head (the pains had just left her). Strands of her black hair lay round her inflamed and perspiring cheeks, her charming rosy mouth with its downy lip was open and she was smiling joyfully. Prince Andrew entered, and paused facing her at the foot of the sofa on which she was lying. Her glittering eyes, filled with child-like fear and excitement, rested on him without changing their expression. 'I love you all and have done no harm to anyone; why must I suffer so? help me!' her look seemed to say. She saw her husband, but did not realize the significance of his appearance before her now. Prince Andrew went round the sofa and kissed her forehead.

'My darling!' he said – a word he had never used to her before. 'God is merciful . . .'

She looked at him inquiringly and with childlike reproach.

'I expected help from you and I get none, none from you either!' said her eyes. She was not surprised at his having come; she did not realize that he had come. His coming had nothing to do with her sufferings or with their relief. The pangs began again and Mary Bogdanovna advised Prince Andrew to leave the room.

The doctor entered. Prince Andrew went out and meeting Princess Mary, again joined her. They began talking in whispers, but their talk broke off at every moment. They waited and listened.

'Go, dear,' said Princess Mary.

Prince Andrew went again to his wife and sat waiting in the room next to hers. A woman came from the bedroom with a frightened face and became confused when she saw Prince Andrew. He covered his face with his hands and remained so for some minutes. Piteous, helpless, animal moans came through the door. Prince Andrew got up, went to the door, and tried to open it. Someone was holding it shut.

'You can't come in! You can't!' said a terrified voice from within.

He began pacing the room. The screaming ceased, and a few more seconds went by. Then suddenly a terrible shriek – it could not be hers, she could not scream like that – came from the bedroom. Prince Andrew ran to the door; the scream ceased and he heard the wail of an infant.

'What have they taken a baby in there for?' thought Prince Andrew in the first second. 'A baby? What baby . . . ? Why is there a baby there? Or is the baby born?'

Then suddenly he realized the joyful significance of that wail; tears choked him, and leaning his elbows on the window-sill he began to cry, sobbing like a child. The door opened. The doctor with his shirt-sleeves tucked up, without a coat, pale and with a trembling jaw, came out of the room. Prince Andrew turned to him, but the doctor gave him a bewildered look and passed by without a word. A woman rushed out and seeing Prince Andrew stopped, hesitating on the threshold. He went into his wife's room. She was lying dead, in the same position he had seen her in five minutes before, and despite the fixed eyes and the pallor of the cheeks, the same expression was on her charming childlike face with its upper lip covered with tiny black hair.

'I love you all, and have done no harm to anyone; and what have you done to me?' – said her charming, pathetic, dead face.

In a corner of the room something red and tiny gave a grunt and squealed in Mary Bogdanovna's trembling white hands.

Two hours later Prince Andrew stepping softly went into his father's room. The old man already knew everything. He was standing close to the door and as soon as it opened his rough old arms closed like a vice round his son's neck, and without a word he began to sob like a child.

*

Three days later the little princess was buried, and Prince Andrew went up the steps to where the coffin stood, to give her the farewell kiss. And there in the coffin was the same face, though with closed eyes. 'Ah, what have you done to me?' it still seemed to say, and Prince Andrew felt that something gave way in his soul, and that he was guilty of a sin he could neither remedy nor forget. He could not weep. The old man too came up and kissed the waxen little hands that lay quietly crossed one on the other on her breast, and to him, too, her face seemed to say: 'Ah, what have you done to me, and why?' And at the sight the old man turned angrily away.

*

Another five days passed, and then the young Prince Nicholas Andreevich was baptized. The wet-nurse supported the coverlet

345

with her chin, while the priest with a goose feather anointed the boy's little red and wrinkled soles and palms.

His grandfather, who was his godfather, trembling and afraid of dropping him, carried the infant round the battered tin font, and handed him over to the godmother, Princess Mary. Prince Andrew sat in another room, faint with fear lest the baby should be drowned in the font, and awaited the termination of the ceremony. He looked up joyfully at the baby when the nurse brought it to him, and nodded approval when she told him that the wax with the baby's hair had not sunk in the font but had floated.*

10

ROSTOV'S share in Dolokhov's duel with Bezukhov was hushed up by the efforts of the old count, and instead of being degraded to the ranks as he expected he was appointed an adjutant to the governor-general of Moscow. As a result he could not go to the country with the rest of the family, but was kept all summer in Moscow by his new duties. Dolokhov recovered, and Rostov became very friendly with him during his convalescence. Dolokhov lay ill at his mother's who loved him passionately and tenderly, and old Mary Ivanovna, who had grown fond of Rostov for his friendship to her Fedya, often talked to him about her son.

'Yes, Count,' she would say, 'he is too noble and pure-souled for our present, depraved world. No one now loves virtue, it seems like a reproach to everyone. Now tell me, Count, was it right, was it honourable, of Bezukhov? And Fedya, with his noble spirit, loved him and even now never says a word against him. Those pranks in Petersburg when they played some tricks on a policeman, didn't they do it together? And there! Bezukhov got off scot free, while Fedya had to bear the whole burden on his shoulders. Fancy what he had to go through! It's true he has been reinstated, but how could they fail to do that? I think there were not many such gallant sons of the fatherland out there as he. And now – this duel! Have these people no feeling, or honour? Knowing him to be an only son, to challenge him and shoot so straight! It's well God had mercy on us. And what was it for? Who doesn't have intrigues nowadays? Why, if he was so jealous, as I see things he should have shown it sooner, but he lets it go on for months. And then to call him out, reckoning on Fedya not fighting because he owed him money! What baseness! What meanness! I know you understand Fedya, my dear Count, that, believe me, is why I am so fond of you. Few people do understand him. His is such a lofty, heavenly soul!'

Dolokhov himself during his convalescence spoke to Rostov in a way no one would have expected of him.

'I know people consider me a bad man!' he said. 'Let them! I don't care a straw about anyone but those I love; but those I love, I love so that I would give my life for them, and the others I'd throttle if they stood in my way. I have an adored, a priceless mother, and two or three friends – you among them, and as for the rest I only care about them in so far as they are harmful or useful. And most of them are harmful, especially the women. Yes, dear boy,' he continued, 'I have met loving, noble, high-minded men, but I have not yet met any women – countesses or cooks – who were not venal. I have not yet met that divine purity and devotion I look for in woman. If I found such a one I'd give my life for her! But those!...' and he made a gesture of contempt. 'And believe me, if I still value my life it is only because I still hope to meet such a divine creature, who will regenerate, purify, and elevate me. But you don't understand it.'

'Oh, yes, I quite understand,' answered Rostov, who was under his new friend's influence.

*

In the autumn the Rostovs returned to Moscow. Early in the winter Denisov also came back and stayed with them. The first half of the winter of 1806 which Nicholas Rostov spent in Moscow, was one of the happiest, merriest times for him and the whole family. Nicholas brought many young men to his parents' house. Vera was a handsome girl of twenty; Sonya a girl of sixteen with all the charm of an opening flower; Natasha, half grown up and half child, was now childishly amusing, now girlishly enchanting.

At that time in the Rostovs' house there prevailed an amorous atmosphere characteristic of homes where there are very young and very charming girls. Every young man who came to the house, seeing those impressionable, smiling, young faces (smiling probably at their own happiness), feeling the eager bustle around him, and hearing the fitful bursts of song and music and the inconsequent but friendly prattle of young girls ready for anything and full of hope – experienced the same feeling; sharing with the young folk of the Rostovs' household a readiness to fall in love and an expectation of happiness.

Among the young men introduced by Rostov one of the first was Dolokhov, whom everyone in the house liked except Natasha. She almost quarrelled with her brother about him. She insisted that he was a bad man, and that in the duel with Bezukhov, Pierre was right and Dolokhov wrong, and further that he was disagreeable and unnatural.

'There's nothing for me to understand,' she cried out with resolute self-will, 'he is wicked and heartless. There now, I like your Denisov though he is a rake and all that, still I like him; so you see I do understand. I don't know how to put it . . . with this one everything is calculated, and I don't like that. But Denisov . . .'

'Oh, Denisov is quite different,' replied Nicholas, implying that even Denisov was nothing compared to Dolokhov – 'you must understand what a soul there is in Dolokhov, you should see him with his mother. What a heart!'

'Well, I don't know about that, but I am uncomfortable with him. And do you know he has fallen in love with Sonya?'

'What nonsense . . .'

'I'm certain of it, you'll see.'

Natasha's prediction proved true. Dolokhov, who did not usually care for the society of ladies, began to come often to the house, and the question for whose sake he came (though no one spoke of it) was soon settled. He came because of Sonya. And Sonya, though she would never have dared to say so, knew it and blushed scarlet every time Dolokhov appeared.

Dolokhov often dined at the Rostovs', never missed a performance at which they were present, and went to Iogel's balls for young people which the Rostovs always attended. He was pointedly attentive to Sonya, and looked at her in such a way that not only could she not bear his glances without colouring, but even the old countess and Natasha blushed when they saw his looks.

It was evident that this strange, strong man was under the irresistible influence of the dark graceful girl who loved another.

Rostov noticed something new in Dolokhov's relations with Sonya, but he did not explain to himself what these new relations were. 'They're always in love with someone,' he thought of Sonya and Natasha. But he was not as much at ease with Sonya and Dolokhov as before, and was less frequently at home.

In the autumn of 1806 everybody had again begun talking of the war with Napoleon* with even greater warmth than the year before. Orders were given to raise recruits, ten men in every thousand for the regular army, and besides this, nine men in every thousand for the militia. Everywhere Bonaparte was anathematized and in Moscow nothing but the coming war was talked of. For the Rostov family the whole interest of these preparations for war lay in the fact that Nicholas would not hear of remaining in Moscow, and only awaited the termination of Denisov's furlough after Christmas, to return with him to their regiment. His approaching departure did not prevent his amusing himself, but rather gave zest to his pleasures. He spent the greater part of his time away from home, at dinners, parties, and balls.

## 11

ON the third day after Christmas Nicholas dined at home, a thing he had rarely done of late. It was a grand farewell dinner, as he and Denisov were leaving to join their regiment after Epiphany. About twenty people were present, including Dolokhov and Denisov.

Never had love been so much in the air, and never had the amorous atmosphere made itself so strongly felt in the Rostovs' house as at this holiday time. 'Seize the moments of happiness, love and be loved! That is the only reality in the world, all else is folly. It is the one thing we are interested in here,' said the spirit of the place.

Nicholas, having as usual exhausted two pairs of horses, without visiting all the places he meant to go to and where he had been invited, returned home just before dinner. As soon as he entered he noticed and felt the tension of the amorous air in the house, and also noticed a curious embarrassment among some of those present. Sonya, Dolokhov, and the old countess were especially disturbed, and to a lesser degree Natasha. Nicholas understood that something must have happened between Sonya and Dolokhov before dinner, and with the kindly sensitiveness natural to him was very gentle and wary with them both at dinner. On that same evening there was to be one of the balls that Iogel (the dancing master) gave for his pupils during the holidays.

'Nicholas, will you come to Iogel's? Please do!' said Natasha. 'He asked you, and Vasili Dmitrich (Denisov) is also going.'

'Where would I not go at the countess's command!' said Denisov, who at the Rostovs' had jocularly assumed the role of Natasha's knight. 'I'm even weady to dance the *pas de châle*.'

'If I have time,' answered Nicholas. 'But I promised the Arkharovs; they have a party.'

'And you?' he asked Dolokhov, but as soon as he had asked the question he noticed that it should not have been put.

'Perhaps,' coldly and angrily replied Dolokhov, glancing at Sonya, and, scowling, he gave Nicholas just such a look as he had given Pierre at the Club dinner.

'There is something up,' thought Nicholas, and he was further confirmed in this conclusion by the fact that Dolokhov left immediately after dinner. He called Natasha and asked her what was the matter.

'And I was looking for you,' said Natasha running out to him. 'I told you, but you would not believe it,' she said triumphantly. 'He has proposed to Sonya!'

Little as Nicholas had occupied himself with Sonya of late, something seemed to give way within him at this news. Dolokhov was a suitable and in some respects a brilliant match for the dowerless, orphan girl. From the point of view of the old countess and of society it was out of the question for her to refuse him. And therefore Nicholas's first feeling on hearing the news was one of anger with Sonya . . . He tried to say, 'That's capital; of course she'll forget her childish promises and accept the offer,' but before he had time to say it Natasha began again.

'And fancy! She refused him quite definitely!' adding, after a pause, 'She told him she loved another.'

'Yes, my Sonya could not have done otherwise!' thought Nicholas.

'Much as Mamma pressed her, she refused, and I know she won't change once she has said . . .'

'And Mamma pressed her!' said Nicholas reproachfully.

'Yes,' said Natasha. 'Do you know, Nicholas – don't be angry – but I know you will not marry her. I know, Heaven knows how, but I know for certain that you won't marry her.'

'Now you don't know that at all!' said Nicholas. 'But I must talk to her. What a darling Sonya is!' he added with a smile.

'Ah, she is indeed a darling! I'll send her to you.'

And Natasha kissed her brother and ran away.

A minute later Sonya came in with a frightened, guilty, and scared look. Nicholas went up to her and kissed her hand. This was the first time since his return that they had talked alone and about their love.

'Sophie,' he began, timidly at first and then more and more boldly, 'if you wish to refuse one who is not only a brilliant and advantageous match but a splendid, noble fellow . . . he is my friend . . .'

Sonya interrupted him.

'I have already refused,' she said hurriedly.

'If you are refusing for my sake, I am afraid that I . . .'

Sonya again interrupted. She gave him an imploring, frightened look.

'Nicholas, don't tell me that!' she said.

'No, but I must. It may be arrogant of me, but still it is best to say it. If you refuse him on my account, I must tell you the whole

350

truth. I love you, and I think I love you more than anyone else . . .'

'That is enough for me,' said Sonya, blushing.

'No, but I have been in love a thousand times and shall fall in love again, though for no one have I such a feeling of friendship, confidence, and love as I have for you. Then I am young. Mamma does not wish it. In a word, I make no promise. And I beg you to consider Dolokhov's offer,' he said, articulating his friend's name with difficulty.

'Don't say that to me! I want nothing. I love you as a brother and always shall, and I want nothing more.'

'You are an angel: I am not worthy of you, but I am afraid of misleading you.'

And Nicholas again kissed her hand.

12

IOGEL'S were the most enjoyable balls in Moscow. So said the mothers as they watched their young people executing their newly-learned steps, and so said the youths and maidens themselves as they danced till they were ready to drop, and so said the grown-up young men and women who came to these balls with an air of condescension, and found them most enjoyable. That year two marriages had come of these balls. The two pretty young Princesses Gorchakov met suitors there and were married, and so further increased the fame of these dances. What distinguished them from others was the absence of host or hostess and the presence of the good-natured Iogel, flying about like a feather and bowing according to the rules of his art, as he collected the tickets from all his visitors. There was the fact that only those came who wished to dance and amuse themselves as girls of thirteen and fourteen do who are wearing long dresses for the first time. With scarcely any exceptions they all were, or seemed to be, pretty – so rapturous were their smiles and so sparkling their eyes. Sometimes the best of the pupils, of whom Natasha, who was exceptionally graceful, was first, even danced the *pas de châle*, but at this last ball only the écossaise, the anglaise, and the mazurka which was just coming into fashion, were danced. Iogel had taken a ballroom in Bezukhov's house, and the ball, as everyone said, was a great success. There were many pretty girls and the Rostov girls were among the prettiest. They were both particularly happy and gay. That evening, proud of Dolokhov's proposal, her refusal, and her explanation with Nicholas, Sonya twirled about before she left home so that the maid could hardly get her hair plaited, and was transparently radiant with impulsive joy.

Natasha no less proud of her first long dress and of being at a real ball was even happier. They were both dresed in white muslin with pink ribbons.

Natasha fell in love the very moment she entered the ballroom. She was not in love with anyone in particular, but with everyone. Whatever person she happened to look at she was in love with for that moment.

'Oh, how delightful it is!' she kept saying, running up to Sonya.

Nicholas and Denisov were walking up and down, looking with kindly patronage at the dancers.

'How sweet she is, – she will be a weal beauty!' said Denisov.

'Who?'

'Countess Natasha,' answered Denisov.

'And how she dances! What gwace!' he said again after a pause.

'Who are you talking about?'

'About your sister,' ejaculated Denisov testily.

Rostov smiled.

'My dear Count, you were one of my best pupils, – you must dance,' said little Iogel coming up to Nicholas. 'Look how many charming young ladies—' He turned with the same request to Denisov who was also a former pupil of his.

'No, my dear fellow, I'll be a wallflower,' said Denisov. 'Don't you wecollect what bad use I made of your lessons?'

'Oh no!' said Iogel, hastening to reassure him. 'You were only inattentive, but you had talent, – oh yes, you had talent!'

The band struck up the newly introduced mazurka. Nicholas could not refuse Iogel, and asked Sonya to dance. Denisov sat down by the old ladies and leaning on his sabre and beating time with his foot, told them something funny and kept them amused, while he watched the young people dancing. Iogel with Natasha, his pride and his best pupil, were the first couple. Noiselessly, skilfully stepping with his little feet in low shoes, Iogel flew first across the hall with Natasha, who though shy, went on carefully executing her steps. Denisov did not take his eyes off her and beat time with his sabre in a way that clearly indicated that if he was not dancing it was because he would not and not because he could not. In the middle of a figure he beckoned to Rostov who was passing:

'This is not at all the thing,' he said. 'What sort of a Polish mazuwka is this? But she does dance splendidly.'

Knowing that Denisov had a reputation even in Poland for the masterly way in which he danced the mazurka, Nicholas ran up to Natasha:

'Go and choose Denisov. He is a real dancer, a wonder!' he said.

When it came to Natasha's turn to choose a partner, she rose and, tripping rapidly across in her little shoes trimmed with bows, ran timidly to the corner where Denisov sat. She saw that everybody was looking at her and waiting. Nicholas saw that Denisov and she were smilingly disputing, and that Denisov was refusing though he smiled delightedly. He ran up to them.

'Please, Vasili Dmitrich,' Natasha was saying, 'do come!'

'Oh no, let me off, Countess,' Denisov replied.

'Now then, Vaska,' said Nicholas.

'They coax me as if I were Vaska the cat!' said Denisov jokingly.

'I'll sing for you a whole evening,' said Natasha.

'Oh, the faiwy! She can do anything with me!' said Denisov, and he unhooked his sabre. He came out from behind the chairs, clasped his partner's hand firmly, threw back his head and advanced his foot, waiting for the beat. Only on horseback and in the mazurka was Denisov's short stature not noticeable and he looked the fine fellow he felt himself to be. At the right beat of the music he looked sideways at his partner with a merry and triumphant air, suddenly stamped with one foot, bounded from the floor like a ball, and flew round the room taking his partner with him. He glided silently on one foot half across the room, and seeming not to notice the chairs was dashing straight at them, when suddenly, clinking his spurs and spreading out his legs, he stopped short on his heels, stood so a second, stamped on the spot clanking his spurs, whirled rapidly round, and striking his left heel against his right, flew round again in a circle. Natasha guessed what he meant to do, and abandoning herself to him followed his lead hardly knowing how. First he spun her round, holding her now with his left now with his right hand, then falling on one knee he twirled her round him, and again jumping up, dashed so impetuously forward that it seemed as if he would rush through the whole suite of rooms without drawing breath, and then he suddenly stopped and performed some new and unexpected steps. When at last, smartly whirling his partner round in front of her chair, he drew up with a click of his spurs and bowed to her, Natasha did not even make him a curtsey. She fixed her eyes on him in amazement, smiling as if she did not recognize him.

'What does this mean?' she brought out.

Although Iogel did not acknowledge this to be the real mazurka, everyone was delighted with Denisov's skill, he was asked again and again as a partner, and the old men began smilingly to talk about Poland and the good old days. Denisov, flushed after the mazurka and mopping himself with his handkerchief, sat down by Natasha and did not leave her for the rest of the evening.

## 13

For two days after that Rostov did not see Dolokhov at his own or at Dolokhov's home: on the third day he received a note from him:

'As I do not intend to be at your house again for reasons you know of, and am going to rejoin my regiment, I am giving a farewell supper to-night to my friends – come to the English Hotel.'

About ten o'clock Rostov went to the English Hotel straight from the theatre, where he had been with his family and Denisov. He was at once shown to the best room, which Dolokhov had taken for that evening. Some twenty men were gathered round a table at which Dolokhov sat between two candles. On the table was a pile of gold and paper money, and he was keeping the bank. Rostov had not seen him since his proposal and Sonya's refusal, and felt uncomfortable at the thought of how they would meet.

Dolokhov's clear cold glance met Rostov as soon as he entered the door, as though he had long expected him.

'It's a long time since we met,' he said. 'Thanks for coming. I'll just finish dealing, and then Ilyushka will come with his chorus.'

'I called once or twice at your house,' said Rostov, reddening.

Dolokhov made no reply.

'You may punt,' he said.

Rostov recalled at that moment a strange conversation he had once had with Dolokhov. 'None but fools trust to luck in play,' Dolokhov had then said.

'Or are you afraid to play with me?' Dolokhov now asked as if guessing Rostov's thought.

Beneath his smile Rostov saw in him the mood he had shown at the Club dinner and at other times, when as if tired of everyday life he had felt a need to escape from it by some strange, and usually cruel, action.

Rostov felt ill at ease. He tried, but failed, to find some joke with which to reply to Dolokhov's words. But before he had thought of anything, Dolokhov, looking straight in his face, said slowly and deliberately so that everyone could hear:

'Do you remember we had a talk about cards . . . "He's a fool who trusts to luck, one should make certain," and I want to try.'

'To try his luck or the certainty?' Rostov asked himself.

'Well you'd better not play,' Dolokhov added, and springing a new pack of cards said: 'Bank, gentlemen!'

Moving the money forward he prepared to deal. Rostov sat down by his side and at first did not play. Dolokhov kept glancing at him.

'Why don't you play?' he asked.

And strange to say Nicholas felt that he could not help taking up a card, putting a small stake on it, and beginning to play.

'I have no money with me,' he said.

'I'll trust you.'

Rostov staked five rubles on a card and lost, staked again, and again lost. Dolokhov 'killed', that is, beat, ten cards of Rostov's running.

'Gentlemen,' said Dolokhov after he had dealt for some time. 'Please place your money on the cards or I may get muddled in the reckoning.'

One of the players said he hoped he might be trusted.

'Yes, you might, but I am afraid of getting the accounts mixed. So I ask you to put the money on your cards,' replied Dolokhov. 'Don't stint yourself, we'll settle afterwards,' he added, turning to Rostov.

The game continued; a waiter kept handing round champagne.

All Rostov's cards were beaten and he had eight hundred rubles scored up against him. He wrote '800 rubles' on a card, but while the waiter filled his glass he changed his mind, and altered it to his usual stake of twenty rubles.

'Leave it,' said Dolokhov, though he did not seem to be even looking at Rostov, 'you'll win it back all the sooner. I lose to the others but win from you. Or are you afraid of me?' he asked again.

Rostov submitted. He let the eight hundred remain and laid down a seven of hearts with a torn corner, which he had picked up from the floor. He well remembered that seven afterwards. He laid down the seven of hearts, on which with a broken bit of chalk he had written '800 rubles' in clear upright figures; he emptied the glass of warm champagne that was handed him, smiled at Dolokhov's words, and with a sinking heart, waiting for a seven to turn up, gazed at Dolokhov's hands which held the pack. Much depended on Rostov's winning or losing on that seven of hearts. On the previous Sunday the old count had given his son two thousand rubles, and though he always disliked speaking of money difficulties had told Nicholas that this was all he could let him have till May, and asked him to be more economical this time. Nicholas had replied that it would be more than enough for him, and that he gave his word of honour not to take anything more till the spring. Now only twelve hundred rubles was left of that money, so that this seven of hearts meant for him not only the loss of sixteen hundred rubles, but the necessity of going back on his word. With a sinking heart he watched Dolokhov's hands and thought, 'Now then, make haste and let me have this card and I'll take my cap and drive home to supper with Denisov, Natasha, and Sonya, and will certainly never touch a card again.' At that moment his home life, jokes with Petya, talks with Sonya, duets with Natasha, picquet with his father, and even his comfortable bed in the house on the Povarskaya, rose before him with such vividness, clearness, and charm that it seemed as if it were all a lost and unappreciated bliss, long past. He could not conceive that a stupid chance, letting the seven be dealt to the right rather than to the left, might deprive him of all this happiness, newly appreciated and newly illumined, and plunge him into the depths of unknown and undefined misery. That could not be, yet he awaited with a sinking heart the movement of Dolokhov's hands. Those broad, reddish hands, with hairy wrists visible from under the shirt-cuffs, laid down the pack and took up a glass and a pipe that were handed him.

'So you are not afraid to play with me?' repeated Dolokhov, and as if about to tell a good story he put down the cards, leant back in his chair, and began deliberately with a smile:

'Yes, gentlemen, I've been told there's a rumour going about Moscow that I'm a sharper, so I advise you to be careful.'

'Come now, deal!' exclaimed Rostov.

'Oh, those Moscow gossips!' said Dolokhov, and he took up the cards with a smile.

'Aah!' Rostov almost screamed lifting both hands to his head. The seven he needed was lying uppermost, the first card in the pack. He had lost more than he could pay.

'Still, don't ruin yourself!' said Dolokhov with a side glance at Rostov as he continued to deal.

14

AN hour and a half later most of the players were but little interested in their own play.

The whole interest was concentrated on Rostov. Instead of sixteen hundred rubles he had a long column of figures scored against him, which he had reckoned up to ten thousand, but that now, as he vaguely supposed, must have risen to fifteen thousand. In reality it already exceeded twenty thousand rubles. Dolokhov was no longer listening to stories or telling them, but followed every movement of Rostov's hands and occasionally ran his eyes over the score against him. He had decided to play until that score reached forty-three thousand. He had fixed on that number because forty-three was the sum of his and Sonya's joint ages. Rostov, leaning his head on both hands, sat at the table which was scrawled over with figures, wet with spilt wine, and littered with cards. One tormenting impression did not leave him: that those broad-boned reddish hands with hairy wrists visible from under the shirt-sleeves, those hands which he loved and hated, held him in their power.

'Six hundred rubles, ace, a corner, a nine . . . winning it back's impossible . . . Oh, how pleasant it was at home! . . . The knave, double or quits . . . it can't be! . . . And why is he doing this to me?' Rostov pondered. Sometimes he staked a large sum, but Dolokhov refused to accept it and fixed the stake himself. Nicholas submitted to him, and at one moment prayed to God as he had done on the battlefield at the bridge over the Enns, and then guessed that the card that came first to hand from the crumpled heap under the table would save him, now counted the cords on his coat and took a card with that number and tried staking the total of his losses on it, then he looked round for aid from the other players, or peered at the now cold face of Dolokhov and tried to read what was passing in his mind.

'He knows of course what this loss means to me. He can't want my ruin. Wasn't he my friend? Wasn't I fond of him? But it's not his fault. What's he to do if he has such luck? . . . And it's not my fault either,' he thought to himself. 'I have done nothing wrong. Have I killed anyone, or insulted or wished harm to anyone? Why such a terrible misfortune? And when did it begin? Such a little while ago I came to this table with the thought of winning a hundred rubles to buy that casket for mamma's name-day and then going home. I was so happy, so free, so light-hearted! And I did not realize how happy I was! When did that end and when did this new, terrible state of things begin? What marked the change? I sat all the time in this same place at this table, chose and placed cards, and watched those broad-boned agile hands in the same way. When did it happen and what has happened? I am well and strong, and still the same and in the same place. No, it can't be! Surely it will all end in nothing!'

He was flushed and bathed in perspiration, though the room was not hot. His face was terrible and piteous to see, especially from its helpless efforts to seem calm.

The score against him reached the fateful sum of forty-three thousand. Rostov had just prepared a card, by bending the corner of which he meant to double the three thousand just put down to his score, when Dolokhov, slamming down the pack of cards, put it aside and began rapidly adding up the total of Rostov's debt, breaking the chalk as he marked the figures in his clear, bold hand.

'Supper, it's time for supper! And here are the gipsies!'

Some swarthy men and women were really entering from the cold outside, and saying something in their gipsy accents. Nicholas understood that it was all over; but he said in an indifferent tone:

'Well, won't you go on? I had a splendid card all ready,' as if it were the fun of the game which interested him most.

'It's all up! I'm lost!' thought he. 'Now a bullet through my brain – that's all that's left me!' And at the same time he said in a cheerful voice:

'Come now, just this one more little card!'

'All right!' said Dolokhov, having finished the addition. 'All right! Twenty-one rubles,' he said, pointing to the figure twenty-one by which the total exceeded the round sum of forty-three thousand; and taking up a pack he prepared to deal. Rostov submissively unbent the corner of his card and, instead of the six thousand he had intended, carefully wrote twenty-one.

'It's all the same to me,' he said. 'I only want to see whether you will let me win this ten, or beat it.'

Dolokhov began to deal seriously. Oh, how Rostov detested at that moment those hands with their short reddish fingers and hairy wrists, which held him in their power... The ten fell to him.

'You owe forty-three thousand, Count,' said Dolokhov, and stretching himself he rose from the table. 'One does get tired sitting so long,' he added.

'Yes, I'm tired too,' said Rostov.

Dolokhov cut him short, as if to remind him that it was not for him to jest.

'When am I to receive the money, Count?'

Rostov, flushing, drew Dolokhov into the next room.

'I cannot pay it all immediately. Will you take an I.O.U.?' he said.

'I say, Rostov,' said Dolokhov clearly, smiling, and looking Nicholas straight in the eyes, 'You know the saying, "Lucky in love unlucky at cards." Your cousin is in love with you, I know.'

'Oh, it's terrible to feel oneself so in this man's power,' thought Rostov. He knew what a shock he would inflict on his father and mother by the news of this loss, he knew what a relief it would be to escape it all, and felt that Dolokhov knew that he could save him from all this shame and sorrow, but wanted now to play with him as a cat does with a mouse.

'Your cousin...' Dolokhov started to say, but Nicholas interrupted him.

'My cousin has nothing to do with this and it's not necessary to mention her!' he exclaimed fiercely.

'Then when am I to have it?'

'To-morrow,' replied Rostov and left the room.

## 15

TO say 'to-morrow' and keep up a dignified tone was not difficult, but to go home alone, see his sisters, brother, mother, and father, confess and ask for money he had no right to after giving his word of honour, was terrible.

At home they had not yet gone to bed. The young people after returning from the theatre had had supper, and were grouped round the clavichord. As soon as Nicholas entered he was enfolded in that poetic atmosphere of love which pervaded the Rostov household that winter, and now after Dolokhov's proposal and Iogel's ball seemed to have grown thicker round Sonya and Natasha as the air does before a thunderstorm. Sonya and Natasha in the light blue dresses they had worn at the theatre, looking pretty and conscious of it, were standing by the clavichord happy and smiling. Vera was playing chess with Shinshin in the drawing-room. The old countess, waiting for the return of her husband and son, sat playing patience with the old gentlewoman who lived in their house. Denisov, with sparkling eyes and ruffled hair, sat at the clavichord striking chords with his short fingers, his legs thrown back and his eyes rolling as he sang, with his small, husky, but true voice, some verses called 'Enchantress'* which he had composed, and to which he was trying to fit music.

> Enchantress say, to my forsaken lyre
> What magic power is this recalls me still?
> What spark has set my inmost soul on fire,
> What is this bliss that makes my fingers thrill?

– He was singing in passionate tones, gazing with his sparkling black agate eyes at the frightened and happy Natasha.

'Splendid! Excellent!' exclaimed Natasha. 'Another verse,' she said without noticing Nicholas.

'Everything's still the same with them,' thought Nicholas, glancing into the drawing-room, where he saw Vera and his mother with the old lady.

'Ah, and here's Nicholas!' cried Natasha running up to him.

'Is papa at home?' he asked.

'I am so glad you've come!' said Natasha without answering him. 'We *are* enjoying ourselves! Vasili Dmitrich is staying a day longer for my sake! Did you know?'

'No, papa is not back yet,' said Sonya.

'Nicholas, have you come? Come here, dear!' called the old countess from the drawing-room.

Nicholas went to her, kissed her hand, and sitting down silently at her table began to watch her hands arranging the cards. From the dancing-room they still heard the laughter, and merry voices trying to persuade Natasha to sing.

"All wight! All wight!' shouted Denisov, 'It's no good making excuses now! It's your turn to sing the ba'cawolle – I entweat you!'

The countess glanced at her silent son.

'What is the matter?' she asked.

'Oh, nothing,' said he as if weary of being continually asked the same question. 'Will Papa be back soon?'

'I expect so.'

'Everything's the same with them. They know nothing about it! Where am I to go?' thought Nicholas, and went again into the dancing-room where the clavichord stood.

Sonya was sitting at the clavichord playing the prelude to Denisov's favourite barcarolle. Natasha was preparing to sing. Denisov was looking at her with enraptured eyes.

Nicholas began pacing up and down the room.

'Why do they want to make her sing? How can she sing? There's nothing to be happy about!' thought he.

Sonya struck the first chord of the prelude.

'My God, I'm a ruined and dishonoured man! A bullet through my brain is the only thing left me – not singing!' his thoughts ran on. 'Go away? But where to? It's all one – let them sing!'

He continued to pace the room looking gloomily at Denisov and the girls and avoiding their eyes.

'Nikolenka, what is the matter?' Sonya's eyes fixed on him seemed to ask. She noticed at once that something had happened to him.

Nicholas turned away from her. Natasha too, with her quick instinct, had instantly noticed her brother's condition. But though she noticed it, she was herself in such high spirits at that moment, so far from sorrow, sadness or self-reproach, that she purposely deceived herself as young people often do. 'No, I am too happy now to spoil my enjoyment by sympathy with anyone's sorrow,' she felt, and she said to herself: 'No, I must be mistaken, he must be feeling happy just as I am.'

'Now Sonya!' she said, going to the very middle of the room where she considered the resonance was best.

Having lifted her head and let her arms droop lifelessly as ballet-dancers do, Natasha, rising energetically from her heels to her toes, stepped to the middle of the room and stood still.

'Yes, that's me!' she seemed to say, answering the rapt gaze with which Denisov followed her.

'And what is she so pleased about?' thought Nicholas, looking at his sister. 'Why isn't she dull and ashamed?'

Natasha took the first note, her throat swelled, her chest rose, her eyes became serious. At that moment she was oblivious of her surroundings, and from her smiling lips flowed sounds which any one may produce at the same intervals and hold for the same time, but which leave you cold a thousand times and the thousand and first time thrill you and make you weep.

Natasha that winter had for the first time begun to sing seriously, mainly because Denisov so delighted in her singing. She no longer sang as a child, there was no longer in her singing that comical, childish, painstaking effect that had been in it before; but she did not yet sing well, as all the connoisseurs who heard her said: 'It is not trained, but it is a beautiful voice that must be trained.' Only they generally said this some time after she had finished singing. While that untrained voice with its incorrect breathing and laboured transitions was sounding, even the connoisseurs said nothing, but only delighted in it and wished to hear it again. In her voice there was a virginal freshness, an unconsciousness of her own powers, and an as yet untrained velvety softness, which so mingled with her lack of art in singing that it seemed as if nothing in that voice could be altered without spoiling it.

'What is this?' thought Nicholas, listening to her with widely opened eyes. 'What has happened to her? How she is singing to-day!' And suddenly the whole world centred for him on anticipation of the next note, the next phrase, and everything in the world was divided into three beats: *Oh mio crudele affetto* ... One, two, three ... one, two, three ... One ... *Oh mio crudele affetto* ... One, two, three ... One. 'Oh, this senseless life of ours!' thought Nicholas. 'All this misery, and money, and Dolokhov, and anger, and honour – it's all nonsense ... but this is real ... Now then, Natasha, now then, dearest! Now then, darling! How will she take that *si*? She's taken it! Thank God!' And without noticing that he was singing, to strengthen the *si* he sung a second, a third below the high note. 'Ah, God! How fine! Did I really take it? How fortunate!' he thought.

Oh, how that chord vibrated, and how moved was something

that was finest in Rostov's soul! And this something was apart from everything else in the world and above everything in the world. 'What were losses, and Dolokhov, and words of honour? ... All nonsense! One might kill and rob and yet be happy ...'

## 16

IT was long since Rostov had felt such enjoyment from music as he did that day. But no sooner had Natasha finished her barcarolle than reality again presented itself. He got up without saying a word and went downstairs to his own room. A quarter of an hour later the old count came in from his Club cheerful and contented. Nicholas, hearing him drive up, went to meet him.

'Well – had a good time?' said the old count, smiling gaily and proudly at his son.

Nicholas tried to say 'Yes,' but could not: and he nearly burst into sobs. The count was lighting his pipe and did not notice his son's condition.

'Ah, it can't be avoided!' thought Nicholas for the first and last time. And suddenly, in the most casual tone, which made him feel ashamed of himself, he said, as if merely asking his father to let him have the carriage to drive into town:

'Papa, I have come on a matter of business. I was nearly forgetting. I need some money.'

'Dear me!' said his father who was in a specially good humour. 'I told you it would not be enough. How much?'

'Very much,' said Nicholas flushing, and with a stupid careless smile for which he was long unable to forgive himself, 'I have lost a little, I mean a good deal, a great deal – forty-three thousand.'

'What! To whom? ... Nonsense!' cried the count, suddenly reddening with an apoplectic flush over neck and nape as old people do.

'I promised to pay to-morrow,' said Nicholas.

'Well! ...' said the old count, spreading out his arms and sinking helplessly on the sofa.

'It can't be helped! It happens to everyone!' said the son with a bold, free and easy tone, while in his soul he regarded himself as a worthless scoundrel whose whole life could not atone for his crime. He longed to kiss his father's hands and kneel to beg his forgiveness, but said, in a careless and even rude voice, that it happens to everyone!

The old count cast down his eyes on hearing his son's words, and began bustlingly searching for something.

'Yes, yes,' he muttered, 'it will be difficult, I fear, difficult to raise.... happens to everybody! Yes, who has not done it?'

And with a furtive glance at his son's face the count went out of the room...Nicholas had been prepared for resistance, but had not at all expected this.

'Papa! Pa-pa!' he called after him sobbing, 'forgive me!' And seizing his father's hand, he pressed it to his lips and burst into tears.

*

While father and son were having their explanation, the mother and daughter were having one not less important. Natasha came running to her mother quite excited.

'Mamma!...Mamma!...He has made me...'

'Made what?'

'Made, made me an offer, mamma! Mamma!' she exclaimed.

The countess did not believe her ears. Denisov had proposed. To whom? To this chit of a girl, Natasha, who not so long ago was playing with dolls and who was still having lessons.

'Don't, Natasha! What nonsense!' she said, hoping it was a joke.

'Nonsense indeed! I am telling you the fact,' said Natasha indignantly. 'I come to ask you what to do, and you call it "nonsense!"'

The countess shrugged her shoulders.

'If it is true that Monsieur Denisov has made you a proposal, tell him he is a fool, that's all!'

'No, he's not a fool!' replied Natasha indignantly and seriously.

'Well then, what do you want? You're all in love nowadays. Well, if you are in love, marry him!' said the countess with a laugh of annoyance. 'Good luck to you!'

'No, mamma, I'm not in love with him, I suppose I'm not in love with him.'

'Well then, tell him so.'

'Mamma, are you cross? Don't be cross, dear! Is it my fault?'

'No, but what is it, my dear? Do you want me to go and tell him?' said the countess smiling.

'No, I will do it myself, only tell me what to say. It's all very well for you,' said Natasha, with a responsive smile. 'You should have seen how he said it! I know he did not mean to say it, but it came out accidentally.'

'Well, all the same, you must refuse him.'

'No, I mustn't. I am so sorry for him! He's so nice.'

'Well then, accept his offer. It's high time for you to be married,' answered the countess sharply and sarcastically.

'No, mamma, but I'm so sorry for him. I don't know how I'm to say it.'

'And there's nothing for you to say. I shall speak to him myself,' said the countess, indignant that they should have dared to treat this little Natasha as grown up.

'No, not on any account! I will tell him myself, and you'll listen at the door,' and Natasha ran across the drawing-room to the dancing-hall, where Denisov was sitting on the same chair by the clavichord with his face in his hands.

He jumped up at the sound of her light step.

'Natalie,' he said, moving with rapid steps towards her, 'decide my fate. It is in your hands.'

'Vasili Dmitrich, I'm so sorry for you!... No, but you are so nice... but it won't do... not that... but as a friend I shall always love you.'

Denisov bent over her hand and she heard strange sounds she did not understand. She kissed his rough curly black head. At this instant they heard the quick rustle of the countess's dress. She came up to them.

'Vasili Dmitrich, I thank you for the honour,' she said, with an embarrassed voice, though it sounded severe to Denisov '– but my daughter is so young, and I thought that, as my son's friend, you would have addressed yourself first to me. In that case you would not have obliged me to give this refusal.'

'Countess...' said Denisov with downcast eyes and a guilty face. He tried to say more, but faltered.

Natasha could not remain calm seeing him in such a plight. She began to sob aloud.

'Countess, I have done w'ong,' Denisov went on in an unsteady voice, 'but believe me, I so adore your daughter and all your family that I would give my life twice over...' He looked at the countess, and seeing her severe face said: 'Well, good-bye, Countess,' and kissing her hand, he left the room with quick resolute strides, without looking at Natasha.

*

Next day Rostov saw Denisov off. He did not wish to stay another day in Moscow. All Denisov's Moscow friends gave him a farewell entertainment at the gipsies', with the result that he had no recollection of how he was put in the sledge or of the first three stages of his journey.

After Denisov's departure Rostov spent another fortnight in Moscow, without going out of the house, waiting for the money his father could not at once raise, and he spent most of his time in the girls' room.

Sonya was more tender and devoted to him than ever. It was as if she wanted to show him that his losses were an achievement that made her love him all the more, but Nicholas now considered himself unworthy of her.

He filled the girls' albums with verses and music, and having at last sent Dolokhov the whole forty-three thousand rubles and received his receipt, he left at the end of November without taking leave of any of his acquaintances, to overtake his regiment which was already in Poland.

END OF PART ONE

# PART TWO

## 1

AFTER his interview with his wife Pierre left for Petersburg. At
the Torzhok post-station either there were no horses or the post-
master would not supply them. Pierre was obliged to wait. Without
undressing, he lay down on the leather sofa in front of a round
table, put his big feet in their over-boots on the table and began to
reflect.

'Will you have the portmanteaux brought in? And a bed got
ready, and tea?' asked his valet.

Pierre gave no answer, for he neither heard nor saw anything.
He had begun to think at the last station and was still pondering
on the same question – one so important that he took no notice
of what went on around him. Not only was he indifferent as to
whether he got to Petersburg earlier or later, or whether he secured
accommodation at this station, but compared to the thoughts that
now occupied him it was a matter of indifference whether he
remained there for a few hours or for the rest of his life.

The post-master, his wife, the valet, and a peasant woman selling
Torzhok embroidery, came into the room offering their services.
Without changing his careless attitude Pierre looked at them over
his spectacles unable to understand what they wanted or how
they could go on living without having solved the problems that
so absorbed him. He had been engrossed by the same thoughts
ever since the day he returned from Sokolniki after the duel and
had spent that first agonizing, sleepless night. But now in the
solitude of the journey they seized him with special force. No
matter what he thought about, he always returned to these same
questions which he could not solve and yet could not cease to ask
himself. It was as if the thread of the chief screw which held his
life together were stripped, so that the screw could not get in or
out, but went on turning uselessly in the same place.

The post-master came in and began obsequiously to beg his
Excellency to wait only two hours, when, come what might, he
would let his Excellency have the courier-horses. It was plain that

he was lying and only wanted to get more money from the traveller.

'Is this good or bad?' Pierre asked himself. 'It is good for me, bad for another traveller, and for himself it's unavoidable because he needs money for food; the man said an officer had once given him a thrashing for letting a private traveller have the courier-horses. But the officer thrashed him because he had to get on as quickly as possible. And I,' continued Pierre, 'shot Dolokhov because I considered myself injured, and Louis XVI was executed because they considered him a criminal, and a year later they executed those who had executed him – also for some reason. What is bad? What is good? What should one love and what hate? What does one live for? And what am I? What is life, and what is death? What Power governs it all?'

There was no answer to any of these questions, except one, and that not a logical answer and not at all a reply to them. The answer was: 'You'll die and all will end. You'll die and know all, or cease asking.' But dying was also dreadful.

The Torzhok pedlar woman in a whining voice went on offering her wares, especially a pair of goat-skin slippers. 'I have hundreds of rubles I don't know what to do with, and she stands in her tattered cloak looking timidly at me,' he thought. 'And what does she want the money for? As if that money could add a hair's breadth to her happiness or peace of mind. Can anything in the world make her or me less a prey to evil and death? – death which ends all and must come to-day or to-morrow – at any rate in an instant as compared with eternity.' And again he twisted the screw with the stripped thread, and again it turned uselessly in the same place.

His servant handed him a half-cut novel, in the form of letters, by Madame de Souza.* He began reading about the sufferings and virtuous struggles of a certain Émilie de Mansfeld. 'And why did she resist her seducer when she loved him?' he thought. 'God could not have put into her heart an impulse that was against His will. My wife – as she once was – did not struggle, and perhaps she was right. Nothing has been found out, nothing discovered,' Pierre again said to himself. 'All we can know is that we know nothing. And that's the height of human wisdom.'

Everything within and around him seemed confused, senseless, and repellent. Yet in this very repugnance to all his circumstances Pierre found a kind of tantalizing satisfaction.

'I make bold to ask your Excellency to move a little for this gentleman,' said the post-master, entering the room followed by another traveller also detained for lack of horses.

The newcomer was a short, large-boned, yellow-faced, wrinkled old man, with grey bushy eyebrows overhanging bright eyes of an indefinite greyish colour.

Pierre took his feet off the table, stood up, and lay down on a bed that had been got ready for him, glancing now and then at the newcomer, who with a gloomy and tired face was wearily taking off his wraps with the aid of his servant, and not looking at Pierre. With a pair of felt boots on his thin bony legs, and keeping on a worn, nankeen-covered sheep-skin coat, the traveller sat down on the sofa, leant back his big head with its broad temples and close-cropped hair, and looked at Bezukhov. The stern, shrewd, and penetrating expression of that look struck Pierre. He felt a wish to speak to the stranger, but by the time he had made up his mind to ask him a question about the roads, the traveller had closed his eyes. His shrivelled old hands were folded and on the finger of one of them Pierre noticed a large cast-iron ring with a seal representing a death's head. The stranger sat without stirring, either resting or, as it seemed to Pierre, sunk in profound and calm meditation. His servant was also a yellow, wrinkled old man, without beard or moustache, evidently not because he was shaven but because they had never grown. The active old servant was unpacking the traveller's canteen and preparing tea. He brought in a boiling samovar. When everything was ready, the stranger opened his eyes, moved to the table, filled a tumbler with tea for himself and one for the beardless old man to whom he passed it. Pierre began to feel a sense of uneasiness, and the need, even the inevitability, of entering into conversation with this stranger.

The servant brought back his tumbler turned upside down with an unfinished bit of nibbled sugar, and asked if anything more would be wanted.*

'No. Give me the book,' said the stranger.

The servant handed him a book which Pierre took to be a devotional work, and the traveller became absorbed in it. Pierre looked at him. All at once the stranger closed the book, putting in a marker, and again, leaning with his arms on the back of the sofa, sat in his former position with his eyes shut. Pierre looked at him and had not time to turn away when the old man, opening his eyes, fixed his steady and severe gaze straight on Pierre's face.

Pierre felt confused, and wished to avoid that look, but the bright old eyes attracted him irresistibly.

## 2

'I HAVE the pleasure of addressing Count Bezukhov if I am not mistaken,' said the stranger in a deliberate and loud voice.

Pierre looked silently and inquiringly at him over his spectacles.

'I have heard of you, my dear sir,' continued the stranger, 'and of your misfortune.' He seemed to emphasize the last word, as if to say – 'Yes, misfortune! Call it what you please, I know that what happened to you in Moscow was a misfortune.' – 'I regret it very much, my dear sir.'

Pierre flushed, and hurriedly putting his legs down from the bed, bent forward towards the old man with a forced and timid smile.

'I have not referred to this out of curiosity, my dear sir, but for graver reasons.'

He paused, his gaze still on Pierre, and moved aside on the sofa by way of inviting the other to take a seat beside him. Pierre felt reluctant to enter into conversation with this old man, but submitting to him involuntarily, came up and sat down beside him.

'You are unhappy, my dear sir,' the stranger continued. 'You are young and I am old. I should like to help you as far as lies in my power.'

'Oh, yes!' said Pierre, with a forced smile. 'I am very grateful to you. Where are you travelling from?'

The stranger's face was not genial, it was even cold and severe, but in spite of this, both the face and words of his new acquaintance were irresistibly attractive to Pierre.

'But if for any reason you don't feel inclined to talk to me,' said the old man, 'say so, my dear sir.' And he suddenly smiled in an unexpected and tenderly paternal way.

'Oh no, not at all! On the contrary I am very glad to make your acquaintance,' said Pierre. And again glancing at the stranger's hands he looked more closely at the ring with its skull – a masonic sign.

'Allow me to ask,' he said, 'are you a mason?'

'Yes, I belong to the Brotherhood of the Freemasons,'* said the stranger, looking deeper and deeper into Pierre's eyes. 'And in their name and my own I hold out a brotherly hand to you.'

'I am afraid,' said Pierre, smiling, and wavering between the confidence the personality of the freemason inspired in him and his own habit of ridiculing the masonic beliefs '– I am afraid I am very far from understanding – how am I to put it? – I am afraid my way of looking at the world is so opposed to yours that we shall not understand one another.'

'I know your outlook,' said the mason, 'and the view of life you mention, and which you think is the result of your own mental efforts, is the one held by the majority of people, and is the invariable fruit of pride, indolence, and ignorance. Forgive me, my dear sir, but if I had not known it I should not have addressed you. Your view of life is a regrettable delusion.'

'Just as I may suppose you to be deluded,' said Pierre with a faint smile.

'I should never dare to say that I know the truth,' said the mason, whose words struck Pierre more and more by their precision and firmness. 'No one can attain to truth by himself. Only by laying stone on stone with the co-operation of all, by the millions of generations from our forefather Adam to our own times, is that temple reared which is to be a worthy dwelling-place of the Great God,' he added, and closed his eyes.

'I ought to tell you that I do not believe ... do not believe in God,' said Pierre regretfully and with an effort, feeling it essential to speak the whole truth.

The mason looked intently at Pierre and smiled as a rich man with millions in hand might smile at a poor fellow who told him that he, poor man, had not the five rubles that would make him happy.

'Yes, you do not know Him, my dear sir,' said the mason. 'You cannot know Him. You do not know Him and that is why you are unhappy.'

'Yes, yes, I am unhappy,' assented Pierre. 'But what am I to do?'

'You know Him not, my dear sir, and so you are very unhappy. You do not know Him, but He is here. He is in me, He is in my words, He is in thee, and even in those blasphemous words thou hast just uttered!' pronounced the mason in a stern and tremulous voice.

He paused and sighed, evidently trying to calm himself.

'If He were not,' he said quietly, 'you and I would not be speaking of Him, my dear sir. Of what, of whom, are we speaking? Whom hast thou denied?' he suddenly asked with exulting austerity and authority in his voice. 'Who invented Him, if He does not exist? Whence came thy conception of the existence of such an incomprehensible Being? Why didst thou, and why did the whole world, conceive the idea of the existence of such an incomprehensible Being, a Being all-powerful, eternal, and infinite in all His attributes? ...'

He stopped and remained silent for a long time.

Pierre could not and did not wish to break this silence.

'He exists, but to understand Him is hard,' the mason began again, looking not at Pierre but straight before him, and turning the leaves of his book with his old hands which from excitement he could not keep still. 'If it were a man whose existence thou didst doubt I could bring him to thee, could take him by the hand and show him to thee. But how can I, an insignificant mortal, show His omnipotence, His infinity, and all His mercy to one who is blind, or who shuts his eyes that he may not see or understand Him and may not see or understand his own vileness and sinfulness?' He paused again. 'Who art thou? Thou dreamest that thou art wise because thou couldst utter those blasphemous words,' he went on with a sombre and scornful smile. 'And thou art more foolish and unreasonable than a little child, who playing with the parts of a skilfully made watch dares to say that, as he does not understand its use, he does not believe in the master who made it. To know Him is hard . . . For ages, from our forefather Adam to our own day, we labour to attain that knowledge and are still infinitely far from our aim; but in our lack of understanding we see only our weakness and His greatness . . .'

Pierre listened with swelling heart, gazing into the mason's face with shining eyes, not interrupting or questioning him but believing with his whole soul what the stranger said. Whether he accepted the wise reasoning contained in the mason's words, or believed as a child believes, in the speaker's tone of conviction and earnestness or the tremor of the speaker's voice – which sometimes almost broke – or those brilliant aged eyes grown old in this conviction, or the calm firmness and certainty of his vocation, which radiated from his whole being (and which struck Pierre especially by contrast with his own dejection and hopelessness) – at any rate Pierre longed with his whole soul to believe and he did believe, and felt a joyful sense of comfort, regeneration, and return to life.

'He is not to be apprehended by reason, but by life,' said the mason.

'I do not understand,' said Pierre, feeling with dismay doubts reawakening. He was afraid of any want of clearness, any weakness, in the mason's arguments, he dreaded not to be able to believe in him. 'I don't understand,' he said, 'how it is that the mind of man cannot attain the knowledge of which you speak?'

The mason smiled with his gentle fatherly smile.

'The highest wisdom and truth are like the purest liquid we may wish to imbibe,' he said. 'Can I receive that pure liquid into an impure vessel and judge of its purity? Only by the inner purification of myself can I retain in some degree of purity the liquid I receive.'

'Yes, yes, that is so,' said Pierre joyfully.

'The highest wisdom is not founded on reason alone, not on those worldly sciences of physics, history, chemistry, and the like, into which intellectual knowledge is divided. The highest wisdom is one. The highest wisdom has but one science – the science of the whole – the science explaining the whole creation and man's place in it. To receive that science it is necessary to purify and renew one's inner self, and so before one can know, it is necessary to believe and to perfect one's self. And to attain this end we have the light called conscience, that God has implanted in our souls.'

'Yes, yes,' assented Pierre.

'Look then at thy inner self with the eyes of the spirit, and ask thyself whether thou art content with thyself. What hast thou attained relying on reason only? What art thou? You are young, you are rich, you are clever, you are well educated. And what have you done with all these good gifts? Are you content with yourself and with your life?'

'No, I hate my life,' Pierre muttered, wincing.

'Thou hatest it. Then change it, purify thyself; and as thou art purified thou wilt gain wisdom. Look at your life, my dear sir. How have you spent it? In riotous orgies and debauchery, receiving everything from society and giving nothing in return. You have become the possessor of wealth. How have you used it? What have you done for your neighbour? Have you ever thought of your tens of thousands of slaves? Have you helped them physically and morally? No! You have profited by their toil to lead a profligate life. That is what you have done. Have you chosen a post in which you might be of service to your neighbour? No! You have spent your life in idleness. Then you married, my dear sir – took on yourself responsibility for the guidance of a young woman, and what have you done? You have not helped her to find the way of truth, my dear sir, but have thrust her into an abyss of deceit and misery. A man offended you and you shot him, and you say you do not know God and hate your life. There is nothing strange in that, my dear sir!'

After these words the mason, as if tired by his long discourse, again leant his arms on the back of the sofa and closed his eyes. Pierre looked at that aged, stern, motionless, almost lifeless face, and moved his lips without uttering a sound. He wished to say, 'Yes, a vile, idle, vicious life!' but dared not break the silence.

The mason cleared his throat huskily as old men do, and called his servant.

373

'How about the horses?' he asked, without looking at Pierre.

'The exchange horses have just come,' answered the servant. 'Will you not rest here?'

'No, tell them to harness.'

'Can he really be going away and leaving me alone without having told me all, and without promising to help me?' thought Pierre rising with downcast head; and he began to pace the room, glancing occasionally at the mason. 'Yes, I never thought of it, but I have led a contemptible and profligate life though I did not like it and did not want to,' thought Pierre. 'But this man knows the truth, and if he wished to, could disclose it to me.'

Pierre wished to say this to the mason, but did not dare to. The traveller, having packed his things with his practised hands, began fastening his coat. When he had finished he turned to Bezukhov, and said in a tone of indifferent politeness:

'Where are you going now, my dear sir?'

'I? ... I'm going to Petersburg,' answered Pierre in a childlike hesitating voice. 'I thank you. I agree with all you have said. But do not suppose me to be so bad. With my whole soul I wish to be what you would have me be, but I have never had help from anyone ... But it is I, above all, who am to blame for everything. Help me, teach me, and perhaps I may ...'

Pierre could not go on. He gulped and turned away.

The mason remained silent for a long time, evidently considering.

'Help comes from God alone,' he said, 'but such measure of help as our Order can bestow it will render you, my dear sir. You are going to Petersburg. Hand this to Count Willarski' (he took out his notebook and wrote a few words on a large sheet of paper folded in four). 'Allow me to give you a piece of advice. When you reach the capital, first of all devote some time to solitude and self-examination and do not resume your former way of life. And now I wish you a good journey, my dear sir,' he added, seeing that his servant had entered ... 'and success.'

The traveller was Joseph Alexeevich Bazdeev, as Pierre saw from the post-master's book. Bazdeev had been one of the best-known freemasons and Martinists even in Novikov's time.* For a long while after he had gone Pierre did not go to bed or order horses but paced up and down the room pondering over his vicious past, and with a rapturous sense of beginning anew pictured to himself the blissful irreproachable virtuous future that seemed to him so easy. It seemed to him that he had been vicious only because he had somehow forgotten how good it is to be virtuous. Not a trace of his former doubts remained in his soul. He firmly believed in the

possibility of the brotherhood of men united in the aim of supporting one another in the path of virtue, and that is how freemasonry
presented itself to him.

## 3

ON reaching Petersburg Pierre did not let anyone know of his
arrival, he went nowhere and spent whole days in reading Thomas
à Kempis,* whose book had been sent him by someone unkown.
One thing he continually realized as he read that book: the joy,
hitherto unknown to him, of believing in the possibility of attaining perfection and in the possibility of active brotherly love among
men, which Joseph Alexeevich had revealed to him. A week after
his arrival the young Polish count Willarski, whom Pierre had
known slightly in Petersburg society, came into his room one
evening in the official and ceremonious manner with which Dolokhov's second had called on him, and having closed the door
behind him and satisfied himself that there was nobody else in
the room, addressed Pierre.

'I have come to you with a message and an offer, Count,' he
said without sitting down. 'A person of very high standing in our
Brotherhood has made application for you to be received into our
Order before the usual term, and has proposed to me to be your
sponsor. I consider it a sacred duty to fulfil that person's wishes.
Do you wish to enter the Brotherhood of Freemasons under my
sponsorship?'

The cold austere tone of this man, whom he had almost always
before met at balls amiably smiling in the society of the most
brilliant women, surprised Pierre.

'Yes, I do wish it,' said he.

Willarski bowed his head.

'One more question, Count,' he said, 'which I beg you to
answer in all sincerity – not as a future mason but as an honest
man: have you renounced your former convictions – do you believe
in God?'

Pierre considered.

'Yes . . . yes, I believe in God,' he said.

'In that case . . .' began Willarski, but Pierre interrupted him.

'Yes, I do believe in God,' he repeated.

'In that case we can go,' said Willarski. 'My carriage is at your
service.'

Willarski was silent throughout the drive. To Pierre's inquiries
as to what he must do and how he should answer, Willarski only

replied that brothers more worthy than he would test him, and that Pierre had only to tell the truth.*

Having entered the courtyard of a large house where the Lodge had its quarters, and having ascended a dark staircase, they entered a small well-lit ante-room where they took off their cloaks without the aid of a servant. From there they passed into another room. A man in strange attire appeared at the door. Willarski, stepping towards him, said something to him in French in an undertone and then went up to a small wardrobe in which Pierre noticed garments such as he had never seen before. Having taken a kerchief from the cupboard, Willarski bound Pierre's eyes with it and tied it in a knot behind, catching some hairs painfully in the knot. Then he drew his face down, kissed him, and taking him by the hand led him forward. The hairs tied in the knot hurt Pierre and there were lines of pain on his face and a shamefaced smile. His huge figure, with arms hanging down and with a puckered though smiling face, moved after Willarski with uncertain timid steps.

Having led him about ten paces, Willarski stopped.

'Whatever happens to you,' he said, 'you must bear it all manfully if you have firmly resolved to join our Brotherhood.' (Pierre nodded affirmatively.) 'When you hear a knock at the door you will uncover your eyes,' added Willarski. 'I wish you courage and success,' and pressing Pierre's hand, he went out.

Left alone, Pierre went on smiling in the same way. Once or twice he shrugged his shoulders and raised his hand to the kerchief as if wishing to take it off, but let it drop again. The five minutes spent with his eyes bandaged seemed to him an hour. His arm felt numb, his legs almost gave way, it seemed to him that he was tired out. He experienced a variety of most complex sensations. He felt afraid of what would happen to him, and still more afraid of showing his fear. He felt curious to know what was going to happen and what would be revealed to him; but most of all he felt joyful that the moment had come when he would at last start on that path of regeneration and on the actively virtuous life of which he had been dreaming since he met Joseph Alexeevich. Loud knocks were heard at the door. Pierre took the bandage off his eyes and glanced around him. The room was in black darkness, only a small lamp was burning inside something white. Pierre went nearer and saw that the lamp stood on a black table on which lay an open book. The book was the Gospel, and the white thing with the lamp inside was a human skull with its cavities and teeth. After reading the first words of the Gospel: 'In the beginning was the Word, and the Word was with God', Pierre went round the table and saw a large open box filled with something. It was a coffin with bones inside. He was not at all surprised by what he saw. Hoping to enter on an entirely new life quite unlike the old one, he expected everything to be unusual, even more unusual than what he was seeing. A skull, a coffin, the Gospel – it seemed to him that he had expected all this and even more. Trying to stimulate his emotions he looked around. 'God, death, love, the brotherhood of man,' he kept saying to himself, associating these words with vague yet joyful ideas. The door opened and someone came in.

By the dim light to which Pierre had already become accustomed, he saw a rather short man. Having evidently come from the light into the darkness, the man paused, then moved with cautious steps towards the table and placed on it his small leather-gloved hands.

This short man had on a white leather apron which covered his chest and part of his legs, and a kind of necklace above which rose a high white ruffle, outlining his rather long face which was lit up from below.

'For what have you come hither?' asked the newcomer turning in Pierre's direction at a slight rustle made by the latter. 'Why have you, who do not believe in the truth of the light and who have not seen the light, come here? What do you seek from us? Wisdom, virtue, enlightenment?'

At the moment the door opened and the stranger came in Pierre felt a sense of awe and veneration such as he had experienced in his boyhood at confession; he felt himself in the presence of one socially a complete stranger, yet near to him through the brotherhood of man. With bated breath and beating heart he moved towards the Rhetor (by which name the brother who prepared a seeker for entrance into the Brotherhood was known). Drawing nearer, he recognized in the Rhetor a man he knew, Smolyaninov, and it mortified him to think that the newcomer was an acquaintance – he wished him simply a brother and a virtuous instructor. For a long time he could not utter a word, so that the Rhetor had to repeat his question.

'Yes . . . I . . . I . . . desire regeneration,' Pierre uttered with difficulty.

'Very well,' said Smolyaninov, and went on at once: 'Have you any idea of the means by which our holy Order will help you to reach your aim?' said he quietly and quickly.

'I . . . hope . . . for guidance . . . help . . . in regeneration,' said Pierre with a trembling voice and some difficulty in utterance, due to his excitement and to being unaccustomed to speak of abstract matters in Russian.

'What is your conception of Freemasonry?'

377

'I imagine that Freemasonry is the fraternity and equality of men who have virtuous aims,' said Pierre, feeling ashamed of the inadequacy of his words for the solemnity of the moment, as he spoke. 'I imagine . . .'

'Good!' said the Rhetor quickly, apparently quite satisfied with this answer. 'Have you sought for means of attaining your aim in religion?'

'No, I considered it erroneous and did not follow it,' said Pierre, so softly that the Rhetor did not hear him and asked him what he was saying. 'I have been an atheist,' answered Pierre.

'You are seeking for truth in order to follow its laws in your life, therefore you seek wisdom and virtue. Is that not so?' said the Rhetor after a moment's pause.

'Yes, yes,' assented Pierre.

The Rhetor cleared his throat, crossed his gloved hands on his breast and began to speak.

'Now I must disclose to you the chief aim of our Order,' he said, 'and if this aim coincides with yours, you may enter our Brotherhood with profit. The first and chief object of our Order, the foundation on which it rests and which no human power can destroy, is the preservation and handing on to posterity of a certain important mystery . . . which has come down to us from the remotest ages, even from the first man – a mystery on which perhaps the fate of mankind depends. But since this mystery is of such a nature that nobody can know or use it unless he be prepared by long and diligent self-purification, not everyone can hope to attain it quickly. Hence we have a secondary aim, that of preparing our members as much as possible to reform their hearts, to purify and enlighten their minds, by means handed on to us by tradition from those who have striven to attain this mystery, and thereby to render them capable of receiving it.

'By purifying and regenerating our members we try, thirdly, to improve the whole human race, offering it in our members an example of piety and virtue, and thereby try with all our might to combat the evil which sways the world. Think this over and I will come to you again.'

'To combat the evil which sways the world . . .' Pierre repeated, and a mental image of his future activity in this direction rose in his mind. He imagined men such as he had himself been a fortnight ago, and he addressed an edifying exhortation to them. He imagined to himself vicious and unfortunate people whom he would assist by word and deed, imagined oppressors whose victims he would rescue. Of the three objects mentioned by the Rhetor this last, that of improving mankind, specially appealed to Pierre.

The important mystery mentioned by the Rhetor, though it aroused his curiosity, did not seem to him essential, and the second aim, that of purifying and regenerating himself, did not much interest him because at that moment he felt with delight that he was already perfectly cured of his former faults and was ready for all that was good.

Half an hour later the Rhetor returned to inform the seeker of the seven virtues, corresponding to the seven steps of Solomon's temple, which every freemason should cultivate in himself. These virtues were: 1. *Discretion*, the keeping of the secrets of the Order. 2. *Obedience* to those of higher ranks in the Order. 3. *Morality*. 4. *Love of mankind*. 5. *Courage*. 6. *Generosity*. 7. *The love of death*.

'In the *seventh* place, try by the frequent thought of death,' the Rhetor said, 'to bring yourself to regard it not as a dreaded foe, but as a friend that frees the soul grown weary in the labours of virtue from this distressful life, and leads it to its place of recompense and peace.'

'Yes, that must be so,' thought Pierre when after these words the Rhetor went away leaving him to solitary meditation. 'It must be so, but I am still so weak that I love my life, the meaning of which is only now gradually opening before me.' But five of the other virtues, which Pierre recalled, counting them on his fingers, he felt already in his soul: *Courage, generosity, morality, love of mankind*, and especially *obedience* – which did not even seem to him a virtue, but a joy. (He now felt so glad to be free from his own lawlessness and to submit his will to those who knew the indubitable truth.) He forgot what the seventh virtue was, and could not recall it.

The third time the Rhetor came back more quickly, and asked Pierre whether he was still firm in his intention and determined to submit to all that would be required of him.

'I am ready for everything,' said Pierre.

'I must also inform you,' said the Rhetor, 'that our Order delivers its teaching not in words only but also by other means, which may perhaps have a stronger effect on the sincere seeker after wisdom and virtue than mere words. This chamber with what you see therein, should already have suggested to your heart, if it is sincere, more than words could do. You will perhaps also see in your further initiation a like method of enlightenment. Our Order imitates the ancient societies that explained their teaching by hieroglyphics. A hieroglyph,' said the Rhetor, 'is an emblem of something not cognizable by the senses but which possesses qualities resembling those of the symbol.'

Pierre knew very well what a hieroglyph was, but dared not

speak. He listened to the Rhetor in silence, feeling from all he said that his ordeal was about to begin.

'If you are resolved, I must begin your initiation,' said the Rhetor coming closer to Pierre. 'In token of generosity I ask you to give me all your valuables.'

'But I have nothing here,' replied Pierre, supposing that he was asked to give up all he possessed.

'What you have with you: watch, money, rings ...'

Pierre quickly took out his purse and watch, but could not manage for some time to get the wedding ring off his fat finger. When that had been done the Rhetor said:

'In token of obedience I ask you to undress.'

Pierre took off his coat, waistcoat, and left boot according to the Rhetor's instructions. The mason drew the shirt back from Pierre's left breast, and stooping down pulled up the left leg of his trousers to above the knee. Pierre hurriedly began taking off his right boot also and was going to tuck up the other trouser-leg to save this stranger the trouble, but the mason told him that was not necessary and gave him a slipper for his left foot. With a childlike smile of embarrassment, doubt, and self-derision, which appeared on his face against his will, Pierre stood with his arms hanging down and legs apart before his brother Rhetor, and awaited his further commands.

'And now in token of candour, I ask you to reveal to me your chief passion,' said the latter.

'My passion! I have had so many,' replied Pierre.

'That passion which more than all others caused you to waver on the path of virtue,' said the mason.

Pierre paused, seeking a reply.

'Wine? Gluttony? Idleness? Laziness? Irritability? Anger? Women?' He went over his vices in his mind not knowing to which of them to give the pre-eminence.

'Women,' he said in a low, scarcely audible voice.

The mason did not move and for a long time said nothing after this answer. At last he moved up to Pierre and, taking the kerchief that lay on the table, again bound his eyes.

'For the last time I say to you – turn all your attention upon yourself, put a bridle on your senses, and seek blessedness not in passion but in your own heart. The source of blessedness is not without us but within ...'

Pierre had already long been feeling in himself that refreshing source of blessedness which now flooded his heart with glad emotion.

SOON after this there came into the dark chamber to fetch Pierre, not the Rhetor but Pierre's sponsor Willarski, whom he recognized by his voice. To fresh questions as to the firmness of his resolution Pierre replied: 'Yes, yes, I agree,' and with a beaming, childlike smile, his fat chest uncovered, stepping unevenly and timidly in one slippered and one booted foot, he advanced, while Willarski held a sword to his bare chest. He was conducted from that room along passages that turned backwards and forwards, and was at last brought to the doors of the Lodge. Willarski coughed, he was answered by the masonic knock with mallets, the doors opened before them. A bass voice (Pierre was still blindfold) questioned him as to who he was, when and where he was born, and so on. Then he was again led somewhere still blindfold, and as they went along he was told allegories of the toils of his pilgrimage, of holy friendship, of the Eternal Architect of the universe, and of the courage with which he should endure toils and dangers. During these wanderings Pierre noticed that he was spoken of now as the 'Seeker', now as the 'Sufferer', and now as the 'Postulant', to the accompaniment of various knockings with mallets and swords. As he was being led up to some object he noticed a hesitation and uncertainty among his conductors. He heard those around him disputing in whispers and one of them insisting that he should be led along a certain carpet. After that they took his right hand, placed it on something, and told him to hold a pair of compasses to his left breast with the other hand and to repeat, after someone who read aloud, an oath of fidelity to the laws of the Order. The candles were then extinguished and some spirit lighted, as Pierre knew by the smell, and he was told that he would now see the lesser light. The bandage was taken off his eyes and by the faint light of the burning spirit Pierre, as in a dream, saw several men standing before him, wearing aprons like the Rhetor's and holding swords in their hands pointed at his breast. Among them stood a man whose white shirt was stained with blood. On seeing this Pierre moved forward with his breast towards the swords, meaning them to pierce it. But the swords were drawn back from him and he was at once blindfolded again.

'Now thou hast seen the lesser light,' uttered a voice. Then the candles were relit and he was told that he would see the full light; the bandage was again removed and more than ten voices said together: '*Sic transit gloria mundi.*'

Pierre gradually began to recover himself, and looked about at the room and at the people in it. Round a long table covered with black sat some twelve men in garments like those he had already seen. Some of them Pierre had met in Petersburg society. In the President's chair sat a young man he did not know, with a peculiar cross hanging from his neck. On his right sat the Italian abbé whom Pierre had met at Anna Pavlovna's two years before. There were also present a very distinguished dignitary, and a Swiss who had formerly been tutor at the Kuragins. All maintained a solemn silence, listening to the words of the President, who held a mallet in his hand. Let into the wall was a star-shaped light. At one side of the table was a small carpet with various figures worked upon it, at the other was something resembling an altar on which lay a Testament and a skull. Round it stood seven large candlesticks like those used in churches. Two of the brothers led Pierre up to the altar, placed his feet at right angles, and bade him lie down, saying that he must prostrate himself at the Gates of the Temple.

'He must first receive the trowel,' whispered one of the brothers.

'Oh, hush, please!' said another.

Pierre, perplexed, looked round with his short-sighted eyes without obeying, and suddenly doubts rose in his mind. 'Where am I? What am I doing? Aren't they laughing at me? Shan't I be ashamed to remember this?' But these doubts only lasted a moment. Pierre glanced at the serious faces of those around, remembered all he had already gone through, and realized that he could not stop half-way. He was aghast at his hesitation, and trying to arouse his former devotional feeling, prostrated himself before the Gates of the Temple. And really the feeling of devotion returned to him even more strongly than before. When he had lain there some time he was told to get up, and a white leather apron such as the others wore was put on him; he was given a trowel and three pairs of gloves, and then the Grand Master addressed him. He told him that he should try to do nothing to stain the whiteness of that apron, which symbolized strength and purity; then of the unexplained trowel, he told him to toil with it to cleanse his own heart from vice, and indulgently to smooth with it the heart of his neighbour. As to the first pair of gloves, a man's, he said that Pierre could not know their meaning but must keep them. The second pair of man's gloves he was to wear at the meetings, and finally of the third, a pair of women's gloves, he said: 'Dear brother, these woman's gloves are intended for you too. Give them to the woman whom you shall honour most of all. This gift will be a pledge of your purity of heart to her whom you select to be your worthy helpmeet in masonry.' And after a pause he added:

'But beware, dear brother, that these gloves do not deck hands that are unclean.' While the Grand Master said these last words it seemed to Pierre that he grew embarrassed. Pierre himself grew still more confused, blushed like a child till tears came into his eyes, began looking about him uneasily, and an awkward pause followed.

This silence was broken by one of the Brethren who led Pierre up to the rug and began reading to him from a manuscript book an explanation of all the figures on it: the sun, the moon, a hammer, a plumb-line, a trowel, a rough stone and a squared stone, a pillar, three windows, and so on. Then a place was assigned to Pierre, he was shown the signs of the Lodge, told the password, and at last was permitted to sit down. The Grand Master began reading the statutes. They were very long, and Pierre, from joy, agitation, and embarrassment, was not in a state to understand what was being read. He managed to follow only the last words of the statutes and these remained in his mind.

'In our temples we recognize no other distinctions,' read the Grand Master, 'but those between virtue and vice. Beware of making any distinctions which may infringe equality. Fly to a brother's aid whoever he may be, exhort him who goeth astray, raise him that falleth, and never bear malice or enmity towards thy brother. Be kindly and courteous. Kindle in all hearts the flame of virtue. Share thy happiness with thy neighbour, and may envy never dim the purity of that bliss. Forgive thy enemy, do not avenge thyself except by doing him good. Thus fulfilling the highest law thou shalt regain traces of the ancient dignity which thou hast lost.'

He finished, and getting up embraced and kissed Pierre, who with tears of joy in his eyes looked round him, not knowing how to answer the congratulations and greetings from acquaintances that met him on all sides. He acknowledged no acquaintances but saw in all these men only brothers, and burnt with impatience to set to work with them.

The Grand Master rapped with his mallet. All the masons sat down in their places, and one of them read an exhortation on the necessity of humility.

The Grand Master proposed that the last duty should be performed, and the distinguished dignitary who bore the title of 'Collector of Alms', went round to all the brothers. Pierre would have liked to subscribe all he had, but fearing that it might look like pride, subscribed the same amount as the others.

The meeting was at an end, and on reaching home Pierre felt as if he had returned from a long journey on which he had spent dozens of years, had become completely changed, and had quite left behind his former habits and way of life.

## 5

THE day after he had been received into the Lodge Pierre was sitting at home reading a book and trying to fathom the significance of the Square, one side of which symbolized God, another moral things, a third physical things, and the fourth a combination of these. Now and then his attention wandered from the book and the Square and he formed in imagination a new plan of life. On the previous evening at the Lodge he had heard that a rumour of his duel had reached the Emperor, and that it would be wiser for him to leave Petersburg. Pierre proposed going to his estates in the south and there attending to the welfare of his serfs. He was joyfully planning this new life, when Prince Vasili suddenly entered the room.

'My dear fellow, what have you been up to in Moscow? Why have you quarrelled with Hélène, *mon cher*? You are under a delusion,' said Prince Vasili as he entered. 'I know all about it, and I can tell you positively that Hélène is as innocent before you as Christ was before the Jews.'

Pierre was about to reply but Prince Vasili interrupted him.

'And why didn't you simply come straight to me as to a friend? I know all about it and understand it all,' he said. 'You behaved as becomes a man who values his honour, perhaps too hastily, but we won't go into that. But consider the position in which you are placing her and me in the eyes of society, and even of the Court,' he added, lowering his voice. 'She is living in Moscow and you are here. Remember, dear boy,' and he drew Pierre's arm downwards, 'it is simply a misunderstanding. I expect you feel it so yourself. Let us write her a letter at once, and she'll come here and all will be explained, or else, my dear boy, let me tell you it's quite likely you'll have to suffer for it.'

Prince Vasili gave Pierre a significant look.

'I know from reliable sources that the Dowager Empress is taking a keen interest in the whole affair. You know she is very gracious to Hélène.'

Pierre tried several times to speak, but on one hand Prince Vasili did not let him and on the other Pierre himself feared to begin to speak in the tone of decided refusal and disagreement in which he had firmly resolved to answer his father-in-law. Moreover the words of the masonic statutes, 'be kindly and courteous', recurred to him. He blinked, went red, got up and sat down again, struggling with himself to do what was for him the most difficult thing in life – to say an unpleasant thing to a man's face, to say what the other, whoever he might be, did not expect. He was so used to submitting to Prince Vasili's tone of careless self-assurance that he felt he would be unable to withstand it now, but he also felt that on what he said now his future depended – whether he would follow the same old road, or that new path so attractively shown him by the masons, on which he firmly believed he would be reborn to a new life.

'Now, dear boy,' said Prince Vasili playfully, 'say "yes", and I'll write to her myself, and we will kill the fatted calf.'

But before Prince Vasili had finished his playful speech, Pierre without looking at him, and with a kind of fury that made him like his father, muttered in a whisper:

'Prince, I did not ask you here. Go, please go!' And he jumped up and opened the door for him.

'Go!' he repeated, amazed at himself and glad to see the look of confusion and fear that showed itself on Prince Vasili's face.

'What's the matter with you? Are you ill?'

'Go!' the quivering voice repeated. And Prince Vasili had to go without receiving any explanation.

A week later Pierre, having taken leave of his new friends, the masons, and leaving large sums of money with them for alms, went away to his estates. His new brethren gave him letters to the Kiev and Odessa masons and promised to write to him and guide him in his new activity.

6

THE duel between Pierre and Dolokhov was hushed up and, in spite of the Emperor's severity regarding duels at that time, neither the principals nor their seconds suffered for it. But the story of the duel, confirmed by Pierre's rupture with his wife, was the talk of society. Pierre, who had been regarded with patronizing condescension when he was an illegitimate son, and petted and extolled when he was the best match in Russia, had sunk greatly in the esteem of society after his marriage – when the marriageable daughters and their mothers had nothing to hope from him – especially as he did not know how, and did not wish, to court society's favour. Now he alone was blamed for what had happened, he was said to be insanely jealous, and subject like his father to fits of bloodthirsty rage. And when after Pierre's departure Hélène returned to Petersburg, she was received by all her acquaintances not only cordially, but even with a shade of deference due to her misfortune. When conversation turned on her husband Hélène assumed a dignified expression, which with characteristic tact she had acquired though she did not understand its significance. This expression suggested that she had resolved to endure her troubles uncomplainingly, and that her husband was a cross laid upon her by God. Prince Vasili expressed his opinion more openly. He shrugged his shoulders when Pierre was mentioned and pointing to his forehead, remarked:

'A bit touched – I always said so.'

'I said from the first,' declared Anna Pavlovna referring to Pierre, 'I said at the time and before anyone else' (she insisted on her priority), 'that that senseless young man was spoilt by the depraved ideas of these days. I said so even at the time when everybody was in raptures about him, when he had just returned from abroad and when, if you remember, he posed as a sort of Marat at one of my soirées. And how has it ended? I was against this marriage even then, and foretold all that has happened.'

Anna Pavlovna continued to give on free evenings the same kind of soirées as before – such as she alone had the gift of arranging – at which was to be found 'the cream of really good society, the bloom of the intellectual essence of Petersburg', as she herself put it. Besides this refined selection of society Anna Pavlovna's receptions were also distinguished by the fact that she always presented some new and interesting persons to the visitors, and that nowhere else was the state of the political thermometer of legitimate Petersburg Court society so clearly and distinctly indicated.

Towards the end of 1806, when all the sad details of Napoleon's destruction of the Prussian Army at Jena and Auerstadt and the surrender of most of the Prussian fortresses had been received, when our troops had already entered Prussia and our second war with Napoleon was beginning, Anna Pavlovna gave one of her soirées. The 'cream of really good society' consisted of the fascinating Hélène, forsaken by her husband, Mortemart, the delightful Prince Hippolyte who had just returned from Vienna, two diplomatists, the old aunt, a young man referred to in that drawing-room as 'a man of great merit' (*un homme de beaucoup de mérite*), a newly-appointed maid of honour and her mother, and several other less noteworthy persons.

The novelty Anna Pavlovna was setting before her guests that evening was Boris Drubetskoy, who had just arrived as a special messenger from the Prussian army and was aide-de-camp to a very important personage.

The temperature shown by the political thermometer to the company that evening was this:

'Whatever the European sovereigns and commanders may do to countenance Bonaparte, and to cause *me*, and *us* in general, annoyance and mortification, our opinion of Bonaparte cannot alter. We shall not cease to express our sincere views on that subject, and can only say to the King of Prussia and others: "So much the worse for you. *Tu l'as voulu, George Dandin*",* that's all we have to say about it!'

When Boris who was to be served up to the guests entered the drawing-room, almost all the company had assembled, and the conversation, guided by Anna Pavlovna, was about our diplomatic relations with Austria and the hope of an alliance with her.

Boris, grown more manly and looking fresh, rosy, and self-possessed, entered the drawing-room elegantly dressed in the uniform of an aide-de-camp, and was duly conducted to pay his respects to the aunt and then brought back to the general circle.

Anna Pavlovna gave him her shrivelled hand to kiss, and introduced him to several persons whom he did not know, giving him a whispered description of each.

'Prince Hippolyte Kuragin – charming young fellow; M. Krug – *chargé d'affaires* from Copenhagen – a profound intellect,' and simply, 'Mr Shitov – a man of great merit,' – this of the man usually so described.

Thanks to Anna Mikhaylovna's efforts, his own tastes, and the peculiarities of his reserved nature, Boris had managed during his service to place himself very advantageously. He was aide-de-camp to a very important personage, had been sent on a very important mission to Prussia, and had just returned from there as a special messenger. He had become thoroughly conversant with that unwritten code with which he had been so pleased at Olmütz and according to which an ensign might rank incomparably higher than a general, and according to which what was needed for success in the service was not effort or work, or courage, or perseverance, but only the knowledge of how to get on with those who can grant rewards, and he was himself often surprised at the rapidity of his success, and at the inability of others to understand these things. In consequence of this discovery his whole manner of life, all his relations with old friends, all his plans for his future, were completely altered. He was not rich, but would spend his last groat to be better dressed than others, and would rather deprive himself of many pleasures than allow himself to be seen in a shabby equipage or appear in the streets of Petersburg in an old uniform. He made friends with and sought the acquaintance of only those above him in position and who could therefore be of use to him. He liked Petersburg and despised Moscow. The remembrance of the Rostovs' house and of his childish love for Natasha was unpleasant to him and he had not once been to see the Rostovs since the day of his departure for the army. To be in Anna Pavlovna's drawing-room he considered an important step up in the service, and he at once understood his rôle, letting his hostess make use of whatever interest he had to offer. He himself carefully scanned each face, appraising the possibilities of establishing intimacy with each of those present, and the advantages that might accrue. He took the seat indicated to him beside the fair Hélène, and listened to the general conversation.

'Vienna considers the bases of the proposed treaty so unattainable* that not even a continuity of most brilliant successes would secure them, and she doubts the means we have of gaining them. That is the actual phrase used by the Vienna cabinet,' said the Danish *chargé d'affaires*.

'The doubt is flattering,' said 'the man of profound intellect',* with a subtle smile.

'We must distinguish between the Vienna cabinet and the Emperor of Austria,' said Mortemart. 'The Emperor of Austria can never have thought of such a thing, it is only the cabinet that says it.'

'Ah, my dear Vicomte,' put in Anna Pavlovna, '*L'Urope*' (for some reason she called it *Urope* as if that were a specially refined French pronunciation which she could allow herself when conversing with a Frenchman), '*L'Urope ne sera jamais notre alliée sincère.*'

After that Anna Pavlovna led up to the courage and firmness of the King of Prussia, in order to draw Boris into the conversation.

Boris listened attentively to each of the speakers, awaiting his turn, but managed meanwhile to look round repeatedly at his neighbour, the beautiful Hélène, whose eyes several times met those of the handsome young aide-de-camp with a smile.

Speaking of the position of Prussia, Anna Pavlovna very naturally asked Boris to tell them about his journey to Glogau and in what state he found the Prussian army. Boris, speaking with deliberation, told them in pure correct French many interesting details about the armies and the Court, carefully abstaining from expressing an opinion of his own about the facts he was recounting. For some time he engrossed the general attention, and Anna Pavlovna felt that the novelty she had served up was received with pleasure by all her visitors. The greatest attention of all to Boris's narrative was shown by Hélène. She asked him several questions about his journey and seemed greatly interested in the state of the Prussian army. As soon as he had finished she turned to him with her usual smile.

'You absolutely must come and see me,' she said in a tone that implied that for certain considerations he could not know of this was absolutely necessary. 'On Tuesday, between eight and nine. It will give me great pleasure.'

Boris promised to fulfil her wish and was about to begin a conversation with her, when Anna Pavlovna called him away on the pretext that her aunt wished to hear him.

'You know her husband, of course?' said Anna Pavlovna, closing her eyes and indicating Hélène with a sorrowful gesture. 'Ah, she is such an unfortunate and charming woman! Don't mention him before her – please don't! It is too painful for her!'

## 7

WHEN Boris and Anna Pavlovna returned to the others Prince Hippolyte had the ear of the company. Bending forward in his arm-chair he said: *'Le Roi de Prusse!'* and having said this laughed. Everyone turned towards him.

*'Le Roi de Prusse?'* Hippolyte said interrogatively, again laughing, and then calmly and seriously sat back in his chair. Anna Pavlovna waited for him to go on, but as he seemed quite decided to say no more she began to tell of how at Potsdam the impious Bonaparte had stolen the sword of Frederick the Great.

'It is the sword of Frederick the Great which I . . .' she began, but Hippolyte interrupted her with the words: *'Le Roi de Prusse . . .'* and again as soon as all turned towards him, excused himself and said no more.

Anna Pavlovna frowned. Mortemart, Hippolyte's friend, addressed him firmly.

'Come now, what about your *Roi de Prusse?*'

Hippolyte laughed as if ashamed of laughing.

'Oh, it's nothing. I only wished to say . . .' (He wanted to repeat a joke he had heard in Vienna and which he had been trying all that evening to get in) 'I only wished to say that we are wrong to fight, *pour le Roi de Prusse!*'*

Boris smiled circumspectly, so that it might be taken as ironical or appreciative according to the way the joke was received. Everybody laughed.

'Your joke is too bad, it's witty but unjust,' said Anna Pavlovna, shaking her little shrivelled finger at him.

'We are not fighting *pour le Roi de Prusse*, but for right principles. Oh, that wicked Prince Hippolyte!' she said.

The conversation did not flag all evening and turned chiefly on the political news. It became particularly animated towards the end of the evening when the rewards bestowed by the Emperor were mentioned.

'You know N— N— received a snuff-box with the portrait last year?' said 'the man of profound intellect'. 'Why shouldn't S— S— get the same distinction?'

'Pardon me! A snuff-box with the Emperor's portrait is a reward but not a distinction,' said the diplomatist – 'A gift, rather.'

'There are precedents, I may mention Schwarzenberg.'

'It's impossible,' replied another.

'Will you bet? The ribbon of the order is a different matter . . .'

When everybody rose to go, Hélène who had spoken very little all the evening again turned to Boris, asking him in a tone of caressing significant command, to come to her on Tuesday.

'It is of great importance to me,' she said, turning with a smile towards Anna Pavlovna, and Anna Pavlovna with the same sad smile with which she spoke of her exalted patroness, supported Hélène's wish.

It seemed as if from some words Boris had spoken that evening about the Prussian army, Hélène had suddenly found it necessary to see him. She seemed to promise to explain that necessity to him when he came on Tuesday.

But on Tuesday evening, having come to Hélène's splendid salon, Boris received no clear explanation of why it had been necessary for him to come. There were other guests and the countess talked little to him, and only as he kissed her hand on taking leave, said unexpectedly and in a whisper, with a strangely unsmiling face: 'Come to dinner to-morrow . . . in the evening. You must come . . . Come!'

During that stay in Petersburg, Boris became an intimate in the countess's house.

8

THE war was flaming up and nearing the Russian frontier. Everywhere one heard curses on Bonaparte, 'the enemy of mankind'. Militiamen and recruits were being enrolled in the villages, and from the seat of war came contradictory news, false as usual and therefore variously interpreted.

The life of old Prince Bolkonsky, Prince Andrew, and Princess Mary, had greatly changed since 1805.

In 1806 the old prince was made one of the eight commanders-in-chief then appointed to supervise the enrolment decreed throughout Russia. Despite the weakness of age, which had become particularly noticeable since the time when he thought his son had been killed, he did not think it right to refuse a duty to which he had been appointed by the Emperor himself, and this fresh opportunity for action gave him new energy and strength. He was continually travelling through the three provinces entrusted to him, was pedantic in the fulfilment of his duties, severe to cruelty with his subordinates, and went into everything down to the minutest details himself. Princess Mary had ceased taking lessons in mathematics from her father, and when the old prince was at home went to his study with the wet-nurse and little Prince Nicholas (as his grandfather called him). The baby Prince Nicholas lived with his wet-nurse and nurse Savishna in the late princess's rooms and Princess Mary spent most of the day in the nursery, taking a mother's place to her little nephew as best she could. Mademoiselle Bourienne, too, seemed passionately fond of the boy, and Princess Mary often deprived herself to give her friend the pleasure of dandling the little *angel* – as she called her nephew – and playing with him.

Near the altar of the church at Bald Hills there was a chapel over the tomb of the little princess, and in this chapel was a marble monument brought from Italy, representing an angel with outspread wings ready to fly upwards. The angel's upper lip was slightly raised as though about to smile, and once on coming out of the chapel Prince Andrew and Princess Mary admitted to one another that the angel's face reminded them strangely of the little princess. But what was still stranger, though of this Prince Andrew said nothing to his sister, was that in the expression the sculptor had happened to give the angel's face, Prince Andrew read the same mild reproach he had read on the face of his dead wife: 'Ah, why have you done this to me?'

Soon after Prince Andrew's return the old prince made over to him a large estate, Bogucharovo, about twenty-five miles from Bald Hills. Partly because of the depressing memories associated with Bald Hills, partly because Prince Andrew did not always feel equal to bearing with his father's peculiarities, and partly because he needed solitude, Prince Andrew made use of Bogucharovo, began building, and spent most of his time there.

After the Austerlitz campaign Prince Andrew had firmly resolved not to continue his military service, and when the war recommenced and everybody had to serve, he took a post under his father in the recruitment so as to avoid active service. The old prince and his son seemed to have changed rôles since the campaign of 1805. The old man, roused by activity, expected the best results from the new campaign, while Prince Andrew on the contrary, taking no part in the war and secretly regretting this, saw only the dark side.

On 26th February 1807 the old prince set off on one of his circuits. Prince Andrew remained at Bald Hills as usual during his father's absence. Little Nicholas had been unwell for four days. The coachman who had driven the old prince to town returned bringing papers and letters for Prince Andrew.

Not finding the young prince in his study the valet went with the letters to Princess Mary's apartments, but did not find him there. He was told that the prince had gone to the nursery.

'If you please, your Excellency, Petrusha has brought some papers,' said one of the nursemaids to Prince Andrew who was sitting on a child's little chair while, frowning and with trembling hands, he poured drops from a medicine bottle into a wineglass half full of water.

'What is it?' he said crossly, and his hand shaking unintentionally, he poured too many drops into the glass. He threw the mixture onto the floor and asked for some more water. The maid brought it.

There were in the room a child's cot, two boxes, two arm-chairs, a table, a child's table, and the little chair on which Prince Andrew was sitting. The curtains were drawn, and a single candle was burning on the table, screened by a bound music-book so that the light did not fall on the cot.

'My dear,' said Princess Mary, addressing her brother from beside the cot where she was standing, 'better wait a bit... later...'

'Oh, leave off, you always talk nonsense and keep putting things off – and this is what comes of it!' said Prince Andrew in an exasperated whisper, evidently meaning to wound his sister.

'My dear, really... it's better not to wake him... he's asleep,' said the princess in a tone of entreaty.

Prince Andrew got up, and went on tiptoe up to the little bed, wineglass in hand.

'Perhaps we'd really better not wake him,' he said hesitating.

'As you please... really... I think so... but as you please,' said Princess Mary, evidently intimidated and confused that her opinion had prevailed. She drew her brother's attention to the maid who was calling him in a whisper.

It was the second night that neither of them had slept, watching the boy who was in a high fever. These last days, mistrusting their household doctor and expecting another for whom they had sent to town, they had been trying first one remedy and then another. Worn out by sleeplessness and anxiety they threw their burden of sorrow on one another, and reproached and disputed with each other.

'Petrusha has come with papers from your father,' whispered the maid.

Prince Andrew went out.

'Devil take them!' he muttered, and after listening to the verbal instructions his father had sent and taking the correspondence and his father's letter, he returned to the nursery.

'Well?' he asked.

'Still the same. Wait, for heaven's sake. Karl Ivanich always says that sleep is more important than anything,' whispered Princess Mary with a sigh.

Prince Andrew went up to the child and felt him. He was burning hot.

'Confound you and your Karl Ivanich!' He took the glass with the drops and again went up to the cot.

'Andrew, don't!' said Princess Mary.

But he scowled at her angrily though also with suffering in his eyes, and stooped glass in hand over the infant.

'But I wish it,' he said. 'I beg you – give it him!'

Princess Mary shrugged her shoulders but took the glass submissively, and calling the nurse began giving the medicine. The child screamed hoarsely. Prince Andrew winced, and clutching his head went out and sat down on a sofa in the next room.

He still had all the letters in his hand. Opening them mechanically he began reading. The old prince, now and then using abbreviations, wrote in his large elongated hand on blue paper as follows:

'Have just this moment received by special messenger very joyful news – if it's not false. Bennigsen seems to have obtained a complete victory over Buonaparte at Eylau.* In Petersburg everyone is rejoicing, and the rewards sent to the army are innumerable. Though he is a German – I congratulate him! I can't make out what the commander at Korchevo – a certain Khandrikov – is up to; till now the additional men and provisions have not arrived. Gallop off to him at once and say I'll have his head off if everything is not here in a week. Have received another letter about the Prussisch-Eylau battle from Petenka – he took part in it – and it's all true. When mischief-makers don't meddle even a German beats Buonaparte. He is said to be fleeing in great disorder. Mind you gallop off to Korchevo without delay and carry out instructions!'

Prince Andrew sighed and broke the seal of another envelope. It was a closely written letter of two sheets from Bilibin. He folded it up without reading it and re-read his father's letter, ending with the words: 'Gallop off to Korchevo and carry out instructions!'

'No, pardon me, I won't go now till the child is better,' thought he, going to the door and looking into the nursery.

Princess Mary was still standing by the cot, gently rocking the baby.

'Ah yes, and what else did he say that's unpleasant?' thought Prince Andrew, recalling his father's letter. 'Yes, we have gained a victory over Bonaparte, just when I'm not serving. Yes, yes, he's always poking fun at me...Ah, well! Let him!' And he began reading Bilibin's letter which was written in French. He read without understanding half of it, read only to forget, if but for a moment, what he had too long been thinking of so painfully to the exclusion of all else.

9

BILIBIN was now at army head-quarters in a diplomatic capacity, and though he wrote in French and used French jests and French idioms, he described the whole campaign with a fearless self-censure and self-derision genuinely Russian. Bilibin wrote that the obligation of diplomatic discretion tormented him, and he was happy to have in Prince Andrew a reliable correspondent to whom he could pour out the bile he had accumulated at the sight of all that was being done in the army. The letter was old, having been written before the battle at Prussisch-Eylau.

Since the day of our brilliant success at Austerlitz, [wrote Bilibin] as you know, my dear Prince, I never leave head-quarters. I have certainly acquired a taste for war, and it is just as well for me; what I have seen during these last three months is incredible.

I begin *ab ovo*. 'The enemy of the human race', as you know, attacks the Prussians. The Prussians are our faithful allies who have only betrayed us three times in three years. We take up their cause, but it turns out that 'the enemy of the human race' pays no heed to our fine speeches and in his rude and savage way throws himself on the Prussians without giving them time to finish the parade they had begun, and in two twists of the hand he breaks them to smithereens and installs himself in the palace at Potsdam.

'I most ardently desire,' writes the King of Prussia to Bonaparte, 'that your Majesty should be received and treated in my palace in a manner agreeable to yourself, and in so far as circumstances allowed,

I have hastened to take all steps to that end. May I have succeeded!'
The Prussian generals pride themselves on being polite to the French
and lay down their arms at the first demand.

The head of the garrison at Glogau, with ten thousand men, asks
the King of Prussia what he is to do if he is summoned to surrender ...
All this is absolutely true.

In short, hoping to settle matters by taking up a war-like attitude,
it turns out that we have landed ourselves in war, and what is more,
in war on our own frontiers, with and for the King of Prussia. We
have everything in perfect order, only one little thing is lacking,
namely, a commander-in-chief. As it was considered that the Austerlitz
success might have been more decisive had the commander-in-chief
not been so young, all our octogenarians were reviewed, and of
Prozorovsky and Kamensky the latter was preferred. The general comes
to us, Suvorov-like, in a kibitka,* and is received with acclamations
of joy and triumph.

On the 4th, the first courier arrives from Petersburg. The mails are
taken to the field-marshal's room, for he likes to do everything himself.
I am called in to help sort the letters and take those meant for us.
The field-marshal looks on and waits for letters addressed to him. We
search, but none are to be found. The field-marshal grows impatient
and sets to work himself, and finds letters from the Emperor to Count
T., Prince V., and others. Then he bursts into one of his wild furies
and rages at everyone and everything, seizes the letters, opens them,
and reads those from the Emperor addressed to others. 'Ah! So that's
the way they treat me! No confidence in me! Ah, ordered to keep an
eye on me! Very well then! Get along with you!' So he writes the
famous order of the day to General Bennigsen:

'I am wounded and cannot ride, and consequently cannot command
the army. You have brought your army corps to Pultusk, routed: here
it is exposed, and without fuel or forage, so something must be done,
and, as you yourself reported to Count Buxhöwden yesterday, you
must think of retreating to our frontier – which do to-day.'

'From all my riding,' he writes to the Emperor, 'I have got a saddle-
sore, which coming after all my previous journeys quite prevents my
riding and commanding so vast an army, so I have passed on the command to the general next in seniority, Count Buxhöwden, having sent
him my whole staff and all that belongs to it, advising him if there is a
lack of bread, to move farther into the interior of Prussia, for only
one day's ration of bread remains, and in some regiments none at all,
as reported by the division commanders, Ostermann and Sedmoretzky,
and all that the peasants had has been eaten up. I myself will remain
in hospital at Ostrolenka till I recover. In regard to which I humbly
submit my report, with the information that if the army remains in
its present bivouac another fortnight there will not be a healthy man
left in it by spring.

'Grant leave to retire to his country seat to an old man who is
already in any case dishonoured by being unable to fulfil the great
and glorious task for which he was chosen. I shall await your most

395

gracious permission here in hospital, that I may not have to play the part of a *secretary* rather than *commander* in the army. My removal from the army does not produce the slightest stir – a blind man has left it. There are thousands such as I in Russia.'

The field-marshal is angry with the Emperor and he punishes us all, isn't it logical?

This is the first act. Those that follow are naturally increasingly interesting and entertaining. After the field-marshal's departure it appears that we are within sight of the enemy and must give battle. Buxhöwden is commander-in-chief by seniority, but General Bennigsen does not quite see it; more particularly as it is he and his corps who are within sight of the enemy and he wishes to profit by the opportunity to fight a battle 'on his own hand' as the Germans say. He does so. This is the battle of Pultusk, which is considered a great victory but in my opinion was nothing of the kind. We civilians, as you know, have a very bad way of deciding whether a battle was won or lost. Those who retreat after a battle have lost it, is what we say; and according to that it is we who lost the battle of Pultusk. In short, we retreat after the battle but send a courier to Petersburg with news of a victory, and General Bennigsen hoping to receive from Petersburg the post of commander-in-chief as a reward for his victory, does not give up the command of the army to General Buxhöwden. During this interregnum we begin a very original and interesting series of manœuvres. Our aim is no longer, as it should be, to avoid or attack the enemy, but solely to avoid General Buxhöwden who by right of seniority should be our chief. So energetically do we pursue this aim that after crossing an unfordable river we burn the bridges to separate ourselves from our enemy, who at the moment is not Bonaparte but Buxhöwden. General Buxhöwden was all but attacked and captured by a superior enemy force as a result of one of these manœuvres that enabled us to escape him. Buxhöwden pursues us – we scuttle. He hardly crosses the river to our side before we recross to the other. At last our enemy, Buxhöwden, catches us and attacks. Both generals are angry, and the result is a challenge on Buxhöwden's part and an epileptic fit on Bennigsen's. But at the critical moment the courier, who carried the news of our victory at Pultusk to Petersburg, returns bringing our appointment as commander-in-chief, and our first foe, Buxhöwden, is vanquished; we can now turn our thoughts to the second, Bonaparte. But as it turns out, just at that moment a third enemy rises before us – namely the *Orthodox Russian soldiers*, loudly demanding bread, meat, biscuits, fodder, and what not! The stores are empty, the roads impassable. The Orthodox begin looting, and in a way of which our last campaign can give you no idea. Half the regiments form bands and scour the countryside and put everything to fire and sword. The inhabitants are totally ruined, the hospitals overflow with sick, and famine is everywhere. Twice the marauders even attack our head-quarters and the commander-in-chief has to ask for a battalion to disperse them. During one of these attacks they carried off my empty portmanteau and my dressing-gown. The

Emperor proposes to give all commanders of divisions the right to shoot marauders, but I much fear this will oblige one-half the army to shoot the other.

At first Prince Andrew read with his eyes only, but after a while in spite of himself (although he knew how far it was safe to trust Bilibin) what he read began to interest him more and more. When he had read thus far, he crumpled the letter up and threw it away. It was not what he had read that vexed him, but the fact that the life out there in which he had now no part could perturb him. He shut his eyes, rubbed his forehead as if to rid himself of all interest in what he had read, and listened to what was passing in the nursery. Suddenly he thought he heard a strange noise through the door. He was seized with alarm lest something should have happened to the child while he was reading the letter. He went on tiptoe to the nursery door and opened it.

Just as he went in he saw that the nurse was hiding something from him with a scared look, and that Princess Mary was no longer by the cot.

'My dear,' he heard what seemed to him her despairing whisper behind him.

As often happens after long sleeplessness and long anxiety, he was seized by an unreasoning panic – it occurred to him that the child was dead. All that he saw and heard seemed to confirm this terror.

'All is over,' he thought, and a cold sweat broke out on his forehead. He went to the cot in confusion, sure that he would find it empty and that the nurse had been hiding the dead baby. He drew the curtain aside and for some time his frightened, restless eyes could not find the baby. At last he saw him: the rosy boy had tossed about till he lay across the bed with his head lower than the pillow, and was smacking his lips in his sleep and breathing evenly.

Prince Andrew was as glad to find the boy like that as if he had already lost him. He bent over him and, as his sister had taught him, tried with his lips whether the child was still feverish. The soft forehead was moist. Prince Andrew touched the head with his hand; even the hair was wet, so profusely had the child perspired. He was not dead: evidently the crisis was over and he was convalescent. Prince Andrew longed to snatch up, to squeeze, to hold to his heart, this helpless little creature, but dared not do so. He stood over him, gazing at his head and at the little arms and legs which showed under the blanket. He heard a rustle behind him and a shadow appeared under the curtain of the cot. He did not look round, but still gazing at the infant's face listened to his regular breathing. The dark shadow was Princess Mary, who had come up to the cot with noiseless steps, lifted the curtain, and dropped it again behind her. Prince Andrew recognized her without looking and held out his hand to her. She pressed it.

'He has perspired,' said Prince Andrew.

'I was coming to tell you so.'

The child moved slightly in his sleep, smiled, and rubbed his forehead against the pillow.

Prince Andrew looked at his sister. In the dim shadow of the curtain her luminous eyes shone more brightly than usual from the tears of joy that were in them. She leaned over to her brother and kissed him, slightly catching the curtain of the cot. Each made the other a warning gesture, and stood still in the dim light beneath the curtain as if not wishing to leave that seclusion where they three were shut off from all the world. Prince Andrew was the first to move away, ruffling his hair against the muslin of the curtain.

'Yes, this is the one thing left me now,' he said with a sigh.

10

SOON after his admission to the Masonic Brotherhood Pierre went to the Kiev province, where he had the greatest number of serfs, taking with him full directions which he had written down for his own guidance as to what he should do on his estates.

When he reached Kiev he sent for all his stewards to the head office and explained to them his intentions and wishes. He told them that steps would be taken immediately to free his serfs – and that till then they were not to be overburdened with labour, women while nursing their babies were not to be sent to work, assistance was to be given to the serfs, punishments were to be admonitory and not corporal, and hospitals, asylums, and schools were to be established on all the estates. Some of the stewards (there were semi-literate foremen among them) listened with alarm, supposing these words to mean that the young count was displeased with their management and embezzlement of money, some after their first fright were amused by Pierre's lisp and the new words they had not heard before, others simply enjoyed hearing how the master talked, while the cleverest among them, including the chief steward, understood from this speech how they could best handle the master for their own ends.

The chief steward expressed great sympathy with Pierre's intentions, but remarked that besides these changes it would be necessary to go into the general state of affairs which was far from satisfactory.

Despite Count Bezukhov's enormous wealth, since he had come into an income which was said to amount to five hundred thousand rubles a year, Pierre felt himself far poorer than when his father had made him an allowance of ten thousand rubles. He had a dim perception of the following budget:

About 80,000 went in payments on all the estates to the Land Bank; about 30,000 went for the upkeep of the estate near Moscow, the town house, and the allowance to the three princesses; about 15,000 was given in pensions and the same amount for asylums; 150,000 alimony was sent to the countess; about 70,000 went for interest on debts. The building of a new church previously begun, had cost about 10,000 in each of the last two years, and he did not know how the rest, about 100,000 rubles, was spent, and almost every year he was obliged to borrow. Besides this the chief steward wrote every year telling him of fires and bad harvests, or of the necessity of rebuilding factories and workshops. So the first task Pierre had to face was one for which he had very little aptitude or inclination – practical business.

He discussed estate affairs every day with his chief steward. But he felt that this did not forward matters at all. He felt that these consultations were detached from real affairs and did not link up with them or make them move. On the one hand the chief steward put the state of things to him in the very worst light, pointing out the necessity of paying off the debts and undertaking new activities with serf-labour, to which Pierre did not agree. On the other hand Pierre demanded that steps should be taken to liberate the serfs, which the steward met by showing the necessity of first paying off the loans from the Land Bank, and the consequent impossibility of a speedy emancipation.

The steward did not say it was quite impossible, but suggested selling the forests in the province of Kostroma, the land lower down the river, and the Crimean estate, in order to make it possible: all of which operations according to him were connected with such complicated measures – the removal of injunctions, petitions, permits, and so on – that Pierre became quite bewildered and only replied:

'Yes, yes, do so.'

Pierre had none of the practical persistence that would have enabled him to attend to the business himself, and so he disliked it and only tried to pretend to the steward that he was attending to it. The steward for his part tried to pretend to the count that he considered these consultations very valuable for the proprietor and troublesome to himself.

In Kiev Pierre found some people he knew, and strangers hastened to make his acquaintance and joyfully welcomed the rich newcomer, the largest landowner of the province. Temptations to Pierre's greatest weakness – the one to which he had confessed when admitted to the Lodge – were so strong that he could not resist them. Again whole days, weeks, and months of his life passed in as great a rush, and were as much occupied with evening parties, dinners, lunches and balls, giving him no time for reflection, as in Petersburg. Instead of the new life he had hoped to lead he still lived the old life, only in new surroundings.

Of the three precepts of freemasonry Pierre realized that he did not fulfil the one which enjoined every mason to set an example of moral life, and that of the seven virtues he lacked two – morality and the love of death. He consoled himself with the thought that he fulfilled another of the precepts – that of reforming the human race – and had other virtues – love of his neighbour and especially generosity.

In the spring of 1807 he decided to return to Petersburg. On the way he intended to visit all his estates and see for himself how far his orders had been carried out and in what state were the serfs whom God had entrusted to his care and whom he intended to benefit.

The chief steward, who considered the young count's attempts almost insane – unprofitable to himself, to the count, and to the serfs – made some concessions. Continuing to represent the liberation of the serfs as impracticable, he arranged for the erection of large buildings – schools, hospitals, and asylums – on all the estates before the master arrived. Everywhere preparations were made not for ceremonious welcomes (which he knew Pierre would not like), but for just such gratefully religious ones, with offerings of icons and the bread and salt of hospitality, as according to his understanding of his master would touch and delude him.

The southern spring, the comfortable rapid travelling in a Vienna carriage and the solitude of the road, all had a gladdening effect on Pierre. The estates he had not before visited were each more picturesque than the other; the serfs everywhere seemed thriving and touchingly grateful for the benefits conferred on them. Everywhere were receptions, which though they embarrassed Pierre awakened a joyful feeling in the depth of his heart. In one place the peasants presented him with bread and salt and an icon of St Peter and St Paul, asking permission, as a mark of their gratitude for the benefits he had conferred on them, to build a new chantry to the church at their own expense in honour of Peter and Paul, his patron saints. In another place the women with infants in arms met him to thank him for releasing them from hard work. On a third estate the priest, bearing a cross, came to meet him surrounded by children whom, by the count's generosity, he was instructing in reading, writing, and religion. On all his estates Pierre saw with his own eyes brick buildings erected or in course of erection, all on one plan, for hospitals, schools, and almshouses, which were soon to be opened. Everywhere he saw the stewards' accounts, according to which the serfs' manorial labour had been diminished, and heard the touching thanks of deputations of serfs in their full-skirted blue coats.

What Pierre did not know was that the place where they presented him with bread and salt and wished to build a chantry in honour of Peter and Paul was a market-village where a fair was held on St Peter's day,* and that the richest peasants (who formed the deputations) had begun the chantry long before, and that nine-tenths of the peasants in that village were in a state of the greatest poverty. He did not know that since the nursing mothers were no longer sent to work on his land, they did still harder work on their own land. He did not know that the priest who met him with the cross oppressed the peasants by his exactions, and that the pupils' parents wept at having to let him take their children and secured their release by heavy payments. He did not know that the brick buildings, built to plan, were being built by serfs whose manorial labour was thus increased, though lessened on paper. He did not know that where the steward had shown him in the accounts that the serfs' payments had been diminished by a third, their obligatory manorial work had been increased by a half. And so Pierre was delighted with his visit to his estates and quite recovered the philanthropic mood in which he had left Petersburg, and wrote enthusiastic letters to his 'brother-instructor' as he called the Grand Master.

'How easy it is, how little effort it needs, to do so much good,' thought Pierre, 'and how little attention we pay to it!'

He was pleased at the gratitude he received, but felt abashed at receiving it. This gratitude reminded him of how much more he might do for these simple kindly people.

The chief steward, a very stupid but cunning man who saw perfectly through the naïve and intelligent count and played with him as with a toy, seeing the effect these prearranged receptions had on Pierre, pressed him still harder with proofs of the impossibility and above all the uselessness of freeing the serfs, who were quite happy as it was.

Pierre in his secret soul agreed with the steward that it would be difficult to imagine happier people, and that God only knew what would happen to them when they were free, but he insisted, though reluctantly, on what he thought right. The steward promised to do all in his power to carry out the count's wishes, seeing clearly that not only would the count never be able to find out whether all measures had been taken for the sale of the land and forests and to release them from the Land Bank, but would probably never even inquire, and would never know that the newly-erected buildings were standing empty, and that the serfs continued to give in money and work all that other people's serfs gave – that is to say, all that could be got out of them.

11

RETURNING from his journey through South Russia in the happiest state of mind, Pierre carried out an intention he had long had of visiting his friend Bolkonsky whom he had not seen for two years.

Bogucharovo lay in a flat uninteresting part of the country among fields and forests of fir and birch, which were partly cut down. The house lay behind a newly-dug pond filled with water to the brink and with banks still bare of grass. It was at the end of a village that stretched along the high road in the midst of a young copse in which were a few fir trees.

The homestead consisted of a threshing floor, outhouses, stables, a bath-house, a lodge, and a large brick house with semicircular façade still in course of construction. Round the house was a garden newly laid out. The fences and gates were new and solid; two fire pumps and a water-cart, painted green, stood in a shed; the paths were straight, the bridges were strong and had hand-rails. Everything bore an impress of tidiness and good management. Some domestic serfs Pierre met, in reply to inquiries as to where the prince lived, pointed out a small newly-built lodge close to the pond. Anton, a man who had looked after Prince Andrew in his boyhood, helped Pierre out of his carriage, said that the prince was at home, and showed him into a clean little ante-room.

Pierre was struck by the modesty of the small though clean house after the brilliant surroundings in which he had last met his friend in Petersburg.

He quickly entered the small reception-room with its still un-plastered wooden walls redolent of pine, and would have gone farther, but Anton ran ahead on tiptoe and knocked at a door.

'Well, what is it?' came a sharp, unpleasant voice.

'A visitor,' answered Anton.

'Ask him to wait,' and the sound was heard of a chair being pushed back.

Pierre went with rapid steps to the door and suddenly came face to face with Prince Andrew, who came out frowning and looking old. Pierre embraced him, and lifting his spectacles kissed his friend on the cheek and looked at him closely.

'Well, I did not expect you, I am very glad,' said Prince Andrew.

Pierre said nothing; he looked fixedly at his friend with surprise. He was struck by the change in him. His words were kindly and there was a smile on his lips and face, but his eyes were dull and lifeless and in spite of his evident wish to do so he could not give them a joyous and glad sparkle. Prince Andrew had grown thinner, paler, and more manly looking, but what amazed and estranged Pierre till he got used to it was his inertia and a wrinkle on his brow indicating prolonged concentration on some one thought.

As is usually the case with people meeting after a prolonged separation, it was long before their conversation could settle on anything. They put questions and gave brief replies about things they knew ought to be talked over at length. At last the conversation gradually settled on some of the topics at first lightly touched on: their past life, plans for the future, Pierre's journeys and occupations, the war, and so on. The preoccupation and despondency which Pierre had noticed in his friend's look was now still more clearly expressed in the smile with which he listened to Pierre, especially when he spoke with joyful animation of the past or the future. It was as if Prince Andrew would have liked to sympathize with what Pierre was saying, but could not. The latter began to feel that it was in bad taste to speak of his enthusiasms, dreams, and hopes of happiness or goodness, in Prince Andrew's presence. He was ashamed to express his new masonic views, which had been particularly revived and strengthened by his late tour. He checked himself, fearing to seem naïve, yet he felt an irresistible desire to show his friend as soon as possible that he was now a quite different, and better, Pierre than he had been in Petersburg.

'I can't tell you how much I have lived through since then. I hardly know myself again.'

'Yes, we have altered much, very much, since then,' said Prince Andrew.

'Well, and you? What are your plans?'

403

'Plans!' repeated Prince Andrew ironically. 'My plans?' he said, as if astonished at the word. 'Well, you see, I'm building. I mean to settle here altogether next year ...'

Pierre looked silently and searchingly into Prince Andrew's face, which had grown much older.

'No, I meant to ask ...' Pierre began, but Prince Andrew interrupted him.

'But why talk of me? ... Talk to me, yes, tell me about your travels and all you have been doing on your estates.'

Pierre began describing what he had done on his estates, trying as far as possible to conceal his own part in the improvements that had been made. Prince Andrew several times prompted Pierre's story of what he had been doing, as though it were all an old-time story, and he listened not only without interest but even as if ashamed of what Pierre was telling him.

Pierre felt uncomfortable and even depressed in his friend's company and at last became silent.

'I'll tell you what, my dear fellow,' said Prince Andrew, who evidently also felt depressed and constrained with his visitor. 'I am only bivouacking here, and have just come to look round. I am going back to my sister to-day. I will introduce you to her. But of course you know her already,' he said, evidently trying to entertain a visitor with whom he now found nothing in common. 'We will go after dinner. And would you now like to look round my place?'

They went out and walked about till dinner-time, talking of the political news and common acquaintances, like people who do not know each other intimately. Prince Andrew spoke with some animation and interest only of the new homestead he was constructing and its buildings, but even here, while on the scaffolding, in the midst of a talk explaining the future arrangements of the house, he interrupted himself:

'However, this is not at all interesting. Let us have dinner, and then we'll set off.'

At dinner conversation turned on Pierre's marriage.

'I was very much surprised when I heard of it,' said Prince Andrew.

Pierre blushed, as he always did when it was mentioned, and said hurriedly:

'I will tell you some time how it all happened. But you know it is all over, and for ever.'

'For ever?' said Prince Andrew. 'Nothing's for ever.'

'But you know how it all ended, don't you? You heard of the duel?'

'And so you had to go through that too!'

'One thing I thank God for, is that I did not kill that man,' said Pierre.

'Why so?' asked Prince Andrew. 'To kill a vicious dog is a very good thing really.'

'No, to kill a man is bad – wrong.'

'Why is it wrong?' urged Prince Andrew. 'It is not given to man to know what is right and what is wrong. Men always did and always will err and in nothing more than in what they consider right and wrong.'

'What does harm to another is wrong,' said Pierre, feeling with pleasure that for the first time since his arrival Prince Andrew was roused, had begun to talk, and wanted to express what had brought him to his present state.

'And who has told you what is bad for another man?' he asked.

'Bad! Bad!' exclaimed Pierre. 'We all know what is bad for ourselves.'

'Yes we know that, but the harm I am conscious of in myself is something I cannot inflict on others,' said Prince Andrew, growing more and more animated and evidently wishing to express his new outlook to Pierre. He spoke in French. 'I only know two very real evils in life: remorse and illness. The only good is the absence of those evils. To live for myself avoiding those two evils is my whole philosophy now.'

'And love of one's neighbour, and self-sacrifice?' began Pierre. 'No, I can't agree with you! To live only so as not to do evil and not to have to repent, is not enough. I lived like that, I lived for myself and ruined my life. And only now when I am living, or at least trying' (Pierre's modesty made him correct himself) 'to live for others, only now have I understood all the happiness of life. No, I shall not agree with you, and you do not really believe what you are saying.'

Prince Andrew looked silently at Pierre with an ironic smile.

'When you see my sister, Princess Mary, you'll get on with her,' he said. 'Perhaps you are right for yourself,' he added after a short pause, 'but everyone lives in his own way. You lived for yourself and say you nearly ruined your life and only found happiness when you began living for others. I experienced just the reverse. I lived for glory. – And after all what is glory? The same love of others, a desire to do something for them, a desire for their approval. – So I lived for others, and not almost, but quite, ruined my life. And I have become calmer since I began to live only for myself.'

'But what do you mean by living only for yourself?' asked

Pierre growing excited. 'What about your son, your sister, and your father?'

'But that's just the same as myself – they are not *others*,' explained Prince Andrew. 'The others, one's neighbours, *le prochain*, as you and Princess Mary call it, are the chief source of all error and evil. *Le prochain* – your Kiev peasants to whom you want to do good.'

And he looked at Pierre with a mocking, challenging expression. He evidently wished to draw him on.

'You are joking,' replied Pierre, growing more and more excited. 'What error or evil can there be in my wishing to do good, and even doing a little – though I did very little and did it very badly? – What evil can there be in it if unfortunate people, our serfs, people like ourselves, were growing up and dying with no idea of God and truth beyond ceremonies and meaningless prayers, and are now instructed in a comforting belief in future life, retribution, recompense, and consolation? What evil and error is there in it, if people were dying of disease without help while material assistance could so easily be rendered, and I supplied them with a doctor, a hospital, and an asylum for the aged? And is it not a palpable, unquestionable good if a peasant, or a woman with a baby has no rest day or night, and I give them rest and leisure?' said Pierre, hurrying and lisping. 'And I have done that though badly and to a small extent, but I have done something towards it, and you cannot persuade me that it was not a good action, and more than that, you can't make me believe that you do not think so yourself. And the main thing is,' he continued, 'that I know, and know for certain, that the enjoyment of doing this good is the only sure happiness in life.'

'Yes, if you put it like that it's quite a different matter,' said Prince Andrew. 'I build a house and lay out a garden, and you build hospitals. The one and the other may serve as a pastime. But what's right and what's good must be judged by one who knows all, but not by us. Well, you want an argument,' he added, 'come on then.'

They rose from the table and sat down in the entrance porch which served as a verandah.

'Come, let's argue then,' said Prince Andrew. 'You talk of schools,' he went on, crooking a finger, 'education and so forth; that is, you want to raise him' (pointing to a peasant who passed by them taking off his cap) 'from his animal condition and awaken in him spiritual needs, while it seems to me that animal happiness is the only happiness possible, and that is just what you want to deprive him of. I envy him, but you want to make him what I am,

406

without giving him my means. Then you say, "lighten his toil". But as I see it, physical labour is as essential to him, as much a condition of his existence, as mental activity is to you or me. You can't help thinking. I go to bed after two in the morning, thoughts come and I can't sleep but toss about till dawn, because I think and can't help thinking, just as he can't help ploughing and mowing; if he didn't he would go to the drink shop or fall ill. Just as I could not stand his terrible physical labour but should die of it in a week, so he could not stand my physical idleness, but would grow fat and die. The third thing – what else was it you talked about?' and Prince Andrew crooked a third finger, 'Ah, yes, hospitals, medicine. He has a fit, he is dying, and you come and bleed him and patch him up. He will drag about as a cripple, a burden to everybody, for another ten years. It would be far easier and simpler for him to die. Others are being born and there are plenty of them as it is. It would be different if you grudged losing a labourer – that's how I regard him – but you want to cure him from love of him. And he does not want that. And besides, what a notion that medicine ever cured anyone! Killed them, yes!' said he, frowning angrily and turning away from Pierre.

Prince Andrew expressed his ideas so clearly and distinctly that it was evident he had reflected on this subject more than once, and he spoke readily and rapidly like a man who has not talked for a long time. His glance became more animated as his conclusions became more hopeless.

'Oh, that is dreadful, dreadful!' said Pierre. 'I don't understand how one can live with such ideas. I had such moments myself not long ago, in Moscow and when travelling, but at such times I collapse so that I don't live at all – everything seems hateful to me ... myself most of all. Then I don't eat, don't wash ... and how is it with you? ...'

'Why not wash? That is not cleanly,' said Prince Andrew; 'on the contrary one must try to make one's life as pleasant as possible. I'm alive; that is not my fault, so I must live out my life as best I can, without hurting others.'

'But with such ideas what motive have you for living? One would sit without moving, undertaking nothing ...'

'Life as it is leaves one no peace. I should be thankful to do nothing, but here on the one hand the local nobility have done me the honour to choose me to be their marshal;* it was all I could do to get out of it. They could not understand that I have not the necessary qualifications for it – the kind of good-natured, fussy shallowness necessary for the position. Then there's this house, which must be built in order to have a nook of one's own in which to be quiet. And now there's this recruiting.'

'Why aren't you serving in the army?'

'After Austerlitz!' said Prince Andrew gloomily. 'No, thank you very much! I have promised myself not to serve again in the active Russian army. And I won't – not even if Bonaparte were here at Smolensk threatening Bald Hills – even then I wouldn't serve in the Russian army! Well, as I was saying,' he continued, recovering his composure, 'now there's this recruiting. My father is chief in command of the 3rd District, and my only way of avoiding active service is to serve under him.'

'Then you are serving?'

'I am.'

He paused a little while.

'And why do you serve?'

'Why, for this reason! My father is one of the most remarkable men of his time. But he is growing old, and though not exactly cruel, he has too energetic a character. He is so accustomed to unlimited power that he is terrible, and now he has this authority of a commander-in-chief of the recruiting, granted by the Emperor. If I had been two hours late a fortnight ago he would have had a paymaster's clerk at Yukhnova hanged,' said Prince Andrew with a smile. 'So I am serving because I alone have any influence with my father, and now and then can save him from actions which would torment him afterwards.'

'Well, there you see!'

'Yes, but it is not as you imagine,' Prince Andrew continued, 'I did not, and do not, in the least care about that scoundrel of a clerk who had stolen some boots from the recruits, I should even have been very glad to see him hanged, but I was sorry for my father – that again is for myself.'

Prince Andrew grew more and more animated. His eyes glittered feverishly while he tried to prove to Pierre that in his actions there was no desire to do good to his neighbour.

'There now, you wish to liberate your serfs,' he continued, 'that is a very good thing, but not for you – I don't suppose you ever had anyone flogged or sent to Siberia – and still less for your serfs. If they are beaten, flogged, or sent to Siberia, I don't suppose they are any the worse off. In Siberia they lead the same animal life, and the stripes on their bodies heal, and they are happy as before. But it is a good thing for proprietors who perish morally, bring remorse upon themselves, stifle this remorse and grow callous, as a result of being able to inflict punishments justly and unjustly. It is those people I pity, and for their sake I should like to liberate the serfs. You may not have seen, but I have seen, how good men brought up in those traditions of unlimited power, in time when they grow more irritable, become cruel and harsh, are conscious of it, but cannot restrain themselves and grow more and more miserable.'

Prince Andrew spoke so earnestly that Pierre could not help thinking that these thoughts had been suggested to Prince Andrew by his father's case.

He did not reply.

'So that's what I am sorry for – human dignity, peace of mind, purity, and not the serfs' backs and foreheads, which, beat and shave as you may,* always remain the same backs and foreheads.'

'No, no! A thousand times no! I shall never agree with you,' said Pierre.


12

IN the evening Andrew and Pierre got into an open carriage and drove to Bald Hills. Prince Andrew, glancing at Pierre, broke the silence now and then with remarks which showed that he was in a good temper.

Pointing to the fields, he spoke of the improvements he was making in his husbandry.

Pierre remained gloomily silent, answering in monosyllables and apparently immersed in his own thoughts.

He was thinking that Prince Andrew was unhappy, had gone astray, did not see the true light, and that he, Pierre, ought to aid, enlighten, and raise him. But as soon as he thought of what he should say, he felt that Prince Andrew with one word, one argument, would upset all his teaching, and he shrank from beginning, afraid of exposing to possible ridicule what to him was precious and sacred.

'No, but why do you think so?' Pierre suddenly began, lowering his head and looking like a bull about to charge, 'why do you think so? You should not think so.'

'Think? What about?' asked Prince Andrew with surprise.

'About life, about man's destiny. It can't be so. I myself thought like that, and do you know what saved me? Freemasonry! No, don't smile. Freemasonry is not a religious ceremonial sect, as I thought it was: freemasonry is the best expression of the best, the eternal, aspects of humanity.'

And he began to explain freemasonry as he understood it to Prince Andrew. He said that freemasonry is the teaching of

Christianity freed from the bonds of State and Church, a teaching of equality, brotherhood, and love.

'Only our holy Brotherhood has the real meaning of life, all the rest is a dream,' said Pierre. 'Understand, my dear fellow, that outside this union all is filled with deceit and falsehood and I agree with you that nothing is left for an intelligent and good man but to live out his life, like you, merely trying not to harm others. But make our fundamental convictions your own, join our Brotherhood, give yourself up to us, let yourself be guided, and you will at once feel yourself, as I have felt myself, a part of that vast invisible chain the beginning of which is hidden in Heaven,' said Pierre.

Prince Andrew looking straight in front of him listened in silence to Pierre's words. More than once when the noise of the wheels prevented his catching what Pierre said, he asked him to repeat it, and by the peculiar glow that came into Prince Andrew's eyes and by his silence, Pierre saw that his words were not in vain and that Prince Andrew would not interrupt him nor laugh at what he said.

They reached a river that had overflowed its banks and which they had to cross by ferry. While the carriage and horses were being placed on it, they also stepped on the raft.

Prince Andrew leaning his arms on the raft railing, gazed silently at the flooding waters glittering in the setting sun.

'Well, what do you think about it?' Pierre asked. 'Why are you silent?'

'What do I think about it? I am listening to you. It's all very well . . . You say: join our Brotherhood and we will show you the aim of life, the destiny of man, and the laws which govern the world. But who are *we*? Men. How is it you know everything? Why do I alone not see what you see? You see a reign of goodness and truth on earth, but I don't see it.'

Pierre interrupted him.

'Do you believe in a future life?' he asked.

'A future life?' Prince Andrew repeated, but Pierre, giving him no time to reply, took the repetition for a denial, the more readily as he knew Prince Andrew's former atheistic convictions.

'You say you can't see a reign of goodness and truth on earth. Nor could I, and it cannot be seen if one looks on our life here as the end of everything. On *earth*, here on this earth' (Pierre pointed to the fields), 'there is no truth, all is false and evil; but in the universe, in the whole universe, there is a kingdom of truth, and we who are now the children of earth are – eternally – children of the whole universe. Don't I feel in my soul that I am part of this vast harmonious whole? Don't I feel that I form one link, one step, between the lower and higher beings, in this vast harmonious multitude of beings in whom the Deity – the Supreme Power if you prefer the term – is manifest? If I see, clearly see, that ladder leading from plant to man, why should I suppose it breaks off at me and does not go farther and farther? I feel that I cannot vanish, since nothing vanishes in this world, but that I shall always exist and always have existed. I feel that beyond me and above me there are spirits, and that in this world there is truth.'

'Yes, that is Herder's theory,' said Prince Andrew, 'but it is not that which can convince me, dear friend – life and death are what convince. What convinces is when one sees a being dear to one, bound up with one's own life, before whom one was to blame and had hoped to make it right' (Prince Andrew's voice trembled and he turned away), 'and suddenly that being is seized with pain, suffers, and ceases to exist . . . Why? It cannot be that there is no answer. And I believe there is . . . That's what convinces, that is what has convinced me,' said Prince Andrew.

'Yes, yes, of course,' said Pierre, 'isn't that what I'm saying?'

'No. All I say is that it is not argument that convinces me of the necessity of a future life, but this: when you go hand in hand with someone and all at once that person vanishes *there, into nowhere*, and you yourself are left facing that abyss, and look in. And I have looked in . . .'

'Well, that's it then! You know that there is a *there* and there is a *Someone*? *There* is the future life. The *Someone* is – God.'

Prince Andrew did not reply. The carriage and horses had long since been taken off, onto the farther bank, and reharnessed. The sun had sunk half below the horizon and an evening frost was starring the puddles near the ferry, but Pierre and Andrew, to the astonishment of the footmen, coachmen, and ferrymen, still stood on the raft and talked.

'If there is a God and future life there is truth and good, and man's highest happiness consists in striving to attain them. We must live, we must love, and we must believe that we live not only to-day on this scrap of earth but have lived and shall live for ever, there, in the Whole,' said Pierre, and he pointed to the sky.

Prince Andrew stood leaning on the railing of the raft listening to Pierre, and he gazed with his eyes fixed on the red reflection of the sun gleaming on the blue waters. There was perfect stillness. Pierre became silent. The raft had long since stopped, and only the waves of the current beat softly against it below. Prince

Andrew felt as if the sound of the waves kept up a refrain to Pierre's words, whispering:

'It is true, believe it.'

He sighed, and glanced with a radiant, childlike, tender look at Pierre's face, flushed and rapturous, but yet shy before his superior friend.

'Yes, if only it were so!' said Prince Andrew. 'However, it is time to get on,' he added, and stepping off the raft he looked up at the sky to which Pierre had pointed, and for the first time since Austerlitz saw that high everlasting sky he had seen while lying on that battlefield; and something that had long been slumbering, something that was best within him, suddenly awoke, joyful and youthful, in his soul. It vanished as soon as he returned to the customary conditions of his life, but he knew that this feeling which he did not know how to develop, existed within him. His meeting with Pierre formed an epoch in Prince Andrew's life. Though outwardly he continued to live in the same old way, inwardly he began a new life.

13

IT was getting dusk when Prince Andrew and Pierre drove up to the front entrance of the house at Bald Hills. As they approached the house Prince Andrew with a smile drew Pierre's attention to a commotion going on at the back porch. A woman bent with age, with a wallet on her back, and a short, long-haired young man in a black garment, had rushed back to the gate on seeing the carriage driving up. Two women ran out after them, and all four, looking round at the carriage, ran in dismay up the steps of the back porch.

'Those are Mary's "God's folk",'* said Prince Andrew. 'They have mistaken us for my father. This is the one matter in which she disobeys him. He orders these pilgrims to be driven away, but she receives them.'

'But what are "God's folk"?' asked Pierre.

Prince Andrew had no time to answer. The servants came out to meet them, and he asked where the old prince was and whether he was expected back soon.

The old prince had gone to the town and was expected back any minute.

Prince Andrew led Pierre to his own apartments, which were always kept in perfect order and readiness for him in his father's house; he himself went to the nursery.

'Let us go and see my sister,' he said to Pierre when he returned. 'I have not found her yet, she is hiding now, sitting with her "God's folk". It will serve her right, she will be confused, but you will see her "God's folk". It's really very curious.'

'What are "God's folk"?' asked Pierre.

'Come, and you'll see for yourself.'

Princess Mary really was disconcerted and red patches came on her face when they went in. In her snug rooms, with lamps burning before the icon-stand, a young lad with a long nose and long hair, wearing a monk's cassock, sat on the sofa beside her, behind a samovar. Near them in an arm-chair sat a thin, shrivelled old woman, with a meek expression on her childlike face.

'Andrew, why didn't you warn me?' said the princess with mild reproach, as she stood before her pilgrims like a hen before her chickens.

'*Charmée de vous voir. Je suis très contente de vous voir,*' she said to Pierre as he kissed her hand. She had known him as a child, and now his friendship with Andrew, his misfortune with his wife, and above all, his kindly simple face, disposed her favourably towards him. She looked at him with her beautiful radiant eyes and seemed to say, 'I like you very much, but please don't laugh at my people.' After exchanging the first greetings they sat down.

'Ah, and Ivanushka is here too!' said Prince Andrew, glancing with a smile at the young pilgrim.

'Andrew!' said Princess Mary imploringly.

'*Il faut que vous sachiez que c'est une femme,*' said Prince Andrew to Pierre.

'Andrew, *au nom de Dieu!*' Princess Mary repeated.

It was evident that Prince Andrew's ironical tone towards the pilgrims, and Princess Mary's helpless attempts to protect them, were their customary long-established relations on the matter.

'*Mais, ma bonne amie,*' said Prince Andrew, '*vous devriez au contraire m'être reconnaissante de ce que j'explique à Pierre votre intimité avec ce jeune homme.*'*

'Really?' said Pierre, gazing over his spectacles with curiosity and seriousness (for which Princess Mary was specially grateful to him) into Ivanushka's face, who seeing that she was being spoken about, looked round at them all with crafty eyes.

Princess Mary's embarrassment on *her people*'s account was quite unnecessary. They were not in the least abashed. The old woman, lowering her eyes but casting side-glances at the newcomers, had turned her cup upside down and placed a nibbled bit of sugar beside it, and sat quietly in her arm-chair, though hoping to be offered another cup of tea. Ivanushka, sipping out of her saucer, looked with sly womanish eyes from under her brows at the young men.

'Where have you been? To Kiev?' Prince Andrew asked the old woman.

'I have, good sir,' she answered garrulously. 'Just at Christmas time I was deemed worthy to partake of the holy and heavenly sacrament at the shrine of the saint. And now I'm from Kolyazin, master, where a great and wonderful blessing has been revealed.'

'And was Ivanushka with you?'

'I go by myself, benefactor,' said Ivanushka, trying to speak in a bass voice. 'I only came across Pelageya in Yukhnovo ...'

Pelageya interrupted her companion; she evidently wished to tell of what she had seen.

'In Kolyazin, master, a wonderful blessing has been revealed.'

'What is it? Some new relics?' asked Prince Andrew.

'Andrew, do leave off,' said Princess Mary. 'Don't tell him, Pelageya.'

'No ... why not, my dear, why shouldn't I? I like him. He is kind, he is one of God's chosen, he's a benefactor, he once gave me ten rubles, I remember. When I was in Kiev, Crazy Cyril says to me (he's one of God's own and goes barefoot summer and winter), he says, "Why are you not going to the right place? Go to Kolyazin where a wonder-working icon of the holy Mother of God has been revealed." On hearing these words I said good-bye to the holy folk and went.'

All were silent, only the pilgrim woman went on in measured tones, drawing in her breath.

'So I come, master, and the people say to me: "A great blessing has been revealed, holy oil trickles from the cheeks of our blessed Mother, the holy Virgin Mother of God." ...'

'All right, all right, you can tell us afterwards,' said Princess Mary flushing.

'Let me ask her,' said Pierre. 'Did you see it yourselves?' he inquired.

'Oh, yes, master, I was found worthy. Such a brightness on the face like the light of heaven, and from the blessed Mother's cheek it drops and drops ...'

'But, dear me, that must be a fraud!' said Pierre naïvely, who had listened attentively to the pilgrim.

'Oh, master, what are you saying?' exclaimed the horrified Pelageya, turning to Princess Mary for support.

'They impose on the people,' he repeated.

'Lord Jesus Christ!' exclaimed the pilgrim woman crossing herself. 'Oh, don't speak so, master! There was a general who did not

414

believe, and said, "The monks cheat," and as soon as he'd said it he went blind. And he dreamt that the Holy Virgin Mother of the Kiev catacombs came to him and said, "Believe in me and I will make you whole." So he begged: "Take me to her, take me to her." It's the real truth I'm telling you, I saw it myself. So he was brought, quite blind, straight to her, and he goes up to her and falls down and says, "Make me whole," says he, "and I'll give thee what the Tsar bestowed on me." I saw it myself, master; the star is fixed into the icon. Well, and what do you think? He received his sight! It's a sin to speak so. God will punish you,' she said admonishingly, turning to Pierre.

'How did the star get into the icon?' Pierre asked.

'And was the Holy Mother promoted to the rank of general?' said Prince Andrew with a smile.

Pelageya suddenly grew quite pale and clasped her hands.

'Oh, master, master, what a sin! And you who have a son!' she began, her pallor suddenly turning to a vivid red. 'Master, what have you said? God forgive you!' And she crossed herself. 'Lord forgive him! My dear, what does it mean? . . .' she asked, turning to Princess Mary. She got up and, almost crying, began to arrange her wallet. She evidently felt frightened and ashamed to have accepted charity in a house where such things could be said, and was at the same time sorry to have now to forgo the charity of this house.

'Now, why need you do it?' said Princess Mary. 'Why did you come to me? . . .'

'Come, Pelageya, I was joking,' said Pierre. '*Princesse, ma parole, je n'ai pas voulu l'offenser.* I did not mean anything, I was only joking,' he said, smiling shyly and trying to efface his offence. 'It was all my fault, and Andrew was only joking.'

Pelageya stopped doubtfully, but in Pierre's face there was such a look of sincere penitence, and Prince Andrew glanced so meekly now at her and now at Pierre, that she was gradually reassured.

14

THE pilgrim woman was appeased, and being encouraged to talk gave a long account of Father Amphilochus, who led so holy a life that his hands smelt of incense, and how on her last visit to Kiev some monks she knew let her have the keys of the catacombs, and how she, taking some dried bread with her, had spent two days in the catacombs with the saints. 'I'd pray awhile to one, ponder awhile, then go on to another. I'd sleep a bit and then again go and kiss the relics, and there was such peace all around, such blessedness, that you don't want to come out even into the light of heaven again.'

Pierre listened to her attentively and seriously. Prince Andrew went out of the room, and then, leaving 'God's folk' to finish their tea, Princess Mary took Pierre into the drawing-room.

'You are very kind,' she said to him.

'Oh, I really did not mean to hurt her feelings. I understand them so well and have the greatest respect for them.'

Princess Mary looked at him silently and smiled affectionately.

'I have known you a long time, you see, and am as fond of you as of a brother,' she said. 'How do you find Andrew?' she added hurriedly, not giving him time to reply to her affectionate words. 'I am very anxious about him. His health was better in the winter, but last spring his wound reopened and the doctor said he ought to go away for a cure. And I am also very much afraid for him spiritually. He has not a character like us women who when we suffer can weep away our sorrows. He keeps it all within him. To-day he is cheerful and in good spirits, but that is the effect of your visit – he is not often like that. If you could persuade him to go abroad! He needs activity, and this quiet regular life is very bad for him. Others don't notice it, but I see it.'

Towards ten o'clock the menservants rushed to the front door hearing the bells of the old prince's carriage approaching. Prince Andrew and Pierre also went out into the porch.

'Who's that?' asked the old prince, noticing Pierre as he got out of the carriage.

'Ah! Very glad! Kiss me,' he said, having learnt who the young stranger was.

The old prince was in a good temper and very gracious to Pierre.

Before supper Prince Andrew, coming back to his father's study, found him disputing hotly with his visitor. Pierre was maintaining that a time would come when there would be no more wars. The old prince disputed it chaffingly, but without getting angry.

'Drain the blood from men's veins and put in water instead, then there will be no more war! Old women's nonsense – old women's nonsense!' he repeated, but still he patted Pierre affectionately on the shoulder, and then went up to the table where Prince Andrew, evidently not wishing to join in the conversation, was looking over the papers his father had brought from town. The old prince went up to him and began to talk business.

'The marshal, a Count Rostov, hasn't sent half his contingent. He came to town and wanted to invite me to dinner – I gave him a pretty dinner!...And there, look at this...Well, my boy,' the

416

old prince went on, addressing his son and patting Pierre on the shoulder. 'A fine fellow – your friend – I like him! He stirs me up. Another says clever things and one doesn't care to listen, but this one talks rubbish yet stirs an old fellow up. Well, go! Get along! Perhaps I'll come and sit with you at supper. We'll have another dispute. Make friends with my little fool, Princess Mary,' he shouted after Pierre through the door.

Only now on his visit to Bald Hills did Pierre fully realize the strength and charm of his friendship with Prince Andrew. That charm was not expressed so much in his relations with him, as with all his family and with the household. With the stern old prince and the gentle timid Princess Mary, though he had scarcely known them, Pierre at once felt like an old friend. They were all fond of him already. Not only Princess Mary, who had been won by his gentleness with the pilgrims, gave him her most radiant looks, but even the one-year-old 'Prince Nicholas' (as his grandfather called him) smiled at Pierre and let himself be taken in his arms, and Michael Ivanovich and Mademoiselle Bourienne looked at him with pleasant smiles when he talked to the old prince.

The old prince came in to supper; this was evidently on Pierre's account. And during the two days of the young man's visit he was extremely kind to him, and told him to visit them again.

When Pierre had gone and the members of the household met together, they began to express their opinions of him as people always do after a new acquaintance has left, but as seldom happens, no one said anything but good of him.

## 15

WHEN returning from his leave Rostov felt for the first time how close was the bond that united him to Denisov and the whole regiment.

On approaching it Rostov felt as he had done when approaching his home in Moscow. When he saw the first hussar with the unbuttoned uniform of his regiment, when he recognized red-haired Dementyev and saw the picket ropes of the roan horses, when Lavrushka gleefully shouted to his master, 'The Count has come!' and Denisov, who had been asleep on his bed, ran all dishevelled out of the mud hut to embrace him, and the officers collected round to greet the new arrival, Rostov experienced the same feeling as when his mother, his father, and his sister had embraced him, and tears of joy choked him so that he could not speak. The regiment was also a home, and as unalterably dear and precious as his parents' house.

When he had reported himself to the commander of the regiment and been re-assigned to his former squadron, had been on duty and gone out foraging, when he had again entered into all the little interests of the regiment and felt himself deprived of liberty and bound in one narrow unchanging frame, he experienced the same sense of peace, of moral support, and the same sense of being at home here in his own place, as he had felt under the parental roof. But here was none of all that turmoil of the world at large where he did not know his right place and took mistaken decisions, here was no Sonya with whom he ought, or ought not, to have an explanation; here was no possibility of going there or not going there; here there were not twenty-four hours in the day which could be spent in such a variety of ways; there was not that innumerable crowd of people of whom not one was nearer to him or farther from him than another; there were none of those uncertain and undefined money relations with his father, and nothing to recall that terrible loss to Dolokhov. Here in the regiment all was clear and simple. The whole world was divided into two unequal parts: one, our Pavlograd regiment; the other, all the rest. And the rest was no concern of his. In the regiment everything was definite: who was lieutenant, who captain, who was a good fellow, who a bad one, and most of all, who was a comrade. The canteen-keeper gave one credit, one's pay came every four months, there was nothing to think out or decide, you had only to do nothing that was considered bad in the Pavlograd regiment and, when given an order, to do what was clearly, distinctly, and definitely ordered – and all would be well.

Having once more entered into the definite conditions of this regimental life, Rostov felt the joy and relief a tired man feels on lying down to rest. Life in the regiment during this campaign was all the pleasanter for him because after his loss to Dolokhov (for which, in spite of all his family's efforts to console him, he could not forgive himself) he had made up his mind to atone for his fault by serving not as he had done before, but really well, and by being a perfectly first-rate comrade and officer – in a word, a splendid man altogether, a thing which seemed so difficult out in the world, but so possible in the regiment.

After his losses he had determined to pay back his debt to his parents in five years. He received ten thousand rubles a year, but now resolved to take only two thousand and leave the rest to repay the debt to his parents.

Our army, after repeated retreats and advances and battles at Pultusk and Preussisch-Eylau, was concentrated near Bartenstein. It was awaiting the Emperor's arrival and the beginning of a new campaign.

The Pavlograd regiment, belonging to that part of the army which had served in the 1805 campaign, had been recruiting up to strength in Russia, and arrived too late to take part in the first actions of the campaign. It had been neither at Pultusk nor at Preussisch-Eylau, and, when it joined the army in the field in the second half of the campaign, was attached to Platov's division.*

Platov's division was acting independently of the main army. Several times parts of the Pavlograd regiment had exchanged shots with the enemy, had taken prisoners, and once had even captured Marshal Oudinot's carriages. In April the Pavlograds were stationed immovably for some weeks near a totally ruined and deserted German village.

A thaw had set in, it was muddy and cold, the ice on the river broke, and the roads became impassable. For days neither provisions for the men nor fodder for the horses had been issued.* As no transports could arrive the men dispersed about the abandoned and deserted villages searching for potatoes, but found few even of these.

Everything had been eaten up and the inhabitants had all fled – if any remained they were worse than beggars and nothing more could be taken from them; even the soldiers, usually pitiless enough, instead of taking anything from them often gave them the last of their rations.

The Pavlograd regiment had had only two men wounded in action but had lost nearly half its men from hunger and sickness. In the hospitals death was so certain that soldiers suffering from fever, or the swelling that came from bad food, preferred to remain on duty, and hardly able to drag their legs went to the front rather than to the hospitals. When spring came on the soldiers found a plant just showing out of the ground that looked like asparagus, which for some reason they called 'Mashka's sweet root'. It was very bitter, but they wandered about the fields seeking it and dug it out with their sabres and ate it, though they were ordered not to do so as it was a noxious plant. That spring a new disease broke out among the soldiers, a swelling of the arms, legs, and face, which the doctors attributed to eating this root. But in spite of all this, the soldiers of Denisov's squadron fed chiefly on 'Mashka's sweet root', because it was the second week that the last of the biscuits were being doled out at the rate of half a pound a man, and the last potatoes received had sprouted and frozen.

The horses also had been fed for a fortnight on straw from the thatched roofs, and had become terribly thin, though still covered with tufts of felty winter hair.

Despite this destitution the soldiers and officers went on living just as usual. Despite their pale swollen faces and tattered uniforms, the hussars formed line for roll-call, kept things in order, groomed their horses, polished their arms, brought in straw from the thatched roofs in place of fodder, and sat down to dine round the cauldrons from which they rose up hungry, joking about their nasty food and their hunger. As usual in their spare time they lit bonfires, steamed themselves before them naked, smoked, picked out and baked sprouting rotten potatoes, told and listened to stories of Potëmkin's and Suvorov's campaigns, or to legends of Alësha the Sly, or the priest's labourer Mikolka.

The officers as usual lived in twos and threes in the roofless half-ruined houses. The seniors tried to collect straw and potatoes, and in general food for the men. The younger ones occupied themselves as before, some playing cards (there was plenty of money though there was no food), some with more innocent games such as quoits and skittles.* The general trend of the campaign was rarely spoken of partly because nothing certain was known about it, partly because there was a vague feeling that in the main it was going badly.

Rostov lived as before with Denisov, and since their furlough they had become more friendly than ever. Denisov never spoke of Rostov's family, but by the tender friendship his commander showed him, Rostov felt that the elder hussar's luckless love for Natasha played a part in strengthening their friendship. Denisov evidently tried to expose Rostov to danger as seldom as possible, and after an action greeted his safe return with evident joy. On one of his foraging expeditions, in a deserted and ruined village to which he had come in search of provisions, Rostov found a family consisting of an old Pole and his daughter with an infant in arms. They were half-clad, hungry, too weak to get away on foot, and had no means of obtaining a conveyance. Rostov brought them to his quarters, placed them in his own lodging, and kept them for some weeks while the old man was recovering. One of his comrades, talking of women, began chaffing Rostov, saying that he was more wily than any of them and that it would not be a bad thing if he introduced to them the pretty Polish girl he had saved. Rostov took the joke as an insult, flared up, and said such unpleasant things to the officer that it was all Denisov could do to prevent a duel. When the officer had gone away, Denisov, who did not himself know what Rostov's relations with the Polish girl might be, began to upbraid him for his quickness of temper, and Rostov replied:

'Say what you like ... She is like a sister to me, and I can't tell you how it offended me ... because ... well, for that reason ...'

Denisov patted him on the shoulder, and began rapidly pacing the room without looking at Rostov, as was his way at moments of deep feeling.

'Ah, what a mad bweed you Wostovs are!' he muttered, and Rostov noticed tears in his eyes.

## 16

IN April the troops were enlivened by news of the Emperor's arrival, but Rostov had no chance of being present at the review he held at Bartenstein, as the Pavlograds were at the outposts far beyond that place.

They were bivouacking. Denisov and Rostov were living in an earth hut, dug out for them by the soldiers and roofed with branches and turf. The hut was made in the following manner, which had then come into vogue. A trench was dug three and a half feet wide, four feet eight inches deep, and eight feet long. At one end of the trench steps were cut out and these formed the entrance and vestibule. The trench itself was the room, in which the lucky ones, such as the squadron-commander, had a board lying on piles at the end opposite the entrance, to serve as a table. On each side of the trench the earth was cut out to a breadth of about two and a half feet, and this did duty for bedsteads and couches. The roof was so constructed that one could stand up in the middle of the trench, and could even sit up on the beds if one drew close to the table. Denisov, who was living luxuriously because the soldiers of his squadron liked him, had also a board in the roof at the farther end, with a piece of (broken but mended) glass in it for a window. When it was very cold, embers from the soldiers' camp fire were placed on a bent sheet of iron on the steps in the 'reception room' – as Denisov called that part of the hut – and it was then so warm that the officers, of whom there were always some with Denisov and Rostov, sat in their shirt-sleeves.

In April Rostov was on orderly duty. One morning between seven and eight, returning after a sleepless night, he sent for embers, changed his rain-soaked underclothes, said his prayers, drank tea, got warm, then tidied up the things on the table and in his own corner and, his face glowing from exposure to the wind and with nothing on but his shirt, lay down on his back putting his arms under his head. He was pleasantly considering the probability of being promoted in a few days for his last reconnoitring expedition, and was awaiting Denisov, who had gone out somewhere and with whom he wanted a talk.

Suddenly he heard Denisov shouting in a vibrating voice behind the hut, evidently much excited. Rostov moved to the window to see whom he was speaking to, and saw the quartermaster Topcheenko.

'I ordered you not to let them eat that Mashka woot stuff!' Denisov was shouting. 'And I saw with my own eyes how Lazarchuk bwought some fwom the fields.'

'I have given the order again and again, your honour, but they don't obey,' answered the quartermaster.

Rostov lay down again on his bed, and thought complacently: 'Let him fuss and bustle now, my job's done and I'm lying down – capitally!' He could hear that Lavrushka – that sly, bold orderly of Denisov's – was talking, as well as the quartermaster. Lavrushka was saying something about loaded wagons, biscuits and oxen, he had seen when he had gone out for provisions.

Then Denisov's voice was heard shouting farther and farther away. 'Saddle! Second platoon!'

'Where are they off to now?' thought Rostov.

Five minutes later Denisov came into the hut, climbed with muddy boots on the bed, lit his pipe, furiously scattered his things about, took his leaded whip, buckled on his sabre, and went out again. In answer to Rostov's inquiry where he was going, he answered vaguely and crossly that he had some business.

'Let God and our great monarch judge me afterwards!' said Denisov going out, and Rostov heard the hoofs of several horses splashing through the mud. He did not even trouble to find out where Denisov had gone. Having got warm in his corner he fell asleep and did not leave the hut till towards evening. Denisov had not yet returned. The weather had cleared up, and near the next hut two officers and a cadet were playing svayka, laughing as they threw their missiles which buried themselves in the soft mud. Rostov joined them. In the middle of the game the officers saw some wagons approaching with fifteen hussars on their skinny horses behind them. The wagons escorted by the hussars drew up to the picket ropes and a crowd of hussars surrounded them.

'There now, Denisov has been worrying,' said Rostov, 'and here are the provisions.'

'So they are!' said the officers. 'Won't the soldiers be glad!'

A little behind the hussars came Denisov, accompanied by two infantry officers with whom he was talking.

Rostov went to meet them.

'I warn you, Captain,' one of the officers, a short thin man, evidently very angry, was saying.

'Haven't I told you I won't give them up?' replied Denisov.

'You will answer for it, Captain. It is mutiny – seizing the transport of one's own army. Our men have had nothing to eat for two days.'

'And mine have had nothing for two weeks,' said Denisov.

'It is robbery! You'll answer for it, sir!' said the infantry officer raising his voice.

'Now what are you pestewing me for?' cried Denisov, suddenly losing his temper. 'I shall answer for it and not you, and you'd better not buzz about here till you get hurt. Be off! Go!' he shouted at the officers.

'Very well, then!' shouted the little officer, undaunted and not riding away. 'If you are determined to rob, I'll . . .'

'Go to the devil! Quick ma'ch, while you're safe and sound!' and Denisov turned his horse on the officer.

'Very well, very well!' muttered the officer threateningly, and turning his horse he trotted away, jolting in his saddle.

'A dog astwide a fence! A weal dog astwide a fence!' shouted Denisov after him (the most insulting expression a cavalryman can address to a mounted infantryman) and riding up to Rostov he burst out laughing.

'I've taken twansports from the infantwy by force!' he said. 'After all, can't let our men starve.'

The wagons that had reached the hussars had been consigned to an infantry regiment, but learning from Lavrushka that the transport was unescorted, Denisov with his hussars had seized it by force. The soldiers had biscuits dealt out to them freely, and they even shared them with the other squadrons.

The next day the regimental commander sent for Denisov, and holding his fingers spread out before his eyes said:

'This is how I look at this affair: I know nothing about it and won't begin proceedings, but I advise you to ride over to the staff, and settle the business there in the commissariat department, and if possible sign a receipt for such and such stores received. If not, as the demand was booked against an infantry regiment, there will be a row and the affair may end badly.'

From the regimental commander's Denisov rode straight to the staff with a sincere desire to act on this advice. In the evening he came back to his dug-out in a state such as Rostov had never yet seen him in. Denisov could not speak, and gasped for breath. When Rostov asked what was the matter, he only uttered some incoherent oaths and threats in a hoarse feeble voice.

Alarmed at Denisov's condition, Rostov suggested that he should undress, drink some water and send for the doctor.

'Twy me for wobbewy ... oh! Some more water ... Let them twy me, but I'll always thwash scoundwels ... and I'll tell the Empewo' ... Ice ...' he muttered.

The regimental doctor when he came said it was absolutely necessary to bleed Denisov. A deep saucer of black blood was taken from his hairy arm, and only then was he able to relate what had happened to him.

'I get there,' began Denisov. '"Now then, where's your chief's quarters?" They were pointed out. "Please to wait." "I've widden twenty miles and have duties to attend to and no time to wait. Announce me." Vewy well, so out comes their head thief – also took it into his head to lecture me: "It's wobbewy!" – "Wobbewy," I say, "is not done by a man who seizes pwovisions to feed his soldiers, but by him who takes them to fill his own pockets!" "Will you please be silent?" "Vewy good!" Then he says: "Go and give a weceipt to the commissioner, but your affair will be passed on to head-quarters." I go to the commissioner. I enter, and at the table ... who do you think? No, but wait a bit! ... Who is it that's starving us?' shouted Denisov, hitting the table with the fist of his newly-bled arm so violently that the table nearly broke down and the tumblers on it jumped about. 'Telyanin! "What? So it's you who's starving us to death! Is it? Take this and this!" and I hit him so pat, stwaight on his snout ... "Ah, what a ... what a ... !" and I sta'ted fwashing him ... Well I've had a bit of fun I can tell you!' cried Denisov, gleeful and yet angry, his white teeth showing under his black moustache. 'I'd have killed him if they hadn't taken him away!'

'But what are you shouting for? Calm yourself,' said Rostov. 'You've set your arm bleeding afresh. Wait, we must tie it up again.'

Denisov was bandaged up again and put to bed. Next day he woke calm and cheerful.

But at noon the adjutant of the regiment came into Rostov's and Denisov's dug-out with a grave and serious face, and regretfully showed them a paper addressed to Major Denisov from the regimental commander, in which inquiries were made about yesterday's occurrence. The adjutant told them that the affair was likely to take a very bad turn: that a court-martial had been appointed, and that in view of the severity with which marauding and insubordination were now regarded, degradation to the ranks would be the best that could be hoped for.

The case as presented by the offended parties was that after seizing the transports, Major Denisov, being drunk, went to the chief quartermaster and without any provocation called him a thief, threatened to strike him, and on being led out had rushed into the office and given two officials a thrashing, and dislocated the arm of one of them.

In answer to Rostov's renewed questions, Denisov said, laughing, that he thought he remembered that some other fellow had got mixed up in it, but that it was all nonsense and rubbish, and he did not in the least fear any kind of trial, and that if those scoundrels dared attack him he would give them an answer they would not easily forget.

Denisov spoke contemptuously of the whole matter, but Rostov knew him too well not to detect that (while hiding it from others) at heart he feared a court-martial and was worried over the affair, which was evidently taking a bad turn. Every day letters of inquiry and notices from the Court arrived, and on the first of May Denisov was ordered to hand the squadron over to the next in seniority and appear before the staff of his division to explain his violence at the commissariat office. On the previous day Platov reconnoitred with two Cossack regiments and two squadrons of hussars. Denisov, as was his wont, rode out in front of the outposts parading his courage. A bullet fired by a French sharpshooter hit him in the fleshy part of his leg. Perhaps at another time Denisov would not have left the regiment for so slight a wound, but now he took advantage of it to excuse himself from appearing at the staff, and went into hospital.

## 17

In June the battle of Friedland was fought, in which the Pavlograds did not take part, and after that an armistice was proclaimed. Rostov, who felt his friend's absence very much, having no news of him since he left and feeling anxious about his wound and the progress of his affairs, took advantage of the armistice to get leave to visit Denisov in hospital.

The hospital was in a small Prussian town that had been twice devastated by Russian and French troops. Because it was summer, when it is so beautiful out in the fields, the little town presented a particularly dismal appearance with its broken roofs and fences, its foul streets, tattered inhabitants, and the sick and drunken soldiers wandering about.

The hospital was in a brick building with some of the window frames and panes broken, and a courtyard surrounded by the remains of a wooden fence that had been pulled to pieces. Several bandaged soldiers, with pale swollen faces, were sitting or walking about in the sunshine in the yard.

Directly Rostov entered the door he was enveloped by a smell of putrefaction and hospital air. On the stairs he met a Russian army doctor smoking a cigar. The doctor was followed by a Russian assistant.

'I can't tear myself in pieces,' the doctor was saying. 'Come to Makar Alexeevich in the evening. I shall be there.'

The assistant asked some further questions.

'Oh, do the best you can! Isn't it all the same?' The doctor noticed Rostov coming upstairs.

'What do you want, sir?' said the doctor. 'What do you want? The bullets having spared you, do you want to try typhus? This is a pest-house, sir.'

'How so?' asked Rostov.

'Typhus, sir. It's death to go in. Only we two, Makeev and I' (he pointed to the assistant) 'keep on here. Some five of us doctors have died in this place . . . When a new one comes he is done for in a week,' said the doctor with evident satisfaction. 'Prussian doctors have been invited here but our allies don't like it at all.'

Rostov explained that he wanted to see Major Denisov of the hussars, who was wounded.

'I don't know. I can't tell you, sir. Only think! I am alone in charge of three hospitals with more than four hundred patients! It's well that the charitable Prussian ladies send us two pounds of coffee and some lint each month or we should be lost!' he laughed. 'Four hundred, sir, and they're always sending me fresh ones. There *are* four hundred? Eh?' he asked, turning to his assistant.

The assistant looked fagged out. He was evidently vexed, and impatient for the talkative doctor to go.

'Major Denisov,' Rostov said again. 'He was wounded at Molliten.'

'Dead, I fancy. Eh, Makeev?' queried the doctor in a tone of indifference.

The assistant however did not confirm the doctor's words.

'Is he tall and with reddish hair?' asked the doctor.

Rostov described Denisov's appearance.

'There was one like that,' said the doctor, as if pleased. 'That one is dead, I fancy. However, I'll look up our list. We had a list. Have you got it, Makeev?'

'Makar Alexeevich has the list,' answered the assistant. 'But if

426

you'll step into the officers' wards you'll see for yourself,' he added, turning to Rostov.

'Ah, you'd better not go, sir,' said the doctor, 'or you may have to stay here yourself.'

But Rostov bowed himself away from the doctor and asked the assistant to show him the way.

'Only don't blame me!' the doctor shouted up after him.

Rostov and the assistant went into the dark corridor. The smell was so strong there that Rostov held his nose, and had to pause and collect his strength before he could go on. A door opened to the right, and an emaciated sallow man on crutches, barefoot and in underclothing, limped out, and leaning against the doorpost looked with glittering envious eyes at those who were passing. Glancing in at the door, Rostov saw that the sick and wounded were lying on the floor on straw and overcoats.

'May I go in and look?'

'What is there to see?' said the assistant.

But just because the assistant evidently did not want him to go in, Rostov entered the soldiers' ward. The foul air to which he had already begun to get used in the corridor was still stronger here. It was a little different, more pungent, and one felt that this was where it originated.

In the long room, brightly lit up by the sun through the large windows, the sick and wounded lay in two rows with their heads to the walls, and leaving a passage in the middle. Most of them were unconscious and paid no attention to the newcomers. Those who were conscious raised themselves or lifted their thin yellow faces, and all looked intently at Rostov with the same expression of hope, of relief, reproach, and envy of another's health. Rostov went to the middle of the room, and looking through the open doors into the two adjoining rooms saw the same thing there. He stood still looking silently around. He had not at all expected such a sight. Just before him, almost across the middle of the passage on the bare floor, lay a sick man, probably a Cossack to judge by the cut of his hair. The man lay on his back, his huge arms and legs outstretched. His face was purple, his eyes were rolled back so that only the whites were seen, and on his bare legs and arms which were still red, the veins stood out like cords. He was knocking the back of his head against the floor, hoarsely uttering some word which he kept repeating. Rostov listened and made out the word. It was 'drink, drink, a drink!' Rostov glanced round, looking for someone who would put this man back in his place and bring him water.

'Who looks after the sick here?' he asked the assistant.

Just then a commissariat soldier, a hospital orderly, came in from the next room, marching stiffly, and drew up in front of Rostov.

'Good day, your honour!' he shouted, rolling his eyes at Rostov and evidently mistaking him for one of the hospital authorities.

'Get him to his place and give him some water,' said Rostov, pointing to the Cossack.

'Yes, your honour,' the soldier replied complacently, and rolling his eyes more than ever he drew himself up still straighter, but did not move.

'No, it's impossible to do anything here,' thought Rostov, lowering his eyes, and he was going out, but became aware of an intense look fixed on him on his right, and he turned. Close to the corner, on an overcoat, sat an old unshaven grey-bearded soldier as thin as a skeleton, with a stern sallow face and eyes intently fixed on Rostov. The man's neighbour on one side whispered something to him, pointing at Rostov, who noticed that the old man wanted to speak to him. He drew nearer and saw that the old man had only one leg bent under him, the other had been amputated above the knee. His neighbour on the other side, who lay motionless some distance from him with his head thrown back, was a young soldier with a snub nose. His pale waxen face was still freckled, and his eyes were rolled back. Rostov looked at the young soldier and a cold chill ran down his back.

'Why, this one seems...' he began, turning to the assistant.

'And how we've been begging, your honour,' said the old soldier, his jaw quivering. 'He's been dead since morning. After all we're men, not dogs.'

'I'll send someone at once. He shall be taken away – taken away at once,' said the assistant hurriedly. 'Let us go, your honour.'

'Yes, yes, let us go,' said Rostov hastily, and lowering his eyes and shrinking, he tried to pass unnoticed between the rows of reproachful envious eyes that were fixed upon him, and went out of the room.

18

GOING along the corridor the assistant led Rostov to the officers' wards, consisting of three rooms, the doors of which stood open. There were beds in these rooms and the sick and wounded officers were lying or sitting on them. Some were walking about the rooms in hospital dressing-gowns. The first person Rostov met in the officers' ward was a thin little man with one arm, who was walking about the first room in a nightcap and a hospital dressing-gown with a pipe between his teeth. Rostov looked at him trying to remember where he had seen him before.

'See where we've met again!' said the little man. 'Tushin, Tushin, don't you remember, who gave you a lift at Schön Graben? And I've had a bit cut off, you see . . .' he went on with a smile, pointing to the empty sleeve of his dressing-gown. 'Looking for Vasili Dmitrich Denisov? My neighbour,' he added when he heard who Rostov wanted. 'Here, here', and Tushin led him into the next room, from whence came sounds of several laughing voices.

'How can they laugh, or even live at all here?' thought Rostov, still aware of that smell of decomposing flesh that had been so strong in the soldiers' ward, and still seeming to see fixed on him those envious looks which had followed him out from both sides, and the face of that young soldier with eyes rolled back.

Denisov lay asleep on his bed with his head under the blanket, though it was nearly noon.

'Ah, Wostov? How are you, how are you?' he called out, still in the same voice as in the regiment, but Rostov noticed sadly that under this habitual ease and animation some new, sinister, hidden feeling showed itself in the expression of Denisov's face and the intonations of his voice.

His wound, though such a slight one, had not yet healed even now six weeks after he had been hit. His face had the same swollen pallor as the faces of the other hospital patients, but it was not this that struck Rostov. What struck him was that Denisov did not seem glad to see him, and smiled at him unnaturally. He did not ask about the regiment, nor about the general state of affairs, and when Rostov spoke of these matters did not listen.

Rostov even noticed that Denisov did not like to be reminded of the regiment, or in general of that other, free life which was going on outside the hospital. He seemed to try to forget that old life and was only interested in the affair with the commissariat officers. On Rostov's inquiry as to how that matter stood, he at once produced from under his pillow a paper he had received from the commission and the rough draft of his answer to it. He became animated when he began reading his paper, and specially drew Rostov's attention to the stinging rejoinders he made to his enemies. His hospital companions, who had gathered round Rostov – a fresh arrival from the world outside – gradually began to disperse as soon as Denisov began reading his answer. Rostov noticed by their faces that all those gentlemen had already heard that story more than once and were tired of it. Only the man who had the next bed, a stout Uhlan, continued to sit on his bed gloomily frowning and smoking a pipe, and little one-armed Tushin still listened, shaking his head disapprovingly. In the middle of the reading the Uhlan interrupted Denisov.

'But what I say is,' he said, turning to Rostov, 'it would be best simply to petition the Emperor for pardon. They say great rewards will now be distributed, and surely a pardon would be granted...'

'Me petition the Empewo'!' exclaimed Denisov in a voice to which he tried hard to give the old energy and fire, but which sounded like an expression of irritable impotence. 'What for? If I were a wobber I would ask mercy, but I'm being court-martialled for bwinging wobbers to book. Let them twy me, I'm not afwaid of anyone. I've served the Tsar and my countwy honouwably and have not stolen! And am I to be degwaded?... Listen, I'm w'iting to them stwaight. This is what I say: "If I had wobbed the Tweasury..."'

'It's well written certainly,' said Tushin, 'but that's not the point, Vasili Dmitrich,' and he also turned to Rostov. 'One has to submit, and Vasili Dmitrich doesn't want to. You know the auditor told you it was a bad business.'

'Well, let it be bad,' said Denisov.

'The auditor wrote out a petition for you,' continued Tushin, 'and you ought to sign it and ask this gentleman to take it. No doubt he' (indicating Rostov) 'has connexions on the staff. You won't find a better opportunity.'

'Haven't I said I'm not going to gwovel?' Denisov interrupted him, and went on reading his paper.

Rostov had not the courage to persuade Denisov, though he instinctively felt that the way advised by Tushin and the other officers was the safest, and though he would have been glad to be of service to Denisov. He knew his stubborn will and straightforward hasty temper.

When the reading of Denisov's virulent reply, which took more than an hour, was over, Rostov said nothing, and he spent the rest of the day in a most dejected state of mind amid Denisov's hospital comrades who had gathered around him, telling them what he knew and listening to their stories. Denisov was moodily silent all the evening.

Late in the evening when Rostov was about to leave, he asked Denisov whether he had no commission for him.

'Yes, wait a bit,' said Denisov glancing round at the officers, and taking his papers from under his pillow he went to the window where he had an inkpot, and sat down to write.

'It seems it's no use knocking one's head against a wall!' he said, coming from the window and giving Rostov a large envelope.

In it was the petition to the Emperor drawn up by the auditor, in which Denisov without alluding to the offences of the commissariat officials, simply asked for pardon.

'Hand it in. It seems . . .'

He did not finish but gave a painfully unnatural smile.

## 19

HAVING returned to the regiment and told the commander the state of Denisov's affairs, Rostov rode to Tilsit with the letter to the Emperor.

On the 13th of June the French and Russian Emperors arrived in Tilsit.* Boris Drubetskoy had asked the important personage on whom he was in attendance to include him in the suite appointed for the stay at Tilsit.

'I should like to see the great man,' he said alluding to Napoleon, whom hitherto he like everyone else had always called Buonaparte.

'You are speaking of Buonaparte?' asked the general, smiling.

Boris looked at his general inquiringly and immediately saw that he was being tested.

'I am speaking, Prince, of the Emperor Napoleon,' he replied. The general patted him on the shoulder with a smile.

'You will go far,' he said, and took him to Tilsit with him.

Boris was among the few present at the Niemen on the day the two Emperors met. He saw the raft, decorated with monograms, saw Napoleon pass before the French Guards on the farther bank of the river, saw the pensive face of the Emperor Alexander as he sat in silence in a tavern on the bank of the Niemen awaiting Napoleon's arrival, saw both Emperors get into boats, and saw how Napoleon – reaching the raft first – stepped quickly forward to meet Alexander and held out his hand to him, and how they both retired into the pavilion. Since he had begun to move in the highest circles Boris had made it his habit to watch attentively all that went on around him and to note it down. At the time of the meeting at Tilsit he asked the names of those who had come with Napoleon and about the uniforms they wore, and listened attentively to words spoken by important personages. At the moment the Emperors went into the pavilion he looked at his watch, and did not forget to look at it again when Alexander came out. The interview had lasted an hour and fifty-three minutes. He noted this down that same evening among other facts he felt to be of historic importance. As the Emperor's suite was a very small one it was a matter of great importance, for a man who valued his success in the service, to be at Tilsit on the occasion of this interview between the two Emperors, and having succeeded in this, Boris felt that henceforth his position was fully assured. He had not only become known, but people had grown accustomed to him and accepted him. Twice he had executed commissions to the Emperor himself, so that the latter knew his face, and all those at Court, far from cold-shouldering him as at first when they considered him a newcomer, would now have been surprised had he been absent.

Boris lodged with another adjutant, the Polish Count Zhilinski. Zhilinski, a Pole brought up in Paris, was rich, and passionately fond of the French, and almost every day of the stay at Tilsit, French officers of the Guard and from French head-quarters were dining and lunching with him and Boris.

On the evening of the 24th of June, Count Zhilinski was giving a supper to his French friends. The guest of honour was an aide-de-camp of Napoleon's, there were also several French officers of the Guard, and a page of Napoleon's, a young lad of an old aristocratic French family. That very day Rostov, profiting by the darkness to avoid being recognized in civilian dress, came to Tilsit and went to the lodging occupied by Boris and Zhilinski.

Rostov, in common with the whole army from which he came, was far from having experienced the change of feeling towards Napoleon and the French – who from being foes had suddenly become friends – that had taken place at head-quarters and in Boris. In the army, Bonaparte and the French were still regarded with mingled feelings of anger, contempt, and fear. Only recently, talking with one of Platov's Cossack officers, Rostov had argued that if Napoleon were taken prisoner he would be treated not as a sovereign, but as a criminal. Quite lately happening to meet a wounded French colonel on the road, Rostov had maintained with heat that peace was impossible between a legitimate sovereign and the criminal Bonaparte. Rostov was therefore unpleasantly struck by the presence of French officers in Boris's lodgings, dressed in uniforms he had been accustomed to see from quite a different point of view from the outposts of the flank. As soon as he noticed a French officer who thrust his head out of the door, that warlike feeling of hostility which he always experienced at the sight of the enemy, suddenly seized him. He stopped at the threshold and asked in Russian whether Drubetskoy lived there. Boris, hearing a strange voice in the ante-room, came out to meet him. An expression of annoyance showed itself for a moment on his face on first recognizing Rostov.

'Ah, it's you? Very glad, very glad to see you,' he said however, coming towards him with a smile. But Rostov had noticed his first impulse.

'I've come at a bad time I think. I should not have come, but I have business,' he said coldly.

'No, I only wonder how you managed to get away from your regiment. *Dans un moment je suis à vous*,' he said, answering someone who called him.

'I see I'm intruding,' Rostov repeated.

The look of annoyance had already disappeared from Boris's face: having evidently reflected and decided how to act he very quietly took both Rostov's hands and led him into the next room. His eyes, looking serenely and steadily at Rostov, seemed to be veiled by something, as if screened by blue spectacles of conventionality. So it seemed to Rostov.

'Oh come now! As if you could come at a wrong time!' said Boris, and he led him into the room where the supper table was laid and introduced him to his guests, explaining that he was not a civilian, but an hussar officer, and an old friend of his.

'Count Zhilinski – *le Comte* N. N. – *le Capitaine* S. S.' said he, naming his guests. Rostov looked frowningly at the Frenchmen, bowed reluctantly, and remained silent.

Zhilinski evidently did not receive this new Russian person very willingly into his circle, and did not speak to Rostov. Boris did not appear to notice the constraint the newcomer produced, and with the same pleasant composure and the same veiled look in his eyes with which he had met Rostov, tried to enliven the conversation. One of the Frenchmen, with the politeness characteristic of his countrymen, addressed the obstinately taciturn Rostov, saying that the latter had probably come to Tilsit to see the Emperor.

'No, I came on business,' replied Rostov briefly.

Rostov had been out of humour from the moment he noticed the look of dissatisfaction on Boris's face, and as always happens to those in a bad humour, it seemed to him that everyone regarded him with aversion and that he was in everybody's way. He really was in their way, for he alone took no part in the conversation which again became general. The looks the visitors cast on him seemed to say: 'And what is he sitting here for?' He rose and went up to Boris.

'Anyhow I'm in your way,' he said in a low tone. 'Come and talk over my business and I'll go away.'

'Oh, no, not at all,' said Boris. 'But if you are tired, come and lie down in my room and have a rest.'

'Yes, really . . .'

They went into the little room where Boris slept. Rostov without

433

sitting down, began at once, irritably (as if Boris were to blame in some way) telling him about Denisov's affair, asking him whether, through his general, he could and would intercede with the Emperor on Denisov's behalf and get Denisov's petition handed in. When he and Boris were alone, Rostov felt for the first time that he could not look Boris in the face without a sense of awkwardness. Boris, with one leg crossed over the other and stroking his left hand with the slender fingers of his right, listened to Rostov as a general listens to the report of a subordinate, now looking aside and now gazing straight into Rostov's eyes with the same veiled look. Each time this happened Rostov felt uncomfortable and cast down his eyes.

'I have heard of such cases and know that his Majesty is very severe in such affairs. I think it would be best not to bring it before the Emperor, but to apply to the commander of the corps . . . But in general, I think . . .'

'So you don't want to do anything? Well then, say so!' Rostov almost shouted, not looking Boris in the face.

Boris smiled.

'On the contrary I will do what I can. Only I thought . . .'

At that moment Zhilinski's voice was heard calling Boris.

'Well then, go, go, go . . .' said Rostov, and refusing supper and remaining alone in the little room, he walked up and down for a long time hearing the light-hearted French conversation from the next room.

20

ROSTOV had come to Tilsit on the day least suitable for a petition on Denisov's behalf. He could not himself go to the general in attendance as he was in mufti and had come to Tilsit without permission to do so, and Boris, even had he wished to, could not have done so on the following day. On that day, June 27th, the preliminaries of peace were signed. The Emperors exchanged decorations: Alexander received the Cross of the Legion of Honour, and Napoleon the Order of St Andrew of the First Degree, and a dinner had been arranged for the evening, given by a battalion of the French Guards to the Preobrazhensk battalion. The Emperors were to be present at that banquet.

Rostov felt so ill at ease and uncomfortable with Boris, that when the latter looked in after supper he pretended to be asleep, and early next morning went away, avoiding Boris. In his civilian clothes and a round hat he wandered about the town, staring at the

French and their uniforms and at the streets and houses where the Russian and French Emperors were staying. In a square he saw tables being set up and preparations made for the dinner, he saw the Russian and French colours draped from side to side of the streets with huge monograms A. and N. In the windows of the houses also, flags and bunting were displayed.

'Boris doesn't want to help me and I don't want to ask him. That's settled,' thought Nicholas. 'All is over between us, but I won't leave here without having done all I can for Denisov and certainly not without getting his letter to the Emperor. The Emperor! . . . He is here!' thought Rostov who had unconsciously returned to the house where Alexander lodged.

Saddled horses were standing before the house and the suite were assembling, evidently preparing for the Emperor to come out.

'I may see him at any moment,' thought Rostov. 'If only I were to hand the letter direct to him and tell him all . . . could they really arrest me for my civilian clothes? Surely not! He would understand on whose side justice lies. He understands everything, knows everything. Who can be more just, more magnanimous than he? And even if they did arrest me for being here, what would it matter?' thought he, looking at an officer who was entering the house the Emperor occupied. 'After all, people do go in . . . It's all nonsense! I'll go in and hand the letter to the Emperor myself, so much the worse for Drubetskoy who drives me to it!' And suddenly with a determination he himself did not expect, Rostov felt for the letter in his pocket and went straight to the house.

'No, I won't miss my opportunity now as I did after Austerlitz,' he thought, expecting every moment to meet the monarch, and conscious of the blood that rushed to his heart at the thought. 'I will fall at his feet and beseech him. He will lift me up, will listen, and will even thank me. "I am happy when I can do good, but to remedy injustice is the greatest happiness,"' Rostov fancied the sovereign saying. And passing people who looked after him with curiosity, he entered the porch of the Emperor's house.

A broad staircase led straight up from the entry, and to the right he saw a closed door. Below, under the staircase, was a door leading to the lower floor.

'Whom do you want?' someone inquired.

'To hand in a letter, a petition, to his Majesty,' said Nicholas, with a tremor in his voice.

'A petition? This way, to the officer on duty' (he was shown the door leading downstairs) 'only it won't be accepted.'

On hearing this indifferent voice Rostov grew frightened at what he was doing; the thought of meeting the Emperor at any moment was so fascinating and consequently so alarming, that he was ready to run away, but the official who had questioned him opened the door, and Rostov entered.

A short stout man of about thirty, in white breeches and high boots and a batiste shirt that he had evidently only just put on, was standing in that room, and his valet was buttoning onto the back of his breeches a new pair of handsome silk-embroidered braces that for some reason attracted Rostov's attention. This man was speaking to someone in the adjoining room.

'A good figure and in her first bloom,' he was saying, but on seeing Rostov he stopped short and frowned.

'What is it? A petition?'

'What is it?' asked the person in the other room.

'Another petitioner,' answered the man with the braces.

'Tell him to come later. He'll be coming out directly, we must go.'

'Later ... later! To-morrow. It's too late ...'

Rostov turned and was about to go, but the man in the braces stopped him.

'Whom have you come from? Who are you?'

'I come from Major Denisov,' answered Rostov.

'Are you an officer?'

'Lieutenant Count Rostov.'

'What audacity! Hand it in through your commander. And go along with you ... go'; and he continued to put on the uniform the valet handed him.

Rostov went back into the hall and noticed that in the porch there were many officers and generals in full parade uniform whom he had to pass.

Cursing his temerity, his heart sinking at the thought of finding himself at any moment face to face with the Emperor and being put to shame and arrested in his presence, fully alive now to the impropriety of his conduct and repenting of it, Rostov with downcast eyes was making his way out of the house through the brilliant suite, when a familiar voice called him and a hand detained him.

'What are you doing here, sir, in civilian dress?' asked a deep voice.

It was a cavalry general who had obtained the Emperor's special favour during this campaign, and who had formerly commanded the division in which Rostov was serving.

Rostov in dismay began justifying himself, but seeing the kindly, jocular face of the general, he took him aside and in an excited voice told him the whole affair, asking him to intercede for Denisov, whom the general knew. Having heard Rostov to the end the general shook his head gravely.

'I'm sorry, sorry for that fine fellow. Give me the letter.'

Hardly had Rostov handed him the letter and finished explaining Denisov's case, when hasty steps and the jingling of spurs was heard on the stairs, and the general, leaving him, went to the porch. The gentlemen of the Emperor's suite ran down the stairs and went to their horses. Hayne, the same groom who had been at Austerlitz, led up the Emperor's horse, and the faint creak of a footstep Rostov knew at once, was heard on the stairs. Forgetting the danger of being recognized, Rostov went close to the porch together with some inquisitive civilians, and again after two years saw those features he adored: that same face and same look and step, and the same union of majesty and mildness ... And the feeling of enthusiasm and love for his sovereign rose again in Rostov's soul in all its old force. In the uniform of the Preobrazhensk regiment – white chamios-leather breeches and high boots – and wearing a star Rostov did not know (it was that of the *Légion d'honneur*), the monarch came out into the porch, putting on his gloves and carrying his hat under his arm. He stopped and looked about him, brightening everything around by his glance. He spoke a few words to some of the generals, and recognizing the former commander of Rostov's division smiled and beckoned to him.

All the suite drew back, and Rostov saw the general talking for some time to the Emperor.

The Emperor said a few words to him and took a step towards his horse. Again the crowd of members of the suite and street-gazers (among whom was Rostov) moved nearer to the Emperor. Stopping beside his horse with his hand on the saddle, the Emperor turned to the cavalry general and said in a loud voice, evidently wishing to be heard by all:

'I cannot do it, General. I cannot, because the law is stronger than I,' and he raised his foot to the stirrup.

The general bowed his head respectfully, and the monarch mounted and rode down the street at a gallop. Beside himself with enthusiasm Rostov ran after him with the crowd.

21

THE Emperor rode to the square where, facing one another, a battalion of the Preobrazhensk regiment stood on the right and a battalion of the French Guards in their bearskin caps on the left.

As the Tsar rode up to one flank of the battalions, which presented arms, another group of horsemen galloped up to the opposite flank, and at the head of them Rostov recognized Napoleon. It could be no one else. He came at a gallop, wearing a small hat, a blue uniform open over a white vest, and the St Andrew ribbon over his shoulder. He was riding a very fine thoroughbred grey Arab horse with a crimson gold-embroidered saddle-cloth. On approaching Alexander he raised his hat, and as he did so Rostov, with his cavalryman's eye, could not help noticing that Napoleon did not sit well or firmly in the saddle. The battalions shouted 'Hurrah!' and 'Vive l'Empereur!' Napoleon said something to Alexander, and both Emperors dismounted and took each other's hands. Napoleon's face wore an unpleasant and artificial smile. Alexander was saying something affable to him.

In spite of the trampling of the French gendarmes' horses which were pushing back the crowd, Rostov kept his eyes on every movement of Alexander and Bonaparte. It struck him as a surprise that Alexander treated Bonaparte as an equal and that the latter was quite at ease with the Tsar, as if such relations with an Emperor were an everyday matter to him.

Alexander and Napoleon, with the long train of their suites, approached the right flank of the Preobrazhensk battalion and came straight up to the crowd standing there. The crowd unexpectedly found itself so close to the Emperors that Rostov, standing in the front row, was afraid he might be recognized.

'Sire, I ask your permission to present the Legion of Honour to the bravest of your soldiers,' said a sharp, precise voice articulating every letter.

This was said by the undersized Napoleon, looking up straight into Alexander's eyes. Alexander listened attentively to what was said to him, and bending his head smiled pleasantly.

'To him who has borne himself most bravely in this last war,' added Napoleon, accentuating each syllable, as with a composure and assurance exasperating to Rostov he ran his eye over the Russian ranks drawn up before him, who all presented arms with their eyes fixed on their Emperor.

'Will your Majesty allow me to consult the colonel?' said Alexander and took a few hasty steps towards Prince Kozlovsky, the commander of the battalion.

Bonaparte meanwhile began taking the glove off his small white hand, tore it in so doing and threw it away. An aide-de-camp behind him rushed forward and picked it up.

'To whom shall it be given?' the Emperor Alexander asked Kozlovsky in Russian in a low voice.

'To whomever your Majesty commands.'

The Emperor knit his brows with dissatisfaction, and glancing back remarked:

'But we must give him an answer.'

Kozlovsky scanned the ranks resolutely, and included Rostov in his scrutiny.

'Can it be me?' thought Rostov.

'Lazarev!' the colonel called with a frown, and Lazarev, the first soldier in the rank, stepped briskly forward.

'Where are you off to? Stop here!' voices whispered to Lazarev who did not know where to go. Lazarev stopped, casting a sidelong look at his colonel in alarm. His face twitched, as often happens to soldiers called before the ranks.

Napoleon slightly turned his head, and put his plump little hand out behind him as if to take something. The members of his suite, guessing at once what he wanted, moved about and whispered as they passed something from one to another, and a page – the same one Rostov had seen the previous evening at Boris's – ran forward, and bowing respectfully over the outstretched hand and not keeping it waiting a moment, laid in it an Order on a red ribbon. Napoleon without looking pressed two fingers together and the badge was between them. Then he approached Lazarev (who rolled his eyes and persistently gazed at his own monarch), looked round at the Emperor Alexander to imply that what he was now doing was done for the sake of his ally, and the small white hand holding the Order touched one of Lazarev's buttons. It was as if Napoleon knew that it was only necessary for his hand to deign to touch that soldier's breast for the soldier to be for ever happy, rewarded, and distinguished from everyone else in the world. Napoleon merely laid the cross on Lazarev's breast and, dropping his hand, turned towards Alexander as though sure that the cross would adhere there. And it really did.

Officious hands, Russian and French, immediately seized the cross and fastened it to the uniform. Lazarev glanced morosely at the little man with white hands who was doing something to him, and still standing motionless presenting arms, looked again straight into Alexander's eyes as if asking whether he should stand there, or go away, or do something else. But receiving no orders he remained for some time in that rigid position.

The Emperors remounted and rode away. The Preobrazhensk battalion, breaking rank, mingled with the French Guards and sat down at the tables prepared for them.

Lazarev sat in the place of honour. Russian and French officers embraced him, congratulated him, and pressed his hands. Crowds of officers and civilians drew near merely to see him. A rumble of

439

Russian and French voices and laughter filled the air round the tables in the square. Two officers with flushed faces, looking cheerful and happy, passed by Rostov.

'What d'you think of the treat? All on silver plate,' one of them was saying. 'Have you seen Lazarev?'

'I have.'

'To-morrow, I hear, the Preobrazhenskys will give them a dinner.'

'Yes, but what luck for Lazarev! Twelve hundred francs pension for life.'

'Here's a cap, lads!' shouted a Preobrazhensk soldier, donning a shaggy French cap.

'It's a fine thing! First rate!'

'Have you heard the password?' asked one Guards' officer of another. 'The day before yesterday it was, "Napoléon, France, bravoure"; yesterday, "Alexandre, Russie, grandeur". One day our Emperor gives it and next day Napoleon. To-morrow our Emperor will send a St George's Cross to the bravest of the French Guards. It has to be done. He must respond in kind.'

Boris too with his friend Zhilinski, came to see the Preobrazhensk banquet. On his way back he noticed Rostov standing by the corner of a house.

'Rostov! How d'you do? We missed one another,' he said, and could not refrain from asking what was the matter, so strangely dismal and troubled was Rostov's face.

'Nothing, nothing,' replied Rostov.

'You'll call round?'

'Yes, I will.'

Rostov stood at that corner for a long time, watching the feast from a distance. In his mind a painful process was going on which he could not bring to a conclusion. Terrible doubts rose in his soul. Now he remembered Denisov with his changed expression, his submission, and the whole hospital, with arms and legs torn off and its dirt and disease. So vividly did he recall that hospital stench of dead flesh that he looked round to see where the smell came from. Next he thought of that self-satisfied Bonaparte with his small white hand, who was now an Emperor, liked and respected by Alexander. Then why those severed arms and legs and those dead men? ... Then again he thought of Lazarev rewarded and Denisov punished and unpardoned. He caught himself harbouring such strange thoughts that he was frightened.

The smell of food the Preobrazhenskys were eating, and a sense of hunger, recalled him from these reflections; he had to get something to eat before going away. He went to an hotel he had noticed that morning. There he found so many people, among them officers who like himself had come in civilian clothes, that he had difficulty in getting a dinner. Two officers of his own division joined him. The conversation naturally turned on the peace. The officers, his comrades, like most of the army, were dissatisfied with the peace concluded after the battle of Friedland. They said that had we held out a little longer Napoleon would have been done for, as his troops had neither provisions nor ammunition. Nicholas ate and drank (chiefly the latter) in silence. He finished a couple of bottles of wine by himself. The process in his mind went on tormenting him without reaching a conclusion. He feared to give way to his thoughts yet he could not get rid of them. Suddenly, on one of the officers saying that it was humiliating to look at the French, Rostóv began shouting with uncalled-for warmth, and therefore much to the surprise of the officers:

'How can you judge what's best?' he cried, the blood suddenly rushing to his face. 'How can you judge the Emperor's actions? What right have we to argue? We cannot comprehend either the Emperor's aims or his actions!'

'But I never said a word about the Emperor!' said the officer, justifying himself, and unable to understand Rostóv's outburst except on the supposition that he was drunk.

But Rostóv did not listen to him.

'We are not diplomatic officials, we are soldiers and nothing more,' he went on. 'If we are ordered to die, we must die. If we're punished, it means that we have deserved it, it's not for us to judge. If the Emperor pleases to recognize Bonaparte as Emperor and to conclude an alliance with him, it means that that is the right thing to do. If once we begin judging and arguing about everything, nothing sacred will be left! That way we shall be saying there is no God – nothing!' shouted Nicholas banging the table – very little to the point as it seemed to his listeners, but quite relevantly to the course of his own thoughts.

'Our business is to do our duty, to fight and not to think! That's all . . .' said he.

'And to drink,' said one of the officers, not wishing to quarrel.

'Yes, and to drink,' assented Nicholas. 'Hullo there! Another bottle!' he shouted.

END OF PART TWO

# PART THREE

## 1

IN 1808 the Emperor Alexander went to Erfurt for a fresh interview with the Emperor Napoleon, and in the upper circles of Petersburg there was much talk of the grandeur of this important meeting.

In 1809 the intimacy between 'the world's two arbiters', as Napoleon and Alexander were called, was such that when Napoleon declared war on Austria a Russian corps crossed the frontier to co-operate with our old enemy Bonaparte against our old ally the Emperor of Austria, and in court circles the possibility of marriage between Napoleon and one of Alexander's sisters was spoken of. But besides considerations of foreign policy the attention of Russian society was at that time keenly directed on the internal changes that were being undertaken in all the departments of government.

Life meanwhile – real life, with its essential interests of health and sickness, toil and rest, and its intellectual interests in thought, science, poetry, music, love, friendship, hatred, and passions – went on as usual, independently of and apart from political friendship or enmity with Napoleon Bonaparte and from all the schemes of reconstruction.

\*

Prince Andrew had spent two years continuously in the country.

All the plans Pierre had attempted on his estates – and constantly changing from one thing to another had never accomplished – were carried out by Prince Andrew without display and without perceptible difficulty.

He had in the highest degree a practical tenacity which Pierre lacked, and without fuss or strain on his part this set things going.

On one of his estates the three hundred serfs were liberated and became free agricultural labourers – this being one of the first examples of the kind in Russia. On other estates the serfs' compulsory labour was commuted for a quit-rent. A trained midwife was engaged for Bogucharovo at his expense, and a priest was paid to teach reading and writing to the children of the peasants and household serfs.

Prince Andrew spent half his time at Bald Hills with his father and his son, who was still in the care of nurses. The other half he spent in 'Bogucharovo Cloister', as his father called Prince Andrew's estate. Despite the indifference to the affairs of the world he had expressed to Pierre, he diligently followed all that went on, received many books, and to his surprise noticed that when he or his father had visitors from Petersburg, the very vortex of life, these people lagged behind himself – who never left the country – in knowledge of what was happening in home and foreign affairs.

Besides being occupied with his estates, and reading a great variety of books, Prince Andrew was at this time busy with a critical survey of our last two unfortunate campaigns, and with drawing up a proposal for a reform of the army rules and regulations.

In the spring of 1809 he went to visit the Ryazan estates which his son, whose guardian he was, had inherited.

Warmed by the spring sunshine he sat in the calèche looking at the new grass, the first leaves on the birches and the first puffs of white spring clouds floating across the clear blue sky. He was not thinking of anything, but looked absent-mindedly and cheerfully from side to side.

They crossed the ferry where he had talked with Pierre the year before. They went through the muddy village, past threshing-floors and green fields of winter rye, downhill where snow still lodged near the bridge, uphill where the clay had been liquefied by the rain, past strips of stubble land and bushes touched with green here and there, and into a birch forest growing on both sides of the road. In the forest it was almost hot, no wind could be felt. The birches with their sticky green leaves were motionless, and lilac-coloured flowers and the first blades of green grass were pushing up and lifting last year's leaves. The coarse evergreen colour of the small fir-trees scattered here and there among the birches was an unpleasant reminder of winter. On entering the forest the horses began to snort, and sweated visibly.

Peter the footman made some remark to the coachman; the latter assented. But apparently the coachman's sympathy was not enough for Peter, and he turned on the box towards his master.

'How pleasant it is, your Excellency!' he said with a respectful smile.

'What?'

'It's pleasant, your Excellency!'

'What is he talking about?' thought Prince Andrew. 'Oh, the spring, I suppose,' he thought as he turned round. 'Yes, really everything is green already ... How early! The birches and cherry and alders too are coming out ... But the oaks show no sign yet. Ah, here is one oak!'

At the edge of the road stood an oak. Probably ten times the age of the birches that formed the forest, it was ten times as thick and twice as tall as they. It was an enormous tree, its girth twice as great as a man could embrace, and evidently long ago some of its branches had been broken off and its bark scarred. With its huge ungainly limbs sprawling unsymmetrically, and its gnarled hands and fingers, it stood an aged, stern, and scornful monster among the smiling birch-trees. Only the dead-looking evergreen firs dotted about in the forest, and this oak, refused to yield to the charm of spring, or notice either the spring or the sunshine.

'Spring, love, happiness!' this oak seemed to say. 'Are you not weary of that stupid, meaningless, constantly repeated fraud? Always the same and always a fraud! There is no spring, no sun, no happiness! Look at those cramped dead firs, ever the same, and at me too, sticking out my broken and barked fingers just where they have grown, whether from my back or my sides: as they have grown so I stand, and I do not believe in your hopes and your lies.'

As he passed through the forest Prince Andrew turned several times to look at that oak, as if expecting something from it. Under the oak, too, were flowers and grass, but it stood among them scowling, rigid, misshapen, and grim as ever.

'Yes, the oak is right, a thousand times right,' thought Prince Andrew. 'Let others – the young – yield afresh to that fraud, but we know life, our life is finished!'

A whole sequence of new thoughts, hopeless but mournfully pleasant, rose in his soul in connexion with that tree. During this journey he, as it were, considered his life afresh and arrived at his old conclusion, restful in its hopelessness: that it was not for him to begin anything anew – but that he must live out his life, content to do no harm, and not disturbing himself or desiring anything.

2

PRINCE ANDREW had to see the Marshal of the Nobility for the district in connexion with the affairs of the Ryazan estate of which he was trustee. This Marshal was Count Ilya Rostov, and in the middle of May Prince Andrew went to visit him.

It was now hot spring weather. The whole forest was already

clothed in green. It was dusty, and so hot that on passing near water one longed to bathe.

Prince Andrew, depressed, and preoccupied with the business about which he had to speak to the Marshal, was driving up the avenue in the grounds of the Rostovs' house at Otradnoe. He heard merry girlish cries behind some trees on the right, and saw a group of girls running to cross the path of his calèche. Ahead of the rest and nearer to him ran a dark-haired, remarkably slim, pretty girl in a yellow chintz dress, with a white handkerchief on her head from under which loose locks of hair escaped. The girl was shouting something, but seeing that he was a stranger, ran back laughing without looking at him.

Suddenly, he did not know why, he felt a pang. The day was so beautiful, the sun so bright, everything around so gay, but that slim pretty girl did not know, or wish to know, of his existence and was contented and cheerful in her own separate – probably foolish – but bright and happy life. 'What is she so glad about? What is she thinking of? Not of the military regulations or of the arrangement of the Ryazan serfs' quit-rents. Of what is she thinking? Why is she so happy?' Prince Andrew asked himself with instinctive curiosity.

In 1809 Count Ilya Rostov was living at Otradnoe just as he had done in former years, that is, entertaining almost the whole province with hunts, theatricals, dinners, and music. He was glad to see Prince Andrew, as he was to see any new visitor, and insisted on his staying the night.

During the dull day, in the course of which he was entertained by his elderly hosts and by the more important of the visitors (the old count's house was crowded on account of an approaching name-day), Prince Andrew repeatedly glanced at Natasha, gay and laughing among the younger members of the company, and asked himself each time, 'What is she thinking about? Why is she so glad?'

That night, alone in new surroundings, he was long unable to sleep. He read awhile and then put out his candle, but relit it. It was hot in the room, the inside shutters of which were closed. He was cross with the stupid old man (as he called Rostov), who had made him stay by assuring him that some necessary documents had not yet arrived from town, and he was vexed with himself for having stayed.

He got up and went to the window to open it. As soon as he opened the shutters the moonlight, as if it had long been watching for this, burst into the room. He opened the casement. The night was fresh, bright, and very still. Just before the window was a row of pollard-trees, looking black on one side and with a silvery light

on the other. Beneath the trees grew some kind of lush, wet, bushy
vegetation with silver-lit leaves and stems here and there. Farther
back beyond the dark trees a roof glittered with dew, to the right
was a leafy tree with brilliantly white trunk and branches, and
above it shone the moon, nearly at its full, in a pale, almost starless,
spring sky. Prince Andrew leaned his elbows on the window-ledge
and his eyes rested on that sky.

His room was on the first floor. Those in the rooms above were
also awake. He heard female voices overhead.

'Just once more,' said a girlish voice above him which Prince
Andrew recognized at once.

'But when are you coming to bed?' replied another voice.

'I won't, I can't sleep, what's the use? Come now, for the last
time.'

Two girlish voices sang a musical passage – the end of some
song.

'Oh, how lovely! Now go to sleep, and there's an end of it.'

'You go to sleep, but I can't,' said the first voice, coming nearer
to the window. She was evidently leaning right out, for the rustle
of her dress and even her breathing could be heard. Everything was
stone-still, like the moon and its light and the shadows. Prince
Andrew, too, dared not stir, for fear of betraying his unintentional
presence.

'Sonya! Sonya!' he again heard the first speaker. 'Oh, how can
you sleep? Only look how glorious it is! Ah, how glorious! Do wake
up, Sonya!' she said almost with tears in her voice. 'There never,
never was such a lovely night before!'

Sonya made some reluctant reply.

'Do just come and see what a moon!... Oh, how lovely! Come
here... Darling, sweetheart, come here! There, you see? I feel like
sitting down on my heels, putting my arms round my knees like
this, straining tight, as tight as possible, and flying away! Like
this...'*

'Take care, you'll fall out.'

He heard the sound of a scuffle and Sonya's disapproving voice:
'It's past one o'clock.'

'Oh, you only spoil things for me. All right, go, go!'

Again all was silent, but Prince Andrew knew she was still sitting there. From time to time he heard a soft rustle, and at times a
sigh.

'O God, O God! What does it mean?' she suddenly exclaimed.
'To bed then, if it must be!' and she slammed the casement.

'For her I might as well not exist!' thought Prince Andrew while
he listened to her voice, for some reason expecting yet fearing that

she might say something about him. 'There she is again! As if it were on purpose,' thought he.

In his soul there suddenly arose such an unexpected turmoil of youthful thoughts and hopes, contrary to the whole tenor of his life, that unable to explain his condition to himself he lay down and fell asleep at once.

3

NEXT morning, having taken leave of no one but the count, and not waiting for the ladies to appear, Prince Andrew set off for home.

It was already the beginning of June when on his return journey he drove into the birch forest where the gnarled old oak had made so strange and memorable an impression on him. In the forest the harness-bells sounded yet more muffled than they had done six weeks before, for now all was thick, shady and dense, and the young firs dotted about in the forest did not jar on the general beauty but, lending themselves to the mood around, were delicately green with fluffy young shoots.

The whole day had been hot. Somewhere a storm was gathering, but only a small cloud had scattered some rain-drops lightly, sprinkling the road and the sappy leaves. The left side of the forest was dark in the shade, the right side glittered in the sunlight, wet and shiny and scarcely swayed by the breeze. Everything was in blossom, the nightingales trilled, and their voices reverberated now near now far away.

'Yes, here in this forest was that oak with which I agreed,' thought Prince Andrew. 'But where is it?' he again wondered, gazing at the left side of the road, and without recognizing it he looked with admiration at the very oak he sought. The old oak, quite transfigured, spreading out a canopy of sappy dark-green foliage, stood rapt and slightly trembling in the rays of the evening sun. Neither gnarled fingers nor old scars nor old doubts and sorrows were any of them in evidence now. Through the hard century-old bark, even where there were no twigs, leaves had sprouted such as one could hardly believe the old veteran could have produced.

'Yes, it is the same oak,' thought Prince Andrew, and all at once he was seized by an unreasoning spring-time feeling of joy and renewal. All the best moments of his life suddenly rose to his memory. Austerlitz with the lofty heavens, his wife's dead reproachful face, Pierre at the ferry, that girl thrilled by the beauty of the

448

night, and that night itself and the moon, and ... all this rushed suddenly to his mind.

'No, life is not over at thirty-one!' Prince Andrew suddenly decided finally and decisively. 'It is not enough for me to know what I have in me – everyone must know it: Pierre, and that young girl who wanted to fly away into the sky, everyone must know me, so that my life may not be lived for myself alone while others live so apart from it, but so that it may be reflected in them all, and they and I may live in harmony.'

On reaching home Prince Andrew decided to go to Petersburg that autumn and found all sorts of reasons for this decision. A whole series of sensible and logical considerations showing it to be essential for him to go to Petersburg, and even to re-enter the service, kept springing up in his mind. He could not now understand how he could ever even have doubted the necessity of taking an active share in life, just as a month before he had not understood how the idea of leaving the quiet country could ever enter his head. It now seemed clear to him that all his experience of life must be senselessly wasted unless he applied it to some kind of work and again played an active part in life. He did not even remember how formerly, on the strength of similar wretched logical arguments, it had seemed obvious that he would be degrading himself if he now, after the lessons he had had in life, allowed himself to believe in the possibility of being useful and in the possibility of happiness or love. Now reason suggested quite the opposite. After that journey to Ryazan he found the country dull; his former pursuits no longer interested him, and often when sitting alone in his study he got up, went to the mirror and gazed a long time at his own face. Then he would turn away to the portrait of his dead Lise, who with hair curled *à la grecque* looked tenderly and gaily at him out of the gilt frame. She did not now say those former terrible words to him, but looked simply, merrily, and inquisitively at him. And Prince Andrew, crossing his arms behind him, long paced the room, now frowning now smiling, as he reflected on those irrational, inexpressible thoughts, secret as a crime, which altered his whole life and were connected with Pierre, with fame, with the girl at the window, the oak, and woman's beauty and love. And if anyone came into his room at such moments he was particularly cold, stern, and above all, unpleasantly logical.

'My dear,' Princess Mary entering at such a moment would say, 'little Nicholas can't go out to-day, it's very cold.'

'If it were hot,' Prince Andrew would reply at such times very drily to his sister, 'he could go out in his smock, but as it is cold he must wear warm clothes, which were designed for that purpose. That is what follows from the fact that it is cold; and not that a child who needs fresh air should remain at home,' he would add with extreme logic, as if punishing someone for those secret illogical emotions that stirred within him.

At such moments Princess Mary would think how intellectual work dries men up.

4

PRINCE ANDREW arrived in Petersburg in August 1809. It was the time when the youthful Speransky was at the zenith of his fame* and his reforms were being pushed forward with the greatest energy. That same August the Emperor was thrown from his calèche, injured his leg, and remained three weeks at Peterhof, receiving Speransky every day and no one else. At that time the two famous decrees were being prepared that so agitated society – abolishing court ranks and introducing examinations to qualify for the grades of Collegiate Assessor and State Councillor* – and not merely these but a whole State constitution, intended to change the existing order of government in Russia: legal, administrative, and financial, from the Council of State down to the district tribunals. Now those vague liberal dreams with which the Emperor Alexander had ascended the throne, and which he had tried to put into effect with the aid of his associates, Czartoryski, Novosiltsev, Kochubey, and Stroganov – whom he himself in jest had called his *Comité de salut public* – were taking shape and being realized.

Now all these men were replaced by Speransky on the civil side and Arakcheev* on the military. Soon after his arrival Prince Andrew, as a gentleman of the chamber, presented himself at court and at a levée. The Emperor, though he met him twice, did not favour him with a single word. It had always seemed to Prince Andrew before that he was antipathetic to the Emperor and that the latter disliked his face and personality generally, and in the cold, repellent glance the Emperor gave him, he now found further confirmation of this surmise. The courtiers explained the Emperor's neglect of him by his Majesty's displeasure at Bolkonsky's not having served since 1805.

'I know myself that one cannot help one's sympathies and antipathies,' thought Prince Andrew, 'so it will not do to present my proposal for the reform of the army regulations to the Emperor personally, but the project will speak for itself.'

He mentioned what he had written to an old field-marshal, a

friend of his father's. The field-marshal made an appointment to see him, received him graciously, and promised to inform the Emperor. A few days later Prince Andrew received notice that he was to go to see the Minister of War, Count Arakcheev.

On the appointed day Prince Andrew entered Count Arakcheev's waiting-room at nine in the morning.

He did not know Arakcheev personally, had never seen him, and all he had heard of him inspired him with but little respect for the man.

'He is Minister of War, a man trusted by the Emperor, and I need not concern myself about his personal qualities: he has been commissioned to consider my project, so he alone can get it adopted,' thought Prince Andrew as he waited among a number of important and unimportant people in Count Arakcheev's waiting-room.

During his service, chiefly as an adjutant, Prince Andrew had seen the ante-rooms of many important men, and the different types of such rooms were well known to him. Count Arakcheev's ante-room had quite a special character. The faces of the unimportant people awaiting their turn for an audience showed embarrassment and servility; the faces of those of higher rank expressed a common feeling of awkwardness, covered by a mask of unconcern and ridicule of themselves, their situation, and the person for whom they were waiting. Some walked thoughtfully up and down, others whispered and laughed. Prince Andrew heard the nickname 'Sila Andreevich'* and the words, '*Uncle* will give it us hot,' in reference to Count Arakcheev. One general (an important personage) evidently feeling offended at having to wait so long, sat crossing and uncrossing his legs and smiling contemptuously to himself.

But the moment the door opened one feeling alone appeared on all faces – that of fear. Prince Andrew for the second time asked the adjutant on duty to take in his name, but received an ironical look and was told that his turn would come in due course. After some others had been shown in and out of the minister's room by the adjutant on duty, an officer who struck Prince Andrew by his humiliated and frightened air was admitted at that terrible door. This officer's audience lasted a long time. Then suddenly the grating sound of a harsh voice was heard from the other side of the door, and the officer – with pale face and trembling lips – came out and passed through the waiting-room clutching his head.

After this Prince Andrew was conducted to the door and the officer on duty said in a whisper. 'To the right, at the window.'

Prince Andrew entered a plain tidy room, and saw at the table

451

a man of forty with a long waist, a long closely cropped head, deep wrinkles, scowling brows above dull greenish-hazel eyes, and an overhanging red nose. Arakcheev turned his head towards him without looking at him.

'What is your petition?' asked Arakcheev.

'I am not petitioning, your Excellency,' returned Prince Andrew quietly.

Arakcheev's eyes turned towards him.

'Sit down,' said he. 'Prince Bolkonsky?'

'I am not petitioning about anything. His Majesty the Emperor has deigned to send your Excellency a project submitted by me...'

'You see, my dear sir, I have read your project,' interrupted Arakcheev, uttering only the first words amiably and then – again without looking at Prince Andrew – relapsing gradually into a tone of grumbling contempt. 'You are proposing new military laws? There are many laws but no one to carry out the old ones. Nowadays everybody designs laws, it is easier writing than doing.'

'I came at his Majesty the Emperor's wish to learn from your Excellency how you propose to deal with the memorandum I have presented,' said Prince Andrew politely.

'I have endorsed a resolution on your memorandum and sent it to the Committee. I do *not* approve of it,' said Arakcheev rising and taking a paper from his writing-table. 'Here!' and he handed it to Prince Andrew.

Across the paper was scrawled in pencil, without capital letters, misspelt, and without punctuation: 'Unsoundly constructed because resembles an imitation of the French military code and from the Articles of War needlessly deviating.'

'To what Committee has the memorandum been referred?' inquired Prince Andrew.

'To the Committee on Army Regulations, and I have recommended that your honour should be appointed a member, but without a salary.'

Prince Andrew smiled.

'I don't want one.'

'A member without salary,' repeated Arakcheev. 'I have the honour... Eh! Call the next one! Who else is there?' he shouted, bowing to Prince Andrew.

WHILE waiting for the announcement of his appointment to the Committee, Prince Andrew looked up his former acquaintances, particularly those he knew to be in power and whose aid he might need. In Petersburg he now experienced the same feeling he had had on the eve of a battle, when troubled by anxious curiosity and irresistibly attracted to the ruling circles where the future, on which the fate of millions depended, was being shaped. From the irritation of the older men, the curiosity of the uninitiated, the reserve of the initiated, the hurry and preoccupation of everyone, and the innumerable committees and commissions of whose existence he learnt every day, he felt that now, in 1809, here in Petersburg a vast civil conflict was in preparation, the commander-in-chief of which was a mysterious person he did not know, but who was supposed to be a man of genius – Speransky. And this movement of reconstruction of which Prince Andrew had a vague idea, and Speransky its chief promoter, began to interest him so keenly that the question of the army regulations quickly receded to a secondary place in his consciousness.

Prince Andrew was most favourably placed to secure a good reception in the highest and most diverse Petersburg circles of the day. The reforming party cordially welcomed and courted him, in the first place because he was reputed to be clever and very well-read, and secondly because by liberating his serfs he had obtained the reputation of being a liberal. The party of the old and dissatisfied, who censured the innovations, turned to him expecting his sympathy in their disapproval of the reforms, simply because he was the son of his father. The feminine society world welcomed him gladly, because he was rich, distinguished, a good match, and almost a newcomer, with a halo of romance on account of his supposed death and the tragic loss of his wife. Besides this the general opinion of all who had known him previously was that he had greatly improved during these last five years, having softened and grown more manly, lost his former affectation, pride and contemptuous irony, and acquired the serenity that comes with years. People talked about him, were interested in him, and wanted to meet him.

The day after his interview with Count Arakcheev, Prince Andrew spent the evening at Count Kochubey's.* He told the count of his interview with *Sila Andreevich* (Kochubey spoke of Arakcheev by that nickname with the same vague irony Prince Andrew had noticed in the Minister of War's ante-room).

'*Mon cher*, even in this case you can't do without Michael Mikhaylovich Speransky. He manages everything. I'll speak to him. He has promised to come this evening.'

'What has Speransky to do with the army regulations?' asked Prince Andrew.

Kochubey shook his head smilingly, as if surprised at Bolkonsky's simplicity.

'We were talking to him about you a few days ago,' Kochubey continued, 'and about your free ploughmen.'

'Oh, is it you, Prince, who have freed your serfs?' said an old man of Catherine's day, turning contemptuously towards Bolkonsky.

'It was a small estate that brought in no profit,' replied Prince Andrew, trying to extenuate his action so as not to irritate the old man uselessly.

'Afraid of being late . . .' said the old man, looking at Kochubey.

'There's one thing I don't understand,' he continued. 'Who will plough the land if they are set free? It is easy to write laws, but difficult to rule . . . Just the same as now – I ask you, Count – who will be heads of the departments when everybody has to pass examinations?'

'Those who pass the examinations, I suppose,' replied Kochubey crossing his legs and glancing round.

'Well, I have Pryanichnikov serving under me, a splendid man, a priceless man, but he's sixty. Is he to go up for examination?'

'Yes, that's a difficulty, as education is not at all general, but . . .'

Count Kochubey did not finish. He rose, took Prince Andrew by the arm, and went to meet a tall, bald, fair man of about forty with a large open forehead and a long face of unusual and peculiar whiteness, who was just entering. The newcomer wore a blue swallow-tail coat with a cross suspended from his neck and a star on his left breast. It was Speransky. Prince Andrew recognized him at once, and felt a throb within him, as happens at critical moments of life. Whether it was from respect, envy, or anticipation, he did not know. Speransky's whole figure was of a peculiar type that made him easily recognizable. In the society in which Prince Andrew lived he had never seen anyone who together with awkward and clumsy gestures possessed such calmness and self-assurance; he had never seen so resolute yet gentle an expression as that in those half-closed, rather humid eyes, or so firm a smile that expressed nothing; nor had he heard such a refined, smooth, soft voice; above all he had never seen such delicate whiteness of face or hands – hands which were broad, but very plump, soft, and white. Such whiteness and softness Prince Andrew had only seen on the faces of soldiers who had been long in hospital. This was

454

Speransky, Secretary of State, reporter to the Emperor and his companion at Erfurt, where he had more than once met and talked with Napoleon.

Speransky did not shift his eyes from one face to another as people involuntarily do on entering a large company, and was in no hurry to speak. He spoke slowly, with assurance that he would be listened to, and he looked only at the person with whom he was conversing.

Prince Andrew followed Speransky's every word and movement with particular attention. As happens to some people, especially to men who judge those near to them severely, he always on meeting anyone new – especially anyone whom, like Speransky, he knew by reputation – expected to discover in him the perfection of human qualities.

Speransky told Kochubey he was sorry he had been unable to come sooner, as he had been detained at the palace. He did not say that the Emperor had kept him, and Prince Andrew noticed this affectation of modesty. When Kochubey introduced Prince Andrew, Speransky slowly turned his eyes to Bolkonsky with his customary smile, and looked at him in silence.

'I am very glad to make your acquaintance. I had heard of you, as everyone has,' he said after a pause.

Kochubey said a few words about the reception Arakcheev had given Bolkonsky. Speransky smiled more markedly.

'The chairman of the Committee on Army Regulations is my good friend Monsieur Magnitsky,' he said, fully articulating every word and syllable, 'and if you like I can put you in touch with him.' He paused at the full stop. 'I hope you will find him sympathetic, and ready to co-operate in promoting all that is reasonable.'

A circle soon formed round Speransky, and the old man who had talked about his subordinate Pryanichnikov addressed a question to him.

Prince Andrew without joining in the conversation watched every movement of Speransky's: this man, not long since an insignificant divinity student, who now, Bolkonsky thought, held in his hands – those plump white hands – the fate of Russia. Prince Andrew was struck by the extraordinarily disdainful composure with which Speransky answered the old man. He appeared to address condescending words to him from an immeasurable height. When the old man began to speak too loud, Speransky smiled and said he could not judge of the advantage or disadvantage of what pleased the sovereign.

Having talked for a little while in the general circle, Speransky rose and coming up to Prince Andrew took him along to the other end of the room. It was clear that he thought it necessary to interest himself in Bolkonsky.

'I had no chance to talk with you, Prince, during the animated conversation in which that venerable gentleman involved me,' he said with a mildly contemptuous smile, as if intimating by that smile that he and Prince Andrew understood the insignificance of the people with whom he had just been talking. This flattered Prince Andrew. 'I have known of you for a long time: first from your action with regard to your serfs, a first example, of which it is very desirable that there should be more imitators; and secondly because you are one of those gentlemen of the chamber who have not considered themselves offended by the new decree concerning the ranks allotted to courtiers, which is causing so much gossip and tittle-tattle.'

'No,' said Prince Andrew, 'my father did not wish me to take advantage of the privilege. I began the service from the lower grade.'

'Your father, a man of the last century, evidently stands above our contemporaries who so condemn this measure which merely re-establishes natural justice.'

'I think, however, that these condemnations have some ground,' returned Prince Andrew, trying to resist Speransky's influence, of which he began to be conscious. He did not like to agree with him in everything and felt a wish to contradict. Though he usually spoke easily and well, he felt a difficulty in expressing himself now while talking with Speransky. He was too much absorbed in observing the famous man's personality.

'Grounds of personal ambition maybe,' Speransky put in quietly.

'And of state-interest to some extent,' said Prince Andrew.

'What do you mean?' asked Speransky quietly, lowering his eyes.

'I am an admirer of Montesquieu,'* replied Prince Andrew, 'and his idea that *le principe des monarchies est l'honneur, me paraît incontestable. Certains droits et privilèges de la noblesse me paraissent être des moyens de soutenir ce sentiment.*'

The smile vanished from Speransky's white face, which was much improved by the change. Probably Prince Andrew's thought interested him.

'*Si vous envisagez la question sous ce point de vue,*' he began, pronouncing French with evident difficulty, and speaking even slower than in Russian but quite calmly.

Speransky went on to say that honour, *l'honneur,* cannot be upheld by privileges harmful to the service; that honour, *l'honneur,* is either a negative concept of not doing what is blameworthy, or it is a source of emulation in pursuit of commendation and rewards, which recognize it. His arguments were concise, simple, and clear.

456

'An institution upholding honour, the source of emulation, is one similar to the *Légion d'honneur* of the great Emperor Napoleon, not harmful but helpful to the success of the service, but not a class or court privilege.'

'I do not dispute that, but it cannot be denied that court privileges have attained the same end,' returned Prince Andrew. 'Every courtier considers himself bound to maintain his position worthily.'

'Yet you do not care to avail yourself of the privilege, Prince,' said Speransky, indicating by a smile that he wished to finish amiably an argument which was embarrassing for his companion. 'If you will do me the honour of calling on me on Wednesday,' he added, 'I will, after talking with Magnitsky, let you know what may interest you, and shall also have the pleasure of a more detailed chat with you.'

Closing his eyes, he bowed *à la française*, without taking leave, and trying to attract as little attention as possible, he left the room.

## 6

DURING the first weeks of his stay in Petersburg Prince Andrew felt the whole trend of thought he had formed during his life of seclusion quite overshadowed by the trifling cares that engrossed him in that city.

On returning home in the evening he would jot down in his notebook four or five necessary calls or appointments for certain hours. The mechanism of life, the arrangement of the day so as to be in time everywhere, absorbed the greater part of his vital energy. He did nothing, did not even think or find time to think, but only talked, and talked successfully, of what he had thought while in the country.

He sometimes noticed with dissatisfaction that he repeated the same remark on the same day in different circles. But he was so busy for whole days together that he had no time to notice that he was thinking of nothing.

As he had done on their first meeting at Kochubey's, Speransky produced a strong impression on Prince Andrew on the Wednesday, when he received him *tête-a-tête* at his own house and talked to him long and confidentially.

To Bolkonsky so many people appeared contemptible and insignificant creatures, and he so longed to find in someone the living ideal of that perfection towards which he strove, that he readily believed that in Speransky he had found this ideal of a perfectly rational and virtuous man. Had Speransky sprung from the same class as himself and possessed the same breeding and traditions, Bolkonsky would soon have discovered his weak, human, unheroic sides; but as it was, Speransky's strange and logical turn of mind inspired him with respect all the more because he did not quite understand him. Moreover Speransky, either because he appreciated the other's capacity or because he considered it necessary to win him to his side, showed off his dispassionate calm reasonableness before Prince Andrew and flattered him with that subtle flattery which goes hand in hand with self-assurance, and consists in a tacit assumption that one's companion is the only man besides oneself capable of understanding the folly of the rest of mankind, and the reasonableness and profundity of one's own ideas.

During their long conversation on Wednesday evening, Speransky more than once remarked: 'We regard everything that is above the common level of rooted custom'...; or, with a smile: 'But we want the wolves to be fed and the sheep to be safe...' or: 'They cannot understand this...' and all in a way that seemed to say: 'We, you and I, understand what they are and who we are.'

This first long conversation with Speransky only strengthened in Prince Andrew the feeling he had experienced towards him at their first meeting. He saw in him a remarkable, clear-thinking man of vast intellect who by his energy and persistence had attained power, which he was using solely for the welfare of Russia. In Prince Andrew's eyes Speransky was the man he would himself have wished to be – one who explained all the facts of life reasonably, considered important only what was rational, and was capable of applying the standard of reason to everything. Everything seemed so simple and clear in Speransky's exposition that Prince Andrew involuntarily agreed with him about everything. If he replied and argued, it was only because he wished to maintain his independence and not submit to Speransky's opinions entirely. Everything was right and everything was as it should be: only one thing disconcerted Prince Andrew. This was Speransky's cold, mirror-like look, which did not allow one to penetrate to his soul, and his delicate white hands, which Prince Andrew involuntarily watched as one does watch the hands of those who possess power. This mirror-like gaze and those delicate hands irritated Prince Andrew, he knew not why. He was unpleasantly struck, too, by the excessive contempt for others that he observed in Speransky, and by the diversity of lines of argument he used to support his opinions. He made use of every kind of mental device, except analogy, and passed too boldly, it seemed to Prince Andrew, from one to another. Now he would take up the position of a practical man and condemn dreamers; now that of a satirist, and laugh ironically at his opponents; now grow severely logical, or suddenly rise to the realm of metaphysics. (This last resource was one he very frequently employed.) He would transfer a question to metaphysical heights, pass on to definitions of space, time, and thought, and having deduced the refutation he needed, would again descend to the level of the original discussion.

In general the trait of Speransky's mentality which struck Prince Andrew most was his absolute and unshakable belief in the power and authority of reason. It was evident that the thought could never occur to him which to Prince Andrew seemed so natural, namely, that it is after all impossible to express all one thinks; and that he had never felt the doubt, 'Is not all I think and believe nonsense?' And it was just this peculiarity of Speransky's mind that particularly attracted Prince Andrew.

During the first period of their acquaintance Bolkonsky felt a passionate admiration for him similar to that which he had once felt for Bonaparte. The fact that Speransky was the son of a village priest, and that stupid people might meanly despise him on account of his humble origin (as in fact many did), caused Prince Andrew to cherish his sentiment for him the more, and unconsciously to strengthen it.

On that first evening Bolkonsky spent with him, having mentioned the Commission for the Revision of the Code of Laws, Speransky told him sarcastically that the Commission had existed for a hundred and fifty years, had cost millions, and had done nothing except that Rosenkampf had stuck labels on the corresponding paragraphs of the different codes.

'And that is all the State has for the millions it has spent,' said he. 'We want to give the Senate new juridical powers, but we have no laws. That is why it is a sin for men like you, Prince, not to serve in these times!'

Prince Andrew said that for that work an education in jurisprudence was needed which he did not possess.

'But nobody possesses it, so what would you have? It is a vicious circle from which we must break a way out.'

A week later Prince Andrew was a member of the Committee on Army Regulations, and – what he had not at all expected – was chairman of a section of the Committee for the revision of the laws. At Speransky's request he took the first part of the Civil Code that was being drawn up, and with the aid of the *Code Napoléon* and the Institutes of Justinian he worked at formulating the section on Personal Rights.

## 7

NEARLY two years before this, in 1808, Pierre on returning to Petersburg after visiting his estates had involuntarily found himself in a leading position among the Petersburg Freemasons. He arranged dining and funeral Lodge meetings, enrolled new members, and busied himself uniting various Lodges and acquiring authentic charters. He gave money for the erection of temples, and supplemented as far as he could the collection of alms, in regard to which the majority of members were stingy and irregular. He supported almost single-handed a poorhouse the Order had founded in Petersburg.

His life meanwhile continued as before, with the same infatuations and dissipations. He liked to dine and drink well, and though he considered it immoral and humiliating could not resist the temptations of the bachelor circles in which he moved.

Amid the turmoil of his activities and distractions, however, Pierre at the end of a year began to feel that the more firmly he tried to rest upon it, the more the masonic ground on which he stood gave way under him. At the same time he felt that the deeper the ground sank under him the closer bound he involuntarily became to the Order. When he had joined the Freemasons he had experienced the feeling of one who confidently steps onto the smooth surface of a bog. When he put his foot down it sank in. To make quite sure of the firmness of the ground, he put his other foot down and sank deeper still, became stuck in it, and involuntarily waded knee-deep in the bog.

Joseph Alexeevich was not in Petersburg – he had of late stood aside from the affairs of the Petersburg Lodges and lived almost entirely in Moscow. All the members of the Lodges were men Pierre knew in ordinary life, and it was difficult for him to regard them merely as Brothers in Freemasonry and not as Prince B. or Ivan Vasilevich D., whom he knew in society mostly as weak and insignificant men. Under the masonic aprons and insignia he saw the uniforms and decorations at which they aimed in ordinary life. Often after collecting alms, and reckoning up twenty to thirty rubles received for the most part in promises from a dozen members, of whom half were as well able to pay as himself, Pierre remembered the masonic vow in which each Brother promised to devote all his belongings to his neighbour, and doubts, on which he tried not to dwell, arose in his soul.

He divided the Brothers he knew into four categories. In the first he put those who did not take an active part in the affairs of the Lodges or in human affairs, but were exclusively occupied with the mystical science of the Order: with questions of the threefold designation of God, the three primordial elements – sulphur, mercury, and salt* – or the meaning of the square and all the various figures of the temple of Solomon. Pierre respected this class of Brothers, to which the elder ones chiefly belonged, including, Pierre thought, Joseph Alexeevich himself, but he did not share their interests. His heart was not in the mystical aspect of Freemasonry.

In the second category Pierre reckoned himself and others like him, seeking and vacillating, who had not yet found in Freemasonry a straight and comprehensible path, but hoped to do so.

In the third category he included those Brothers (the majority) who saw nothing in Freemasonry but the external forms and ceremonies, and prized the strict performance of these forms without troubling about their purport or significance. Such were Willarski and even the Grand Master of the principal Lodge.

Finally, to the fourth category also a great many Brothers belonged, particularly those who had lately joined. These according to Pierre's observation were men who had no belief in anything, nor desire for anything, but joined the Freemasons merely to associate with the wealthy young Brothers who were influential through their connexions or rank, and of whom there were very many in the Lodge.

Pierre began to feel dissatisfied with what he was doing. Freemasonry, at any rate as he saw it here, sometimes seemed to him based merely on externals. He did not think of doubting Freemasonry itself, but suspected that Russian Masonry had taken a wrong path and deviated from its original principles. And so towards the end of the year he went abroad to be initiated into the higher secrets of the Order.

In the summer of 1809 Pierre returned to Petersburg. Our Freemasons knew from correspondence with those abroad that Bezukhov had obtained the confidence of many highly placed persons, had been initiated into many mysteries, had been raised to a higher grade, and was bringing back with him much that might conduce to the advantage of the masonic cause in Russia. The Petersburg Freemasons all came to see him, tried to ingratiate themselves with him, and it seemed to them all that he was preparing something for them and concealing it.

A solemn meeting of the Lodge of the second degree was convened, at which Pierre promised to communicate to the Petersburg Brothers what he had to deliver to them from the highest

461

leaders of their Order. The meeting was a full one. After the usual ceremonies Pierre rose and began his address.

'Dear Brothers,' he began, blushing and stammering, with a written speech in his hand, 'it is not sufficient to observe our mysteries in the seclusion of our Lodge – we must act – act! We are drowsing, but we must act.' Pierre raised his notebook and began to read.

'For the dissemination of pure truth and to secure the triumph of virtue,' he read, 'we must cleanse men from prejudice, diffuse principles in harmony with the spirit of the times, undertake the education of the young, unite ourselves in indissoluble bonds with the wisest men, boldly yet prudently overcome superstitions, infidelity, and folly, and form of those devoted to us a body linked together by unity of purpose and possessed of authority and power.

'To attain this end we must ensure a preponderance of virtue over vice, and must endeavour to secure that the honest man may, even in this world, receive a lasting reward for his virtue. But in these great endeavours we are gravely hampered by the political institutions of to-day. What is to be done in these circumstances? To favour revolutions, overthrow everything, repel force by force? ...No! We are very far from that. Every violent reform deserves censure, for it quite fails to remedy evil while men remain what they are, and also because wisdom needs no violence.

'The whole plan of our Order should be based on the idea of preparing men of firmness and virtue bound together by unity of conviction – aiming at the punishment of vice and folly, and patronizing talent and virtue: raising worthy men from the dust and attaching them to our Brotherhood. Only then will our Order have the power unobtrusively to bind the hands of the protectors of disorder and to control them without their being aware of it. In a word, we must found a form of government holding universal sway, which should be diffused over the whole world without destroying the bonds of citizenship, and beside which all other governments can continue in their customary course and do everything except what impedes the great aim of our Order, which is to obtain for virtue the victory over vice. This aim was that of Christianity itself. It taught men to be wise and good, and for their own benefit to follow the example and instruction of the best and wisest men.

'At that time, when everything was plunged in darkness, preaching alone was of course sufficient. The novelty of Truth endowed her with special strength, but now we need much more powerful methods. It is now necessary that man governed by his senses should find in virtue a charm palpable to those senses. It is im-

462

possible to eradicate the passions; but we must strive to direct them to a noble aim, and it is therefore necessary that everyone should be able to satisfy his passions within the limits of virtue. Our Order should provide means to that end.

'As soon as we have a certain number of worthy men in every State, each of them again training two others and all being closely united, everything will be possible for our Order, which has already in secret accomplished much for the welfare of mankind.'

This speech not only made a strong impression, but created excitement in the Lodge. The majority of the Brothers, seeing in it dangerous designs of Illuminism,* met it with a coldness that surprised Pierre. The Grand Master began answering him, and Pierre began developing his views with more and more warmth. It was long since there had been so stormy a meeting. Parties were formed, some accusing Pierre of Illuminism, others supporting him. At that meeting he was struck for the first time by the endless variety of men's minds, which prevents a truth from ever presenting itself identically to two persons. Even those members who seemed to be on his side understood him in their own way, with limitations and alterations he could not agree to, as what he always wanted most was to convey his thought to others just as he himself understood it.

At the end of the meeting the Grand Master reproved Bezukhov with irony and ill will for his vehemence, and said it was not love of virtue alone, but also a love of strife that had moved him in the dispute. Pierre did not answer him, and asked briefly whether his proposal would be accepted. He was told that it would not, and without waiting for the usual formalities he left the Lodge and went home.

8

AGAIN Pierre was overtaken by the depression he so dreaded. For three days after the delivery of his speech at the Lodge* he lay on a sofa at home receiving no one and going nowhere.

It was just then that he received a letter from his wife, who implored him to see her, telling him how grieved she was about him and how she wished to devote her whole life to him.

At the end of the letter she informed him that in a few days she would return to Petersburg from abroad.

Following this letter one of the masonic Brothers whom Pierre respected less than the others forced his way in to see him and turning the conversation upon Pierre's matrimonial affairs, by way of fraternal advice expressed the opinion that his severity to his wife was wrong, and that he was neglecting one of the first rules of Freemasonry by not forgiving the penitent.

At the same time his mother-in-law, Prince Vasili's wife, sent to him imploring him to come if only for a few minutes to discuss a most important matter. Pierre saw that there was a conspiracy against him and that they wanted to reunite him with his wife, and in the mood he then was in, this was not even unpleasant to him. Nothing mattered to him. Nothing in life seemed to him of much importance, and under the influence of the depression that possessed him he valued neither his liberty nor his resolution to punish his wife.

'No one is right and no one is to blame; so she too is not to blame,' he thought.

If he did not at once give his consent to a reunion with his wife, it was only because in his state of depression he did not feel able to take any step. Had his wife come to him, he would not have turned her away. Compared to what preoccupied him, was it not a matter of indifference whether he lived with his wife or not?

Without replying either to his wife or his mother-in-law, Pierre late one night prepared for a journey and started for Moscow to see Joseph Alexeevich. This is what he noted in his diary:

*Moscow, 17th November.*
I have just returned from my benefactor, and hasten to write down what I have experienced. Joseph Alexeevich is living poorly and has for three years been suffering from a painful disease of the bladder. No one has ever heard him utter a groan or a word of complaint. From morning till late at night, except when he eats his very plain food, he is working at science. He received me graciously and made me sit down on the bed on which he lay. I made the sign of the Knights of the East and of Jerusalem, and he responded in the same manner, asking me with a mild smile what I had learned and gained in the Prussian and Scottish Lodges. I told him everything as best I could, and told him what I had proposed to our Petersburg Lodge, of the bad reception I had encountered, and of my rupture with the Brothers. Joseph Alexeevich, having remained silent and thoughtful for a good while, told me his view of the matter, which at once lit up for me my whole past, and the future path I should follow. He surprised me by asking whether I remembered the threefold aim of the Order: (1) The preservation and study of the mystery. (2) The purification and reformation of oneself for its reception, and (3) The improvement of the human race by striving for such purification. Which is the principal *aim* of these three? Certainly self-reformation and self-purification. Only to this aim can we always strive independently of circumstances. But at the same time, just this aim demands

the greatest efforts of us; and so, led astray by pride, losing sight of this aim, we occupy ourselves either with the mystery which in our impurity we are unworthy to receive, or seek the reformation of the human race while ourselves setting an example of baseness and profligacy. Illuminism is not a pure doctrine just because it is attracted by social activity and puffed up by pride. On this ground Joseph Alexeevich condemned my speech and my whole activity, and in the depth of my soul I agreed with him. Talking of my family affairs he said to me, 'the chief duty of a true Mason, as I have told you, lies in perfecting himself. We often think that by removing all the difficulties of our life we shall more quickly reach our aim, but on the contrary, my dear sir, it is only in the midst of worldly cares that we can attain our three chief aims: (1) Self-knowledge – for man can only know himself by comparison. (2) Self-perfecting, which can only be attained by conflict, and (3) The attainment of the chief virtue – love of death. Only the vicissitudes of life can show us its vanity, and develop our innate love of death or of rebirth to a new life.' These words are all the more remarkable because, in spite of his great physical sufferings, Joseph Alexeevich is never weary of life though he loves death, for which – in spite of the purity and loftiness of his inner man – he does not yet feel himself sufficiently prepared. My benefactor then explained to me fully the meaning of the Great Square of creation, and pointed out to me that the numbers three and seven are the basis of everything. He advised me not to avoid intercourse with the Petersburg Brothers, but to take up only second-grade posts in the Lodge, to try, while diverting the Brothers from pride, to turn them towards the true path of self-knowledge and self-perfecting. Besides this he advised me for myself personally above all to keep a watch over myself, and to that end he gave me a notebook, the one I am now writing in, and in which I will in future note down all my actions.

*Petersburg, 23rd November.*
I am again living with my wife. My mother-in-law came to me in tears and said that Hélène was here and that she implored me to hear her; that she was innocent and unhappy at my desertion, and much more. I knew that if I once let myself see her I should not have strength to go on refusing what she wanted. In my perplexity I did not know whose aid and advice to seek. Had my benefactor been here he would have told me what to do. I went to my room and re-read Joseph Alexeevich's letters and recalled my conversations with him, and deduced from it all that I ought not to refuse a suppliant, and ought to reach out a helping hand to everyone – especially to one so closely bound to me – and that I must bear my cross. But if I forgive her for the sake of doing right, then let union with her have only a spiritual aim. That is what I decided, and what I wrote to Joseph Alexeevich. I told my wife that I begged her to forget the past, to forgive me whatever wrong I may have done her, and that I had nothing to forgive. It gave me joy to tell her this. She need not

465

know how hard it was for me to see her again. I have settled on the upper floor of this big house, and am experiencing a happy feeling of regeneration.

## 9

AT that time, as always happens, the highest society that met at Court and at the grand balls was divided into several circles, each with its own particular tone. The largest of these was the French circle of the Napoleonic alliance, the circle of Count Rumyantsev and Caulaincourt.* In this group Hélène, as soon as she had settled in Petersburg with her husband, took a very prominent place. She was visited by the members of the French embassy and by many belonging to that circle and noted for their intellect and polished manners.

Hélène had been at Erfurt* during the famous meeting of the Emperors, and had brought from there these connexions with the Napoleonic notabilities. At Erfurt her success had been brilliant. Napoleon himself had noticed her in the theatre, and said of her: 'C'est un superbe animal.' Her success as a beautiful and elegant woman did not surprise Pierre, for she had become even handsomer than before. What did surprise him was that during these last two years his wife had succeeded in gaining the reputation 'd'une femme charmante, aussi spirituelle que belle'. The distinguished Prince de Ligne* wrote her eight-page letters. Bilibin saved up his epigrams to produce them in Countess Bezukhova's presence. To be received in the Countess Bezukhova's salon was regarded as a diploma of intellect. Young men read books before attending Hélène's evenings, to have something to say in her salon, and secretaries of the embassy, and even ambassadors, confided diplomatic secrets to her, so that in a way Hélène was a power. Pierre, who knew she was very stupid, sometimes attended, with a strange feeling of perplexity and fear, her evenings and dinner parties, where politics, poetry, and philosophy were discussed. At these parties his feelings were like those of a conjuror who always expects his trick to be found out at any moment. But whether because stupidity was just what was needed to run such a salon, or because those who were deceived found pleasure in the deception, at any rate it remained unexposed and Hélène Bezukhova's reputation as a lovely and clever woman became so firmly established that she could say the emptiest and stupidest things and yet everybody would go into raptures over every word of hers, and look for a profound meaning in it of which she herself had no conception.

Pierre was just the husband needed for a brilliant society woman. He was that absent-minded crank, a *grand seigneur* husband who was in no one's way, and far from spoiling the high tone and general impression of the drawing-room, he served, by the contrast he presented to her, as an advantageous background to his elegant and tactful wife. Pierre during the last two years, as a result of his continual absorption in abstract interests and his sincere contempt for all else, had acquired in his wife's circle, which did not interest him, that air of unconcern, indifference, and benevolence towards all, which cannot be acquired artificially, and therefore inspires involuntary respect. He entered his wife's drawing-room as one enters a theatre, was acquainted with everybody, equally pleased to see everyone and equally indifferent to them all. Sometimes he joined in a conversation which interested him and, regardless of whether any 'gentlemen of the embassy' were present or not, lispingly expressed his views, which were sometimes not at all in accord with the accepted tone of the moment. But the general opinion concerning the queer husband of 'the most distinguished woman in Petersburg' was so well established that no one took his freaks seriously.

Among the many young men who frequented her house every day, Boris Drubetskoy, who had already achieved great success in the service, was the most intimate friend of the Bezukhov household since Hélène's return from Erfurt. Hélène spoke of him as '*mon page*', and treated him like a child. Her smile for him was the same as for everybody, but sometimes that smile made Pierre uncomfortable. Towards him, Boris behaved with a particularly dignified and sad deference. This shade of deference also disturbed Pierre. He had suffered so painfully three years before from the mortification to which his wife had subjected him, that he now protected himself from the danger of its repetition, first by not being a husband to his wife, and secondly by not allowing himself to suspect.

'No, now that she has become a blue-stocking she has finally renounced her former infatuations,' he told himself. 'There has never been an instance of a blue-stocking being carried away by affairs of the heart' – a statement which, though gathered from an unknown source, he believed implicitly. Yet strange to say Boris's presence in his wife's drawing-room (and he was almost always there) had a physical effect upon Pierre; it constricted his limbs and destroyed the unconsciousness and freedom of his movements.

'What a strange antipathy,' thought Pierre, 'yet I used to like him very much.'

In the eyes of the world Pierre was a great gentleman, the rather

467

blind and absurd husband of a distinguished wife, a clever crank who did nothing, but harmed nobody, and was a first-rate, good-natured fellow. But a complex and difficult process of internal development was taking place all this time in Pierre's soul, revealing much to him and causing him many spiritual doubts and joys.

## 10

PIERRE went on with his diary, and this is what he wrote in it during that time:

*24th November.*
Got up at eight, read the Scriptures, then went to my duties.

(By Joseph Alexeevich's advice Pierre had entered the service of the State and served on one of the committees.)

Returned home for dinner and dined alone – the countess had many visitors I do not like. I ate and drank moderately, and after dinner copied out some passages for the Brothers. In the evening I went down to the countess and told a funny story about B., and only remembered that I ought not to have done so when everybody laughed loudly at it.

I am going to bed with a happy and tranquil mind. Great God, help me to walk in Thy paths, (1) to conquer anger by calmness and deliberation, (2) to vanquish lust by self-restraint and repulsion, (3) to withdraw from worldliness, but not avoid (a) the service of the State, (b) family duties, (c) relations with my friends, and (d) the management of my affairs.

*27th November.*
I got up late. On waking I lay long in bed yielding to sloth. O God, help and strengthen me that I may walk in Thy ways! Read the Scriptures, but without proper feeling. Brother Urusov came and we talked about worldly vanities. He told me of the Emperor's new projects. I began to criticize them, but remembered my rules and my benefactor's words – that a true Freemason should be a zealous worker for the State when his aid is required and a quiet onlooker when not called on to assist. My tongue is my enemy. Brothers G. V. and O. visited me and we had a preliminary talk about the reception of a new Brother. They laid on me the duty of Rhetor. I feel myself weak and unworthy. Then our talk turned to the interpretation of the seven pillars and steps of the Temple, the seven sciences, the seven virtues, the seven vices, and the seven gifts of the Holy Spirit. Brother O. was very eloquent. In the evening the admission took place. The new decoration of the premises contributed much to the magnificence of the spectacle. It was Boris Drubetskoy who was admitted. I nominated him and was the Rhetor. A strange feeling agitated me all the time I was alone with him in the dark chamber. I caught myself harbour-

ing a feeling of hatred towards him which I vainly tried to overcome. That is why I should really like to save him from evil and lead him into the path of truth, but evil thoughts of him did not leave me. It seemed to me that his object in entering the Brotherhood was merely to be intimate and in favour with members of our Lodge. Apart from the fact that he had asked me several times whether N. and S. were members of our Lodge (a question to which I could not reply) and that according to my observation he is incapable of feeling respect for our holy Order and is too preoccupied and satisfied with the outer man to desire spiritual improvement, I had no cause to doubt him, but he seemed to me insincere, and all the time I stood alone with him in the dark temple it seemed to me that he was smiling contemptuously at my words, and I wished really to stab his bare breast with the sword I held to it. I could not be eloquent, nor could I frankly mention my doubts to the Brothers and to the Grand Master. Great Architect of Nature, help me to find the true path out of the labyrinth of lies!

After this three pages were left blank in the diary, and then the following was written:

I have had a long and instructive talk alone with Brother V., who advised me to hold fast by Brother A. Though I am unworthy, much was revealed to me. Adonai is the name of the creator of the world. Elohim is the name of the ruler of all. The third name is the name unutterable which means the All. Talks with Brother V. strengthen, refresh, and support me in the path of virtue. In his presence doubt has no place. The distinction between the poor teachings of mundane science and our sacred all-embracing teaching is clear to me. Human sciences dissect everything to comprehend it, and kill everything to examine it. In the holy science of our Order all is one, all is known in its entirety and life. The Trinity – the three elements of matter – are sulphur, mercury, and salt. Sulphur is of an oily and fiery nature; in combination with salt by its fiery nature it arouses a desire in the latter by means of which it attracts mercury, seizes it, holds it, and in combination produces other bodies. Mercury is a fluid, volatile, spiritual essence. Christ, the Holy Spirit, Him! . . .

*3rd December.*
Awoke late, read the Scriptures but was apathetic. Afterwards went and paced up and down the large hall. I wished to meditate, but instead my imagination pictured an occurrence of four years ago, when Dolokhov, meeting me in Moscow after our duel, said he hoped I was enjoying perfect peace of mind in spite of my wife's absence. At the time I gave him no answer. Now I recalled every detail of that meeting and in my mind gave him the most malevolent and bitter replies. I recollected myself and drove away that thought only when I found myself glowing with anger, but I did not sufficiently repent. Afterwards Boris Drubetskoy came and began relating various adventures. His coming vexed me from the first, and I said

469

something disagreeable to him. He replied. I flared up and said much that was unpleasant and even rude to him. He became silent, and I recollected myself only when it was too late. My God, I cannot get on with him at all. The cause of this is my egotism. I set myself above him and so become much worse than he, for he is lenient to my rudeness while I on the contrary nourish contempt for him. O God, grant that in his presence I may rather see my own vileness, and behave so that he too may benefit. After dinner I fell asleep and as I was drowsing off I clearly heard a voice saying in my left ear, 'Thy day!'

I dreamt that I was walking in the dark and was suddenly surrounded by dogs, but I went on undismayed. Suddenly a smallish dog seized my left thigh with its teeth and would not let go. I began to throttle it with my hands. Scarcely had I torn it off before another, a bigger one, began biting me. I lifted it up but the higher I lifted it the bigger and heavier it grew. And suddenly Brother A. came and, taking my arm, led me to a building, to enter which we had to pass along a narrow plank. I stepped on it, but it bent and gave way and I began to clamber up a fence which I could scarcely reach with my hands. After much effort I dragged myself up, so that my legs hung down on one side and my body on the other. I looked round and saw Brother A. standing on the fence and pointing me to a broad avenue and garden, and in the garden was a large and beautiful building. I woke up. O Lord, great Architect of Nature, help me to tear from myself these dogs – my passions – especially the last, which unites in itself the strength of all the former ones, and aid me to enter that temple of virtue to a vision of which I attained in my dream.

*7th December.*

I dreamt that Joseph Alexeevich was sitting in my house, and that I was very glad, and wished to entertain him. It seemed as if I chattered incessantly with other people and suddenly remembered that this could not please him, and I wished to come close to him and embrace him. But as soon as I drew near, I saw that his face had changed and grown young, and he was quietly telling me something about the teaching of our Order, but so softly that I could not hear it. Then it seemed that we all left the room and something strange happened. We were sitting or lying on the floor. He was telling me something, and I wished to show him my sensibility, and not listening to what he was saying, I began picturing to myself the condition of my inner man and the grace of God sanctifying me. And tears came into my eyes, and I was glad he noticed this. But he looked at me with vexation and jumped up, breaking off his remarks. I felt abashed and asked whether what he had been saying did not concern me; but he did not reply, gave me a kind look, and then we suddenly found ourselves in my bedroom where there is a double bed. He lay down on the edge of it and I burned with longing to caress him and lie down too. And he said, 'Tell me frankly what is your chief temptation? Do you know it? I think you know it already.' Abashed by this question, I replied that sloth was my chief temptation. He shook his head incredulously; and even more abashed, I said that though I was living with my wife as he advised, I was not living with her as her husband. To this he replied that one should not deprive a wife of one's embraces, and gave me to understand that that was my duty. But I replied that I should be ashamed to do it, and suddenly everything vanished. And I awoke and found in my mind the text from the Gospel: 'The life was the light of men. And the light shineth in darkness; and the darkness comprehended it not.' Joseph Alexeevich's face had looked young and bright. That day I received a letter from my benefactor in which he wrote about 'conjugal duties'.

9th December.

I had a dream from which I awoke with a throbbing heart. I saw that I was in Moscow in my house, in the big sitting-room, and Joseph Alexeevich came in from the drawing-room. I seemed to know at once that the process of regeneration had already taken place in him, and I rushed to meet him. I embraced him and kissed his hands, and he said, 'Hast thou noticed that my face is different?' I looked at him, still holding him in my arms, and saw that his face was young, but that he had no hair on his head and his features were quite changed. And I said, 'I should have known you had I met you by chance,' and I thought to myself, 'Am I telling the truth?' And suddenly I saw him lying like a dead body; then he gradually recovered and went with me into my study carrying a large book of sheets of drawing paper; I said, 'I drew that,' and he answered by bowing his head. I opened the book, and on all the pages there were excellent drawings. And in my dream I knew that these drawings represented the love adventures of the soul with its beloved. And on its pages I saw a beautiful representation of a maiden in transparent garments and with a transparent body, flying up to the clouds. And I seemed to know that this maiden was nothing else than a representation of the Song of Songs. And looking at those drawings I dreamed I felt that I was doing wrong, but could not tear myself away from them. Lord, help me! My God, if Thy forsaking me is Thy doing, Thy will be done; but if I am myself the cause, teach me what I should do! I shall perish of my debauchery if Thou utterly desertest me!

11

THE Rostovs' monetary affairs had not improved during the two years they had spent in the country.

Though Nicholas Rostov had kept firmly to his resolution and was still serving modestly in an obscure regiment spending comparatively little, the way of life at Otradnoe – Mitinka's management of affairs, in particular – was such that the debts inevitably increased every year. The only resource obviously presenting itself to the old count was to apply for an official post, so he had come to Petersburg to look for one and also, as he said, to let the lassies enjoy themselves for the last time.

Soon after their arrival in Petersburg, Berg proposed to Vera and was accepted.

Though in Moscow the Rostovs belonged to the best society without themselves giving it a thought, yet in Petersburg their circle of acquaintances was a mixed and indefinite one. In Petersburg they were provincials, and the very people they had entertained in Moscow without inquiring to what set they belonged, here looked down on them.

The Rostovs lived in the same hospitable way in Petersburg as in Moscow, and the most diverse people met at their suppers. Country neighbours from Otradnoe, impoverished old squires and their daughters, Peronskaya a maid of honour, Pierre Bezukhov, and the son of their district postmaster, who had obtained a post in Petersburg. Among the men who very soon became frequent visitors at the Rostovs' house in Petersburg were Boris, Pierre whom the count had met in the street and dragged home with him, and Berg who spent whole days at the Rostovs' and paid the eldest daughter, Countess Vera, the attentions a young man pays when he intends to propose.

Not in vain had Berg shown everybody his right hand wounded at Austerlitz and held a perfectly unnecessary sword in his left. He narrated that episode so persistently and with so important an air that everyone believed in the merit and usefulness of his deed, and he had obtained two decorations for Austerlitz.

In the Finnish war he also managed to distinguish himself. He had picked up the scrap of a grenade that had killed an aide-de-camp standing near the commander-in-chief, and had taken it to his commander. Just as he had done after Austerlitz, he related this occurrence at such length and so insistently that everyone again believed it had been necessary to do this, and he received two decorations for the Finnish war also. In 1809 he was a captain in the Guards, wore medals, and held some special lucrative posts in Petersburg.

Though some sceptics smiled when told of Berg's merits, it could not be denied that he was a painstaking and brave officer, on excellent terms with his superiors, and a moral young man with a brilliant career before him and an assured position in society.

Four years before, meeting a German comrade in the stalls of a Moscow theatre, Berg had pointed out Vera Rostova to him and had said in German, '*das soll mein Weib werden*', and from that moment had made up his mind to marry her. Now in Petersburg, having considered the Rostovs' position and his own, he decided that the time had come to propose.

Berg's proposal was at first received with a perplexity that was not flattering to him. At first it seemed strange that the son of an obscure Livonian gentleman should propose marriage to a Countess Rostova; but Berg's chief characteristic was such a naïve and good-natured egotism that the Rostovs involuntarily came to think it would be a good thing, since he himself was so firmly convinced that it was good, indeed excellent. Moreover, the Rostovs' affairs were seriously embarrassed, as the suitor could not but know; and above all, Vera was twenty-four, had been taken out everywhere, and though she was certainly good-looking and sensible, no one up to now had proposed to her. So they gave their consent.

'You see,' said Berg to his comrade, whom he called 'friend' only because he knew that everyone has friends, 'You see, I have considered it all, and should not marry if I had not thought it all out or if it were in any way unsuitable. But on the contrary, my papa and mamma are now provided for – I have arranged that rent for them in the Baltic Provinces* – and I can live in Petersburg on my pay, and with her fortune and my good management we can get along nicely. I am not marrying for money – I consider that dishonourable – but a wife should bring her share and a husband his. I have my position in the service, she has connexions and some means. In our times that is worth something, isn't it? But above all, she is a handsome, estimable girl, and she loves me . . .'

Berg blushed and smiled.

'And I love her, because her character is sensible and very good. Now the other sister, though they are the same family, is quite different – an unpleasant character and has not the same intelligence. She is so . . . you know? . . . Unpleasant . . . But my fiancée . . .! Well, you will be coming' – he was going to say 'to dine', but changed his mind and said 'to take tea with us', and quickly doubling up his tongue he blew a small round ring of tobacco smoke, perfectly embodying his dream of happiness.

After the first feeling of perplexity aroused in the parents by Berg's proposal, the holiday tone of joyousness usual at such times took possession of the family, but the rejoicing was external and insincere. In the family's feeling towards this wedding a certain awkwardness and constraint was evident: as if they were ashamed of not having loved Vera sufficiently and of being so ready to get her off their hands. The old count felt this most. He would probably have been unable to state the cause of his embarrassment, but it resulted from the state of his affairs. He did not know at all how

473

much he had, what his debts amounted to, or what dowry he could give Vera. When his daughters were born he had assigned to each of them, for her dowry, an estate with three hundred serfs; but one of those estates had already been sold, and the other was mortgaged, and the interest so much in arrears that it would have to be sold, so that it was impossible to give it to Vera. Nor had he any money.

Berg had already been engaged a month, and only a week remained before the wedding, but the count had not yet decided in his own mind the question of the dowry, nor spoken to his wife about it. At one time the count thought of giving her the Ryazan estate, or of selling a forest, at another time of borrowing money on a note of hand. A few days before the wedding Berg entered the count's study early one morning, and with a pleasant smile respectfully asked his future father-in-law to let him know what Vera's dowry would be. The count was so disconcerted by this long-foreseen inquiry that without consideration he gave the first reply that came into his head. 'I like your being business-like about it . . . I like it. You shall be satisfied . . .'

And patting Berg on the shoulder he got up, wishing to end the conversation. But Berg, smiling pleasantly, explained that if he did not know for certain how much Vera would have and did not receive at least part of the dowry in advance, he would have to break matters off.

'Because, consider, Count – if I allowed myself to marry now without having definite means to maintain my wife, I should be acting badly . . .'

The conversation ended by the count, who wished to be generous and to avoid further importunity, saying that he would give a note of hand for eighty thousand rubles. Berg smiled meekly, kissed the count on the shoulder, and said that he was very grateful, but that it was impossible for him to arrange his new life without receiving thirty thousand in ready money. 'Or at least twenty thousand, Count,' he added, 'and then a note of hand for only sixty thousand.'

'Yes, yes, all right!' said the count hurriedly. 'Only excuse me, my dear fellow, I'll give you twenty thousand and a note of hand for eighty thousand as well. Yes, yes! Kiss me.'

12

NATASHA was sixteen and it was the year 1809, the very year to which she had counted on her fingers with Boris after they had kissed four years ago. Since then she had not once seen him. Before Sonya and her mother, if Boris happened to be mentioned, she spoke quite freely of that episode as of some childish, long-forgotten matter that was not worth mentioning. But in the secret depths of her soul the question whether her engagement to Boris was a jest or an important, binding promise tormented her.

Since Boris left Moscow in 1805 to join the army he had not seen the Rostovs. He had been in Moscow several times, and had passed near Otradnoe, but had never been to see them.

Sometimes it occurred to Natasha that he did not wish to see her, and this conjecture was confirmed by the sad tone in which her elders spoke of him.

'Nowadays old friends are not remembered,' the countess would say when Boris was mentioned.

Anna Mikhaylovna also had of late visited them less frequently, seemed to hold herself with particular dignity, and always spoke rapturously and gratefully of the merits of her son and the brilliant career on which he had entered. When the Rostovs came to Petersburg, Boris called on them.

He drove to their house in some agitation. The memory of Natasha was his most poetic recollection. But he went with the firm intention of letting her and her parents feel that the childish relations between himself and Natasha could not be binding either on her or on him. He had a brilliant position in society thanks to his intimacy with Countess Bezukhova, a brilliant position in the service thanks to the patronage of an important personage whose complete confidence he enjoyed, and he was beginning to make plans for marrying one of the richest heiresses in Petersburg, plans which might very easily be realized. When he entered the Rostovs' drawing-room Natasha was in her own room. When she heard of his arrival she almost ran into the drawing-room, flushed, and beaming with a more than cordial smile.

Boris remembered Natasha in a short dress, with dark eyes shining from under her curls and boisterous, childish laughter, as he had known her four years before; and so he was taken aback when quite a different Natasha entered, and his face expressed rapturous astonishment. This expression on his face pleased Natasha.

'Well, do you recognize your little madcap playmate?' asked the countess.

Boris kissed Natasha's hand and said that he was astonished at the change in her.

'How handsome you have grown!'

'I should think so!' replied Natasha's laughing eyes.

'And is papa older?' she asked.

Natasha sat down and, without joining in Boris's conversation with the countess, silently and minutely studied her childhood's suitor. He felt the weight of that resolute and affectionate scrutiny, and glanced at her occasionally.

Boris's uniform, spurs, tie, and the way his hair was brushed, were all *comme il faut* and in the latest fashion. This Natasha noticed at once. He sat rather sideways in the arm-chair next to the countess, arranging with his right hand the cleanest of gloves that fitted his left hand like a skin, and he spoke with a particularly refined compression of his lips about the amusements of the highest Petersburg society, recalling with mild irony old times in Moscow and Moscow acquaintances. It was not accidentally, Natasha felt, that he alluded, when speaking of the highest aristocracy, to an ambassador's ball he had attended, and to invitations he had received from N. N. and S. S.

All this time Natasha sat silent, glancing up at him from under her brows. This gaze disturbed and confused Boris more and more. He looked round more frequently towards her, and broke off in what he was saying. He did not stay more than ten minutes, then rose and took his leave. The same inquisitive, challenging, and rather mocking eyes still looked at him. After his first visit Boris said to himself that Natasha attracted him just as much as ever, but that he must not yield to that feeling, because to marry her, a girl almost without fortune, would mean ruin to his career, while to renew their former relations without intending to marry her would be dishonourable. Boris made up his mind to avoid meeting Natasha, but despite that resolution he called again a few days later, and began calling often and spending whole days at the Rostovs'. It seemed to him that he ought to have an explanation with Natasha and tell her that the old times must be forgotten, that in spite of everything . . . she could not be his wife, that he had no means, and they would never let her marry him. But he failed to do so, and felt awkward about entering on such an explanation. From day to day he became more and more entangled. It seemed to her mother and Sonya that Natasha was in love with Boris as of old. She sang him his favourite songs, showed him her album, making him write in it, did not allow him to allude to the past, letting it be understood how delightful was the present; and every day he went away in a fog, without having said what he meant to, and not knowing what he was doing or why he came, or how it would all end. He left off visiting Hélène and received reproachful notes from her every day, and yet he continued to spend whole days with the Rostovs.

## 13

ONE night when the old countess, in night-cap and dressing-jacket, without her false curls, and with her poor little knob of hair showing under her white cotton cap, knelt sighing and groaning on a rug and bowing to the ground in prayer, her door creaked and Natasha, also in a dressing-jacket with slippers on her bare feet and her hair in curl-papers, ran in. The countess – her prayerful mood dispelled – looked round and frowned. She was finishing her last prayer: 'Can it be that this couch will be my grave?' Natasha, flushed and eager, seeing her mother in prayer suddenly checked her rush, half sat down, and unconsciously put out her tongue as if chiding herself. Seeing that her mother was still praying she ran on tiptoe to the bed and, rapidly slipping one little foot against the other, pushed off her slippers and jumped onto the bed the countess had feared might become her grave. This couch was high, with a feather-bed and five pillows each smaller than the one below. Natasha jumped on it, sank into the feather-bed, rolled over to the wall, and began snuggling up the bedclothes as she settled down, raising her knees to her chin, kicking out and laughing almost inaudibly, now covering herself up head and all, and now peeping at her mother. The countess finished her prayers and came to the bed with a stern face, but seeing that Natasha's head was covered, she smiled in her kind, weak way.

'Now then, now then!' said she.

'Mamma, can we have a talk? Yes?' said Natasha. 'Now, just one on your throat and another . . . that'll do!' And seizing her mother round the neck, she kissed her on the throat. In her behaviour to her mother Natasha seemed rough, but she was so sensitive and tactful that however she clasped her mother, she always managed to do it without hurting her, or making her feel uncomfortable or displeased.

'Well, what is it to-night?' said the mother, having arranged her pillows and waited until Natasha, after turning over a couple of times, had settled down beside her under the quilt, spread out her arms, and assumed a serious expression.

These visits of Natasha's at night, before the count returned from his club, were one of the greatest pleasures of both mother and daughter.

'What is it to-night? – But I have to tell you . . .'

Natasha put her hand on her mother's mouth.

'About Boris . . . I know,' she said seriously; 'that's what I have come about. Don't say it – I know. No, do tell me!' and she removed her hand. 'Tell me, mamma! He's nice?'

'Natasha, you are sixteen. At your age I was married. You say Boris is nice. He is very nice, and I love him like a son. But what then . . . ? What are you thinking about? You have quite turned his head, I can see that . . .'

As she said this the countess looked round at her daughter. Natasha was lying looking steadily straight before her at one of the mahogany sphinxes carved on the corners of the bedstead, so that the countess only saw her daughter's face in profile. That face struck her by its peculiarly serious and concentrated expression.

Natasha was listening and considering.

'Well, what then?' said she.

'You have quite turned his head, and why? What do you want of him? You know you can't marry him.'

'Why not?' said Natasha, without changing her position.

'Because he is young, because he is poor, because he is a relation . . . and because you yourself don't love him.'

'How do you know?'

'I know. It is not right, darling!'

'But if I want to . . .' said Natasha.

'Leave off talking nonsense,' said the countess.

'But if I want to . . .'

'Natasha, I am in earnest . . .'

Natasha did not let her finish. She drew the countess's large hand to her, kissed it on the back and then on the palm, then again turned it over and began kissing first one knuckle,* then the space between the knuckles, then the next knuckle, whispering, 'January, February, March, April, May. Speak, mamma, why don't you say anything? Speak!' said she, turning to her mother, who was tenderly gazing at her daughter and in that contemplation seemed to have forgotten all she had wished to say.

'It won't do, my love! Not everyone will understand this friendship dating from your childish days, and to see him so intimate with you may injure you in the eyes of other young men who visit us, and above all, it torments him for nothing. He may already have found a suitable and wealthy match, and now he's half crazy.'

'Crazy?' repeated Natasha.

'I'll tell you some things about myself. I had a cousin . . .'

'I know! Cyril Matveich . . . but he is old.'

'He was not always old. But this is what I'll do, Natasha, I'll have a talk with Boris. He need not come so often . . .'

'Why not, if he likes to?'

'Because I know it will end in nothing . . .'

478

'How can you know? No, mamma, don't speak to him! What nonsense!' said Natasha in the tone of one being deprived of her property. 'Well, I won't marry, but let him come if he enjoys it and I enjoy it.' Natasha smiled and looked at her mother. 'Not to marry, but just *so*,' she added.

'How *so*, my pet?'

'Just *so*. There's no need for me to marry him. But ... just *so*.'

'Just so, just so,' repeated the countess, and shaking all over, she went off into a good-humoured, unexpected, elderly laugh.

'Don't laugh, stop!' cried Natasha. 'You're shaking the whole bed! You're awfully like me, just such another giggler ... Wait ...' and she seized the countess's hands and kissed a knuckle of the little finger, saying, 'June,' and continued, kissing, 'July, August' on the other hand. 'But, mamma, is he very much in love? What do you think? Was anybody ever so much in love with you? And he's very nice, very, very, very nice. Only not quite my taste – he is so narrow, like the dining-room clock ... Don't you understand? Narrow, you know – grey, light grey ...'

'What rubbish you're talking!' said the countess.

Natasha continued:

'Don't you really understand? Nicholas would understand ... Bezukhov, now, is blue, dark blue and red, and he is square.'

'You flirt with him too,' said the countess, laughing.

'No, he is a Freemason, I have found out. He is fine, dark blue and red ... How can I explain it to you?'

'Little Countess!' the count's voice called from behind the door. 'You're not asleep?' Natasha jumped up, snatched up her slippers, and ran barefoot to her own room.

It was a long time before she could sleep. She kept thinking that no one could understand all that she understood and all there was in her.

'Sonya?' she thought, glancing at that curled-up, sleeping little kitten with her enormous plait of hair. 'No, how could she? She's virtuous. She fell in love with Nicholas and does not wish to know anything more. Even mamma does not understand. It is wonderful how clever I am and how ... charming she is,' she went on, speaking of herself in the third person, and imagining it was some very wise man – the wisest and best of men – who was saying it of her. 'There is everything, everything in her,' continued this man. 'She is unusually intelligent, charming ... and then she is pretty, uncommonly pretty, and agile – she swims and rides splendidly ... and her voice! One can really say it's a wonderful voice!'

She hummed a scrap from her favourite opera by Cherubini, threw herself on her bed, laughed at the pleasant thought that she would immediately fall asleep, called Dunyasha, the maid, to put out the candle, and before Dunyasha had left the room had already passed into another yet happier world of dreams, where everything was as light and beautiful as in reality, and even more so because it was different.

Next day the countess called Boris aside and had a talk with him, after which he ceased coming to the Rostovs.

14

On the 31st of December, New Year's Eve 1810, an old grandee of Catherine's day was giving a ball and midnight supper. The diplomatic corps and the Emperor himself were to be present.

The grandee's well-known mansion on the English Quay glittered with innumerable lights. Police were stationed at the brightly lit entrance which was carpeted with red baize, and not only gendarmes but dozens of police officers and even the police-master himself stood at the porch. Carriages kept driving away and fresh ones arriving, with red-liveried footmen and footmen in plumed hats. From the carriages emerged men wearing uniforms, stars, and ribbons, while ladies in satin and ermine cautiously descended the carriage steps which were let down for them with a clatter, and then walked hurriedly and noiselessly over the baize at the entrance.

Almost every time a new carriage drove up a whisper ran through the crowd and caps were doffed.

'The Emperor? . . . No, a minister . . . prince . . . ambassador. Don't you see the plumes? . . .' was whispered among the crowd.

One person, better dressed than the rest, seemed to know everyone and mentioned by name the greatest dignitaries of the day.

A third of the visitors had already arrived, but the Rostovs, who were to be present, were still hurrying to get dressed.

There had been many discussions and preparations for this ball in the Rostov family, many fears that the invitation would not arrive, that the dresses would not be ready, or that something would not be arranged as it should be.

Marya Ignatevna Peronskaya, a thin and sallow maid of honour at the court of the Dowager Empress, who was a friend and relation of the countess and piloted the provincial Rostovs in Petersburg high society, was to accompany them to the ball.

They were to call for her at her house in the Taurida Gardens at ten o'clock, but it was already five minutes to ten and the girls were not yet dressed.

Natasha was going to her first grand ball. She had got up at eight that morning and had been in a fever of excitement and activity all day. All her powers since morning had been concentrated on ensuring that they all – she herself, mamma, and Sonya – should be as well dressed as possible. Sonya and her mother put themselves entirely in her hands. The countess was to wear a claret-coloured velvet dress, and the two girls white gauze over pink silk slips, with roses on their bodices and their hair dressed à la grecque.

Everything essential had already been done; feet, hands, necks, and ears washed, perfumed, and powdered, as befits a ball; the open-work silk stockings and white satin shoes with ribbons were already on; the hairdressing was almost done. Sonya was finishing dressing and so was the countess, but Natasha, who had bustled about helping them all, was behindhand. She was still sitting before a looking-glass with a dressing-jacket thrown over her slender shoulders. Sonya stood ready dressed in the middle of the room, and pressing the head of a pin till it hurt her dainty finger, was fixing on a last ribbon that squeaked as the pin went through it.

'That's not the way, that's not the way, Sonya!' cried Natasha turning her head and clutching with both hands at her hair which the maid, who was dressing it, had not time to release. 'That bow is not right. Come here!'

Sonya sat down and Natasha pinned the ribbon on differently.

'Allow me, Miss! I can't do it like that,' said the maid who was holding Natasha's hair.

'Oh dear! Well then, wait. That's right, Sonya.'

'Aren't you ready? It is nearly ten,' came the countess's voice.

'Directly! Directly! And you, mamma?'

'I have only my cap to pin on.'

'Don't do it without me!' called Natasha. 'You won't do it right.'

'But it's already ten.'

They had decided to be at the ball by half-past ten, and Natasha had still to get dressed and they had to call at the Taurida Gardens.

When her hair was done, Natasha, in her short petticoat from under which her dancing shoes showed, and in her mother's dressing-jacket, ran up to Sonya, scrutinized her, and then ran to her mother. Turning her mother's head this way and that, she fastened on the cap and hurriedly kissing her grey hair ran back to the maids who were turning up the hem of her skirt.

The cause of the delay was Natasha's skirt, which was too long. Two maids were turning up the hem and hurriedly biting off the ends of thread. A third with pins in her mouth was running about between the countess and Sonya, and a fourth held the whole of the gossamer garment up high on one uplifted hand.

'Mavra, quicker, darling!'

'Give me my thimble, Miss, from there . . .'

'Whenever will you be ready?' asked the count coming to the door. 'Here is some scent. Peronskaya must be tired of waiting.'

'It's ready, Miss,' said the maid, holding up the shortened gauze dress with two fingers, and blowing and shaking something off it, as if by this to express a consciousness of the airiness and purity of what she held.

Natasha began putting on the dress.

'In a minute! In a minute! Don't come in, papa!' she cried to her father as he opened the door – speaking from under the filmy skirt which still covered her whole face.

Sonya slammed the door to. A minute later they let the count in. He was wearing a blue swallow-tail coat, shoes and stockings, and was perfumed and his hair pomaded.

'Oh, papa! how nice you look! Charming!' cried Natasha, as she stood in the middle of the room smoothing out the folds of the gauze.

'If you please, Miss! allow me,' said the maid, who on her knees was pulling the skirt straight and shifting the pins from one side of her mouth to the other with her tongue.

'Say what you like,' exclaimed Sonya, in a despairing voice as she looked at Natasha, 'say what you like, it is still too long.'

Natasha stepped back to look at herself in the pier-glass. The dress *was* too long.

'Really, madam, it is not at all too long,' said Mavra, crawling on her knees after her young lady.

'Well, if it's too long we'll tack it up . . . we'll tack it up in one minute,' said the resolute Dunyasha taking a needle that was stuck on the front of her little shawl and, still kneeling on the floor, set to work once more.

At that moment, with soft steps, the countess came in shyly, in her cap and velvet gown.

'Oo-oo, my beauty!' exclaimed the count, 'she looks better than any of you!'

He would have embraced her but, blushing, she stepped aside fearing to be rumpled.

'Mamma, your cap, more to this side,' said Natasha. 'I'll arrange it,' and she rushed forward so that the maids who were tacking up her skirt could not move fast enough and a piece of gauze was torn off.

'Oh, goodness! What has happened? Really it was not my fault!'

'Never mind, I'll run it up, it won't show,' said Dunyasha.

'What a beauty – a very queen!' said the nurse as she came to the door. 'And Sonya! They are lovely!'

At a quarter past ten they at last got into their carriages and started. But they had still to call at the Taurida Gardens.

Peronskaya was quite ready. In spite of her age and plainness she had gone through the same process as the Rostovs, but with less flurry – for to her it was a matter of routine. Her ugly old body was washed, perfumed, and powdered, in just the same way. She had washed behind her ears just as carefully, and when she entered her drawing-room in her yellow dress, wearing her badge as maid of honour, her old lady's maid was as full of rapturous admiration as the Rostovs' servants had been.

She praised the Rostovs' toilettes. They praised her taste and toilette, and at eleven o'clock, careful of their *coiffures* and dresses, they settled themselves in their carriages and drove off.

## 15

NATASHA had not had a moment free since early morning and had not once had time to think of what lay before her.

In the damp chill air and crowded closeness of the swaying carriage, she for the first time vividly imagined what was in store for her there at the ball, in those brightly lighted rooms – with music, flowers, dances, the Emperor, and all the brilliant young people of Petersburg. The prospect was so splendid that she hardly believed it would come true, so out of keeping was it with the chill darkness and closeness of the carriage. She understood all that awaited her only when, after stepping over the red baize at the entrance, she entered the hall, took off her fur cloak and, beside Sonya and in front of her mother, mounted the brightly illuminated stairs between the flowers. Only then did she remember how she must behave at a ball, and tried to assume the majestic air she considered indispensable for a girl on such an occasion. But, fortunately for her, she felt her eyes growing misty, she saw nothing clearly, her pulse beat a hundred to the minute and the blood throbbed at her heart. She could not assume that pose, which would have made her ridiculous, and she moved on almost fainting from excitement and trying with all her might to conceal it. And this was the very attitude that became her best. Before and behind them other visitors were entering, also talking in low tones and wearing ball-dresses. The mirrors on the landing reflected ladies in white, pale-blue, and pink dresses, with diamonds and pearls on their bare necks and arms.

Natasha looked in the mirrors and could not distinguish her reflection from the others. All was blent into one brilliant procession. On entering the ball-room the regular hum of voices, footsteps, and greetings deafened Natasha, and the light and glitter dazzled her still more. The host and hostess, who had already been standing at the door for half an hour repeating the same words to the various arrivals, '*Charmé de vous voir,*' greeted the Rostovs and Peronskaya in the same manner.

The two girls in their white dresses, each with a rose in her black hair, both curtsied in the same way, but the hostess's eye involuntarily rested longer on the slim Natasha. She looked at her and gave her alone a special smile, in addition to her usual smile as hostess. Looking at her she may have recalled the golden, irrevocable days of her own girlhood and her own first ball. The host also followed Natasha with his eyes and asked the count which was his daughter.

'Charming!' said he, kissing the tips of his fingers.

In the ball-room guests stood crowding at the entrance doors awaiting the Emperor. The countess took up a position in one of the front rows of that crowd. Natasha heard and felt that several people were asking about her and looking at her. She realized that those noticing her liked her, and this observation helped to calm her.

'There are some like ourselves and some worse,' she thought.

Peronskaya was pointing out to the countess the most important people at the ball.

'That is the Dutch ambassador, do you see? That grey-haired man,' she said, indicating an old man with a profusion of silver-grey curly hair, who was surrounded by ladies laughing at something he said.

'Ah, here she is, the Queen of Petersburg, Countess Bezukhova,' said Peronskaya, indicating Hélène who had just entered. 'How lovely! She is quite equal to Marya Antonovna.* See how the men, young and old, pay court to her. Beautiful and clever . . . they say Prince —— is quite mad about her. But see, those two, though not good-looking, are even more run after.'

She pointed to a lady who was crossing the room followed by a very plain daughter.

'She is a splendid match, a millionairess,' said Peronskaya. 'And look, here come her suitors.'

'That is Bezukhova's brother, Anatole Kuragin,' she said, indicating a handsome officer of the Horse Guards who passed by them with head erect, looking at something over the heads of the ladies. 'He's handsome, isn't he? I hear they will marry him to that rich girl. But your cousin, Drubetskoy, is also very attentive to her. They say she has millions. Oh yes, that's the French ambassador himself!' she replied to the countess's inquiry about Caulaincourt. 'Looks as if he were a king! All the same, the French are charming, very charming. No one more charming in society. Ah, here she is! Yes, she is still the most beautiful of them all, our Marya Antonovna! And how simply she is dressed! Lovely! And that stout one in spectacles is the universal Freemason,' she went on, indicating Pierre. 'Put him beside his wife and he looks a regular buffoon!'

Pierre, swaying his stout body, advanced making way through the crowd and nodding to right and left as casually and good-naturedly as if he were passing through a crowd at a fair. He pushed through, evidently looking for someone.

Natasha looked joyfully at the familiar face of Pierre, 'the buffoon', as Peronskaya had called him, and knew he was looking for them, and for her in particular. He had promised to be at the ball and introduce partners to her.

But before he reached them Pierre stopped beside a very handsome, dark man of middle height, and in a white uniform, who stood by a window talking to a tall man wearing stars and a ribbon. Natasha at once recognized the shorter and younger man in the white uniform: it was Bolkonsky, who seemed to her to have grown much younger, happier, and better-looking.

'There's someone else we know – Bolkonsky, do you see, mamma?' said Natasha, pointing out Prince Andrew. 'You remember, he stayed a night with us at Otradnoe.'

'Oh, you know him?' said Peronskaya. 'I can't bear him. *Il fait à présent la pluie et le beau temps.* He's too proud for anything. Takes after his father. And he's hand in glove with Speransky, writing some projects or other. Just look how he treats the ladies! There's one talking to him, and he has turned away,' she said, pointing at him. 'I'd give it him if he treated me as he does those ladies.'


16


SUDDENLY everybody stirred, began talking, and pressed forward and then back, and between the two rows, which separated, the Emperor entered to the sounds of music that had immediately struck up. Behind him walked his host and hostess. He walked in rapidly, bowing to right and left as if anxious to get the first moments of the reception over. The band played the polonaise in vogue at that time on account of the words that had been set to it, beginning: 'Alexander, Elisaveta, all our hearts you ravish quite . . .' The Emperor passed on to the drawing-room, the crowd made a rush for the doors, and several persons with excited faces hurried there and back again. Then the crowd hastily retired from the drawing-room door, at which the Emperor reappeared talking to the hostess. A young man, looking distraught, pounced down on the ladies, asking them to move aside. Some ladies, with faces betraying complete forgetfulness of all the rules of decorum, pushed forward to the detriment of their toilettes. The men began to choose partners and take their places for the polonaise.

Everyone moved back, and the Emperor came smiling out of the drawing-room leading his hostess by the hand but not keeping time to the music. The host followed with Marya Antonovna Naryshkina; then came ambassadors, ministers, and various generals, whom Peronskaya diligently named. More than half the ladies already had partners and were taking up, or preparing to take up, their positions for the polonaise. Natasha felt that she would be left with her mother and Sonya among a minority of women who crowded near the wall, not having been invited to dance. She stood with her slender arms hanging down, her scarcely defined bosom rising and falling regularly, and with bated breath and glittering, frightened eyes gazed straight before her, evidently prepared for the height of joy or misery. She was not concerned about the Emperor, or any of those great people whom Peronskaya was pointing out – she had but one thought: 'Is it possible no one will ask me, that I shall not be among the first to dance? Is it possible that not one of all these men will notice me? They do not even seem to see me, or if they do, they look as if they were saying, "Ah, she's not the one I'm after, so it's not worth looking at her!" No, it's impossible,' she thought. 'They must know how I long to dance, how splendidly I dance, and how they would enjoy dancing with me.'

The strains of the polonaise, which had continued for a considerable time, had begun to sound like a sad reminiscence in Natasha's ears. She wanted to cry. Peronskaya had left them. The count was at the other end of the room. She and the countess and Sonya were standing by themselves as in the depths of a forest, amid that crowd of strangers, with no one interested in them and not wanted by anyone. Prince Andrew with a lady passed by, evidently not recognizing them. The handsome Anatole was smilingly talking to a partner on his arm, and looked at Natasha as one looks at a wall. Boris passed them twice and each time turned away. Berg and his wife, who were not dancing, came up to them.

This family gathering seemed humiliating to Natasha – as if there were nowhere else for the family to talk but here at the ball. She did not listen to or look at Vera, who was telling her something about her own green dress.

At last the Emperor stopped beside his last partner (he had danced with three) and the music ceased. A worried aide-de-camp ran up to the Rostovs requesting them to stand farther back, though as it was they were already close to the wall, and from the gallery resounded the distinct, precise, enticingly rhythmical strains of a valse. The Emperor looked smilingly down the room. A minute passed but no one had yet begun dancing. An aide-de-camp, the Master of Ceremonies, went up to Countess Bezukhova and asked her to dance. She smilingly raised her hand and laid it on his shoulder without looking at him. The aide-de-camp, an adept in his art, grasping his partner firmly round her waist, with confident deliberation started smoothly, gliding first round the edge of the circle, then at the corner of the room he caught Hélène's left hand and turned her, the only sound audible, apart from the ever-quickening music, being the rhythmic click of the spurs on his rapid, agile feet, while at every third beat his partner's velvet dress spread out and seemed to flash as she whirled round. Natasha gazed at them and was ready to cry because it was not she who was dancing that first turn of the valse.

Prince Andrew, in the white uniform of a cavalry colonel, wearing stockings and dancing-shoes, stood looking animated and bright in the front row of the circle not far from the Rostovs. Baron Firhoff was talking to him about the first sitting of the Council of State to be held next day. Prince Andrew, as one closely connected with Speransky and participating in the work of the legislative commission, could give reliable information about that sitting, concerning which various rumours were current. But not listening to what Firhoff was saying, he was gazing now at the sovereign, and now at the men intending to dance who had not yet gathered courage to enter the circle.

Prince Andrew was watching these men abashed by the Emperor's presence, and the women who were breathlessly longing to be asked to dance.

Pierre came up to him and caught him by the arm.

'You always dance. I have a protégée, the young Rostova, here. Ask her,' he said.

'Where is she?' asked Bolkonsky. 'Excuse me!' he added, turning to the baron, 'we will finish this conversation elsewhere – at a ball one must dance.' He stepped forward in the direction Pierre indicated. The despairing, dejected expression of Natasha's face caught his eye. He recognized her, guessed her feelings, saw that it was her début, remembered her conversation at the window, and with an expression of pleasure on his face approached Countess Rostova.

'Allow me to introduce you to my daughter,' said the countess, with heightened colour.

'I have the pleasure of being already acquainted, if the Countess remembers me,' said Prince Andrew with a low and courteous bow quite belying Peronskaya's remarks about his rudeness, and approaching Natasha he held out his arm to grasp her waist before he had completed his invitation. He asked her to valse. That tremulous expression on Natasha's face, prepared either for despair or rapture, suddenly brightened into a happy, grateful, childlike smile.

'I have long been waiting for you,' that frightened happy little girl seemed to say by the smile that replaced the threatened tears, as she raised her hand to Prince Andrew's shoulder. They were the second couple to enter the circle. Prince Andrew was one of the best dancers of his day and Natasha danced exquisitely. Her little feet in their white satin dancing-shoes did their work swiftly, lightly, and independently of herself, while her face beamed with ecstatic happiness. Her slender bare arms and neck were not beautiful – compared to Hélène's her shoulders looked thin and her bosom undeveloped. But Hélène seemed, as it were, hardened by a varnish left by the thousands of looks that had scanned her person, while Natasha was like a girl exposed for the first time, who would have felt very much ashamed had she not been assured that this was absolutely necessary.

Prince Andrew liked dancing, and wishing to escape as quickly as possible from the political and clever talk which everyone addressed to him, wishing to break up the circle of restraint he disliked, caused by the Emperor's presence, he danced, and had chosen Natasha because Pierre pointed her out to him and because she was the first pretty girl who caught his eye; but scarcely had he embraced that slender supple figure, and felt her stirring so close to him and smiling so near him, than the wine of her charm rose to his head, and he felt himself revived and rejuvenated when after leaving her he stood breathing deeply and watching the other dancers.

## 17

AFTER Prince Andrew, Boris came up to ask Natasha for a dance, and then the aide-de-camp who had opened the ball, and several other young men, so that, flushed and happy, and passing on her superfluous partners to Sonya, she did not cease dancing all the evening. She noticed and saw nothing of what occupied everyone else. Not only did she fail to notice that the Emperor talked a long time with the French ambassador, and how particularly gracious he was to a certain lady, or that Prince So-and-so and So-and-so did and said this and that, and that Hélène had great success and was honoured by the special attention of So-and-so, but she did not even see the Emperor, and only noticed that he had gone because the ball became livelier after his departure. For one of the merry cotillions before supper Prince Andrew was again her partner. He reminded her of their first encounter in the Otradnoe avenue, and how she had been unable to sleep that moonlight night, and told her how he had involuntarily overheard her. Natasha blushed at that recollection and tried to excuse herself, as if there had been something to be ashamed of in what Prince Andrew had overheard.

Like all men who have grown up in society, Prince Andrew liked meeting someone there not of the conventional society stamp. And such was Natasha, with her surprise, her delight, her shyness, and even her mistakes in speaking French. With her he behaved with special care and tenderness, sitting beside her and talking of the simplest and most unimportant matters; he admired the joyous brightness of her eyes and smile, which related not to what was said but to her own happiness. When she was chosen by a dancer, and rose with a smile and danced round the room, Prince Andrew particularly admired her shy grace. In the middle of the cotillion, having completed one of the figures, Natasha, still out of breath, was returning to her seat when another dancer chose her. She was tired and panting and evidently thought of declining, but immediately put her hand gaily on the man's shoulder, smiling at Prince Andrew.

'I'd be glad to sit beside you and rest: I'm tired; but you see how they keep asking me, and I'm glad of it, I'm happy and I love everybody, and you and I understand it all,' and much, much more was said in her smile. When her partner left her, Natàsha ran across the room to choose two ladies for the figure.

'If she goes to her cousin first and then to another lady, she will be my wife,' said Prince Andrew to himself, quite to his own surprise, as he watched her. She did go first to her cousin.

'What rubbish sometimes enters one's head!' thought Prince Andrew, 'but what is certain is that that girl is so charming, so original, that she won't be dancing here a month before she will be married ... Such as she are rare here,' he thought, as Natasha, readjusting a rose that was slipping on her bodice, settled herself beside him.

When the cotillion was over the old count in his blue coat came up to the dancers. He invited Prince Andrew to come and see them, and asked his daughter whether she was enjoying herself. Natasha did not answer at once, but only looked up with a smile that said reproachfully: 'How can you ask such a question?'

'I have never enjoyed myself so much before!' she said, and Prince Andrew noticed how her thin arms rose quickly as if to embrace her father, and instantly dropped again. Natasha was happier than she had ever been in her life. She was at that height of bliss when one becomes completely kind and good, and does not believe in the possibility of evil, unhappiness, or sorrow.

At that ball Pierre for the first time felt humiliated by the position his wife occupied in court circles. He was gloomy and absent-minded. A deep furrow ran across his forehead, and standing by a window he stared over his spectacles seeing no one.

On her way to supper Natasha passed him.

Pierre's gloomy, unhappy look struck her. She stopped in front of him. She wished to help him, to bestow on him the super-abundance of her own happiness.

'How delightful it is, Count!' said she. 'Isn't it?'

Pierre smiled absent-mindedly, evidently not grasping what she said.

'Yes, I am very glad,' he said.

'How can people be dissatisfied with anything?' thought Natasha. 'Especially such a capital fellow as Bezukhov!' In Natasha's eyes all the people at the ball alike were good, kind, and splendid people, loving one another; none of them capable of injuring another – and so they ought all to be happy.

## 18

NEXT day Prince Andrew thought of the ball, but his mind did not dwell on it long. 'Yes, it was a very brilliant ball,' and then . . . 'Yes, that little Rostova is very charming. There's something fresh, original, unPetersburg-like about her that distinguishes her.' That was all he thought about yesterday's ball, and after his morning tea he set to work.

But either from fatigue or want of sleep he was ill-disposed for work and could get nothing done. He kept criticizing his own work as he often did, and was glad when he heard someone coming.

The visitor was Bitsky, who served on various committees, frequented all the societies in Petersburg, and was a passionate devotee of the new ideas and of Speransky, and a diligent Petersburg newsmonger – one of those men who choose their opinions like their clothes, according to the fashion, but who for that very reason appear to be the warmest partisans. Hardly had he got rid of his hat before he ran into Prince Andrew's room with a preoccupied air and at once began talking. He had just heard particulars of that morning's sitting of the Council of State opened by the Emperor, and he spoke of it enthusiastically. The Emperor's speech had been extraordinary. It had been a speech such as only constitutional monarchs deliver. 'The sovereign plainly said that the Council and Senate are *estates* of the realm, he said that the government must rest not on authority but on secure bases. The Emperor said that the fiscal system must be reorganized and the accounts published,' recounted Bitsky, emphasizing certain words and opening his eyes significantly.

'Ah, yes. To-day's events mark an epoch, the greatest epoch in our history,' he concluded.

Prince Andrew listened to the account of the opening of the Council of State, which he had so impatiently awaited and to which he had attached such importance, and was surprised that this event, now that it had taken place, did not affect him, and even seemed quite insignificant. He listened with quiet irony to Bitsky's enthusiastic account of it. A very simple thought occurred to him: 'What does it matter to me or to Bitsky what the Emperor was pleased to say at the Council? Can all that make me any happier or better?'

And this simple reflection suddenly destroyed all the interest Prince Andrew had felt in the impending reforms. He was going to dine that evening at Speransky's, 'with only a few friends', as the host had said when inviting him. The prospect of that dinner in the intimate home circle of the man he so admired had greatly interested Prince Andrew, especially as he had not yet seen Speransky in his domestic surroundings, but now he felt disinclined to go to it.

At the appointed hour, however, he entered the modest house Speransky owned in the Taurida Gardens. In the parqueted dining-room of this small house, remarkable for its extreme cleanliness (suggesting that of a monastery), Prince Andrew, who was rather late, found the friendly gathering of Speransky's intimate acquaintances already assembled at five o'clock. There were no ladies present except Speransky's little daughter (long-faced like her father) and her governess. The other guests were Gervais, Magnitsky, and Stolypin.* While still in the ante-room, Prince Andrew heard loud voices and a ringing staccato laugh – a laugh such as one hears on the stage. Someone – it sounded like Speransky – was distinctly ejaculating *ha-ha-ha*. Prince Andrew had never before heard Speransky's famous laugh, and this ringing, high-pitched laughter from a statesman made a strange impression on him.

He entered the dining-room. The whole company were standing

491

between two windows, at a small table laid with hors-d'œuvres. Speransky, wearing a grey swallow-tail coat with a star on the breast, and evidently still the same waistcoat and high white stock he had worn at the meeting of the Council of State, stood at the table with a beaming countenance. His guests surrounded him. Magnitsky, addressing himself to Speransky, was relating an anecdote, and Speransky was laughing in advance at what Magnitsky was going to say. When Prince Andrew entered the room Magnitsky's words were again drowned by laughter. Stolypin gave a deep bass guffaw as he munched a piece of bread and cheese. Gervais laughed softly with a hissing chuckle, and Speransky in a high-pitched staccato manner.

Still laughing, Speransky held out his soft white hand to Prince Andrew.

'Very pleased to see you, Prince,' he said. 'One moment . . .' he went on, turning to Magnitsky and interrupting his story. 'We have agreed that this is a dinner for recreation, with not a word about business!' and turning again to the narrator he began to laugh afresh.

Prince Andrew looked at the laughing Speransky with astonishment, regret, and disillusionment. It seemed to him that this was not Speransky but someone else. Everything that had formerly appeared mysterious and fascinating in Speransky suddenly became plain and unattractive.

At dinner the conversation did not cease for a moment, and seemed to consist of the contents of a book of funny anecdotes. Before Magnitsky had finished his story, someone else was anxious to relate something still funnier. Most of the anecdotes, if not relating to the State service, related to people in the service. It seemed that in this company the insignificance of those people was so definitely accepted that the only possible attitude towards them was one of good-humoured ridicule. Speransky related how at the Council that morning, a deaf dignitary, when asked his opinion, replied that he thought so too. Gervais gave a long account of an official revision, remarkable for the stupidity of everybody concerned. Stolypin, stuttering, broke into the conversation and began excitedly talking of the abuses that existed under the former order of things – threatening to give a serious turn to the conversation. Magnitsky starting quizzing Stolypin about his vehemence. Gervais intervened with a joke, and the talk reverted to its former lively tone.

Evidently Speransky liked to rest after his labours and find amusement in a circle of friends, and his guests, understanding his wish, tried to enliven him and amuse themselves. But their gaiety seemed to Prince Andrew mirthless and tiresome. Speransky's high-pitched voice struck him unpleasantly, and the incessant laughter grated on him like a false note. Prince Andrew did not laugh and feared that he would be a damper on the spirits of the company, but no one took any notice of his being out of harmony with the general mood. They all seemed very gay.

He tried several times to join in the conversation, but his remarks were tossed aside each time like a cork thrown out of the water, and he could not jest with them.

There was nothing wrong or unseemly in what they said, it was witty, and might have been funny, but it lacked just that something which is the salt of mirth, and they were not even aware that such a thing existed.

After dinner Speransky's daughter and her governess rose. He patted the little girl with his white hand and kissed her. And that gesture, too, seemed unnatural to Prince Andrew.

The men remained at table over their port – English fashion. In the midst of a conversation that was started about Napoleon's Spanish affairs,* which they all agreed in approving, Prince Andrew began to express a contrary opinion. Speransky smiled and, with an evident wish to prevent the conversation from taking an unpleasant course, told a story that had no connexion with the previous conversation. For a few moments all were silent.

Having sat some time at table, Speransky corked a bottle of wine, and remarking, 'Nowadays good wine rides in a carriage and pair,' passed it to the servant and got up. All rose, and continuing to talk loudly went into the drawing-room. Two letters brought by a courier were handed to Speransky, and he took them to his study. As soon as he had left the room the general merriment stopped and the guests began to converse sensibly and quietly with one another.

'Now for the recitation!' said Speransky on returning from his study. 'A wonderful talent!' he said to Prince Andrew and Magnitsky immediately assumed a pose and began reciting some humorous verses in French which he had composed about various well-known Petersburg people. He was interrupted several times by applause. When the verses were finished, Prince Andrew went up to Speransky and took his leave.

'Where are you off to so early?' asked Speransky.

'I promised to go to a reception.'

They said no more. Prince Andrew looked closely into those mirror-like, impenetrable eyes, and felt that it had been ridiculous of him to have expected anything from Speransky and from any of his own activities connected with him, or ever to have attributed importance to what Speransky was doing. That precise, mirthless laughter rang in Prince Andrew's ears long after he had left the house.

When he reached home Prince Andrew began thinking of his life in Petersburg during those last four months, as if it were something new. He recalled his exertions and solicitations, and the history of his project of army reform, which had been accepted for consideration and which they were trying to pass over in silence simply because another, a very poor one, had already been prepared and submitted to the Emperor. He thought of the meetings of a committee of which Berg was a member. He remembered how carefully and at what length everything relating to form and procedure was discussed at those meetings, and how sedulously and promptly all that related to the gist of the business was evaded. He recalled his labours on the Legal Code, and how painstakingly he had translated the articles of the Roman and French codes into Russian, and he felt ashamed of himself. Then he vividly pictured to himself Bogucharovo, his occupations in the country, his journey to Ryazan, he remembered the peasants, and Dron the village elder, and mentally applying to them the Personal Rights he had divided into paragraphs, he felt astonished that he could have spent so much time on such useless work.

19

NEXT day Prince Andrew called at a few houses he had not visited before, and among them at the Rostovs' with whom he had renewed acquaintance at the ball. Apart from considerations of politeness which demanded the call, he wanted to see that original, eager girl who had left such a pleasant impression on his mind, in her own home.

Natasha was one of the first to meet him. She was wearing a dark-blue house-dress, in which Prince Andrew thought her even prettier than in her ball-dress. She and all the Rostov family welcomed him as an old friend, simply and cordially. The whole family, whom he had formerly judged severely, now seemed to him to consist of excellent, simple, and kindly people. The old count's hospitality and good nature, which struck one especially in Petersburg as a pleasant surprise, were such that Prince Andrew could not refuse to stay to dinner. 'Yes,' he thought, 'they are capital people, who of course have not the slightest idea what a treasure they possess in Natasha; but they are kindly folk and form the best possible setting for this strikingly poetic, charming girl, overflowing with life!'

In Natasha Prince Andrew was conscious of a strange world completely alien to him and brimful of joys unknown to him, a different world that in the Otradnoe avenue and at the window that moonlight night had already begun to disconcert him. Now this world disconcerted him no longer and was no longer alien to him, but he himself, having entered it, found in it a new enjoyment.

After dinner Natasha, at Prince Andrew's request, went to the clavichord and began singing. Prince Andrew stood by a window talking to the ladies and listened to her. In the midst of a phrase he ceased speaking and suddenly felt tears choking him, a thing he had thought impossible for him. He looked at Natasha as she sang, and something new and joyful stirred in his soul. He felt happy and at the same time sad. He had absolutely nothing to weep about yet he was ready to weep. What about? His former love? The little princess? His disillusionments? . . . His hopes for the future? . . . Yes and no. The chief reason was a sudden, vivid sense of the terrible contrast between something infinitely great and illimitable within him, and that limited and material something that he, and even she, was. This contrast weighed on and yet cheered him while she sang.

As soon as Natasha had finished she went up to him and asked how he liked her voice. She asked this and then became confused, feeling that she ought not to have asked it. He smiled, looking at her, and said he liked her singing as he liked everything she did.

Prince Andrew left the Rostovs' late in the evening. He went to bed from habit, but soon realized that he could not sleep. Having lit his candle he sat up in bed, then got up, then lay down again not at all troubled by his sleeplessness: his soul was as fresh and joyful as if he had stepped out of a stuffy room into God's own fresh air. It did not enter his head that he was in love with Natasha, he was not thinking about her, but only picturing her to himself, and in consequence all life appeared in a new light. 'Why do I strive, why do I toil in this narrow, confined frame, when life, all life with all its joys, is open to me?' said he to himself. And for the first time for a very long while he began making happy plans for the future. He decided that he must attend to his son's education by finding a tutor and putting the boy in his charge, then he ought to retire from the service and go abroad, and see England, Switzerland, and Italy. 'I must use my freedom while I feel so much strength and youth in me,' he said to himself. 'Pierre was right when he said one must believe in the possibility of happiness in order to be happy, and now I do believe in it. Let the dead bury their dead, but while one has life one must live and be happy!' thought he.

20

ONE morning Colonel Adolf Berg, whom Pierre knew as he knew everybody in Moscow and Petersburg, came to see him. Berg arrived in an immaculate brand-new uniform, with his hair pomaded and brushed forward over his temples as the Emperor Alexander wore his hair.

'I have just been to see the countess, your wife. Unfortunately she could not grant my request, but I hope, Count, I shall be more fortunate with you,' he said with a smile.

'What is it you wish, Colonel? I am at your service.'

'I have now quite settled in my new rooms, Count, (Berg said this with perfect conviction that this information could not but be agreeable) 'and so I wish to arrange just a small party for my own and my wife's friends.' (He smiled still more pleasantly.) 'I wished to ask the countess and you to do me the honour of coming to tea and to supper.'

Only Countess Hélène, considering the society of such people as the Bergs beneath her, could be cruel enough to refuse such an invitation. Berg explained so clearly why he wanted to collect at his house a small but select company, and why this would give him pleasure, and why though he grudged spending money on cards or anything harmful, he was prepared to run into some expense for the sake of good society – that Pierre could not refuse, and promised to come.

'But don't be late, Count, if I may venture to ask; about ten minutes to eight, please. We shall make up a rubber. Our general is coming. He is very good to me. We shall have supper, Count. So you will do me the favour.'

Contrary to his habit of being late, Pierre on that day arrived at the Bergs' house, not at ten but at fifteen minutes to eight.

Having prepared everything necessary for the party, the Bergs were ready for their guests' arrival.

In their new, clean, and light study, with its small busts and pictures and new furniture, sat Berg and his wife. Berg, closely buttoned up in his new uniform, sat beside his wife, explaining to her that one always could and should be acquainted with people above one, because only then does one get satisfaction from acquaintances.

496

'You can get to know something, you can ask for something. See how I managed from my first promotion.' (Berg measured his life not by years but by promotions.) 'My comrades are still nobodies, while I am only waiting for a vacancy to command a regiment, and have the happiness to be your husband.' (He rose and kissed Vera's hand, and on the way to her straightened out a turned-up corner of the carpet.) 'And how have I obtained all this? Chiefly by knowing how to choose my acquaintances. It goes without saying that one must be conscientious and methodical.'

Berg smiled with a sense of his superiority over a weak woman, and paused, reflecting that this dear wife of his was after all but a weak woman who could not understand all that constitutes a man's dignity, what it was *ein Mann zu sein*. Vera at the same time was smiling with a sense of superiority over her good, conscientious husband, who all the same understood life wrongly as, according to Vera, all men did. Berg, judging by his wife, thought all women weak and foolish. Vera, judging only by her husband and generalizing from that observation, supposed that all men, though they understand nothing and are conceited and selfish, ascribe common sense to themselves alone.

Berg rose and embraced his wife carefully, so as not to crush her lace fichu for which he had paid a good price, kissing her straight on the lips.

'The only thing is, we mustn't have children too soon,' he continued, following an unconscious sequence of ideas.

'Yes,' answered Vera, 'I don't at all want that. We must live for society.'

'Princess Yusupova wore one exactly like this,' said Berg, pointing to the fichu with a happy and kindly smile.

Just then Count Bezukhov was announced. Husband and wife glanced at one another, both smiling with self-satisfaction, and each mentally claiming the honour of this visit.

'This is what comes of knowing how to make acquaintances,' thought Berg. 'This is what comes of knowing how to conduct oneself.'

'But please don't interrupt me when I am entertaining the guests,' said Vera, 'because I know what interests each of them and what to say to different people.'

Berg smiled again.

'It can't be helped: men must sometimes have masculine conversation,' said he.

They received Pierre in their small, new drawing-room, where it was impossible to sit down anywhere without disturbing its symmetry, neatness, and order; so it was quite comprehensible and not strange that Berg, having generously offered to disturb the symmetry of an arm-chair or of the sofa for his dear guest, but being apparently painfully undecided on the matter himself, eventually left the visitor to settle the question of selection. Pierre disturbed the symmetry by moving a chair for himself, and Berg and Vera immediately began their evening party, interrupting each other in their efforts to entertain their guest.

Vera, having decided in her own mind that Pierre ought to be entertained with conversation about the French embassy, at once began accordingly. Berg, having decided that masculine conversation was required, interrupted his wife's remarks and touched on the question of the war with Austria, and unconsciously jumped from the general subject to personal considerations as to the proposals made him to take part in the Austrian campaign, and the reasons why he had declined them. Though the conversation was very incoherent and Vera was angry at the intrusion of the masculine element, both husband and wife felt with satisfaction that, even if only one guest was present, their evening had begun very well and was as like as two peas to every other evening party with its talk, tea, and lighted candles.

Before long Boris, Berg's old comrade, arrived. There was a shade of condescension and patronage in his treatment of Berg and Vera. After Boris came a lady with the colonel, then the general himself, then the Rostovs, and the party became unquestionably exactly like all other evening parties. Berg and Vera could not repress their smiles of satisfaction at the sight of all this movement in their drawing-room, at the sound of the disconnected talk, the rustling of dresses, and the bowing and scraping. Everything was just as everybody always has it, especially so the general, who admired the apartment, patted Berg on the shoulder, and with parental authority superintended the setting-out of the table for boston.* The general sat down by Count Ilya Rostov, who was next to himself the most important guest. The old people sat with the old, the young with the young, and the hostess at the tea-table, on which stood exactly the same kind of cakes in a silver cake-basket as the Panins had at their party. Everything was just as it was everywhere else.

21

PIERRE, as one of the principal guests, had to sit down to boston with Count Rostov, the general, and the colonel. At the card-table he happened to be directly facing Natasha, and was struck by a

498

curious change that had come over her since the ball. She was silent, and not only less pretty than at the ball, but only redeemed from plainness by her look of gentle indifference to everything around.

'What's the matter with her?' thought Pierre, glancing at her. She was sitting by her sister at the tea-table, and reluctantly, without looking at him, made some reply to Boris who sat down beside her. After playing out a whole suit and to his partner's delight taking five tricks, Pierre, hearing greetings and the steps of someone who had entered the room while he was picking up his tricks, glanced again at Natasha.

'What has happened to her?' he asked himself with still greater surprise.

Prince Andrew was standing before her, saying something to her with a look of tender solicitude. She having raised her head, was looking up at him, flushed and evidently trying to master her rapid breathing. And the bright glow of some inner fire that had been suppressed was again alight in her. She was completely transformed, and from a plain girl had again become what she had been at the ball.

Prince Andrew went up to Pierre, and the latter noticed a new and youthful expression in his friend's face.

Pierre changed places several times during the game, sitting now with his back to Natasha and now facing her, but during the whole of the six rubbers he watched her and his friend.

'Something very important is happening between them,' thought Pierre, and a feeling that was both joyful and painful agitated him and made him neglect the game.

After six rubbers the general got up, saying that it was no use playing like that, and Pierre was released. Natasha on one side was talking with Sonya and Boris, and Vera with a subtle smile was saying something to Prince Andrew. Pierre went up to his friend, and asking whether they were talking secrets, sat down beside them. Vera having noticed Prince Andrew's attentions to Natasha, decided that at a party, a real evening party, subtle allusions to the tender passion were absolutely necessary, and seizing a moment when Prince Andrew was alone, began a conversation with him about feelings in general and about her sister. With so intellectual a guest as she considered Prince Andrew to be, she felt that she had to employ her diplomatic tact.

When Pierre went up to them he noticed that Vera was being carried away by her self-satisfied talk, but that Prince Andrew seemed embarrassed, a thing that rarely happened with him.

'What do you think?' Vera was saying with an arch smile. 'You are so discerning, Prince, and understand people's characters so well at a glance. What do you think of Natalie? Could she be constant in her attachments? Could she, like other women' (Vera meant herself) 'love a man once for all and remain true to him for ever? That is what I consider true love. What do you think, Prince?'

'I know your sister too little,' replied Prince Andrew, with a sarcastic smile under which he wished to hide his embarrassment, 'to be able to solve so delicate a question, and then I have noticed that the less attractive a woman is the more constant she is likely to be,' he added, and looked up at Pierre who was just approaching them.

'Yes, that is true, Prince. In our days,' continued Vera – mentioning 'our days' as people of limited intelligence are fond of doing, imagining that they have discovered and appraised the peculiarities of 'our days' and that human characteristics change with the times – 'In our days a girl has so much freedom that the pleasure of being courted often stifles real feeling in her. And it must be confessed that Natalie is very susceptible.' This return to the subject of Natalie caused Prince Andrew to knit his brows with discomfort: he was about to rise, but Vera continued with a still more subtle smile:

'I think no one has been more courted than she,' she went on, 'but till quite lately she never cared seriously for anyone. Now you know, Count,' she said to Pierre, 'even our dear cousin Boris, who, between ourselves, was very far gone in the land of tenderness...' (alluding to a map of love much in vogue at that time).

Prince Andrew frowned and remained silent.

'You are friendly with Boris, aren't you?' asked Vera.

'Yes, I know him...'

'I expect he has told you of his childish love for Natasha?'

'Oh, there was a childish love?' suddenly asked Prince Andrew, blushing unexpectedly.

'Yes, you know between cousins intimacy often leads to love. *Le cousinage est un dangereux voisinage.* Don't you think so?'

'Oh, undoubtedly!' said Prince Andrew, and with sudden and unnatural liveliness he began chaffing Pierre about the need to be very careful with his fifty-year-old Moscow cousins, and in the midst of these jesting remarks he rose, taking Pierre by the arm, and drew him aside.

'Well?' asked Pierre, seeing his friend's strange animation with surprise, and noticing the glance he turned on Nastasha as he rose.

'I must... I must have a talk with you,' said Prince Andrew. 'You know that pair of women's gloves?' (He referred to the masonic gloves given to a newly initiated Brother to present to the woman he loved.) 'I . . . but no, I will talk to you later on,' and with a strange light in his eyes and restlessness in his movements, Prince Andrew approached Natasha and sat down beside her. Pierre saw how Prince Andrew asked her something and how she flushed as she replied.

But at that moment Berg came to Pierre and began insisting that he should take part in an argument between the general and the colonel on the affairs in Spain.

Berg was satisfied and happy. The smile of pleasure never left his face. The party was very successful and quite like other parties he had seen. Everything was similar: the ladies' subtle talk, the cards, the general raising his voice at the card-table, and the samovar and the tea-cakes; only one thing was lacking that he had always seen at the evening parties he wished to imitate. They had not yet had a loud conversation among the men and a dispute about something important and clever. Now the general had begun such a discussion and so Berg drew Pierre to it.

22

NEXT day, having been invited by the count, Prince Andrew dined with the Rostovs and spent the rest of the day there.

Everyone in the house realized for whose sake Prince Andrew came, and without concealing it he tried to be with Natasha all day. Not only in the soul of the frightened yet happy and enraptured Natasha, but in the whole house, there was a feeling of awe at something important that was bound to happen. The countess looked with sad and sternly serious eyes at Prince Andrew when he talked to Natasha, and timidly started some artificial conversation about trifles as soon as he looked her way. Sonya was afraid to leave Natasha and afraid of being in the way when she was with them. Natasha grew pale, in a panic of expectation, when she remained alone with him for a moment. Prince Andrew surprised her by his timidity. She felt that he wanted to say something to her but could not bring himself to do so.

In the evening, when Prince Andrew had left, the countess went up to Natasha and whispered:

'Well, what?'

'Mamma! For heaven's sake don't ask me anything now! One can't talk about that,' said Natasha.

But all the same that night Natasha, now agitated and now frightened, lay a long time in her mother's bed gazing straight before her. She told her how he had complimented her, how he told her he was going abroad, asked her where they were going to spend the summer, and then how he had asked her about Boris.

'But such a . . . such a . . . never happened to me before!' she said. 'Only I feel afraid in his presence. I am always afraid when I'm with him. What does that mean? Does it mean that it's the real thing? Yes? Mamma, are you asleep?'

'No, my love; I am frightened myself,' answered her mother. 'Now go!'

'All the same I shan't sleep. What silliness, to sleep! Mummy! Mummy! such a thing never happened to me before,' she said, surprised and alarmed at the feeling she was aware of in herself. 'And could we ever have thought! . . .'

It seemed to Natasha that even at the time she first saw Prince Andrew at Otradnoe, she had fallen in love with him. It was as if she feared this strange, unexpected happiness of meeting again the very man she had then chosen (she was firmly convinced she had done so), and of finding him, as it seemed, not indifferent to her.

'And it had to happen that he should come specially to Petersburg while we are here. And it had to happen that we should meet at that ball. It is fate. Clearly it is fate, that everything led up to this! Already *then*, directly I saw him I felt something peculiar.'

'What else did he say to you? What are those verses? Read them, . . .' said her mother, thoughtfully, referring to some verses Prince Andrew had written in Natasha's album.

'Mamma, one need not be ashamed of his being a widower?'

' 'Don't, Natasha! Pray to God. "Marriages are made in heaven",' said her mother.

At that very time Prince Andrew was sitting with Pierre and telling him of his love for Natasha and his firm resolve to make her his wife.

That day Countess Hélène had a reception at her house. The French ambassador was there, and a foreign Prince of the Blood who had of late become a frequent visitor of hers, and many brilliant ladies and gentlemen. Pierre, who had come downstairs, walked through the rooms and struck everyone by his preoccupied, absent-minded and morose air.

Since the ball he had felt the approach of a fit of nervous depression and had made desperate efforts to combat it. Since the intimacy of his wife with the royal prince, Pierre had unexpectedly been made a gentleman of the bedchamber, and from that time he had begun to feel oppressed and ashamed in court society, and dark thoughts of the vanity of all things human came to him oftener than before. At the same time the feeling he had noticed between his protégée Natasha and Prince Andrew accentuated his gloom by the contrast between his own position and his friend's. He tried equally to avoid thinking about his wife, and about Natasha and Prince Andrew; and again everything seemed to him insignificant in comparison with eternity; again the question: For what? presented itself; and he forced himself to work day and night at masonic labours, hoping to drive away the evil spirit that threatened him. Towards midnight, after he had left the countess's apartments, he was sitting upstairs in a shabby dressing-gown, copying out the original transactions of the Scottish Lodge of Freemasons, at a table in his low room cloudy with tobacco smoke, when someone came in. It was Prince Andrew.

'Ah, it's you!' said Pierre with a preoccupied, dissatisfied air. 'And I, you see, am hard at it,' he pointed to his manuscript-book with that air of escaping from the ills of life with which unhappy people look at their work.

Prince Andrew, with a beaming, ecstatic expression of renewed life on his face, paused in front of Pierre and, not noticing his sad look, smiled at him with the egotism of joy.

'Well, dear heart,' said he, 'I wanted to tell you about it yester-day, and I have come to do so to-day. I never experienced anything like it before. I am in love, my friend!'

Suddenly Pierre heaved a deep sigh and dumped his heavy person down on the sofa beside Prince Andrew.

'With Natasha Rostova, yes?' said he.

'Yes, yes! Who else should it be? I should never have believed it, but the feeling is stronger than I. Yesterday I tormented myself and suffered, but I would not exchange even that torment for anything in the world, I have not lived till now. At last I live, but I can't live without her! But can she love me? . . . I am too old for her . . . Why don't you speak?'

'I? I? What did I tell you?' said Pierre suddenly, rising and beginning to pace up and down the room. 'I always thought it . . . That girl is such a treasure . . . she is a rare girl . . . My dear friend, I entreat you, don't philosophize, don't doubt, marry, marry, marry . . . And I am sure there will not be a happier man than you.'

'But what of her?'

'She loves you.'

'Don't talk rubbish, . . .' said Prince Andrew, smiling and looking into Pierre's eyes.

'She does, I know,' Pierre cried fiercely.

'But do listen,' returned Prince Andrew, holding him by the arm. 'Do you know the condition I am in? I must talk about it to some-one.'

'Well, go on, go on. I am very glad,' said Pierre, and his face really changed, his brow became smooth, and he listened gladly to Prince Andrew. Prince Andrew seemed, and really was, quite a different, quite a new man. Where was his spleen, his contempt for life, his disillusionment? Pierre was the only person to whom he made up his mind to speak openly; and to him he told all that was in his soul. Now he boldly and lightly made plans for an extended future, said he could not sacrifice his own happiness to his father's caprice, and spoke of how he would either make his father consent to this marriage and love her, or would do without his consent; then he marvelled at the feeling that had mastered him, as at something strange, apart from and independent of himself.

'I should not have believed anyone who told me that I was capable of such love,' said Prince Andrew. 'It is not at all the same feeling that I knew in the past. The whole world is now for me divided into two halves: one half is she, and there all is joy, hope, light; the other half is everything where she is not, and there all is gloom and darkness . . .'

'Darkness and gloom,' reiterated Pierre; 'yes, yes, I understand that.'

'I cannot help loving the light, it is not my fault. And I am very happy! You understand me? I know you are glad for my sake.'

'Yes, yes,' Pierre assented, looking at his friend with a touched and sad expression in his eyes. The brighter Prince Andrew's lot appeared to him, the gloomier seemed his own.

23

PRINCE ANDREW needed his father's consent to his marriage, and to obtain this he started for the country next day.

His father received his son's communication with external composure, but inward wrath. He could not comprehend how anyone could wish to alter his life or introduce anything new into it, when his own life was already ending. 'If only they would let me end my days as I want to,' thought the old man, 'then they might do as they please.' With his son, however, he employed the diplomacy he reserved for important occasions and, adopting a quiet tone, discussed the whole matter.

In the first place the marriage was not a brilliant one as regards birth, wealth, or rank. Secondly, Prince Andrew was no longer as young as he had been and his health was poor (the old man laid special stress on this), while she was very young. Thirdly, he had a son whom it would be a pity to entrust to a chit of a girl. 'Fourthly and finally,' the father said, looking ironically at his son, 'I beg you to put it off for a year: go abroad, take a cure, look out, as you wanted to, for a German tutor for Prince Nicholas. Then if your love or passion or obstinacy – as you please – is still as great, marry! And that's my last word on it. Mind, the last! . . .' concluded the prince, in a tone which showed that nothing would make him alter his decision.

Prince Andrew saw clearly that the old man hoped that his feelings, or his fiancée's, would not stand a year's test, or that he (the old prince himself) would die before then, and he decided to conform to his father's wish – to propose, and postpone the wedding for a year.

Three weeks after the last evening he had spent with the Rostovs, Prince Andrew returned to Petersburg.

Next day after her talk with her mother Natasha expected Bolkonsky all day, but he did not come. On the second and third day it was the same. Pierre did not come either and Natasha, not knowing that Prince Andrew had gone to see his father, could not explain his absence to herself.

Three weeks passed in this way. Natasha had no desire to go out anywhere, and wandered from room to room like a shadow, idle and listless; she wept secretly at night and did not go to her mother in the evenings. She blushed continually and was irritable. It seemed to her that everybody knew about her disappointment, and was laughing at her and pitying her. Strong as was her inward grief, this wound to her vanity intensified her misery.

Once she came to her mother, tried to say something, and suddenly began to cry. Her tears were those of an offended child who does not know why it is being punished.

The countess began to soothe Natasha, who after first listening to her mother's words, suddenly interrupted her:

'Leave off, mamma! I don't think, and don't want to think about it! He just came and then left off, left off . . .'

Her voice trembled, and she again nearly cried, but recovered and went on quietly:

'And I don't at all want to get married. And I am afraid of him; I have now become quite, quite calm.'

The day after this conversation Natasha put on the old dress which she knew had the peculiar property of conducing to cheerfulness in the mornings, and that day she returned to the old way of life which she had abandoned since the ball. Having finished her morning tea she went to the ball-room, which she particularly liked for its loud resonance, and began singing her solfeggio. When she had finished her first exercise she stood still in the middle of the room and sang a musical phrase that particularly pleased her. She listened joyfully (as though she had not expected it) to the charm of the notes reverberating, filling the whole empty ball-room, and slowly dying away; and all at once she felt cheerful. 'What's the good of making so much of it? Things are nice as it is,' she said to herself, and she began walking up and down the room, not stepping simply on the resounding parquet but treading with each step from the heel to the toe (she had on a new and favourite pair of shoes) and listening to the regular tap of the heel and creak of the toe as gladly as she had to the sounds of her own voice. Passing a mirror she glanced into it. 'There, that's me!' the expression of her face seemed to say as she caught sight of herself. 'Well, and very nice too! I need nobody.'

A footman wanted to come in to clear away something in the room, but she would not let him, and having closed the door behind him continued her walk. That morning she had returned to her favourite mood – love of, and delight in, herself. 'How charming that Natasha is!' she said again, speaking as some third, collective, male person. 'Pretty, a good voice, young, and in nobody's way if only they leave her in peace.' But however much they left her in peace, she could not now be at peace, and immediately felt this.

In the hall the porch-door opened, and someone asked, 'At home?' and then footsteps were heard. Natasha was looking at the mirror, but did not see herself. She listened to the sounds in the hall. When she saw herself, her face was pale. It was *he*. She knew this for certain, though she hardly heard his voice through the closed doors.

Pale and agitated, Natasha ran into the drawing-room.

'Mamma! Bolkonsky has come!' she said. 'Mamma, it is awful, it is unbearable! I don't want . . . to be tormented! What am I to do? . . .'

Before the countess could answer, Prince Andrew entered the room with an agitated and serious face. As soon as he saw Natasha his face brightened. He kissed the countess's hand and Natasha's, and sat down beside the sofa.

'It is long since we had the pleasure . . .' began the countess, but Prince Andrew interrupted her by answering her intended question, obviously in haste to say what he had to.

'I have not been to see you all this time because I have been at my father's. I had to talk over a very important matter with him. I only got back last night,' he said, glancing at Natasha; 'I want to have a talk with you, Countess,' he added after a moment's pause.

The countess lowered her eyes, sighing deeply.

'I am at your disposal,' she murmured.

Natasha knew that she ought to go away, but was unable to do so: something gripped her throat, and regardless of manners she stared straight at Prince Andrew with wide-open eyes.

'At once? This instant! ... No, it can't be!' she thought.

Again he glanced at her, and that glance convinced her that she was not mistaken. Yes, at once, that very instant, her fate would be decided.

'Go, Natasha! I will call you,' said the countess in a whisper.

Natasha glanced with frightened imploring eyes at Prince Andrew and at her mother, and went out.

'I have come, Countess, to ask for your daughter's hand,' said Prince Andrew.

The countess's face flushed hotly, but she said nothing.

'Your offer ...' she began at last sedately. He remained silent, looking into her eyes. 'Your offer ...' (she grew confused) 'is agreeable to us, and ... I accept your offer. I am glad. And my husband ... I hope ... but it will depend on her ...'

'I will speak to her when I have your consent ... Do you give it to me?' said Prince Andrew.

'Yes,' replied the countess. She held out her hand to him, and with a mixed feeling of estrangement and tenderness pressed her lips to his forehead as he stooped to kiss her hand. She wished to love him as a son, but felt that to her he was a stranger and a terrifying man. 'I am sure my husband will consent,' said the countess, 'but your father ...'

'My father, to whom I have told my plans, has made it an express condition of his consent that the wedding is not to take place for a year. And I wished to tell you of that,' said Prince Andrew.

'It is true that Natasha is still young, but – so long as that? ...'

'It is unavoidable,' said Prince Andrew with a sigh.

'I will send her to you,' said the countess, and left the room.

'Lord have mercy upon us!' she repeated while seeking her daughter.

Sonya said that Natasha was in her bedroom. Natasha was sitting on the bed, pale and dry-eyed, and was gazing at the icons and whispering something as she rapidly crossed herself. Seeing her mother, she jumped up and flew to her.

'Well, mamma? ... Well? ...'

'Go, go to him. He is asking for your hand,' said the countess, coldly it seemed to Natasha. 'Go ... go,' said the mother, sadly and reproachfully, with a deep sigh, as her daughter ran away.

Natasha never remembered how she entered the drawing-room. When she came in and saw him she paused. 'Is it possible that this stranger has now become *everything* to me?' she asked herself, and immediately answered, 'Yes, everything! He alone is now dearer to me than everything in the world.' Prince Andrew came up to her with downcast eyes.

'I have loved you from the very first moment I saw you. May I hope?'

He looked at her and was struck by the serious impassioned expression of her face. Her face said: 'Why ask? Why doubt what you cannot but know? Why speak, when words cannot express what one feels?'

She drew near to him and stopped. He took her hand and kissed it.

'Do you love me?'

'Yes, yes!' Natasha murmured as if in vexation. Then she sighed loudly and, catching her breath more and more quickly, began to sob.

'What is it? What's the matter?'

'Oh, I am so happy!' she replied, smiled through her tears, bent over closer to him, paused for an instant as if asking herself whether she might, and then kissed him.

Prince Andrew held her hands, looked into her eyes, and did not find in his heart his former love for her. Something in him had suddenly changed; there was no longer the former poetic and mystic charm of desire, but there was pity for her feminine and childish weakness, fear at her devotion and trustfulness, and an oppressive yet joyful sense of the duty that now bound him to her for ever. The present feeling, though not so bright and poetic as the former, was stronger and more serious.

'Did your mother tell you that it cannot be for a year?' asked Prince Andrew, still looking into her eyes.

'Is it possible that I – the "chit of a girl", as everybody called me,' thought Natasha, 'is it possible that I am now to be the *wife* and the equal of this strange, dear, clever man, whom even my father looks up to? Can it be true? Can it be true that there can be no more playing with life, that now I am grown up, that on me now lies a responsibility for my every word and deed? Yes, but what did he ask me?'

'No,' she replied, but she had not understood his question.

'Forgive me!' he said. 'But you are so young, and I have already been through so much in life. I am afraid for you, you do not yet know yourself.'

Natasha listened with concentrated attention, trying but failing to take in the meaning of his words.

'Hard as this year which delays my happiness will be,' continued

508

Prince Andrew, 'it will give you time to be sure of yourself. I ask you to make me happy in a year, but you are free: our engagement shall remain a secret, and should you find that you do not love me, or should you come to love...' said Prince Andrew with an unnatural smile.

'Why do you say that?' Natasha interrupted him. 'You know that from the very day you first came to Otradnoe I have loved you,' she cried, quite convinced that she spoke the truth.

'In a year you will learn to know yourself...'

'A whole year!' Natasha repeated suddenly, only now realizing that the marriage was to be postponed for a year. 'But why a year? Why a year?...'

Prince Andrew began to explain to her the reasons for this delay. Natasha did not hear him.

'And can't it be helped?' she asked. Prince Andrew did not reply, but his face expressed the impossibility of altering that decision.

'It's awful! Oh, it's awful! awful!' Natasha suddenly cried, and again burst into sobs. 'I shall die, waiting a year: it's impossible, it's awful!' She looked into her lover's face and saw in it a look of commiseration and perplexity.

'No, no! I'll do anything!' she said, suddenly checking her tears. 'I am so happy.'

The father and mother came into the room and gave the betrothed couple their blessing.

From that day Prince Andrew began to frequent the Rostovs' as Natasha's affianced lover.

24

No betrothal ceremony took place and Natasha's engagement to Bolkonsky was not announced; Prince Andrew insisted on that. He said that as he was responsible for the delay, he ought to bear the whole burden of it; that he had given his word and bound himself for ever, but that he did not wish to bind Natasha and gave her perfect freedom. If after six months she felt that she did not love him, she would have full right to reject him. Naturally neither Natasha nor her parents wished to hear of this, but Prince Andrew was firm. He came every day to the Rostovs', but did not behave to Natasha as an affianced lover: he did not use the familiar *thou*, but said *you* to her, and kissed only her hand. After their engagement, quite different, intimate, and natural relations sprang up between them. It was as if they had not known each other till now. Both liked to recall how they had regarded each other when as yet they were *nothing* to one another; they felt themselves now quite different beings: then they were artificial, now natural and sincere. At first the family felt some constraint in intercourse with Prince Andrew; he seemed a man from another world, and for a long time Natasha trained the family to get used to him, proudly assuring them all that he only appeared to be different, but was really just like all of them, and that she was not afraid of him and no one else ought to be. After a few days they grew accustomed to him, and without restraint in his presence pursued their usual way of life, in which he took his part. He could talk about rural economy with the count, fashions with the countess and Natasha, and about albums and fancy-work with Sonya. Sometimes the household both among themselves and in his presence expressed their wonder at how it had all happened, and at the evident omens there had been of it: Prince Andrew's coming to Otradnoe and their coming to Petersburg, and the likeness between Natasha and Prince Andrew which her nurse had noticed on his first visit, and Andrew's encounter with Nicholas in 1805, and many other incidents betokening that it had to be.

In the house that poetic dullness and quiet reigned which always accompanies the presence of a betrothed couple. Often when all sitting together everyone kept silent. Sometimes the others would get up and go away and the couple, left alone, still remained silent. They rarely spoke of their future life. Prince Andrew was afraid and ashamed to speak of it. Natasha shared this as she did all his feelings, which she constantly divined. Once she began questioning him about his son. Prince Andrew blushed, as he often did now – Natasha particularly liked it in him – and said that his son would not live with them.

'Why not?' asked Natasha in a frightened tone.

'I cannot take him away from his grandfather, and besides . . .'

'How I should have loved him!' said Natasha, immediately guessing his thought; 'but I know you wish to avoid any pretext for finding fault with us.'

Sometimes the old count would come up, kiss Prince Andrew, and ask his advice about Petya's education or Nicholas's service. The old countess sighed as she looked at them; Sonya was always getting frightened lest she should be in the way, and tried to find excuses for leaving them alone, even when they did not wish it. When Prince Andrew spoke (he could tell a story very well) Natasha listened to him with pride; when she spoke, she noticed with fear and joy that he gazed attentively and scrutinizingly at her. She asked herself in perplexity: 'What does he look for in me? He is trying to discover something by looking at me! What if what he seeks in me is not there?' Sometimes she fell into one of the mad, merry moods characteristic of her, and then she particularly loved to hear and see how Prince Andrew laughed. He seldom laughed, but when he did he abandoned himself entirely to his laughter, and after such a laugh she always felt nearer to him. Natasha would have been completely happy if the thought of the separation awaiting her and drawing near had not terrified her, just as the mere thought of it made him turn pale and cold.

On the eve of his departure from Petersburg Prince Andrew brought with him Pierre, who had not been to the Rostovs' once since the ball. Pierre seemed disconcerted and embarrassed. He was talking to the countess, and Natasha sat down beside a little chess-table with Sonya, thereby inviting Prince Andrew to come too. He did so.

'You have known Bezukhov a long time?' he asked. 'Do you like him?'

'Yes, he's a dear, but very absurd.'

And, as usual when speaking of Pierre, she began to tell anecdotes of his absent-mindedness, some of which had even been invented about him.

'Do you know I have entrusted him with our secret? I have known him from childhood. He has a heart of gold. I beg you, Natalie,' Prince Andrew said with sudden seriousness – 'I am going away, and heaven knows what may happen. You may cease to ... all right, I know I am not to say that. Only this, then: whatever may happen to you when I am not there ...'

'What can happen?'

'Whatever trouble may come,' Prince Andrew continued, 'I beg you, Mademoiselle Sophie, whatever may happen, to turn to him alone for advice and help! He is a most absent-minded and absurd fellow, but he has a heart of gold.'

Neither her father, nor her mother, nor Sonya, nor Prince Andrew himself, could have foreseen how the separation from her lover would act on Natasha. Flushed and agitated she went about the house all that day, dry-eyed, occupied with most trivial matters as if not understanding what awaited her. She did not even cry when, on taking leave, he kissed her hand for the last time. 'Don't go!' she said in a tone that made him wonder whether he really ought not to stay and which he remembered long afterwards. Nor did she cry when he was gone; but for several days she sat in her room dry-eyed, taking no interest in anything and only saying now and then, 'Oh, why did he go away?'

But a fortnight after his departure, to the surprise of those around her, she recovered from her mental sickness just as suddenly and became her old self again, but with a change in her moral physiognomy, as a child gets up after a long illness with a changed expression of face.

## 25

DURING that year after his son's departure, Prince Nicholas Bolkonsky's health and temper became much worse. He grew still more irritable, and it was Princess Mary who generally bore the brunt of his frequent fits of unprovoked anger. He seemed carefully to seek out her tender spots so as to torture her mentally as harshly as possible. Princess Mary had two passions and consequently two joys – her nephew, little Nicholas, and religion – and these were the favourite subjects of the prince's attacks and ridicule. Whatever was spoken of he would bring round to the superstitiousness of old maids, or the petting and spoiling of children. 'You want to make him' – little Nicholas – 'into an old maid like yourself! A pity! Prince Andrew wants a son and not an old maid,' he would say. Or, turning to Mademoiselle Bourienne, he would ask her in Princess Mary's presence how she liked our village priests and icons, and would joke about them.

He continually hurt Princess Mary's feelings and tormented her, but it cost her no effort to forgive him. Could he be to blame towards her, or could her father, who she knew loved her in spite of it all, be unjust? And what is justice? The princess never thought of that proud word 'justice'. All the complex laws of man centred for her in one clear and simple law – the law of love and self-sacrifice taught us by Him who lovingly suffered for mankind though He Himself was God. What had she to do with the justice or injustice of other people? She had to endure and love, and that she did.

During the winter Prince Andrew had come to Bald Hills, and had been gay, gentle, and more affectionate than Princess Mary had known him for a long time past. She felt that something had happened to him, but he said nothing to her about his love. Before he left he had a long talk with his father about something, and Princess Mary noticed that before his departure they were dissatisfied with one another.

Soon after Prince Andrew had gone, Princess Mary wrote to her friend Julie Karagina in Petersburg, whom she had dreamed (as all girls dream) of marrying to her brother, and who was at that time in mourning for her own brother, killed in Turkey.*

512

Sorrow, it seems, is our common lot, my dear, tender friend Julie.

Your loss is so terrible that I can only explain it to myself as a special providence of God who, loving you, wishes to try you and your excellent mother. Oh, my friend! Religion, and religion alone, can – I will not say comfort us – but save us from despair. Religion alone can explain to us what without its help man cannot comprehend: why, for what cause, kind and noble beings, able to find happiness in life – not merely harming no one, but necessary to the happiness of others – are called away to God, while cruel, useless, harmful persons, or such as are a burden to themselves and to others, are left living. The first death I saw, and one I shall never forget – that of my dear sister-in-law – left that impression on me. Just as you ask destiny why your splendid brother had to die, so I asked why that angel Lise, who not only never wronged anyone, but in whose soul there were never any unkind thoughts, had to die. And what do you think, dear friend? Five years have passed since then, and already I, with my petty understanding, begin to see clearly why she had to die, and in what way that death was but an expression of the infinite goodness of the Creator, whose every action, though generally incomprehensible to us, is but a manifestation of His infinite love for His creatures. Perhaps, I often think, she was too angelically innocent to have the strength to perform all a mother's duties. As a young wife she was irreproachable; perhaps she could not have been so as a mother. As it is, not only has she left us, and particularly Prince Andrew, with the purest regrets and memories, but probably she will *there* receive a place I dare not hope for myself. But not to speak of her alone, that early and terrible death has had the most beneficent influence on me and on my brother in spite of all our grief. Then, at the moment of our loss, these thoughts could not occur to me; I should then have dismissed them with horror, but now they are very clear and certain. I write all this to you, dear friend, only to convince you of the Gospel truth which has become for me a principle of life: not a single hair of our heads will fall without His will. And His will is governed only by infinite love for us, and so whatever befalls us is for our good.

You ask whether we shall spend next winter in Moscow. In spite of my wish to see you, I do not think so and do not want to do so. You will be surprised to hear that the reason for this is Buonaparte! The case is this: my father's health is growing noticeably worse, he cannot stand any contradiction and is becoming irritable. This irritability is, as you know, chiefly directed to political questions. He cannot endure the notion that Buonaparte is negotiating on equal terms with all the sovereigns of Europe, and particularly with our own, the grandson of the Great Catherine! As you know, I am quite indifferent to politics, but from my father's remarks and his talks with Michael Ivanovich I know all that goes on in the world, and especially about the honours conferred on Buonaparte, who only at Bald Hills in the whole world, it seems, is not accepted as a great man, still less as Emperor of France. And my father cannot stand this. It seems to me that it is chiefly because of his political views that my father is reluctant to speak of going to Moscow; for he foresees the encounters that would result from his way of expressing his views regardless of anybody. All the benefit he might derive from a course of treatment, he would lose as a result of the disputes about Buonaparte which would be inevitable. In any case it will be decided very shortly.

Our family life goes on in the old way except for my brother Andrew's absence. He, as I wrote you before, has changed very much of late. After his sorrow he only this year quite recovered his spirits. He has again become as I used to know him when a child: kind, affectionate, with that heart of gold to which I know no equal. He has realized, it seems to me, that life is not over for him. But together with this mental change he has grown physically much weaker. He has become thinner and more nervous. I am anxious about him and glad he is taking this trip abroad which the doctors recommended long ago. I hope it will cure him. You write that in Petersburg he is spoken of as one of the most active, cultivated, and capable of the young men. Forgive my vanity as a relation, but I never doubted it. The good he has done to everybody here, from his peasants up to the gentry, is incalculable. On his arrival in Petersburg he received only his due. I always wonder at the way rumours fly from Petersburg to Moscow, especially such false ones as that you write about – I mean the report of my brother's betrothal to the little Rostova. I do not think my brother will ever marry again, and certainly not her; and this is why: first, I know that though he rarely speaks about the wife he has lost, the grief of that loss has gone too deep in his heart for him ever to decide to give her a successor and our little angel a step-mother. Secondly because, as far as I know, that girl is not the kind of girl who could please Prince Andrew. I do not think he would choose her for a wife, and frankly I do not wish it. But I am running on too long and am at the end of my second sheet. Good-bye, my dear friend. May God keep you in His holy and mighty care. My dear friend, Mademoiselle Bourienne, sends you kisses.

Mary.

## 26

In the middle of the summer Princess Mary received an unexpected letter from Prince Andrew in Switzerland in which he gave her strange and surprising news. He informed her of his engagement to Natasha Rostova. The whole letter breathed loving rapture for his betrothed and tender and confiding affection for his sister. He wrote that he had never loved as he did now, and that only now did he understand and know what life was. He asked his sister to forgive him for not having told her of his resolve when he had last visited Bald Hills, though he had spoken of it to his father. He had not done so for fear Princess Mary should ask her father to give his consent, irritating him and having to bear the brunt of his displeasure without attaining her object.

Besides [he wrote] the matter was not then so definitely settled as it is now. My father then insisted on a delay of a year and now already *six months*, half of that period, has passed, and my resolution is firmer than ever. If the doctors did not keep me here at the spas I should be back in Russia, but as it is I have to postpone my return for three months. You know me and my relations with father. I want nothing from him. I have been and always shall be independent; but to go against his will and arouse his anger, now that he may perhaps remain with us such a short time, would destroy half my happiness. I am now writing to him about the same question, and beg you to choose a good moment to hand him the letter, and to let me know how he looks at the whole matter and whether there is hope that he may consent to reduce the term by four months.

After long hesitations, doubts and prayers, Princess Mary gave the letter to her father. The next day the old prince said to her quietly:

'Write and tell your brother to wait till I am dead ... It won't be long – I shall soon set him free.'

The princess was about to reply, but her father would not let her speak and raising his voice more and more, cried:

'Marry, marry, my boy! ... A good family! ... Clever people, eh? Rich, eh? Yes, a nice step-mother little Nicholas will have! Write and tell him that he may marry to-morrow if he likes. She will be little Nicholas's step-mother and I'll marry Bourienne! ... Ha, ha, ha! He mustn't be without a step-mother either! Only one thing, no more women are wanted in my house – let him marry and live by himself. Perhaps you will go and live with him too?' he added, turning to Princess Mary. 'Go in heaven's name! Go out into the frost ... the frost ... the frost!'

After this outburst the prince did not speak any more about the matter. But repressed vexation at his son's poor-spirited behaviour found expression in his treatment of his daughter. To his former pretexts for irony a fresh one was now added – allusions to stepmothers, and amiabilities to Mademoiselle Bourienne.

'Why shouldn't I marry her?' he asked his daughter. 'She'll make a splendid princess!'

And latterly, to her surprise and bewilderment, Princess Mary noticed that her father was really associating more and more with the Frenchwoman. She wrote to Prince Andrew about the reception of his letter, but comforted him with hopes of reconciling their father to the idea.

Little Nicholas and his education, her brother Andrew, and

religion, were Princess Mary's joys and consolations; but besides that, since everyone must have personal hopes, Princess Mary in the profoundest depths of her heart had a hidden dream and hope that supplied the chief consolation of her life. This comforting dream and hope were given her by God's folk – the half-witted and other pilgrims who visited her without the prince's knowledge. The longer she lived, the more experience and observation she had of life, the greater was her wonder at the short-sightedness of men who seek enjoyment and happiness here on earth: toiling, suffering, struggling, and harming one another, to obtain that impossible, visionary, sinful happiness. Prince Andrew had loved his wife, she died, but that was not enough, he wanted to bind his happiness to another woman. Her father objected to this because he wanted a more distinguished and wealthier match for Andrew. And they all struggled and suffered and tormented one another and injured their souls, their eternal souls, for the attainment of benefits which endure but for an instant. Not only do we know this ourselves, but Christ, the Son of God, came down to earth and told us that this life is but for a moment and is a probation; yet we cling to it and think to find happiness in it. 'How is it that no one realizes this?' thought Princess Mary. 'No one except these despised God's folk who, wallet on back, come to me by the back door, afraid of being seen by the prince, not for fear of ill-usage by him but for fear of causing him to sin. To leave family, home, and all the cares of worldly welfare, in order without clinging to anything to wander in hempen rags from place to place under an assumed name, doing no one any harm but praying for all – for those who drive one away as well as for those who protect one: higher than that life and truth there is no life or truth!'

There was one pilgrim, a quiet pock-marked little woman of fifty called Theodosia, who for over thirty years had gone about barefoot and worn heavy chains. Princess Mary was particularly fond of her. Once when in a room with a lamp dimly lit before the icon Theodosia was talking of her life, the thought that Theodosia alone had found the true path of life suddenly came to Princess Mary with such force that she resolved to become a pilgrim herself. When Theodosia had gone to sleep Princess Mary thought about this for a long time, and at last made up her mind that, strange as it might seem, she must go on pilgrimage. She disclosed this thought to no one but to her confessor, Father Akinfi, the monk, and he approved of her intention. Under guise of a present for the pilgrims, Princess Mary prepared a pilgrim's complete costume for herself: a coarse smock, bast shoes, a rough coat and a black kerchief. Often, approaching the chest of drawers containing this secret treasure,

Princess Mary paused, uncertain whether the time had not already come to put her project into execution.

Often listening to the pilgrims' tales she was so stimulated by their simple speech, mechanical to them but to her so full of deep meaning, that several times she was on the point of abandoning everything and running away from home. In imagination she already pictured herself by Theodosia's side, dressed in coarse rags, walking with a staff, a wallet on her back, along the dusty road, directing her wanderings from one saint's shrine to another, free from envy, earthly love, or desire, and reaching at last the place where there is no more sorrow or sighing, but eternal joy and bliss.

'I shall come to a place and pray there, and before having time to get used to it or getting to love it, I shall go farther. I will go on till my legs fail, and I'll lie down and die somewhere, and shall at last reach that eternal, quiet haven, where there is neither sorrow nor sighing . . .' thought Princess Mary.

But afterwards, when she saw her father and especially little Koko (Nicholas) her resolve weakened. She wept quietly, and felt that she was a sinner who loved her father and little nephew more than God.

END OF PART THREE

# PART FOUR

## 1

THE Bible legend tells us that the absence of labour – idleness – was a condition of the first man's blessedness before the Fall. Fallen man has retained a love of idleness, but the curse weighs on the race not only because we have to seek our bread in the sweat of our brows, but because our moral nature is such that we cannot be both idle and at ease. An inner voice tells us we are in the wrong if we are idle. If man could find a state in which he felt that though idle he was fulfilling his duty, he would have found one of the conditions of man's primitive blessedness. And such a state of obligatory and irreproachable idleness is the lot of a whole class – the military. The chief attraction of military service has consisted and will consist in this compulsory and irreproachable idleness.

Nicholas Rostov experienced this blissful condition to the full when after 1807 he continued to serve in the Pavlograd regiment, in which he already commanded the squadron he had taken over from Denisov.

Rostov had become a bluff, good-natured fellow, whom his Moscow acquaintances would have considered rather bad form, but who was liked and respected by his comrades, subordinates, and superiors, and was well contented with his life. Of late, in 1809, he found in letters from home more frequent complaints from his mother that their affairs were falling into greater and greater disorder, and that it was time for him to come back to gladden and comfort his old parents.

Reading these letters Nicholas felt a dread of their wanting to take him away from surroundings in which, protected from all the entanglements of life, he was living so calmly and quietly. He felt that sooner or later he would have to re-enter that whirlpool of life, with its embarrassments and affairs to be straightened out, its accounts with stewards, quarrels, and intrigues, its ties, society, and with Sonya's love and his promise to her. It was all dreadfully difficult and complicated; and he replied to his mother in cold, formal letters in French, beginning: 'My dear mamma' and ending: 'Your obedient son', which said nothing of when he would return.

In 1810 he received letters from his parents in which they told him of Natasha's engagement to Bolkonsky, and that the wedding would be in a year's time because the old prince made difficulties. This letter grieved and mortified Nicholas. In the first place he was sorry that Natasha, for whom he cared more than for anyone else in the family, should be lost to the home; and secondly, from his hussar point of view, he regretted not to have been there to show that fellow Bolkonsky that connexion with him was no such great honour after all, and that if he loved Natasha he might dispense with permission from his dotard father. For a moment he hesitated whether he should not apply for leave in order to see Natasha before she was married, but then came the manœuvres, and considerations about Sonya and about the confusion of their affairs, and Nicholas again put it off. But in the spring of that year he received a letter from his mother, written without his father's knowledge, and that letter persuaded him to return. She wrote that if he did not come and take matters in hand, their whole property would be sold by auction and they would all have to go begging. The count was so weak, and trusted Mitenka so much, and was so good-natured, that everybody took advantage of him and things were going from bad to worse. 'For God's sake, I implore you, come at once, if you do not wish to make me and the whole family wretched,' wrote the countess.

This letter touched Nicholas. He had that common sense of a matter-of-fact man which showed him what he ought to do.

The right thing now was, if not to retire from the service, at any rate to go home on leave. Why he had to go he did not know; but after his after-dinner nap he gave orders to saddle Mars, an extremely vicious grey stallion that had not been ridden for a long time, and when he returned with the horse all in a lather, he informed Lavrushka (Denisov's servant who had remained with him) and his comrades who turned up in the evening, that he was applying for leave and was going home. Difficult and strange as it was for him to reflect that he would go away without having heard from the staff – and this interested him extremely – whether he was promoted to a captaincy or would receive the Order of St Anne for the last manœuvres; strange as it was to think that he would go away without having sold his three roans to the Polish Count Goluchowski, who was bargaining for the horses Rostov had betted he would sell for two thousand rubles; incomprehensible as it seemed that the ball the hussars were giving in honour of the Polish Mademoiselle Przazdziecka (out of rivalry to the uhlans, who had given one in honour of their Polish Mademoiselle Borzozowska) would take place without him – he knew he must go away from this good, bright world, to somewhere where everything was stupid and confused. A week later he obtained his leave. His hussar comrades – not only those of his own regiment, but the whole brigade – gave Rostov a dinner to which the subscription was fifteen rubles a head, and at which there were two bands and two choirs of singers. Rostov danced the Trepak with Major Basov; the tipsy officers tossed, embraced, and dropped Rostov; the soldiers of the third squadron tossed him too, and shouted 'hurrah!', and then they put him in his sledge and escorted him as far as the first post-station.

During the first half of the journey – from Kremenchug to Kiev – all Rostov's thoughts, as is usual in such cases, were behind him, with the squadron; but when he had gone more than half-way he began to forget his three roans and Dozhoyveyko, his quartermaster, and to wonder anxiously how things would be at Otradnoe and what he would find there. Thoughts of home grew stronger the nearer he approached it – far stronger, as though this feeling of his was subject to the law by which the force of attraction is in inverse proportion to the square of the distance. At the last post-station before Otradnoe he gave the driver a three-ruble tip, and on arriving he ran breathlessly, like a boy, up the steps of his home.

After the rapture of meeting, and after that odd feeling of un-satisfied expectation – the feeling that 'everything is just the same, so why did I hurry?' – Nicholas began to settle down in his old home world. His father and mother were much the same, only a little older. What was new in them was a certain uneasiness and occasional discord, which there used not to be, and which, as Nicholas soon found out, was due to the bad state of their affairs. Sonya was nearly twenty, she had stopped growing prettier and promised nothing more than she was already, but that was enough. She exhaled happiness and love from the time Nicholas returned, and the faithful, unalterable love of this girl had a gladdening effect on him. Petya and Natasha surprised Nicholas most. Petya was a big, handsome boy of thirteen, merry, witty, and mischievous, with a voice that was already breaking. As for Natasha, for a long while Nicholas wondered and laughed whenever he looked at her.

'You're not the same at all,' he said.

'How? Am I uglier?'

'On the contrary, but what dignity! A princess!' he whispered to her.

'Yes, yes, yes!' cried Natasha joyfully.

She told him all about her romance with Prince Andrew and of his visit to Otradnoe, and showed him his last letter.

'Well, are you glad?' Natasha asked. 'I am so tranquil and happy now.'

'Very glad,' answered Nicholas. 'He is an excellent fellow ... And are you very much in love?'

'How shall I put it?' replied Natasha. 'I was in love with Boris, with my teacher, and with Denisov, but this is quite different. I feel at peace and settled. I know that no better man than he exists, and I am calm and contented now. Not at all as before.'

Nicholas expressed his disapproval of the postponement of the marriage for a year; but Natasha attacked her brother with exasperation, proving to him that it could not be otherwise, and that it would be a bad thing to enter a family against the father's will, and that she herself wished it so.

'You don't at all understand,' she said.

Nicholas was silent and agreed with her.

Her brother often wondered as he looked at her. She did not seem at all like a girl in love and parted from her affianced husband. She was even-tempered and calm, and quite as cheerful as of old. This amazed Nicholas and even made him regard Bolkonsky's courtship sceptically. He could not believe that her fate was sealed, especially as he had not seen her with Prince Andrew. It always seemed to him that there was something not quite right about this intended marriage.

'Why this delay? Why no betrothal?' he thought. Once, when he had touched on this topic with his mother, he discovered, to his surprise and somewhat to his satisfaction, that in the depth of her soul she too had doubts about this marriage.

'You see he writes,' said she, showing her son a letter of Prince Andrew's with that latent grudge a mother always has in regard to a daughter's future married happiness, 'he writes that he won't come before December. What can be keeping him? Illness, probably! His health is very delicate. Don't tell Natasha. And don't attach importance to her being so bright: that's because she's living through the last days of her girlhood, but I know what she is like every time we receive a letter from him! However, God grant that everything turns out well!' (she always ended with these words). 'He is an excellent man!'

2

AFTER reaching home Nicholas was at first serious and even dull. He was worried by the impending necessity of interfering in the stupid business matters for which his mother had called him home. To throw off this burden as quickly as possible, on the third day

522

after his arrival he went, angry and scowling and without answering questions as to where he was going, to Mitenka's lodge, and demanded an *account of everything*. But what an *account of everything* might be Nicholas knew even less than the frightened and bewildered Mitenka. The conversation and the examination of the accounts with Mitenka did not last long. The village elder, a peasant delegate, and the village clerk, who were waiting in the passage, heard with fear and delight first the young count's voice roaring and snapping and rising louder and louder, and then words of abuse, dreadful words, ejaculated one after the other.

'Robber!... Ungrateful wretch!... I'll hack the dog to pieces! I'm not my father!... Robbing us!...' and so on.

Then with no less fear and delight they saw how the young count, red in the face and with bloodshot eyes, dragged Mitenka out by the scruff of the neck and applied his foot and knee to him behind with great agility at convenient moments between his words, shouting, 'Be off! Never let me see your face here again, you villain!'

Mitenka flew headlong down the six steps and ran away into the shrubbery. (This shrubbery was a well-known haven of refuge for culprits at Otradnoe. Mitenka himself, returning tipsy from the town, used to hide there, and many of the residents at Otradnoe, hiding from Mitenka, knew of its protective qualities.)

Mitenka's wife and sister-in-law thrust their heads and frightened faces out of the door of a room where a bright samovar was boiling and where the steward's high bedstead stood with its patchwork quilt.

The young count paid no heed to them, but breathing hard passed by with resolute strides and went into the house.

The countess, who heard at once from the maids what had happened at the lodge, was calmed by the thought that now their affairs would certainly improve, but on the other hand felt anxious as to the effect this excitement might have on her son. She went several times to his door on tiptoe and listened, as he lighted one pipe after another.

Next day the old count called his son aside and with an embarrassed smile said to him:

'But you know, my dear boy, it's a pity you got excited! Mitenka has told me all about it.'

'I knew,' thought Nicholas, 'that I should never understand anything in this crazy world.'

'You were angry that he had not entered those 700 rubles. But they were carried forward – and you did not look at the other page.'

'Papa, he is a blackguard and a thief! I know he is! And what I have done, I have done; but if you like I won't speak to him again.'

'No, my dear boy' (the count, too, felt embarrassed. He knew he had mismanaged his wife's property and was to blame towards his children, but he did not know how to remedy it). 'No, I beg you to attend to the business. I am old. I . . .'

'No, papa. Forgive me if I have caused you unpleasantness. I understand it all less than you do.'

'Devil take all these peasants, and money matters, and carryings forward from page to page,' he thought. 'I used to understand what a "corner" and the stakes at cards meant, but carrying forward to another page I don't understand at all,' said he to himself, and after that he did not meddle in business affairs. But once the countess called her son and informed him that she had a promissory note from Anna Mikhaylovna for two thousand rubles, and asked him what he thought of doing with it.

'This,' answered Nicholas. 'You say it rests with me. Well, I don't like Anna Mikhaylovna, and I don't like Boris, but they were our friends and poor. Well then, this!' and he tore up the note, and by so doing caused the old countess to weep tears of joy. After that, young Rostov took no further part in any business affairs, but devoted himself with passionate enthusiasm to what was to him a new pursuit – the chase – for which his father kept a large establishment.

3

THE weather was already growing wintry, and morning frosts congealed an earth saturated by autumn rains. The verdure had thickened, and its bright green stood out sharply against the brownish strips of winter rye trodden down by the cattle, and against the pale yellow stubble of the spring sowing and the reddish strips of buckwheat. The wooded ravines and the copses, which at the end of August had still been green islands amid black fields and stubble, had become golden and bright-red islands amid the green winter rye. The hares had already half changed their summer coats, the fox-cubs were beginning to scatter, and the young wolves were bigger than dogs. It was the best time of year for the chase. The hounds of that ardent young sportsman Rostov had not merely reached hard winter condition, but were so jaded that at a meeting of the huntsmen it was decided to give them a three days' rest and then, on the 16th of September, to go on a distant expedition, starting from the oak grove where there was an undisturbed litter of wolf-cubs.

All that day the hounds remained at home. It was frosty and the air was sharp, but towards evening the sky became overcast and it began to thaw. On the 15th, when young Rostov in his dressing-gown looked out of the window, he saw it was an unsurpassable morning for hunting:* it was as if the sky were melting and sinking to the earth without any wind. The only motion in the air was that of the dripping, microscopic particles of drizzling mist. The bare twigs in the garden were hung with transparent drops which fell on the freshly fallen leaves. The earth in the kitchen-garden looked wet and black and glistened like poppy-seed and at a short distance merged into the dull moist veil of mist. Nicholas went out into the wet and muddy porch. There was a smell of decaying leaves and of dog. Milka, a black-spotted broad-haunched bitch with prominent black eyes, got up on seeing her master, stretched her hind legs, lay down like a hare and then suddenly jumped up and licked him right on his nose and moustache. Another borzoi, a dog, catching sight of his master from the garden path, arched his back and rushing headlong towards the porch with lifted tail began rubbing himself against his legs.

'O-hoy!' came at that moment that inimitable huntsman's call which unites the deepest bass with the shrillest tenor, and round the corner came Daniel the head huntsman and head kennel-man, a grey, wrinkled old man with hair cut straight over his forehead, Ukrainian fashion, a long bent whip in his hand, and that look of independence and scorn of everything that is only seen in huntsmen. He doffed his Circassian cap to his master and looked at him scornfully. This scorn was not offensive to his master. Nicholas knew that this Daniel, disdainful of everybody and who considered himself above them, was all the same his serf and huntsman.

'Daniel!' Nicholas said timidly, conscious at the sight of the weather, the hounds, and the huntsman, that he was being carried away by that irresistible passion for sport which makes a man forget all his previous resolutions, as a lover forgets in the presence of his mistress.

'What orders, your Excellency?' said the huntsman in his deep bass, deep as a proto-deacon's and hoarse with hallooing – and two flashing black eyes gazed from under his brows at his master, who was silent. 'Can you resist it?' those eyes seemed to be asking.

'It's a good day, eh? For a hunt and a gallop, eh?' asked Nicholas, scratching Milka behind the ears.

Daniel did not answer, but winked instead.

'I sent Uvarka at dawn to listen,' his bass boomed out after a minute's pause. 'He says *she's moved them* into the Otradnoe enclosure. They were howling there.' (This meant that the she-wolf, about whom they both knew, had moved with her cubs to the Otradnoe copse, a small place two versts from the house.)

'We ought to go, don't you think so?' said Nicholas. 'Come to me with Uvarka.'

'As you please.'

'Then put off feeding them.'

'Yes, sir.'

Five minutes later Daniel and Uvarka were standing in Nicholas's big study. Though Daniel was not a big man, to see him in a room was like seeing a horse or a bear on the floor among the furniture and surroundings of human life. Daniel himself felt this, and as usual stood just inside the door, trying to speak softly and not move, for fear of breaking something in the master's apartment, and he hastened to say all that was necessary so as to get from under that ceiling, out into the open under the sky once more.

Having finished his inquiries and extorted from Daniel an opinion that the hounds were fit (Daniel himself wished to go hunting), Nicholas ordered the horses to be saddled. But just as Daniel was about to go, Natasha came in with rapid steps, not having done up her hair or finished dressing, and with her old nurse's big shawl wrapped round her. Petya ran in at the same time.

'You are going?' asked Natasha. 'I knew you would! Sonya said you wouldn't go, but I knew that to-day is the sort of day when you couldn't help going.'

'Yes, we are going,' replied Nicholas reluctantly, for to-day as he intended to hunt seriously he did not want to take Natasha and Petya. 'We are going, but only wolf-hunting: it would be dull for you.'

'You know it is my greatest pleasure,' said Natasha. 'It's not fair; you are going by yourself, are having the horses saddled, and said nothing to us about it.'

'"No barrier bars a Russian's path" – we'll go!' shouted Petya.

'But you can't. Mamma said you mustn't,' said Nicholas to Natasha.

'Yes, I'll go. I shall certainly go,' said Natasha decisively. 'Daniel, tell them to saddle for us, and Michael must come with my dogs,' she added to the huntsman.

It seemed to Daniel irksome and improper to be in a room at all, but to have anything to do with a young lady seemed to him impossible. He cast down his eyes and hurried out as if it were none of his business, careful as he went not to inflict any accidental injury on the young lady.

THE old count, who had always kept up an enormous hunting establishment but had now handed it all completely over to his son's care, being in very good spirits on this 15th of September, prepared to go out with the others.

In an hour's time the whole hunting party was at the porch. Nicholas, with a stern and serious air which showed that now was no time for attending to trifles, went past Natasha and Petya who were trying to tell him something. He had a look at all the details of the hunt, sent a pack of hounds and huntsmen on ahead to find the quarry, mounted his chestnut Donets, and whistling to his own leash of borzois, set off across the threshing-ground to a field leading to the Otradnoe wood. The old count's horse, a sorrel gelding called Viflyanka, was led by the groom in attendance on him, while the count himself was to drive in a small trap straight to a spot reserved for him.

They were taking fifty-four hounds with six hunt-attendants and whippers-in. Besides the family there were eight borzoi kennel-men and more than forty borzois, so that, with the borzois on leash belonging to members of the family, there were about a hundred and thirty dogs and twenty horsemen.

Each dog knew its master and its call. Each man in the hunt knew his business, his place, and what he had to do. As soon as they had passed the fence they all spread out evenly and quietly without noise or talk, along the road and field leading to the Otradnoe covert.

The horses stepped over the field as over a thick carpet, now and then splashing into puddles as they crossed a road. The misty sky still seemed to descend evenly and imperceptibly towards the earth, the air was still, warm, and silent. Occasionally the whistle of a huntsman, the snort of a horse, the crack of a whip, or the whine of a straggling hound, could be heard.

When they had gone about a verst, five more riders with dogs appeared out of the mist, approaching the Rostovs. In front rode a fresh-looking handsome old man with a large grey moustache.

'Good morning, Uncle!' said Nicholas when the old man drew near.

'That's it. Come on!...I was sure of it,' began 'Uncle'. (He was a distant relative of the Rostovs', a man of small means, and their neighbour.) 'I knew you wouldn't be able to resist it and it's a good thing you're going. That's it! Come on!' (This was 'Uncle's' favourite expression.) 'Take the covert at once, for my Girchik says the Ilagins are at Korniki with their hounds. That's it. Come on! . . . They'll take the cubs from under your very nose.'

'That's where I'm going. Shall we join up our packs?' asked Nicholas.

The hounds were joined into one pack, and 'Uncle' and Nicholas rode on side by side. Natasha, muffled up in shawls which did not hide her eager face and shining eyes, galloped up to them. She was followed by Petya who always kept close to her, by Michael a huntsman, and by a groom appointed to look after her. Petya, who was laughing, whipped and pulled at his horse. Natasha sat easily and confidently on her black Arabchick and reined him in without effort with a firm hand.

'Uncle' looked round disapprovingly at Petya and Natasha. He did not like to combine frivolity with the serious business of hunting.

'Good morning, Uncle! We are going too!' shouted Petya.

'Good morning, good morning! But don't go overriding the hounds,' said 'Uncle' sternly.

'Nicholas, what a fine dog Trunila is! He knew me,' said Natasha, referring to her favourite hound.

'In the first place Trunila is not a "dog" but a harrier,' thought Nicholas, and looked sternly at his sister, trying to make her feel the distance that ought to separate them at that moment. Natasha understood it.

'You mustn't think we'll be in anyone's way, Uncle,' she said. 'We'll go to our places and won't budge.'

'A good thing too, little Countess,' said 'Uncle', 'only mind you don't fall off your horse,' he added, 'because – that's it, come on! – you've nothing to hold on to.'

The oasis of the Otradnoe covert came in sight a couple of hundred yards off, the huntsmen were already nearing it. Rostov, having finally settled with 'Uncle' where they should set on the hounds, and having shown Natasha where she was to stand – a spot where nothing could possibly run out – went round above the ravine.

'Well, nephew, you're going for a big wolf,' said 'Uncle'. 'Mind and don't let her slip!'

'That's as may happen,' answered Rostov. 'Karay, here!' he shouted, answering 'Uncle's' remark by this call to his borzoi. Karay was a shaggy old dog with a hanging jowl, famous for having tackled a big wolf unaided. They all took up their places.

The old count, knowing his son's ardour in the hunt, hurried so as not to be late, and the huntsmen had not yet reached their places when Count Ilya Rostov, cheerful, flushed, and with quivering cheeks, drove up with his black horses over the winter rye to the place reserved for him where a wolf might come out. Having straightened his coat and fastened on his hunting-knives and horn, he mounted his good, sleek, well-fed and comfortable horse, Viflyanka, which was turning grey like himself. His horses and trap were sent home. Count Ilya Rostov, though not at heart a keen sportsman, knew the rules of the hunt well, and rode to the bushy edge of the wood where he was to stand, arranged his reins, settled himself in the saddle and, feeling that he was ready, looked about with a smile.

Beside him was Simon Chekmar, his personal attendant, an old horseman now somewhat stiff in the saddle. Chekmar held in leash three formidable wolf-hounds, who had, however, grown fat like their master and his horse. Two wise old dogs lay down unleashed. Some hundred paces farther along the edge of the wood stood Mitka, the count's other groom, a daring horseman and keen rider to hounds. Before the hunt, by old custom, the count had drunk a silver cupful of mulled brandy, taken a snack, and washed it down with half a bottle of his favourite Bordeaux.

He was somewhat flushed with the wine and the drive. His eyes were rather moist and glittered more than usual, and as he sat in his saddle wrapped up in his fur coat he looked like a child taken for an outing.

The thin, hollow-cheeked Chekmar, having got everything ready, kept glancing at his master with whom he had lived on the best of terms for thirty years, and understanding the mood he was in, expected a pleasant chat. A third person rode up circumspectly through the wood (it was plain that he had had a lesson) and stopped behind the count. This person was a grey-bearded old man in a woman's cloak with a tall peaked cap on his head. He was the buffoon, who went by a woman's name, Nastasya Ivanovna.*

'Well, Nastasya Ivanovna!' whispered the count, winking at him. 'If you scare away the beast, Daniel'll give it you!'

'I know a thing or two myself!' said Nastasya Ivanovna.

'Hush!' whispered the count and turned to Simon. 'Have you seen the young countess?' he asked. 'Where is she?'

'With young Count Peter, by the Zharov rank grass,' answered Simon, smiling. 'Though she's a lady she's very fond of hunting.'

'And you're surprised at the way she rides, Simon, eh?' said the count. 'She's as good as many a man!'

'Of course! It's marvellous. So bold, so easy!'

'And Nicholas? Where is he? By the Lyadov upland, isn't he?'

'Yes sir. He knows where to stand. He understands the matter so well that Daniel and I are often quite astounded,' said Simon, well knowing what would please his master.

'Rides well, eh? And how well he looks on his horse, eh?'

'A perfect picture! How he chased a fox out of the rank grass by the Zavarzinsk thicket the other day! Leapt a fearful place; what a sight when they rushed from the covert ... the horse worth a thousand rubles and the rider beyond all price! Yes, one would have to search far to find another as smart.'

'To search far ...' repeated the count, evidently sorry Simon had not said more. 'To search far,' he said, turning back the skirt of his coat to get at his snuff-box.

'The other day when he came out from Mass in full uniform, Michael Sidorych ...' Simon did not finish, for on the still air he had distinctly caught the music of the hunt with only two or three hounds giving tongue. He bent down his head and listened, shaking a warning finger at his master. 'They are on the scent of the cubs ...' he whispered, 'straight to the Lyadov uplands.'

The count, forgetting to smooth out the smile on his face, looked into the distance straight before him, down the narrow open space, holding the snuff-box in his hand but not taking any. After the cry of the hounds came the deep tones of the wolf-call from Daniel's hunting-horn; the pack joined the first three hounds and they could be heard in full cry, with that peculiar lift in the note that indicates that they are after a wolf. The whippers-in no longer set on the hounds, but changed to the cry of *ulyulyu*, and above the others rose Daniel's voice, now a deep bass, now piercingly shrill. His voice seemed to fill the whole wood and carried far beyond out into the open field.

After listening a few moments in silence the count and his attendant convinced themselves that the hounds had separated into two packs: the sound of the larger pack, eagerly giving tongue, began to die away in the distance, the other pack rushed by the wood past the count, and it was with this that Daniel's voice was heard calling *ulyulyu*. The sounds of both packs mingled and broke apart again, but both were becoming more distant.

Simon sighed and stooped to straighten the leash a young borzoi had entangled, the count too sighed, and noticing the snuff-box in his hand opened it and took a pinch. 'Back!' cried Simon to a borzoi that was pushing forward out of the wood. The count started and dropped the snuff-box. Nastasya Ivanovna dismounted to pick it up. The count and Simon were looking at him.

Then unexpectedly, as often happens, the sounds of the hunt suddenly approached, as if the hounds in full cry and Daniel *ulyulyuing* were just in front of them.

The count turned and saw on his right Mitka, staring at him with eyes starting out of his head, raising his cap and pointing before him to the other side.

'Look out!' he shouted in a voice plainly showing that he had long fretted to utter that word, and letting the borzois slip he galloped towards the count.

The count and Simon galloped out of the wood, and saw on their left a wolf which, softly swaying from side to side was coming at a quiet lope farther to the left to the very place where they were standing. The angry borzois whined, and getting free of the leash rushed past the horses' feet at the wolf.

The wolf paused, turned its heavy forehead towards the dogs awkwardly, like a man suffering from the quinsy, and still slightly swaying from side to side, gave a couple of leaps and with a swish of its tail disappeared into the skirt of the wood. At the same instant, with a cry like a wail, first one hound, then another, and then another, sprang out helter-skelter from the wood opposite and the whole pack rushed across the field towards the very spot where the wolf had disappeared. The hazel bushes parted behind the hounds, and Daniel's chestnut horse appeared, dark with sweat. On its long back sat Daniel, hunched forward, capless, his dishevelled grey hair hanging over his flushed, perspiring face.

'Ulyulyulyu! ulyulyu! . . .' he cried. When he caught sight of the count his eyes flashed lightning.

'Blast you!' he shouted, holding up his whip threateningly at the count.

'You've let the wolf go! . . . What sportsmen!' and as if scorning to say more to the frightened and shamefaced count, he lashed the heaving flanks of his sweating chestnut gelding with all the anger the count had aroused, and flew off after the hounds. The count, like a punished schoolboy, looked round trying by a smile to win Simon's sympathy for his plight. But Simon was no longer there. He was galloping round by the bushes while the field was coming up on both sides, all trying to head the wolf, but it vanished into the wood before they could do so.

5

NICHOLAS ROSTOV meanwhile remained at his post waiting for the wolf. By the way the hunt approached and receded, by the cries of the dogs whose notes were familiar to him, by the way the voices of the huntsmen approached, receded, and rose, he realized what was happening at the copse. He knew that young and old wolves were there, that the hounds had separated into two packs, that somewhere a wolf was being chased, and that something had gone wrong. He expected the wolf to come his way any moment. He made thousands of different conjectures as to where and from what side the beast would come and how he would set upon it. Hope alternated with despair. Several times he addressed a prayer to God that the wolf should come his way. He prayed with that passionate and shamefaced feeling with which men pray at moments of great excitement arising from trivial causes. 'What would it be to Thee to do this for me?' he said to God. 'I know Thou art great, and that it is a sin to ask this of Thee, but for God's sake do let the old wolf come my way and let Karay spring at it – in sight of "Uncle" who is watching from over there – and seize it by the throat in a death-grip!' A thousand times during that half-hour Rostov cast eager and restless glances over the edge of the wood, with the two scraggy oaks rising above the aspen undergrowth and the gully with its water-worn side and 'Uncle's' cap just visible above the bush on his right.

'No, I shan't have such luck,' thought Rostov, 'yet what wouldn't it be worth! It is not to be! Everywhere, at cards and in war, I am always unlucky.' Memories of Austerlitz and of Dolokhov flashed rapidly and clearly through his mind. 'Only once in my life to get an old wolf, I want only that!' thought he, straining eyes and ears and looking to the left and then to the right, and listening to the slightest variation of note in the cries of the dogs.

Again he looked to the right, and saw something running towards him across the deserted field. 'No, it can't be!' thought Rostov taking a deep breath, as a man does at the coming of something long hoped for. The height of happiness was reached – and so simply, without warning, or noise, or display, that Rostov could not believe his eyes and remained in doubt for over a second. The wolf ran forward and jumped heavily over a gully that lay in her path. She was an old animal, with a grey back and big reddish belly. She ran without hurry, evidently feeling sure that no one saw her. Rostov, holding his breath, looked round at the borzois. They stood or lay not seeing the wolf or understanding the situation. Old Karay had turned his head and was angrily searching for fleas, baring his yellow teeth and snapping at his hind legs.

'Ulyulyulyu!' whispered Rostov pouting his lips. The borzois jumped up, jerking the rings of the leashes and pricking their ears. Karay finished scratching his hind quarters, and cocking his ears, got up with quivering tail from which tufts of matted hair hung down.

'Shall I loose them or not?' Nicholas asked himself as the wolf approached him coming from the copse. Suddenly the wolf's whole physiognomy changed; she shuddered, seeing what she had probably never seen before – human eyes fixed upon her, and turning her head a little towards Rostov she paused.

'Back or forward? Eh, no matter, forward . . .' the wolf seemed to say to herself, and she moved forward without again looking round, and with a quiet, long, easy yet resolute lope.

'*Ulyulyu!*' cried Nicholas in a voice not his own, and of its own accord his good horse darted headlong downhill leaping over gullies to head off the wolf, and the borzois passed it running faster still. Nicholas did not hear his own cry nor feel that he was galloping, nor see the borzois, nor the ground over which he went: he saw only the wolf, who increasing her speed bounded on in the same direction along the hollow. The first to come into view was Milka, with her black markings and powerful quarters, gaining upon the wolf. Nearer and nearer . . . now she was ahead of it; but the wolf turned its head to face her, and instead of putting on speed as she usually did Milka suddenly raised her tail and stiffened her forelegs.

'*Ulyulyulyulyu!*' shouted Nicholas.

The reddish Lyubim rushed forward from behind Milka, sprang impetuously at the wolf and seized it by its hind quarters, but immediately jumped aside in terror. The wolf crouched, gnashed her teeth, and again rose and bounded forward, followed at the distance of a couple of feet by all the borzois, who did not get any closer to her.

'She'll get away! No, it's impossible!' thought Nicholas, still shouting with a hoarse voice.

'Karay, *ulyulyu!* . . .' he shouted, looking round for the old borzoi who was now his only hope. Karay, with all the strength age had left him, stretched himself to the utmost, and watching the wolf galloped heavily aside to intercept it. But the quickness of the wolf's lope and the borzoi's slower pace made it plain that Karay had miscalculated. Nicholas could already see not far in front of him the wood, where the wolf would certainly escape should she reach it. But coming towards him he saw hounds and a huntsman galloping almost straight at the wolf. There was still hope. A long yellowish young borzoi, one Nicholas did not know, from another leash, rushed impetuously at the wolf from in front and almost knocked her over. But the wolf jumped up more quickly than anyone could have expected and, gnashing her teeth, flew at the yellowish borzoi, which with a piercing yelp fell with its head on the ground, bleeding from a gash in its side.

'Karay! Old fellow! . . .' wailed Nicholas.

Thanks to the delay caused by this crossing of the wolf's path, the old dog with its felted hair hanging from its thigh was within five paces of it. As if aware of her danger the wolf turned her eyes on Karay, tucked her tail yet further between her legs, and increased her speed. But here Nicholas only saw that something happened to Karay – the borzoi was suddenly on the wolf, and they rolled together down into a gully just in front of them.

That instant when Nicholas saw the wolf struggling in the gully with the dogs, while from under them could be seen her grey hair and outstretched hind leg and her frightened choking head with ears laid back (Karay was pinning her by the throat), was the happiest moment of his life. With his hand on his saddle-bow he was ready to dismount and stab the wolf, when she suddenly thrust her head up from among that mass of dogs, and then her fore-paws were on the edge of the gully. She clicked her teeth (Karay no longer had her by the throat), leapt with a movement of her hind legs out of the gully, and having disengaged herself from the dogs, with tail tucked in again went forward. Karay, his hair bristling, and probably bruised or wounded, climbed with difficulty out of the gully.

'Oh my God! Why?' Nicholas cried in despair.

'Uncle's' huntsman was galloping from the other side across the wolf's path and his borzois once more stopped the animal's advance. She was again hemmed in.

Nicholas and his attendant, with 'Uncle' and his huntsman, were all riding round the wolf, crying *'ulyulyu!'*, shouting and preparing to dismount each moment that the wolf crouched back, and starting forward again every time she shook herself and moved towards the wood where she would be safe.

Already at the beginning of this chase Daniel, hearing the *ulyulyuing*, had rushed out from the wood. He saw Karay seize the wolf, and checked his horse supposing the affair to be over. But when he saw that the horsemen did not dismount and that the wolf shook herself and ran for safety, Daniel set his chestnut galloping not at the wolf but straight towards the wood, just as Karay had run to cut the animal off. As a result of this he galloped up to the wolf just when she had been stopped a second time by 'Uncle's' borzois.

Daniel galloped up silently, holding a naked dagger in his left hand and thrashing the labouring sides of his chestnut horse with his whip as if it were a flail.

Nicholas neither saw nor heard Daniel until the chestnut, breathing heavily, panted past him, and he heard the fall of a body and saw Daniel lying on the wolf's back among the dogs trying to seize her by the ears. It was evident to the dogs, the hunters, and to the wolf herself, that all was now over. The terrified wolf pressed back her ears and tried to rise, but the borzois stuck to her. Daniel rose a little, took a step, and with his whole weight, as if lying down to rest, fell on the wolf, seizing her by the ears. Nicholas was about to stab her, but Daniel whispered, 'Don't, we'll gag her!' and changing his position set his foot on the wolf's neck. A stick was thrust between her jaws and she was fastened with a leash, as if bridled, her legs were bound together, and Daniel rolled her over once or twice from side to side.

With happy, exhausted faces they laid the old wolf, alive, on a shying and snorting horse, and accompanied by the dogs yelping at her, took her to the place where they were all to meet. The hounds had killed two of the cubs and the borzois three. The huntsmen assembled with their booty and their stories, and all came to look at the wolf, which with her broad-browed head hanging down and the bitten stick between her jaws, gazed with great glassy eyes at this crowd of dogs and men surrounding her. When she was touched, she jerked her bound legs and looked wildly yet simply at everybody. Old Count Rostov also rode up and touched the wolf.

'Oh, what a formidable one!' said he. 'A formidable one, eh?' he asked Daniel, who was standing near.

'Yes, your Excellency,' answered Daniel quickly doffing his cap.

The count remembered the wolf he had let slip and his encounter with Daniel.

'Ah, but you are a crusty fellow, friend!' said the count.

For sole reply Daniel gave him a shy, childlike, meek and amiable smile.

6

THE old count went home and Natasha and Petya promised to return very soon, but as it was still early the hunt went farther. At midday they put the hounds into a ravine thickly overgrown with young trees. Nicholas standing in a fallow field could see all his whips.

Facing him lay a field of winter rye, and there his own huntsman stood alone in a hollow behind a hazel bush. The hounds had scarcely been loosed before Nicholas heard one he knew, Voltorn, giving tongue at intervals, other hounds joined in, now pausing and now again giving tongue. A moment later he heard a cry from the wooded ravine that a fox had been found, and the whole pack, joining together, rushed along the ravine towards the rye-field and away from Nicholas.

He saw the whips in their red caps galloping along the edge of the ravine, he even saw the hounds, and was expecting a fox to show itself at any moment on the rye-field opposite.

The huntsman standing in the hollow moved and loosed his borzois, and Nicholas saw a queer, short-legged red fox with a fine brush going hard across the field. The borzois bore down on it . . . Now they drew close to the fox which began to dodge between the field in sharper and sharper curves, trailing its brush, when suddenly a strange white borzoi dashed in followed by a black one, and everything was in confusion; the borzois formed a star-shaped figure, scarcely swaying their bodies and with tails turned away from the centre of the group. Two huntsmen galloped up to the dogs, one in a red cap, the other, a stranger, in a green coat.

'What's this?' thought Nicholas. 'Where's that huntsman from? He is not "Uncle's" man.'

The huntsman got the fox, but stayed there a long time without strapping it to the saddle. Their horses, bridled and with high saddles, stood near them and there too the dogs were lying. The huntsmen waved their arms and did something to the fox. Then from that spot came the sound of a horn, with the signal agreed on in case of a fight.

'That's Ilagin's huntsman having a row with our Ivan,' said Nicholas's groom.

Nicholas sent the man to call Natasha and Petya to him, and rode at a foot-pace to the place where the whips were getting the hounds together. Several of the field galloped to the spot where the fight was going on.

Nicholas dismounted, and with Natasha and Petya who had ridden up, stopped near the hounds, waiting to see how the matter would end. Out of the bushes came the huntsman who had been fighting, and rode towards his young master with the fox tied to his crupper. While still at a distance he took off his cap and tried to speak respectfully, but he was pale and breathless and his face was angry. One of his eyes was black, but he probably was not even aware of it.

'What has happened?' asked Nicholas.

'A likely thing, killing a fox our dogs had hunted! And it was my grey bitch that caught it! Go to law, indeed! . . . He snatches at the fox! I gave him one with the fox. Here it is on my saddle! Do you want a taste of this? . . .' said the huntsman, pointing to his dagger and probably imagining himself still speaking to his foe.

Nicholas, not stopping to talk to the man, asked his sister and Petya to wait for him and rode to the spot where the enemy's, Ilagin's, hunting-party was.

The victorious huntsman rode off to join the field, and there, surrounded by inquiring sympathizers, recounted his exploits.

The facts were that Ilagin, with whom the Rostovs had a quarrel and were at law, hunted over places that belonged by custom to the Rostovs, and had now, as if purposely, sent his men to the very woods the Rostovs were hunting, and let his man snatch a fox their dogs had chased.

Nicholas, though he had never seen Ilagin, with his usual absence of moderation in judgement, hated him cordially from reports of his arbitrariness and violence, and regarded him as his bitterest foe. He rode in angry agitation towards him, firmly grasping his whip and fully prepared to take the most resolute and desperate steps to punish his enemy.

Hardly had he passed an angle of the wood before a stout gentleman in a beaver cap came riding towards him on a handsome raven-black horse, accompanied by two hunt-servants.

Instead of an enemy, Nicholas found in Ilagin a stately and courteous gentleman who was particularly anxious to make the young count's acquaintance. Having ridden up to Nicholas, Ilagin raised his beaver cap and said he much regretted what had occurred and would have the man punished who had allowed himself to seize a fox hunted by someone else's borzois. He hoped to become better acquainted with the count and invited him to draw his covert.

Natasha, afraid that her brother would do something dreadful, had followed him in some excitement. Seeing the enemies exchanging friendly greetings she rode up to them. Ilagin lifted his beaver cap still higher to Natasha, and said with a pleasant smile that the young countess resembled Diana in her passion for the chase as well as in her beauty, of which he had heard much.

To expiate his huntsman's offence Ilagin pressed the Rostovs to come to an upland of his about a verst away which he usually kept for himself and which, he said, swarmed with hares. Nicholas agreed, and the hunt, now doubled, moved on.

The way to Ilagin's upland was across the fields. The hunt-servants fell into line. The masters rode together, 'Uncle', Rostov, and Ilagin, kept stealthily glancing at one another's dogs, trying not to be observed by their companions and searching uneasily for rivals to their own borzois.

Rostov was particularly struck by the beauty of a small, pure bred, red-spotted bitch on Ilagin's leash, slender but with muscles like steel, a delicate muzzle and prominent black eyes. He had heard of the swiftness of Ilagin's borzois, and in that beautiful bitch saw a rival to his own Milka.

In the middle of a sober conversation begun by Ilagin about the year's harvest, Nicholas pointed to the red-spotted bitch.

'A fine little bitch, that!' said he in a careless tone. 'Is she swift?'

'That one? Yes, she's a good dog, gets what she's after,' answered Ilagin indifferently of the red-spotted bitch Erza, for which a year before he had given a neighbour three families of house-serfs. 'So in your parts, too, the harvest is nothing to boast of, Count?' he went on, continuing the conversation they had begun. And considering it polite to return the young count's compliment, Ilagin looked at his borzois and picked out Milka, who attracted his attention by her breadth. 'That black-spotted one of yours is fine – well-shaped!' said he.

'Yes, she's fast enough,' replied Nicholas, and thought: 'If only a full-grown hare would cross the field now, I'd show you what sort of a borzoi she is,' and turning to his groom he said he would give a ruble to anyone who found a hare.

'I don't understand,' continued Ilagin, 'how some sportsmen can be so jealous about game and dogs. For myself, I can tell you, Count, I enjoy riding in company such as this . . . what could be better?' (he again raised his cap to Natasha), 'but as for counting skins and what one takes, I don't care about that.'

'Of course not!'

'Or being upset because someone else's borzoi and not mine catches something. All I care about is to enjoy seeing the chase, is it not so, Count? For I consider that . . .'

'A-tu!' came the long-drawn cry of one of the borzoi-whippers-in who had halted. He stood on a knoll in the stubble holding his whip aloft, and again repeated his long-drawn cry, 'a-tu!' (This call and the uplifted whip meant that he saw a sitting hare.)

'Ah, he has found one, I think,' said Ilagin carelessly. 'Well, let us course it, Count. '

'Yes, we must ride up . . . Shall we both course it?' answered Nicholas, seeing in Erza and 'Uncle's' red Rugay two rivals he had never yet had a chance of pitting against his own borzois. 'And suppose they outdo my Milka at once!' he thought, as he rode with 'Uncle' and Ilagin towards the hare.

'A full-grown one?' asked Ilagin as he approached the whip who had sighted the hare – and not without agitation he looked round and whistled to Erza.

'And you, Michael Nikanorovich?' he said, addressing 'Uncle'.

The latter was riding with a sullen expression on his face.

'How can I join in? Why you've given a village for each of your borzois! That's it, come on! Yours are worth thousands. Try yours against one another, you two, and I'll look on!'

'Rugay, hey, hey!' he shouted. 'Rugayushka!' he added, involuntarily by this diminutive expressing his affection and the hopes he placed on this red borzoi. Natasha saw and felt the agitation the two elderly men and her brother were trying to conceal, and was herself excited by it.

The huntsman stood half-way up the knoll holding up his whip and the gentlefolk rode up to him at a foot-pace; the hounds that were far off on the horizon turned away from the hare, and the whips, but not the gentlefolk, also moved away. All were moving slowly and sedately.

'How is it pointing?' asked Nicholas, riding a hundred paces towards the whip who had sighted the hare.

But before the whip could reply, the hare, scenting the frost coming next morning, was unable to rest and leapt up. The pack on leash rushed downhill in full cry after the hare, and from all sides the borzois that were not on leash darted after the hounds and the hare. All the hunt, who had been moving slowly, shouted 'Stop!', calling in the hounds, while the borzoi-whips, with a cry of '*a-tu!*', galloped across the field setting the borzois on the hare. The tranquil Ilagin, Nicholas, Natasha, and 'Uncle', flew, reckless of where or how they went, seeing only the borzois and the hare and fearing only to lose sight even for an instant of the chase. The hare they had started was a strong and swift one. When he jumped up he did not run at once, but pricked his ears listening to the shouting and trampling that resounded from all sides at once. He took a dozen bounds not very quickly, letting the borzois gain on him, and finally, having chosen his direction and realized his danger, laid back his ears and rushed off headlong. He had been lying in the stubble, but in front of him was the autumn-sowing where the ground was soft. The two borzois of the huntsman who had sighted him, having been the nearest, were the first to see and pursue him, but they had not gone far before Ilagin's red-spotted Erza passed them, got within a length, flew at the hare with terrible swiftness aiming at his scut, and thinking she had seized him rolled over like a ball. The hare arched his back and bounded off yet more swiftly. From behind Erza rushed the broad-haunched black-spotted Milka and began rapidly gaining on the hare.

'Milashka, dear!' rose Nicholas's triumphant cry. It looked as if Milka would immediately pounce on the hare, but she overtook him and flew past. The hare had squatted. Again the beautiful Erza reached him, but when close to the hare's scut paused as if measuring the distance so as not to make a mistake this time but seize his hind leg.

'Erza, darling!' Ilagin wailed in a voice unlike his own. Erza did

539

not hearken to his appeal. At the very moment when she would have seized her prey, the hare moved and darted along the balk between the winter rye and the stubble. Again Erza and Milka were abreast, running like a pair of carriage horses, and began to overtake the hare, but it was easier for the hare to run on the balk and the borzois did not overtake him so quickly.

'Rugay, Rugayushka! That's it, come on!' came a third voice just then, and 'Uncle's' red borzoi, straining and curving its back, caught up with the two foremost borzois, pushed ahead of them, regardless of the terrible strain put on speed close to the hare, knocked it off the balk onto the rye-field, again put on speed still more viciously, sinking to his knees in the muddy field, and all one could see was how, muddying his back, he rolled over with the hare. A ring of borzois surrounded him. A moment later everyone had drawn up around the crowd of dogs. Only the delighted 'Uncle' dismounted, and cut off a pad, shaking the hare for the blood to drip off, and anxiously glancing round with restless eyes while his arms and legs twitched. He spoke without himself knowing whom to or what about. 'That's it, come on! That's a dog! . . . There, it has beaten them all, the thousand-ruble as well as the one-ruble borzois. That's it, come on!' said he, panting and looking wrathfully around as if he were abusing someone, and as if they were all his enemies, had insulted him, and only now had he at last succeeded in justifying himself. 'There are your thousand-ruble ones . . . That's it, come on! . . .'

'Rugay, here's a pad for you!' he said, throwing down the hare's muddy pad. 'You've deserved it, that's it, come on!'

'She'd tired herself out, she'd run it down three times by herself,' said Nicholas, also not listening to anyone and regardless of whether he were heard or not.

'But what is there in running across it like that?' said Ilagin's groom.

'Once she had missed it and turned it away, any mongrel could take it,' Ilagin was saying at the same time, breathless from his gallop and his excitement. At the same moment Natasha, without drawing breath, screamed joyously, ecstatically, and so piercingly that it set everyone's ears tingling. By that shriek she expressed what the others expressed by all talking at once, and it was so strange that she must herself have been ashamed of so wild a cry, and everyone else would have been amazed at it, at any other time. 'Uncle' himself twisted up the hare, threw it neatly and smartly across his horse's back as if by that gesture he meant to rebuke everybody, and with an air of not wishing to speak to anyone mounted his bay and rode off. The others all followed dispirited and shamefaced, and only much later were they able to regain their former affectation of indifference. For a long time they continued to look at red Rugay who, his arched back spattered with mud and clanking the ring of his leash, walked along just behind 'Uncle's' horse with the serene air of a conqueror.

'Well, I am like any other dog as long as it's not a question of coursing. But when it is, then look out!' his appearance seemed to Nicholas to be saying.

When, much later, 'Uncle' rode up to Nicholas and began talking to him, he felt flattered that, after what had happened, 'Uncle' deigned to speak to him.

## 7

TOWARDS evening Ilagin took leave of Nicholas, who found that they were so far from home that he accepted 'Uncle's' offer that the hunting-party should spend the night in his little village of Mikhaylovna.

'And if you put up at my house that will be better still. That's it, come on!' said 'Uncle'. 'You see it's damp weather, and you could rest, and the little countess could be driven home in a trap.'

'Uncle's' offer was accepted. A huntsman was sent to Otradnoe for a trap, while Nicholas rode with Natasha and Petya to 'Uncle's' house.

Some five male domestic serfs, big and little, rushed out to the front porch to meet their master. A score of women serfs old and young, as well as children, popped out from the back entrance to have a look at the hunters who were arriving. The presence of Natasha – a woman, a lady, and on horseback – raised the curiosity of the serfs to such a degree that many of them came up to her, stared her in the face, and unabashed by her presence made remarks about her as though she were some prodigy on show, and not a human being able to hear or understand what was said about her.

'Arinka! Look, she sits sideways! There she sits and her skirt dangles . . . See, she's got a little hunting-horn!'

'Goodness gracious! See her knife? . . .'

'Isn't she a Tartar!'

'How is it you didn't go head over heels?' asked the boldest of all, addressing Natasha directly.

'Uncle' dismounted at the porch of his little wooden house, which stood in the midst of an overgrown garden, and after a glance at his retainers shouted authoritatively that the superfluous ones should take themselves off and that all necessary preparations should be made to receive the guests and the visitors.

The serfs all dispersed. 'Uncle' lifted Natasha off her horse, and taking her hand led her up the rickety wooden steps of the porch. The house with its bare unplastered log-walls was not over-clean – it did not seem that those living in it aimed at keeping it spotless – but neither was it noticeably neglected. In the entry there was a smell of fresh apples, and wolf and fox skins hung about.

'Uncle' led his visitors through the ante-room into a small hall with a folding table and red chairs, then into the drawing-room with a round birch-wood table and a sofa, and finally into his private room, where there was a tattered sofa, a worn carpet, and portraits of Suvorov, of the host's father and mother, and of himself in military uniform. The study smelt strongly of tobacco and dogs. 'Uncle' asked his visitors to sit down and make themselves at home, and then went out of the room. Rugay, his back still muddy, came into the room and lay down on the sofa, cleaning himself with his tongue and teeth. Leading from the study was a passage in which a partition with ragged curtains could be seen. From behind this came women's laughter and whispers. Natasha, Nicholas, and Petya took off their wraps and sat down on the sofa. Petya, leaning on his elbow, fell asleep at once. Natasha and Nicholas were silent. Their faces glowed, they were hungry and very cheerful. They looked at one another (now that the hunt was over and they were in the house, Nicholas no longer considered it necessary to show his manly superiority over his sister), Natasha gave him a wink, and neither refrained long from bursting into a peal of ringing laughter even before they had a pretext ready to account for it.

After a while 'Uncle' came in, in a Cossack coat, blue trousers, and small top-boots. And Natasha felt that this costume, the very one she had regarded with surprise and amusement at Otradnoe, was just the right thing and not at all worse than a swallow-tail or frock coat. 'Uncle' too was in high spirits, and far from being offended by the brother's and sister's laughter (it could never enter his head that they might be laughing at his way of life), he himself joined in their spontaneous merriment.

'That's right, young Countess, that's it, come on! I never saw anyone like her!' said he, offering Nicholas a pipe with a long stem and with a practised motion of three fingers taking down another that had been cut short. 'She's ridden all day like a man, and is as fresh as ever!'

Soon after 'Uncle's' reappearance the door was opened, evidently from the sound by a bare-footed girl, and a stout, rosy, good-looking woman of about forty, with a double chin and full red lips, entered carrying a large loaded tray. With hospitable dignity and cordiality in her glance and in every motion, she looked at the visitors and,

with a pleasant smile, bowed respectfully. In spite of her exceptional stoutness, which caused her to protrude her chest and
stomach and throw back her head, this woman (who was 'Uncle's'
housekeeper) trod very lightly. She went to the table, set down the
tray, and with her plump white hands deftly took from it the bottles
and various hors-d'œuvre and dishes, and arranged them on the table.
When she had finished, she stepped aside and stopped at the door
with a smile on her face. 'Here I am. I am she! Now do you understand "Uncle"?' her expression said to Rostov. How could one help
understanding? Not only Nicholas but even Natasha understood the
meaning of his puckered brow and the happy complacent smile that
slightly puckered his lips when Anisya Fëdorovna entered. On the
tray was a bottle of herb-wine, different kinds of vodka, pickled
mushrooms, rye-cakes made with buttermilk, honey in the comb,
still mead and sparkling mead, apples, nuts (raw and roasted), and
nut-and-honey sweets. Afterwards she brought a freshly roasted
chicken, ham, preserves made with honey, and preserves made with
sugar.

All this was the fruit of Anisya Fëdorovna's housekeeping,
gathered and prepared by her. The smell and taste of it all had a
smack of Anisya Fëdorovna herself; a savour of juiciness, cleanliness,
whiteness, and pleasant smiles.

'Take this, little Lady-Countess!' she kept saying, as she offered
Natasha first one thing and then another.

Natasha ate of everything and thought she had never seen or
eaten such buttermilk-cakes, such aromatic jam, such honey-and-nut
sweets, or such a chicken anywhere. Anisya Fëdorovna left the
room.

After supper over their cherry brandy Rostov and 'Uncle' talked
of past and future hunts, of Rugay and Ilagin's dogs, while Natasha
sat upright on the sofa and listened with sparkling eyes. She tried
several times to wake Petya that he might eat something, but he
only muttered incoherent words without waking up. Natasha felt
so light-hearted and happy in these novel surroundings that she
only feared the trap would come for her too soon. After a casual
pause such as often occurs when receiving friends for the first time
in one's own house, 'Uncle', answering a thought that was in his
visitors' minds, said:

'This, you see, is how I am finishing my days ... Death will
come. That's it, come on! Nothing will remain. Then why harm
anyone?'

'Uncle's' face was very significant and even handsome as he said
this. Involuntarily Rostov recalled all the good he had heard about
him from his father and the neighbours. Throughout the whole

543

province 'Uncle' had the reputation of being the most honourable and disinterested of cranks. They called him in to decide family disputes, chose him as executor, confided secrets to him, elected him to be a justice and to other posts; but he always persistently refused public appointments, passing the autumn and spring in the fields on his bay gelding, sitting at home in winter, and lying in his overgrown garden in summer.

'Why don't you enter the service, Uncle?'

'I did once, but gave it up. I am not fit for it. That's it, come on! I can't make head or tail of it. That's for you – I haven't brains enough. Now hunting is another matter – that's it, come on! Open the door, there!' he shouted. 'Why have you shut it?'

The door at the end of the passage led to the huntsmen's room, as they called the room for the hunt-servants.

There was a rapid patter of bare feet, and an unseen hand opened the door into the huntsmen's room, from which came the clear sounds of a balalayka, on which someone who was evidently a master of the art was playing. Natasha had been listening to those strains for some time and now went out into the passage to hear better.

'That's Mitka, my coachman . . . I have got him a good balalayka. I'm fond of it,' said 'Uncle'.

It was the custom for Mitka to play the balalayka in the huntsmen's room when 'Uncle' returned from the chase. 'Uncle' was fond of such music.

'How good! Really very good!' said Nicholas with some unintentional superciliousness, as if ashamed to confess that the sounds pleased him very much.

'Very good?' said Natasha reproachfully, noticing her brother's tone. 'Not "very good" – it's simply delicious!'

Just as 'Uncle's' pickled mushrooms, honey, and cherry brandy had seemed to her the best in the world, so also that song, at that moment, seemed to her the acme of musical delight.

'More, please, more!' cried Natasha at the door as soon as the balalayka ceased. Mitka tuned up afresh, and recommenced thrumming the balalayka to the air of *My Lady*, with trills and variations. 'Uncle' sat listening, slightly smiling with his head on one side. The air was repeated a hundred times. The balalayka was retuned several times and the same notes were thrummed again, but the listeners did not grow weary of it and wished to hear it again and again. Anisya Fëdorovna came in and leaned her portly person against the door-post.

'You like listening?' she said to Natasha, with a smile extremely like 'Uncle's'. 'That's a good player of ours,' she added.

'He doesn't play that part right!' said 'Uncle' suddenly, with an energetic gesture. 'Here he ought to burst out – that's it, come on! – ought to burst out.'

'Do you play then?' asked Natasha.

'Uncle' did not answer, but smiled.

'Anisya, go and see if the strings of my guitar are all right. I haven't touched it for a long time. That's it – come on! I've given it up.'

Anisya Fëdorovna with her light step willingly went to fulfil her errand, and brought back the guitar.

Without looking at anyone, 'Uncle' blew the dust off it, and tapping the case with his bony fingers tuned the guitar and settled himself in his arm-chair. He took the guitar a little above the finger-board, arching his left elbow with a somewhat theatrical gesture, and with a wink at Anisya Fëdorovna struck a single chord, pure and sonorous, and then quietly, smoothly, and confidently began playing in very slow time not *My Lady*, but the well-known song *Came a maiden down the street*. The tune played with precision and in exact time began to thrill in the hearts of Nicholas and Natasha, arousing in them the same kind of sober mirth as radiated from Anisya Fëdorovna's whole being. Anisya Fëdorovna flushed, and drawing her kerchief over her face went laughing out of the room. 'Uncle' continued to play correctly, carefully, with energetic firmness, looking with a changed and inspired expression at the spot where Anisya Fëdorovna had just stood. Something seemed to be laughing a little on one side of his face under his grey moustaches, especially as the song grew brisker and the time quicker, and when, here and there, as he ran his fingers over the strings, something seemed to snap.

'Lovely, lovely! Go on, Uncle, go on!' shouted Natasha as soon as he had finished. She jumped up and hugged and kissed him. 'Nicholas, Nicholas!' she said, turning to her brother, as if asking him: 'What is it moves me so?'

Nicholas too was greatly pleased by 'Uncle's' playing, and 'Uncle' played the piece over again. Anisya Fëdorovna's smiling face re-appeared in the doorway and behind hers other faces ...

> Fetching water clear and sweet,
> Stop, dear maiden, I entreat –

played 'Uncle' once more, running his fingers skilfully over the strings, and then he stopped short and jerked his shoulders.

'Go on, Uncle dear,' Natasha wailed in an imploring tone as if her life depended on it.

'Uncle' rose, and it was as if there were two men in him: one of them smiled seriously at the merry fellow, while the merry fellow struck a naïve and precise attitude preparatory to a folk-dance.

'Now then, niece!' he exclaimed, waving to Natasha the hand that had just struck a chord.

Natasha threw off the shawl from her shoulders, ran forward to face 'Uncle', and setting her arms akimbo, also made a motion with her shoulders and struck an attitude.

Where, how, and when had this young countess, educated by an *émigrée* French governess, imbibed from the Russian air she breathed that spirit, and obtained that manner which the *pas de châle** would, one would have supposed, long ago have effaced? But the spirit and the movements were those inimitable and unteachable Russian ones that 'Uncle' had expected of her. As soon as she had struck her pose and smiled triumphantly, proudly, and with sly merriment, the fear that had at first seized Nicholas and the others that she might not do the right thing was at an end, and they were already admiring her.

She did the right thing with such precision, such complete precision, that Anisya Fëdorovna, who had at once handed her the handkerchief she needed for the dance, had tears in her eyes, though she laughed as she watched this slim, graceful countess, reared in silks and velvets and so different from herself, who yet was able to understand all that was in Anisya and in Anisya's father and mother and aunt, and in every Russian man and woman.

'Well, little Countess; that's it – come on!' cried 'Uncle' with a joyous laugh, having finished the dance. 'Well done, niece! Now a fine young fellow must be found as husband for you. That's it – come on!'

'He's chosen already,' said Nicholas smiling.

'Oh?' said 'Uncle' in surprise, looking inquiringly at Natasha, who nodded her head with a happy smile.

'And such a one!' she said. But as soon as she had said it a new train of thoughts and feelings arose in her. 'What did Nicholas's smile mean when he said "chosen already"? Is he glad of it or not? It is as if he thought my Bolkonsky would not approve of or understand our gaiety. But he would understand it all. Where is he now?' she thought, and her face suddenly became serious. But this lasted only a second. 'Don't dare to think about it,' she said to herself, and sat down again smilingly beside 'Uncle', begging him to play something more.

'Uncle' played another song and a valse; then after a pause he cleared his throat, and sang his favourite hunting song:

> As 'twas growing dark last night
> Fell the snow so soft and light . . .

'Uncle' sang as peasants sing, with full and naïve conviction that the whole meaning of a song lies in the words, and that the tune comes of itself, and that apart from the words there is no tune, which exists only to give measure to the words. As a result of this the unconsidered tune, like the song of a bird, was extraordinarily good. Natasha was in ecstasies over 'Uncle's' singing. She resolved to give up learning the harp, and to play only the guitar. She asked 'Uncle' for his guitar and at once found the chords of the song.

After nine o'clock two traps and three mounted men, who had been sent to look for them, arrived to fetch Natasha and Petya. The count and countess did not know where they were and were very anxious, said one of the men.

Petya was carried out like a log and laid in the larger of the two traps. Natasha and Nicholas got into the other. 'Uncle' wrapped Natasha up warmly, and took leave of her with quite a new tenderness. He accompanied them on foot as far as a bridge that could not be crossed, so that they had to go round by the ford, and he sent huntsmen to ride in front with lanterns.

'Good-bye, dear niece,' his voice called out of the darkness – not the voice Natasha had known previously, but the one that had sung *As 'twas growing dark last night.*

In the village through which they passed there were red lights and a cheerful smell of smoke.

'What a darling "Uncle" is!' said Natasha, when they had come out onto the high road.

'Yes,' returned Nicholas. 'You're not cold?'

'No. I'm quite, quite all right. I feel so comfortable!' answered Natasha, almost perplexed by her feelings. They remained silent a long while. The night was dark and damp. They could not see the horses, but only heard them splashing through the unseen mud.

What was passing in that receptive childlike soul that so eagerly caught and assimilated all the diverse impressions of life? How did they all find place in her? But she was very happy. As they were nearing home she suddenly struck up the air of *As 't was growing dark last night* – the tune of which she had all the way been trying to get, and had at last caught.

'Got it?' said Nicholas.

'What were you thinking about just now, Nicholas?' inquired Natasha.

They were fond of asking one another that question.

'I?' said Nicholas, trying to remember. 'Well, you see, first I thought that Rugay, the red hound, was like "Uncle", and that if he were a man he would always keep "Uncle" near him, if not for

547

his riding then for his manner. What a good fellow "Uncle" is! Don't you think so? Well, and you?'

'I?' Wait a bit, wait. Yes, first I thought that we are driving along and imagining that we are going home, but that heaven knows where we are really going in the darkness, and that we shall arrive and suddenly find that we are not in Otradnoe but in Fairyland. And then I thought . . . No, nothing else.'

'I know, I expect you thought of him,' said Nicholas, smiling as Natasha knew by the sound of his voice.

'No,' said Natasha, though she had in reality been thinking about Prince Andrew at the same time as of the rest, and of how he would have liked 'Uncle'. 'And then I was saying to myself all the way, "How well Anisya carried herself, how well!"' And Nicholas heard her spontaneous, happy, ringing laughter. 'And do you know,' she suddenly said, 'I know that I shall never again be as happy and tranquil as I am now.'

'Rubbish, nonsense, humbug!' exclaimed Nicholas, and he thought: 'How charming this Natasha of mine is! I have no other friend like her, and never shall have. Why should she marry? We might always drive about together!'

'What a darling this Nicholas of mine is!' thought Natasha.

'Ah, there are still lights in the drawing-room!' she said, pointing to the windows of the house that gleamed invitingly in the moist velvety darkness of the night.

8

COUNT Ilya Rostov had resigned the position of Marshal of the Nobility because it involved him in too much expense, but still his affairs did not improve. Natasha and Nicholas often noticed their parents conferring together anxiously and privately, and heard suggestions of selling the fine ancestral house and estate near Moscow. It was not necessary to entertain so freely as when the count had been Marshal, and life at Otradnoe was quieter than in former years, but still the enormous house and its lodges were full of people, and more than twenty sat down to table every day. These were all their own people who had settled down in the house almost as members of the family, or persons who were, it seemed, obliged to live in the count's house. Such were Dimmler the musician* and his wife, Vogel the dancing-master and his family, Belova, an old maiden lady, an inmate of the house, and many others such as Petya's tutors, the girls' former governess, and other people who simply found it preferable and more advantageous to live in the count's house than at home. They had not as many visitors as before, but the old habits of life, without which the count and countess could not conceive of existence, remained unchanged. There was still the hunting establishment which Nicholas had even enlarged, the same fifty horses and fifteen grooms in the stables, the same expensive presents and dinner-parties to the whole district on name-days; there were still the count's games of whist and boston, at which – spreading out his cards so that everyone could see them – he let himself be plundered of hundreds of rubles every day by neighbours, who looked upon an opportunity to play a rubber with Count Rostov as a most profitable source of income.

The count moved in his affairs as in a huge net, trying not to believe that he was entangled but becoming more and more so at every step, and feeling too feeble to break the meshes or to set to work carefully and patiently to disentangle them. The countess with her loving heart felt that her children were being ruined, that it was not the count's fault, for he could not help being what he was – that (though he tried to hide it) he himself suffered from the consciousness of his own and his children's ruin, and she tried to find means of remedying the position. From her feminine point of view she could see only one solution, namely, for Nicholas to marry a rich heiress. She felt this to be their last hope, and that if Nicholas refused the match she had found for him, she would have to abandon the hope of ever getting matters right. This match was with Julie Karagina, the daughter of excellent and virtuous parents, a girl the Rostovs had known from childhood, and who had now become a wealthy heiress through the death of the last of her brothers.

The countess had written direct to Julie's mother in Moscow, suggesting a marriage between their children, and had received a favourable answer from her. Karagina had replied that for her part she was agreeable, and everything would depend on her daughter's inclination. She invited Nicholas to come to Moscow.

Several times the countess, with tears in her eyes, told her son that now that both her daughters were settled her only wish was to see him married. She said she could lie down in her grave peacefully if that were accomplished. Then she told him that she knew of a splendid girl, and tried to discover what he thought about marriage.

At other times she praised Julie to him, and advised him to go to Moscow during the holidays to amuse himself. Nicholas guessed what his mother's remarks were leading to, and during one of these conversations induced her to speak quite frankly. She told him

549

that her only hope of getting their affairs disentangled, now lay in his marrying Julie Karagina.

'But, mamma, suppose I loved a girl who has no fortune, would you expect me to sacrifice my feelings and my honour for the sake of money?' he asked his mother, not realizing the cruelty of his question and only wishing to show his noble-mindedness.

'No, you have not understood me,' said his mother, not knowing how to justify herself. 'You have not understood me, Nikolenka. It is your happiness I wish for,' she added, feeling that she was telling an untruth and was becoming entangled. She began to cry.

'Mamma, don't cry. Only tell me that you wish it, and you know I will give my life, anything, to put you at ease,' said Nicholas. 'I would sacrifice anything for you – even my feelings.'

But the countess did not want the question put like that: she did not want a sacrifice from her son, she herself wished to make a sacrifice for him.

'No, you have not understood me, don't let us talk about it,' she replied, wiping away her tears.

'Maybe I do love a poor girl,' said Nicholas to himself. 'Am I to sacrifice my feelings and my honour for money? I wonder how mamma could speak so to me. Because Sonya is poor I must not love her,' he thought, 'must not respond to her faithful, devoted love? Yet I should certainly be happier with her than with some doll-like Julie. I can always sacrifice my feelings for my family's welfare,' he said to himself, 'but I can't coerce my feelings. If I love Sonya, that feeling is for me stronger and higher than all else.'

Nicholas did not go to Moscow, and the countess did not renew the conversation with him about marriage. She saw with sorrow, and sometimes with exasperation, symptoms of a growing attachment between her son and the portionless Sonya. Though she blamed herself for it, she could not refrain from grumbling at and worrying Sonya, often pulling her up without reason, addressing her stiffly as 'my dear', and using the formal 'you' instead of the intimate 'thou' in speaking to her. The kind-hearted countess was the more vexed with Sonya because that poor, dark-eyed niece of hers was so meek, so kind, so devotedly grateful to her benefactors, and so faithfully, unchangingly and unselfishly in love with Nicholas, that there were no grounds for finding fault with her.

Nicholas was spending the last of his leave at home. A fourth letter had come from Prince Andrew, from Rome, in which he wrote that he would have been on his way back to Russia long ago had not his wound unexpectedly reopened in the warm climate, which obliged him to defer his return till the beginning of the new year. Natasha was still as much in love with her betrothed, found the same comfort in that love, and was still as ready to throw herself into all the pleasures of life as before; but at the end of the fourth month of their separation she began to have fits of depression which she could not master. She felt sorry for herself; sorry that she was being wasted all this time, and of no use to anyone – while she felt herself so capable of loving and being loved.

Things were not cheerful in the Rostovs' home.

## 9

CHRISTMAS came, and except for the ceremonial Mass, the solemn and wearisome Christmas congratulations from neighbours and servants, and the new dresses everyone put on, there were no special festivities, though the calm frost of twenty degrees Réaumur,* the dazzling sunshine by day, and the starlight of the winter nights, seemed to call for some special celebration of the season.

On the third day of Christmas week, after the midday dinner all the inmates of the house dispersed to various rooms. It was the dullest time of the day. Nicholas, who had been visiting some neighbours that morning, was asleep on the sitting-room sofa. The old count was resting in his study. Sonya sat in the drawing-room at the round table, copying a design for embroidery. The countess was playing patience. Nastasya Ivanovna, the buffoon, sat with a sad face at the window with two old ladies. Natasha came into the room, went up to Sonya, glanced at what she was doing, and then went up to her mother and stood without speaking.

'Why are you wandering about like an outcast?' asked her mother. 'What do you want?'

'Him . . . I want him . . . now, this minute! I want *him!*' said Natasha, with glittering eyes and no sign of a smile.

The countess lifted her head and looked attentively at her daughter.

'Don't look at me, mamma! Don't look; I shall cry directly.'

'Sit down with me a little,' said the countess.

'Mamma, I want *him*. Why should I be wasted like this, mamma?'

Her voice broke, tears gushed from her eyes, and she turned quickly to hide them and left the room.

She passed into the sitting-room, stood there thinking awhile, and then went into the maids' room. There an old maid-servant was grumbling at a young girl who stood panting, having just run in through the cold from the serfs' quarters.

'Stop playing – there's a time for everything,' said the old woman.

'Let her alone, Kondratevna,' said Natasha. 'Go, Mavrusha, go.'

Having released Mavrusha, Natasha crossed the dancing-hall and went to the vestibule. There an old footman and two young ones were playing cards. They broke off and rose as she entered.

'What can I do with them?' thought Natasha.

'Oh, Nikita, please go ... where can I send him? ... Yes, go to the yard and fetch a fowl, please, a cock, and you, Misha, bring me some oats.'*

'Just a few oats?' said Misha cheerfully and readily.

'Go, go quickly,' the old man urged him.

'And you, Theodore, get me a piece of chalk.'

On her way past the butler's pantry she told them to set a samovar, though it was not at all the time for tea.

Foka, the butler, was the most ill-tempered person in the house. Natasha liked to test her power over him. He distrusted the order and asked whether the samovar was really wanted.

'Oh dear, what a young lady!' said Foka, pretending to frown at Natasha.

No one in the house sent people about or gave them as much trouble as Natasha did. She could not see people unconcernedly, but had to send them on some errand. She seemed to be trying whether any of them would get angry or sulky with her; but the serfs fulfilled no one's orders so readily as they did hers. 'What can I do, where can I go?' thought she, as she went slowly along the passage.

'Nastasya Ivanovna, what sort of children shall I have?' she asked the buffoon, who was coming towards her in a woman's jacket.

'Why, fleas, crickets, grasshoppers,' answered the buffoon.

'O Lord, O Lord, it's always the same! Oh, where am I to go? What am I to do with myself?' And tapping with her heels she ran quickly upstairs to see Vogel and his wife who lived on the upper storey.

Two governesses were sitting with the Vogels at a table on which were plates of raisins, walnuts, and almonds. The governesses were discussing whether it was cheaper to live in Moscow or Odessa. Natasha sat down, listened to their talk with a serious and thoughtful air, and then got up again.

'The island of Madagascar,' she said, 'Ma-da-gas-car,' she repeated, articulating each syllable distinctly, and, not replying to Madame Schoss who asked what she was saying, she went out of the room.

Her brother Petya was upstairs too; with the man in attendance on him he was preparing fireworks to let off that night.

'Petya! Petya!' she called to him. 'Carry me downstairs.'

Petya ran up and offered her his back. She jumped on it putting her arms round his neck, and he pranced along with her.

'No don't . . . the island of Madagascar!' she said, and jumping off his back she went downstairs.

Having as it were reviewed her kingdom, tested her power, and made sure that everyone was submissive, but that all the same it was dull, Natasha betook herself to the ball-room, picked up her guitar, sat down in a dark corner behind a bookcase and began to run her fingers over the strings in the bass, picking out a passage she recalled from an opera she had heard in Petersburg with Prince Andrew. What she drew from the guitar would have had no meaning for other listeners, but in her imagination a whole series of reminiscences arose from those sounds. She sat behind the bookcase with her eyes fixed on a streak of light escaping from the pantry door, and listened to herself and pondered. She was in a mood for brooding on the past.

Sonya passed to the pantry with a glass in her hand. Natasha glanced at her and at the crack in the pantry door, and it seemed to her that she remembered the light falling through that crack once before and Sonya passing with a glass in her hand. 'Yes, it was exactly the same,' thought Natasha.

'Sonya, what is this?' she cried, twanging a thick string.

'Oh, you are there!' said Sonya with a start, and came near and listened. 'I don't know. A storm?' she ventured timidly, afraid of being wrong.

'There! That's just how she started and just how she came up smiling timidly when all this happened before,' thought Natasha, 'and in just the same way I thought there was something lacking in her.'

'No, it's the chorus from the *Water-Carrier*, listen!' and Natasha sang the air of the chorus so that Sonya should catch it. 'Where were you going?' she asked.

'To change the water in this glass. I am just finishing the design.'

'You always find something to do, but I can't,' said Natasha. 'And where's Nicholas?'

'Asleep, I think.'

'Sonya, go and wake him,' said Natasha. 'Tell him I want him to come and sing.'

She sat awhile, wondering what the meaning of it all having happened before could be, and without solving this problem, or at all regretting not having done so, she again passed in fancy to the time when she was with *him* and he was looking at her with a lover's eyes.

'Oh, if only he would come quicker! I am so afraid it will never be! And worst of all, I am growing old – that's the thing! There won't then be in me what there is now. But perhaps he'll come to-day, will come immediately. Perhaps he has come and is sitting in the drawing-room. Perhaps he came yesterday and I have forgotten it.' She rose, put down the guitar, and went to the drawing-room.

All the domestic circle, tutors, governesses, and guests, were already at the tea-table. The servants stood round the table – but Prince Andrew was not there and life was going on as before.

'Ah, here she is!' said the old count when he saw Natasha enter. 'Well, sit down by me.' But Natasha stayed by her mother and glanced round as if looking for something.

'Mamma!' she muttered, 'give him to me, give him, mamma, quickly, quickly!' and she again had difficulty in repressing her sobs.

She sat down at the table and listened to the conversation between the elders and Nicholas, who had also come to the table. 'My God, my God! The same faces, the same talk, papa holding his cup and blowing in the same way!' thought Natasha, feeling with horror a sense of repulsion rising up in her for the whole household because they were always the same.

After tea Nicholas, Sonya, and Natasha went to the sitting-room, to their favourite corner where their most intimate talks always began.

10

'DOES it ever happen to you,' said Natasha to her brother when they had settled down in the sitting-room, 'does it ever happen to you to feel as if there were nothing more to come – nothing; that everything good is past? And to feel not exactly dull, but sad?'

'I should think so!' he replied. 'I have felt like that when everything was all right and everyone was cheerful. The thought has come into my mind that I was already tired of it all, and that we must all die. Once in the regiment I had not gone to some merry-making where there was music ... and suddenly I felt so depressed ...'

'Oh yes, I know, I know!' Natasha interrupted him. 'When I was quite little that used to be so with me. Do you remember when I was punished once about some plums? You were all dancing, and I sat sobbing in the school-room? I shall never forget it: I felt sad and sorry for everyone, for myself, and for everyone.

And I was innocent – that was the chief thing,' said Natasha. 'Do you remember?'

'I remember,' answered Nicholas. 'I remember that I came to you afterwards and wanted to comfort you but, do you know, I felt ashamed to. We were terribly absurd. I had a funny doll then and wanted to give it you. Do you remember?'

'And do you remember,' Natasha asked with a pensive smile, 'how once, long long ago, when we were quite little, uncle called us into the study – that was in the old house – and it was dark – we went in and suddenly there stood . . .'

'A negro,' chimed in Nicholas with a smile of delight. 'Of course I remember. Even now I don't know whether there really was a negro, or if we only dreamt it or were told about him.'

'He was grey, you remember, and had white teeth, and stood and looked at us . . .'

'Sonya, do you remember?' asked Nicholas.

'Yes, yes, I do remember something too,' Sonya answered timidly.

'You know I have asked papa and mamma about that negro,' said Natasha, 'and they say there was no negro at all. But you see, you remember!'

'Of course I do, I remember his teeth as if I had just seen them.'

'How strange it is! It's as if it were a dream! I like that.'

'And do you remember how we rolled hard-boiled eggs in the ball-room, and suddenly two old women began spinning round on the carpet? Was that real or not? Do you remember what fun it was?'

'Yes, and you remember how papa in his blue overcoat fired a gun in the porch?'

So they went through their memories, smiling with pleasure: not the sad memories of old age, but poetic, youthful ones – those impressions of one's most distant past in which dreams and realities blend – and they laughed with quiet enjoyment.

Sonya, as always, did not quite keep pace with them, though they shared the same reminiscences.

Much that they remembered had slipped from her mind, and what she recalled did not arouse the same poetic feeling as they experienced. She simply enjoyed their pleasure and tried to fit in with it.

She only really took part when they recalled Sonya's first arrival. She told them how afraid she had been of Nicholas because he had on a corded jacket, and her nurse had told her that she, too, would be sewn up with cords.

'And I remember their telling me that you had been born under a cabbage,' said Natasha, 'and I remember that I dared not disbelieve it then, but knew it was not true, and I felt so uncomfortable.'

555

While they were talking a maid thrust her head in at the other door of the sitting-room.

'They have brought the cock, Miss,' she said in a whisper.

'It isn't wanted, Polya. Tell them to take it away,' replied Natasha.

In the middle of their talk in the sitting-room, Dimmler came in and went up to the harp that stood there in a corner. He took off its cloth covering, and the harp gave out a jarring sound.

'Mr Dimmler, please play my favourite nocturne by Field,'* came the old countess's voice from the drawing-room.

Dimmler struck a chord, and turning to Natasha, Nicholas and Sonya, remarked: 'How quiet you young people are!'

'Yes, we're philosophizing,' said Natasha, glancing round for a moment and then continuing the conversation. They were now discussing dreams.

Dimmler began to play, Natasha went on tiptoe noiselessly to the table, took up a candle, carried it out and returned, seating herself quietly in her former place. It was dark in the room, especially where they were sitting on the sofa, but through the big windows the silvery light of the full moon fell on the floor. Dimmler had finished the piece but still sat softly running his fingers over the strings, evidently uncertain whether to stop or to play something else.

'Do you know,' said Natasha in a whisper, moving closer to Nicholas and Sonya, 'that when one goes on and on recalling memories, one at last begins to remember what happened before one was in the world ...'

'That is metempsychosis,' said Sonya, who had always learned well, and remembered everything. 'The Egyptians believed that our souls have lived in animals, and will go back into animals again.'

'No, I don't believe we ever were in animals,' said Natasha, still in a whisper though the music had ceased. 'But I am certain that we were angels somewhere *there*, and have been here, and that is why we remember ...'

'May I join you?' said Dimmler who had come up quietly, and he sat down by them.

'If we have been angels, why have we fallen lower?' said Nicholas. 'No, that can't be!'

'Not lower, who said we were lower? ... How do I know what I was before?' Natasha rejoined with conviction. 'The soul is immortal – well then, if I shall always live I must have lived before, lived for a whole eternity.'

'Yes, but it is hard for us to imagine eternity,' remarked Dimmler, who had joined the young folk with a mildly condescending smile but now spoke as quietly and seriously as they.

'Why is it hard to imagine eternity?' said Natasha. 'It is now to-day, and it will be to-morrow, and always; and there was yester-day, and the day before ...'

'Natasha! Now it's your turn. Sing me something,' they heard the countess say. 'Why are you sitting there like conspirators?'

'Mamma, I don't at all want to,' replied Natasha, but all the same she rose.

None of them, not even the middle-aged Dimmler, wanted to break off their conversation and quit that corner in the sitting-room, but Natasha got up and Nicholas sat down at the clavichord. Standing as usual in the middle of the hall, and choosing the place where the resonance was best, Natasha began to sing her mother's favourite song.

She had said she did not want to sing, but it was long since she had sung, and long before she again sang as she did that evening. The count, from his study where he was talking to Mitenka, heard her, and like a schoolboy in a hurry to run out to play, blundered in his talk while giving orders to the steward, and at last stopped, while Mitenka stood in front of him, also listening and smiling. Nicholas did not take his eyes off his sister and drew breath in time with her. Sonya, as she listened, thought of the immense difference there was between herself and her friend, and how impossible it was for her to be anything like as bewitching as her cousin. The old countess sat with a blissful yet sad smile and with tears in her eyes, occasionally shaking her head. She thought of Natasha and of her own youth, and of how there was something unnatural and dreadful in this impending marriage of Natasha and Prince Andrew.

Dimmler, who had seated himself beside the countess, listened with closed eyes.

'Ah, Countess,' he said at last, 'that's a European talent, she has nothing to learn – what softness, tenderness, and strength ...'

'Ah, how afraid I am for her, how afraid I am!' said the countess, not realizing to whom she was speaking. Her maternal instinct told her that Natasha had too much of something, and that because of this she would not be happy. Before Natasha had finished singing, fourteen-year-old Petya rushed in delightedly to say that some mummers had arrived.

Natasha stopped abruptly.

'Idiot!' she screamed at her brother and running to a chair threw herself on it sobbing so violently that she could not stop for a long time.

'It's nothing, mamma, really it's nothing; only Petya startled me,' she said trying to smile, but her tears still flowed and sobs still choked her.

The mummers (some of the house-serfs), dressed up as bears, Turks, inn-keepers, and ladies – frightening and funny – bringing in with them the cold from outside and a feeling of gaiety, crowded, at first timidly, in the ante-room, then hiding behind one another they pushed into the ball-room where, shyly at first and then more and more merrily and heartily, they started singing, dancing, and playing Christmas games. The countess, when she had identified them and laughed at their costumes, went into the drawing-room. The count sat in the ball-room smiling radiantly and applauding the players. The young people had disappeared.

Half an hour later there appeared among the other mummers in the ball-room an old lady in a hooped skirt – this was Nicholas. A Turkish girl was Petya. A clown was Dimmler. An hussar was Natasha, and a Circassian was Sonya with burnt-cork moustache and eyebrows.

After the condescending surprise, non-recognition, and praise, of those who were not themselves dressed up, the young people decided that their costumes were so good that they ought to be shown elsewhere.

Nicholas, who as the roads were in splendid condition wanted to take them all for a drive in his troyka, proposed to take with them about a dozen of the serf-mummers and drive to 'Uncle's'.

'No, why disturb the old fellow?' said the countess, 'besides, you wouldn't have room to turn round there. If you must go, go to the Melyukovs'.'

Melyukova was a widow, who with her family and their tutors and governesses lived three miles from the Rostovs.

'That's right, my dear,' chimed in the old count, thoroughly aroused. I'll dress up at once and go with them. I'll make Pashette open her eyes.'

But the countess would not agree to his going; he had had a bad leg all these days. It was decided that the count must not go, but that if Louisa Ivanovna (Madame Schoss) would go with them, the young ladies might go to the Melyukovs', Sonya, generally so timid and shy, begging Louisa Ivanovna not to refuse more urgently than anyone.

Sonya's costume was the best of all. Her moustache and eyebrows were extraordinarily becoming. Everyone told her she looked very handsome, and she was in a spirited and energetic mood unusual with her. Some inner voice told her that now or never her fate would be decided, and in her male attire she seemed quite a different person. Louisa Ivanovna consented to go, and in half an hour four troyka-sledges with large and small bells, their runners squeaking and whistling over the frozen snow, drove up to the porch.

Natasha was foremost in setting a merry holiday tone, which passing from one to another grew stronger and stronger and reached its climax when they all came out into the frost and got into the sledges, talking, calling to one another, laughing and shouting.

Two of the troykas were the usual household sledges, the third was the old count's with a trotter from the Orlov stud as shaft-horse, the fourth was Nicholas's own with a short shaggy black shaft-horse. Nicholas, in his old lady's dress, over which he had belted his hussar overcoat, stood in the middle of the sledge reins in hand.

It was so light that he could see the moonlight reflected from the metal harness disks and from the eyes of the horses, who looked round in alarm at the noisy party under the shadow of the porch-roof.

Natasha, Sonya, Madame Schoss and two maids got into Nicholas's sledge, Dimmler, his wife, and Petya into the old count's, and the rest of the mummers seated themselves in the other two sledges.

'You go ahead, Zakhar!' shouted Nicholas to his father's coach-man, wishing for a chance to race past him.

The old count's troyka, with Dimmler and his party, started forward squeaking on its runners as though freezing to the snow, its deep-toned bell clanging. The side-horses, pressing against the shafts of the middle horse, sank in the snow which was dry and glittered like sugar, and threw it up.

Nicholas set off following the first sledge: behind him the others moved noisily, their runners squeaking. At first they drove at a steady trot along the narrow road. While they drove past the garden, the shadows of the bare trees fell across the road and hid the brilliant moonlight, but as soon as they were past the fence, the snowy plain, bathed in moonlight and motionless, spread out before them glittering like diamonds and dappled with bluish shadows. *Bang, bang!* went the first sledge over a cradle-hole in the snow of the road, and each of the other sledges jolted in the same way, and rudely breaking the frost-bound stillness the troykas began to speed along the road one after the other.

'A hare's track, a lot of tracks!' rang out Natasha's voice through the frost-bound air.

'How light it is, Nicholas!' came Sonya's voice.

Nicholas glanced round at Sonya, and bent down to see her

face closer. Quite a new, sweet face with black eyebrows and moustaches peeped up at him from her sable furs – so close and yet so distant – in the moonlight.

'That used to be Sonya,' thought he, and looked at her closer and smiled.

'What is it, Nicholas?'

'Nothing,' said he and turned again to the horses.

When they came out onto the beaten high road – polished by sledge-runners and cut up by rough-shod hoofs, the marks of which were visible in the moonlight – the horses began to tug at the reins of their own accord and increased their pace. The near side-horse, arching his head and breaking into a short canter, tugged at his traces. The shaft-horse swayed from side to side moving his ears as if asking: 'Isn't it time to begin now?' In front, already far ahead, the deep bell of the sledge ringing farther and farther off, the black horses driven by Zakhar could be clearly seen against the white snow. From that sledge one could hear the shouts, laughter, and voices of the mummers.

'Gee up, my darlings!' shouted Nicholas pulling the reins to one side and flourishing the whip.

It was only by the keener wind that met them and the jerks given by the side-horses who pulled harder – ever increasing their gallop – that one noticed how fast the troyka was flying. Nicholas looked back. With screams, squeals, and waving of whips, that caused even the shaft-horses to gallop – the other sledges followed. The shaft-horse swung steadily beneath the bow over its head, with no thought of slackening pace and ready to put on speed when required.

Nicholas overtook the first sledge. They were driving down hill and coming out upon a broad trodden track across a meadow near a river.

'Where are we?' thought he. 'It's the Kosoy meadow, I suppose. But no – this is something new I've never seen before. This isn't the Kosoy meadow, nor the Dëmkin hill, and heaven only knows what it is! It is something new and enchanted. Well, whatever it may be ...' And shouting to his horses he began to pass the first troyka.

Zakhar held back his horses and turned his face, which was already covered with hoar-frost to his eyebrows.

Nicholas gave the horses the rein, and Zakhar, stretching out his arms, clucked his tongue and let his horses go.

'Now, look out, Master!' he cried.

Faster still the two troykas flew, side by side, and faster moved the feet of the galloping side-horses. Nicholas began to draw ahead. Zakhar, while still keeping his arms extended, raised one hand with the reins.

'No you won't, Master!' he shouted.

Nicholas put all his horses to a gallop and passed Zakhar. The horses showered the fine dry snow on the faces of those in the sledge – beside them sounded quick ringing bells and they caught confused glimpses of swiftly moving legs and the shadows of the troyka they were passing. The whistling sound of the runners on the snow and the voices of girls shrieking, were heard from different sides.

Again checking his horses, Nicholas looked around him. They were still surrounded by the magic plain bathed in moonlight and spangled with stars.

'Zakhar is shouting that I should turn to the left, but why to the left?' thought Nicholas. 'Are we getting to the Melyukovs'? Is this Melyukovka? Heaven only knows where we are going, and heaven knows what is happening to us – but it is very strange and pleasant whatever it is.' And he looked round in the sledge.

'Look, his moustache and eyelashes are all white!' said one of the strange, pretty, unfamiliar people – the one with fine eyebrows and moustache.

'I think this used to be Natasha,' thought Nicholas, 'and that was Madame Schoss, but perhaps it's not, and this Circassian with the moustache I don't know, but I love her.'

'Aren't you cold?' he asked.

They did not answer but began to laugh. Dimmler from the sledge behind shouted something – probably something funny – but they could not make out what he said.

'Yes, yes!' some voices answered, laughing.

'But here was a fairy forest with black moving shadows, and a glitter of diamonds and a flight of marble steps and the silver roofs of fairy buildings and the shrill yells of some animals. And if this is really Melyukovka it is still stranger that we drove heaven knows where and have come to Melyukovka,' thought Nicholas.

It really was Melyukovka, and maids and footmen with merry faces came running out to the porch, carrying candles.

'Who is it?' asked someone in the porch.

'The mummers from the count's. I know by the horses,' replied some voices.

11

PELAGEYA Danilovna Melyukova, a broadly built, energetic woman wearing spectacles, sat in the drawing-room in a loose dress surrounded by her daughters whom she was trying to keep from feeling dull. They were quietly dropping melted wax into snow and looking at the shadows the wax figures would throw on the wall, when they heard the steps and voices of new arrivals in the vestibule.

Hussars, ladies, witches, clowns and bears, after clearing their throats and wiping the hoar-frost from their faces in the vestibule, came into the ball-room where candles were hurriedly lighted. The clown – Dimmler – and the lady – Nicholas – started a dance. Surrounded by the screaming children the mummers, covering their faces and disguising their voices, bowed to their hostess and arranged themselves about the room.

'Dear me! there's no recognizing them! And Natasha! See whom she looks like! She really reminds me of somebody. But Herr Dimmler – isn't he good! I didn't know him! And how he dances. Dear me, there's a Circassian. Really how becoming it is to dear Sonya. And who is that? Well you have cheered us up! Nikita and Vanya – clear away the tables! And we were sitting so quietly. Ha, ha, ha! . . . The hussar, the hussar! Just like a boy! And the legs! . . . I can't look at him . . .' different voices were saying.

Natasha, the young Melyukovs' favourite, disappeared with them into the back rooms where a cork, and various dressing-gowns and male garments were called for, and received from the footman by bare girlish arms from behind the door. Ten minutes later all the young Melyukovs joined the mummers.

Pelageya Danilovna, having given orders to clear the rooms for the visitors, and arranged about refreshments for the gentry and the serfs, went about among the mummers without removing her spectacles, peering into their faces with a suppressed smile and failing to recognize any of them. It was not merely Dimmler and the Rostovs she failed to recognize, she did not even recognize her own daughters, or her late husband's dressing-gowns and uniforms, which they had put on.

'And who is this?' she asked her governess, peering into the face of her own daughter dressed up as a Kazan-Tartar. 'I suppose it is one of the Rostovs! Well, Mr Hussar, and what regiment do you serve in?' she asked Natasha. 'Here, hand some fruit-jelly to the Turk!' she ordered the butler who was handing things round. 'That's not forbidden by his law.'

Sometimes, as she looked at the strange but amusing capers cut by the dancers, who – having decided once for all that being disguised no one would recognize them – were not at all shy, Pelageya Danilovna hid her face in her handkerchief, and her whole stout body shook with irrepressible, kindly, elderly laughter.

'My little Sasha! Look at Sasha!' she said.

After Russian country-dances and chorus-dances, Pelageya Danilovna made the serfs and gentry join in one large circle: a ring, a string, and a silver ruble were fetched, and they all played games together.

In an hour all the costumes were crumpled and disordered. The corked eyebrows and moustaches were smeared over the perspiring, flushed, and merry faces. Pelageya Danilovna began to recognize the mummers, admired their cleverly contrived costumes, and particularly how they suited the young ladies, and she thanked them all for having entertained her so well. The visitors were invited to supper in the drawing-room, and the serfs had something served to them in the ball-room.

'Now to tell one's fortune in the empty bath-house is frightening!' said an old maid who lived with the Melyukovs, during supper.

'Why?' asked the eldest Melyukov girl.

'You wouldn't go, it takes courage ...'

'I'll go,' said Sonya.

'Tell what happened to the young lady!' said the second Melyukov girl.

'Well,' began the old maid, 'a young lady once went out, took a cock, laid the table for two, all properly, and sat down. After sitting a while, she suddenly hears someone coming ... a sledge drives up with harness bells; she hears him coming! He comes in, just in the shape of a man, like an officer – comes in and sits down to table with her.'

'Ah! ah!' screamed Natasha, rolling her eyes with horror.

'Yes? And how ... did he speak?'

'Yes, like a man. Everything quite all right, and he began persuading her; and she should have kept him talking till cock-crow, but she got frightened, just got frightened and hid her face in her hands. Then he caught her up. It was lucky the maids ran in just then ...'

'Now, why frighten them?' said Pelageya Danilovna.

'Mamma, you used to try your fate yourself ...' said her daughter.

'And how does one do it in a barn?' inquired Sonya.

'Well, say you went to the barn now, and listened. It depends on what you hear; hammering and knocking – that's bad; but a sound of shifting grain is good, and one sometimes hears that, too.'

'Mamma, tells us what happened to you in the barn.'

Pelageya Danilovna smiled.

'Oh, I've forgotten ...' she replied. 'But none of you would go?'

'Yes, I will, Pelageya Danilovna, let me! I'll go,' said Sonya.

'Well why not, if you're not afraid?'

'Louisa Ivanovna, may I?' asked Sonya.

Whether they were playing the ring and string game, or the ruble game, or talking as now, Nicholas did not leave Sonya's side, and gazed at her with quite new eyes. It seemed to him that it was only to-day, thanks to that burnt-cork moustache, that he had fully learnt to know her. And really that evening Sonya was brighter, more animated, and prettier, than Nicholas had ever seen her before.

'So that's what she is like; what a fool I have been!' he thought, gazing at her sparkling eyes, and under the moustache a happy, rapturous smile dimpled her cheeks, a smile he had never seen before.

'I'm not afraid of anything,' said Sonya. 'May I go at once?' She got up.

They told her where the barn was and how she should stand silent and listen, and they handed her a fur cloak. She threw this over her head and shoulders and glanced at Nicholas.

'What a darling that girl is!' thought he. 'And what have I been thinking of till now?'

Sonya went out into the passage to go to the barn. Nicholas went hastily to the front porch, saying he felt too hot. The crowd of people really had made the house stuffy.

Outside there was the same cold stillness, and the same moon, but even brighter than before. The light was so strong and the snow sparkled with so many stars, that one did not wish to look up at the sky and the real stars were unnoticed. The sky was black and dreary, while the earth was gay.

'I am a fool, a fool! what have I been waiting for?' thought Nicholas, and running out from the porch he went round the corner of the house and along the path that led to the back porch. He knew Sonya would pass that way. Half-way lay some snow-covered piles of firewood, and across and along them a network of shadows from the bare old lime trees fell on the snow and on the path. This path led to the barn. The log walls of the barn and its snow-covered roof, that looked as if hewn out of some precious stone, sparkled in the moonlight. A tree in the garden snapped with the frost, and then all was again perfectly silent. His bosom seemed to inhale not air, but the strength of eternal youth and gladness.

From the back porch came the sound of feet descending the steps, the bottom step, upon which snow had fallen, gave a ringing creak and he heard the voice of an old maidservant saying, 'Straight, straight along the path, Miss. Only don't look back.'

'I am not afraid,' answered Sonya's voice, and along the path towards Nicholas came the crunching, whistling sound of Sonya's feet in her thin shoes.

Sonya came along wrapped in her cloak. She was only a couple of paces away when she saw him, and to her too he was not the Nicholas she had known and always slightly feared. He was in a woman's dress, with tousled hair and a happy smile new to Sonya. She ran rapidly towards him.

'Quite different and yet the same,' thought Nicholas looking at her face all lit up by the moonlight. He slipped his arms under the cloak that covered her head, embraced her, pressed her to him, and kissed her on the lips that wore a moustache and had a smell of burnt cork. Sonya kissed him full on the lips, and disengaging her little hands, pressed them to his cheeks.

'Sonya!' . . . 'Nicholas!' . . . was all they said. They ran to the barn and then back again, re-entering, he by the front and she by the back porch.

12

WHEN they all drove back from Pelageya Danilovna's, Natasha, who always saw and noticed everything, arranged that she and Madame Schoss should go back in the sledge with Dimmler, and Sonya with Nicholas and the maids.

On the way back Nicholas drove at a steady pace instead of racing, and kept peering by that fantastic all-transforming light into Sonya's face and searching beneath the eyebrows and moustache for his former and his present Sonya from whom he had resolved never to be parted again. He looked, and recognizing in her both the old and the new Sonya, and being reminded by the smell of burnt cork of the sensation of her kiss, inhaled the frosty air with a full breast and, looking at the ground flying beneath him and at the sparkling sky, felt himself again in fairyland.

'Sonya, is it well with *thee*?' he asked from time to time.

'Yes!' she replied. 'And with *thee*?'

When half-way home, Nicholas handed the reins to the coachman and ran for a moment to Natasha's sledge and stood on its wing.

'Natasha!' he whispered in French, 'do you know I have made up my mind about Sonya?'

'Have you told her?' asked Natasha, suddenly beaming all over with joy.

'Oh, how strange you are with that moustache and those eyebrows! . . . Natasha – are you glad?'

'I am so glad, so glad! I was beginning to be vexed with you.

565

I did not tell you, but you have been treating her badly. What a heart she has, Nicholas! I am horrid sometimes but I was ashamed to be happy while Sonya was not,' continued Natasha. 'Now I am so glad! Well, run back to her.'

'No, wait a bit . . . Oh, how funny you look!' cried Nicholas peering into her face and finding in his sister too something new, unusual, and bewitchingly tender, that he had not seen in her before. 'Natasha, it's magical, isn't it?'

'Yes,' she replied. 'You have done splendidly.'

'Had I seen her before as she is now,' thought Nicholas, 'I should long ago have asked her what to do, and have done whatever she told me, and all would have been well.'

'So you are glad, and I have done right?'

'Oh, quite right! I had a quarrel with mamma some time ago about it. Mamma said she was angling for you. How could she say such a thing! I nearly stormed at mamma. I will never let anyone say anything bad of Sonya, for there is nothing but good in her.'

'Then it's all right?' said Nicholas again scrutinizing the expression of his sister's face to see if she was in earnest. Then he jumped down and, his boots scrunching the snow, ran back to his sledge. The same happy smiling Circassian with moustache and beaming eyes looking up from under a sable hood, was still sitting there, and that Circassian was Sonya, and that Sonya was certainly his future happy and loving wife.

When they reached home and had told their mother how they had spent the evening at the Melyukovs', the girls went to their bed-room. When they had undressed, but without washing off the cork moustaches, they sat a long time talking of their happiness. They talked of how they would live when they were married, how their husbands would be friends, and how happy they would be. On Natasha's table stood two looking-glasses which Dunyasha had prepared beforehand.

'Only when will all that be? I am afraid never . . . It would be too good!' said Natasha, rising and going to the looking-glasses.

'Sit down, Natasha; perhaps you'll see him,' said Sonya.

Natasha lit the candles, one on each side of one of the looking-glasses, and sat down.

'I see someone with a moustache,' said Natasha, seeing her own face.

'You mustn't laugh, Miss,' said Dunyasha.

With Sonya's help and the maid's, Natasha got the glass she held into the right position opposite the other; her face assumed a serious expression, and she sat silent. She sat a long time looking at the receding line of candles reflected in the glasses and expecting (from tales she had heard) to see a coffin, or *him*, Prince Andrew, in that last dim, indistinctly outlined, square. But ready as she was to take the smallest speck for the image of a man or of a coffin, she saw nothing. She began blinking rapidly and moved away from the looking-glasses.

'Why is it others see things and I don't?' she said. 'You sit down now, Sonya. You absolutely must, to-night! Do it for me ... To-day I feel so frightened!'

Sonya sat down before the glasses, got the right position, and began looking.

'Now, Miss Sonya is sure to see something,' whispered Dunyasha; 'while you do nothing but laugh.'

Sonya heard this and Natasha's whisper:

'I know she will. She saw something last year.'

For about three minutes all were silent.

'Of course she will!' whispered Natasha, but did not finish ... suddenly Sonya pushed away the glass she was holding and covered her eyes with her hand.

'Oh, Natasha!' she cried.

'Did you see? Did you? What was it?' exclaimed Natasha, holding up the looking-glass.

Sonya had not seen anything, she was just wanting to blink and to get up when she heard Natasha say, 'Of course she will!' She did not wish to disappoint either Dunyasha or Natasha, but it was hard to sit still. She did not herself know how or why the exclamation escaped her when she covered her eyes.

'You saw him?' urged Natasha, seizing her hand.

'Yes. Wait a bit ... I ... saw him,' Sonya could not help saying, not yet knowing whom Natasha meant by *him*, Nicholas or Prince Andrew.

'But why shouldn't I say I saw something? Others do see! Besides, who can tell whether I saw anything or not?' flashed through Sonya's mind.

'Yes, I saw him,' she said.

'How? Standing or lying?'

'No, I saw ... At first there was nothing, then I saw him lying down.'

'Andrew lying? Is he ill?' asked Natasha, her frightened eyes fixed on her friend.

'No, on the contrary, on the contrary! His face was cheerful, and he turned to me.' And when saying this she herself fancied she had really seen what she described.

'Well and then, Sonya? ...'

'After that, I could not make out what there was; something blue and red . . .'

'Sonya! When will he come back? When shall I see him! O, God, how afraid I am for him and for myself and about everything! . . .' Natasha began, and without replying to Sonya's words of comfort she got into bed, and long after her candle was out lay open-eyed and motionless, gazing at the moonlight through the frosty window-panes.

## 13

SOON after the Christmas holidays Nicholas told his mother of his love for Sonya and of his firm resolve to marry her. The countess who had long noticed what was going on between them and was expecting this declaration, listened to him in silence, and then told her son that he might marry whom he pleased, but that neither she nor his father would give their blessing to such a marriage. Nicholas, for the first time, felt that his mother was displeased with him and that, despite her love for him, she would not give way. Coldly, without looking at her son, she sent for her husband, and when he came tried briefly and coldly to inform him of the facts, in her son's presence, but unable to restrain herself she burst into tears of vexation and left the room. The old count began irresolutely to admonish Nicholas and beg him to abandon his purpose. Nicholas replied that he could not go back on his word, and his father, sighing and evidently disconcerted, very soon became silent and went in to the countess. In all his encounters with his son the count was always conscious of his own guilt towards him for having wasted the family fortune, and so he could not be angry with him for refusing to marry an heiress and choosing the dowerless Sonya. On this occasion he was only more vividly conscious of the fact that if his affairs had not been in disorder, no better wife for Nicholas than Sonya could have been wished for, and that no one but himself, with his Mitenka and his unconquerable habits, was to blame for the condition of the family finances.

The father and mother did not speak of the matter to their son again, but a few days later the countess sent for Sonya and, with a cruelty neither of them expected, reproached her niece for trying to catch Nicholas and for ingratitude. Sonya listened silently with downcast eyes to the countess's cruel words, without understanding what was required of her. She was ready to sacrifice everything for her benefactors. Self-sacrifice was her most cherished idea; but in this case she could not see what she ought to sacrifice, or for whom.

She could not help loving the countess and the whole Rostov family, but neither could she help loving Nicholas and knowing that his happiness depended on that love. She was silent and sad, and did not reply. Nicholas felt the situation to be intolerable and went to have an explanation with his mother. He first implored her to forgive him and Sonya and consent to their marriage, then he threatened that if she molested Sonya he would at once marry her secretly.

The countess, with a coldness her son had never seen in her before, replied that he was of age, that Prince Andrew was marrying without his father's consent, and he could do the same, but that she would never receive that *intriguer* as her daughter.

Exploding at the word *intriguer*, Nicholas, raising his voice, told his mother he had never expected her to try to force him to sell his feelings, but if that were so, he would say for the last time... But he had no time to utter the decisive word which the expression of his face caused his mother to await with terror, and which would perhaps have for ever remained a cruel memory to them both. He had not time to say it, for Natasha, with a pale and set face, entered the room from the door at which she had been listening.

'Nicholas, you are talking nonsense! Be quiet, be quiet, be quiet, I tell you!...' she almost screamed, so as to drown his voice.

'Mamma darling, it's not at all so... my poor, sweet darling,' she said to her mother, who conscious that they had been on the brink of a rupture, gazed at her son with terror, but in the obstinacy and excitement of the conflict could not and would not give way.

'Nicholas, I'll explain to you. Go away! Listen, mamma darling,' said Natasha.

Her words were incoherent, but they attained the purpose at which she was aiming.

The countess, sobbing heavily, hid her face on her daughter's breast, while Nicholas rose, clutching his head, and left the room.

Natasha set to work to effect a reconciliation, and so far succeeded that Nicholas received a promise from his mother that Sonya should not be troubled, while he on his side promised not to undertake anything without his parents' knowledge.

Firmly resolved, after putting his affairs in order in the regiment, to retire from the army and return and marry Sonya, Nicholas, serious, sorrowful, and at variance with his parents, but as it seemed to him passionately in love, left at the beginning of January to rejoin his regiment.

After Nicholas had gone things in the Rostov household were

more depressing than ever, and the countess fell ill from mental agitation.

Sonya was unhappy at the separation from Nicholas, and still more so on account of the hostile tone the countess could not help adopting towards her. The count was more perturbed than ever by the condition of his affairs, which called for some decisive action. Their town house and estate near Moscow had inevitably to be sold, and for this they had to go to Moscow. But the countess's health obliged them to delay their departure from day to day.

Natasha, who had borne the first period of separation from her betrothed lightly and even cheerfully, now grew more agitated and impatient every day. The thought that her best days, which she would have employed in loving him, were being vainly wasted with no advantage to anyone, tormented her incessantly. His letters for the most part irritated her. It hurt her to think that while she lived only in the thought of him, he was living a real life, seeing new places and new people that interested him. The more interesting his letters were the more vexed she felt. Her letters to him, far from giving her any comfort, seemed to her a wearisome and artificial obligation. She could not write, because she could not conceive the possibility of expressing sincerely in a letter even a thousandth part of what she expressed by voice, smile, and glance. She wrote to him formal, monotonous, and dry letters, to which she attached no importance herself, and in the rough copies of which the countess corrected her mistakes in spelling.

There was still no improvement in the countess's health, but it was impossible to defer the journey to Moscow any longer. Natasha's trousseau had to be ordered and the house sold. Moreover Prince Andrew was expected in Moscow, where old Prince Bolkonsky was spending the winter, and Natasha felt sure he had already arrived.

So the countess remained in the country, and the count, taking Sonya and Natasha with him, went to Moscow at the end of January.

### END OF PART FOUR

# PART FIVE

## 1

AFTER Prince Andrew's engagement to Natasha, Pierre without any apparent cause suddenly felt it impossible to go on living as before. Firmly convinced as he was of the truths revealed to him by his benefactor, and happy as he had been in perfecting his inner man, to which he had devoted himself with such ardour – all the zest of such a life vanished after the engagement of Andrew and Natasha, and the death of Joseph Alexeevich, the news of which reached him almost at the same time. Only the skeleton of life remained: his house, a brilliant wife who now enjoyed the favours of a very important personage, acquaintance with all Petersburg, and his Court service with its dull formalities. And this life suddenly seemed to Pierre unexpectedly loathsome. He ceased keeping a diary, avoided the company of the Brothers, began going to the club again, drank a great deal, and came once more in touch with the bachelor sets, leading such a life that the Countess Hélène thought it necessary to speak severely to him about it. Pierre felt that she was right, and to avoid compromising her went away to Moscow.

In Moscow as soon as he entered his huge house in which the faded and fading princesses still lived, with its enormous retinue: as soon as, driving through the town, he saw the Iberian shrine with innumerable tapers burning before the golden settings of the icons, the Kremlin Square with its snow undisturbed by vehicles, the sledge-drivers and hovels of the Sivtsev Vrazhok,* those old Moscovites who desired nothing, hurried nowhere, and were ending their days leisurely; when he saw those old Moscow ladies, the Moscow balls and the English Club, he felt himself at home in a quiet haven. In Moscow he felt at peace, at home, warm and dirty as in an old dressing-gown.

Moscow society, from the old women down to the children, received Pierre like a long-expected guest whose place was always ready, awaiting him. For Moscow society Pierre was the nicest, kindest, most intellectual, merriest, and most magnanimous of cranks, a heedless, genial nobleman of the old Russian type. His purse was always empty because it was open to everyone.

Benefit performances, poor pictures, statues, benevolent societies, gipsy choirs, schools, subscription dinners, sprees, Freemasons, churches, and books – no one and nothing met with a refusal from him, and had it not been for two friends who had borrowed large sums from him and taken him under their protection, he would have given everything away. There was never a dinner or soirée at the club without him. As soon as he sank into his place on the sofa after two bottles of Margaux he was surrounded, and talking, disputing, and joking began. When there were quarrels, his kindly smile and well-timed jests reconciled the antagonists. The masonic dinners were dull and dreary when he was not there.

When after a bachelor supper he rose with his amiable and kindly smile, yielding to the entreaties of the festive company to drive off somewhere with them, shouts of delight and triumph arose among the young men. At balls he danced if a partner was needed. Young ladies, married and unmarried, liked him because, without making love to any one of them, he was equally amiable to all, especially after supper. '*Il est charmant; il n'a pas de sexe*,' they said of him.

Pierre was one of those retired gentlemen-in-waiting of whom there were hundreds, good-humouredly ending their days in Moscow.

How horrified he would have been seven years before, when he first arrived from abroad, had he been told that there was no need for him to seek or plan anything, that his rut had long been shaped, eternally predetermined, and that wriggle as he might, he would be what all in his position were. He could not have believed it! Had he not at one time longed with all his heart to establish a republic in Russia; then himself to be a Napoleon; then to be a philosopher; and then a strategist and the conqueror of Napoleon? Had he not seen the possibility of, and passionately desired, the regeneration of the sinful human race, and his own progress to the highest degree of perfection? Had he not established schools and hospitals and liberated his serfs?

But instead of all that – here he was, the wealthy husband of an unfaithful wife, a retired gentleman-in-waiting, fond of eating and drinking and, as he unbuttoned his waistcoat, of abusing the government a bit, a member of the Moscow English Club and a universal favourite in Moscow society. For a long time he could not reconcile himself to the idea that he was one of those same retired Moscow gentlemen-in-waiting he had so despised seven years before.

Sometimes he consoled himself with the thought that he was only living this life temporarily; but then he was shocked by the thought of how many, like himself, had entered that life and that club temporarily, with all their teeth and hair, and had only left it when not a single tooth or hair remained.

In moments of pride, when he thought of his position it seemed to him that he was quite different and distinct from those other retired gentlemen-in-waiting he had formerly despised: they were empty, stupid, contented fellows, satisfied with their position, 'while I am still discontented and want to do something for mankind. But perhaps all these comrades of mine struggled just like me and sought something new, a path in life of their own, and like me were brought by force of circumstances, society, and race – by that elemental force against which man is powerless – to the condition I am in,' said he to himself in moments of humility; and after living some time in Moscow he no longer despised, but began to grow fond of, to respect, and to pity, his comrades in destiny, as he pitied himself.

Pierre no longer suffered moments of despair, hypochondria, and disgust with life, but the malady that had formerly found expression in such acute attacks was driven inwards and never left him for a moment. 'What for? Why? What is going on in the world?' he would ask himself in perplexity several times a day, involuntarily beginning to reflect anew on the meaning of the phenomena of life; but knowing by experience that there were no answers to these questions he made haste to turn away from them, and took up a book, or hurried off to the club or to Apollon Nikolaevich's, to exchange the gossip of the town.

'Hélène, who has never cared for anything but her own body and is one of the stupidest women in the world,' thought Pierre, 'is regarded by people as the acme of intelligence and refinement, and they pay homage to her. Napoleon Bonaparte was despised by all as long as he was great, but now that he has become a wretched comedian the Emperor Francis wants to offer him his daughter in an illegal marriage.* The Spaniards, through the Catholic clergy, offer praise to God for their victory over the French on the 14th of June,* and the French, also through the Catholic clergy, offer praise because on that same 14th of June they defeated the Spaniards. My brother Masons swear by the blood that they are ready to sacrifice everything for their neighbour, but they do not give a ruble each to the collections for the poor, and they intrigue, the Astræa Lodge against the Manna Seekers,* and fuss about an authentic Scotch carpet* and a charter that nobody needs, and the meaning of which the very man who wrote it does not understand. We all profess the Christian law of forgiveness of injuries and love of our neighbours, the law in honour of which we have built in Moscow forty times forty churches – but yesterday a deserter was knouted to death and a minister of that same law of love and forgiveness, a priest, gave the soldier a cross to kiss before his execution.' So thought Pierre, and the whole of this general deception which everyone accepts, accustomed as he was to it, astonished him each time as if it were something new. 'I understand the deception and confusion,' he thought, 'but how am I to tell them all that I see? I have tried, and have always found that they too in the depths of their souls understand it as I do, and only try not to see it. So it appears that it must be so! But I – what is to become of me?' thought he. He had the unfortunate capacity many men, especially Russians, have of seeing and believing in the possibility of goodness and truth, but of seeing the evil and falsehood of life too clearly to be able to take a serious part in it. Every sphere of work was connected, in his eyes, with evil and deception. Whatever he tried to be, whatever he engaged in, the evil and falsehood of it repulsed him and blocked every path of activity. Yet he had to live and to find occupation. It was too dreadful to be under the burden of these insoluble problems, so he abandoned himself to any distraction in order to forget them. He frequented every kind of society, drank much, bought pictures, engaged in building, and above all – read.

He read, and read everything that came to hand. On coming home, while his valets were still taking off his things, he picked up a book and began to read. From reading he passed to sleeping, from sleeping to gossip in drawing-rooms of the club, from gossip to carousals and women; from carousals back to gossip, reading, and wine. Drinking became more and more a physical and also a moral necessity. Though the doctors warned him that with his corpulence wine was dangerous for him, he drank a great deal. He was only quite at ease when, having poured several glasses of wine mechanically into his large mouth, he felt a pleasant warmth in his body, an amiability towards all his fellows, and a readiness to respond superficially to every ideal without probing it deeply. Only after emptying a bottle or two did he feel dimly that the terribly tangled skein of life which previously had terrified him was not as dreadful as he had thought. He was always conscious of some aspect of that skein, as with a buzzing in his head after dinner or supper he chatted or listened to conversation, or read. But under the influence of wine he said to himself: 'It doesn't matter. I'll get it unravelled. I have a solution ready, but have no time now – I'll think it all out later on!' But the *later on* never came.

In the morning, on an empty stomach, all the old questions

appeared as insoluble and terrible as ever, and Pierre hastily picked up a book, and if anyone came to see him he was glad.

Sometimes he remembered how he had heard that soldiers in war when entrenched under the enemy's fire, if they have nothing to do, try hard to find some occupation the more easily to bear the danger. To Pierre all men seemed like those soldiers, seeking refuge from life: some in ambition, some in cards, some in framing laws, some in women, some in toys, some in horses, some in politics, some in sport, some in wine, and some in governmental affairs. 'Nothing is trivial, and nothing is important, it's all the same – only to save oneself from it as best one can,' thought Pierre. 'Only not to see *it*, that dreadful *it*!'

2

AT the beginning of winter Prince Nicholas Bolkonsky and his daughter moved to Moscow. At that time enthusiasm for the Emperor Alexander's regime had weakened, and a patriotic and anti-French tendency prevailed there, and this together with his past and his intellect and his originality, at once made Prince Nicholas Bolkonsky an object of particular respect to the Moscovites, and the centre of the Moscow opposition to the government.

The prince had aged very much that year. He showed marked signs of senility by a tendency to fall asleep, forgetfulness of quite recent events, remembrance of remote ones, and the childish vanity with which he accepted the role of head of the Moscow opposition. In spite of this the old man inspired in all his visitors alike a feeling of respectful veneration – especially of an evening when he came in to tea in his old-fashioned coat and powdered wig and, aroused by anyone, told his abrupt stories of the past, or uttered yet more abrupt and scathing criticisms of the present. For them all, that old-fashioned house with its gigantic mirrors, pre-Revolution furniture, powdered footmen, and the stern shrewd old man (himself a relic of the past century) with his gentle daughter and the pretty Frenchwoman who were reverently devoted to him, presented a majestic and agreeable spectacle. But the visitors did not reflect that besides the couple of hours during which they saw their host, there were also twenty-two hours in the day during which the private and intimate life of the house continued.

Latterly that private life had become very trying for Princess Mary. There in Moscow she was deprived of her greatest pleasures – talks with the pilgrims and the solitude which refreshed her at Bald Hills – and she had none of the advantages and pleasures of city life. She did not go out into society; everyone knew that her father would not let her go anywhere without him, and his failing health prevented his going out himself, so that she was not invited to dinners and evening parties. She had quite abandoned the hope of getting married. She saw the coldness and malevolence with which the old prince received and dismissed the young men, possible suitors, who sometimes appeared at their house. She had no friends: during this visit to Moscow she had been disappointed in the two who had been nearest to her. Mademoiselle Bourienne, with whom she had never been able to be quite frank, had now become unpleasant to her, and for various reasons Princess Mary avoided her. Julie, with whom she had corresponded for the last five years, was in Moscow, but proved to be quite alien to her when they met. Just then Julie, who by the death of her brothers had become one of the richest heiresses in Moscow, was in the full whirl of society pleasures. She was surrounded by young men who, she fancied, had suddenly learnt to appreciate her worth. Julie was at that stage in the life of a society woman when she feels that her last chance of marrying has come, and that her fate must be decided now or never. On Thursdays Princess Mary remembered with a mournful smile that she now had no one to write to, since Julie – whose presence gave her no pleasure – was here and they met every week. Like the old *émigré* who declined to marry the lady with whom he had spent his evenings for years, she regretted Julie's presence and having no one to write to. In Moscow Princess Mary had no one to talk to, no one to whom to confide her sorrow, and much sorrow fell to her lot just then. The time for Prince Andrew's return and marriage was approaching, but his request to her to prepare his father for it had not been carried out; in fact it seemed as if matters were quite hopeless, for at every mention of the young Countess Rostova the old Prince (who apart from that was usually in a bad temper) lost control of himself. Another lately added sorrow arose from the lessons she gave her six-year-old nephew. To her consternation she detected in herself in relation to little Nicholas some symptoms of her father's irritability. However often she told herself that she must not get irritable when teaching her nephew, almost every time that, pointer in hand, she sat down to show him the French alphabet, she so longed to pour her own knowledge quickly and easily into the child – who was already afraid that Auntie might at any moment get angry – that at his slightest inattention she trembled, became flustered and heated, raised her voice, and sometimes pulled him by the arm and put him in the corner. Having put him in the corner she would herself begin to cry over her cruel, evil nature, and little Nicholas, following her example, would sob, and without permission would leave his corner, come to her, pull her wet hands from her face, and comfort her. But what distressed the princess most of all was her father's irritability, which was always directed against her and had of late amounted to cruelty. Had he forced her to prostrate herself to the ground all night, had he beaten her, or made her fetch wood or water, it would never have entered her mind to think her position hard; but this loving despot – the more cruel because he loved her and for that reason tormented himself and her – knew how not merely to hurt and humiliate her deliberately, but to show her that she was always to blame for everything. Of late he had exhibited a new trait that tormented Princess Mary more than anything else; this was his ever-increasing intimacy with Mademoiselle Bourienne. The idea that at the first moment of receiving the news of his son's intentions had occurred to him in jest – that if Andrew got married, he himself would marry Bourienne – had evidently pleased him, and latterly he had persistently, and as it seemed to Princess Mary merely to offend her, shown special endearments to the companion, and expressed his dissatisfaction with his daughter by demonstrations of love for Bourienne.

One day in Moscow in Princess Mary's presence (she thought her father did it purposely when she was there) the old prince kissed Mademoiselle Bourienne's hand and, drawing her to him, embraced her affectionately. Princess Mary flushed and ran out of the room. A few minutes later Mademoiselle Bourienne came into Princess Mary's room smiling and making cheerful remarks in her agreeable voice. Princess Mary hastily wiped away her tears, went resolutely up to Mademoiselle Bourienne, and evidently unconscious of what she was doing began shouting in angry haste at the Frenchwoman, her voice breaking: 'It's horrible, vile, inhuman, to take advantage of the weakness . . .' She did not finish. 'Leave my room,' she exclaimed, and burst into sobs.

Next day the prince did not say a word to his daughter, but she noticed that at dinner he gave orders that Mademoiselle Bourienne should be served first. After dinner, when the footman handed coffee, and from habit began with the princess, the prince suddenly grew furious, threw his stick at Philip, and instantly gave instructions to have him conscripted for the army.

'He doesn't obey . . . I said it twice . . . and he doesn't obey! She is the first person in this house; she's my best friend,' cried the prince. 'And if you allow yourself,' he screamed in a fury, addressing Princess Mary for the first time, 'to forget yourself again before her as you dared to do yesterday, I will show you who is master in this house. Go! Don't let me set eyes on you; beg her pardon!'

Princess Mary asked Mademoiselle Bourienne's pardon, and also her father's pardon for herself and for Philip the footman, who had begged for her intervention.

At such moments something like a pride of sacrifice gathered in her soul. And suddenly that father, whom she had judged, would look for his spectacles in her presence, fumbling near them and not seeing them, or would forget something that had just occurred, or take a false step with his failing legs and turn to see if anyone had noticed his feebleness, or, worst of all, at dinner when there were no visitors to excite him, would suddenly fall asleep, letting his napkin drop and his shaking head sink over his plate. 'He is old and feeble, and I dare to condemn him!' she thought at such moments, with a feeling of revulsion against herself.

## 3

In 1811 there was living in Moscow a French doctor – Métivier – who had rapidly become the fashion. He was enormously tall, handsome, amiable as Frenchmen are, and was, as all Moscow said, an extraordinarily clever doctor. He was received in the best houses not merely as a doctor, but as an equal.

Prince Nicholas had always ridiculed medicine, but latterly on Mademoiselle Bourienne's advice had allowed this doctor to visit him and had grown accustomed to him. Métivier came to see the prince about twice a week.

On December 6th – St Nicholas's day and the prince's name-day – all Moscow came to the prince's front door, but he gave orders to admit no one, and to invite to dinner only a small number, a list of whom he gave to Princess Mary.

Métivier, who came in the morning with his felicitations, considered it proper in his quality of doctor *de forcer la consigne,* as he told Princess Mary, and went in to see the prince. It happened that on that morning of his name-day the prince was in one of his worst moods. He had been going about the house all the morning finding fault with everyone and pretending not to understand what was said to him and not to be understood himself. Princess Mary well knew this mood of quiet absorbed querulousness, which generally culminated in a burst of rage, and she went about all that morning as though facing a cocked and loaded gun and awaited the inevitable explosion. Until the doctor's arrival the morning had passed off safely. After admitting the doctor, Princess Mary sat down with a book in the drawing-room near the door through which she could hear all that passed in the study.

At first she only heard Métivier's voice, then her father's, then both voices began speaking at the same time, the door was flung open, and on the threshold appeared the handsome figure of the terrified Métivier with his shock of black hair, and the prince in his dressing-gown and fez, his face distorted with fury and the pupils of his eyes rolled downwards.

'You don't understand?' shouted the prince, 'but I do! French spy, slave of Buonaparte, spy, get out of my house! Be off, I tell you . . .' and he slammed the door.

Métivier, shrugging his shoulders, went up to Mademoiselle Bourienne, who at the sound of shouting had run in from an adjoining room.

'The prince is not very well: bile and rush of blood to the head. Keep calm, I will call again to-morrow,' said Métivier, and putting his fingers to his lips he hastened away.

Through the study-door came the sound of slippered feet and the cry: 'Spies, traitors, traitors everywhere! Not a moment's peace in my own house!'

After Métivier's departure the old prince called his daughter in, and the whole weight of his wrath fell on her. She was to blame that a spy had been admitted. Had he not told her, yes, told her to make a list, and not to admit anyone who was not on that list? Then why was that scoundrel admitted? She was the cause of it all. With her, he said, he could not have a moment's peace, and could not die quietly.

'No, ma'am! We must part, we must part! Understand that, understand it! I cannot endure any more,' he said, and left the room. Then, as if afraid she might find some means of consolation, he returned and trying to appear calm added: 'And don't imagine I have said this in a moment of anger. I am calm, I have thought it over, and it will be carried out – we must part; so find some place for yourself! . . .' But he could not restrain himself and, with the virulence of which only one who loves is capable, evidently suffering himself, he shook his fists at her and screamed:

'If only some fool would marry her!' Then he slammed the door, sent for Mademoiselle Bourienne and subsided in his study.

At two o'clock the six chosen guests assembled for dinner.

These guests – the famous Count Rostopchin, Prince Lopukhin and his nephew, General Chatrov, an old war comrade of the prince's, and of the younger generation Pierre and Boris Drubetskoy – awaited the prince in the drawing-room.

Boris, who had come to Moscow on leave a few days before, had been anxious to be presented to Prince Nicholas Bolkonsky, and had contrived to ingratiate himself so well that the old prince in his case made an exception to the rule of not receiving bachelors in his house.

The prince's house did not belong to what is known as *fashionable society*, but his little circle – though not much talked about in town – was one it was more flattering to be received in than any other. Boris had realized this the week before, when the commander-in-chief in his presence invited Rostopchin to dinner on St Nicholas's day, and Rostopchin had replied that he could not come:

'On that day I always go to pay my devotions to the relics of Prince Nicholas Bolkonsky.'

'Oh, yes, yes!' replied the commander-in-chief. 'How is he? . . .'

The small group that assembled before dinner in the lofty old-fashioned drawing-room, with its old furniture, resembled the solemn gathering of a Court of Justice. All were silent or talked in low tones. Prince Nicholas came in serious and taciturn. Princess Mary seemed even quieter and more diffident than usual. The guests were reluctant to address her, feeling that she was in no mood for their conversation. Count Rostopchin alone kept the conversation going, now relating the latest town news, and now the latest political gossip.

Lopukhin and the old general occasionally took part in the conversation. Prince Bolkonsky listened as a presiding judge receives a report, only now and then, silently or by a brief word, showing that he took heed of what was being reported to him. The tone of the conversation was such as indicated that no one approved of what was being done in the political world. Incidents were related evidently confirming the opinion that everything was going from bad to worse, but whether telling a story or giving an opinion the speaker always stopped, or was stopped, at the point beyond which his criticism might touch the sovereign himself.

At dinner the talk turned on the latest political news: Napoleon's seizure of the Duke of Oldenburg's territory,* and the Russian Note, hostile to Napoleon, which had been sent to all the European courts.

'Bonaparte treats Europe as a pirate does a captured vessel,' said Count Rostopchin, repeating a phrase he had uttered several times before. 'One only wonders at the long-suffering or blindness of the crowned heads. Now the Pope's turn has come, and Bonaparte doesn't scruple to depose the head of the Catholic Church – yet all keep silent! Our sovereign alone has protested against the seizure of the Duke of Oldenburg's territory, and even . . .' Count Rostopchin paused, feeling that he had reached the limit beyond which censure was impossible.

'Other territories have been offered in exchange for the Duchy of Oldenburg,' said Prince Bolkonsky. 'He shifts the Dukes about as I might move my serfs from Bald Hills to Bogucharovo or my Ryazan estates.'

'The Duke of Oldenburg bears his misfortunes with admirable strength of character and resignation,' remarked Boris, joining in respectfully.

He said this because on his journey from Petersburg he had had the honour of being presented to the Duke. Prince Bolkonsky glanced at the young man as if about to say something in reply, but changed his mind, evidently considering him too young.

'I have read our protest about the Oldenburg affair and was surprised how badly the Note was worded,' remarked Count Rostopchin in the casual tone of a man dealing with a subject quite familiar to him.

Pierre looked at Rostopchin with naïve astonishment, not understanding why he should be disturbed by the bad composition of the Note.

'Does it matter, Count, how the Note is worded,' he asked, 'so long as its substance is forceful?'

'My dear fellow, with our five hundred thousand troops it should be easy to have a good style,' returned Count Rostopchin.

Pierre now understood the count's dissatisfaction with the wording of the Note.

'One would have thought quill-drivers enough had sprung up,' remarked the old prince. 'There in Petersburg they are always writing – not Notes only but even new laws. My Andrew there has written a whole volume of laws for Russia. Nowadays they are always writing!' and he laughed unnaturally.

There was a momentary pause in the conversation; the old general cleared his throat to draw attention.

'Did you hear of the last event at the review in Petersburg? The figure cut by the new French ambassador.'

'Eh? Yes, I heard something: he said something awkward in his Majesty's presence.'

'His Majesty drew his attention to the Grenadier division and to the march past,' continued the general, 'and it seems the ambassador took no notice and allowed himself to reply that: "We in France pay no attention to such trifles!" The Emperor did not condescend to reply. At the next review, they say, the Emperor did not once deign to address him.'

All were silent. On this fact relating to the Emperor personally, it was impossible to pass any judgment.

'Impudent fellows!' said the prince. 'You know Métivier? I turned him out of my house this morning. He was here; they admitted him in spite of my request that they should let no one in,' he went on, glancing angrily at his daughter.

And he narrated his whole conversation with the French doctor and the reasons that convinced him that Métivier was a spy. Though these reasons were very insufficient and obscure, no one made any rejoinder.

After the roast, champagne was served. The guests rose to congratulate the old prince. Princess Mary, too, went round to him.

He gave her a cold, angry look, and offered her his wrinkled, clean-shaven cheek to kiss. The whole expression of his face told her that he had not forgotten the morning's talk, that his decision remained in force, and only the presence of visitors hindered his speaking of it to her now.

When they went into the drawing-room where coffee was served, the old men sat together.

Prince Nicholas grew more animated and expressed his views on the impending war.

He said that our wars with Bonaparte would be disastrous so long as we sought alliances with the Germans and thrust ourselves into European affairs, into which we had been drawn by the Peace of Tilsit. 'We ought not to fight either for or against Austria. Our political interests are all in the East, and in regard to Bonaparte the only thing is to have an armed frontier and a firm policy, and he will never dare to cross the Russian frontier, as was the case in 1807!'

'How can we fight the French, Prince?' said Count Rostopchin. 'Can we arm ourselves against our teachers and divinities? Look at our youths, look at our ladies! The French are our Gods: Paris is our Kingdom of Heaven.'

He began speaking louder, evidently to be heard by everyone.

'French dresses, French ideas, French feelings! There now, you turned Métivier out by the scruff of his neck because he is a Frenchman and a scoundrel, but our ladies crawl after him on their knees. I went to a party last night, and there out of five ladies three were Roman Catholics and had the Pope's indulgence for doing wool-work on Sundays. And they themselves sit there nearly naked, like the sign-boards at our Public Baths, if I may say so. Ah, when one looks at our young people, Prince, one would like to take Peter the Great's old cudgel out of the museum and belabour them in the Russian way till all the nonsense jumps out of them.'

All were silent. The old prince looked at Rostopchin with a smile and wagged his head approvingly.

'Well, good-bye, your Excellency, keep well!' said Rostopchin, getting up with characteristic briskness and holding out his hand to the prince.

'Good-bye, my dear fellow...His words are music, I never tire of hearing him!' said the old prince, keeping hold of the hand and offering his cheek to be kissed.

Following Rostopchin's example the others also rose.

## 4

PRINCESS MARY, as she sat listening to the old men's talk and fault-finding, understood nothing of what she heard; she only wondered whether the guests had all observed her father's hostile attitude towards her. She did not even notice the special attentions and amiabilities shown her during dinner by Boris Drubetskoy, who was visiting them for the third time already.

Princess Mary turned with an absent-minded questioning look to Pierre, who hat in hand and with a smile on his face was the last of the guests to approach her after the old prince had gone out and they were left alone in the drawing-room.

'May I stay a little longer?' he said, letting his stout body sink into an arm-chair beside her.

'Oh yes,' she answered. 'You noticed nothing?' her look asked.

Pierre was in an agreeable after-dinner mood. He looked straight before him and smiled quietly.

'Have you known that young man long, Princess?' he asked.

'Who?'

'Drubetskoy.'

'No, not long...'

'Do you like him?'

'Yes, he is an agreeable young man... Why do you ask me that?' said Princess Mary, still thinking of that morning's conversation with her father.

'Because I have noticed that when a young man comes on leave from Petersburg to Moscow it is usually with the object of marrying an heiress.'

'You have observed that?' said Princess Mary.

'Yes,' returned Pierre with a smile, 'and this young man now manages matters so that where there is a wealthy heiress, there he is too. I can read him like a book. At present he is hesitating whom to lay siege to – you or Mademoiselle Julie Karagina. He is very attentive to her.'

'He visits them?'

'Yes, very often. And do you know the new way of courting?'

said Pierre with an amused smile, evidently in that cheerful mood of good-humoured raillery for which he so often reproved himself in his diary.

'No,' replied Princess Mary.

'To please Moscow girls nowadays one has to be melancholy. He is very melancholy with Mademoiselle Karagina,' said Pierre.

'Really?' asked Princess Mary, looking into Pierre's kindly face and still thinking of her own sorrow. 'It would be a relief,' thought she, 'if I ventured to confide what I am feeling to someone. I should like to tell everything to Pierre. He is kind and generous. It would be a relief. He would give me advice.'

'Would you marry him?'

'Oh, my God, Count, there are moments when I would marry anybody!' she cried suddenly to her own surprise and with tears in her voice. 'Ah, how bitter it is to love someone near to you and to feel that...' she went on in a trembling voice, 'that you can do nothing for him but grieve him, and to know that you cannot alter this. Then there is only one thing left – to go away, but where could I go?'

'What is wrong? What is it, Princess?'

But without finishing what she was saying, Princess Mary burst into tears.

'I don't know what is the matter with me to-day. Don't take any notice – forget what I have said!'

Pierre's gaiety vanished completely. He anxiously questioned the princess, asked her to speak out fully and confide her grief to him; but she only repeated that she begged him to forget what she had said, that she did not remember what she had said, and that she had no trouble except the one he knew of – that Prince Andrew's marriage threatened to cause a rupture between father and son.

'Have you any news of the Rostovs?' she asked, to change the subject. 'I was told they are coming soon. I am also expecting Andrew any day. I should like them to meet here.'

'And how does he now regard the matter?' asked Pierre, referring to the old prince.

Princess Mary shook her head.

'What is to be done? In a few months the year will be up. The thing is impossible. I only wish I could spare my brother the first moments. I wish they would come sooner. I hope to be friends with her. You have known them a long time,' said Princess Mary. 'Tell me honestly the whole truth: what sort of a girl is she, and what do you think of her? – The real truth, because you know Andrew is risking so much doing this against his father's will, that I should like to know . . .'

An undefined instinct told Pierre that these explanations, and repeated requests to be told the *whole truth*, expressed ill will on the princess's part towards her future sister-in-law, and a wish that he should disapprove of Andrew's choice; but in reply he said what he felt rather than what he thought.

'I don't know how to answer your question,' he said, blushing without knowing why. 'I really don't know what sort of girl she is; I can't analyse her at all. She is enchanting, but what makes her so I don't know. That is all one can say about her.'

Princess Mary sighed, and the expression on her face said: 'Yes, that's what I expected and feared.'

'Is she clever?' she asked.

Pierre considered.

'I think not,' he said, 'and yet – yes. She does not deign to be clever . . . Oh no, she is simply enchanting, and that is all.'

Princess Mary again shook her head disapprovingly.

'Ah, I so long to like her! Tell her so, if you see her before I do.'

'I hear they are expected very soon,' said Pierre.

Princess Mary told Pierre of her plan to become intimate with her future sister-in-law as soon as the Rostovs arrived and to try to accustom the old prince to her.

5

BORIS had not succeeded in making a wealthy match in Petersburg, so with the same object in view he came to Moscow. There he wavered between the two richest heiresses, Julie and Princess Mary. Though Princess Mary despite her plainness seemed to him more attractive than Julie, he, without knowing why, felt awkward about paying court to her. When they had last met, on the old prince's name-day, she had answered at random all his attempts to talk sentimentally, evidently not listening to what he was saying.

Julie on the contrary accepted his attentions readily, though in a manner peculiar to herself.

She was twenty-seven. After the death of her brothers she had become very wealthy. She was by now decidedly plain, but thought herself not merely as good-looking as before but even far more attractive. She was confirmed in this delusion by the fact that she had become a very wealthy heiress and also by the fact that the older she grew the less dangerous she became to men, and the more freely they could associate with her and avail themselves of her suppers, soirées, and the animated company that assembled at her house, without incurring any obligation. A man who would have been afraid ten years before of going every day to the house when there was a girl of seventeen there, for fear of compromising her and committing himself, would now go boldly every day and treat her not as a marriageable girl but as a sexless acquaintance.

That winter the Karagins' house was the most agreeable and hospitable in Moscow. In addition to the formal evening and dinner parties, a large company, chiefly of men, gathered there every day, supping at midnight and staying till three in the morning. Julie never missed a ball, a promenade, or a play. Her dresses were always of the latest fashion. But in spite of that she seemed to be disillusioned about everything, and told everyone that she did not believe either in friendship or in love, or any of the joys of life, and expected peace only 'yonder'. She adopted the tone of one who has suffered a great disappointment, like a girl who has either lost the man she loved or been cruelly deceived by him. Though nothing of the kind had happened to her, she was regarded in that light and had even herself come to believe that she had suffered much in life. This melancholy, which did not prevent her amusing herself, did not hinder the young people who came to her house from passing the time pleasantly. Every visitor who came to the house paid his tribute to the melancholy mood of the hostess, and then amused himself with society gossip, dancing, intellectual games, and *bouts rimés*, which were in vogue at the Karagins'. Only a few of these young men, among them Boris, entered more deeply into Julie's melancholy, and with these she had prolonged conversations in private on the vanity of all worldly things, and to them she showed her albums, filled with mournful sketches, maxims, and verses.

To Boris Julie was particularly gracious: she regretted his early disillusionment with life, offered him such consolation of friendship as she, who had herself suffered so much, could render, and showed him her album. Boris sketched two trees in the album, and wrote: 'Rustic trees, your dark branches shed gloom and melancholy upon me.'

On another page he drew a tomb, and wrote:

> *La mort est secourable et la mort est tranquille.*
> *Ah! contre les douleurs il n'y a pas d'autre asile.*

Julie said this was charming.

'There is something so enchanting in the smile of melancholy,' she said to Boris, repeating word for word a passage she had copied from a book. 'It is a ray of light in the darkness, a shade between sadness and despair, showing the possibility of consolation.'

586

In reply Boris wrote these lines:

> Aliment de poison d'une âme trop sensible,
> Toi, sans qui le bonheur me serait impossible,
> Tendre mélancolie, ah, viens me consoler,
> Viens calmer les tourments de ma sombre retraite
> Et mêle une douceur secrète
> A ces pleurs, que je sens couler.

For Boris Julie played most doleful nocturnes on her harp. Boris read *Poor Liza* aloud to her, and more than once interrupted the reading because of the emotions that choked him. Meeting at large gatherings Julie and Boris looked on one another as the only souls who understood one another in a world of indifferent people.

Anna Mikhaylovna, who often visited the Karagins, while playing cards with the mother made careful inquiries as to Julie's dowry (she was to have two estates in Penza and the Nizhegorod forests). Anna Mikhaylovna regarded the refined sadness that united her son to the wealthy Julie with emotion and resignation to the Divine will.

'You are always charming and melancholy, my dear Julie,' she said to the daughter. 'Boris says his soul finds repose at your house. He has suffered so many disappointments and is so sensitive,' said she to the mother. 'Ah, my dear, I can't tell you how fond I have grown of Julie latterly,' she said to her son. 'But who could help loving her? She is an angelic being! Ah, Boris, Boris!' – she paused. 'And how I pity her mother,' she went on; 'to-day she showed me her accounts and letters from Penza (they have enormous estates there) and she, poor thing, has no one to help her, and they do cheat her so!'

Boris smiled almost imperceptibly while listening to his mother. He laughed blandly at her naïve diplomacy but listened to what she had to say, and sometimes questioned her carefully about the Penza and Nizhegorod estates.

Julie had long been expecting a proposal from her melancholy adorer and was ready to accept it; but some secret feeling of repulsion for her, for her passionate desire to get married, for her artificiality, and a feeling of horror at renouncing the possibility of real love, still restrained Boris. His leave was expiring. He spent every day and whole days at the Karagins', and every day on thinking the matter over told himself that he would propose to-morrow. But in Julie's presence, looking at her red face and chin (nearly always powdered), her moist eyes, and her expression of continual readiness to pass at once from melancholy to an unnatural rapture of married bliss, Boris could not utter the decisive words, though in imagination he had long regarded himself as the possessor of those Penza and Nizhegorod estates and had apportioned the use of the income from them. Julie saw Boris's indecision and sometimes the thought occurred to her that she was repulsive to him, but her feminine self-deception immediately supplied her with consolation, and she told herself that he was only shy from love. Her melancholy however began to turn to irritability, and not long before Boris's departure she formed a definite plan of action. Just as Boris's leave of absence was expiring, Anatole Kuragin made his appearance in Moscow, and of course in the Karagins' drawing-room, and Julie, suddenly abandoning her melancholy, became cheerful and very attentive to Kuragin.

'My dear,' said Anna Mikhaylovna to her son, 'I know from a reliable source that Prince Vasili has sent his son to Moscow to get him married to Julie. I am so fond of Julie that I should be sorry for her. What do you think of it, my dear?'

The idea of being made a fool of, and of having thrown away that whole month of arduous melancholy service to Julie, and of seeing all the revenue from the Penza estates, which he had already mentally apportioned and put to proper use, fall into the hands of another, and especially into the hands of that idiot Anatole, pained Boris. He drove to the Karagins' with the firm intention of proposing. Julie met him in a gay, careless manner, spoke casually of how she had enjoyed yesterday's ball, and asked when he was leaving. Though Boris had come intentionally to speak of his love and therefore meant to be tender, he began speaking irritably of feminine inconstancy, of how easily women can turn from sadness to joy, and how their moods depend solely on who happens to be paying court to them. Julie was offended, and replied that it was true that a woman needs variety, and the same thing over and over again would weary anyone.

'Then I should advise you ...' Boris began, wishing to sting her; but at that instant the galling thought occurred to him that he might have to leave Moscow without having accomplished his aim, and have vainly wasted his efforts – which was a thing he never allowed to happen.

He checked himself in the middle of the sentence, lowered his eyes to avoid seeing her unpleasantly irritated and irresolute face, and said:

'I did not come here at all to quarrel with you. On the contrary ...'

He glanced at her to make sure that he might go on. Her irritability had suddenly quite vanished, and her anxious, imploring eyes were fixed on him with greedy expectation. 'I can always arrange so as not to see her often,' thought Boris. 'The affair has been begun and must be finished!' He blushed hotly, raised his eyes to hers, and said:

'You know my feelings for you!'

There was no need to say more: Julie's face shone with triumph and self-satisfaction; but she forced Boris to say all that is said on such occasions – that he loved her and had never loved any other woman more than her. She knew that for the Penza estates and Nizhegorod forests she could demand this, and she received what she demanded.

The affianced couple, no longer alluding to trees that shed gloom and melancholy upon them, planned the arrangements of a splendid house in Petersburg, paid calls, and prepared everything for a brilliant wedding.

6

AT the end of January old Count Rostov went to Moscow with Natasha and Sonya. The countess was still unwell and unable to travel but it was impossible to wait for her recovery. Prince Andrew was expected in Moscow any day, the trousseau had to be ordered and the estate near Moscow had to be sold, besides which the opportunity of presenting his future daughter-in-law to old Prince Bolkonsky while he was in Moscow could not be missed. The Rostovs' Moscow house had not been heated that winter and, as they had come only for a short time and the countess was not with them, the count decided to stay with Marya Dmitrievna Akhrosimova, who had long been pressing her hospitality on them.

Late one evening the Rostovs' four sledges drove into Marya Dmitrievna's courtyard in the old Konyusheny Street. Marya Dmitrievna lived alone. She had already married off her daughter, and her sons were all in the service.

She held herself as erect, told everyone her opinion as candidly, loudly, and bluntly, as ever, and her whole bearing seemed a reproach to others for any weakness, passion, or temptation – the possibility of which she did not admit. From early in the morning, wearing a dressing-jacket, she attended to her household affairs, and then she drove out: on holy days to church, and after the service to jails and prisons on affairs of which she never spoke to anyone.* On ordinary days, after dressing, she received petitioners of various classes, of whom there were always some. Then she had dinner, a substantial and appetizing meal at which there were always three or four guests; after dinner she played a game of boston, and at night she had the newspapers or a new book read to her while she knitted. She rarely made an exception and went out to pay visits, and then only to the most important persons in the town.

She had not yet gone to bed when the Rostovs arrived and the pulley of the hall-door squeaked as it let in the Rostovs and their servants from the cold. Marya Dmitrievna, with her spectacles hanging down on her nose and her head flung back, stood in the hall doorway looking with a stern, grim face at the new arrivals. One might have thought she was angry with the travellers and would immediately turn them out, had she not at the same time been giving careful instructions to the servants for the accommodation of the visitors and their belongings.

'The Count's things? Bring them here,' she said, pointing to the portmanteaux and not greeting anyone. 'The young ladies? There to the left. Now what are you dawdling for?' she cried to the maids. 'Get the samovar ready!... You've grown plumper and prettier,' she remarked, drawing Natasha (whose cheeks were glowing from the cold) to her by the hood. 'Foo! You *are* cold! Now take off your things, quick!' she shouted to the count who was going to kiss her hand. 'You're half frozen, I'm sure! Bring some rum for tea!... *Bonjour*, Sonya dear!' she added, turning to Sonya and indicating by this French greeting her slightly contemptuous though affectionate attitude towards her.

When they came in to tea, having taken off their outdoor things and tidied themselves up after their journey, Marya Dmitrievna kissed them all in due order.

'I'm heartily glad you have come and are staying with me. It was high time,' she said, giving Natasha a significant look. 'The old man is here and his son's expected any day. You'll have to make his acquaintance. But we'll speak of that later on,' she added, glancing at Sonya with a look that showed she did not want to speak of it in her presence. 'Now listen,' she said to the count. 'What do you want to-morrow? Whom will you send for? Shinshin?' She crooked one of her fingers. 'The snivelling Anna Mikhaylovna? That's two. She's here with her son. The son is getting married! Then Bezukhov, eh? He is here too, with his wife. He ran away from her and she came galloping after him. He dined with me on Wednesday. As for them' – and she pointed to the girls – 'to-morrow I'll take them first to the Iberian shrine of the Mother of God, and then we'll drive to the Super-Rogue's.* I suppose you'll have everything new. Don't judge by me: sleeves nowadays are this size! The other day young Princess Irina Vasilevna came to see me; she was an awful sight – looked as if she had put two barrels on her arms. You know not a day passes now without some new fashion. And what have you to do yourself?' she asked the count sternly.

'One thing has come on top of another: her rags to buy, and now a purchaser has turned up for the Moscow estate and for the house. If you will be so kind, I'll fix a time and go down to the estate just for a day, and leave my lassies with you.'

'All right. All right. They'll be safe with me, as safe as in Chancery! I'll take them where they must go, scold them a bit, and pet them a bit,' said Marya Dmitrievna, touching her god-daughter and favourite, Natasha, on the cheek with her large hand.

Next morning Marya Dmitrievna took the young ladies to the Iberian shrine of the Mother of God and to Madame Suppert-Roguet, who was so afraid of Marya Dmitrievna that she always let her have costumes at a loss merely to get rid of her. Marya Dmitrievna ordered almost the whole trousseau. When they got home she turned everybody out of the room except Natasha, and then called her pet to her arm-chair.

'Well, now we'll talk. I congratulate you on your betrothed. You've hooked a fine fellow! I am glad for your sake, and I've known him since he was so high.' She held her hand a couple of feet from the ground. Natasha blushed happily. 'I like him and all his family. Now listen! You know that old Prince Nicholas much dislikes his son's marrying. The old fellow's crotchety! Of course Prince Andrew is not a child and can shift without him, but it's not nice to enter a family against a father's will. One wants to do it peacefully and lovingly. You're a clever girl and you'll know how to manage. Be kind, and use yours wits. Then all will be well.'

Natasha remained silent, from shyness Marya Dmitrievna supposed, but really because she disliked anyone interfering in what touched her love of Prince Andrew, which seemed to her so apart from all human affairs that no one could understand it. She loved and knew Prince Andrew, he loved her only, and was to come one of these days and take her. She wanted nothing more.

'You see, I have known him a long time and am also fond of Mary, your future sister-in-law. "Husbands' sisters bring up blisters", but this one wouldn't hurt a fly. She has asked me to bring you two together. To-morrow you'll go with your father to see her. Be very nice and affectionate to her: you're younger than she. When *he* comes, he'll find you already know his sister and father and are liked by them. Am I right or not? Won't that be best?'

'Yes, it will,' Natasha answered reluctantly.

NEXT day, on Marya Dmitrievna's advice, Count Rostov took Natasha to call on Prince Nicholas Bolkonsky. The count did not set out cheerfully on this visit, at heart he felt afraid. He well remembered the last interview he had had with the old prince, at the time of the enrolment, when in reply to an invitation to dinner he had had to listen to an angry reprimand for not having provided his full quota of men. Natasha, on the other hand, having put on her best gown was in the highest spirits. 'They can't help liking me,' she thought. 'Everybody always has liked me, and I am so willing to do anything they wish, so ready to be fond of him – for being *his* father – and of her – for being *his* sister – that there is no reason for them not to like me . . .'

They drove up to the gloomy old house on the Vozdvizhenka and entered the vestibule.

'Well, the Lord have mercy on us!' said the count, half in jest, half in earnest; but Natasha noticed that her father was flurried on entering the ante-room, and inquired timidly and softly whether the prince and princess were at home.

When they had been announced a perturbation was noticeable among the servants. The footman who had gone to announce them was stopped by another in the large hall and they whispered to one another. Then a maidservant ran into the hall and hurriedly said something, mentioning the princess. At last an old, cross-looking footman came and announced to the Rostovs that the prince was not receiving, but that the princess begged them to walk up. The first person who came to meet the visitors was Mademoiselle Bourienne. She greeted the father and daughter with special politeness, and showed them to the princess's room. The princess, looking excited and nervous, her face flushed in patches, ran in to meet the visitors, treading heavily, and vainly trying to appear cordial and at ease. From the first glance Princess Mary did not like Natasha. She thought her too fashionably dressed, frivolously gay, and vain. She did not at all realize that before having seen her future sister-in-law she was prejudiced against her by involuntary envy of her beauty, youth, and happiness, as well as by jealousy of her brother's love for her. Apart from this insuperable antipathy to her, Princess Mary was agitated just then because on the Rostovs being announced, the old prince had shouted that he did not wish to see them, that Princess Mary might do so if she chose, but they were not to be admitted to him. She had decided to receive them, but feared lest the prince might at any moment indulge in some freak, as he seemed much upset by the Rostovs' visit.

'There, my dear Princess, I've brought you my songstress,' said the count, bowing, and looking round uneasily as if afraid the old prince might appear. 'I am so glad you should get to know one another ... very sorry the prince is still ailing,' and after a few more commonplace remarks he rose. 'If you'll allow me to leave my Natasha in your hands for a quarter of an hour, Princess, I'll drive round to see Anna Semënovna, it's quite near, in the Dogs' Square, and then I'll come back for her.'

The count had devised this diplomatic ruse (as he afterwards told his daughter) to give the future sisters-in-law an opportunity to talk to one another freely, but another motive was to avoid the danger of encountering the old prince, of whom he was afraid. He did not mention this to his daughter, but Natasha noticed her father's nervousness and anxiety and felt mortified by it. She blushed for him, grew still angrier at having blushed, and looked at the princess with a bold and defiant expression which said that she was not afraid of anybody. The princess told the count that she would be delighted, and only begged him to stay longer at Anna Semënovna's, and he departed.

Despite the uneasy glances thrown at her by Princess Mary – who wished to have a tête-à-tête with Natasha – Mademoiselle Bourienne remained in the room and persistently talked about Moscow amusements and theatres. Natasha felt offended by the hesitation she had noticed in the ante-room, by her father's nervousness, and by the unnatural manner of the princess who – she thought – was making a favour of receiving her, and so everything displeased her. She did not like Princess Mary, whom she thought very plain, affected, and dry. Natasha suddenly shrank into herself, and involuntarily assumed an off-hand air which alienated Princess Mary still more. After five minutes of irksome, constrained conversation, they heard the sound of slippered feet rapidly approaching. Princess Mary looked frightened. The door opened, and the old prince, in a dressing-gown and a white night-cap, came in.

'Ah, madam!' he began. 'Madam, Countess ... Countess Rostova, if I am not mistaken ... I beg you to excuse me, to excuse me ... I did not know, madam. God is my witness, I did not know you had honoured us with a visit, and I came in such a costume only to see my daughter. I beg you to excuse me ... God is my witness, I didn't know –' he repeated, stressing the word 'God' so unnaturally and so unpleasantly that Princess Mary stood with downcast eyes, not daring to look either at her father or at Natasha.

Nor did the latter, having risen and curtsied, know what to do. Mademoiselle Bourienne alone smiled agreeably.

'I beg you to excuse me, excuse me! God is my witness, I did not know,' muttered the old man, and after looking Natasha over from head to foot he went out.

Mademoiselle Bourienne was the first to recover herself after this apparition, and began speaking about the prince's indisposition. Natasha and Princess Mary looked at one another in silence, and the longer they did so, without saying what they wanted to say, the greater grew their antipathy to one another.

When the count returned, Natasha was impolitely pleased, and hastened to get away: at that moment she hated the stiff, elderly princess, who could place her in such an embarrassing position and had spent half an hour with her without once mentioning Prince Andrew. 'I couldn't begin talking about him in the presence of that Frenchwoman,' thought Natasha. The same thought was meanwhile tormenting Princess Mary. She knew what she ought to have said to Natasha, but she had been unable to say it because Mademoiselle Bourienne was in the way, and because, without knowing why, she felt it very difficult to speak of the marriage. When the count was already leaving the room, Princess Mary went up hurriedly to Natasha, took her by the hand, and said with a deep sigh:

'Wait, I must . . .'

Natasha glanced at her ironically, without knowing why.

'Dear Natalie,' said Princess Mary, 'I want you to know that I am glad my brother has found happiness . . .'

She paused, feeling that she was not telling the truth. Natasha noticed this and guessed its reason.

'I think, Princess, it is not convenient to speak of that now,' she said with external dignity and coldness, though she felt the tears choking her.

'What have I said and what have I done?' thought she, as soon as she was out of the room.

They waited a long time for Natasha to come to dinner that day. She sat in her room crying like a child, blowing her nose and sobbing. Sonya stood beside her, kissing her hair.

'Natasha, what is it about?' she asked. 'What do they matter to you? It will all pass, Natasha.'

'But if you only knew how offensive it was . . . as if I . . .'

'Don't talk about it, Natasha. It wasn't your fault, so why should you mind? Kiss me,' said Sonya.

Natasha raised her head and, kissing her friend on the lips, pressed her wet face against her.

'I can't tell you, I don't know. No one's to blame,' said Natasha – 'It's my fault. But it all hurts terribly. Oh, why doesn't he come? . . .'

She came in to dinner with red eyes. Marya Dmitrievna, who

knew how the prince had received the Rostovs, pretended not to notice how upset Natasha was, and jested resolutely and loudly at table with the count and the other guests.

## 8

THAT evening the Rostovs went to the Opera, for which Marya Dmitrievna had taken a box.

Natasha did not want to go, but could not refuse Marya Dmitrievna's kind offer which was intended expressly for her. When she came ready dressed into the ball-room to await her father and looking in the large mirror there saw that she was pretty, very pretty, she felt even more sad, but it was a sweet, tender sadness.

'O, God, if he were here now I would not behave as I did then, but differently. I would not be silly and afraid of things, I would simply embrace him, cling to him, and make him look at me with those searching inquiring eyes with which he has so often looked at me, and then I would make him laugh as he used to laugh. And his eyes – how I see those eyes!' thought Natasha. 'And what do his father and sister matter to me? I love him alone, him, him, with that face and those eyes, with his smile, manly and yet child-like ... No, I had better not think of him; not think of him but forget him, quite forget him for the present. I can't bear this waiting and I shall cry in a minute!' and she turned away from the glass, making an effort not to cry. 'And how can Sonya love Nicholas so calmly and quietly and wait so long and so patiently?' thought she, looking at Sonya, who also came in quite ready, with a fan in her hand. 'No, she's altogether different. I can't!'

Natasha at that moment felt so softened and tender that it was not enough for her to love and know she was beloved, she wanted now, at once, to embrace the man she loved, to speak and hear from him words of love such as filled her heart. While she sat in the carriage beside her father, pensively watching the lights of the street-lamps flickering on the frozen window, she felt still sadder and more in love, and forgot where she was going and with whom. Having fallen into the line of carriages, the Rostovs' carriage drove up to the theatre, its wheels squeaking over the snow. Natasha and Sonya, holding up their dresses, jumped out quickly. The count got out helped by the footmen, and, passing among men and women who were entering, and the programme sellers, they all three went along the corridor to the first row of boxes. Through the closed doors the music was already audible.

'Natasha, your hair!' . . . whispered Sonya.

An attendant deferentially and quickly slipped before the ladies and opened the door of their box. The music sounded louder, and through the door rows of brightly lit boxes in which ladies sat with bare arms and shoulders, and noisy stalls brilliant with uniforms, glittered before their eyes. A lady entering the next box shot a glance of feminine envy at Natasha. The curtain had not yet risen and the overture was being played. Natasha, smoothing her gown, went in with Sonya and sat down, scanning the brilliant tiers of boxes opposite. A sensation she had not experienced for a long time – that of hundreds of eyes looking at her bare arms and neck – suddenly affected her both agreeably and disagreeably and called up a whole crowd of memories, desires, and emotions associated with that feeling.

The two remarkably pretty girls, Natasha and Sonya, with Count Rostov who had not been seen in Moscow for a long time, attracted general attention. Moreover, everybody knew vaguely of Natasha's engagement to Prince Andrew, and knew that the Rostovs had lived in the country ever since, and all looked with curiosity at a fiancée who was making one of the best matches in Russia.

Natasha's looks, as everyone told her, had improved in the country, and that evening thanks to her agitation she was particularly pretty. She struck those who saw her by her fullness of life and beauty, combined with her indifference to everything about her. Her black eyes looked at the crowd without seeking anyone, and her delicate arm, bare to above the elbow, lay on the velvet edge of the box, while, evidently unconsciously, she opened and closed her hand in time to the music, crumpling her programme.

'Look, there's Alenina,' said Sonya, 'with her mother, isn't it?'

'Dear me, Michael Kirilovich has grown still stouter!' remarked the count.

'Look at our Anna Mikhaylovna – what a head-dress she has on!'

'The Karagins, Julie – and Boris with them. One can see at once that they're engaged . . .'

'Drubetskoy has proposed?'

'Oh, yes, I heard it to-day,' said Shinshin, coming into the Rostovs' box.

Natasha looked in the direction in which her father's eyes were turned, and saw Julie sitting beside her mother with a happy look on her face and a string of pearls round her thick red neck – which Natasha knew was covered with powder. Behind them, wearing a smile and leaning over with an ear to Julie's mouth, was Boris's handsome smoothly brushed head. He looked at the Rostovs from under his brows and said something, smiling, to his betrothed.

596

'They are talking about us, about me and him!' thought Natasha. 'And he no doubt is calming her jealousy of me. They needn't trouble themselves! If only they knew how little I am concerned about any of them.'

Behind them sat Anna Mikhaylovna wearing a green head-dress, and with a happy look of resignation to the will of God on her face. Their box was pervaded by that atmosphere of an affianced couple which Natasha knew so well and liked so much. She turned away and suddenly remembered all that had been so humiliating in her morning's visit.

'What right has he not to wish to receive me into his family? Oh, better not think of it – not till he comes back!' she told herself, and began looking at the faces, some strange and some familiar, in the stalls. In the front, in the very centre, leaning back against the orchestra-rail, stood Dolokhov in a Persian dress, his curly hair brushed up into a huge shock. He stood in full view of the audience, well aware that he was attracting everyone's attention, yet as much at ease as though he were in his own room. Around him thronged Moscow's most brilliant young men, whom he evidently dominated.

The count, laughing, nudged the blushing Sonya and pointed to her former adorer.

'Do you recognize him?' said he. 'And where has he sprung from?' he asked, turning to Shinshin. 'Didn't he vanish somewhere?'

'He did,' replied Shinshin. 'He was in the Caucasus and ran away from there. They say he has been acting as minister to some ruling prince in Persia, where he killed the Shah's brother. Now all the Moscow ladies are mad about him! It's "Dolokhov the Persian" that does it! We never hear a word but Dolokhov is mentioned. They swear by him, they offer him to you as they would a dish of choice sterlet. Dolokhov and Anatole Kuragin have turned all our ladies' heads.'

A tall, beautiful woman with a mass of plaited hair and much exposed plump white shoulders and neck, round which she wore a double string of large pearls, entered the adjoining box rustling her heavy silk dress, and took a long time settling into her place.

Natasha involuntarily gazed at that neck, those shoulders and pearls and *coiffure*, and admired the beauty of the shoulders and the pearls. While Natasha was fixing her gaze on her for the second time the lady looked round, and meeting the count's eyes nodded to him and smiled. She was the Countess Bezukhova, Pierre's wife, and the count, who knew everyone in society, leaned over and spoke to her.

'Have you been here long, Countess?' he inquired. 'I'll call, I'll call to kiss your hand. I'm here on business and have brought my

597

girls with me. They say Semënova acts marvellously. Count Pierre never used to forget us. Is he here?'

'Yes, he meant to look in,' answered Hélène, and glanced attentively at Natasha.

Count Rostov resumed his seat.

'Handsome, isn't she?' he whispered to Natasha.

'Wonderful!' answered Natasha. 'She's a woman one could easily fall in love with.'

Just then the last chords of the overture were heard and the conductor tapped with his stick. Some latecomers took their seats in the stalls and the curtain rose.

As soon as it rose everyone in the boxes and stalls became silent, and all the men, old and young, in uniform and evening dress, and all the women with gems on their bare flesh, turned their whole attention with eager curiosity to the stage. Natasha too began to look at it.

9

THE floor of the stage consisted of smooth boards, at the sides was some painted cardboard representing trees, and at the back was a cloth stretched over boards. In the centre of the stage sat some girls in red bodices and white skirts. One very fat girl in a white silk dress sat apart on a low bench, to the back of which a piece of green cardboard was glued. They all sang something. When they had finished their song the girl in white went up to the prompter's box, and a man with tight silk trousers over his stout legs, and holding a plume and a dagger, went up to her and began singing, waving his arms about.

First the man in the tight trousers sang alone, then she sang, then they both paused while the orchestra played and the man fingered the hand of the girl in white, obviously awaiting the beat to start singing with her. They sang together and everyone in the theatre began clapping and shouting, while the man and woman on the stage – who represented lovers – began smiling, spreading out their arms, and bowing.

After her life in the country, and in her present serious mood, all this seemed grotesque and amazing to Natasha. She could not follow the opera nor even listen to the music, she saw only the painted cardboard and the queerly dressed men and women who moved, spoke, and sang so strangely in that brilliant light. She knew what it was all meant to represent, but it was so pretentiously false and unnatural that she first felt ashamed for the actors and then amused at them. She looked at the faces of the audience, seeking in them the same sense of ridicule and perplexity she herself experienced, but they all seemed attentive to what was happening on the stage, and expressed delight which to Natasha seemed feigned. 'I suppose it has to be like this!' she thought. She kept looking round in turn at the rows of pomaded heads in the stalls and then at the semi-nude women in the boxes, especially at Hélène in the next box, who – apparently quite unclothed – sat with a quiet tranquil smile, not taking her eyes off the stage. And feeling the bright light that flooded the whole place and the warm air heated by the crowd, Natasha little by little began to pass into a state of intoxication she had not experienced for a long while. She did not realize who and where she was, nor what was going on before her. As she looked and thought, the strangest fancies unexpectedly and disconnectedly passed through her mind: the idea occurred to her of jumping onto the edge of the box and singing the air the actress was singing, then she wished to touch with her fan an old gentleman sitting not far from her, then to lean over to Hélène and tickle her.

At a moment when all was quiet before the commencement of a song, a door leading to the stalls on the side nearest the Rostovs' box creaked, and the steps of a belated arrival were heard. 'There's Kuragin!' whispered Shinshin. Countess Bezukhova turned smiling to the newcomer, and Natasha, following the direction of that look, saw an exceptionally handsome adjutant approaching their box with a self-assured yet courteous bearing. This was Anatole Kuragin whom she had seen and noticed long ago at the ball in Petersburg. He was now in an adjutant's uniform with one epaulette and a shoulder-knot. He moved with a restrained swagger which would have been ridiculous had he not been so good-looking and had his handsome face not worn such an expression of good-humoured complacency and gaiety. Though the performance was proceeding, he walked deliberately down the carpeted gangway, his sword and spurs slightly jingling and his handsome perfumed head held high. Having looked at Natasha he approached his sister, laid his well-gloved hand on the edge of her box, nodded to her, and leaning forward asked a question, with a motion towards Natasha.

'*Mais charmante!*' said he, evidently referring to Natasha, who did not exactly hear his words but understood them from the movement of his lips. Then he took his place in the first row of the stalls and sat down beside Dolokhov, nudging with his elbow in a friendly and off-hand way that Dolokhov whom others treated so fawningly. He winked at him gaily, smiled, and rested his foot against the orchestra-screen.

'How like the brother is to the sister,' remarked the count. 'And how handsome they both are!'

Shinshin, lowering his voice, began to tell the count of some intrigue of Kuragin's in Moscow, and Natasha tried to overhear it just because he had said she was *'charmante'*.

The first act was over. In the stalls everyone began moving about, going out and coming in.

Boris came to the Rostovs' box, received their congratulations very simply, and raising his eyebrows with an absent-minded smile conveyed to Natasha and Sonya his fiancée's invitation to her wedding, and went away. Natasha with a gay coquettish smile talked to him, and congratulated on his approaching wedding that same Boris with whom she had formerly been in love. In the state of intoxication she was in everything seemed simple and natural.

The scantily clad Hélène was sitting near her, smiling at everyone with the same smile and Natasha gave Boris just such a smile.

Hélène's box was filled, and surrounded from the stalls, by the most distinguished and intellectual men, who seemed to vie with one another in their wish to let everyone see that they knew her.

During the whole of that *entr'acte* Kuragin stood with Dolokhov in front of the orchestra partition looking at the Rostovs' box. Natasha knew he was talking about her and this afforded her pleasure. She even turned so that he should see her profile in what she thought was its most becoming aspect. Before the beginning of the second act Pierre appeared in the stalls. The Rostovs had not seen him since their arrival. His face looked sad, and he had grown still stouter since Natasha last saw him. He passed up to the front rows not noticing anyone. Anatole went up to him and began speaking to him, looking at and indicating the Rostovs' box. On seeing Natasha Pierre grew animated and, hastily passing between the rows, came towards their box. When he got there he leaned on his elbows and, smiling, talked to her for a long time. While conversing with Pierre Natasha heard a man's voice in Countess Bezukhova's box and something told her it was Kuragin. She turned and their eyes met. Almost smiling, he gazed straight into her eyes with such an enraptured caressing look that it seemed strange to be so near him, to look at him like that, to be so sure he admired her, and not to be acquainted with him.

In the second act there was scenery representing tombstones, and there was a round hole in the canvas to represent the moon, shades were raised over the footlights, and from horns and contrabass came deep notes while many people appeared from right and left wearing black cloaks and holding things like daggers in their

hands. They began waving their arms. Then some other people
ran in and began dragging away the maiden who had been in
white and was now in light blue. They did not drag her away at
once, but sang with her for a long time, and then at last dragged
her off, and behind the scenes something metallic was struck three
times and everyone knelt down and sang a prayer. All these things
were repeatedly interrupted by the enthusiastic shouts of the
audience.

During this act every time Natasha looked towards the stalls
she saw Anatole Kuragin, with an arm thrown across the back of
his chair, staring at her. She was pleased to see that he was
captivated by her and it did not occur to her that there was anything wrong in it.

When the second act was over Countess Bezukhova rose, turned
to the Rostovs' box – her whole bosom completely exposed –
beckoned the old count with a gloved finger, and paying no attention to those who had entered her box, began talking to him with
an amiable smile.

'Do make me acquainted with your charming daughters,' said
she. 'The whole town is singing their praises and I don't even
know them.'

Natasha rose and curtsied to the splendid countess. She was so
pleased by praise from this brilliant beauty that she blushed with
pleasure.

'I want to become a Moscovite too, now,' said Hélène. 'How is it
you're not ashamed to bury such pearls in the country?'

Countess Bezukhova quite deserved her reputation of being a
fascinating woman. She could say what she did not think – especially what was flattering – quite simply and naturally.

'Dear Count, you must let me look after your daughters! Though
I am not staying here long this time – nor are you – I will try
to amuse them. I have already heard much of you in Petersburg
and wanted to get to know you,' said she to Natasha with her
stereotyped and lovely smile. 'I had heard about you from my
page, Drubetskoy. Have you heard he is getting married? And also
from my husband's friend, Bolkonsky, Prince Andrew Bolkonsky,'
she went on with special emphasis, implying that she knew of his
relation to Natasha. To get better acquainted she asked that one of
the young ladies should come into her box for the rest of the
performance, and Natasha moved over to it.

The scene of the third act represented a palace in which many
candles were burning and pictures of knights with short beards
hung on the walls. In the middle stood what were probably a
king and a queen. The king waved his right arm and, evidently

nervous, sang something badly and sat down on a crimson throne. The maiden who had been first in white and then in light blue, now wore only a smock, and stood beside the throne with her hair down. She sang something mournfully, addressing the queen, but the king waved his arm severely, and men and women with bare legs came in from both sides and began dancing all together. Then the violins played very shrilly and merrily and one of the women with thick bare legs and thin arms, separating from the others, went behind the wings, adjusted her bodice, returned to the middle of the stage, and began jumping and striking one foot rapidly against the other. In the stalls everyone clapped and shouted 'bravo!' Then one of the men went into a corner of the stage. The cymbals and horns in the orchestra struck up more loudly, and this man with bare legs jumped very high and waved his feet about very rapidly. (He was Duport, who received sixty thousand rubles a year for this art.) Everybody in the stalls, boxes, and galleries began clapping and shouting with all their might, and the man stopped and began smiling and bowing to all sides. Then other men and women danced with bare legs. Then the king again shouted to the sound of music and they all began singing. But suddenly a storm came on, chromatic scales and diminished sevenths were heard in the orchestra, everyone ran off, again dragging one of their number away, and the curtain dropped. Once more there was a terrible noise and clatter among the audience, and with rapturous faces everyone began shouting: 'Duport! Duport! Duport!' Natasha no longer thought this strange. She looked about with pleasure, smiling joyfully.

'Isn't Duport delightful?' Hélène asked her.

'Oh yes,' replied Natasha.

10

DURING the *entr'acte* a whiff of cold air came into Hélène's box, the door opened and Anatole entered, stooping and trying not to brush against anyone.

'Let me introduce my brother to you,' said Hélène, her eyes shifting uneasily from Natasha to Anatole.

Natasha turned her pretty little head towards the elegant young officer, and smiled at him over her bare shoulder. Anatole, who was as handsome at close quarters as at a distance, sat down beside her and told her he had long wished to have this happiness – ever since the Naryshkins' ball, in fact, at which he had had the well-remembered pleasure of seeing her. Kuragin was much more sensible

602

and simple with women than among men. He talked boldly and naturally, and Natasha was strangely and agreeably struck by the fact that there was nothing formidable in this man about whom there was so much talk, but that on the contrary his smile was most naïve, cheerful, and good-natured.

Kuragin asked her opinion of the performance, and told her how at a previous performance Semënova had fallen down on the stage.

'And do you know, Countess,' he said, suddenly addressing her as an old, familiar acquaintance, 'we are getting up a costume-tournament; you ought to take part in it! It will be great fun. We shall all meet at the Karagins! Please come! No! Really, eh?' said he.

While saying this he never removed his smiling eyes from her face, her neck, and her bare arms. Natasha knew for certain that he was enraptured by her. This pleased her, yet his presence made her feel constrained and oppressed. When she was not looking at him she felt that he was looking at her shoulders, and she involuntarily caught his eye so that he should look into hers rather than this. But looking into his eyes she was frightened, realizing that there was not that barrier of modesty she had always felt between herself and other men. She did not know how it was that within five minutes she had come to feel herself terribly near to this man. When she turned away she feared he might seize her from behind by her bare arm and kiss her on the neck. They spoke of most ordinary things, yet she felt that they were closer to one another than she had ever been to any man. Natasha kept turning to Hélène and to her father, as if asking what it all meant, but Hélène was engaged in conversation with a general, and did not answer her look, and her father's eyes said nothing but what they always said: 'Having a good time? Well, I'm glad of it!'

During one of these moments of awkward silence when Anatole's prominent eyes were gazing calmly and fixedly at her, Natasha, to break the silence, asked him how he liked Moscow. She asked the question and blushed. She felt all the time that by talking to him she was doing something improper. Anatole smiled as though to encourage her.

'At first I did not like it much, because what makes a town pleasant *ce sont les jolies femmes*, isn't that so? But now I like it very much indeed,' he said, looking at her significantly. 'You'll come to the costume-tournament, Countess? Do come!' and putting out his hand to her bouquet and dropping his voice, he added, 'You will be the prettiest there. Do come, dear Countess, and give me this flower as a pledge!'

Natasha did not understand what he was saying any more than he did himself, but she felt that his incomprehensible words had an improper intention. She did not know what to say, and turned away as if she had not heard his remark. But as soon as she had turned away she felt that he was there, behind, so close behind her.

'How is he now? Confused? Angry? Ought I to put it right?' she asked herself, and she could not refrain from turning round. She looked straight into his eyes, and his nearness, self-assurance, and the good-natured tenderness of his smile, vanquished her. She smiled just as he was doing, gazing straight into his eyes. And again she felt with horror that no barrier lay between him and her.

The curtain rose again. Anatole left the box, serene and gay. Natasha went back to her father in the other box, now quite submissive to the world she found herself in. All that was going on before her now seemed quite natural, but on the other hand all her previous thoughts of her betrothed, of Princess Mary, or of life in the country, did not once recur to her mind and were as if belonging to a remote past.

In the fourth act there was some sort of a devil who sang, waving his arm about, till the boards were withdrawn from under him and he disappeared down below. That was the only part of the fourth act that Natasha saw. She felt agitated and tormented, and the cause of this was Kuragin, whom she could not help watching. As they were leaving the theatre Anatole came up to them, called their carriage and helped them in. As he was putting Natasha in he pressed her arm above the elbow. Agitated and flushed she turned round. He was looking at her with glittering eyes, smiling tenderly.

Only after she had reached home was Natasha able clearly to think over what had happened to her, and suddenly remembering Prince Andrew she was horrified, and at tea to which all had sat down after the opera, she gave a loud exclamation, flushed, and ran out of the room.

'O God! I am lost!' she said to herself. 'How could I let him?' She sat for a long time hiding her flushed face in her hands trying to realize what had happened to her, but was unable either to understand what had happened or what she felt. Everything seemed dark, obscure, and terrible. There in that enormous, illuminated theatre where the bare-legged Duport, in a tinsel-decorated jacket, jumped about to the music on wet boards, and young girls and old men, and the nearly naked Hélène with her proud, calm smile, rapturously cried 'bravo!' – there in the presence of that Hélène it had all seemed clear and simple; but now, alone, by herself, it was incomprehensible. 'What is it? What was that terror I felt of him? What is this gnawing of conscience I am feeling now?' she thought.

Only to the old countess at night in bed could Natasha have told all she was feeling. She knew that Sonya with her severe and simple views would either not understand it at all or would be horrified at such a confession. So Natasha tried to solve what was torturing her by herself.

'Am I spoilt for Andrew's love or not?' she asked herself, and with soothing irony replied: 'What a fool I am to ask that! What did happen to me? Nothing! I have done nothing, I didn't lead him on at all. Nobody will know and I shall never see him again,' she told herself. 'So it is plain that nothing has happened and there is nothing to repent of, and Andrew can love me still. But why "still"? O God, O God, why isn't he here?' Natasha quieted herself for a moment but again some instinct told her that though all this was true, and though nothing had happened, yet the former purity of her love for Prince Andrew had perished. And again in imagination she went over her whole conversation with Kuragin, and again saw the face, gestures, and tender smile of that bold handsome man when he pressed her arm.

## 11

ANATOLE KURAGIN was staying in Moscow because his father had sent him away from Petersburg, where he had been spending twenty thousand rubles a year in cash, besides running up debts for as much more which his creditors demanded from his father.

His father announced to him that he would now pay half his debts for the last time, but only on condition that he went to Moscow as adjutant to the commander-in-chief – a post his father had procured for him – and would at last try to make a good match there. He indicated to him Princess Mary and Julie Karagina.

Anatole consented and went to Moscow, where he put up at Pierre's house. Pierre received him unwillingly at first, but got used to him after a while, sometimes even accompanied him on his carousals, and gave him money under the guise of loans.

As Shinshin had remarked, from the time of his arrival Anatole had turned the heads of the Moscow ladies, especially by the fact that he slighted them and plainly preferred the gipsy-girls and French actresses – with the chief of whom, Mademoiselle George, he was said to be in intimate relations. He never missed a carousal at Danilov's or other Moscow revellers, drank whole nights through, outvying everyone else, and was at all the balls and parties of the best society. There was talk of his intrigues with some of the ladies, and he flirted with a few of them at the balls. But he did not run after the unmarried girls, especially the rich heiresses who were most of them plain. There was a special reason for this, as he had got married two years before – a fact known only to his most intimate friends. At that time, while with his regiment in Poland, a Polish landowner of small means had forced him to marry his daughter. Anatole had very soon abandoned his wife, and for a payment which he agreed to send to his father-in-law had arranged to be free to pass himself off as a bachelor.

Anatole was always content with his position, with himself, and with others. He was instinctively and thoroughly convinced that it was impossible for him to live otherwise than as he did, and that he had never in his life done anything base. He was incapable of considering how his actions might affect others, or what the consequences of this or that action of his might be. He was convinced that, as a duck is so made that it must live in water, so God had made him such that he must spend thirty thousand rubles a year and always occupy a prominent position in society. He believed this so firmly that others, looking at him, were persuaded of it too, and did not refuse him either a leading place in society, or money, which he borrowed from anyone and everyone and evidently would not repay.

He was not a gambler, at any rate he did not care about winning. He was not vain. He did not mind what people thought of him. Still less could he be accused of ambition. More than once he had vexed his father by spoiling his own career, and he laughed at distinctions of all kinds. He was not mean, and did not refuse anyone who asked of him. All he cared about was gaiety and women, and as according to his ideas there was nothing dishonourable in these tastes, and he was incapable of considering what the gratification of his tastes entailed for others, he honestly considered himself irreproachable, sincerely despised rogues and bad people, and with a tranquil conscience carried his head high.

Rakes, those male Magdalenes, have a secret feeling of innocence similar to that which female Magdalenes have, based on the same hope of forgiveness. 'All will be forgiven her, for she loved much; and all will be forgiven him, for he enjoyed much.'

Dolokhov, who had reappeared that year in Moscow after his exile and his Persian adventures, and was leading a life of luxury, gambling and dissipation, associated with his old Petersburg comrade Kuragin and made use of him for his own ends.

Anatole was sincerely fond of Dolokhov for his cleverness and audacity. Dolokhov, who needed Anatole Kuragin's name, position, and connexions as a bait to draw rich young men into his gambling set, made use of him and amused himself at his expense without letting the other feel it. Apart from the advantage he derived from Anatole, the very process of dominating another's will was in itself a pleasure, a habit, and a necessity to Dolokhov.

Natasha had made a strong impression on Kuragin. At supper after the opera he described to Dolokhov, with the air of a connoisseur, the attractions of her arms, shoulders, feet and hair, and expressed his intention of making love to her. Anatole had no notion, and was incapable of considering, what might come of such love-making, as he never had any notion of the outcome of any of his actions.

'She's first-rate, my dear fellow, but not for us,' replied Dolokhov.

'I will tell my sister to ask her to dinner,' said Anatole, 'Eh?'

'You'd better wait till she's married ...'

'You know, I adore little girls, they lose their heads at once,' pursued Anatole.

'You have been caught once already by a "little girl",' said Dolokhov, who knew of Kuragin's marriage. 'Take care!'

'Well, that can't happen twice! Eh?' said Anatole, with a good-humoured laugh.

12

THE day after the opera the Rostovs went nowhere and nobody came to see them. Marya Dmitrievna talked to the count about something which they concealed from Natasha. Natasha guessed they were talking about the old prince and planning something, and this disquieted and offended her. She was expecting Prince Andrew any moment, and twice that day sent a manservant to the Vozdvizhenka to ascertain whether he had come. He had not arrived. She suffered more now than during her first days in Moscow. To her impatience and pining for him were now added the unpleasant recollection of her interview with Princess Mary and the old prince, and a fear and anxiety of which she did not understand the cause. She continually fancied that either he would never come, or that something would happen to her before he came. She could no longer think of him by herself calmly and continuously as she had done before. As soon as she began to think of him, the recollection of the old prince, of Princess Mary, of the theatre, and of Kuragin, mingled with her thoughts. The question again presented itself whether she was not guilty, whether she had not already broken faith with Prince Andrew, and again she found herself recalling to the minutest detail, every word, every gesture, and every shade in the play of expression on the face of the man who had been able to arouse in her such an incomprehensible and terrifying feeling. To the family Natasha seemed livelier than usual, but she was far less tranquil and happy than before.

On Sunday morning Marya Dmitrievna invited her visitors to Mass at her parish church – the Church of the Assumption built over the graves of victims of the plague.

'I don't like those fashionable churches,' she said, evidently priding herself on her independence of thought. 'God is the same everywhere. We have an excellent priest, he conducts the service decently and with dignity, and the deacon is the same. What holiness is there in giving concerts in the choir? I don't like it, it's just self-indulgence!'

Marya Dmitrievna liked Sundays and knew how to keep them. Her whole house was scrubbed and cleaned on Saturdays; neither she nor the servants worked, and they all wore holiday dress and went to church. At her table there were extra dishes at dinner, and the servants had vodka and roast goose or sucking-pig. But in nothing in the house was the holiday so noticeable as in Marya Dmitrievna's broad, stern face, which on that day wore an invariable look of solemn festivity.

After Mass, when they had finished their coffee, in the dining-room where the loose covers had been removed from the furniture, a servant announced that the carriage was ready, and Marya Dmitrievna rose with a stern air. She wore her holiday shawl, in which she paid calls, and announced that she was going to see Prince Nicholas Bolkonsky to have an explanation with him about Natasha.

After she had gone, a dressmaker from Madame Suppert-Roguet waited on the Rostovs, and Natasha, very glad of this diversion, having shut herself into a room adjoining the drawing-room, occupied herself trying on the new dresses. Just as she had put on a bodice without sleeves and only tacked together, and was turning her head to see in the glass how the back fitted, she heard in the drawing-room the animated sounds of her father's voice and another's – a woman's – that made her flush. It was Hélène. Natasha had not time to take off the bodice before the door opened and Countess Bezukhova, dressed in a purple velvet gown with a high collar, came into the room beaming with good-humoured amiable smiles.

'Oh, my enchantress!' she cried to the blushing Natasha. 'Charming! No, this is really beyond anything, my dear Count,' said she to Count Rostov who had followed her in. 'How can you live in Moscow and go nowhere? No, I won't let you off! Mademoiselle George will recite at my house to-night, and there'll be some people, and if you don't bring your lovely girls – who are prettier than Mademoiselle George – I won't know you! My husband is away in Tver or I would send him to fetch you. You must come. You positively must! Between eight and nine.'

She nodded to the dressmaker, whom she knew and who had curtsied respectfully to her, and seated herself in an arm-chair beside the looking-glass draping the folds of her velvet dress picturesquely. She did not cease chattering good-naturedly and gaily, continually praising Natasha's beauty. She looked at Natasha's dresses and praised them, as well as a new dress of her own, made of 'metallic gauze', which she had received from Paris, and advised Natasha to have one like it.

'But anything suits you, my charmer!' she remarked.

A smile of pleasure never left Natasha's face. She felt happy and as if she were blossoming, under the praise of this dear Countess Bezukhova who had formerly seemed to her so unapproachable and important and was now so kind to her. Natasha brightened up and felt almost in love with this woman, who was so beautiful and so kind. Hélène for her part was sincerely delighted with Natasha and wished to give her a good time. Anatole had asked her to bring him and Natasha together, and she was calling on the Rostovs for that purpose. The idea of throwing her brother and Natasha together amused her.

Though at one time, in Petersburg, she had been annoyed with Natasha for drawing Boris away, she did not think of that now, and in her own way heartily wished Natasha well. As she was leaving the Rostovs she called her protégée aside.

'My brother dined with me yesterday – we nearly died of laughter – he ate nothing and kept sighing for you, my charmer! He is madly, quite madly, in love with you, my dear.'

Natasha blushed scarlet when she heard this.

'How she blushes, how she blushes, my pretty!' said Hélène. 'You must certainly come. If you love somebody, my charmer, that is not a reason to shut yourself up. Even if you are engaged, I am sure your fiancé would wish you to go into society rather than be bored to death.'

'So she knows I am engaged, and she and her husband Pierre – that good Pierre – have talked and laughed about this. So it's all right.' And again, under Hélène's influence, what had seemed terrible now seemed simple and natural. 'And she is such a *grande dame*, so kind, and evidently likes me so much. And why not enjoy myself?' thought Natasha gazing at Hélène with wide-open, wondering eyes.

Marya Dmitrievna came back to dinner taciturn and serious.

having evidently suffered a defeat at the old prince's. She was still too agitated by the encounter to be able to talk of the affair calmly. In answer to the count's inquiries she replied that things were all right and that she would tell about it next day. On hearing of Countess Bezukhova's visit and the invitation for that evening, Marya Dmitrievna remarked:

'I don't care to have anything to do with Bezukhova and don't advise you to; however, if you've promised – go. It will divert your thoughts,' she added, addressing Natasha.

## 13

COUNT ROSTOV took the girls to Countess Bezukhova's. There were a good many people there, but nearly all strangers to Natasha. Count Rostov was displeased to see that the company consisted almost entirely of men and women known for the freedom of their conduct. Mademoiselle George was standing in a corner of the drawing-room surrounded by young men. There were several Frenchmen present, among them Métivier, who from the time Hélène reached Moscow had been an intimate in her house. The count decided not to sit down to cards or let his girls out of his sight, and to get away as soon as Mademoiselle George's performance was over.

Anatole was at the door, evidently on the look-out for the Rostovs. Immediately after greeting the count he went up to Natasha and followed her. As soon as she saw him she was seized by the same feeling she had had at the opera – gratified vanity at his admiration of her, and fear at the absence of a moral barrier between them.

Hélène welcomed Natasha delightedly and was loud in admiration of her beauty and her dress. Soon after their arrival Mademoiselle George went out of the room to change her costume. In the drawing-room people began arranging the chairs and taking their seats. Anatole moved a chair for Natasha and was about to sit down beside her, but the count, who never lost sight of her, took the seat himself. Anatole sat down behind her.

Mademoiselle George, with her bare, fat, dimpled arms, and a red shawl draped over one shoulder, came into the space left vacant for her, and assumed an unnatural pose. Enthusiastic whispering was audible.

Mademoiselle George looked sternly and gloomily at the audience, and began reciting some French verses describing her guilty love for her son. In some places she raised her voice, in others she whispered, lifting her head triumphantly, sometimes she paused and uttered hoarse sounds, rolling her eyes.

'Adorable! divine! delicious!' was heard from every side.

Natasha looked at the fat actress, but neither saw nor heard nor understood anything of what went on before her. She only felt herself again completely borne away into this strange senseless world – so remote from her old world – a world in which it was impossible to know what was good or bad, reasonable or senseless. Behind her sat Anatole, and conscious of his proximity she experienced a frightened sense of expectancy.

After the first monologue the whole company rose and surrounded Mademoiselle George, expressing their enthusiasm.

'How beautiful she is!' Natasha remarked to her father, who had also risen and was moving through the crowd towards the actress.

'I don't think so when I look at you!' said Anatole, following Natasha. He said this at a moment when she alone could hear him. 'You are enchanting ... from the moment I saw you I have never ceased ...'

'Come, come, Natasha!' said the count, as he turned back for his daughter. 'How beautiful she is!'

Natasha without saying anything stepped up to her father and looked at him with surprised inquiring eyes.

After giving several recitations, Mademoiselle George left, and Countess Bezukhova asked her visitors into the ball-room.

The count wished to go home, but Hélène entreated him not to spoil her improvised ball, and the Rostovs stayed on. Anatole asked Natasha for a valse and as they danced he pressed her waist and hand and told her she was bewitching and that he loved her. During the Écossaise, which she also danced with him, Anatole said nothing when they happened to be by themselves, but merely gazed at her. Natasha lifted her frightened eyes to him, but there was such confident tenderness in his affectionate look and smile that she could not, whilst looking at him, say what she had to say. She lowered her eyes.

'Don't say such things to me. I am betrothed and love another,' she said rapidly ... She glanced at him.

Anatole was not upset or pained by what she had said.

'Don't speak to me of that! What can I do?' said he. 'I tell you I am madly, madly, in love with you! Is it my fault that you are enchanting? ... It's our turn to begin.'

Natasha, animated and excited, looked about her with wide-open frightened eyes and seemed merrier than usual. She understood hardly anything that went on that evening. They danced the

Écossaise and the *Grossvater*. Her father asked her to come home, but she begged to remain. Wherever she went and whomever she was speaking to, she felt *his* eyes upon her. Later on she recalled how she had asked her father to let her go to the dressing-room to rearrange her dress, that Hélène had followed her and spoken laughingly of her brother's love, and that she again met Anatole in the little sitting-room. Hélène had disappeared leaving them alone, and Anatole had taken her hand and said in a tender voice:

'I cannot come to visit you but is it possible that I shall never see you? I love you madly. Can I never . . . ?' and, blocking her path, he brought his face close to hers.

His large, glittering, masculine eyes were so close to hers that she saw nothing but them.

'Natalie?' he whispered inquiringly while she felt her hands being painfully pressed. 'Natalie?'

'I don't understand. I have nothing to say,' her eyes replied.

Burning lips were pressed to hers, and at the same instant she felt herself released, and Hélène's footsteps and the rustle of her dress were heard in the room. Natasha looked round at her, and then, red and trembling, threw a frightened look of inquiry at Anatole and moved towards the door.

'One word, just one, for God's sake!' cried Anatole.

She paused. She so wanted a word from him that would explain to her what had happened, and to which she could find an answer.

'Natalie, just a word, only one!' he kept repeating, evidently not knowing what to say – and he repeated it till Hélène came up to them.

Hélène returned with Natasha to the drawing-room. The Rostovs went away without staying for supper.

After reaching home Natasha did not sleep all night. She was tormented by the insoluble question whether she loved Anatole or Prince Andrew. She loved Prince Andrew – she remembered distinctly how deeply she loved him. But she also loved Anatole, of that there was no doubt. 'Else how could all this have happened?' thought she. 'If, after that, I could return his smile when saying good-bye, if I was able to let it come to that, it means that I loved him from the first. It means that he is kind, noble, and splendid, and I could not help loving him. What am I to do if I love him and the other one too?' she asked herself, unable to find an answer to these terrible questions.

## 14

MORNING came with its cares and bustle. Everyone got up and began to move about and talk, dressmakers came again, Marya Dmitrievna appeared, and they were called to breakfast. Natasha kept looking uneasily at everybody with wide-open eyes, as if wishing to intercept every glance directed towards her, and tried to appear the same as usual.

After breakfast, which was her best time, Marya Dmitrievna sat down in her arm-chair and called Natasha and the count to her.

'Well, friends, I have now thought the whole matter over and this is my advice,' she began. 'Yesterday, as you know, I went to see Prince Bolkonsky. Well, I had a talk with him ... He took it into his head to begin shouting, but I am not one to be shouted down. I said what I had to say!'

'Well, and he?' asked the count.

'He? He's crazy ... he did not want to listen. But what's the use of talking? As it is we have worn the poor girl out,' said Marya Dmitrievna. 'My advice to you is, finish your business and go back home to Otradnoe ... and wait there.'

'Oh, no!' exclaimed Natasha.

'Yes, go back,' said Marya Dmitrievna, 'and wait there. If your betrothed comes here now – there will be no avoiding a quarrel; but alone with the old man he will talk things over and then come on to you.'

Count Rostov approved of this suggestion, appreciating its reasonableness. If the old man came round it would be all the better to visit him in Moscow or at Bald Hills later on; and if not, the wedding, against his wishes, could only be arranged at Otradnoe.

'That is perfectly true. And I am sorry I went to see him and took her,' said the old count.

'No, why be sorry! Being here you had to pay your respects. But if he won't – that's his affair,' said Marya Dmitrievna, looking for something in her reticule. 'Besides, the trousseau is ready, so there is nothing to wait for; and what is not ready I'll send after you. Though I don't like letting you go, it is the best way. So go, with God's blessing!'

Having found what she was looking for in the reticule she handed it to Natasha. It was a letter from Princess Mary.

'She has written to you. How she torments herself, poor thing! She's afraid you might think that she does not like you.'

'But she doesn't like me,' said Natasha.

'Don't talk nonsense!' cried Marya Dmitrievna.

'I shan't believe anyone, I know she doesn't like me,' replied

Natasha boldly as she took the letter, and her face expressed a cold and angry resolution that caused Marya Dmitrievna to look at her more intently and to frown.

'Don't answer like that, my good girl!' she said. 'What I say is true! Write an answer!'

Natasha did not reply, and went to her own room to read Princess Mary's letter.

Princess Mary wrote that she was in despair at the misunderstanding that had occurred between them. Whatever her father's feelings might be, she begged Natasha to believe that she could not help loving her as the one chosen by her brother, for whose happiness she was ready to sacrifice everything.

'Do not think, however,' she wrote, 'that my father is ill-disposed towards you. He is an invalid and an old man who must be forgiven; but he is good and magnanimous, and will love her who makes his son happy.' Princess Mary went on to ask Natasha to fix a time when she could see her again.

After reading the letter Natasha sat down at the writing-table to answer it. 'Dear Princess,' she wrote in French quickly and mechanically, and then paused. What more could she write after all that had happened the evening before? 'Yes, yes! All that has happened, and now all is changed,' she thought as she sat with the letter she had begun before her. 'Must I break off with him? Must I really? That's awful! . . .' and to escape from these dreadful thoughts she went to Sonya and began sorting patterns with her.

After dinner Natasha went to her room and again took up Princess Mary's letter. 'Can it be that it is all over?' she thought. 'Can it be that all this has happened so quickly and has destroyed all that went before?' She recalled her love for Prince Andrew in all its former strength, and at the same time felt that she loved Kuragin. She vividly pictured herself as Prince Andrew's wife, and the scenes of happiness with him she had so often repeated in her imagination, and at the same time, aglow with excitement, recalled every detail of yesterday's interview with Anatole.

'Why could that not be as well?' she sometimes asked herself in complete bewilderment. 'Only so could I be completely happy; but now I have to choose, and I can't be happy without either of them. Only,' she thought, 'to tell Prince Andrew what has happened or to hide it from him are both equally impossible. But with *that one* nothing is spoilt. But am I really to abandon for ever the joy of Prince Andrew's love, in which I have lived so long?'

'Please, Miss!' whispered a maid entering the room with a mysterious air. 'A man told me to give you this –' and she handed Natasha a letter.

'Only, for Christ's sake . . .' the girl went on, as Natasha, without thinking, mechanically broke the seal and read a love-letter from Anatole, of which, without taking in a word, she understood only that it was a letter from him – from the man she loved. Yes, she loved him, or else how could that have happened which had happened? And how could she have a love-letter from him in her hand?

With trembling hands Natasha held that passionate love-letter which Dolokhov had composed for Anatole, and as she read it, she found in it an echo of all that she herself imagined she was feeling.

'Since yesterday evening my fate has been sealed; to be loved by you or to die. There is no other way for me,' the letter began. Then he went on to say that he knew her parents would not give her to him – for this there were secret reasons he could reveal only to her – but that if she loved him, she need only say the word *Yes*, and no human power could hinder their bliss. Love would conquer all. He would steal her away and carry her off to the ends of the earth.

'Yes, yes! I love him!' thought Natasha, reading the letter for the twentieth time and finding some peculiarly deep meaning in each word of it.

That evening Marya Dmitrievna was going to the Akharovs' and proposed to take the girls with her. Natasha, pleading a headache, remained at home.

## 15

ON returning late in the evening Sonya went to Natasha's room, and to her surprise found her still dressed, and asleep on the sofa. Open on the table beside her lay Anatole's letter. Sonya picked it up and read it.

As she read she glanced at the sleeping Natasha, trying to find in her face an explanation of what she was reading, but did not find it. Her face was calm, gentle, and happy. Clutching her breast to keep herself from choking, Sonya, pale and trembling with fear and agitation, sat down in an arm-chair and burst into tears.

'How was it I noticed nothing? How could it go so far? Can she have left off loving Prince Andrew? And how could she let Kuragin go to such lengths? He is a deceiver and a villain, that's plain! What will Nicholas, dear noble Nicholas, do when he hears of it? So this is the meaning of her excited, resolute, unnatural look the the day before yesterday, yesterday, and to-day,' thought Sonya. 'But it can't be that she loves him! She probably opened the letter

615

without knowing whom it was from. Probably she is offended by it. She could not do such a thing!'

Sonya wiped away her tears and went up to Natasha, again scanning her face.

'Natasha!' she said, just audibly.

Natasha awoke and saw Sonya.

'Ah, you're back?'

And with the decision and tenderness that often come at the moment of awakening, she embraced her friend, but noticing Sonya's look of embarrassment, her own face expressed confusion and suspicion.

'Sonya, you've read that letter?' she demanded.

'Yes,' answered Sonya softly.

Natasha smiled rapturously.

'No, Sonya, I can't any longer!' she said. 'I can't hide it from you any longer. You know we love one another! Sonya, darling, he writes ... Sonya ...'

Sonya stared open-eyed at Natasha, unable to believe her ears.

'And Bolkonsky?' she asked.

'Ah, Sonya, if you only knew how happy I am!' cried Natasha. 'You don't know what love is ...'

'But, Natasha, can *that* be all over?'

Natasha looked at Sonya with wide-open eyes as if she could not grasp the question.

'Well then, are you refusing Prince Andrew?' said Sonya.

'Oh, you don't understand anything! Don't talk nonsense, just listen!' said Natasha, with momentary vexation.

'But I can't believe it,' insisted Sonya. 'I don't understand. How is it you have loved a man for a whole year and suddenly ... Why, you have only seen him three times! Natasha, I don't believe you, you're joking! In three days to forget everything and so ...'

'Three days?' said Natasha. 'It seems to me I've loved him a hundred years. It seems to me that I have never loved anyone before. You can't understand it. Sonya, wait a bit, sit here,' and Natasha embraced and kissed her.

'I had heard that it happens like this, and you must have heard it too, but it's only now that I feel such love. It's not the same as before. As soon as I saw him I felt he was my master and I his slave, and that I could not help loving him. Yes, his slave! Whatever he orders I shall do. You don't understand that. What can I do? What can I do, Sonya?' cried Natasha with a happy yet frightened expression.

'But think what you are doing,' cried Sonya. 'I can't leave it like this. This secret correspondence ... How could you let him go so far?' she went on, with a horror and disgust she could hardly conceal.

'I told you that I have no will,' Natasha replied. 'Why can't you understand? I love him!'

'Then I won't let it come to that . . . I shall tell!' cried Sonya, bursting into tears.

'What do you mean? For God's sake . . . If you tell, you are my enemy!' declared Natasha. 'You want me to be miserable, you want us to be separated . . .'

When she saw Natasha's fright, Sonya shed tears of shame and pity for her friend.

'But what has happened between you?' she asked. 'What has he said to you? Why doesn't he come to the house?'

Natasha did not answer her questions.

'For God's sake, Sonya, don't tell anyone, don't torture me,' Natasha entreated. 'Remember no one ought to interfere in such matters! I have confided in you . . .'

'But why this secrecy? Why doesn't he come to the house?' asked Sonya. 'Why doesn't he openly ask for your hand? You know Prince Andrew gave you complete freedom – if it is really so; but I don't believe it! Natasha, have you considered what these *secret reasons* can be?'

Natasha looked at Sonya with astonishment. Evidently this question presented itself to her mind for the first time and she did not know how to answer it.

'I don't know what the reasons are. But there must be reasons!'

Sonya sighed and shook her head incredulously.

'If there were reasons . . .' she began.

But Natasha, guessing her doubts, interrupted her in alarm.

'Sonya, one can't doubt him! One can't, one can't! Don't you understand?' she cried.

'Does he love you?'

'Does he love me?' Natasha repeated with a smile of pity at her friend's lack of comprehension. 'Why, you have read his letter and you have seen him.'

'But if he is dishonourable?'

'*He*! dishonourable? If you only knew!' exclaimed Natasha.

'If he is an honourable man he should either declare his intentions, or cease seeing you; and if you won't do this, I will. I will write to him, and I will tell papa!' said Sonya resolutely.

'But I can't live without him!' cried Natasha.

'Natasha, I don't understand you. And what are you saying! Think of your father and of Nicholas.'

'I don't want anyone, I don't love anyone but him. How dare

617

you say he is dishonourable? Don't you know that I love him?' screamed Natasha. 'Go away, Sonya! I don't want to quarrel with you, but go, for God's sake go! You see how I am suffering!' Natasha cried angrily, in a voice of despair and repressed irritation. Sonya burst into sobs and ran from the room.

Natasha went to the table and without a moment's reflection wrote that answer to Princess Mary which she had been unable to write all the morning. In this letter she said briefly that all their misunderstandings were at an end; that availing herself of the magnanimity of Prince Andrew, who when he went abroad had given her her freedom, she begged Princess Mary to forget everything and forgive her if she had been to blame towards her, but that she could not be his wife. At that moment this all seemed quite easy, simple, and clear to Natasha.

On Friday the Rostovs were to return to the country, but on Wednesday the count went with the prospective purchaser to his estate near Moscow.

On the day the count left, Sonya and Natasha were invited to a big dinner-party at the Karagins', and Marya Dmitrievna took them there. At that party Natasha again met Anatole, and Sonya noticed that she spoke to him, trying not to be overheard, and that all through dinner she was more agitated than ever. When they got home Natasha was the first to begin the explanation Sonya expected.

'There, Sonya, you were talking all sorts of nonsense about him,' Natasha began in a mild voice such as children use when they wish to be praised. 'We have had an explanation to-day.'

'Well, what happened? What did he say? Natasha, how glad I am you're not angry with me! Tell me everything – the whole truth. What did he say?'

Natasha became thoughtful.

'Oh, Sonya, if you knew him as I do! He said . . . He asked me what I had promised Bolkonsky. He was glad I was free to refuse him.'

Sonya sighed sorrowfully.

'But you haven't refused Bolkonsky?' said she.

'Perhaps I have. Perhaps all is over between me and Bolkonsky. Why do you think so badly of me?'

'I don't think anything, only I don't understand this . . .'

'Wait a bit, Sonya, you'll understand everything. You'll see what a man he is! Don't think badly of me or of him. I don't think badly of anyone: I love and pity everybody. But what am I to do?'

Sonya did not succumb to the tender tone Natasha used towards her. The more emotional and ingratiating the expression of Natasha's face became, the more serious and stern grew Sonya's.

'Natasha,' said she, 'you asked me not to speak to you, and I haven't spoken, but now you yourself have begun. I don't trust him, Natasha. Why this secrecy?'

'Again, again!' interrupted Natasha.

'Natasha, I am afraid for you!'

'Afraid of what?'

'I am afraid you're going to your ruin,' said Sonya resolutely, and was herself horrified at what she had said.

Anger again showed in Natasha's face.

'And I'll go to my ruin, I will, as soon as possible! It's not your business! It won't be you, but I, who'll suffer. Leave me alone, leave me alone! I hate you!'

'Natasha!' moaned Sonya, aghast.

'I hate you, I hate you! You're my enemy for ever!' And Natasha ran out of the room.

Natasha did not speak to Sonya again, and avoided her. With the same expression of agitated surprise and guilt she went about the house, taking up now one occupation, now another, and at once abandoning them.

Hard as it was for Sonya, she watched her friend and did not let her out of her sight.

The day before the count was to return, Sonya noticed that Natasha sat by the drawing-room window all the morning, as if expecting something, and that she made a sign to an officer who drove past, whom Sonya took to be Anatole.

Sonya began watching her friend still more attentively, and noticed that at dinner and all that evening Natasha was in a strange and unnatural state. She answered questions at random, began sentences she did not finish, and laughed at everything.

After tea Sonya noticed a housemaid at Natasha's door timidly waiting to let her pass. She let the girl go in, and then listening at the door, learnt that another letter had been delivered.

Then suddenly it became clear to Sonya that Natasha had some dreadful plan for that evening. Sonya knocked at her door. Natasha did not let her in.

'She will run away with him!' thought Sonya. 'She is capable of anything. There was something particularly pathetic and resolute in her face to-day. She cried as she said good-bye to uncle,' Sonya remembered. 'Yes, that's it, she means to elope with him, but what am I to do?' thought she, recalling all the signs that clearly indicated that Natasha had some terrible intention. 'The count is away.

619

What am I to do? Write to Kuragin demanding an explanation? But what is there to oblige him to reply? Write to Pierre, as Prince Andrew asked me to in case of some misfortune? ... But perhaps she really has already refused Bolkonsky – she sent a letter to Princess Mary yesterday. And uncle is away...' To tell Marya Dmitrievna who had such faith in Natasha, seemed to Sonya terrible. 'Well anyway,' thought Sonya as she stood in the dark passage, 'now or never I must prove that I remember the family's goodness to me and that I love Nicholas. Yes! If I don't sleep for three nights I'll not leave this passage, and will hold her back by force and not let the family be disgraced,' she thought.

16

ANATOLE had lately moved to Dolokhov's. The plan for Natalie Rostova's abduction had been arranged and the preparations made by Dolokhov a few days before, and on the day that Sonya, after listening at Natasha's door, resolved to safeguard her, it was to have been put into execution. Natasha had promised to come out to Kuragin at the back porch at ten that evening. Kuragin was to put her into a troyka he would have ready, and to drive her forty miles to the village of Kamenka, where an unfrocked priest was in readiness to perform a marriage ceremony over them. At Kamenka a relay of horses was to wait which would take them to the Warsaw high road, and from there they would hasten abroad with post-horses.

Anatole had a passport, an order for post-horses, ten thousand rubles he had taken from his sister and another ten thousand borrowed with Dolokhov's help.

Two witnesses for the mock marriage – Khvostikov, a retired petty official whom Dolokhov made use of in his gambling transactions, and Makarin, a retired hussar, a kindly, weak fellow who had an unbounded affection for Kuragin – were sitting at tea in Dolokhov's front room.

In his large study, the walls of which were hung to the ceiling with Persian rugs, bearskins, and weapons, sat Dolokhov in a travelling cloak and high boots, at an open desk on which lay an abacus and some bundles of paper money. Anatole, with uniform unbuttoned, walked to and fro between the room where the witnesses were sitting, the study, and the room behind, where his French valet and others were packing the last of his things. Dolokhov was counting the money and noting something down.

'Well,' he said, 'Khvostikov must have two thousand.'

'Give it him, then,' said Anatole.

'Makarka' (their name for Makarin) 'will go through fire and water for you for nothing. So here are our accounts all settled,' said Dolokhov, showing him the memorandum. 'Is that right?'

'Yes, of course,' returned Anatole, evidently not listening to Dolokhov and looking straight before him with a smile that did not leave his face.

Dolokhov banged down the lid of his desk, and turned to Anatole with an ironic smile:

'Do you know? You'd really better drop it all. There's still time!'

'Fool,' retorted Anatole. 'Don't talk nonsense! If you only knew ... it's the devil knows what!'

'No, really, give it up!' said Dolokhov. 'I am speaking seriously. It's no joke, this plot you've hatched.'

'What, teasing again? Go to the devil! Eh?' said Anatole, making a grimace. 'Really it's no time for your stupid jokes,' and he left the room.

Dolokhov smiled contemptuously and condescendingly when Anatole had gone out.

'You wait a bit,' he called after him. 'I'm not joking, I'm talking sense. Come here, come here!'

Anatole returned and looked at Dolokhov, trying to give him his attention and evidently submitting to him involuntarily.

'Now listen to me. I'm telling you this for the last time. Why should I joke about it? Did I hinder you? Who arranged everything for you? Who found the priest and got the passport? Who raised the money? I did it all.'

'Well, thank you for it. Do you think I am not grateful?' And Anatole sighed and embraced Dolokhov.

'I helped you, but all the same I must tell you the truth; it is a dangerous business, and if you think about it – a stupid business. Well, you'll carry her off – all right! Will they let it stop at that? It will come out that you're already married. Why, they'll have you in the criminal court . . .'

'Oh, nonsense, nonsense!' Anatole ejaculated and again made a grimace. 'Didn't I explain to you? What?' And Anatole, with the partiality dull-witted people have for any conclusion they have reached by their own reasoning, repeated the argument he had already put to Dolokhov a hundred times. 'Didn't I explain to you that I have come to this conclusion: if this marriage is invalid,' he went on, crooking one finger, 'then I have nothing to answer for; but if it is valid, no matter! Abroad no one will know anything about it. Isn't that so? And don't talk to me, don't don't!'

'Seriously, you'd better drop it! You'll only get yourself into a mess!'

'Go to the devil!' cried Anatole and clutching his hair left the room, but returned at once and dropped into an arm-chair in front of Dolokhov with his feet tucked under him. 'It's the very devil! What? Feel how it beats!' He took Dolokhov's hand and put it on his heart. 'What a foot, my dear fellow! What a glance! A goddess!' he added in French. 'What?'

Dolokhov with a cold smile and a gleam in his handsome insolent eyes looked at him – evidently wishing to get some more amusement out of him.

'Well, and when the money's gone, what then?'

'What then? Eh?' repeated Anatole, sincerely perplexed by a thought of the future. 'What then? . . . Then, I don't know . . . But why talk nonsense!' He glanced at his watch. 'It's time!'

Anatole went into the back room.

'Now then! Nearly ready? You're dawdling!' he shouted to the servants.

Dolokhov put away the money, called a footman whom he ordered to bring something for them to eat and drink before the journey, and went into the room where Khvostikov and Makarin were sitting.

Anatole lay on the sofa in the study leaning on his elbow and smiling pensively, while his handsome lips muttered tenderly to himself.

'Come and eat something. Have a drink!' Dolokhov shouted to him from the other room.

'I don't want to,' answered Anatole continuing to smile.

'Come! Balaga is here.'

Anatole rose and went into the dining-room. Balaga was a famous troyka driver who had known Dolokhov and Anatole some six years and had given them good service with his troykas. More than once when Anatole's regiment was stationed at Tver he had taken him from Tver in the evening, brought him to Moscow by daybreak, and driven him back again the next night. More than once he had enabled Dolokhov to escape when pursued. More than once he had driven them through the town with gipsies and 'ladykins' as he called the *cocottes*. More than once in their service he had run over pedestrians and upset vehicles in the streets of Moscow, and had always been protected from the consequences by 'my gentlemen' as he called them. He had ruined more than one horse in their service. More than once they had beaten him, and more than once they had made him drunk on champagne and madeira, which he loved; and he knew more than one thing about each of them which would long ago have sent an ordinary man to Siberia. They often called Balaga into their orgies and made him drink and dance at the gipsies', and more than one thousand rubles of their money had passed through his hands. In their service he risked his skin and his life twenty times a year, and in their service had lost more horses than the money he had from them would buy. But he liked them; liked that mad driving at twelve miles an hour, liked upsetting a driver, or running down a pedestrian, and flying at full gallop through the Moscow streets. He liked to hear those wild, tipsy shouts behind him: 'Get on! Get on!' when it was impossible to go any faster. He liked giving a painful lash on the neck to some peasant who, more dead than alive, was already hurrying out of his way. 'Real gentlemen!' he considered them.

Anatole and Dolokhov liked Balaga too, for his masterly driving and because he liked the things they liked. With others Balaga bargained, charging twenty-five rubles for a two-hours' drive, and rarely drove himself, generally letting his young men do so. But with 'his gentlemen' he always drove himself, and never demanded anything for his work. Only a couple of times a year – when he knew from their valets that they had money in hand – he would turn up of a morning quite sober, and with a deep bow would ask them to help him. The gentlemen always made him sit down.

'Do help me out, Theodore Ivanych, sir,' or 'your Excellency,' he would say. 'I am quite out of horses. Let me have what you can to go to the fair.'

And Anatole and Dolokhov, when they had money, would give him a thousand or a couple of thousand rubles.

Balaga was a fair-haired, short, and snub-nosed peasant of about twenty-seven, red-faced, with a particularly red thick neck, glittering little eyes, and a small beard. He wore a fine, dark-blue, silk-lined cloth coat over a sheepskin.

On entering the room now, he crossed himself, turning towards the front corner of the room, and went up to Dolokhov holding out a small, black hand.

'Theodore Ivanych!' he said, bowing.

'How d'you do, friend? Well, here he is!'

'Good day, your Excellency!' he said, again holding out his hand to Anatole who had just come in.

'I say, Balaga,' said Anatole, putting his hands on the man's shoulders, 'do you care for me or not? Eh? Now, do me a service . . . What horses have you come with? Eh?'

'As your messenger ordered, your special beasts,' replied Balaga.

623

'Well, listen, Balaga! Drive all three to death, but get me there in three hours. Eh?'

'When they are dead, what shall I drive?' said Balaga with a wink.

'Mind, I'll smash your face in! Don't make jokes!' cried Anatole, suddenly rolling his eyes.

'Why joke?' said the driver, laughing. 'As if I'd grudge my gentlemen anything! As fast as ever the horses can gallop, so fast we'll go!'

'Ah!' said Anatole. 'Well, sit down.'

'Yes, sit down!' said Dolokhov.

'I'll stand, Theodore Ivanych.'

'Sit down; nonsense! Have a drink!' said Anatole, and filled a large glass of madeira for him.

The driver's eyes sparkled at the sight of the wine. After refusing it for manners' sake, he drank it and wiped his mouth with a red silk handkerchief he took out of his cap.

'And when are we to start, your Excellency?'

'Well...' Anatole looked at his watch. 'We'll start at once. Mind, Balaga! You'll get there in time? Eh?'

'That depends on our luck in starting, else why shouldn't we be there in time?' replied Balaga. 'Didn't we get you to Tver in seven hours? I think you remember that, your Excellency?'

'Do you know, one Christmas I drove from Tver,' said Anatole, smiling at the recollection and turning to Makarin who gazed rapturously at him with wide-open eyes. 'Will you believe it, Makarka, it took one's breath away, the rate we flew. We came across a train of loaded sledges, and drove right over two of them. Eh?'

'Those were horses!' Balaga continued the tale. 'That time I'd harnessed two young side-horses with the bay in the shafts,' he went on, turning to Dolokhov. 'Will you believe it, Theodore Ivanych, those animals flew forty miles? I couldn't hold them in, my hands grew numb in the sharp frost so that I threw down the reins – "Catch hold yourself, your Excellency!" says I, and I just tumbled on the bottom of the sledge and sprawled there. It wasn't a case of urging them on, there was no holding them in till we reached the place. The devils took us there in three hours! Only the near one died of it.'

## 17

ANATOLE went out of the room and returned a few minutes later wearing a fur coat girt with a silver belt and a sable cap jauntily set on one side and very becoming to his handsome face. Having looked in a mirror, and standing before Dolokhov in the same pose he had assumed before it, he lifted a glass of wine.

'Well, good-bye, Theodore. Thank you for everything and farewell!' said Anatole. 'Well, comrades and friends...' he considered for a moment, '...of my youth, farewell!' he said, turning to Makarin and the others.

Though they were all going with him, Anatole evidently wished to make something touching and solemn out of this address to his comrades. He spoke slowly in a loud voice, and throwing out his chest slightly swayed one leg.

'All take glasses; you too, Balaga. Well, comrades and friends of my youth, we've had our fling and lived and revelled. Eh? And now, when shall we meet again? I am going abroad. We have had a good time – now farewell, lads! To our health! Hurrah!...' he cried, and emptying his glass flung it on the floor.

'To your health!' said Balaga who also emptied his glass, and wiped his mouth with his handkerchief.

Makarin embraced Anatole with tears in his eyes.

'Ah, Prince, how sorry I am to part from you?'

'Let's go. Let's go!' cried Anatole.

Balaga was about to leave the room.

'No, stop!' said Anatole. 'Shut the door; we have first to sit down.* That's the way.'

They shut the door and all sat down.

'Now, quick march, lads!' said Anatole, rising.

Joseph, his valet, handed him his sabretache and sabre, and they all went out into the vestibule.

'And where's the fur cloak?' asked Dolokhov. 'Hey, Ignatka! Go to Matrëna Matrevna and ask her for the sable cloak. I have heard what elopements are like,' continued Dolokhov with a wink. 'Why, she'll rush out more dead than alive just in the things she is wearing; if you delay at all, there'll be tears and "papa" and "mamma", and she's frozen in a minute and must go back – but you wrap the fur cloak round her first thing and carry her to the sledge.'

The valet brought a woman's fox-lined cloak.

'Fool, I told you the sable one! Hey, Matrëna, the sable!' he shouted, so that his voice rang far through the rooms.

A handsome, slim, and pale-faced gipsy-girl with glittering black eyes and curly blue-black hair, wearing a red shawl, ran out with a sable mantle on her arm.

'Here, I don't grudge it – take it!' she said, evidently afraid of her master and yet regretful of her cloak.

Dolokhov, without answering, took the cloak, threw it over Matrëna and wrapped her up in it.

'That's the way,' said Dolokhov, 'and then so!' and he turned the collar up round her head, leaving only a little of the face uncovered. 'And then so, do you see?' and he pushed Anatole's head forward to meet the gap left by the collar, through which Matrëna's brilliant smile was seen.

'Well, good-bye, Matrëna,' said Anatole, kissing her. 'Ah, my revels here are over. Remember me to Stëshka.* There, good-bye! Good-bye, Matrëna, wish me luck!'

'Well, Prince, may God give you great luck!' said Matrëna in her gipsy accent.

Two troykas were standing before the porch and two young drivers were holding the horses. Balaga took his seat in the front one, and holding his elbows high arranged the reins deliberately. Anatole and Dolokhov got in with him. Makarin, Khvostikov, and a valet seated themselves in the other sledge.

'Well, are you ready?' asked Balaga.

'Go!' he cried, twisting the reins round his hands, and the troyka tore down the Nikitsky Boulevard.

'Tproo! Get out of the way! Hi!...Tproo!...' The shouting of Balaga and of the sturdy young fellow seated on the box was all that could be heard. On the Arbat Square the troyka caught against a carriage; something cracked, shouts were heard, and the troyka flew along the Arbat Street.

After taking a turn along the Podnovinsky Boulevard, Balaga began to rein in, and turning back drew up at the crossing of the old Konyusheny Street.

The young fellow on the box jumped down to hold the horses, and Anatole and Dolokhov went along the pavement. When they reached the gate Dolokhov whistled. The whistle was answered, and a maidservant ran out.

'Come into the courtyard or you'll be seen; she'll come out directly,' said she.

Dolokhov stayed by the gate. Anatole followed the maid into the courtyard, turned the corner, and ran up into the porch.

He was met by Gabriel, Marya Dmitrievna's gigantic footman.

'Come to the mistress, please,' said the footman in his deep bass, intercepting any retreat.

'To what mistress? Who are you?' asked Anatole in a breathless whisper.

'Kindly step in, my orders are to bring you in.'

'Kuragin! Come back!' shouted Dolokhov. 'Betrayed! Back!'

Dolokhov, after Anatole entered, had remained at the wicket-gate, and was struggling with the yard-porter who was trying to lock it. With a last desperate effort Dolokhov pushed the porter aside, and when Anatole ran back seized him by the arm, pulled him through the wicket, and ran back with him to the troyka.

## 18

MARY DMITRIEVNA having found Sonya weeping in the corridor, made her confess everything, and intercepting the note to Natasha she read it and went into Natasha's room with it in her hand.

'You shameless good-for-nothing!' said she. 'I won't hear a word.'

Pushing back Natasha, who looked at her with astonished but tearless eyes, she locked her in, and having given orders to the yard-porter to admit the persons who would be coming that evening, but not to let them out again, and having told the footman to bring them up to her, she seated herself in the drawing-room to await the abductors.

When Gabriel came to inform her that the men who had come had run away again, she rose frowning, and clasping her hands behind her paced through the rooms a long time considering what she should do. Towards midnight she went to Natasha's room finger-ing the key in her pocket. Sonya was sitting sobbing in the corridor. 'Marya Dmitrievna, for God's sake let me in to her!' she pleaded, but Marya Dmitrievna unlocked the door and went in without giving her an answer ... 'Disgusting, abominable ... In my house ... horrid girl, hussy! I'm only sorry for her father!' thought she, trying to restrain her wrath. 'Hard as it may be, I'll tell them all to hold their tongues, and will hide it from the count.' She entered the room with resolute steps. Natasha was lying on the sofa, her head hidden in her hands, and she did not stir. She was in just the same position in which Marya Dmitrievna had left her.

'A nice girl! Very nice!' said Marya Dmitrievna. 'Arranging meetings with lovers in my house! It's no use pretending: you listen when I speak to you!' And Marya Dmitrievna touched her arm. 'Listen when I speak! You've disgraced yourself like the lowest of hussies. I'd treat you differently, but I'm sorry for your father, so I will conceal it.'

Natasha did not change her position, but her whole body heaved with noiseless, convulsive sobs which choked her. Marya Dmitrievna glanced round at Sonya and seated herself on the sofa beside Natasha.

'It's lucky for him that he escaped me; but I'll find him!' she said in her rough voice. 'Do you hear what I am saying or not?' she added.

She put her large hand under Natasha's face and turned it towards her. Both Marya Dmitrievna and Sonya were amazed when they saw how Natasha looked. Her eyes were dry and glistening, her lips compressed, her cheeks sunken.

'Let me be! . . . What is it to me? . . . I shall die!' she muttered, wrenching herself from Marya Dmitrievna's hands with a vicious effort and sinking down again into her former position.

'Natalie!' said Marya Dmitrievna. 'I wish for your good. Lie still, stay like that then, I won't touch you. But listen. I won't tell you how guilty you are. You know that yourself. But when your father comes back to-morrow – what am I to tell him? Eh?'

Again Natasha's body shook with sobs.

'Suppose he finds out, and your brother, and your betrothed?'

'I have no betrothed: I have refused him!' cried Natasha.

'That's all the same,' continued Marya Dmitrievna. 'If they hear of this will they let it pass? He, your father, I know him . . . if he challenges him to a duel will that be all right? Eh?'

'Oh, let me be! Why have you interfered at all? Why? Why? Who asked you to?' shouted Natasha, raising herself on the sofa and looking malignantly at Marya Dmitrievna.

'But what did you want?' cried Marya Dmitrievna, growing angry again. 'Were you kept under lock and key? Who hindered his coming to the house? Why carry you off as if you were some gipsy singing-girl? . . . Well, if he had carried you off . . . do you think they wouldn't have found him? Your father, or brother, or your betrothed? And he's a scoundrel, a wretch – that's a fact!'

'He is better than any of you!' exclaimed Natasha getting up. 'If you hadn't interfered . . . Oh, my God! What is it all? What is it? Sonya, why . . . ? Go away!'

And she burst into sobs with the despairing vehemence with which people bewail disasters they feel they have themselves caused. Marya Dmitrievna was about to speak again, but Natasha cried out:

'Go away! Go away! You all hate and despise me!' and she threw herself back on the sofa.

Marya Dmitrievna went on admonishing her for some time, enjoining on her that it must all be kept from her father and assuring her that nobody would know anything about it if only Natasha herself would undertake to forget it all and not let anyone

628

see that something had happened. Natasha did not reply, nor did she sob any longer, but she grew cold and had a shivering fit. Marya Dmitrievna put a pillow under her head, covered her with two quilts, and herself brought her some lime-flower water, but Natasha did not respond to her.

'Well, let her sleep,' said Marya Dmitrievna as she went out of the room supposing Natasha to be asleep.

But Natasha was not asleep; with pale face and fixed wide-open eyes she looked straight before her. All that night she did not sleep or weep, and did not speak to Sonya who got up and went to her several times.

Next day Count Rostov returned from his estate near Moscow in time for lunch as he had promised. He was in very good spirits; the affair with the purchaser was going on satisfactorily, and there was nothing to keep him any longer in Moscow, away from the countess whom he missed. Marya Dmitrievna met him and told him that Natasha had been very unwell the day before and that they had sent for the doctor, but that she was better now. Natasha had not left her room that morning. With compressed and parched lips, and dry fixed eyes, she sat at the window, uneasily watching the people who drove past, and hurriedly glancing round at anyone who entered the room. She was evidently expecting news of him and that he would come or would write to her.

When the count came to see her she turned anxiously round at the sound of a man's footstep, and then her face resumed its cold and malevolent expression. She did not even get up to greet him.

'What is the matter with you, my angel? Are you ill?' asked the count.

After a moment's silence Natasha answered: 'Yes, ill.'

In reply to the count's anxious inquiries as to why she was so dejected and whether anything had happened to her betrothed, she assured him that nothing had happened and asked him not to worry. Marya Dmitrievna confirmed Natasha's assurances that nothing had happened. From the pretence of illness, from his daughter's distress, and by the embarrassed faces of Sonya and Marya Dmitrievna, the count saw clearly that something had gone wrong during his absence, but it was so terrible for him to think that anything disgraceful had happened to his beloved daughter, and he so prized his own cheerful tranquillity, that he avoided inquiries and tried to assure himself that nothing particular had happened, and he was only dissatisfied that her indisposition delayed their return to the country.

## 19

FROM the day his wife arrived in Moscow Pierre had been intending to go away somewhere, so as not to be near her. Soon after the Rostovs came to Moscow the effect Natasha had on him made him hasten to carry out his intention. He went to Tver to see Joseph Alexeevich's widow, who had long since promised to hand over to him some papers of her deceased husband's.

When he returned to Moscow Pierre was handed a letter from Marya Dmitrievna asking him to come and see her on a matter of great importance relating to Andrew Bolkonsky and his betrothed. Pierre had been avoiding Natasha because it seemed to him that his feeling for her was stronger than a married man's should be for his friend's fiancée. Yet some fate constantly threw them together.

'What can have happened? And what can they want with me?' thought he as he dressed to go to Marya Dmitrievna's. 'If only Prince Andrew would hurry up and come and marry her!' thought he on his way to the house.

On the Tverskoy Boulevard a familiar voice called to him.

'Pierre! Been back long?' someone shouted. Pierre raised his head. In a sledge drawn by two grey trotting-horses that were bespattering the dashboard with snow, Anatole and his constant companion Makarin dashed past. Anatole was sitting upright in the classic pose of military dandies, the lower part of his face hidden by his beaver collar and his head slightly bent. His face was fresh and rosy, his white-plumed hat, tilted to one side, disclosed his curled and pomaded hair besprinkled with powdery snow.

'Yes, indeed, that's a true sage,' thought Pierre. 'He sees nothing beyond the pleasure of the moment, nothing troubles him and so he is always cheerful, satisfied, and serene. What wouldn't I give to be like him!' he thought enviously.

In Marya Dmitrievna's ante-room the footman who helped him off with his fur coat said that the mistress asked him to come to her bedroom.

When he opened the ball-room door Pierre saw Natasha sitting at the window, with a thin, pale, and spiteful face. She glanced round at him, frowned, and left the room with an expression of cold dignity.

'What has happened?' asked Pierre, entering Marya Dmitrievna's room.

'Fine doings!' answered Marya Dmitrievna. 'For fifty-eight years have I lived in this world and never known anything so disgraceful.'

And having put him on his honour not to repeat anything she

told him, Marya Dmitrievna informed him that Natasha had refused Prince Andrew without her parents' knowledge, and that the cause of this was Anatole Kuragin into whose society Pierre's wife had thrown her, and with whom Natasha had tried to elope during her father's absence, in order to be married secretly.

Pierre raised his shoulders and listened open-mouthed to what was told him, scarcely able to believe his own ears. That Prince Andrew's deeply loved affianced wife – the same Natasha Rostova who used to be so charming – should give up Bolkonsky for that fool Anatole who was already secretly married (as Pierre knew), and should be so in love with him as to agree to run away with him, was something Pierre could not conceive and could not imagine.

He could not reconcile the charming impression he had of Natasha, whom he had known from a child, with this new conception of her baseness, folly, and cruelty. He thought of his wife. 'They are all alike!' he said to himself, reflecting that he was not the only man unfortunate enough to be tied to a bad woman. But still he pitied Prince Andrew to the point of tears and sympathized with his wounded pride, and the more he pitied his friend the more did he think with contempt and even with disgust of that Natasha who had just passed him in the ball-room with such a look of cold dignity. He did not know that Natasha's soul was overflowing with despair, shame, and humiliation, and that it was not her fault that her face happened to assume an expression of calm dignity and severity.

'But how get married?' said Pierre, in answer to Marya Dmitrievna. 'He could not marry – he is married!'

'Things get worse from hour to hour!' ejaculated Marya Dmitrievna. 'A nice youth! What a scoundrel! And she's expecting him – expecting him since yesterday. She must be told! Then at least she won't go on expecting him.'

After hearing the details of Anatole's marriage from Pierre, and giving vent to her anger against Anatole in words of abuse, Marya Dmitrievna told Pierre why she had sent for him. She was afraid that the count or Bolkonsky, who might arrive at any moment, if they knew of this affair (which she hoped to hide from them) might challenge Anatole to a duel, and she therefore asked Pierre to tell his brother-in-law in her name to leave Moscow and not dare to let her set eyes on him again. Pierre – only now realizing the danger to the old count, Nicholas, and Prince Andrew – promised to do as she wished. Having briefly and exactly explained her wishes to him, she let him go to the drawing-room.

'Mind, the count knows nothing. Behave as if you know nothing either,' she said. 'And I will go and tell her it is no use expecting him! And stay to dinner if you care to!' she called after Pierre.

Pierre met the old count, who seemed nervous and upset. That morning Natasha had told him that she had rejected Bolkonsky.

'Troubles, troubles, my dear fellow!' he said to Pierre. 'What troubles one has with these girls without their mother! I do so regret having come here. I will be frank with you. Have you heard she has broken off her engagement without consulting anybody? It's true this engagement never was much to my liking. Of course he is an excellent man, but still, with his father's disapproval they wouldn't have been happy, and Natasha won't lack suitors. Still, it has been going on so long, and to take such a step without father's or mother's consent! And now she's ill, and God knows what! It's hard, Count, hard to manage daughters in their mother's absence . . .'

Pierre saw that the count was much upset, and tried to change the subject, but the count returned to his troubles.

Sonya entered the room with an agitated face.

'Natasha is not quite well; she's in her room and would like to see you. Marya Dmitrievna is with her and she too asks you to come.'

'Yes, you are a great friend of Bolkonsky's, no doubt she wants to send him a message,' said the count. 'Oh dear! Oh dear! How happy it all was!'

And clutching the spare grey locks on his temples the count left the room.

When Marya Dmitrievna told Natasha that Anatole was married, Natasha did not wish to believe it, and insisted on having it confirmed by Pierre himself. Sonya told Pierre this as she led him along the corridor to Natasha's room.

Natasha, pale and stern, was sitting beside Marya Dmitrievna, and her eyes, glittering feverishly, met Pierre with a questioning look the moment he entered. She did not smile or nod, but only gazed fixedly at him, and her look asked only one thing: was he a friend, or like the others an enemy in regard to Anatole? As for himself, Pierre evidently did not exist for her.

'He knows all about it,' said Marya Dmitrievna pointing to Pierre and addressing Natasha. 'Let him tell you whether I have told you the truth.'

Natasha looked from one to the other as a hunted and wounded animal looks at the approaching dogs and sportsmen.

'Natalya Ilynichna,' Pierre began, dropping his eyes with a feeling of pity for her and loathing for the thing he had to do, 'whether it is true or not should make no difference to you, because . . .'

'Then it is not true that he's married!'

'Yes, it is true.'

'Has he been married long?' she asked. 'On your honour? . . .'
Pierre gave his word of honour.
'Is he still here?' she asked, quickly.
'Yes, I have just seen him.'
She was evidently unable to speak, and made a sign with her hands that they should leave her alone.

20

PIERRE did not stay for dinner, but left the room and went away at once. He drove through the town seeking Anatole Kuragin, at the thought of whom now the blood rushed to his heart and he felt a difficulty in breathing. He was not at the ice-hills, nor at the gipsies', nor at Komoneno's. Pierre drove to the club. In the club all was going on as usual. The members who were assembling for dinner were sitting about in groups; they greeted Pierre and spoke of the town news. The footman having greeted him, knowing his habits and his acquaintances, told him there was a place left for him in the small dining-room, and that Prince Michael Zakharych was in the library, but Paul Timofeevich had not yet arrived. One of Pierre's acquaintances, while they were talking about the weather, asked if he had heard of Kuragin's abduction of Rostova which was talked of in the town, and was it true? Pierre laughed and said it was nonsense for he had just come from the Rostovs'. He asked everyone about Anatole. One man told him he had not come yet, and another that he was coming to dinner. Pierre felt it strange to see this calm, indifferent crowd of people unaware of what was going on in his soul. He paced through the ball-room, waited till everyone had come, and as Anatole had not turned up, did not stay for dinner but drove home.

Anatole, for whom Pierre was looking, dined that day with Dolokhov, consulting him as to how to remedy this unfortunate affair. It seemed to him essential to see Natasha. In the evening he drove to his sister's to discuss with her how to arrange a meeting. When Pierre returned home after vainly hunting all over Moscow, his valet informed him that Prince Anatole was with the countess. The countess's drawing-room was full of guests.

Pierre without greeting his wife whom he had not seen since his return – at that moment she was more repulsive to him than ever – entered the drawing-room and seeing Anatole went up to him.

'Ah, Pierre,' said the countess going up to her husband. 'You don't know what a plight our Anatole . . .'

She stopped, seeing in the forward thrust of her husband's head,

633

in his glowing eyes and his resolute gait, the terrible indications of that rage and strength which she knew, and had herself experienced after his duel with Dolokhov.

'Where you are, there is vice and evil!' said Pierre to his wife. 'Anatole, come with me! I must speak to you,' he added in French.

Anatole glanced round at his sister and rose submissively, ready to follow Pierre. Pierre, taking him by the arm, pulled him towards himself and was leading him from the room.

'If you allow yourself in my drawing-room . . .' whispered Hélène, but Pierre did not reply and went out of the room.

Anatole followed him with his usual jaunty step but his face betrayed anxiety.

Having entered his study Pierre closed the door, and addressed Anatole without looking at him.

'You promised Countess Rostova to marry her and were about to elope with her, is that so?'

'Mon cher,' answered Anatole (their whole conversation was in French), 'I don't consider myself bound to answer questions put to me in that tone.'

Pierre's face, already pale, became distorted by fury. He seized Anatole by the collar of his uniform with his big hand, and shook him from side to side till Anatole's face showed a sufficient degree of terror.

'When I tell you that I must talk to you! . . .' repeated Pierre.

'Come now, this is stupid. What?' said Anatole, fingering a button of his collar that had been wrenched loose with a bit of the cloth.

'You're a scoundrel and a blackguard, and I don't know what restrains me from the pleasure of smashing your head with this,' said Pierre, expressing himself so artificially because he was talking French.

He took a heavy paper-weight and lifted it threateningly, but at once put it back in its place.

'Did you promise to marry her?'

'I . . . I . . . I didn't think of it. I never promised, because . . .'

Pierre interrupted him.

'Have you any letters of hers? Any letters?' he said, moving towards Anatole.

Anatole glanced at him and immediately thrust his hand into his pocket and drew out his pocket-book.

Pierre took the letter Anatole handed him, and pushing aside a table that stood in his way, threw himself on the sofa.

'I shan't be violent, don't be afraid,' said Pierre in answer to a frightened gesture of Anatole's. 'First, the letters,' said he, as if repeating a lesson to himself. 'Secondly,' he continued after a short pause, again rising and again pacing the room, 'to-morrow you must get out of Moscow.'

'But how can I . . . ?'

'Thirdly,' Pierre continued without listening to him, 'you must never breathe a word of what has passed between you and Countess Rostova. I know I can't prevent your doing so, but if you have a spark of conscience . . .' Pierre paced the room several times in silence.

Anatole sat at the table frowning and biting his lips.

'After all, you must understand that besides your pleasure there is such a thing as other people's happiness and peace, and that you are ruining a whole life for the sake of amusing yourself! Amuse yourself with women like my wife – with them you are within your rights, for they know what you want of them. They are armed against you by the same experience of debauchery; but to promise *a maid* to marry her . . . to deceive, to kidnap . . . Don't you understand that it is as mean as beating an old man or a child? . . .'

Pierre paused and looked at Anatole no longer with an angry, but with a questioning look.

'I don't know about that, eh?' said Anatole, growing more confident as Pierre mastered his wrath. 'I don't know that and don't want to,' he said, not looking at Pierre, and with a slight tremor of his lower jaw, 'but you have used such words to me – "mean" and so on, which as a man of honour I can't allow anyone to use.'

Pierre glanced at him with amazement, unable to understand what he wanted.

'Though it was tête-à-tête,' Anatole continued, 'still I can't . . .'

'Is it satisfaction you want?' said Pierre ironically.

'You could at least take back your words. What? If you want me to do as you wish, eh?'

'I take them back, I take them back!' said Pierre, 'and I ask you to forgive me.' Pierre involuntarily glanced at the loose button. 'And if you require money for your journey . . .'

Anatole smiled. The expression of that base and cringing smile, which Pierre knew so well in his wife, revolted him.

'Oh, vile and heartless brood!' he exclaimed, and left the room.

Next day Anatole left for Petersburg.

21

PIERRE drove to Marya Dmitrievna's to tell her of the fulfilment of her wish that Kuragin should be banished from Moscow. The whole house was in a state of alarm and commotion. Natasha was very ill, having, as Marya Dmitrievna told him in secret, poisoned herself the night after she had been told that Anatole was married, with some arsenic she had stealthily procured. After swallowing a little she had been so frightened that she woke Sonya and told her what she had done. The necessary antidotes had been administered in time and she was now out of danger, though still so weak that it was out of the question to move her to the country, and so the countess had been sent for. Pierre saw the distracted count and Sonya, who had a tear-stained face, but he could not see Natasha.

Pierre dined at the club that day and heard on all sides gossip about the attempted abduction of Rostova. He resolutely denied these rumours, assuring everyone that nothing had happened except that his brother-in-law had proposed to her and been refused. It seemed to Pierre that it was his duty to conceal the whole affair and re-establish Natasha's reputation.

He was awaiting Prince Andrew's return with dread, and went every day to the old prince's for news of him.

Old Prince Bolkonsky heard all the rumours current in the town from Mademoiselle Bourienne, and had read the note to Princess Mary in which Natasha had broken off her engagement. He seemed in better spirits than usual and awaited his son with great impatience.

Some days after Anatole's departure Pierre received a note from Prince Andrew, informing him of his arrival and asking him to come to see him.

Directly he reached Moscow Prince Andrew had received from his father Natasha's note to Princess Mary breaking off her engagement (Mademoiselle Bourienne had purloined it from Princess Mary and given it to the old prince) and he heard from him the story of Natasha's elopement, with additions.

Prince Andrew had arrived in the evening and Pierre came to see him next morning. Pierre expected to find Prince Andrew in almost the same state as Natasha, and was therefore surprised on entering the drawing-room to hear him in the study talking in a loud animated voice about some intrigue going on in Petersburg. The old prince's voice and another now and then interrupted him. Princess Mary came out to meet Pierre. She sighed, looking towards the door of the room where Prince Andrew was, evidently intending to express her sympathy with his sorrow, but Pierre saw by her face that she was glad both at what had happened and at the way her brother had taken the news of Natasha's faithlessness.

'He says he expected it,' she remarked. 'I know his pride will not let him express his feelings, but still he has taken it better, far better, than I expected. Evidently it had to be . . .'

'But is it possible that all is really ended?' asked Pierre.

Princess Mary looked at him with astonishment. She did not understand how he could ask such a question. Pierre went into the study. Prince Andrew, greatly changed and plainly in better health, but with a fresh horizontal wrinkle between his brows, stood in civilian dress facing his father and Prince Meshchersky, warmly disputing and vigorously gesticulating. The conversation was about Speransky – the news of whose sudden exile and alleged treachery had just reached Moscow.*

'Now he is censured and accused by all who were enthusiastic about him a month ago,' Prince Andrew was saying, 'and by those who were unable to understand his aims. To judge a man who is in disfavour and to throw on him all the blame of other men's mistakes is very easy, but I maintain that if anything good has been accomplished in this reign it was done by him, by him alone.'

He paused at the sight of Pierre. His face quivered and immediately assumed a vindictive expression.

'Posterity will do him justice,' he concluded, and at once turned to Pierre.

'Well, how are you? Still getting stouter?' he said with animation, but the new wrinkle on his forehead deepened. 'Yes, I am well,' he said in answer to Pierre's question, and smiled.

To Pierre that smile said plainly: 'I am well, but my health is now of no use to anyone.'

After a few words to Pierre about the awful roads from the Polish frontier, about people he had met in Switzerland who knew Pierre, and about M. Dessalles, whom he had brought from abroad to be his son's tutor, Prince Andrew again joined warmly in the conversation about Speransky which was still going on between the two old men.

'If there were treason, or proofs of secret relations with Napoleon, they would have been made public,' he said with warmth and haste. 'I do not, and never did, like Speransky personally, but I like justice!'

Pierre now recognized in his friend a need with which he was only too familiar, to get excited and to have arguments about extraneous matters in order to stifle thoughts that were too oppressive and too intimate.

When Prince Meshchersky had left, Prince Andrew took Pierre's arm and asked him into the room that had been assigned him. A bed had been made up there, and some open portmanteaux and trunks stood about. Prince Andrew went to one and took out a small casket, from which he drew a packet wrapped in paper. He did it all silently and very quickly. He stood up and coughed. His face was gloomy and his lips compressed.

'Forgive me for troubling you . . .'

Pierre saw that Prince Andrew was going to speak of Natasha, and his broad face expressed pity and sympathy. This expression irritated Prince Andrew, and in a determined, ringing, and unpleasant tone he continued:

'I have received a refusal from Countess Rostova, and have heard reports of your brother-in-law having sought her hand, or something of that kind. Is that true?'

'Both true and untrue,' Pierre began; but Prince Andrew interrupted him.

'Here are her letters and her portrait,' said he.

He took the packet from the table and handed it to Pierre.

'Give this to the countess . . . if you see her.'

'She is very ill,' said Pierre.

'Then she is here still?' said Prince Andrew. 'And Prince Kuragin?' he added quickly.

'He left long ago. She has been at death's door.'

'I much regret her illness,' said Prince Andrew; and he smiled like his father, coldly, maliciously, and unpleasantly.

'So Monsieur Kuragin has not honoured Countess Rostova with his hand?' said Prince Andrew, and he snorted several times.

'He could not marry, for he was married already,' said Pierre.

Prince Andrew laughed disagreeably, again reminding one of his father.

'And where is your brother-in-law now, if I may ask?' he said.

'He has gone to Peters. . . . But I don't know,' said Pierre.

'Well, it doesn't matter,' said Prince Andrew. 'Tell Countess Rostova that she was and is perfectly free, and that I wish her all that is good.'

Pierre took the packet. Prince Andrew, as if trying to remember whether he had something more to say, or waiting to see if Pierre would say anything, looked fixedly at him.

'I say, do you remember our discussion in Petersburg?' asked Pierre, 'about . . .'

'Yes,' returned Prince Andrew hastily. 'I said that a fallen woman should be forgiven, but I didn't say I could forgive her. I can't.'

'But can this be compared . . . ?' said Pierre.

Prince Andrew interrupted him, and cried sharply:

'Yes, ask her hand again, be magnanimous, and so on? . . . Yes, that would be very noble, but I am unable to follow in that gentleman's footsteps. If you wish to be my friend never speak to me of that . . . of all that! Well, good-bye. So you'll give her the packet?'

Pierre left the room and went to the old prince and Princess Mary. The old man seemed livelier than usual. Princess Mary was the same as always, but beneath her sympathy for her brother Pierre noticed her satisfaction that the engagement had been broken off. Looking at them Pierre realized what contempt and animosity they all felt for the Rostovs, and that it was impossible in their presence even to mention the name of her who could give up Prince Andrew for anyone else.

At dinner the talk turned on the war, the approach of which was becoming evident. Prince Andrew talked incessantly, arguing now with his father, now with the Swiss tutor Dessalles, and showing an unnatural animation, the cause of which Pierre so well understood.

## 22

That same evening Pierre went to the Rostovs' to fulfil the commission entrusted to him. Natasha was in bed, the count at the club, and Pierre, after giving the letters to Sonya, went to Marya Dmitrievna who was interested to know how Prince Andrew had taken the news. Ten minutes later Sonya came to Marya Dmitrievna.

'Natasha insists on seeing Count Peter Kirilovich,' said she.

'But how? Are we to take him up to her? The room there has not been tidied up.'

'No, she has dressed and gone into the drawing-room,' said Sonya.

Marya Dmitrievna only shrugged her shoulders.

'When will her mother come? She has worried me to death! Now mind, don't tell her everything!' said she to Pierre. 'One hasn't the heart to scold her, she is so much to be pitied, so much to be pitied.'

Natasha was standing in the middle of the drawing-room, emaciated, with a pale set face, but not at all shamefaced as Pierre expected to find her. When he appeared at the door she grew flurried, evidently undecided whether to go to meet him or to wait till he came up.

Pierre hastened to her. He thought she would give him her hand as usual; but she, stepping up to him, stopped, breathing heavily, her arms hanging lifelessly just in the pose she used to stand in when she went to the middle of the ball-room to sing, but with quite a different expression of face.

'Peter Kirilovich,' she began rapidly, 'Prince Bolkonsky was your friend – is your friend,' she corrected herself. (It seemed to her that everything that had once been, must now be different.) 'He told me once to apply to you . . .'

Pierre sniffed as he looked at her, but did not speak. Till then he had reproached her in his heart and tried to despise her, but he now felt so sorry for her that there was no room in his soul for reproach.

'He is here now: tell him . . . to for . . . forgive me!'

She stopped and breathed still more quickly, but did not shed tears.

'Yes . . . I will tell him,' answered Pierre; 'but . . .'

He did not know what to say.

Natasha was evidently dismayed at the thought of what he might think she had meant.

'No, I know all is over,' she said hurriedly. 'No, that can never be. I'm only tormented by the wrong I have done him. Tell him only that I beg him to forgive, forgive, forgive me for everything . . .'

She trembled all over and sat down on a chair.

A sense of pity he had never before known overflowed Pierre's heart.

'I will tell him, I will tell him everything once more,' said Pierre. 'But . . . I should like to know one thing . . .'

'Know what?' Natasha's eyes asked.

'I should like to know, did you love . . .' Pierre did not know how to refer to Anatole and flushed at the thought of him – 'did you love that bad man?'

'Don't call him bad!' said Natasha. 'But I don't know, don't know at all . . .'

She began to cry, and a still greater sense of pity, tenderness, and love, welled up in Pierre. He felt the tears trickle under his spectacles and hoped they would not be noticed.

'We won't speak of it any more, my dear,' said Pierre, and his gentle, cordial tone suddenly seemed very strange to Natasha.

'We won't speak of it, my dear – I'll tell him everything; but one thing I beg of you, consider me your friend and if you want help, advice, or simply to open your heart to someone – not now but when your mind is clearer – think of me!' He took her hand and kissed it. 'I shall be happy if it's in my power . . .'

Pierre grew confused.

'Don't speak to me like that. I am not worth it!' exclaimed Natasha and turned to leave the room, but Pierre held her hand.

He knew he had something more to say to her. But when he said it he was amazed at his own words.

'Stop, stop! You have your whole life before you,' said he to her.

'Before me? No! All is over for me,' she replied with shame and self-abasement.

'All over?' he repeated. 'If I were not myself, but the handsomest, cleverest, and best man in the world, and were free, I would this moment ask on my knees for your hand and your love!'

For the first time for many days Natasha wept tears of gratitude and tenderness, and glancing at Pierre she went out of the room.

Pierre, too, when she had gone almost ran into the ante-room, restraining tears of tenderness and joy that choked him, and without finding the sleeves of his fur cloak threw it on and got into his sledge.

'Where to now, your Excellency?' asked the coachman.

'Where to?' Pierre asked himself. 'Where can I go now? Surely not to the club or to pay calls?' All men seemed so pitiful, so poor, in comparison with this feeling of tenderness and love he experienced: in comparison with that softened, grateful, last look she had given him through her tears.

'Home!' said Pierre, and despite ten degrees of frost he threw open the bearskin cloak from his broad chest and inhaled the air with joy.

It was clear and frosty. Above the dirty ill-lit streets, above the black roofs, stretched the dark starry sky. Only looking up at the sky did Pierre cease to feel how sordid and humiliating were all mundane things compared with the heights to which his soul had just been raised. At the entrance to the Arbat Square an immense expanse of dark starry sky presented itself to his eyes. Almost in the centre of it, above the Prechistenka Boulevard, surrounded and sprinkled on all sides by stars but distinguished from them all by its nearness to the earth, its white light, and its long uplifted tail, shone the enormous and brilliant comet of the year 1812 – the comet which was said to portend all kinds of woes and the end of the world. In Pierre, however, that comet with its long luminous tail aroused no feeling of fear. On the contrary he gazed joyfully, his eyes moist with tears, at this bright comet which, having travelled in its orbit with inconceivable velocity through immeasurable space, seemed suddenly – like an arrow piercing the earth – to remain fixed in a chosen spot, vigorously holding its tail erect, shining, and displaying its white light amid countless other scintillating stars. It seemed to Pierre that this comet fully responded to what was passing in his own softened and uplifted soul, now blossoming into a new life.

END OF BOOK TWO

# NOTES

## BOOK ONE

### PART ONE

3 *Genoa and Lucca are now just family estates of the Buonapartes*: Napoleon seized them in June 1805. He had made himself Emperor of the French in December 1804, but Anna Scherer and her associates refer to him slightingly as 'Buonaparte' (the Corsican upstart).

4 *Novosiltsev's dispatch*: a new coalition which included England, Russia, Austria, and Prussia was being formed against France. Napoleon unexpectedly proposed peace to England. At the latter's request Tsar Alexander had sent N. N. Novosiltsev as intermediary, but on hearing at Berlin about the seizure of Genoa he turned back.

11 *the murder of the Duc d'Enghien*: the young duke, a member of the Bourbon family, was alleged to have taken part in a conspiracy of 1804 to assassinate Napoleon, then First Consul. He was kidnapped on neutral territory, tried by an irregular court martial, and shot.

13 *Mademoiselle George*: this celebrated French tragic actress (who failed to impress Pushkin) appeared in Petersburg and Moscow during the years 1808–12. Natasha hears her declaim in Hélène's drawing room (II v 13).

17 In 1805 M. I. Kutuzov (1745–1813) already enjoyed a great military reputation. He had taken part in the Turkish wars in Catherine's reign and together with Suvorov had captured the fortresses of Ochakov and Ismail, but had been seriously wounded and lost an eye. Having displeased Alexander in the post of Governor-General of Petersburg, he had been living for three years in disfavour in the country, but was now recalled to lead an army of 50,000 men to the aid of Austria [M].

17 *Dieu me la donne, gare à qui la touche!*: 'God has given it to me, let him beware who shall touch it'.

18 Maude dismisses Hippolyte's heraldry as 'untranslatable nonsense'.

20 *The prisoners he killed in Africa*: they were massacred in reprisal by Napoleon after the taking of Jaffa in 1799.

21 *the bridge of Arcole*: where, in 1796, Napoleon, fighting against the Austrians, seized the flag and led his troops across.

28 *and he waved his arm*: a forceful gesture employed by Russians to signify dismissal, 'giving it up as a bad job'.

31 *you part our hands*: the Russian custom was to shake hands on a bet, and for some third person, acting as a witness, to separate the hands [M].

35 Radzivilov was on the frontier between Russia and Galicia. Count Ilya Rostov bears a strong likeness to Count Ilya Tolstoy, the author's grandfather, and the Countess to his grandmother. Nicholas has some features of Tolstoy's father. Natasha is closer to his sister-in-law Tanya Behrs than to his wife. Vera resembles another sister-in-law. Sonya's relations with Nicholas are not unlike those between Tolstoy's father and his guardian Tatyana Ergolskaya. Maude remarks that 'the atmosphere of the Rostov family reproduces much that was characteristic of the Behrs' family circle.'

52 *performed his final duty*: i.e. to receive Unction.

59 Marya Dmitrievna Akhrosimova has much in common with N. D. Ofrosimova (1753–1826), a conspicuous figure of the time in Moscow society, though Tolstoy denies the derivation in 'Some Words about *War and Peace*' (p. 1323 below).

61 *summons to zakuska*: an *hors d'œuvre* eaten before the main meal, and consisting of caviare, salt fish etc., with vodka.

65 *Suvorov ... they beat him à plate couture* (hollow): A. S. Suvorov (1729–1800), owing to the failure of his Austrian allies in 1799 to supply him, was hard pressed in Switzerland. But although surrounded by 80,000 French, his army of not many more than 20,000 escaped from encirclement.

68 In the Russian Church cousins come within the prohibited degrees of affinity and a special permission has to be obtained for their marriage [M].

70 The *anglaise* was a contredanse with many figures to which arbitrary and fantastic names were given. Tolstoy obtained his knowledge of it from family tradition [M].

89 Prince Nicholas Andreevich Bolkonsky has many characteristics of Tolstoy's grandfather, Prince Nikolay Sergeevich Volkonsky (1753–1812), though it is suggested that he may derive more closely from Field Marshal M. F. Kamensky, another veteran of Catherine's wars. Princess Mary was modelled on Tolstoy's mother, Marya Nikolaevna Volkonskaya (who died when he was two

years old). Mlle Bourienne portrays a Frenchwoman who was her companion.

91 *From Heloise*: alluding to Rousseau's novel, *La Nouvelle Héloïse* (1761). The correspondence between Princess Mary and Julie (the name of Rousseau's heroine) was suggested by that between M. A. Volkova and V. I. Lanskaya between 1812 and 1818. Tolstoy read it in manuscript.

92 *Some sort of Key to the Mysteries*: The book in question was a mystical one by Eckartshausen (1752–1803) – *A Key to the Mysteries of Nature*. In 1805 it had been recently translated into Russian and was being eagerly read, especially among the Freemasons [M].

96 *grasseyement*: burring the *r*'s in the French manner.

100 *About Michelsen's army I understand*: The old prince is asking about Wintzingerode's plan for an attack on the French from three sides. Mikhelson with Russian and Austrian troops would advance from the east, to bring in Prussia; Tolstoy from the north; Kutuzov with the southern Russian army and Bavarians would fight in Galicia. There would be an Austrian army in northern Italy, and in central Italy a Russian corps with British and Neapolitans.

103 *Hofs-kriegs-wurst-schnapps-Rath*: 'Court-war-sausage-schnapps-councils'.

104 *The German, Pahlen ... to fetch the Frenchman Moreau.* P. A. Pahlen had been Governor-General of Petersburg under Paul, and took part in his assassination (1801). General Moreau had been exiled by Napoleon after the conspiracy of 1804.

105 *the siege of Ochakov*: a Turkish fort at the mouth of the Dnieper, stormed by Kutuzov in the war of 1787–91.

109 *Countess Zubova ... her mouth full of false teeth*: *zub* in Russian means 'tooth'.

111 *Michael Ilarionovich*: Kutuzov.

111 *Lombard-bond*: an interest-bearing bond from a state-run pawn-shop, or Lombard.

## PART TWO

114 *The Tsaritsin Meadow*: subsequently the 'Field of Mars', a parade ground in Petersburg.

121 *leg-bands*: strips of linen wound round in place of stockings.

121 *Wasn't it fine when those Germans gave us lifts?*: Kutuzov's army had moved very slowly from Radzivilov. Napoleon reached the Rhine early in September, and the Austrians supplied carts to speed up the arrival of the Russians.

130 *Schon fleissig?...Hoch Oestreicher! Hoch Russen! Kaiser Alex-*
*ander hoch!*: 'Busy already? Hurrah for the Austrians! Hurrah for
the Russians! Hurrah for the Emperor Alexander!'
*Und die ganze Welt hoch!*: 'And hurrah for the whole world!'

139 After Mack's surrender, Kutuzov began to retreat towards Vienna,
beating back as he went the attacks of the French advanced
guard under Murat. On 23 October, O.S., he crossed the rapid
river Enns. Murat was pressing all day on the troops under
Bagration, trying to intercept him and cut him off from the
crossing. Failing to do this, he reached the river almost simultaneously with Bagration and tried to seize the bridge. As
described in the novel, the Pavlograd hussars managed to fire it
after the Russian troops had crossed [M].

Murat had been with Napoleon in Egypt; he took part in the
*coup d'état* of 18 Brumaire 1799 which established Napoleon as
Consul; and married his sister in 1800. Napoleon made him
King of Naples in 1808 – a title which failed to satisfy his
ambition, and which Tolstoy constantly treats with sarcasm.

148 Colonel Schubert, as Maude points out, is one of many Russo-
Germans serving the Tsar, and he speaks very poor Russian,
which the translation indicates.

153 *actions at Lambach, Amstetten, and Melk*: all three were delay-
ing actions under Bagration in late October, O.S., against the
French advanced guard under Murat.

160 *Murat et tout le tremblement*: in the Tolstoy family *le tremblement* had long been ironically used to denote the bustle usually
accompanying official celebrations and rejoicings ... [M].

161 The Berlin Conference in October 1805 was an attempt by
Alexander I to bring Prussia into the war. A secret treaty was
accorded by the sovereigns, with a solemn oath taken over the
grave of Frederick the Great, but nothing followed.

161 *il faut lui faire grâce de l'u*: 'We must let him off the u' in
Buonaparte (see note to p. 3 above).

161 *His Sardinian Majesty*: Prussia had wanted Napoleon to be made
to compensate the king for his seizure in 1796 of Nice and Savoy.

167 *the Toulon that would lift him from the ranks*: like Napoleon,
who was a young artillery captain at the siege of this Royalist
stronghold in 1793. He gained his first military success and was
promoted general.

176 Tolstoy quotes the letter to Murat from Thiers's *Histoire du
Consulat et de l'Empire* (1845–62).

184 *my Toulon*: see note to p. 167 above.

184 *uttering his words with an oriental accent*: Prince Bagration was

a Georgian, Bagrationi being the dynastic name of former Georgian kings.

191 'This was the attack of which Thiers says: "The Russians behaved courageously, and, what seldom happens in war, two bodies of infantry were seen marching resolutely against one another without either of them giving way before meeting." And Napoleon at St Helena said: "Some Russian battalions showed entire fearlessness." ' [Tolstoy's note.]

200 The 'unicorn', like all other guns of the period, was a smooth-bore muzzle-loader, but was peculiar in the way it narrowed towards the muzzle [M].

## PART THREE

209 *Councillor of State*: in the fifth of the eleven classes in the civil service.

216 *Lëlya*: affectionate diminutive for Elena (Hélène).

247 *the Ismaylov regiment*: Tolstoy has made very few slips in this long novel, but here there seems to be one, for in Chapter 7 of Part One we were told that Boris had been transferred to the Semënov Guards [M].

251 Arnauts is a Turkish name of the Albanians, who supplied the Turks with irregular cavalry [M].

264 *sotnya*: company of a hundred men.

271 *Prishprish*: the Polish general Przebyszewski.

273 30 November, N.S. = 18 November, O.S.

276 Maude points out that the problem of death defeating 'man's greatest efforts and best hopes', here evaded by Prince Andrew, was to revolutionize Tolstoy's life sixteen years later, as described in Chapter 3 of *A Confession* (see also II ii 1, 12 and II ii 22).

281 *Hollabrünn*: Tolstoy refers to this battle as Schön Graben, from the neighbouring village (I ii 16–21).

289 The conversation between Kutuzov and Alexander is recorded in Mikhaylovsky-Danilevsky's *War of 1805*. As R. F. Christian comments, Tolstoy reproduces the dialogue exactly, but 'fills in the reactions of the speakers' – the twitching of Kutuzov's upper lip, the shrugging of his 'rather round shoulders'.

# BOOK TWO

## PART ONE

318 The English Club in Moscow dated from the reign of Catherine in the previous century. Moscow, relegated to the standing of second capital by Petersburg, tended to what Maude styles 'informal opposition'. The club was the meeting place of its aristocracy.

321 *The men who set the tone in conversation*: Count F. V. Rostopchin (1763–1826), to become Governor-General and Commander-in-Chief of Moscow (III iii 11, 24–5); Prince Yu. V. Dolgorukov, Commander-in-Chief of Moscow under Paul; P. S. Valuev, an archaeologist; Count I. I. Markov, a general of Catherine's time; Prince A. N. Vyazemsky, high-ranking official and father of the writer Prince P. A. Vyazemsky.

325 The description of the banquet in honour of Bagration enlarges (with a few slips) the entry for 4 March 1806 in the diary of S. P. Zhikharev. The verses, in awkward Russian, were transcribed from there. Their author, Nikolov, was blind by 1806 and could not have read his verses to the company.

327 *Paul Ivanovich Kutuzov*: not to be confused with the general (Michael Ilarionovich).

334 *Anatole used to come to borrow money from her*: in the first drafts of the novel, Tolstoy made it plain that Hélène and her brother had been in guilty relations with one another, but afterwards he altered this so that only some hints remain [M].

335 *Mais que diable . . . dans cette galère*: 'What the dickens did he get himself into that mess for?' or, more literally, 'What the devil was he going to do in that galley?' (*Les Fourberies de Scapin*).

340 *this morning's frushtique*: for *Frühstück*, breakfast.

346 In the Russian baptismal service the priest cuts off a little of the child's hair and sticks it together with wax from a taper. It is considered unlucky if this wax sinks in the font [M].

348 *In the autumn of 1806 everybody had again begun talking of the war with Napoleon*: all through 1806 Napoleon had been making preparations for a new campaign. Charles James Fox, the pacifically inclined British Foreign Secretary, died in September. At the end of the month Napoleon won victories at Jena and Auerstadt over the Prussians and occupied Berlin. Alexander had no time to give aid, with the French on the Vistula. He conscripted men for the army and militia to defend his borders. Maude notes that four-fifths of the militia would have had to carry pikes.

359 *some verses called 'Enchantress'*: Denisov has certain features of

the poet and partisan hero of 1812, Denis Davydov (1784–1839), but these verses cannot be traced to the latter.

### PART TWO

368 *a half-cut novel...by Madame de Souza: Émilie et Alphonse* (1799). Mme de Souza (1761–1836) was mentioned in an earlier draft along with Mrs Radcliffe, as a novelist much admired by women of the same generation as Tolstoy's mother.

369 Russian serfs and peasants often turn their tea-tumblers upside down as an indication that they do not want any more. From economy they do not dissolve the sugar, but nibble a little with their tea [M].

370 *The Brotherhood of the Freemasons:* Freemasonry came to Russia in the late seventeenth or early eighteenth century. By the 1760s many high officials were Masons. The Lodges were German or English by derivation. (The so-called 'Scottish' Lodges of II iii 8 were actually German.) Catherine closed down the order in 1790, by which time the Russian Freemasons had been formed into a province under a German Grandmaster, the Duke of Brunswick. There had been a revival of Freemasonry in Alexander's reign, with some revolutionary implications. (See note to p. 376.)

374 *in Novikov's time.* N. I. Novikov (1744–1818) was an active Mason, a prominent journalist who attacked serfdom, and publisher of Rosicrucian and other literature. One of the works he printed was L. C. de Saint Martin's *Des erreurs et de la vérité* (1785), the inspiration of the so-called Martinists. Novikov was imprisoned in 1792 for fifteen years in Schlüsselburg but released in 1796 following Catherine's death.

375 *Thomas à Kempis:* (1380–1471), the author of *De Imitatione Christi*, a celebrated devotional treatise.

376 Tolstoy took the ceremonies of the Freemasons from his study of books and manuscripts in the rich collection of the Rumyantsev Museum in Moscow. In a letter to his wife in the autumn of 1866 he wrote: 'After drinking my coffee I went to the Rumyantsev Museum and sat there till three o'clock reading very interesting Masonic manuscripts. I can't describe to you why the reading produced on me a depression I have not been able to get rid of all day. What is distressing is that all those Masons were fools.' Tolstoy sympathized with their aims but considered their methods futile [M].

387 *Tu l'as voulu, George Dandin:* a familiar quotation from Molière's comedy *George Dandin* (1668). (It should be 'Vous l'avez voulu'.)

388 *Vienna considers the bases of the proposed treaty so unattainable:* negotiations for the Bartenstein treaty between France and

Prussia, to which Austria was invited to adhere, were going on in April 1807. Napoleon had been discomfited by the battle of Preussisch Eylau (see note to p. 393 below). The treaty was still unconcluded when the battle of Friedland took place in June. After this the Emperors met at Tilsit (II ii 19–21).

388 *The man of profound intellect*: another of Tolstoy's apparent slips. It was the Danish *chargé d'affaires* who was referred to thus (p. 387). The speaker here is presumably Shitov, he who was described (also p. 387) as 'a man of great merit'.

389 'For the King of Prussia', a phrase used in French to denote 'for a trifle of no value' [M].

393 *a complete victory over Buonaparte at Eylau*: the battle of Preussisch Eylau was fought on 27 January 1807, O. S. Bennigsen commanded the Russian army, losing a third of his men, but Napoleon too suffered heavy losses. Both sides claimed a victory.

395 *kibitka*: a covered wagon.

401 'The same day is kept by the Russian Church in honour of St Peter and St Paul, so that Pierre (Peter) had them both as patron saints [M].' Maude further points out that a chantry would bring people from outside to the fair, and the peasants resented having their children taken because they needed them to work on their own plots.

407 *to be their marshal*: Maréchal de la Noblesse, elected by them and the landed gentry as their representative.

409 *the serfs' backs and foreheads, which, beat and shave as you may*: a proprietor could send any of his serfs as exiles to Siberia, and when going there one side of the head was shaved, that the man might more easily be recaptured should he run away [M].

412 *God's folk*: Tolstoy tells of his aunt Alexandra that she harboured at Yasnaya Polyana, and loved to converse with, 'pilgrims, half-crazy devotees, monks and nuns'. These pilgrims wandered over Russia on their way to Holy Places.

413 *Il faut que vous sachiez ... votre intimité avec ce jeune homme*: 'You realize that this is a woman.' ... 'My dear, you ought on the contrary to be pleased I should explain to Pierre your intimacy with this young man.'

419 *Platov's division*: General M. I. Platov (1751–1818), Ataman (Chief) of the Cossack Host, was a former comrade-in-arms of Suvorov and Kutuzov.

419 *neither provisions for the men nor fodder for the horses*: Maude quotes from Mikhaylovsky-Danilevsky's *Description of the Wars of 1806–7*: 'The lack of grain in spring occasioned the slackness

of the higher command and its inability to stop abuses which made their way into the management of the commissariat. In reply to a report of hunger in the army, Bennigsen once replied: "It is necessary to know how to endure. I only have three dishes for my own dinner." Money was issued to buy provisions, but money cannot buy provisions where there are none. Sometimes the generals seized one another's provision waggons almost by assault, and bread seldom reached Bennigsen's advanced guard, Soldiers swelled up and died of hunger. The hospitals were in a wretched condition.'

420 *quoits and skittles*: literally, *svayka* and *gorodki*. In the former a thick-headed nail has to be thrown into a ring. *Gorodki* is a game in which short, thick sticks are arranged in certain figures within squares. Each side has its own square, and each player in turn throws a stick to try to clear out the enemy's square. The side wins which first accomplishes this with the six figures in which the sticks are successively arranged [M].

431 *The French and Russian Emperors arrived in Tilsit*: this was to arrange a peace which lasted for five years. The King of Prussia was excluded from their two hours of discussion, and admitted only the next day when Napoleon treated him with contempt. Maude notes that their want of silver plate prevented the Preobrazhensk regiment from matching the style of hospitality shown by the French Guards.

PART THREE

447 *flying away! Like this*: Tolstoy at the age of seven or eight attempted to fly from a window eighteen yards up and was concussed by the fall.

450 *when the youthful Speransky was at the zenith of his fame*: M. M. Speransky (1772–1839), son of a village priest, whose abilities enabled him to rise rapidly in the civil service, was from 1808 the Tsar's adviser on home affairs. He worked to reform the finances and administration of Russia. His Plan of 1809, which proposed far-reaching reforms, was implemented only in part. Prince Andrew works on his commission for revising the laws (II iii 6). The civil code drafted by Speransky was indebted to the *Code Napoléon*. The Moscow opposition, led by the fanatically anti-French Rostopchin, who believed Speransky to be the evil genius of Russia and a leader of the Freemasons, campaigned for his overthrow. He was dismissed and exiled in 1812, shortly before Napoleon invaded Russia (II v 21).

450 *the grades of Collegiate Assessor and State Councillor*: the sixth and fifth, equivalent to lieutenant-colonel and full colonel.

450 Count Aleksey Arakcheev (1769–1834) was Alexander's military adviser. He is notorious for his military settlements of the 1820s in which state peasants had to combine army service and agriculture under the harshest discipline. Not only the young liberals of Pushkin's day but some of Alexander's leading generals intensely disliked the settlements.

451 *Sila Andreevich*: *sila* means 'force'.

453 Count V. P. Kochubey (1768–1834) was Minister of the Interior from 1802 until 1807.

456 *an admirer of Montesquieu*: Speransky himself approved the ideas of Montesquieu in *De l'esprit des lois* (1748), as he did those of the eighteenth-century English jurist Blackstone. The French here reads: 'That the principle of monarchies is honour seems to me incontestable. Certain rights and privileges for the aristocracy appear to me a means of maintaining that sentiment.'

461 *the three primordial elements – sulphur, mercury, and salt*: the Rosicrucian Masons, including Novikov, were interested in alchemy.

463 *dangerous designs of Illuminism*: the Illuminati were a Bavarian conspiratorial group with republican aims, founded in 1776 and suppressed by their government in 1785. They had followers in the Moscow Martinists.

463 *For three days after the delivery of his speech at the Lodge*: this incident recalls Tolstoy's own experience on the few occasions when he ventured to make a public speech ... [M].

466 *the circle of Count Rumyantsev and Caulaincourt*: Count N. P. Rumyantsev, Minister of Foreign Affairs in 1807, became Chancellor in 1809. The Marquis de Caulaincourt was French ambassador in Petersburg from 1807 until 1811.

466 *Hélène had been at Erfurt*: Alexander, Napoleon and the King of Prussia met there in the autumn of 1808. Napoleon proposed an alliance between France and Russia which Alexander rejected, knowing the strength of feeling at home. For promising not to intervene in Europe he was allowed to annex Finland and, if he could, Turkey's Danubian provinces.

466 The Prince de Ligne (1735–1814), famous as soldier, diplomat and author, spent some time in Russia. He accompanied Catherine on her tour to the Crimea in 1787.

473 *I have arranged that rent for them in the Baltic provinces*: throughout the nineteenth century the Russian government, as a reward for service, or simply by favouritism, used to make grants of 'rents' (*arenda*), that is to say, the usufruct of land [M].

478 *Natasha ... began kissing first one knuckle*: she is reckoning the knuckles of the closed fist as the months that have 31 days, the

652

spaces between as the shorter months, and Maude observes that she has to cheat in order to arrive at August.

484 *Marya Antonovna*: M. A. Naryshkina (1779–1854) was for a long time Alexander's mistress.

491 *Gervais, Magnitsky, and Stolypin*: A. A. Gervais, who served in the Ministry of Foreign Affairs, was a kinsman of Speransky's; M. L. Magnitsky (1778–1855), his friend and collaborator, also arrested and exiled in 1812; Senator A. A. Stolypin, a wealthy landowner. Tolstoy here handles ironically the reminiscences of Speransky's daughter in Baron M. A. Korf's *Life of Count Speransky* (1861).

493 *Napoleon's Spanish affairs*: Napoleon had invaded the Iberian peninsula in 1807. The following year he installed his brother Joseph (then King of Naples) in place of Ferdinand VII as King of Spain. By 1810 the combined pressure of Wellington's army and Spanish guerrillas was forcing the French out of Spain, a process completed in 1813.

498 *the table for boston*: boston was a card game invented by French officers at Boston, Massachusetts, during the Revolutionary war. It has a distant resemblance to auction bridge [M].

512 *her own brother, killed in Turkey*: following Tilsit the Russian army resumed hostilities against Turkey in the Caucasus and on the Danube. They had little success in the latter region until Kutuzov became Commander-in-Chief.


PART FOUR

525 *an unsurpassable morning for hunting*: Maude observes that 'the hounds in hunting of the kind here described were keen-scented but not very swift dogs. They had to find the game by scent and chase it in the desired direction, but the swift and strong borzois caught and killed the game. A borzoi has very poor scent and only chases the game when he sees it. It must be pointed out to him, and even when following it he sometimes loses sight of it. If the game shams dead, a borzoi is often balked and hesitates what to do, as in the case mentioned when the hare suddenly squatted and the borzoi did not seize it' (ch. 6).

529 *the buffoon ... Nastasya Ivanovna*: the practice of keeping a buffoon in country houses lasted till after the abolition of serfdom. 'Alesha the Pot', from whom Tolstoy later made so tragic a story, was a sort of buffoon Tolstoy's wife found at Yasnaya Polyana when she arrived there after her marriage in 1862 [M].

546 *the pas de châle*: a French shawl dance.

548 *Dimmler the musician*: a real person who gave piano lessons at this time in Moscow.

551 Twenty degrees Réaumur is thirteen below zero Fahrenheit.

552 Feeding a fowl with grain arranged on the floor is a way of telling fortunes at Christmas time [M].

556 John Field (1782–1837), Irish-born pianist and composer, famous for his nocturnes, lived in Petersburg from 1804 until 1831. Pasternak in *An Essay in Autobiography* (1959) speaks of Chopin's originality in 'using the old idiom of Mozart and Field' for new purposes.

### PART FIVE

571 *Sivtsev Vrazhok*: a Moscow slum.

573 *the Emperor Francis wants to offer him his daughter in an illegal marriage*: Napoleon had married Joséphine de Beauharnais in 1796. The marriage was childless. He divorced her in 1809, applied unsuccessfully for the hand of Alexander's sister Anna, and married the Archduchess Marie Louise of Austria in March 1810.

573 The Spanish victory over the French on 14 June appears to be Talavera (15–16 July 1809, O.S.)

573 *Astræa Lodge against the Manna Seekers*: they were both in Petersburg, and the intrigues could take the form of denunciations.

573 *an authentic Scotch carpet*: a carpet with symbolic signs on it was considered important for the equipment of each Lodge. The Lodges competed with one another in obtaining such carpets from the most ancient and highly esteemed masonic organizations, as well as copies of the ceremonies and 'acts' – that is, the rules of the Order [M].

580 *Napoleon's seizure of the Duke of Oldenburg's territory*: he annexed it in 1810, along with Hanseatic towns that had infringed the Continental System, his blockade against Britain. The Duke was Alexander's brother-in-law.

589 *to jails and prisons on affairs of which she never spoke to anyone*: Prisoners 'suffered much want, and to contribute to their needs was a recognized Christian duty [M]'.

590 *we'll drive to the Super-Rogue's*: There is a pun in the Russian. Akhrosimova refers to the dressmaker Mme Aubert-Chalmé as 'Ober-Shel'ma' ('arch-rogue').

625 *we have first to sit down*: according to Russian custom before a journey.

626 *Remember me to Stëshka*: she was a celebrated gypsy singer in Moscow at that time.

637 *Speransky – the news of whose sudden exile and alleged treachery had just reached Moscow*: for Speransky, see note to p. 450. He had neglected to find allies and supporters. In 1812 he was exiled, eventually to Perm on the Siberian border, but in 1814 the Tsar allowed him to settle on his small estate near Novgorod. In 1816 he became Governor of Penza, and three years later Governor-General of Siberia. In 1821 he returned to Petersburg. Under Nicholas I Speransky was responsible for the Digest of Russian Law, a great bureaucratic enterprise. A few months before his death he was made a Count.

# THE WORLD'S CLASSICS

SERGEI AKSAKOV: A Russian Gentleman
*Translated by J. D. Duff*
*Edited by Edward Crankshaw*

LUDOVICO ARIOSTO: Orlando Furioso
*Translated by Guido Waldman*

ARISTOTLE: The Nicomachean Ethics
*Translated and with an introduction by David Ross*

JANE AUSTEN: Emma
*Edited by James Kinsley and David Lodge*

Mansfield Park
*Edited by James Kinsley and John Lucas*

Northanger Abbey, Lady Susan, The Watsons,
*and* Sanditon
*Edited by John Davie*

Persuasion
*Edited by John Davie*

Pride and Prejudice
*Edited by James Kinsley and Frank Bradbrook*

Sense and Sensibility
*Edited by James Kinsley and Claire Lamont*

MAX BEERBOHM: Seven Men and Two Others
*With an introduction by Lord David Cecil*

JAMES BOSWELL: Life of Johnson
*The Hill/Powell edition, revised by David Fleeman*
*With an introduction by Pat Rogers*

CHARLOTTE BRONTË: Jane Eyre
*Edited by Margaret Smith*

Shirley
*Edited by Margaret Smith and Herbert Rosengarten*

EMILY BRONTË: Wuthering Heights
*Edited by Ian Jack*

FANNY BURNEY: Evelina
*Edited by Edward A. Bloom*

LEWIS CARROLL: Alice's Adventures in Wonderland
and Through the Looking Glass
*Edited by Roger Lancelyn Green*
*Illustrated by John Tenniel*

IZAAK WALTON and CHARLES COTTON:
The Compleat Angler
*Edited by John Buxton*
*With an introduction by John Buchan*

OSCAR WILDE: Complete Shorter Fiction
*Edited by Isobel Murray*

The Picture of Dorian Gray
*Edited by Isobel Murray*

MARY WOLLSTONECRAFT:
Mary *and* The Wrongs of Woman
*Edited by Gary Kelly*

A complete list of Oxford Paperbacks, including books in The World's Classics, Past Masters, and OPUS Series, can be obtained from the General Publicity Department, Oxford University Press, Walton Street, Oxford OX2 6DP.